Recent Studies in Early Christianity

A Collection of Scholarly Essays

Series Editor

Everett Ferguson

A GARLAND SERIES

Series Contents

Norms of Faith and Life

Edited with an introduction by
Everett Ferguson

GARLAND PUBLISHING, INC.
A MEMBER OF THE TAYLOR & FRANCIS GROUP
New York & London
1999

Library of Congress Cataloging-in-Publication Data

Norms of faith and life / edited, with introductions by Everett Ferguson.
     p.   cm. — (Recent studies in early Christianity ; 3)
    Includes bibliographical references.
    ISBN 0-8153-3070-7 (alk. paper)
    1. Christian life—History—Early church, ca. 30–600.
  2. Theology, Doctrinal—History—Early church, ca. 30–600.
  3. Church history—Primitive and early church, ca. 30–600.
  I. Ferguson, Everett, 1933–   . II. Series.
  BR195.C5N67 1999
  270.1—dc21   99-24677
                                        CIP

Printed on acid-free, 250-year-life paper
Manufactured in the United States of America

Contents

Series Introduction

Garland published in 1993 *Studies in Early Christianity: A Collection of Scholarly Essays*, an eighteen-volume set of classic articles on the early history of Christianity. The present set of six volumes, *Recent Studies in Early Christianity*, continues that first series by selecting articles written during the last decade. The chronological scope is the same, the first six centuries of the common era. The arrangement once more is topical but with a conflation and realignment of topics to fit the smaller number of volumes. The present series of essays will serve as an important supplement for those who possess the first series. For those without the first series, it will introduce key areas of research and debate on the early history of Christianity.

The growing academic interest in Christianity during its early centuries, as noted in the series introduction to *Studies in Early Christianity*, has greatly accelerated. There has been a proliferation of studies during the last decade on the subject of Christianity in late antiquity. The very popularity of the designation "late antiquity" says something about the current intellectual climate in which these studies arise: a shift from a primary emphasis on Christianity itself to the larger cultural setting of which it was a part, a shift from doctrinal studies to the church as a social institution, and a shift from concern for orthodoxy to the popular religious attitudes and expressions.

The increased study of this period finds expression in more doctoral students, record membership in professional organizations, like the North American Patristics Society and the Association internationale d'études patristiques, and large attendance at the International Conferences on Patristic Studies in Oxford (August 16-21, 1999, marks the thirteenth of these meetings that occur every four years), in addition to participation in specialized conferences on Origen, Gregory of Nyssa, Augustine, and others. Expanded literary productivity is evidenced by new journals (*The Journal of Early Christian Studies*, edited by Elizabeth Clark and Everett Ferguson, a continuation of *The Second Century*; *Zeitschrift für Antikes Christentum/Journal of Ancient Christianity*, edited by H.C. Brennecke and C. Markschies), new reference works (*The Encyclopedia of Early Christianity* [New York: Garland], edited by Everett Ferguson, first edition in 1990, second and greatly expanded edition in 1997, paperback edition 1998; *The Encyclopedia of the Early Church* [New York: Oxford University Press, 1992], English translation of *Dizionario Patristico e di Antichità Cristiane*, edited by Angelo Di Berardino), and substantial scholarly monographs in the field.

In some ways the selection of articles for six volumes on a decade of scholarship is more difficult than eighteen volumes on a century: We do not have the perspective of time to judge what is of enduring worth. Although some of these pieces will no doubt become classics, the guiding principle in selection has been to point to areas that are drawing the greatest attention. Some subjects have become virtually independent subdisciplines in the study of religion in late antiquity. This is notably true of Gnosticism, although the very term is under attack as a proper category.

The six volumes of this collection of scholarly essays take up the following broad topics: (1) the social setting of the early church, with attention to such matters as women, family, friendship, funerary practices, education, and slavery; (2) the political, cultural, and religious setting of early Christianity in relation to Romans, Greeks, and Jews; (3) the internal development of the church as it recognized its canon of scriptures, interpreted those scriptures, defined its confession of faith, and articulated standards of conduct; (4) the diversity — geographical, doctrinal, disciplinary — that counterbalanced the efforts to achieve a unified orthodoxy; (5) the many expressions of devotion and spirituality that both nourished and manifested faith; and (6) the varied ways in which early Christians wrestled with the limitations of historical existence and human language yet voiced their hopes for another and better world.

These topics represent the emphases in the modern study of early Christianity: social history and the application of the social sciences to the understanding of the historical texts, women's concerns and gender issues, Christians' relations with their Jewish and pagan neighbors, variety in early Christianity (especially fueled by the Nag Hammadi texts but not exclusively so), types of asceticism, literary forms and criticism, and Christianity's relationship to late antiquity and the transition to the medieval world. Some themes long present in the study of early Christianity continue to gain attention: the creedal definition of the faith, the causes and effects of persecution, different approaches to the interpretation of the Bible, forms of worship and spirituality, Christian morality, and the Christian hope.

One person's judgment and one small set of essays cannot do full justice to the rich flowering of studies in the field of early Christianity. We can only point to the areas of emphasis and call attention to some significant studies. These studies will lead teachers and students into the larger field and, we hope, spark their interest in pursuing some of these questions and related matters more extensively, thereby enlarging the number of researchers in a field not only intellectually challenging but also spiritually significant.

Volume Introduction

This volume brings together under the rubric of the effort to define what was normative in early Christian faith and practice studies that deal with aspects of authority for Christian doctrine, of the functioning of the church, and of the moral expressions of Christianity.

The Bible was foundational and central as early Christians defined their norms for thought and conduct. The letters of Paul were collected by the end of the first century. Recent study shows considerable interest in the collection of the Four Gospel canon, and some scholars argue that it was formed earlier than many have thought, namely in the early second century. New Testament scholars as well as church historians are interested in the recognition of the canon. One of the former, Graham Stanton, in his 1996 presidential address to the Society of New Testament Studies, reproduced here, assembled the evidence in support of an early second-century date for the bringing of the Gospels of Matthew, Mark, Luke, and John together as an authoritative collection. A more recent detailed study of the fragments of Papias, bishop of Hierapolis in Phrygia (ca. 130), adds strong support to this conclusion.[1]

The Muratorian Fragment has come to the forefront of canon studies as the result of efforts to redate it from the late second century to the fourth century, especially since the publication of Geoffrey Hahneman's dissertation.[2] The reviews of that book have been mixed. The most thorough treatment, introducing new arguments as well, is the study included in this volume by Charles Hill,[3] who has given much attention to canon questions.[4] The curious position of the Wisdom of Solomon in the Muratorian Fragment is given a plausible explanation by William Horbury.

The "New Covenant" as a title for the books now found in the New Testament is an important evidence that something resembling a canonical collection was in place by the beginning of the third century. Wolfram Kinzig gives an extensive treatment to the early use of this phrase, which appears not only to have provided the first title for the canonical New Testament but also in its adjectival form, "covenantal," to have continued to be used in the sense of "canonical" until that term supplanted it in ecclesiastical usage. Clement of Alexandria is the earliest writer certainly to use this title, and he is, moreover, an important witness to the stage of canon formation in the church at Alexandria at the end of the second century, although his canon was broader than what would eventually be recognized (Brooks).

The authority of the Bible led to the interpretation of the Bible. Any authority has to be interpreted. And, it is often not sufficiently appreciated the extent to which the church fathers were concerned with the exegesis of scripture.[5] Their writings provide an almost unlimited supply of material for examination.[6] They sought to be "biblical theologians": Their spirituality comes out of their study and meditation on scripture, and their doctrinal debates were conducted as battles over the correct meaning of scripture. Among modern interpreters of the ancient interpreters of the Bible, Frances Young is at the forefront in making sympathetic and original contributions.[7]

Irenaeus is a central figure in the history of the formation and interpretation of the Bible. He appealed to the "canon of truth" (otherwise known as the "rule of faith") as the standard for interpreting the Bible. The interpretation of Paul was at the center of the church's debates with Marcion and some of those called Gnostics. Richard Norris and David Balás give complementary treatment to this subject; both of their papers originated in a conference at Southern Methodist University in Dallas on "Paul and the Legacies of Paul," the published proceedings of which furnish the source for Norris's article.

The most influential figure in the early history of interpretation was Origen. Karen Jo Torjesen has been one of the most creative students of Origen's exegesis.[8] A later figure in the Alexandrian tradition, Athanasius, one of the creators of fourth-century Trinitarian orthodoxy, is a good representative of the importance given by fourth-century interpreters to the *skopos* ("goal" or "purpose") of scripture. For Athanasius this "scope" of scripture, ultimately his only hermeneutical rule, is the incarnation of the Word of God for the sake of human salvation.[9] This purpose, or "goal," of scripture was an important guiding principle for many authors, comparable to the "rule of faith" in earlier writers.

Crucial for early Christian interpreters of the Bible was the problem of how to approach the Jewish scriptures, which they accepted as divine revelation but which they did not follow in its ceremonial and legal parts, at least not in a literal sense. Robert Wilken examines the treatment of one of the important prophetic texts for Christian self-understanding, Isaiah 2:1-4. Different from the literary studies of the theologians and bishops of the cities was the interpretation of the desert ascetics, appropriately called an "oral culture,"[10] which was operative more extensively than modern students often recognize.

Councils and creeds were normative on disciplinary and doctrinal questions respectively. The council of Nicaea in 325 held a special place, in spite of the fact that the western part of the empire had little part in the council and remained largely untouched by the discussions of the Trinity until the 340s.[11] Creedal confessions and the catechetical instruction of new converts interacted with one another.[12] Nicaea's authority as a norm of doctrine was upheld in 451 by the Council of Chalcedon, which saw its Definition of Faith as an exegetical note on the Nicene Creed (R. Norris). Conciliar definitions became not only a norm for the church, but they also became a cause of controversy.

An important support for the authority of bishops was the claim to apostolic succession. The Christian understanding was shaped by the philosophical schools, which had succession lists of their heads and authoritative representatives (Brent). The great churches rivalled each other for preeminence in the Christian world. Another element from the culture, patronage, influenced the language and reality of claims to primacy in the disputes between Rome and Constantinople (Daley).

Outstanding theologians, such as Augustine, exercised a personal authority (O'Donnell). In addition to Augustine's profound theological contributions, he was one of the leading thinkers on moral questions.[13] He represented the work of many who deepened early Christian moral teaching into theological ethics.[14]

Doctrine shaped ethics, and many thinkers wrestled with difficult moral questions that had also been considered by Greek moral philosophers: envy — the "underside of honor" in ancient Mediterranean society (Limberis), proper use of money — a more acute problem for Christians than for pagans, but appeals on behalf of the poor could be couched in very traditional terms of honor (Leyerle), hypocrisy — a special problem after the triumph of the church (Curran), and lying — a perennial human problem (Feehan).[15]

Notes

[1] Charles E. Hill, "What Papias Said about John (and Luke): A 'New' Papian Fragment," *Journal of Theological Studies*, n.s. 49 (1998):582–629.

[2] Geoffrey Hahneman, *The Muratorian Fragment and the Development of the Canon* (Oxford: Clarendon, 1992).

[3] Among other reviewers unpersuaded by Hahneman's arguments are Everett Ferguson, *Journal of Theological Studies*, n.s. 44 (1993):691–97; J.-D. Kaestli, "La place du Fragment de Muratori dans l'histoire du canon: A propos de la these de Sundberg et Hahneman," *Cristianismo nella storia* 15 (1994):609–34; Bruce Metzger, *Critical Review of Books in Religion* 7 (1996):192–94.

[4] Charles E. Hill, "Justin and the New Testament Writings," *Studia Patristica* 30 (1997):42–48.

[5] An important orientation to this vast field is supplied now by David L. Balás and D. Jeffrey Bingham, "Patristic Exegesis of the Books of the Bible," in William R. Farmer, ed., *The International Bible Commentary: A Catholic and Ecumenical Commentary for the Twenty-First Century* (Collegeville: Liturgical Press, 1998), pp. 64–115.

[6] As a sample of modern study of this vast source material, Graham E. Gould, "Basil of Caesarea and Gregory of Nyssa on the Beatitutdes," *Studia Patristica* 22 (1989):14–22; Arthur G. Holder, "The Mosaic Tabernacle in Early Christian Exegesis," *Studia Patristica* 25 (1993):101–106; Robert C. Hill, "Psalms 45 and Patristic Thinking on Biblical Inspiration," *Studia Patristica* 25 (1993):95–100; and see Wilken in this volume.

[7] As a sampling, Frances Young, "Exegetical Method and Scripture Proof: The Bible in Doctrinal Debate," *Studia Patristica* 19 (1989):291–304; idem, *Biblical Exegesis and the Formation of Christian Culture* (New York: Cambridge University Press, 1997) [her Speakers Lectures at Oxford].

[8] Karen Jo Torjesen, *Hermeneutical Procedure and Theological Method in Origen's Exegesis* (Berlin: Walter de Gruyter, 1986); idem, "Hermeneutics and Soteriology in Origen's Peri Archon," *Studia Patristica* 21 (1989):333–48.

[9] James D. Ernest, "Athanasius of Alexandria: The Scope of Scripture in Polemical and Pastoral Context," *Vigiliae Christianae* 47 (1993):341–62.

[10] Douglas Burton-Christie, "Oral Culture and Biblical Interpretation in Early Egyptian Monasticism," *Studia Patristica* 30 (1997):144–50; cf. his "'Practice Makes Perfect': Interpretation of Scripture in the *Apophthegmata Patrum*," *Studia Patristica* 20 (1989):213–18.

[11] Jorg Ulrich, "Nicaea and the West," *Vigiliae Christianae* 51 (1997):10–24.

[12] Alexis Doval, "The Fourth Century Jerusalem Catechesis and the Development of the Creed," *Studia Patristica* 30 (1997):296–305.

[13] Mary T. Clark, "Augustine on Conscience," *Studia Patristica* 33 (1997):63–67.

[14] Ekkehard Mühlenberg, "From Early Christian Morality to Theological Ethics," *Studia Patristica* 19 (1989):203–25.

[15] The last also introduced by R.D. Ray, "Augustine's Two Treatises on Lying," *Studia Patristica* 22 (1989):321–25.

New Test. Stud. vol. 43, 1997, pp. 317–346

THE FOURFOLD GOSPEL*

GRAHAM N. STANTON

(King's College London, Strand, London WC2R 2LS, England)

The origins and the theological significance of the fourfold Gospel raise a set of teasing questions. Why did the early Church eventually accept four partly parallel foundation documents? There is no precedent for this either in the OT Scriptures or elsewhere in earliest Christianity. Did retention of four gospels assist or hinder the early Church in the presentation of its claims concerning Jesus? No doubt to some, insistence that there were four gospels implied that there were basic flaws in the single gospels. Was the second century church's decision to bring together four separate gospels wise? What were, and what are, the theological implications of the fourfold Gospel? A critical theology cannot avoid asking these questions.

In the early decades of the twentieth century, the views of the great giants, Theodore Zahn and Adolf von Harnack, were influential: many scholars accepted their view that the fourfold Gospel emerged *very early* in the second century, well before Marcion.[1] More recently, particularly under the influence of Hans von Campenhausen, most scholars have accepted that the fourfold Gospel emerged in the *second half* of the second century and that the Muratorian Fragment and Irenaeus are our primary witnesses.[2]

However, the current consensus on the emergence of the fourfold Gospel is now being challenged from two entirely different starting

---

* Presidential Address delivered on 7 August 1996 at the 51st General Meeting of SNTS in Strasbourg, France.

[1] A. von Harnack, *The Origin of the New Testament and the Most Important Consequences of the New Creation* (London and New York, 1925) 69–72; Th. Zahn, *Grundriss der Geschichte des neutestamentlichen Kanons* (Leipzig: Deichert, 2nd ed. 1904) 35–41. E. J. Goodspeed dated the origin of the fourfold Gospel to c. 125: see his *The Formation of the New Testament* (Chicago: University of Chicago, 1937) 33–41. Five years later John Knox rejected Goodspeed's arguments and opted for the West between 150 and 175 as the time when 'we get our first glimpse of the existence of the fourfold Gospel', *Marcion and the New Testament* (Chicago: University of Chicago, 1942) 140–67. K. L. Carroll, 'The Creation of the Fourfold Gospel', *BJRL* 37 (1954–5) 68–77 echoed Knox's claim that the fourfold Gospel was an answer to Marcion.

[2] Hans von Campenhausen, *Die Entstehung der christlichen Bibel* (Tübingen: Mohr, 1968); ET *The Formation of the Christian Bible* (Philadelphia: Fortress; London: Black, 1972) chapter 5.

points. The Muratorian Fragment is being assigned by some to the fourth century, and as a corollary, Irenaeus's devotion to the fourfold Gospel is seen as 'something of an innovation' in a time of fluidity of gospel traditions and a proliferation of gospels.[3]

The other challenge to the consensus approaches the question from a fresh angle. Whereas the traditional way of discussing this question focuses on the use early Christian writers made of the four gospels, attention is now being given to the evidence of the earliest copies of the gospels themselves – especially to the predilection of Christian scribes for the codex and for *nomina sacra*.[4]

Theological reflection on the significance of Christianity's commitment to four gospels has been sparse in recent years. Very little has been written since Oscar Cullmann's important article was first published in 1945.[5] However in some circles a strong challenge has been mounted to the pre-eminence of the canonical four in historical reconstructions of the origin and development of early Christianity. Now and again this challenge is accompanied by hints of a theological agenda: we are told that by giving increased attention to non-canonical gospels it may be possible to construct a Jesus more congenial in a post-modernist era.

I shall attempt to take account *both* of the ways second century writers used and referred to the gospels *and* also of the evidence of the earliest manuscripts. I shall work backwards from Irenaeus, for I find that it is often helpful to work back from the full flowering of a concept or a development to its earlier roots. I shall insist that the decision to accept four gospels, along with the earlier acceptance of a plurality of gospels, was one of the most momentous taken within early Christianity, a decision which cries out for continuing theological reflection.

---

[3] See especially G. M. Hahneman, *The Muratorian Fragment and the Development of the Canon* (Oxford: Clarendon, OUP, 1992) 101. Note also, 'It is difficult therefore to acknowledge that the fourfold Gospel was "firmly established" in the last quarter of the second century' (100; and cf. 108). Hahneman develops considerably the arguments for a fourth century date first advanced by A. C. Sundberg in two articles: 'Towards a Revised History of the New Testament Canon', *Studia Evangelica* 4/1 (1968) 452–61; 'Canon Muratori: A Fourth Century List', *HTR* 66 (1973) 1–41.

[4] See below, 326–9.

[5] O. Cullmann, 'Die Pluralität der Evangelien als theologisches Problem im Altertum', *TZ* 1 (1945) 23–42; ET in Cullmann's *The Early Church* (ed. A. J. B. Higgins; London: SCM, 1956) 37–54. See also R. C. Morgan, 'The Hermeneutical Significance of Four Gospels', *Interpretation* 33 (1979) 376–88; R. A. Burridge, *Four Gospels, One Jesus?* (London: SPCK, 1994) 163–79.

1. IRENAEUS

Book III of Irenaeus's *Adversus Haereses* was written about 180 AD. Irenaeus comments on the origin of the four individual gospels, which he clearly accepts as 'Scripture', and sets out the earliest defence of the Church's fourfold Gospel. His main point is clear: there is one Gospel in fourfold form, held together by one Spirit (*Adv. Haer.* III.11.8).

Irenaeus frequently refers to 'the Gospel', 'the Gospel according to . . .' and only very rarely to 'four gospels'.[6] The Gospel is primarily the faith proclaimed and transmitted by the apostles, and only secondarily the written record 'reported' by such and such an evangelist.[7] If there is one Gospel, why are there four written accounts of it? Why four, no more, no less?

Irenaeus's attempt in Book III.11.8 to defend the number 'four' with analogies from both the natural and the spiritual worlds is well-known. His fourfold appeal to the four points of the compass and the four winds, the four-faced cherubim of Ezekiel 1 and the four living creatures of Revelation 4.7, the fourfold activity of the Word of God, and God's four covenants with mankind has been derided as a 'fundamental error'[8] and seen as a quite desperate attempt to defend a recent innovation.[9]

I do not think that this reading of Irenaeus is accurate: his discussion of the fourfold Gospel is much more sophisticated than many writers have supposed. All too often Irenaeus's comments on the number four are wrenched out of context; they are in fact a digression in a lengthy and often perceptive discussion of the authority and reliability of the witness of the Scriptures to one God, the Creator of all.

Irenaeus's views on the four gospels are established long before

---

[6] See A. Benoit, *Saint Irénée. Introduction à l'Étude de sa Théologie* (Paris: Presses Universitaires de France, 1960). Benoit notes that in Book III, 'Gospel' is used in the singular 41 times, 12 times for a particular Gospel, only 6 times in the plural. See also Yves-Marie Blanchard, *Aux Sources du Canon, Le Témoignage d'Irénée* (Paris: Cerf, 1993) 157, who counts 75 occurrences of 'Gospel' in Book III, only five of which are in the plural.

[7] See especially the Preface to Book III, and III.1.1. For a helpful discussion of the verbs used to refer to the 'reporting' or 'recording' activity of the evangelists, see Blanchard (n. 6) 161.

[8] O. Cullmann (n. 5) ET 50–2 claims that Irenaeus's justification of the fourfold Gospel 'is based on the same fundamental error as the Gnostics' "docetic" arguments against it': his appeal to four as a 'divinely ordained number' left out of account the purely human circumstances of the formation of the fourfold Gospel.

[9] Theodor Zahn, *Geschichte des neutestamentlichen Kanons* (Erlangen: Andreas Deichert, 1888) I, 153, scornfully rejects attempts to write off Irenaeus's arguments as 'dogmatic assertions and theosophical trifles'.

he offers reasons why there are four gospels, no more no less, in chapter 11 of Book III. In the opening chapter of Book III Irenaeus states clearly that the Gospel preached by the Apostles has been 'handed on to us in the Scriptures, so that the Gospel may be the foundation and pillar of our faith'. This image of the Gospel as the 'foundation and pillar' of the church, an allusion to 1 Tim 3.15, is repeated in chapter 11 and extended to the four gospels as the four pillars of the church.

In the important paragraphs which follow, Irenaeus comments further on the origins of the four gospels. After Pentecost the apostles proclaimed the Gospel orally; two of the apostles and two of their followers wrote gospels. Discussion of the human origins of the four written gospels is followed by emphasis on their theological unity: 'They have all declared to us that there is one God, Creator of heaven and earth, announced by the law and the prophets; and one Christ, the Son of God.' (III.1.1–2).

So right from the outset of Book III, the reader knows that the Church has the one God-given Gospel as recorded by two apostles and two of their immediate associates. In other words, the Gospel has been given to the Church in fourfold form, and chapter 11 with its set of four arguments, within each of which the number four plays a central role, is hardly necessary. We may even feel that the extended defence of the number 'four' in 11.8 weakens rather than strengthens Irenaeus's case, but his first readers probably thought otherwise, for they were accustomed to seeing hidden meaning in numbers. At the outset of the *Adversus Haereses* Irenaeus summarises the Valentinians' views and shows that the number four played an important role in their speculations.

For Irenaeus's readers, the number four would certainly have evoked solidity and harmonious proportion, precisely his intention. As an example of the evocative nature of the number four in Irenaeus's day, let me mention the Tetrapylon at Aphrodisias, completed just a few years before Irenaeus wrote. In the second century, Aphrodisias was one of the finest and most influential cities of the ancient world. The Tetrapylon, a superb gateway, has four recently re-erected columns, each one of which has four richly decorated faces. So Irenaeus's first readers may well have been impressed by his claims that the outward form of the Gospel should be harmoniously composed and well proportioned, just like God's creation (III.11.9).

Now to a rather different point. Irenaeus is fascinated by the beginnings of the four gospels. He refers to them three times in Book III, beginning at 11.8. Why does he cite and comment on the

4

openings of the four gospels so fully? He could have made his general point concerning one God the Creator from many other passages from the gospels. The considerable variations in the openings of the four gospels must have baffled both Christian and non-Christian alike. Irenaeus does state that the Valentinians seized on the errors and contradictions of the gospels (III.2.1).[10] So, probably with an eye on his opponents, Irenaeus stresses that in spite of their very different starting points, the four gospels do have a theological unity.[11] The Muratorian Fragment, to which we shall come in a moment, makes a similar point.

Although Irenaeus often cites passages from the four gospels accurately, he also regularly introduces sayings of Jesus with 'the Lord said', 'the Lord said in the Gospel', 'the Lord declared' without indicating from which particular Gospel the sayings are taken. At the end of the Preface to Book III, for example, a version of Luke 10.18 is introduced with the words 'the Lord declared'. In this case, the text is cited in abbreviated form: it is difficult to decide whether the variation occurs as the result of faulty memory, Irenaeus's knowledge of an otherwise unattested textual tradition, or his use of oral tradition. In the middle of his extended discussion of the opening chapters of Luke, Irenaeus refers to four verses from John 1, but without indicating that he has switched from Luke to John (III.10.3). Matt 12.18–21 is quoted as part of the discussion of the opening chapters of John's Gospel, but once again the reader is not told about the change of gospels. Similar phenomena occur elsewhere. This is not surprising once we recognize that for Irenaeus, 'the Gospel' and in particular the words of Jesus have a higher authority than the individual writings of the evangelists, even though the gospels are referred to occasionally as 'Scriptures'.

Irenaeus is able to cite the written gospels both carefully and carelessly,[12] to weave together loosely passages from two or more gospels, and to introduce sayings with 'the Lord said', some of which seem to be taken from the written gospels, some from oral tradition. The fact that these various phenomena are found in a writer for whom the fourfold Gospel is fundamental stands as a

---

[10] '. . . in accusationem convertuntur ipsarum Scripturarum, quasi non recte habeant, neque sint ex auctoritate et quia varie sint dictae . . .' I have used the edition of the Latin text in *Irénée de Lyon. Contre les Hérésies*, III.II (eds. A. Rousseau and L. Doutreleau; Sources Chrétiennes 211; Paris: Cerf, 1974) which includes the Greek fragments and a retroversion of the Latin into Greek.

[11] See Th. Zahn (n. 9) II, 43 and H. Merkel, *Die Widersprüche zwischen den Evangelien; Ihre polemische und apologetische Behandlung in der alten Kirche bis zu Augustin* (Tübingen: Mohr, 1971) 42–3.

[12] Matt 11.27 is cited in three different ways in IV.6.1, 3, 7.

warning sign for all students of Gospel traditions in the second century. Earlier Christian writers may also value the written gospels highly even though they appeal directly either to the words of Jesus, or to oral tradition, or even though they link topically sayings of Jesus taken from two or more gospels. Irenaeus was not the only writer who cites 'words of the Lord', and does not tell us whether he is quoting from written gospels or from oral tradition.

By the time Irenaeus wrote in about 180 AD, the fourfold Gospel was very well established. Irenaeus is not defending an innovation, but explaining why, unlike the heretics, the church has four gospels, no more, no less: she has received four written accounts of the one Gospel from the apostles and their immediate followers.[13]

2. THE MURATORIAN FRAGMENT

The second pillar in most discussions of the origin of the fourfold Gospel has been the Muratorian Fragment, generally dated to just before or just after Irenaeus's *Adversus Haereses*. Is this view still tenable, in spite of attempts to date the Fragment to the fourth century? Or is this pillar beginning to crumble?

In 1992 Geoffrey Hahneman picked up and developed a case for a fourth century date first defended by A. Sundberg in 1968.[14] Even though they have now won a handful of converts, especially on the other side of the Atlantic,[15] I do not think that the case for a fourth century date has been made out. I shall do no more than refer briefly to their three main points.

First, the cornerstone of the traditional dating has always been the Fragment's reference to Hermas's composition of the *Shepherd* 'nuperrime', very recently, in our times, in the city of Rome, while bishop Pius, his brother, was occupying the episcopal chair of the church of the city of Rome (lines 73–6), – i.e. not all that long after

[13] Cf. A. Benoit (n. 6, 117): 'La justification irénéenne ne veut pas être une démonstration, elle ne fait qu'augmenter la crédibilité du fait accepté par ailleurs.' T. C. Skeat, 'Irenaeus and the Four-Gospel Canon', *NovT* 34 (1992) 193–9, claims that in his celebrated identification of the four evangelists with the four living creatures of the Apocalypse, Irenaeus has used an earlier source. His case is strong but not conclusive, so I have not drawn on it in this paper.

[14] See n. 3 above.

[15] In his article 'Muratorian Fragment' in *The Anchor Bible Dictionary* (ed. D. N. Freedman; New York: Doubleday, 1992), G. A. Robbins claims that Sundberg's thesis 'has won considerable acceptance and further confirmation' (IV, 929). In his article 'Canon, New Testament' in the same Dictionary, H. Y. Gamble accepts Sundberg's thesis cautiously (I, 856), as does H. Koester, *Ancient Christian Gospels: their History and Development* (London: SCM; Philadelphia: Trinity, 1990) 243.

140 AD.[16] Hahneman, however, claims that all the Fragment's information about the *Shepherd* is 'erroneous or misleading'. He redates the *Shepherd* to c. 100 AD and then argues that the Fragment's attribution of the *Shepherd* to Hermas is fourth century pseudonymity designed to discredit the *Shepherd*. But since the *Shepherd* is still listed in the Fragment as 'recommended reading', this seems implausible.[17]

Secondly, the Fragment is said to fit naturally into fourth century catalogues of canonical writings; it is an anomaly in the second century. This line of argument is well off the mark, for the Fragment is not a canonical list or catalogue at all. Its genre is that of 'Einleitung' comments about the origin and authority of early Christian writings; the only two later uses of the Fragment are in prologues, not lists.[18]

Thirdly, the Fragment is allegedly out of line with other evidence for the development of the canon. In my judgement none of the Fragment's comments is anomalous in a second century setting; many fit much more readily into that setting than into a fourth century context.[19] I shall now explore this point with reference to the Fragment's comments on the gospels.

There is general agreement that the Fragment's comments on Luke were preceded by comments on Matthew and Mark. The second line could well be a title for Luke's Gospel: the third book of the Gospel according to Luke.[20] Just like Irenaeus, the Fragment uses both the formal phrase, 'evangelium secundum Lucam', a direct translation of εὐαγγέλιον κατὰ Λουκᾶν (a phrase to which

[16] I have used the critical edition edited (with a facsimile reproduction) by S. P. Tregelles, *Canon Muratorianus* (Oxford: Clarendon, 1867). Tregelles's learned notes are still worth consulting. See also H. Lietzmann's edition, *Das Muratorische Fragment und die monarchianischen Prologe zu den Evangelien* (Kleine Texte i; Bonn, 1902).

[17] Similarly, E. Ferguson in his critical review of Hahneman's monograph in *JTS* 44 (1993) 691–7: 'The pseudonymity would seem to be of doubtful value in a polemic against the Shepherd in the fourth century.' See also E. Ferguson's discussion of Sundberg's theory in 'Canon Muratori: Date and Provenance', *Studia Patristica* 18 (1982) 677–83.

[18] Cf. J.-D. Kaestli: 'Par son contenu et par sa forme, le *CM* (Canon de Muratori) est plus proche du genre des "prologues" que de celui des "listes canoniques"', 'La place du *Fragment de Muratori* dans l'histoire du canon. À propos de la thèse de Sundberg et Hahneman', *Cristianesimo nella Storia* 15 (1994) 609–34, here 616. Similarly E. Ferguson (n. 17) 696.

[19] For similar conclusions, see E. Ferguson (n. 17); J.-D. Kaestli (n. 18); P. Henne, 'La Datation du *Canon de Muratori*', *RB* 100 (1993) 54–75; and W. Horbury, 'The Wisdom of Solomon in the Muratorian Fragment', *JTS* 45 (1994) 149–59.

[20] A. T. Ehrhardt suggests that the comment about Luke in lines 6–7, 'dominum tamen nec ipse vidit in carne', is sufficient evidence 'to assume that Papias was responsible for the fragmentary remark about St. Mark in the Muratorian Fragment': 'The Gospels in the Muratorian Fragment' in his *The Framework of the New Testament Stories* (Manchester: Manchester University, 1964) 11–36, here 13; this article was first published in German in *Ostkirchen Studien* 2 (1953) 121–38.

I shall return later), and also uses the plural, 'fourth of the gospels' (line 9, and similarly in lines 17 and 20).

The Fragment comments more fully on the origin of 'the fourth of the gospels' than on any other writing.[21] The attempt to link the origin of this Gospel to the whole apostolic circle smacks of apologetic: the Fourth Gospel, it is claimed, stems ultimately from revelation. This thoroughgoing defence of the Fourth Gospel would surely not have been needed in the fourth century, but we do know that in the latter part of the second century there were doubts in some circles about the Fourth Gospel, most notably among the Alogi and the followers of the anti-Montanist Gaius.

Andrew is the only apostle who is named at this point. This is not surprising, since in John 1.40 Andrew is identified by name as the first person to respond to John's witness to Jesus. In the Fourth Gospel Andrew is given prominence which he does not have in the other three gospels. As we shall see shortly, Papias also singles out Andrew for special mention and in so doing reveals his knowledge of the Fourth Gospel.

The Fragment's lengthy defence of the Fourth Gospel includes in lines 16 to 26 an important reference to the fourfold Gospel. The Fragment concedes that different beginnings are taught in the various Gospel books, yet insists that they are held together by one primary Spirit. This is surely a response to critics who have pounced on the different beginnings of the gospels.[22] As in other lines, we are close to Irenaeus, though there is no sign of verbal dependence.

I have already drawn attention to the way Irenaeus comments at length on the beginnings of the gospels, probably partly in response to critics. Similarly in the Fragment.[23] In lines 7–8 the opening of Luke's story is referred to. In lines 16–26 a theological response is made to the criticism that the gospels have different beginnings: by the one primary Spirit, the central themes of the story of Christ are found in all four gospels. As with Irenaeus, the fourfold Gospel is not an innovation, but it does need to be defended against the jibes of critics who poke fun at the different openings of the gospels.

Who did this? As I noted above, Irenaeus refers to the Valentinians. I also suspect that Celsus, or some other pagan critic may well be lurking behind Irenaeus's comments and lines 16–26 of the

---

[21] See especially A. T. Ehrhardt (n. 20) 18–25.

[22] So also, R. M. Grant, *The Earliest Lives of Jesus* (London: SPCK, 1961) 31.

[23] See also Th. Zahn (n. 9) II, 43.

Fragment. Writing between 177 and 180, just a few years before Irenaeus wrote Book III of the *Adversus Haereses*, Celsus knew all four gospels and had a particular interest in their early chapters. According to Origen, Celsus's Jew claimed that some Christians, as if somewhat the worse from drink, 'alter the original text of the Gospel three or four or several times over, and they change its character to enable them to deny difficulties in the face of criticism'.[24] I take this to be a reference to differences between the 'three or four' canonical gospels.[25]

The Fragment refers to the two parousias of Christ and rather optimistically claims that this schema is found in all four gospels. 'Everything is declared in all the gospels . . . concerning his two comings, the first in humility when he was despised, which is past, the second, glorious in royal power, which is still in the future.' This schema is first developed fully by Justin Martyr, though I have argued that it is partly anticipated in Matthew's Gospel.[26] The two parousias schema is very prominent in Justin's writings; it is also found in his *Apology*, in Irenaeus, Tertullian, Hippolytus, Origen, and the *Anabathmoi Iakobou*, but not, as far as I can discover, in fourth century writings.

The Fragment confirms that the fourfold Gospel was well established towards the end of the second century.[27] Quite independently, the Fragment and Irenaeus make similar points concerning the fourfold Gospel: in spite of what critics may say about the different beginnings of the gospels, there is one Gospel in fourfold form, held together by one Spirit.[28] Needless to say, the points I have emphasised are conspicuous by their absence in the recent attempts to locate the Fragment in the fourth century.

---

[24] *Contra Celsum* II.27 (ed. and transl. by H. Chadwick; Cambridge: CUP, 1953) 90. See also V.56 where Origen responds to Celsus's jibes concerning the number of angels at the tomb of Jesus. For other evidence of the problems caused by differences in the gospels, see H. Merkel, *Die Widersprüche* (n. 11) and *Die Pluralität der Evangelien als theologisches und exegetisches Problem in der alten Kirche* (Bern: Peter Lang, 1978).

[25] So too H. Merkel, *Widersprüche* (n. 11) 11. See also T. Baarda, 'ΔΙΑΦΩΝΙΑ–ΣΥΜΦΩΝΙΑ: Factors in the Harmonization of the Gospels, Especially in the Diatessaron of Tatian', in *Gospel Traditions in the Second Century* (ed. W. L. Petersen; Notre Dame and London: University of Notre Dame, 1989) 133–5, reprinted in his *Essays on the Diatessaron* (Kampen: Kok Pharos, 1994) 29–48; R. M. Grant (n. 22) 59–60.

[26] G. N. Stanton, 'The Two Parousias of Christ: Justin Martyr and Matthew', in *From Jesus to John*, FS M. de Jonge (ed. M. C. de Boer; Sheffield: JSOT, 1993) 183–96.

[27] A. T. Ehrhardt (n. 20) 11 suggests that the Fragment was produced at Rome, probably under Zephyrinus, 197–217.

[28] I am not convinced by A. T. Ehrhardt's claim (n. 20, 14–15) that the reference to John as 'ex discipulis' in line 16 betrays its origin from Irenaeus who refers to John the evangelist as 'the disciple of the Lord', but never refers to him as the son of Zebedee; this similarity could have arisen from independent use of the same tradition.

3. EARLY FOUR-GOSPEL CODICES

Could Irenaeus and the writer of the Muratorian Fragment have used codices containing all four gospels? In 1968 von Campenhausen denied vigorously that the references to the fourfold Gospel in Irenaeus and the Muratorian Fragment had anything to do with 'book production' or Christian use of a four-gospel codex.[29] In 1933, however, F. G. Kenyon had edited the recently discovered $\mathfrak{P}^{45}$, the Chester Beatty codex of the four gospels and Acts, and had noted that this new evidence meant that it was possible to believe that Irenaeus may have been accustomed to the sight of codices which contained all four gospels.[30] Kenyon dated the codex to the first half of the third century and concluded that it was the earliest example of a codex containing all four gospels.

Kenyon's dating of $\mathfrak{P}^{45}$ and his general observations on this codex have been widely agreed, though most scholars have overlooked his important comment on Irenaeus's probable knowledge of four-Gospel codices. In recent years our knowledge of Biblical papyri and codices has increased very considerably: we now have fairly solid evidence for two further four-gospel codices which are even earlier than $\mathfrak{P}^{45}$.

$\mathfrak{P}^{75}$, the Bodmer papyrus of Luke and John, has attracted plenty of attention from text critics. There is general agreement that it dates from early in the third century; the editors dated it to between 175 and 225 AD. However, the possibility that its fragments of Luke and John formed the second of two single-quire codices sewn together does not seem to have been considered until 1994.[31] Why would Luke and John be bound together without Matthew and Mark? It is just possible to imagine a codex containing Matthew and John, the two gospels considered to have been written by apostles. But a codex containing only Luke and John is most unexpected. In fact we have no other example of a two-gospel codex.[32] T. C. Skeat has calculated that $\mathfrak{P}^{75}$ contained 72 leaves,

---

[29] H. von Campenhausen (n. 2) ET 173–4.

[30] *The Chester Beatty Biblical Papyri*, Fasciculi I and II, *The Gospels and Acts, General Introduction and Text* (London: Emery Walker, 1933) here I, 13. $\mathfrak{P}^{45}$ is made up of quires of two leaves – a single sheet of papyrus folded in two. The letters are small; the scribe was no calligrapher.

[31] T. C. Skeat, 'The Origin of the Christian Codex', *ZPE* 102 (1994) 263–8, here 264.

[32] $\mathfrak{P}^{53}$, third century, with fragments of Matthew and Acts in the same hand, is an interesting possible partial exception, though the fragments may not be from the same codex. If they are, and if the codex included all four gospels, it would have run to a highly improbable 300 to 350 leaves. So a codex with one or two gospels, plus Acts, is possible. Cf. K. Aland,

and noted that a codex of double this size would have been almost impossible to handle. So he concludes that $\mathfrak{P}^{75}$ may have originally consisted of a single-quire codex containing Matthew and Mark, sewn together with another containing Luke and John, and then bound.[33]

A strong case has recently been made out in this journal by T. C. Skeat for an even earlier four-Gospel codex.[34] $\mathfrak{P}^{64}$, the fragments of Matthew held at Magdalen College Oxford, was first edited by Colin Roberts in 1953 and dated to the late second century on the grounds that its hand is a precursor of the style known as Biblical Uncial or Biblical Majuscule. These are the three fragments which have attracted so much attention in the media since a sensationalist article published in *The Times* of London on 24 December 1994 reported C. P. Thiede's claim that they date from the mid-first century.[35]

There has never been any doubt that $\mathfrak{P}^{67}$, with its further fragments of Matthew now in Barcelona, was from the same codex as $\mathfrak{P}^{64}$. For some six months before the media became interested in $\mathfrak{P}^{64}$, T. C. Skeat had been working intensively on $\mathfrak{P}^{64}$ + $\mathfrak{P}^{67}$, as well as $\mathfrak{P}^4$, fragments of Luke in the Bibliothèque nationale in Paris. Skeat has now shown beyond reasonable doubt that $\mathfrak{P}^{64}$ + $\mathfrak{P}^{67}$ + $\mathfrak{P}^4$ are from the same single-quire codex, probably our earliest four-Gospel codex which may date from the late second century.

In his *NTS* article Skeat does not comment on the significance of one of the codex's most striking features, its double columns.[36]

Repertorium der griechischen christlichen Papyri 1 (Berlin and New York: De Gruyter, 1976) 53 and 283. See also J. van Haelst, *Catalogue des Papyrus littéraires juifs et chrétiens*, Papyrologie 1 (Paris: Publications de la Sorbonne, 1976) Nr 380, 381.

[33] T. C. Skeat (n. 31) 264. In his most recent article, 'The Oldest Manuscript of the Four Gospels?', *NTS* 43 (1997) 31, Skeat mentions in passing the possibility that perhaps there were two volumes, i.e. two single-quire codices bound separately.

[34] T. C. Skeat (1997, n. 33) 1–34.

[35] See G. N. Stanton, *Gospel Truth? New Light on Jesus and the Gospels* (London: Harper-Collins, 1995) 1–19. For Thiede's theory, see his 'Papyrus Magdalen Greek 17 (Gregory–Aland $\mathfrak{P}^{64}$): A Reappraisal', *ZPE* 105 (1995) 13–20; reprinted in *Tyndale Bulletin* 46 (1995) 29–42. The theory has been rejected by numerous scholars, all of whom accept Roberts's original date for $\mathfrak{P}^{64}$, late second century. See especially, J. Neville Birdsall, 'The Dating of the Magdalen Papyrus', *The Church Times*, 6 January 1995; Klaus Wachtel, '$\mathfrak{P}$64/67: Fragmente des Matthäusevangeliums aus dem 1. Jahrhundert?', *ZPE* 107 (1995) 73–80; Peter M. Head, 'The Date of the Magdalen Papyrus of Matthew (P. Magd. Gr. 17 = P64): A Response to C. P. Thiede', *Tyndale Bulletin* 46 (1995) 251–85; D. C. Parker, 'Was Matthew Written before 50 CE? The Magdalen Papyrus of Matthew', *ET* 107 (1995) 40–3; S. R. Pickering in *NT Textual Research Update* 2 (1994) 94–8 and 3 (1995) 22–5; P. Grelot, 'Remarques sur un Manuscrit de l'Évangile de Matthieu', *RSR* 83 (1995) 403–5; J. K. Elliott in *NovT* 38 (1996) 393–9.

[36] After I had completed the research summarized in this paragraph, T. C. Skeat wrote to me (10 July 1996) as follows: 'The two-column format became the standard form throughout

The format of two columns to the page is rare in papyrus codices. This is the only example of a two column Greek NT papyrus manuscript, though there are four examples in early fragments of OT papyri.[37] The narrow columns, with only about 15 letters in each column, would have assisted reading aloud in the context of worship.[38] The columns have about the same number of letters as each of the three columns of Codex Vaticanus, and only about three fewer than the four columns of Codex Sinaiticus. The two great fourth century manuscripts were almost certainly intended for liturgical use. So the use of two columns in $\mathfrak{P}^{64}$ + $\mathfrak{P}^{67}$ + $\mathfrak{P}^4$ is very probably an indication of a high-class codex, a splendid 'pulpit edition' intended for liturgical use.[39]

There are several other indications that this codex was an *édition de luxe*.[40] The codex was planned and executed meticulously: the skill of the scribe in constructing it is most impressive.[41] All these features indicate a most handsome edition of the four gospels which would have been expensive to produce. This codex does not look at all like an experiment by a scribe working out ways to include four gospels in one codex: it certainly had predecessors much earlier in the second century.

The three early codices are not clones of one another, for they are all constructed and executed quite differently.[42] In all probability they had a number of predecessors. So well before the end of the

the whole of the Middle Ages, and has survived almost down to the present day in printed bibles and prayer-books. Why? I have never seen this considered, but I suppose the answer must be that this is the easiest to read. Certainly reading the lessons from $\mathfrak{P}^{45}$ with its very long lines and small script would have been quite difficult, and no doubt it wasn't intended for liturgical use.'

[37] See E. G. Turner's list of papyrus codices written in two columns, *The Typology of the Early Codex* (Pittsburgh: University of Pennsylvania, 1977) 36.

[38] In 1970 the NEB was published with one single wide column on each page. In 1989 the REB reverted to the more traditional two-column format, partly in order to facilitate reading aloud in the context of worship.

[39] Cf. E. G. Turner (n. 37) 36–7. Van Haelst (n. 32) Nr 336, 336, even says that this is the oldest example of a codex with two columns; presumably he means the oldest *Biblical* codex, though in the light of Turner's list, this is a doubtful claim.

[40] This is Skeat's phrase (n. 33) 26.

[41] C. H. Roberts noted that 'in its handsome script as well as in its organization . . . it is a thoroughgoing literary production'. *Manuscript, Society and Belief in Early Christian Egypt* (London: The British Academy, 1979) 23. Although Skeat (n. 33, 2 and 6–7) has been unable to find any trace of two of the examples given by Roberts – three different positions for punctuation as well as omission and quotation signs – he concurs with Roberts's general conclusions.

[42] $\mathfrak{P}^{45}$, the latest of the three, is the least impressive hand. Whereas $\mathfrak{P}^{45}$ is made up of quires of two leaves – a single sheet of papyrus folded in two, $\mathfrak{P}^{75}$ probably contained two single-quire codices bound together. $\mathfrak{P}^{64}$ + $\mathfrak{P}^{67}$ + $\mathfrak{P}^4$ is a two-column, single-quire codex.

second century there was a very well established tradition of four-Gospel codices. All three papyrus codices were found in Egypt; the evidence of Irenaeus and the Muratorian Fragment points towards the west. So the fourfold Gospel seems to have been well established in both east and west at the end of the second century, and probably very much earlier.

However, for two reasons some caution is necessary. First, it is just possible that one or more of these three codices was in fact written in the west. If that seems an unlikely scenario, we need to bear in mind that a fragment of Irenaeus, POxy 405 (from a roll) travelled from Lyon to Oxyrhynchus within twenty years of its production, 'not long after the ink was dry on the author's manuscript' to quote Roberts's memorable comment.[43]

Secondly, papyrologists are always rightly extremely cautious about dating handwriting styles and developments in the production of manuscripts. On the other hand, the recent media attention has ensured that the dating of $\mathfrak{P}^{64} + \mathfrak{P}^{67} + \mathfrak{P}^4$ has been considered carefully by several papyrologists. Working independently, they have all dated this codex to the end of the second century.[44]

4. EARLIER ROOTS

Irenaeus, the Muratorian Fragment, and the three earliest codices of the gospels all suggest that by the latter decades of the second century, and probably much earlier, the fourfold Gospel was well established and widely accepted. At what point, and under what circumstances were four gospels brought together? Since this was a major development within early Christianity, our critical instincts encourage us to search for answers. Before we resume the search, however, it is important to recall that there are no explicit comments on the fourfold Gospel before Irenaeus, and to note that knowledge and use of a plurality of gospels is not necessarily to be equated with acceptance of the fourfold Gospel.

Is it possible to trace the *roots* of the development of the fourfold Gospel to the first half of the second century? In discussion of this question, three issues are particularly important.

(i) I turn first to Justin Martyr, whose knowledge and use of the gospels shortly after the middle of the century is still much

---

[43] C. H. Roberts (n. 41) 53; Roberts notes some similarities with $\mathfrak{P}^{64} + \mathfrak{P}^{67} + \mathfrak{P}^4$, 23.
[44] See above, n. 35.

disputed, in spite of intense research and debate. I am concerned with only one issue: did Justin anticipate the adoption of the four-fold Gospel, or did he anticipate his pupil Tatian's harmony?

In Justin's well-known account of eucharistic worship in *1 Apol.* 67 he refers to the reading of 'the memoirs of the apostles or the writings of the prophets, as long as time allows'. Here apostolic writings are being accorded a similar authority to the writings of the prophets, which, as for Irenaeus, is a Christian short-hand way of referring to the OT Scriptures. But what are the 'memoirs of the apostles'? In the preceding chapter the reader is told explicitly that they are 'the gospels' (*1 Apol.* 66), the first Christian occurrence of the plural. This is not a later gloss, for, as Luise Abramowski has shown, Justin does add similar explanatory phrases for his readers.[45]

In addition to these two references to 'the memoirs of the apostles' in the *Apology*, Justin uses the phrase thirteen times in one section of the *Dialogue*, chapters 98–107, in which he seems to have incorporated his own earlier extended anti-gnostic exposition of Psalm 22, and in which he emphasizes the 'writtenness' of 'the memoirs of the apostles'. At one point in this exposition Justin refers to Peter's memoirs; from the context this is a reference to Mark's Gospel (*Dialogue* 106.3). So in both the *Apology* and the *Dialogue* the 'memoirs' are identified as written gospels.

How many gospels does Justin accept? In *Dialogue* 103.8 he refers to 'the memoirs composed by his apostles and those who followed them' (ἐν γὰρ τοῖς ἀπομνημονεύμασιν, ἅ φημι ὑπὸ τῶν ἀποστόλων αὐτοῦ καὶ τῶν ἐκείνοις παρακολουθησάντων συντετάχθαι . . .). Although Justin never refers to the number of the gospels he accepts, this passage implies that there were at least four. It is surprising how many recent writers have ignored this point.[46] There is general agreement that Justin used Matthew and Luke regularly, and that Mark's Gospel is referred to once (*Dialogue* 106.3). Justin's knowledge of the Fourth Gospel is much disputed, but I am convinced that *1 Apology* 61.4 draws on John 3.3–5, and that *Dialogue* 88.7 shows knowledge of John 1.19–20. Justin's failure to refer to John's Gospel more frequently is puzzling, but it may be related to his strong interest in infancy narratives, and in ethical teaching and futurist eschatological sayings – all in somewhat short supply in this Gospel. Since there is no clear

---

[45] 'Die "Erinnerungen der Apostel" bei Justin', in *Das Evangelium und die Evangelien* (ed. P. Stuhlmacher; Tübingen: Mohr, 1983) 341–54, esp. 341.

[46] It was noted already by S. Tregelles in 1867 (n. 16, 71): 'no smaller number (than four) could be implied by the two groups'.

evidence for Justin's knowledge of any gospels other than the canonical four, we can be all but certain that he had in mind Matthew, Mark, Luke, and John, no more, no less.

Justin uses the singular 'Gospel' in only two passages, but in both cases he is referring to written traditions. At *Dialogue* 10.2 Justin's opponent Trypho states that he has read with appreciation the commands of Jesus 'in the so-called Gospel'. At *Dialogue* 100.1 there is a similar usage: a citation of Matt 11.27 is introduced with the words, ἐν τῷ εὐαγγελίῳ γέγραπται εἰπών. These two references recall Irenaeus's much more frequent use of the phrase, 'in the Gospel'. For Justin, as for Irenaeus, the sayings of Jesus are of special importance: they are recorded 'in the Gospel', 'in the memoirs of the apostles'.

Unlike Irenaeus, Justin is not interested either in the authorship or in the distinctive features of the individual gospels. However, like Irenaeus, Justin knows at least four written 'memoirs' or gospels, which can be referred to collectively as 'the Gospel'. Of course Justin does not have Irenaeus's clear conception of the fourfold Gospel, but the references in his extant writings to written gospels suggest that he may well have had a four-Gospel codex in his catechetical school in Rome by about 150 AD.[47]

At this point account must be taken of the ways Justin cites sayings of Jesus. The textual evidence is undeniably complex, and it is not easy to account for the variations in wording from Matthew and Luke.[48] In his important recent study W. L. Petersen has shown that some of Justin's harmonised traditions can be traced in his pupil Tatian's more thoroughgoing harmony.[49] Helmut Koester has gone further and suggested that 'Justin was composing the *one* inclusive new Gospel which would make its predecessors, Matthew and Luke (and possibly Mark) obsolete'.[50] If one focuses attention on the wording of the citations, Justin's use of, or even composition of, a harmony of sayings of Jesus is undeniable.

But how can such a conclusion be squared with Justin's references to written gospels? I think it is likely that for catechetical

[47] E. J. Goodspeed (n. 1, 38) is much less cautious: 'Justin became a Christian at Ephesus as early as 135 AD, and probably there became attached to the fourfold gospel.'

[48] See especially, A. J. Bellinzoni, *The Sayings of Jesus in the Writings of Justin Martyr* (Leiden: Brill, 1967) and H. Koester (n. 15) 360–402.

[49] See W. L. Petersen, 'Textual Evidence of Tatian's Dependence upon Justin's ΑΠΟΜΝΗΜΟΝΕΥΜΑΤΑ', *NTS* 36 (1990) 512–34.

[50] H. Koester, 'The Text of the Synoptic Gospels in the Second Century', in *Gospel Traditions in the Second Century* (ed. W. L. Petersen; Notre Dame and London: University of Notre Dame, 1989) 30, and cf. 32.

purposes (and possibly even to disarm critics)[51] Justin himself gathered together topically harmonised clusters of sayings of Jesus from written gospels, primarily Matthew and Luke.[52] In this respect he partially anticipates Tatian, but I do not believe that the corollary is an intention to do away with the 'memoirs of the apostles', i.e. the written gospels in which the Saviour's words were recorded (cf. *Dialogue* 8.2).

The opening programmatic exchange between Justin and Trypho in the *Dialogue* strongly suggests that Justin's references to the sayings of Jesus are based on written gospels. Justin recalls his own conversion experience and the passionate desire which possessed him for the prophets, and for those great men who are 'the friends of Christ', surely the apostles (8.2). Justin refers immediately to the 'dreadful majesty' of the Saviour's words and the importance of carrying them out: there is a clear implication that the words of Jesus have been written down by 'the friends of Christ'. Trypho responds with a taunt: Justin has been deceived, for he has been following men (plural) of no account, once again surely a reference to the apostles who have recorded the words of the Saviour.

Like Irenaeus, Justin set great store by the words of Jesus. So for catechetical purposes he seems to have used written gospels to make his own harmonised collections of sayings of Jesus, linking them together topically. On the other hand, Justin's knowledge and use of four written gospels is clear. Although in some respects he anticipates Tatian, in his use of written gospels alongside harmonised sayings of Jesus his successor is Irenaeus. In the light of our earlier conclusions, Justin's reference to at least four written gospels in *Dialogue* 103.8 suggests that he may well have possessed a four-gospel codex in the library of his catechetical school.

(ii) Martin Hengel has drawn attention to Zahn's and Harnack's views on the titles of the gospels.[53] In my judgement all three scholars have correctly insisted that from early in the second century there was a profound conviction that there was *one* Gospel 'according to' individual evangelists. The evidence is so strong and so widespread that here we are surely in touch with another one of the roots of Irenaeus's conviction that there is one Gospel in fourfold form.

---

[51] W. L. Petersen mentioned the latter possibility to me in a letter dated 1.9.1996.

[52] Similarly A. J. Bellinzoni (n. 48); E. Osborn, *Justin Martyr* (Tübingen: Mohr, 1973) 132; and L. Abramowski (n. 45) 352–3.

[53] M. Hengel, 'The Titles of the Gospels and the Gospel of Mark' in his *Studies in the Gospel of Mark* (London: SCM, 1985) 64–84.

Hengel rightly attached weight to the evidence of the papyri. The opening and closing leaves of papyri codices are usually missing, so the clear inscriptio εὐαγγέλιον κατὰ 'Ιωάννην in 𝔓66 from about 200 is striking. It is in the same hand as the rest of the text, but it has been added to the opening page a little awkwardly; the sub-scriptio would have been identical. In 𝔓75, perhaps only a couple of decades later, we have two examples on the same page of εὐαγγέ-λιον κατά . . ., a subscriptio to Luke and an inscriptio to John.54

The evidence of 𝔓66 and 𝔓75 is consistent with the evidence of Irenaeus and the Muratorian Fragment: in the second half of the second century in many circles there was a strong conviction that there was *one* Gospel, according to a particular evangelist. But what about the first half of the second century? Helmut Koester rejects Martin Hengel's theory that from early in the second century the gospels must have had εὐαγγέλιον κατά . . . attached to them as titles by claiming that Hengel has anachronistically read back to the beginning of the century evidence of papyri from the end of the second century.55

However, Koester and Hengel agree on one crucial point: as soon as Christian communities regularly used more than one written account of the actions and teaching of Jesus, it would have been necessary to distinguish them by some form of title, especially in the context of readings at worship.56 That first happened as soon as Matthew had completed his writing, for many Christians then had two accounts of the story of Jesus, Matthew's and Mark's.

There is plenty of evidence for use of a plurality of gospels in many circles in the first half of the second century. Papias, now dated to c. 110 by several scholars, will serve as an example. He certainly knew Matthew and Mark. I am convinced Papias also knew John: there is no other reasonable explanation for his list of disciples in the order, Andrew, Peter, Philip and Thomas – precisely the order in which they appear in the Fourth Gospel, an order found nowhere else, though Andrew is singled out in line 14 of the Muratorian Fragment as the apostle who received the revelation that John, 'ex discipulis', should write down 'quartum evangeliorum'.

---

54 Hengel also notes that a page from 𝔓64 + 𝔓67 + 𝔓4, 'which belong together' has the inscriptio εὐαγγέλιον κατὰ Μαθθαῖον (n. 53, 66). However, this example should not be set alongside the evidence of 𝔓66 and 𝔓75, for the inscriptio (which is now located with the 𝔓4 fragments of Luke) is not in the same hand; it probably comes from a fly-leaf added to the codex at a later point.

55 H. Koester, 'From the Kerygma-Gospel to Written Gospels', *NTS* 35 (1989) 361–81, here 373 n. 2.

56 Cf. H. Koester (n. 55, 381 n. 1) and M. Hengel (n. 53, 74–81).

So when early Christian communities used more than one gospel, how were they differentiated, particularly in the context of worship? What are the possible terms which could have been used to distinguish what we now know as Matthew from Mark? Certainly not βίος, for which there is no evidence; and not Justin's ἀπομνη-μονεύματα, which was not used by any Christian prior to Justin.[57]

As far as I can see, there is only one candidate, εὐαγγέλιον. As is well known, in the first half of the second century it is not always easy to decide whether εὐαγγέλιον refers to oral proclamation or to a written account of the actions and teaching of Jesus. However, we may be confident that εὐαγγέλιον refers to a writing in four passages in the *Didache* (8.2; 11.3; twice in 15.3–4) which cannot be written off as late second century redaction; twice in Ignatius's letter to the Smyrneans (5.1 and 7.2), and also in *2 Clement* 8.5.[58] Once εὐαγγέλιον began to be used to refer to a writing, it was a natural extension to use this term as a title. What more appropriate way was there of referring to individual gospels than as εὐαγγέλιον κατά . . .? So one of the roots of the fourfold Gospel was undoubtedly the very early use of the term εὐαγγέλιον to refer to a written gospel, and the strong conviction that there was one Gospel, 'according to' a particular evangelist.

(iii) The very early separation of Luke and Acts is another indication of the deep roots of the fourfold Gospel.[59] It is generally accepted that Luke and Acts were originally written on two separate rolls: they could not have been squeezed onto one roll; the short Preface to Acts with its rededication to Theophilus was a conventional way of introducing the second roll of a single work. Once Christian scribes began to use the codex early in the second century, it would have been possible for Luke and Acts to have been juxtaposed in the same codex, with or without other writings, but as far as we know, this did not ever happen.[60] Luke and Acts are separated in the Muratorian Fragment, and in all the lists and catalogues of canonical writings. Irenaeus is the first writer to

---

[57] See R. M. Grant (n. 22) 119–20.

[58] For fuller discussion, see G. N. Stanton, 'Matthew: *BIBΛΟΣ, EYAΓΓEΛION*, or *BIOΣ?*', in *The Four Gospels 1992*, FS Frans Neirynck (ed. F. van Segbroeck *et al.*; Leuven: University, 1992) 1187–1202. For a different view, see R. H. Gundry, 'EYAΓΓEΛION: How Soon a Book?', *JBL* 115 (1996) 321–5.

[59] For discussion of the relationship of Luke and Acts, see M. C. Parsons and R. I. Pervo, *Rethinking the Unity of Luke and Acts* (Minneapolis: Augsburg Fortress, 1993).

[60] 𝔓53 is a possible exception; see n. 32 above. B. M. Metzger, *The Canon of the New Testament: its Origin, Development, and Significance* (Oxford: Clarendon, 1987) 296, lists a few late examples of Luke coming fourth in a sequence of the four gospels, perhaps from a desire to bring the two books by Luke side by side.

stress the close relationship between Luke and Acts: he insists that if his opponents accepted Luke's Gospel, they should also accept Acts (*Adv. Haer.* III.14.3 and 4).

We are so accustomed to treating Luke and Acts as one single writing in two parts that it is easy to overlook the fact that in the second century Luke's Gospel and Acts circulated separately. Even in later centuries they were not brought together. Two explanations are currently given for the early separation of Luke and Acts. W. A. Strange has recently proposed that at Luke's death, Acts remained in draft form; it remained in obscurity until published in the third quarter of the second century, following editorial work by both a 'western' and a 'non-western' editor.[61] Even if this is a plausible solution to the textual problems of Acts, I do not think that Acts was unknown until the time of Irenaeus. Neither Irenaeus nor the Muratorian Fragment presses a case for accepting Acts; they both imply that the existence and authority of Acts had long been recognised. Irenaeus's use of Acts in polemic against his opponents would have been self-defeating if Acts had only recently become available, for Irenaeus insists that unlike some of the writings used by heretics, the writings the church accepts are ancient.[62]

I think that an alternative explanation is much more likely: the acceptance of Luke into the fourfold Gospel led to its early separation from Acts, probably before Marcion.[63] There was plenty of interest in the second century in the apostles, but even more interest in the sayings and actions of Jesus recorded 'in the Gospel'. Hence Acts seems to have remained somewhat in the shadow of 'the Gospel'.

Taken cumulatively, this evidence suggests that the adoption of the fourfold Gospel may well have taken place in some circles (though not necessarily everywhere) shortly before Justin's day. Before I comment further on the date of the emergence of the fourfold Gospel, I shall refer to explanations which have been advanced for this momentous development within early Christianity.

---

[61] W. A. Strange, *The Problem of the Text of Acts* (Cambridge: CUP, 1992) esp. 181–9.

[62] See A. Benoit (n. 6) 122–7 for a fuller discussion.

[63] Similarly, W. R. Farmer and D. M. Farkasfalvy, *The Formation of the New Testament Canon* (New York, 1983) 73, though they date the emergence of the fourfold Gospel somewhat later.

What were the key factors which led to emergence of the fourfold Gospel? Which form of explanation is preferable, a 'big bang' theory, or a theory of gradual development?

It has often been urged that the fourfold Gospel was adopted in order to counter the rapid growth and success of various groups of heretics, especially gnostics. Of course the production and use of gospels by gnostics may have encouraged 'the great church' to clarify its position. But if heretics were primarily in view, would it not have been wiser to opt for just one Gospel? Why four? When Irenaeus attacked the Valentinians of his day, he had to show that all four gospels supported the theological point he was making: it is hard to see how four gospels gave him a stronger case than one.

The same point is relevant when assessing whether or not the fourfold Gospel was an answer to Marcion.[64] It is hard to see how four gospels assisted the struggle against Marcion. Von Campenhausen's judgement is surely correct: 'That the new Gospel canon was particularly directed against Marcion cannot be deduced from its composition.'[65]

A political explanation has often been advanced. The fourfold Gospel is said to have been a compromise worked out between different regional preferences.[66] However it is difficult to find any evidence for the second century equivalent of the European parliament! The older view that individual gospels circulated only in limited geographical areas is no longer tenable:[67] the papyri, both Christian and non-Christian, indicate clearly that there was a great deal of contact between different regions around the Mediterranean.[68]

[64] See John Knox, *Marcion and the New Testament* (n. 1); so also K. L. Carroll (n. 1).

[65] H. von Campenhausen (n. 2) ET 171 n. 113. Elsewhere von Campenhausen accepts that Marcion was very influential on the emergence of the NT canon; for discussion, see F. Bovon, 'La structure canonique de l'Évangile et de l'Apôtre', *Cristianesimo nella Storia* 15 (1994) 559–76.

[66] W. R. Farmer and D. M. Farkasfalvy (n. 63) emphasize the importance of the decision taken by Irenaeus and Anicetus to agree to disagree over the date of Easter: 'there was no other moment in Church history when it is more likely that the fourfold Gospel canon was, in principle, implicitly agreed upon', 72. D. Trobisch also emphasizes the importance of this decision, reported by Eusebius, *H.E.* V.24.14: *Die Endredaktion des Neuen Testaments. Eine Untersuchung zur Entstehung der christlichen Bibel* (Freiburg: Universitätsverlag; Göttingen: Vandenhoeck & Ruprecht, 1996) 158–9.

[67] So too H. von Campenhausen (n. 2) ET 123: 'It is highly questionable whether the idea is correct, that originally each individual Gospel had its own territorial domain.'

[68] See especially E. J. Epp, 'New Testament Papyrus Manuscripts and Letter Carrying in Greco-Roman Times', in *The Future of Early Christianity*, FS H. Koester (ed. B. A. Pearson;

A very different view is preferable. I am convinced that the emergence of the fourfold Gospel is related to Christian adoption of the codex, for no roll could contain four gospels. This explanation is hardly new: in 1933 F. G. Kenyon noted that the Chester Beatty papyri confirmed that the Christian community was *addicted* to the codex rather than to the roll, and recognized that by bringing the four gospels into one codex, they were 'marked off as a single unit'.[69] But Kenyon's important observation went largely ignored until C. H. Roberts and T. C. Skeat set out in full the evidence for early Christian use of the codex and showed that Christian scribes borrowed a Roman invention which had not been an immediate success.[70]

The statistics are astonishing: among non-Christian papyri, rolls predominate until early in the fourth century, but Christian papyri are very nearly all fragments of codices. With only one possible exception, every single papyrus copy of the gospels is from a codex.[71]

Why did Christians have such a strong predilection for the codex? Skeat has recently rejected the reasons usually advanced for adoption of the codex and has insisted that the motive for adopting the codex 'must have been infinitely more powerful than anything hitherto considered'.[72] Skeat notes that the codex could contain the texts of all four gospels; no roll could do this. He then asks, 'What can have induced the Church so suddenly, and totally, to abandon rolls, and substitute not just codices but a single codex containing all four gospels?' He accepts that single gospels circulated as codices, but only as 'spin-offs', so to speak, of the four-Gospel codex. In his view, the production of the Fourth Gospel about 100 AD caused a crisis in the church: a formal decision was taken to publish the four gospels in a single codex, and as a result the codex became the norm for Christian writings. 'How the decision was reached we have no means of knowing. Clearly there

---

Minneapolis: Fortress, 1991) 35–56; E. J. Epp, 'The Papyrus Manuscripts of the New Testament', in *The Text of the New Testament in Contemporary Research*, FS B. M. Metzger (ed. B. D. Ehrman and M. W. Holmes; Grand Rapids: Eerdmans, 1995) 3–21, here 8–10.

[69] F. G. Kenyon (n. 30, Fasciculus I, 12f.).

[70] C. H. Roberts and T. C. Skeat, *The Birth of the Codex* (Oxford: The British Academy, 1983).

[71] The possible exception is 𝔓²² (= POxy, 1228) third century fragments of John 15 now in Glasgow with their recto inexplicably blank. It is worth noting that two of the three fragments of the Gospel of Thomas, POxy 654 and POxy 655 are from rolls; POxy 1 is from a papyrus codex. See *Nag Hammadi Codex II,2–7* (ed. B. Layton; Leiden: Brill, 1989) 96–7.

[72] T. C. Skeat (n. 31) 263–8, here 263.

must have been correspondence between the major churches, and perhaps conferences.'[73]

David Trobisch has recently defended a partly similar theory.[74] He claims that the early Christian use of the codex and of *nomina sacra* can be accounted for only by positing deliberate decisions concerning the appropriate format for canonical writings. Trobisch, however, studiously refrains from stating when and where this guideline for the preparation of Christian manuscripts was drawn up.[75]

The strength of the theories advanced by Skeat and Trobisch is that they draw attention to the rapid and universal adoption of the codex for what became in due course canonical writings. However, I am not completely convinced by either theory. Both theories require a much higher level of structure and centralised organization within early second century Christianity than I think likely.[76] If (as Skeat suggests) the four-Gospel codex *preceded* the circulation of single-gospel codices, it must have been adopted soon after the beginning of the second century, for we have in $\mathfrak{P}^{52}$ (usually dated to c. 125 AD) a single-gospel codex. But a date soon after the turn of the century is difficult to square with the ways written gospels and oral gospel traditions were used at that time.

My own view is that Christian scribes first experimented with single-gospel codices by adopting the Roman invention of the use of pocket editions of literary works referred to in 84–86 AD by Martial. In *Epigram* I.2 Martial recommends that travellers should carry his poems in copies with small parchment pages which could be held in one hand, presumably parchment codices. Martial even gives his readers the name and address of the 'publisher'.

Early codices, whether Roman or Christian, were quite small in size and therefore much more portable than rolls. Christian scribes preparing writings to be carried by missionaries, messengers, and

---

[73] Skeat (n. 31) 263, explains that he no longer accepts either of the two theories which he and C. H. Roberts had advanced in *The Birth of the Codex*. For discussion of the various explanations advanced for Christian adoption of the codex, see J. van Haelst, 'Les origines du codex', in *Les débuts du codex* (ed. A. Blanchard; Turnhout: Brepols, 1989) 13–36; and S. R. Llewelyn, *New Documents Illustrating Early Christianity* Vol. VII (Macquarie University Ancient History Documentary Research Centre, 1994) 249–56.

Skeat's reference to the crisis caused by the publication of the Fourth Gospel recalls E. J. Goodspeed's suggestion that the fourfold Gospel emerged a few years after the appearance of the Fourth Gospel; it was intended to win a wider hearing for the Gospel of John than it would otherwise have received (n. 1, 35–6).

[74] D. Trobisch (n. 66).

[75] D. Trobisch (n. 66), especially 12 and 124.

[76] I am not convinced by Trobisch's attempt (n. 66, 67–8) to overturn this generally held view of early second century Christianity.

travellers over long distances would have readily appreciated the advantages of the codex.[77] Their general counter-cultural stance would have made them more willing than their non-Christian counterparts to break with the almost unanimous preference for the roll and experiment with the unfashionable codex.

No doubt the popularity of the codex in Christian circles was enhanced by its distinctive format. The earliest Christian experiments with the codex took place at a time when Christians were adopting a distinctive identity as a *tertium genus* over against both Judaism and the pagan world. Copying and using the OT Scriptures and their foundation writings in a new format was but one of the ways Christians expressed their sense of 'newness'.[78] Some Christians today still cling to a particular translation and format of the Bible as an identifying mark of their group or their theological convictions.

The codex format caught on rapidly in Christian circles.[79] The ability of the codex to hold four gospels seems to have been appreciated at the very time when four gospels were being brought together in some second century circles.

When did this happen? All the evidence I have set out in this address points to the period shortly before 150. Justin's writings confirm that in the decade or so after the Bar Cochba rebellion Christian self-understanding as a *tertium genus* took hold strongly, so perhaps it was during these years that the four-Gospel codex and the fourfold Gospel began to become popular. I make this suggestion with some hesitation. Numerous pieces of the jig-saw

---

[77] See especially M. McCormick, 'The Birth of the Codex and the Apostolic Life-Style', *Scriptorium* 39 (1985) 150–8.

[78] Colette Sirat rejects the claim made by C. H. Roberts and T. C. Skeat (n. 70) that there was a Jewish origin for Christian use of the codex. She notes that in the first centuries of our era, traditional Jewish texts do not make any allusion to the codex: 'Le livre hébreu dans les premiers siècles de nôtre ère: le témoignage des textes', in *Les débuts du codex* (ed. A. Blanchard; Turnhout: Brepols, 1989) 115–24.

[79] Cf. H. W. Gamble, *Books and Readers in the Early Church* (New Haven and London: Yale, 1995, 65): 'To claim the most primitive edition of the Pauline letter collection was put out in a codex and that it was the religious authority of Paul's collected letters that set the standard for the transcription of subsequent Christian literature in codices is not to claim that this marked the first use of the codex in Christian circles. It is possible, perhaps likely, that the codex was first employed in primitive Christianity for collections of texts (*testimonia*) from Jewish scripture.' I accept the latter point, but I am not convinced that it was a collection of the Pauline letters (which Gamble dates in the early second century, 'and probably earlier' [61]) which 'set the standard' for use of the codex. We have far more early codices of individual gospels and codices of the four gospels than we do of collections of Paul's letters; the gospels are quoted much more frequently in the second century than are the Pauline epistles. As I have noted above, early Christian use of the LXX in codices must also have encouraged Christians to adopt the codex as a standard format.

puzzle are missing; the discovery of only one or two new pieces might well alter the whole picture.

Acceptance of the fourfold Gospel did not mean the end of oral tradition; continuing use of oral traditions did not necessarily mean that written gospels were unknown or of marginal import- ance. It is a great mistake to suppose that written traditions and oral traditions were mutually exclusive.[80] And it is equally import- ant to note that the emergence of the fourfold Gospel did not instantly suppress either the use of, or the production of, further gospels. To have a set of four authoritative gospels does not mean that one stops reading anything else. In some circles doubts emerged from time to time about one or more of the four gospels; the universal adoption of a four-Gospel *canon* took much longer. Above all, we need to recall that even in Irenaeus's day, when the fourfold Gospel was axiomatic in many circles, the sayings of Jesus possessed an even higher authority.

It will be clear from the preceding paragraphs that I prefer a theory of gradual development to a 'big bang' theory. I envisage the following stages in the emergence of the fourfold Gospel, though of course I recognize that my summary suggests a neat and tidy development far removed from the reality of continuing debate and diversity of practice. The codex began to be used for individ- ual gospels soon after the turn of the century, a period when a plurality of gospels was known in many circles. During these decades the term 'Gospel' was used both for oral and for written 'Jesus' traditions. Use of the term 'Gospel' for two or more writings raised the question of their relationship to the *one* Gospel about Jesus Christ. This problem was solved by use of the title εὐαγγέλιον κατά . . . for individual gospels. The use of this title facilitated both acceptance of the fourfold Gospel and the use of the codex for four gospels. The four-gospel codex strongly encouraged acceptance of the fourfold Gospel, and vice versa: both are likely to have taken place for the first time shortly before the middle of the second century.

The fourfold Gospel did not gain immediate acceptance: as I shall recall in a moment, there were very strong currents running in the opposite direction. Christian insistence that the church had four equally authoritative stories written by apostles and their

---

[80] See Gamble (n. 79) 28–30; G. N. Stanton, 'Form Criticism Revisited', in *What about the New Testament?* FS C. F. Evans (ed. M. Hooker and C. Hickling; London: SCM, 1975) 13–27. See also Loveday Alexander, 'The Living Voice: Scepticism towards the Written Word in Early Christian and in Graeco-Roman Texts', in *The Bible in Three Dimensions* (ed. D. J. A. Clines, S. E. Fowl, S. E. Porter; Sheffield: JSOT, 1990) 221–47.

followers left doors wide open for both Jewish and pagan critics. The continuing attraction for many Christians and 'heretics' of *one* written Gospel (whether or not a harmony), as well as the jibes of critics, encouraged Irenaeus to mount what seems to have been the first full theological defence of the fourfold Gospel. The *universal* acceptance of four gospels – a four-Gospel *canon* – followed in due course, but not without further vicissitudes.

6. THEOLOGICAL SIGNIFICANCE

The acceptance of the fourfold Gospel does not raise problems for the historian. On the contrary, the historian is happy to have four sources available for reconstruction of the actions, words, and intentions of Jesus. Of course the historian will want to assess all sources critically, but in principle, the more sources the better. However, as soon as the historian considers the broad sweep of the development of the early Christian movement in the period before Constantine, it becomes clear that the four canonical gospels played a greater part in the development of the Christian movement and of Christian theology than any non-canonical Jesus or Gospel traditions.

The fourfold Gospel is of no significance if one wants to make a particular historical reconstruction of the life of Jesus the *sole* focus of religious concern. For example, if one really believes that nothing more can be said about Jesus than that he was a Wisdom or a Cynic teacher, then one is opting for a post-Christian position: in that case, the four evangelists' portraits of Jesus will be of no more than passing historical interest, to be discarded along with numerous later faith images of Jesus. But if one accepts that the evangelists' attempts to tell the story of Jesus and to spell out his significance are in some way normative for Christian faith, then the fourfold Gospel is problematic. Why do Christians need four stories?

The momentous nature of the decision to accept four gospels becomes clear once we recognize that alternative solutions nearly won the day in the first and second centuries. Acceptance and use of one Gospel was a live option again and again. When Matthew wrote his Gospel, he did not intend to supplement Mark: his incorporation of most of Mark's Gospel is surely an indication that he intended that his Gospel should replace Mark's, and that it should become *the* Gospel for Christians of his day. Similarly Luke. Luke's Preface should not be dismissed merely as the evangelist's way of honouring literary convention. There is little doubt that Luke expects that his more complete Gospel will displace his predecessors, even though he may not intend to disparage their earlier efforts. Whether or not John knew of the existence of one or more of the synoptic gospels, he seems to have expected that his Gospel would win wide acceptance as *the* Gospel.

This pattern continued in the second century. Numerous very different Christian groups used only one Gospel. Immediately before his declaration that there can be neither more nor less than four gospels, Irenaeus notes that four groups of heretics, Marcion included, have all fastened on to one of the four gospels (*Adv. Haer.* III.11.7). Irenaeus is painting with plenty of rhetoric on his brush at this point, nonetheless his picture is broadly accurate.

And then there is Tatian, who produced one harmonised Gospel out of four or possibly five gospels. He was almost certainly not the only person to opt for this solution, and his solution was amazingly successful in some circles for a very long time.

In the first and second centuries there were strong tides moving Christian churches towards acceptance of only one Gospel. Acceptance of the fourfold Gospel meant turning back the tidal currents: it carried as a corollary rejection of all the various attempts to opt either for one single Gospel, or for a harmony of known gospels. The tide did not turn back in a hurry, but once it began to turn, there was no going back: we never find manuscript evidence for acceptance of any 'fifth' gospel such as Thomas or Peter alongside one or more of the writings in the fourfold Gospel.[81] The adoption of the four-Gospel codex undoubtedly encouraged this whole process.

Was Irenaeus correct to give such a robust extended theological defence of the fourfold Gospel? Was he wise to give it a privileged theological position? Most of us have difficulty in accepting his view that two of the evangelists were apostles, and two were close associates of apostles. However, a careful reading of his writings reveals that his notion of 'apostolic' is acceptably broad, for Irenaeus emphasizes the lines of continuity of the four written gospels with the oral Gospel proclaimed by the apostles; like the apostles, the four gospels all proclaim one God, one Christ; they are held together by one Spirit.

At about the same time, Serapion bishop of Antioch made a similar theological judgement. The Gospel of Peter should not be

---

[81] So too J. K. Elliott, 'Manuscripts, the Codex and the Canon', *JSNT* 63 (1996) 107.

accepted solely because the great apostle's name was attached to it: continuity with the apostolic faith was the criterion by which it should be judged. So too Luther in his insistence that the test of apostolicity was whether or not a book proclaimed Christ. 'That which does not preach Christ is not apostolic, though it be the work of Peter or Paul, and conversely that which does teach Christ is apostolic even though it be written by Judas, Annas, Pilate, Herod.'[82]

Once we understand 'apostolic' in this extended sense, then we need not hesitate to affirm Irenaeus's defence of the fourfold Gospel. The other gospels which Irenaeus knew, or which appeared after his day, are clearly beyond the limits of acceptable theological diversity at crucial points. For Irenaeus there were three crucial theological points: the doctrine of one God, the Creator of all; continuity with the Scriptures; and Christology. If we consider all the possible rivals to the four gospels which became canonical, they all fall down on one or more of these theological criteria.

At one point Irenaeus attacks the Valentinians for audaciously accepting 'The Gospel of Truth'. He notes that it is totally unlike the gospels of the Apostles, and also that it is a comparatively recent writing (*Adv. Haer.* III.11.9). In modern times some weight has often been attached to this criterion of 'earliness': the four gospels are authoritative for Christian theology because they are the earliest witnesses we have to the actions and teaching of Jesus. Caution is of course necessary, for there are 'non-canonical' traditions which have a good claim to be as early as traditions which found their way into the four 'canonical' gospels. But their importance must not be exaggerated. Even the *Jesus Seminar* accepts as authentic only five of the logia of Thomas which are not found in the canonical four.[83] And as for complete gospels, are any earlier than the canonical four? Surely J. D. Crossan is exercising a vivid historical imagination when he claims that an early version of the Gospel of Peter was written in the fifties, possibly in Sepphoris.[84]

In short, a critical Christian theology need not stumble over the fourfold Gospel. But there are corollaries, four of which I shall single out for brief comment. First, the question of genre. If the four gospels are regarded primarily as theological witnesses to Jesus Christ in narrative form, then it makes good sense to retain these four primary witnesses. But if the four are considered

---

[82] Luther, *Werke* (Erlangen, 1826–57) 63, 156–7. I owe this reference to R. H. Bainton in the *Cambridge History of the Bible* III (ed. S. L. Greenslade; Cambridge: CUP, 1963) 7.

[83] See further, G. N. Stanton (n. 35) 84–93.

[84] See further, G. N. Stanton (n. 35) 78–82.

primarily as historical records, then along with Tatian it would surely be preferable to roll up the four into one. I think it is clear from the brilliant detective work of Tjitze Baarda and William Petersen that Tatian's concerns were primarily historical and included a quest for unity and harmony.[85] By accepting the fourfold Gospel the early church accepted that the gospels are *not histories*; if we follow suit, we are accepting them as witnesses in narrative form in spite of their discrepancies and contradictions. They belong to the broad genre of βίοι, but they are not βίοι *tout court*, they are four witnesses to the one Gospel.

Secondly, the fourfold Gospel has major implications for Christology. I have drawn attention to the way both the Muratorian Fragment and Irenaeus insisted that in spite of the different beginnings of the gospels, they were held together by one Spirit. Their comments may have been fuelled by pagan attacks on inconsistencies in the openings of the gospels, but their fascination with the beginnings of the gospels is surely an indication of awareness of the different Christological perspectives which result. This was seen clearly by Theodore of Mopsuestia at the end of the fourth century. He also commented on the different beginnings of the gospels, and noted that in the synoptic gospels teaching on the divinity of Christ was almost entirely lacking: that is why John opened his Gospel with an immediate reference to the divinity of Christ.[86]

Acceptance of the fourfold Gospel carries with it a commitment to the Christological tension between the synoptics and John. The history of Christological discussion right up to the present day reminds us again and again that we ignore this creative tension in perspective at our peril. The terminology changes – Christology from below and above, implicit and explicit Christology – but the fundamental Christological issue is marked out by the fourfold Gospel: the very different Christological stances of the synoptics and the Fourth Gospel should not be blurred, but should both be taken with the utmost seriousness.[87]

Thirdly, the fourfold Gospel forces us to reflect on a range of hermeneutical issues. By accepting the fourfold Gospel, we are ignoring the intention of two or possibly three of the evangelists, and in a sense we are encouraging the four gospels to interpret one

---

[85] T. Baarda (n. 25); W. L. Petersen (n. 49), and his *Tatian's Diatessaron: Its Creation, Dissemination, Significance, and History in Scholarship* (Leiden: Brill, 1994).

[86] Theodore of Mopsuestia, *Commentary on the Gospel of John*, Prologue (ed. J.-M. Vosté; CSCO 116; 1940). I owe this reference to H. Merkel, *Die Pluralität* (n. 24) § 36.

[87] On this point, see especially R. C. Morgan (n. 5) 380–6.

another. These observations do not lead me, at least, to abandon
the search for the original intention of the evangelists. But they do
remind me that it is the fourfold Gospel which has fed the life of
the church for nearly two thousand years, not any one or more
single gospels. I personally do not want to give hermeneutical
priority to the canonical shape of the gospels over against the
original intention of the evangelists: I want to try to take both
seriously and critically, along with the ways the gospels have been
understood within the on-going Christian tradition.

By accepting that the four are all witnesses to the one Gospel, we
are forced to reflect both on the theological convictions which they
share as well as on the points at which they diverge. Why do we
prefer one evangelist's portrait or emphasis? What are our theological criteria for making such judgements? Has the continuing
scholarly interest in the distinctive features of the individual
gospels blinded us to the theological concerns they have in common?

Fourthly, the fourfold Gospel raises liturgical issues, especially
for contemporary compilers of lectionaries. Most modern lectionaries treat the gospels as individual writings: one year of lectionary
readings is devoted to each Gospel. Most churches in the United
Kingdom are about to adopt a three year cycle in which a whole
year is devoted to each of the synoptic gospels, with passages from
John's Gospel inserted at appropriate points. Is this compromise
satisfactory? Would it not be preferable, as was the case until
modern times, to take seriously in lectionaries Irenaeus's conviction that there is one Gospel in fourfold form? Why should
liturgical priority be given to the evangelists' individual writings at
the expense of the fourfold Gospel?

I end with my beginning, with Irenaeus. I cannot accept some
of the reasons he offers in defence of the fourfold Gospel. But I do
accept his theological conviction that the fourfold Gospel is the
pillar which sustains the church. This is a static image, so perhaps some might prefer the image which appealed to Hippolytus,
Cyprian, Victorinus of Pettau, and very recently, to Rudolf
Schnackenburg: the four gospels are like the rivers of Paradise
which flow from the Garden of Eden into the whole known earth at
that time (Gen 2.10–14).[88] The Biblical image of rivers and living,

---

[88] R. Schnackenburg, *Jesus in the Gospels. A Biblical Christology* (Louisville: Westminster
John Knox, ET 1995) 324–5. Schnackenburg refers to Gen 2.10–14, but does not note that this
image also appealed to the patristic writers listed above. See H. Merkel (n. 11) 7. n. 1, who
gives full references.

flowing waters was often linked to the gift of the Spirit, as it was by the Fourth Evangelist. So perhaps Irenaeus, with his emphasis on the Spirit who holds together the fourfold Gospel, would have been happy with this later more dynamic image. After all, for Irenaeus the foundation and pillar of the church is the fourfold Gospel *and* the Spirit of life (στῦλος δὲ καὶ στήριγμα ἐκκλησίας τὸ εὐαγγέλιον καὶ Πνεῦμα ζωῆς III.11.8).[89]

[89] I have quoted the Greek text from fragment 11 (Anastasius Sinaita), as edited by A. Rousseau and L. Doutreleau (n. 10) 160–2.

WTJ 57 (1995) 437-52

THE DEBATE OVER THE MURATORIAN FRAGMENT AND THE DEVELOPMENT OF THE CANON*

C. E. HILL

In 1740 Lodovico Muratori published a list of NT books from a codex contained in the Ambrosian Library at Milan. The text printed was in badly transcribed Latin; most, though not all, later scholars have presumed a Greek original. Though the beginning of the document is missing, it is clear that the author described or listed the four Gospels, Acts, thirteen letters of Paul, two (or possibly three) letters of John, one of Jude and the book of Revelation. The omission of the rest of the Catholic Epistles, in particular 1 Peter and James, has sometimes been attributed to copyist error. The fragment also reports that the church accepts the *Wisdom of Solomon* while it is bound to exclude the *Shepherd of Hermas*. Scholars have traditionally assigned the Muratorian Fragment (MF) to the end of the second century or the beginning of the third. As such it has been important as providing the earliest known "canon" list, one that has the same "core" of writings which were later agreed upon by the whole church. Geoffrey Hahneman has now written a forceful book in an effort to dismantle this consensus by showing that "The Muratorian Fragment, if traditionally dated, is an extraordinary anomaly in the development of the Christian Bible on numerous counts" (p. 131), arguing instead for the placement of the MF alongside several fourth-century Eastern catalogues (canons) of the Christian Scriptures. The influence of Hahneman's book is likely to be significant. R. M. Grant, familiar with the book in its dissertation form, has already signified his acceptance of its major conclusion.[1]

Before proceeding to examine the argument of the book, it should be noted that Hahneman's study carries with it more than the simple desire to correct a historical misplacement. Hahneman's deliberate aim is to advance the work on canon begun by Albert C. Sundberg, who is said to have shown that the Christian church received from Judaism not a closed OT canon but a "looser collection of sacred writings" (p. 1). According to Sundberg, the process of fixing even an OT canon in the church did not begin until the third century and was not completed until the fourth. It was

---

* Geoffrey Mark Hahneman: *The Muratorian Fragment and the Development of the Canon* (Oxford Theological Monographs; Oxford: Clarendon Press, 1992. xvii, 237. $55.00). A shorter review of this work appeared in *WTJ* 56 (1994) 437-38.
[1] R. M. Grant, *Heresy and Criticism: The Search for Authenticity in Early Christian Literature* (Louisville: Westminster/Knox, 1993) 110.

this struggle to define the OT canon which in turn became the major catalyst for the church also to firm up its own collection of authoritative Christian documents. Before this time, an undefined number of writings had indeed been used with religious authority as Scripture, but the church had been content to leave the boundaries of this collection quite undefined and open. The process of NT canon formation then also has to be shifted correspondingly farther down the timeline. The MF, as traditionally dated, stood in the way of this shift, for it represents a situation far more advanced than the present theory allows for the late second or early third century. Sundberg's own attempt to dislodge the MF, first in a paper at the International Patristics Conference at Oxford in 1965 and more trenchantly in an article printed in the *Harvard Theological Review* in 1973, availed little in the scholarly world.[2] Hahneman now sets out to rehabilitate Sundberg's thesis, to establish "an Eastern provenance and a fourth-century date for the Fragment" and thus to sound again "Sundberg's call for a revised history of the New Testament canon" (p. 4). We shall first address Hahneman's arguments regarding the Fragment itself, then go on to consider the case he makes for a later and more gradual awakening of the church to the concern for an authoritative, closed list of scriptural books.

Hahneman is correct that if the MF is located in the late second or early third century it is by far the earliest such list of NT documents still preserved (we have two OT lists by about this time, in Melito and Origen). But this we have known for a long time. And there is, a priori, a plausible home to be found for the MF in the fourth century, when many lists or catalogues ("canons") of the books of acknowledged Christian Scripture appear. But this a priori is severely mitigated, as Everett Ferguson has pointed out in an early review,[3] by the observation that these fourth-century canons are "bare 'lists' " while the Fragment is full of discursive commentary.[4] The MF is in fact quite different in character from these lists. Further, the anomalies in the MF do not necessarily point to the fourth century, as we shall see below.

Probably the single greatest difficulty for anyone who would want to redate the Fragment is its statement about the *Shepherd of Hermas*, which it rejects as having been written by the brother of Pius, bishop of Rome

---

[2] The main refutation was provided by E. Ferguson, "Canon Muratori: Date and Provenance," *Studia patristica* 17.2 (Oxford: Pergamon, 1982) 677–83. Ferguson "sufficiently refuted (not to say demolished)" Sundberg's thesis, according to B. M. Metzger, *The Canon of the New Testament: Its Origin, Development, and Significance* (New York: Oxford University Press, 1987) 193; but his rebuttal was "brief and dismissive," according to Hahneman (p. 3). An extensive recent review of the debate between Ferguson and Sundberg can be found in P. Henne, "La datation du *canon de Muratori*," *RB* 100 (1993) 54–75, who decides in favor of Ferguson and a second-century date. Hahneman's book appeared apparently too late for Henne to take account of it.

[3] E. Ferguson, "Review of Geoffrey Mark Hahneman, *The Muratorian Fragment and the Development of the Canon*," *JTS* 44 (1993) 696. See also Metzger, *Canon*, 194.

[4] Despite Hahneman's attempt to play this down (p. 131).

(140-155), "most recently in our time" (*nuperrrime temporibus nostris*). Hahneman recognizes the magnitude of this problem and devotes a whole chapter to its solution. He begins by resuscitating Sundberg's argument that "our time" in the Fragment's statement is here not a reference to the lifetime of the author but is being used to distinguish "apostolic time" and "post-apostolic time" and therefore need not indicate that the fragmentist is writing relatively soon after the *Shepherd*. A similar remark of Irenaeus, that the Apocalypse of John was written "not a very long time ago, but almost in our own generation towards the end of the reign of Domitian" (*Against Heresies* 5.30.3), is explained by Sundberg and Hahneman along these same lines. But Irenaeus does not support them here, as he is pointedly identifying, not separating, his time and the apostle's; both are part of "this present time" and "now." Hahneman, however, does not rest on Sundberg's argument. He urges that since the fragmentist's other comments concerning the *Shepherd* are either untrue or unprovable we must therefore reject also his claim to near contemporaneity. But it remains unclear why this is so. Suppose the fragmentist is wrong in his assertion that the *Shepherd* was written during the episcopate of Pius and suppose that it was written much earlier. He could have been mistaken in the second century as well as in the fourth. And it is hard to imagine why a fourth-century author would deliberately adopt a fictitious, second-century persona just for the purpose of debunking the *Shepherd*.[5]

Hahneman says, "There would be no need to deny so emphatically the apostolicity of Hermas in the Fragment, unless a tradition associating Hermas with an apostle was known. Such a tradition is unknown before Origen and may well have originated with him. If the fragmentist betrays an awareness of that tradition then the Fragment would have to be dated after Origen" (p. 51). But Irenaeus had once cited Hermas as Scripture, probably at least partly on the assumption of the reputed author's identity with Paul's associate mentioned in Rom 16:14 and thus his status as an apostolic co-worker.[6] Irenaeus' use of the *Shepherd* forms an entirely plausible setting for the Fragment's specification that it should be read but cannot be classed with the Scriptures and read in public worship. Tertullian tells us that the *Shepherd*'s standing had at least by the second decade of the third century been considered by several councils, with unanimously negative results. He says in *De pudicitia* 10,

> But I would yield my ground to you, if the scripture of 'the Shepherd,' which is the only one which favours adulterers, had deserved to find a place in the Divine canon [*divino instrumento*]; if it had not been habitually judged by every council [*concilio*] of Churches [even of your own] among apocryphal and false [writings].

[5] See Ferguson, "Review," 692.

[6] Similar to his linking of Linus, an early bishop of Rome, with the man mentioned by Paul in 2 Tim 4:21 (*Ag. Her.* 3.3.3).

That these councils declared Hermas not only to be apocryphal but "false" may indicate an indictment as false prophecy, or the refutation of a claim made for the identity of its author. These ecclesiastical gatherings which deliberated on "canon" at least to the extent of pronouncing against Hermas are suspiciously dismissed by Hahneman: "[Tertullian's] statement that it was rejected by every synod of the churches, even those of the non-Montanists, however, cannot be objectively verified, and might be thought of as an example of his famous rhetoric," and, "Tertullian's reasons for rejecting the Shepherd are clearly sectarian and it should not be thought that there was widespread rejection of the work" (p. 63). Tertullian may have been given to flamboyance, but it was hardly his custom to appeal to historical precedents of his own imagination, especially when his appeal entailed an implicit challenge to his opponents to check his sources. It would seem then that the Fragment's reference to the *Shepherd* remains an obstacle which has not been effectively removed by Sundberg or by Hahneman.

Chapter five deals closely with some of the peculiarities of the Fragment which, with varying degrees of probability, Hahneman believes support his conclusion of a late date. The Fragment's peculiarities are numerous, no matter what date is assumed, but that they together point to a fourth-century, Eastern provenance is not so easily shown. The order it gives for the Gospels, for instance, is said to be late and Eastern. Yet it is paralleled once in Irenaeus (*Ag. Her.* 3.1.1). Its mention of "the Acts of all the Apostles" is said to indicate lateness, for, though Acts is certainly known before this time, nobody seems to have a name for it until Tertullian. But Hahneman has missed a reference by name to "the Acts of the Apostles" in Irenaeus (*Ag. Her.* 3.13.3). Hahneman is prepared to accept the explanation of the absence of 1 Peter and James in the MF as accidental (p. 181). This is understandable, for, surprising as their intentional omission might be at the end of the second century, it would be be unthinkable in the fourth.[7]

Hahneman reiterates Sundberg's claim that the Fragment's mention of *Wisdom of Solomon* in a list of NT writings is paralleled only in the fourth century with Eusebius and Epiphanius (pp. 200–205). In reality, neither the MF, nor Eusebius, nor Epiphanius includes *Wisdom* in a list of NT writings. Eusebius, while discussing the books used by Irenaeus, mentions *Wisdom* not as a contender for NT inclusion but simply to show that this disputed book was known to Irenaeus, it being one of Eusebius's intentions to note which ecclesiastical writers used which of the disputed books. The claim that Epiphanius included *Wisdom* and *Sirach* among his NT canon (p. 204, an argument also pioneered by Sundberg) is also misleading. In *Panarion* 76.5 Epiphanius gives a list of NT writings (identical to the present one), then, clearly set off from the rest, he appends also the books called

⁷ Henne, "La datation," 72.

Wisdom, both of Solomon and of the son of Sirach. Earlier in the same treatise (8.6) Epiphanius had mentioned these two as books disputed by the Jews, "apart from some *other* apocryphal books" (emphasis mine). Writing some years later in *De Mens. et Pond.* 4, Epiphanius again expressly sets these two books among OT apocrypha, used and useful to the church but not classed with the others. The MF's mention of the *Wisdom of Solomon* seemingly in the midst of a catalogue of NT writings would indeed be strange, but William Horbury has recently shown that this is not what the MF does.[8] Horbury points to a widespread practice in the early church of listing undoubted books first, then listing disputed ones, including both OT and NT antilegomena together. The mention of *Wisdom* in the MF comes at the conclusion of the list of assured NT books and at the head of a list of disputed ones. After listing the four Gospels, Acts, and thirteen epistles of Paul, the writer mentions the church's acceptance of Jude and the letters of John. Then he begins his list of disputed books, of both testaments, namely, *Wisdom,* and the Apocalypses of Peter and John, and *The Shepherd* by Hermas. Of these he says that the first three are accepted by the church, though some will not have the Apocalypse of Peter read in the church, but that Hermas' writing must be rejected as postapostolic. Then he concludes with a brief list of rejected books.

> The place of Wisdom in the fragment would then imply not that Wisdom was connected with or even included in the New Testament, but that, like the Revelations of John and of Peter, and (to a lesser degree) the Shepherd of Hermas, it was considered an acceptable book not certainly included in the canonical number. This explanation . . . is in full agreement with a known status accorded to Wisdom—that of a leading antilegomenon, commonly put first in lists of the 'outside' or 'ecclesiastical' books from the Old and New Testaments.[9]

Thus according to Horbury the inclusion of *Wisdom* in the MF is not evidence for a fourth-century date.[10]

Hahneman claims that the Fragment's use (line 84) of the Latin *catafrygum,* an obvious transliteration of κατάφρυγας (or κατὰ Φρύγας), a nickname for the Montanists, is indicative of a fourth-century date (pp. 211–12). This is because the designation in Greek does not occur elsewhere until Cyril of Jerusalem (*Catech.* 16.8), and the Latin transliteration is not extant until the late fourth century. But, as P. Henne points out, "toute étude

[8] William Horbury, "The Wisdom of Solomon in the Muratorian Fragment," *JTS* NS 45 (1994) 149-59.

[9] Ibid., 155.

[10] Ibid., 159: "This evidence weighs against the claim that ecclesiastical definition of an Old Testament canon first begins in the fourth century, and that we would hardly expect the similar New Testament definition seen in the fragment to precede it." Cf. also Henne: "Ce livre était souvent placé après les livres néotestamentaires, comme en annexe des deux Testaments. Cette hésitation peut avoir débuté au IIe siècle, comme elle est attestée au IVe" ("La datation," 60).

lexicographique est périlleuse puisqu'elle a pour seul champ d'application la période de traduction, et pas celle de la rédaction originale."[11] That is, a late-fourth-century Latin translator could easily have substituted *cataphrygum*, the term of his day, for an original "Phrygians." Even so, we probably do have two examples of the Greek κατὰ Φρύγας used for the Montanists from near the beginning of the third century. Ps. Tertullian's *Contra haereses*, a document originally written in Greek in the early to middle third century, but surviving only in a Latin translation, refers to *qui dicuntur secundum Phrygas* (7.21). Hahneman concludes it is unlikely that such represents an original Greek κατὰ Φρύγας, "because similar Greek phrases in the same paragraph were simply transliterated into Latin, namely 'kata Proclum' and 'kata Aeschinen' " (p. 212). What he does not tell us is that in the same paragraph we also have both the transliterated *kata Aeschinen* and the translated *secundum Aeschinen*, both presumably from a Greek κατά. Thus *secundum* instead of a transliterated *kata* with *Phrygas* is no evidence against an assumed original κατά. Paired as it is here with *secundum Aeschinen*, what else would *secundum* have translated? Further, Hahneman has not considered an important piece of evidence from Epiphanius's *Panarion*. Since the researches of Lipsius (1865) and Voigt (1891) scholars have recognized that in *Pan.* 48 Epiphanius is citing a late-second or early-third-century (probably Asian) source.[12] We find this writer too already using the phrase κατὰ Φρύγας for the Montanists (48.12.4).

We go on to Hahneman's treatment of the formation of the canon, given in support of the need to redate the MF. Hahneman accepts as a starting point Sundberg's thesis that there was no closed canon of Jewish Scriptures in Jesus' or the apostles' day. Beckwith's *The Old Testament Canon of the New Testament Church*[13] is listed in the bibliography but unfortunately has exercised absolutely no influence on the author. Instead, Sundberg's argument is allowed to sail on as though uncontested. But if the major conclusions of Beckwith's book are accepted—such as, that "the Jewish canon, in all probability, reached its final form in the time of Judas Maccabeus, about 164 BC, and did so for all schools of thought alike"[14]—much of the wind is taken from Sundberg's (and hence Hahneman's) sails. It would appear incumbent upon those who might want to take Hahneman's position to formulate a response to Beckwith.

On coming to consider the evidence for the reception of the NT documents one should like to expect, if not a detailed treatment of the use of NT writings in the early church, at least accurate and balanced summaries. One will find neither here. The conclusions are largely second-hand and

[11] Henne, "La datation," 63–64.
[12] See R. E. Heine, ed., *The Montanist Oracles and Testimonia* (Macon, Ga.: Macon University Press, 1989) x, 28–51.
[13] R. Beckwith, *The Old Testament Canon of the New Testament Church* (Grand Rapids: Eerdmans, 1985).
[14] Ibid., 406.

consistently skeptical. A few examples will convey the tone of the work and the way evidence is evaluated by the author.

> The linguistic agreements between the Pastorals and Polycarp (c. 135) suggest no more than that they both stand in the same ecclesiastical and cultural tradition [p. 117].
>
> H. Koester has shown that the citations of gospel traditions among the Apostolic Fathers are more likely to be drawn from oral tradition than to be free quotations from written gospels, to which no explicit appeals are made [p. 95].

It is indeed a tricky business to try to determine when similar language truly denotes use of another source, especially if not attributed. To illustrate, let us take the last quotation itself. How does one explain the similar wording found in Harry Y. Gamble's book on the NT canon: "It has been shown that the citations of gospel-type traditions among the Apostolic Fathers are much more likely to have been drawn from the ongoing stream of oral tradition than to be free quotations from written gospels, to which no explicit appeals are made"?[15] Possibly both authors came to nearly identical summaries of Koester's book independently. But curiosity compounds when one sees that at least thirteen full sentences and parts of many others from pp. 18, 26, 27, 28, 29, 30, 33, 34 of Gamble's book also appear verbatim or nearly so in chap. 3 of Hahneman's book, without attribution. As just one example, we may adduce the following (italicized letters signify the divergences):

> He seems at numerous points to have relied on oral tradition, or *on* a compilation of sayings of Jesus, or perhaps on gospels not known *to us,* or variously on all of these. Evidently Justin did not invest any exclusive authority in the *G*ospels which ultimately became canonical. [Gamble, 29]
>
>   He seems at numerous points to have relied on oral tradition, or a compilation of sayings of Jesus, or perhaps on gospels not known, or variously on all of these. Evidently Justin did not invest any exclusive authority in the gospels which ultimately became canonical. [Hahneman, 97]

Does this show that Hahneman borrowed from Gamble? To conclude so might be rash; after all, "no explicit appeals are made." And, even though Gamble's book appeared first and is listed in Hahneman's bibliography, it is just possible that it was Gamble who borrowed from Hahneman. Perhaps the material originated in a lecture or seminar given years earlier by Hahneman at which Gamble may have been in attendance. Alternatively, as Hahneman says of Polycarp and the Pastorals, verbal agreements in our modern authors may "suggest no more than that they both stand in the same ecclesiastical and cultural tradition." Hahneman and Gamble then

---

[15] Harry Y. Gamble, *The New Testament Canon: Its Making and Meaning* (Philadelphia: Fortress, 1985) 27; the statement is followed by a reference to H. Koester's *Synoptisch Überlieferung bei den apostolischen Vätern* [TU 65; Berlin: Akademie, 1957]).

444 WESTMINSTER THEOLOGICAL JOURNAL

may be heirs of oral, history-of-the-canon tradition, in this case a tradition which must have come complete with suggestions for footnotes.[16] Or,
are they both indebted to a common written source, a now lost "Ur-
Kanonsgeschichtebuch," which circulated through both authors' respective scholar-communities in the early 1980s? Perhaps less likely, but a viable
critical possibility nonetheless, is that Gamble and Hahneman are in reality
the same person (cf. the theory that Polycarp wrote the Pastorals). So, here,
just as in the case of apparent use of NT writings in the Apostolic Fathers
and others, actual dependence must not be hastily claimed until all the
probabilities are carefully weighed. But when they are, actual dependence,
in both our ancient and modern instances, is still perhaps the best conclusion.

Arguing against the existence of a fourfold Gospel canon at the end of the
second century, Hahneman says, "The Gospel of John is certainly a surprising member of any orthodox gospel canon at the end of the second
century" (p. 101). Why is this? Because of its early and widespread use by
gnostic Christians such as Basilides, Heracleon, and Ptolemaeus, the En-
cratite Tatian, the heretic Montanists, not to mention the scathing criticism
of it by Gaius of Rome at the beginning of the third century. And those
detractors dubbed by Epiphanius the "Alogi"—either Gaius of Rome and
his ilk or perhaps those already known to Irenaeus by about 180—"may not
have been a heretical group rejecting the long-accepted Gospel of John, but
rather an orthodox element protesting against the introduction into the
Church's usage of a gospel which heretics had long used" (p. 102). Surely,
then, Hahneman has greatly understated the case. For by Hahneman's own
admission John's Gospel "from the beginning of the third century . . . has
been generally accepted in the churches." The reader can only marvel at
how this renegade Gospel could have been catapulted into universal ap-
probation in so short a time. What power on earth could have wrested it
from its gnostic origins and first use, its fresh and still reeking Montanist
contaminations, the bold and searching criticism it suffered at the hands of
seemingly loyal churchmen in Rome and perhaps in Asia, and delivered it
safely into the waiting bosom of an expressly anti-gnostic and anti-
Montanist church? Surely not the allegorical defense of the gospel's fourfold
nature by Irenaeus, which Hahneman tells us is "tortured" and suggestive
of innovation (p. 101)! Alas, the only thing John's Gospel had going for it,
according to Hahneman, was its fortuitous linkage with the Apostle John
forged by Irenaeus, a tradition which, Hahneman and many others today
would hasten to add, "is probably based upon a confusion of persons by
him" (p. 102). No, on this presentation of the evidence, the acceptance of
John's Gospel virtually overnight in all regions of the church by the beginning of the third century simply has no causal basis in history. It would

[16] Compare Hahneman, p. 101, the materials surrounding notes 61 and 63, and Gamble,
p. 33, the materials surrounding notes 27 and 28.

appear to require just the sort of supernatural energy, and a generous outpouring of it, which many writers seem anxious to exclude from the process of Scripture and canon formation! If this conclusion causes discomfort, perhaps it will stimulate a reconsideration of the evidence. The way in which the Fourth Gospel was able to overcome such dreadful odds will be much better accounted for if it is appreciated what a widespread conviction of apostolic origin (not only Irenaeus, but at least the author of the *Epistula Apostolorum*, Polycrates, Theophilus, Clement of Alexandria, and Hippolytus by the start of the third century), what a strong and deeply embedded sanction in ecclesiastical usage (Celsus, in the 160s or 170s, already knows the Christian fourfold Gospel and polemicizes against John),[17] and what a sense of agreement with the (nongnostic, by the way) rule of faith must have attended this writing through its tempestuous first century and a half.

Concerning the four Gospels it is said, "The existence of gospel harmonies at the end of the second century suggests that the Fourfold Gospel canon was not yet established" (p. 98). If this is so, then a fourfold Gospel canon is not yet established today. The author repeatedly interprets the use of noncanonical Gospel traditions by a church writer as evidence against a closed, fourfold canon.[18] This might have some weight if the authors in question were not Clement and Origen, who explicitly state their reception of only the four (Eusebius *Hist. eccl.* 6.14.5; 6.25.4).[19]

As to the Pauline corpus, we read that the continued production even into the fourth century of pseudonymous Pauline works "suggests that there was no established Pauline canon, and that the Pauline collection remained open through the third and into the fourth century" (pp. 110–11). This remarkable statement takes no account whatever of the circumstances of composition of the "Pauline" apocrypha, the ecclesial standing of the authors, their intended audience and purpose, the reasons for choosing the name of Paul rather than one's own name, etc. There is, for instance, no evidence at all that the author of the *Acts of Paul* ever intended his work to be considered Scripture with the same authority as Paul's letters. What Tertullian says in *De baptismo* 17 would seem to assure us of the contrary. An open Pauline corpus is not the witness of the manuscript tradition, according to David Trobisch, who has devoted much study to the question.[20] The

---

[17] See M. Hengel, *The Johannine Question* (Philadelphia: Trinity, 1989) 6, 142 n. 23.

[18] As does Gamble, p. 34.

[19] At least by Origen's time, if not well before, there was a concern to give the limitation of the number of the Gospels apostolic authority. Origen says in his homilies on Luke: "But the Church of God has preferred only the four. There is a report noted down in writing that John collected the written gospels in his own lifetime in the reign of Nero, and approved of and recognised those of which the deceit of the devil had not taken possession; but refused and rejected those which he perceived were not truthful" (cited from W Schneemelcher, ed., *New Testament Apocrypha* [2 vols.; rev. ed.; Louisville: Westminster/Knox, 1991] 1.46).

[20] David Trobisch, *Paul's Letter Collection: Tracing the Origins* (Minneapolis: Fortress, 1994), which is a popular summary of his *Die Entstehung der Paulusbriefsammlung: Studien zu den Anfängen*

only variable he finds in the number and identity of the letters has to do with the book of Hebrews, which he believes was not in the original edition of thirteen letters but was added later to it. Despite some arguable conjectures, Trobisch's work is important as it suggests that a collection of at least some of Paul's letters was published by the author himself.[21]

Hahneman echoes the observation of Sundberg, now supported by Gamble and others, that the presence of authoritative Scriptures in the early church does not necessarily imply a closed canon, or even the concept of canon. Ferguson would bring some needed clarity to this discussion by insisting that

> Between 'scripture' and 'closed canon' another stage needs to be inserted, 'open canon'. 'Scripture' implies 'canon', and 'canon' implies 'closed canon', but they are not the same. When the scripture principle is accepted, there will be a concern to identify which writings are authoritative. . . . There is the stage, at least theoretically, when one acknowledges certain writings but does not rule out that there might be others not yet brought to one's attention or still under consideration. This intermediate stage of 'open canon' may be reflected in the Muratorian Fragment.[22]

But even this does not disclose all the possibilities. "Scripture" implies at least an open canon, or could imply a closed canon without needing to imply unanimous agreement. An author may believe in a closed canon but be personally unsure of its extent, or he may himself be confident of its extent but his verdict may not be validated by all of his contemporaries. It is the latter which seems to characterize several writers by at least the second half of the second century. There are Christians who say there is only one mode of baptism. In a purely descriptive sense they are simply wrong, for more than one mode is practiced by Christians. But from a dogmatic perspective, hypothetically at least, they may be right. At any rate they may still believe they are right, no matter how many "false" baptisms are performed. A similar situation seems to be reflected when Origen and Eusebius report on "disputed" books like Revelation, 2 Peter, 2 and 3 John, etc. If "not all say that these are genuine" (i.e., 2 and 3 John, *Hist. eccl.* 6.25.10), then a substantial number do—and they may be right. There may have been at a given time a great deal of agreement, but not unanimity; widespread use of and confidence in a book, but unsettled disputes in some quarters. A case in point is Origen's treatment of Hebrews. He knew it was disputed, but this made no difference in his own regard for and use of the

---

christlicher Publizistik (NTOA 10; Göttingen: Vandenhoeck & Ruprecht, 1989). On the disputed witness of the remains of P[46], compare Hahneman, pp. 115-116, with Trobisch, *Letter Collection*, 13-17, 22.

[21] Gerd Theissen, in the foreword to the English translation of Trobisch's book, states the significance of his conclusion: "With the publication of this letter collection Paul basically gave birth to the concept of a Christian canon" (p. vii).

[22] Ferguson, "Review," 693.

book. If it is not Paul's, its thoughts "are admirable, and not inferior to the acknowledged writings of the apostle, to this also everyone will consent as true who has given attention to reading the apostle." Origen proceeded to write homilies on Hebrews (Eusebius *Hist. eccl.* 6.25.11-14).

Hahneman proposes that we may see the development of a concept of canon in three stages, reflected first in comments on individual books as Scripture, then manifested in collections of groups of books (such as a fourfold Gospel collection), and finally in the production of catalogues or canons, authoritative lists of recognized books. It is not until the last stage, begun allegedly in the early fourth century by Eusebius, that we may properly speak of a concern for a canon, or a closed list of NT Scriptures (pp. 136, 140, 171, etc.). On writers cited by Eusebius, Hahneman says, "The remarks of the earlier authors themselves reflect only the concept of Scripture," not, that is, "an interest in the Canon" (p. 136). "Not until the fourth century did the churches appear to define and restrict that New Testament collection" (p. 129). "An interest in the Canon," then, and attempts to "define and restrict" the NT collection, are what we must look for before the fourth century. Here are a few places where they may be found.

To begin in the early third century, there are the councils mentioned by Tertullian (on which see the comments above). Again it must be stressed that, whatever other functions these councils may have performed, they deliberated on the NT canon at least to the extent of rejecting Hermas "as apocryphal and false." In passing, it might be suggested that more attention be paid to Tertullian's own title for the literary collection of Christian Scripture, the *instrumentum*, a Latin legal term used for "deeds" or other official documents, which he preferred to the designation which was more popular at that time, *testamentum*. On a view such as Hahneman's we might certainly expect appeals to *instrumenta*, for they were, after all, individual documents. There is no evidence that single codices containing the whole collection (anyone's collection) of the Christian Scriptures had yet been produced. But Tertullian uses the singular, as if he is thinking of one book, or one body of books.[23] Is this not most naturally read as indicating the conception of a closed set of documents?

Eusebius tells us that Clement of Alexandria, in his now lost *Hypotyposeis,* "has given concise explanations of all the Canonical Scriptures, not passing over even the disputed writings, I mean the Epistle of Jude and the remaining Catholic Epistles, and the Epistle of Barnabas, and the Apocalypse known as Peter's. And as for the Epistle to the Hebrews . . ." (6.14.1-2). Eusebius's terminology is important. He does not merely say that

---

[23] *Adv. Marc.* 4.2; *Adv. Prax.* 15, 20; *De pudic.* 1; the plural is used in *Adv. Marc.* 4.1 where he speaks of the two testaments. F. F. Bruce, *The Canon of Scripture* (Downers Grove, IL; InterVarsity, 1988) 181 n. 6, points out that Tertullian "also uses, with regard to the Old or New Testament collection, *armarium* ('bookcase') and *paratura* ('equipment')."

Clement used "testimonies" from the canonical Scriptures, as he did in his *Stromateis* (6.13.4, 6). He states that Clement gave explanations or comments (διηγήσεις) on all of them, all in the same work, as if it were his intention in that treatise to survey all of these books. This certainly seems to reflect a concern for the contents of the covenantal Scripture and forms a fitting parallel to what we find, on a smaller scale, in the MF. Eusebius is surely using his own conception of the canonical writings, and in his stating that Clement wrote on all of them there is an indication that all the documents considered assuredly canonical by Eusebius were thus included and commented on by Clement. Besides these, Clement also remarked upon those writings which Eusebius considers disputed (Jude, the rest of the Catholic letters, *Barnabas, Apoc. Pet.*); whether Clement regarded them as disputed in his day, we cannot say.[24]

The objections brought against the Johannine literature in the second century already imply no little concern about "canon" questions. What we know of Gaius of Rome (the only identifiable representative of the opponents of the Johannine literature) confirms this. Eusebius says Gaius "mentions" (μνημονεύει) only thirteen epistles of Paul and does not accept Hebrews. What does this signify? Eusebius can hardly mean that in Gaius' single treatise against Proclus one could find testimonies from all thirteen (even Philemon?) but not from Hebrews. What Eusebius means is that somewhere in the treatise Gaius gave an enumeration (Eusebius uses the word συναριθμήσας) of the genuine or received epistles of St. Paul which included the thirteen but either omitted or rejected Hebrews. Thus he should be regarded as possessing and specifying for others a thirteen-letter collection of Paul's writings. This concern with the number of authoritative new-covenant Scriptures was certainly germane to the controversy with Montanism in which Gaius was engaged.[25] Eusebius says in another place that Gaius was exercised with Proclus and the Montanists for their "recklessness and audacity . . . in composing new Scriptures" (6.20.3). But why should this have particularly bothered him if, as Hahneman implies, the

---

[24] In 3.32 Eusebius had said, "of the Acts bearing his [Peter's] name, and the gospel named according to him and Preaching called his and the so-called Revelation, we have no knowledge at all in Catholic tradition, for no orthodox writer of the ancient time or of our own has used their testimonies." From this we would well conclude that whatever Clement said about the *Apoc. Pet.* he did not give the impression that it was to be treated as Scripture. Hahneman (p. 207) thinks Eusebius is exaggerating here, in light of what he says later in 6.14.1. If the Clementine material translated and preserved by Cassiodorus (sixth cent.) under the title *Adumbrationes* is indeed from Clement's eight books of the *Hypotyposeis*, as is usually supposed, then we may be sure that he regarded at least 1 Peter, Jude, 1 and 2 John as part of the Christian Scriptures. We also know that Clement regarded Revelation as written by the apostle John.

[25] Gamble's comment, "In fact, arguments about scripture and arguments from scripture played a remarkably small role in the whole [Montanist] conflict" (*New Testament Canon,* 64) is quite wide of the mark. See, e.g., R. Heine, "The Role of the Gospel of John in the Montanist Controversy," *The Second Century* 6 (1987–88) 1–19.

canon was still open to augmentation at this time? It looks very much like Gaius believed there was a "closed canon"; his canon was simply narrower than that of the rest of the church. In another quotation preserved by Eusebius, Gaius criticizes Cerinthus for being "an enemy of the Scriptures of God" (3.28.2). All of this harmonizes well with the summaries of Gaius' argument still extant in Dionysius Bar Salibi's commentary on Revelation,[26] which show that Gaius tried to discredit the book of Revelation by pitting it against what is "written" in the Synoptic Gospels and the writings of Paul.[27]

Writing ca. 196, the anonymous anti-Montanist cited by Eusebius says he had long resisted the request to write against the Montanists "not through lack of ability to refute falsehood and bear witness to the truth, but from fear and extreme caution, lest I might seem to some to be adding a new article or clause to the word of the New Covenant of the Gospel [ἐπισυγγράφειν ἢ ἐπιδιατάσσεσθαι τῷ τῆς τοῦ εὐαγγελίου καινῆς διαθήκης λόγῳ], to which no one who has purposed to live according to the simple Gospel may add, from which no one may take away" (Euseb. *Hist. eccl.* 5.16.3). This writer certainly seems to conceive of the new covenant as represented by a "closed" literary corpus, not subject to expansion or diminution. Van Unnik originally read his statement this way[28] but later made a retraction, stating that "this list is not yet water-tight, because there could be a chance that his own book would be reckoned with it. Had a fixed canon existed already by that time, later well-known difficulties about certain books would have been impossible."[29] Surely this takes far too little regard for the rhetoric. The anonymous author says, "lest I might seem *to some* to be adding . . ."—as if he anticipated someone using against him an argument he and others had been deploying (and Gaius shortly, see *Hist. eccl.* 6.20.3 cited above) against the Montanists. It is of course true that the "later well-known difficulties" expose him as naive. This fact notwithstanding, his view is definite, and he writes as if he believes it is the common view on the subject among catholics. Therefore, while we know of no final list of authoritative, new-covenant books that had been agreed upon at this time, this does not mean that churches and church leaders did not believe there was one.

A. F. Walls points out that Dionysius of Corinth, writing probably no later than about 170, "almost apologizes for publishing his letters, declaring that he does so at the request of 'the brethren', and making it clear that

---

[26] I. Sedlacek, *Dionysius bar Salibi in Apocalypsim, Actus et Epistulas Catholicas* (CSCO, Scriptores Syri 2.101; 1909, text; 1910 Latin version).

[27] 2 Timothy, incidentally, is explicitly cited, adding independent weight to Eusebius' testimony that Gaius recognized all thirteen Pauline epistles.

[28] W. C. van Unnik, "De la règle μήτε προσθεῖναι μήτε ἀφελεῖν dans l'histoire du canon," *VC* 3 (1949) 1-36.

[29] " Ἡ καινὴ διαθήκη: A Problem in the Early History of the Canon," *Studia patristica* 4 (Berlin: Akademie-Verlag, 1961) 212-27, at p. 218.

they are to be distinguished from the dominical Scriptures" (Euseb. *Hist. eccl.* 4.23.12).[30] Again, it is true that other Christian literary productions of the period demonstrate less restraint. Yet such a protective stance on the part of church leaders about the publication of anything which might be misunderstood as staking claim to the kind of authority that was commonly attributed to a received apostolic writing is plainly evident,[31] though its documentation is often ignored by recent writers on the history of the canon. Moreover, Dionysius's designation "dominical Scriptures" (τῶν κυριακῶν . . . γραφῶν) is itself probably to be regarded as specifying a definite body of NT writings.[32] That "the Scriptures of the Lord" is a designation of a NT collection[33] is further supported by a quotation recorded just earlier by Eusebius from Dionysius's contemporary, Hegesippus. Hegesippus had come to Rome from the East during the time of bishop Anicetus (155-166) and on his way had spent some time in Corinth, where he may have met Dionysius. Hegesippus (writing ca. 170-180) testified that on his journey he had found the same doctrine among all the churches: "in each city things are as the law preaches, and the prophets and the Lord" (*Hist. eccl.* 4.22.3). Here ὁ κύριος seems to stand for a known set of writings, on a par with "law" and "prophets."[34] "The Lord's Scriptures," or "the Lord" as a category of writings honored alongside the law and the prophets, are therefore forms of reference to authoritative Christian writings known at least by the 160s or 170s.

The contents and limits of this collection are not specified by either writer, at least in what is preserved by Eusebius. But we do know that Hegesippus had more than a passing interest in the identity of the authentic NT Scriptures. Eusebius reports that he discussed "the so-called Apocrypha" and "relates that some of them were fabricated by certain heretics in his own time" (*Hist. eccl.* 4.22.9). About the same time (180s) Serapion of Antioch too rejected books as inauthentic and not attested by tradition

---

[30] A. F. Walls, "The Montanist 'Catholic Epistle' and Its New Testament Prototype," *SE* 3/2.437-446, at p. 445.

[31] See also in this regard Apollonius of Ephesus, who complains about the Montanist Themiso, who "dared, in imitation of the apostle, to compose an epistle general, to instruct those whose faith was better than his" (Eusebius *Hist. eccl.* 5.18.5).

[32] Writing in the same letter to bishop Soter (166-175) he also makes mention of "the Lord's day" (τὴν σήμερον οὖν κυριακὴν ἁγίαν ἡμέραν διηγάγομεν), where "Lord" obviously refers to Jesus.

[33] Bruce allows that "they might conceivably be the Old Testament writings, especially those passages which were used as 'testimonies' concerning Christ" (*Canon*, 123).

[34] The Syrian translation of Clement's two letters to virgins (early third century according to J. Quasten, *Patrology* [3 vols.; 1951; repr. Westminster, MD: Newman, 1984] 1.58) also preserves this classification: "The Law and the Prophets and the Lord Jesus Christ." See B. F. Westcott, *A General Survey of the History of the Canon of the New Testament* (6th ed.; 1889; repr. Grand Rapids, 1980) 186-87. Hippolytus employs a threefold classification: "the prophets, the Lord, and the apostles" (*Commentary on Daniel* 4.49). Clement speaks similarly of the prophets, the Gospel, and the blessed apostles (*Strom.* 7.16). Irenaeus on one occasion reduces "the entire Scriptures" to the two categories prophets and Gospels (*Ag. Her.* 2.27.2).

(*Hist. eccl.* 6.12.3–6). He is quoted as writing, "for our part, brethren, we receive both Peter and the other apostles as Christ, but the writings which falsely bear their names we reject, as men of experience, knowing that such were not handed down to us."[35] The activity of these last two writers corresponds well with that of the MF, which rejects the *Shepherd* for being written "almost in our time" and other writings which were from known heretical sources.

This is enough to show that it is quite wrong to contend that there was no concern for marking out or keeping inviolate the contents of the new covenant Scriptures in the second century, or to claim that there was no generally accepted core canon at least by the end of that century. In fact, at many points it looks as though the orthodox church at this time was if anything overconfident in its assumption of unanimity. Several writers (Dionysius of Corinth, Irenaeus, the Anonymous anti-Montanist cited by Eusebius) seem to manifest an assurance about the contents of the new-covenant Scriptures which, it may have come as a bit of an embarrassment to find out, was not justified by the facts. An agreement was assumed which was not really there. With scholars like Clement and Origen, even with the MF, we begin to have open admission that there is disagreement among the faithful about some of the church's books. Hahneman's contention that "the decisive period of New Testament canonical history" is properly located in the fourth century may be true only if by decisive period we mean the period in which the church could finally claim (virtually) unanimous agreement on those writings which surrounded the "core," and that from then the canon was settled or fixed. With or without the MF, there is ample evidence that the church was operating with a conception of a closed canon at least by the latter half of the second century. For writers of that generation like Irenaeus and Serapion to speak of the NT writings as that which was "passed on" to them from the previous generation (Irenaeus, *Ag. Her.* 3.1.1; Serapion, *Hist. eccl.* 6.12.3–6) shows that they did not conceive the

---

[35] Given this statement by Serapion, it is surprising that Hahneman (p. 100) labors to give the impression that Petrine pseudepigrapha such as *Gosp. Pet.* held the same place as the canonical Gospels in Syria at this time. Before coming to Rhossus, Serapion had never even seen the work in question and, as he later admits, at the time of his visit somewhat carelessly ("without going through" it) assented to its reading among them. This is hardly to be taken as implying that their "reading" of it was in worship or as Scripture. Gamble reads the "fascinating report" about Serapion similarly: "In the community of Rhossus, which lay in Serapion's jurisdiction, the *Gospel of Peter* was in use, and Serapion expressed no reservation about this. But when it was eventually brought to his attention that this Gospel might contain heterodox ideas, Serapion banned its further use. The incident illustrates that a four-Gospel collection had not become normative in the east" (*New Testament Canon,* 35). Once again, it seems to be assumed that as soon as someone receives a set of documents as canonical or normative, he or she must swear off reading anything else forever. Actually, Serapion never did ban the *Gosp. Pet.* from being read. After studying the works of the Docetists who apparently used this Gospel and giving the pseudepigraphon a careful reading, he simply wrote to the Rhossians a list of objectionable passages which were capable of misleading. Gamble's summary of the incident should be compared to the words of Serapion himself quoted above.

question the way Hahneman does. No matter how many new "Gospels" or imitation apostolic epistles continued to appear, there was no chance of any of them making their way into the body of the church's Scriptures. Apart from the occasional rearguard efforts necessitated by controversialists such as Gaius of Rome, the question that rises to face the church by the end of the second century has mostly to do with minor variations that may have existed in the traditonal collections held in the archives of individual apostolic churches. That we do not have more "lists" surviving from this period[36] and that it took more than 150 more years for the church to arrive at unanimity on the disputed books has to be attributed to other factors. For one thing, the church at this time lacked the means to draw itself together and unite officially beyond local councils about this or any other matter. Thus, as in questions such as belief in the Trinity, the two natures of Christ, sacramental traditions, etc., standard usages did not exist without individual and regional eccentricities.[37]

There is no question that Hahneman has beefed up Sundberg's case for a later date and an Eastern origin for the Muratorian Fragment. Still, we are bound to judge that the case is unconvincing and that the traditional dating does far better justice to the evidence. Along with the present reviewer, Ferguson and Horbury have already pointed to some of the major weaknesses of the proposal. Thus, despite early endorsement from R. M. Grant,[38] the theory certainly cannot be said to have carried the day. Though the thesis of Sundberg and Hahneman may be flawed and at many points tendentious, they have turned over old embers which now are certain to glow again. As we note an interest in canon questions being raised from other quarters (notably by some who would like to see the Gospel of Thomas included in future editions of the NT), it would seem that the stage is set for important work to be done in this area.

Reformed Theological Seminary in Orlando
P. O. Box 945120
Maitland, FL 32794-5120

---

[36] From about AD 240 we have a virtual list in Origen's *Homilies on Joshua* 7.1. See Metzger, *Canon*, 139–40. This list is identical with the present canon, with the apparent omission of John's Revelation (the MSS are divided). From elsewhere we know that Origen did receive that book.

[37] "In the 4th century the tendency towards unification grew stronger in every sphere of the Church's life (liturgy, organisation, Church order, etc.). The canon also was affected by this" (Schneemelcher, *New Testament Apocrypha* 1.31).

[38] A largely favorable review has also appeared from J. K. Elliott in *NovT* 36 (1994) 297–99.

THE WISDOM OF SOLOMON IN THE
MURATORIAN FRAGMENT

THE Muratorian fragment is potentially an important witness to early assessment of the book of Wisdom. Moreover, the lines on Wisdom have played a considerable part in modern assessment and redating of the fragment itself.[1] The interpretation of these lines is reviewed below, in the belief that some widely accepted explanations are at least questionable. The points considered are (*a*) the sense of the ascription of Wisdom to 'Solomon's friends'; and (*b*) the significance of Wisdom's place in the book list underlying the fragment, after New Testament writings and before three Christian apocalypses. It is then asked how the results affect estimates (*c*) of the early repute of Wisdom and (*d*) of the date of the fragment.

The relevant passage runs as follows (lines 68–75 = f. 11^r, lines 6–13):[2]

Epistula sane Iudae et superscripti Iohannis duas in catholica habentur; et Sapientia ab amicis Salomonis in honorem ipsius scripta. Apocalypses etiam Iohannis et Petri tantum recipimus, quam quidam ex nostris legi in ecclesia nolunt. Pastorem vero nuperrime temporibus nostris in urbe Roma Hermas conscripsit...

The Epistle of Jude no doubt, and the couple bearing the name of John, are accepted in the catholic church; and the Wisdom written by the friends of Solomon in his honour. The Revelations also of John and of Peter only we receive—although some of our people will not have the latter read in the church. The Shepherd indeed was written very lately in our times in the city of Rome by Hermas...

(*a*) The book of Wisdom was ascribed in antiquity not only to Solomon, but also to Philo and Ben Sira.[3] S. P. Tregelles alluringly conjectured that 'ab amicis' in the fragment represents misunderstanding of Greek ὑπὸ Φίλωνος, 'by Philo'.[4] The fragment's

---

[1] See especially A. C. Sundberg, 'Canon Muratori: A Fourth Century List', HTR lxvi. (1973), 1–41 (15–18), and G. M. Hahneman, *The Muratorian Fragment and the Development of the Canon* (Oxford, 1992), 215–17 and elsewhere (bibliography).

[2] S. P. Tregelles, *Canon Muratorianus* (Oxford, 1867), 20, or Hahneman, 7, as corrected and punctuated by B. F. Westcott, *A General Survey of the History of the Canon of the New Testament* (5th edn., London, 1881), 537; I have not followed Westcott in beginning a new paragraph at *Apocalypses* (see (*b*), below).

[3] C. Larcher, *Le livre de la Sagesse* (3 vols., Paris, 1983, 1984, 1985), i, 132–34.

[4] Tregelles, *Canon*, 53–4 (noting that the conjecture had been independently made by William Fitzgerald), followed by T. Zahn, *Geschichte des neutestamentlichen Kanons* (2 vols. in 4 parts, Erlangen & Leipzig, 1888–92), ii.1 (1890), 103–5, and H. von Campenhausen, *The Formation of the Christian Bible* (E.T.

© Oxford University Press 1994

[Journal of Theological Studies, NS, Vol. 45, Pt. 1, April 1994]

otherwise unknown ascription to Solomon's friends would then disappear, and the clause would attest the Philonic attribution, which was accepted by old authors, according to Jerome's Prologue to the books of Solomon translated from the Hebrew.[5] Tregelles held that this passage in the fragment was in fact known to Jerome. The possibility that the Latin rests on misunderstood Greek might be supported by the view (also debated) that the reference to two Johannine epistles immediately beforehand likewise reflects misunderstanding.[6]

Yet, as has been briefly urged elsewhere, this explanation of the ascription of Wisdom should be treated with caution.[7] The view put forward in the Latin as we have it, that Wisdom was composed by the king's friends, need not have seemed far-fetched. Royal friends gain prominence in the LXX, in accord with Hellenistic court custom, as compared with MT.[8] Among the places where they appear is a verse regularly cited in ancient Jewish and Christian discussion of the Solomonic books, Prov. 25: 1, on the copying or selection of proverbs of Solomon by Hezekiah's company (LXX 'the *friends* of Hezekiah, the king of Judah', οἱ φίλοι Ἐζεκίου τοῦ βασιλέως τῆς Ἰουδαίας). Thus, in a comment on the Song of Songs attributed to Hippolytus by Anastasius of Sinai, the 'friends of Hezekiah, being wise' choose from Solomon's compositions (1 Kings 5: 12 (4: 32)) the most edifying—including Wisdom.[9] Prov. 25: 1 LXX was adduced by Tregelles in his first stage of study; he then held that the Muratorian fragment referred to Proverbs, not Wisdom.[10]

London, 1972), 245 n. 199, 247 n. 207; the view is judged quite probable by E. Schürer, revised by G. Vermes, F. Millar, M. Goodman, M. Black and P. Vermes, *A History of the Jewish People in the Age of Jesus Christ*, iii.1 (Edinburgh, 1986), 574, and by Hahneman, 14, 201–2, 215.

[5] R. Weber and others, *Biblia Sacra iuxta Vulgatam Versionem* (2nd edn., 2 vols., Stuttgart, 1975), ii, 957 (*nonnulli scriptorum veterum hunc Iudaei Filonis adfirmant*).

[6] C. F. D. Moule, *The Birth of the New Testament* (3rd edn., London, 1982), 266, n. 2 (modifying a conjecture of P. Katz by the suggestion that 2, 3 John were included in an original Greek δύο πρὸς καθολικήν); on other explanations, B. M. Metzger, *The Canon of the New Testament* (Oxford, 1987), 197, and n. 20.

[7] W. Horbury, 'The Christian Use and the Jewish Origins of the Wisdom of Solomon', to appear in a *Festschrift*.

[8] P.-M. Bogaert, 'Relecture et refonte historicisante du Livre de Daniel attestées par la première version grecque (papyrus 967)', in R. Kuntzmann and J. Schlosser (eds.), *Études sur le judaïsme hellénistique* (Paris, 1984), 197–224 (223, citing Dan. 3: 91, 94; 5: 23; 6: 13, Esther, and I-IV Maccabees).

[9] N. Bonwetsch, *Hippolytus Werke*, i. 1 (GCS, Leipzig, 1897), 343 (Proverbs, Wisdom, Ecclesiastes and the Canticle are listed in that order as the four surviving Solomonic books).

[10] Tregelles, *Canon*, 51–52, quoting C. C. J. von Bunsen as an independent sponsor of the same opinion; at 55, n. *o*, he allows that some might still prefer this view.

In the Vulgate the 'friends' (*amici*) of Solomon himself appear in the Song of Songs (Cant. 5: 1, LXX πλησίοι), in a context which could evoke, for a reader in the ancient world, a Solomonic symposium with fitting contributions of wise sayings by the friends. Moreover, Josephus calls Hiram, King of Tyre 'a friend of our king Solomon' (cf. 1 Kings 5: 12), and the tale of their sapiential correspondence which he tells was taken up by Theophilus of Antioch and Eusebius.[11] Lastly, it is just possible that Ben Sira, whose book was regularly associated with Wisdom and often treated as Solomonic, might have been covered by the term 'friend' as an imitator of Solomon.[12]

There was, in any case, material for the theory that royal friends composed Wisdom. Such a theory would, in fact, suit the last chapters of Proverbs, with which Wisdom was closely linked and which it sometimes followed. MT allows the view that Proverbs includes contributions from the Wise, from Agur, and from Lemuel (24: 23; 30: 1; 31: 1). In the LXX and rabbinic tradition pains are taken to exclude this view and to make Proverbs fully Solomonic.[13] Were other Greek renderings current, closer to the interpretative tradition attested in MT, which permitted the excluded view? This is suggested by the retention of a proper name answering to Lemuel at 31: 1 in Aquila, Symmachus, and Theodotion, and by the rendering of Ithiel as a proper name, again contrary to LXX, in Aquila and Theodotion at 30: 1.[14] Furthermore, Psalm lxxii (lxxi) appears in the LXX precisely as a poem 'to Solomon'; here the revised Greek versions appear to have understood the Hebrew title as 'by Solomon',[15] but the LXX rendering, no doubt guarding the possibility of Davidic authorship, makes this psalm an analogue to what is suggested of Wisdom in the Fragment.

---

[11] Josephus, *Ant.* viii. 58, 143–49; *Ap.* 109–120; Theophilus, *Aut.* iii. 22; Eusebius, *Chron.* i. 17, 1–3.

[12] W. O. E. Oesterley in R. H. Charles (ed.), *The Apocrypha and Pseudepigrapha of the Old Testament*, i. (Oxford, 1913), 299; Ben Sira is an imitator (ὀπαδός) of Solomon in the pseudo-Athanasian biblical Synopsis, 46 (*PG* 28.377), translated in the first *AV* Prologue to Ecclesiasticus.

[13] Compare LXX (Solomon speaks to the wise in 24: 23, and the proper names are omitted in the later chapters) with Targ. Prov. 24: 23 (as LXX), Cant. R. i 1, 10 (Agur and Lemuel names of Solomon) and other texts cited by L. Ginzberg, *Legends of the Jews*, vi. (repr. Philadelphia, 1968), 277, n. 2.

[14] F. Field, *Origenis Hexaplorum quae supersunt*, ii. (Oxford, 1875), 373.

[15] A comment ascribed to Eusebius (*PG* 28. 789, 792), contrasting LXX with the rest, who ascribe the psalm to Solomon, is noted as relevant to reconstruction of other Greek versions by Field, ii, 211.

Attribution to 'the friends of Solomon' could therefore be linked with the importance of royal friends in general and Solomon's in particular. It ingeniously reconciles existing doubt on authorship (see (c) below) with the traditional ascription, in a manner consonant with the development of the biblical tradition on Solomon in the Graeco-Roman world. Perhaps, then, the fragment as it stands genuinely reflects an otherwise unknown attribution.

(b) Wisdom is widely said to be included here among the New Testament books.[16] The view that the Latin text represents a misunderstanding of an original Philonic ascription has contributed to this position. Thus Zahn, accepting that Philo was regarded as author, judged that Wisdom was deliberately put at the close of a still flexible list of apostolic works because it was known to be recent and by a writer whom Christians revered.[17]

Nevertheless, it would be surprising if Wisdom were indeed treated here as a New Testament work, or among apostolic writings. Despite the currency of the Philonic attribution from early times, Wisdom was consistently linked in quotations, copying, and lists with Solomon and the Solomonic books, especially Proverbs and Ecclesiasticus.[18] B. F. Westcott's explanation of the place of Wisdom in this passage of the fragment seems preferable.[19] He compared Eusebius' practice of treating the disputed books of both Testaments (antilegomena) together. The same practice is found in Athanasius and Rufinus, where Old and New Testament lists precede the combined list of antilegomena, and the disputed books of either Testament are designated 'outside' or 'ecclesiastical' books;[20] it appears in Epiphanius, who similarly

[16] So Sundberg, 15–18; Larcher, i, 146; R. T. Beckwith, *The Old Testament Canon of the New Testament Church* (London, 1985), 347, 390; Schürer revised, iii.1, 574; A. Tuilier, 'Les livres Sapientiaux et le canon de l'Ancien Testament dans l'Église ancienne', in *Letture cristiane dei Libri Sapienzali* (Studia Ephemeridis "Augustinianum", 37, Rome, 1992), 19–34 (20); Hahneman, 200–5, 215–17. von Campenhausen, 244, n. 193 and 247, n. 208 combines this view with the opinion that in the fourth century Wisdom and other doubtful works were mentioned in a kind of appendix to both Testaments; here it is suggested that the Muratorian fragment itself presupposes such an appendix, so that Wisdom in the fragment is not placed in the New Testament.

[17] Zahn, ii.1, 104–5.

[18] See especially H. B. Swete, *An Introduction to the Old Testament in Greek* (2nd Edn., Cambridge, 1914), 228; C. Larcher, *Études sur le livre de la Sagesse* (Paris, 1969), 36–63; W. Thiele, *Sapientia Salomonis* (Vetus Latina 11/1, Freiburg i.B., 1977–85), 231–32 and (on the title) 241–45.

[19] Westcott, 537, n. 8, citing Eusebius, *HE* v.8, 8; vi. 13, 6 (on Irenaeus and Clement of Alexandria, respectively).

[20] Athanasius, Festal Letter 39 and Rufinus, *Expositio Symboli*, 34–36; see Zahn, ii.1, 203–12, 240–44 (Greek and Latin texts, with discussion); Swete, 203–4, 210 (the Old Testament material only); E. Junod, 'La formation et la composition de

lists Old and New Testament antilegomena after he has summarized the whole body of Old and New Testament scripture;[21] it is probably implied in Cyril of Jerusalem,[22] it is reflected in Jerome,[23] and it reappears later, for example, in the Stichometry of Nicephorus.[24] Although many of Eusebius' antilegomena were treated as canonical in the West, the practice still survives vestigially in the constantly reprinted Clementine Vulgate of 1592, where the Old and New Testaments are followed by an appendix comprising the Prayer of Manasses and III–IV Ezra = I–II Esdras. (The addition to this appendix in R. Weber's manual Vulgate (1969) not only of Psalm 151, but also of a New Testament antilegomenon, Laodiceans, further heightens the resemblance to ancient practice.) In the light of the later evidence Eusebius can clearly be seen to have presupposed an Old Testament as well as a New Testament list in his remarks on disputed books, and this point is confirmed not only by the presence of both Old and New Testament items in his antilegomena, but also by his care to report the Old Testament lists of Melito and Origen—which in both cases might otherwise be lost.[25]

In this old-established usage, then, books of either Testament classed as acceptable but outside the canonical number are

l'Ancien Testament dans l'Église grecque des quatres premiers siècles', and O. Wermelinger, 'Le canon des latins au temps de Jérôme et d'Augustin', in J.-D. Kaestli and O. Wermelinger (eds.), Le canon de l'Ancien Testament (Geneva, 1984), 105–51, 152–210 (141–44, translations of Greek and Coptic texts of Athanasius; 197–98, translation of Rufinus).

[21] Pan. lxxvi. 5, printed and discussed by Zahn, ii.1, 219–26; the passage is not simply a New Testament catalogue, remarkable for its inclusion of Wisdom and Ecclesiasticus, as might be supposed from Sundberg, 17–18 and Hahneman, 147, 179, 204, 217.

[22] Cyril of Jerusalem, Cat. iv. 35–36, lists and numbers the Old and New Testament books, without those usually assigned to the 'outside' section, and immediately adds—probably with reference to these—τὰ δὲ λοιπὰ πάντα ἔξω κείσθω ἐν δευτέρῳ (iv. 36). Arguments against and for this interpretation, respectively, are put by Junod, 'Formation', 129–30 and Wermelinger, 'Le canon', 164–65; Wisdom and the Revelation of John, both quoted by Cyril though excluded from his list, are strong candidates for inclusion in his 'outside' section (see Zahn, ii.1, 176, nn. 1–2.)

[23] His Prologus Galeatus to Kings (Weber, i, 365) groups 'outside' books from both Testaments at the end of an Old Testament list (probably not including Hermas in the Old Testament, as urged by Sundberg, 15, 18): (...quicquid extra hos est, inter apocrifa seponendum. Igitur Sapientia, quae vulgo Salomonis inscribitur, et Iesu filii Sirach liber et Iudith et Tobias et Pastor non sunt in canone).

[24] Zahn, ii.1, 295–301.

[25] Eusebius, HE iv. 26, 12–14 and vi. 25, 1–2, respectively; Eusebius is the only witness to Melito's list (S. G. Hall (ed.), Melito of Sardis, On Pascha and Fragments (Oxford, 1979), 64), and Origen's is otherwise attested only in Latin, in Hilary of Poitiers (N. R. M. de Lange, Origen and the Jews (Cambridge, 1976), 52–53).

grouped together after the canonical books of both Testaments. The books put in this class commonly begin with Wisdom and Ecclesiasticus; this is the case in Eusebius, when he is noting the disputed books cited by Clement of Alexandria (Eusebius, *HE* vi. 13, 6–14, 1), and also in lists given by Athanasius, Epiphanius, Rufinus, and Jerome, as cited above. Various New Testament items which are noted as disputed in the fragment also figure in this class of combined Old and New Testament antilegomena. Thus Eusebius names Hebrews and the epistles of Barnabas and Clement—works unmentioned in the fragment—among the disputed books cited in the works of Clement of Alexandria; but he also includes Jude, 'the remaining catholic epistles', and the Revelation of Peter, which all appear in the fragment ('the remaining catholic epistles' in part). Athanasius, Rufinus, and Jerome include in this class the Shepherd of Hermas, the next item in the fragment, and Rufinus also includes the Judgment according to Peter, a book which is comparable, if not identical, with the Revelation of Peter in the fragment.[26] The Revelation of John, named in the fragment between Wisdom and the Revelation of Peter, was counted among the antilegomena by some, according to Eusebius (*HE* iii. 25, 4). Eusebius notes too what Irenaeus has to say about various disputed books, forming a group which again brings Wisdom together with Hermas; here the order is the Revelation of John, 1 John, 1 Peter, Hermas, and Wisdom (*HE* v. 8, 6–8). Cyril of Jerusalem's evidence probably implies that he envisaged a class of antilegomena including Wisdom and the Revelation of John (n. 22, above). These sources have points of contact with the fragment, therefore, in content as well as placing; Eusebius' varying orders for the antilegomena are doubtless affected by the later Christian writings on which he is commenting, but they also suggest that the group of antilegomena from both Testaments could be held in mind in various ways, although the group as a whole was likely to be considered just after enumeration of the assured New Testament books, and Wisdom was an important item in it.

This pattern seems to be reflected in the Muratorian fragment.

---

[26] Rufinus, *Expositio Symboli*, 36, ed. M. Simonetti (CCL 20, Turnhout, 1961), p. 71, lists as New Testament 'ecclesiastical' books *libellus qui dicitur Pastoris sive Hermae, et is qui appellatur Duae viae, vel Iudicium secundum Petrum*; Zahn, ii.1, 243, n. 1, followed here, takes Rufinus to specify the Judgment as a separate book, not as the Two Ways under another name. Jerome, *Vir. Ill.* 1, notes five apocryphal Petrine books, the fourth being the Revelation and the last being called *Iudicium*; but the content of the Revelation suggests that 'the Judgment according to Peter' would have been an apt alternative name, and it seems possible that the Revelation was also known as the Judgment.

The lost beginning of the fragment probably included comments based on an Old Testament list.[27] This list would have been immediately followed by the New Testament list underlying the text which survives in the fragment. It appears that the New Testament list was itself followed, on the pattern illustrated above, by a list of Old and New Testament books which were not of assured authority but were widely accepted. The passage of the fragment which includes the reference to Wisdom and is quoted at the beginning of this article seems to be based on the conclusion of the New Testament list, and on the immediately following list of disputed books.

In the underlying list, within the New Testament a division can tentatively be recognized between the Pauline corpus and Jude. The writer of the text in the fragment makes a fresh beginning with catholic epistles, having expanded on the Pauline corpus immediately before, and also notes their general acceptance, knowing that some put them among the antilegomena. After these catholic epistles—Jude and two Johannine epistles—the New Testament list ends and the list of Old and New Testament antilegomena begins. In comment, however, a remark like that just made on three catholic epistles is immediately required and made on Wisdom first of all, followed by comments on the Revelations of John and Peter, and on Hermas. The form of the comments in the fragment marks the division within the New Testament list rather than the division between the New Testament and the antilegomena, for a new sentence is begun for Jude, and the clause on Wisdom is simply added to it; but the fragment gives comments based on a list, not simply the list itself.[28]

The place of Wisdom in the fragment would then imply not that Wisdom was connected with or even included in the New Testament, but that, like the Revelations of John and of Peter, and (to a lesser degree) the Shepherd of Hermas, it was considered an acceptable book not certainly included in the canonical number. This explanation, unlike the preceding one, is in full agreement with a known status accorded to Wisdom—that of a leading antilegomenon, commonly put first in lists of the 'outside' or 'ecclesiastical' books from the Old and New Testaments.

A. C. Sundberg and G. M. Hahneman urge that Eusebius and

---

[27] J. B. Lightfoot, *The Apostolic Fathers*, Part i, *S. Clement of Rome* (2nd edn., 2 vols., London, 1890), ii, 412–13; the possibility is allowed by A. Harnack, *Die Chronologie der altchristlichen Litteratur bis Eusebius*, ii. (Leipzig, 1904), 333, n. 1, and Hahneman, 181 ('perhaps probable').

[28] Metzger, 194.

Epiphanius—like the fragment, in their view—also include Wisdom among the New Testament books; but this would be surprising for the reason already noted. For Sundberg, Eusebius, and Epiphanius, as cited above, associate Wisdom with the New Testament, while Jerome puts the Shepherd of Hermas—at the end of a list beginning with Wisdom—in the Old Testament (n. 23, above); but in each case it seems more likely that a separate combined list of Old and New Testament antilegomena is in view, as already suggested. Eusebius is concerned with disputed books, and groups antilegomena of both Testaments together; Epiphanius gives a combined list of Old and New Testament antilegomena after treating the Old and New Testament books, on the pattern seen also in Athanasius and Rufinus (n. 21, above); Jerome, in the context of concern with the Old Testament canon, gives the group of Old and New Testament antilegomena after an Old Testament list. The usage met in these three authors can then be compared, as noted already, with the placing of the 'outside' books in Athanasius, Rufinus, and other witnesses. This separate placing probably reflects Jewish practice, for Origen's list of 'the twenty-two books, according to the Hebrews' has at the end of the biblical list a separate section comprising the Maccabees, with their Hebrew title, after the heading ἔξω δὲ τούτων (Eusebius, *HE* vi. 25, 2).[29] Compare the words with which Athanasius introduces his separate 'outside' section, after recital of the canonical Old and New Testament books: ἔστι καὶ ἕτερα βιβλία τούτων ἔξωθεν. This section begins with Wisdom.

The fragment therefore falls in with a practice first clearly attested in Eusebius, but probably current earlier, as Jewish usage reflected in Origen suggests.

(c) The suggestions made so far would confirm the high position of Wisdom in the opinion underlying the fragment. Its status in the fragment, as suggested in (b) above, is that of an acceptable book not comprised in the canonical number, and here it is the only Old Testament book judged worthy of mention in this category. This estimate agrees with the eminent place of Wisdom as the first of the 'outside' books in Athanasius, Epiphanius, Rufinus, and Jerome, and, earlier, as the first in Eusebius's list of those Old and New Testament antilegomena which are quoted by Clement of Alexandria.

Correspondingly with this high estimate, the ascription of Wisdom to the 'friends of Solomon', interpreted as a genuine

[29] Zahn, i.1 (1888), 126, n. 2, affirms Jewish influence, citing M. Sanh. x. 1 and Jerusalem Talmud, Sanh. x. 1–2, 28a, on 'outside books' (further discussed in Horbury, 'Wisdom', n. 16).

ancient attribution in (*a*), above, seeks to reconcile criticism with tradition. Hahneman stresses (questionably) that, apart from the fragment, doubt about the Solomonic authorship of Wisdom is expressed only by fourth-century authors, Jerome and Augustine.[30] Jerome and Augustine, however, both report existing opinion, making it clear that non-Solomonic ascriptions had long been current. Thus some of the 'old' writers (*nonnulli scriptorum veterum*) made the Philonic ascription, according to Jerome; and when he mentions *veteres* in another place, and this time goes on to specify some of them, they belong to the second and third century, and include Tertullian and Irenaeus.[31] Jerome's remark on Wisdom has been plausibly linked, accordingly, with statements on Philo probably drawn by Eusebius from the second-century Hegesippus.[32] Comparably, the ascription to Ben Sira was given by Augustine, *De Doc. Chr.* ii. 8, 13 as a known opinion which he then regarded as standard (*constantissime perhibetur*). His later withdrawal of this view may reflect not only current doubts (Julian of Eclanum viewed both this and the Philonic ascription as uncertain) but also desire to uphold the authority of Wisdom.[33] The background of the attribution to the friends of Solomon is therefore likely to be existing criticism. The early currency of such criticism in the church, despite the deep Christian veneration for Wisdom, indeed suggests that authorship will already have been debated among Jews at the time of Christian origins. The ascription in the fragment is probably in any case an attempt at reconciliation; but its contacts with the outlook attested in the revised Greek versions confirm that the possibility of Jewish origin should be kept open.

The fragment then reflects high esteem for Wisdom as a pre-eminent 'outside' book, and seeks to uphold Wisdom's authority against a background of long-standing doubts on authenticity by a mediating attribution—which is at the same time a valuable

---

[30] Hahneman, 201–2, 216; his view that Origen doubted canonicity, not authenticity is questioned by Origen's regular use of descriptions like ἡ ἐπιγεγραμμένη Σολομῶντος (*Hom. Jer* viii. 1, quoted with other texts in Schürer revised, iii.1, 574–75).

[31] Jerome, *Comm. Isa*, book xviii, Prologue: to reject literal interpretation of the Revelation of John means that *multorum veterum videbimus opinionibus contraire*.

[32] Notably Eusebius, *HE* ii. 17, 1, discussed with other material by P. E. Bruns, 'Philo Christianus: The Debris of a Legend', *HTR* lxvi. (1973), 141–45.

[33] Augustine, *Op. imp. c. Iul.*, iv. 123; *Retr.* ii. 4, 2, discussed by A. M. la Bonnardière, *Biblia Augustiniana, A.T. Le livre de la Sagesse* (Paris, 1970), 46–57 and 'Le canon des divines Écritures', in la Bonnardière and others, *Saint Augustin et la Bible* (Paris, 1986), 287–301.

remnant of early Christian, and perhaps also Jewish, biblical criticism.

(*d*) How do the suggestions made above bear on dating? A. C. Sundberg has proposed an early fourth-century date and G. M. Hahneman a date about 375, on the basis especially of contacts with fourth-century canonical lists—lists abundant in this century, but not found before (at least for the *New Testament*). On the other hand, there is a strong prima facie case, widely accepted in earlier study, for a late second-century or a third-century date for the material reproduced in the fragment; the late second-century Pius is put 'in our times', and there are references or debts to other second-century figures in the fragment, but no mention of later authorities.[34]

The lines on Wisdom are judged by Sundberg and Hahnemann to support a later date, for reasons discussed in (*a*) and (*b*) above; the passage reflects the ascription to Philo attested by Jerome, and includes Wisdom in a New Testament catalogue, as on their view also happens in Eusebius and Epiphanius. It has been urged above that the Latin is better taken at face value; but even if it indirectly attests the Philonic ascription, Jerome says that this is affirmed by *old* authors, and this interpretation too would therefore be fully consonant with an earlier date. Secondly, contacts with Eusebius and Epiphanius (and other fourth-century writers) certainly remain important even when it has been argued (*b*, above) that the placing of Wisdom in Eusebius and Epiphanius should not be interpreted as inclusion in a New Testament catalogue; but the argument has shown that the placing of Wisdom in Eusebius and later writers has a prehistory. Eusebius's grouping of Old and New Testament antilegomena together reflects custom which he will have learned in the third century, and Origen's Old Testament canon 'according to the Hebrews' reflects in the early third century a Jewish recognition, shared by Christians, of a class of books 'outside' the canonical number—a class in which Christians, concerned with New Testament numbers also, placed New Testament as well as Old Testament antilegomena.

The lines on Wisdom would therefore be compatible with earlier dating of the fragment. The evidence reviewed also, however, tends to qualify the broader consideration that, as other New

---

[34] See n. 1, above, E. Ferguson, 'Canon Muratori: Date and Provenance', *Studia Patristica* xviii. (1982), 677–83, and Metzger, 193–94; a second-century or third-century date would well suit, but of course is not required by, the indebtedness to Papias detected in the Muratorian fragment by R. J. Bauckham, 'Papias and Polycrates on the Origin of the Fourth Gospel', *JTS*, (NS) xliv. (1993), 24–69 (53–63).

Testament lists belong to the fourth century, the same may be true of the list underlying the fragment. Thus, the custom learned by Eusebius in the later third century is linked with earlier Christian and Jewish usage, attested by Origen, and presupposes existing Old and New Testament lists. Two such earlier Old Testament lists in fact survive, thanks to Eusebius, from Melito and Origen; but they both came near to being lost, and it is reasonable to suppose that there will have been other pre-Eusebian material of the same kind, including New Testament lists, as other passages in Origen suggest.[35] This evidence weighs against the claim that ecclesiastical definition of an Old Testament canon first begins in the fourth century, and that we would hardly expect the similar New Testament definition seen in the fragment to precede it.[36] It seems, rather, that a combined Old and New Testament list, with a postscript on antilegomena, on the pattern which the lines on Wisdom in the fragment probably reflect, would not be anachronistic at the end of the second or the beginning of the third century.[37]

WILLIAM HORBURY

[35] Metzger, 136–40, 191 (Origen, *Hom. Jos.* vii. 1, and comments on Matthew and John quoted by Eusebius, *HE*, vi. 25, 3–10).

[36] So Hahneman, 83 (cf. Sundberg, 16–18, 35–8); Hahneman's restriction of the lists in Melito and Origen to anti-Jewish polemical needs is questioned by the use soon made of the lists in canonical inquiry, and by the inner-Christian importance of Jewish opinion; so Origen (*Princ.* iv. 33, cf. *Comm. Joh.* xxviii. 15 (13)) and Augustine (CD xvii. 20, *Praed. Sanct.* xiv. 26–29) note in internal debate that Wisdom's authority is doubted.

[37] Since writing the above I have seen P. Henne, O.P., 'La datation du Canon de Muratori', *Revue biblique* 100 (1993), 54–75 (kindly brought to my notice by Dr J. N. B. Carleton Paget); reviewing arguments by Sundberg and Ferguson, Henne favours a second-century date, with further considerations drawn from the New Testament material. Henne (59–60) cites Zahn and von Campenhausen to show that in the fourth century Wisdom was sometimes mentioned after New Testament writings in a kind of appendix to both Testaments (compare n. 16 above), and holds that its position could have been uncertain in the second century (implying a view not far removed in general from that taken above).

Καινὴ διαθήκη: THE TITLE OF THE NEW TESTAMENT IN THE SECOND AND THIRD CENTURIES*

IN 1961 W. C. van Unnik observed, as regards the New Testament canon: 'In the history of the canon much attention is always paid to the question, how these various books were collected into one volume. The various stages of this process varying from one book or groups of books to another is most interesting. Little attention however is given to that other question, why these books were assembled under the title of a διαθήκη. This problem is the more fascinating since this name had such a success, that it remains the standard title in the church ever since.'[1] Not much has changed since then. Most authors who have recently dealt with the formation of the New Testament canon, such as Philipp Vielhauer, Bruce M. Metzger, or Wilhelm Schneemelcher (to name but three), just note the transition in the meaning of διαθήκη/*testamentum* from the theological concept of 'covenant' to the book title, but do not attempt an explanation of how exactly this came about.[2] Yet van Unnik's question has lost none of its fascination, whilst his results, which I shall deal with below, though a great step forward, have not yet provided us with a sufficient answer.

So I propose to ask once again: Why is the New Testament called 'New Testament'? The origin of the English title is obvious and well known. It is a translation of *novum testamentum* in the Latin Vulgate which itself is a translation of the Greek καινὴ διαθήκη. Διαθήκη in turn is the Greek rendering of Hebrew בְּרִית. The precise meaning of that term has been admirably elucidated by Ernst Kutsch. It may suffice here to resume his main results: בְּרִית does not originally signify a covenant of two

---

* I am indebted to Professor Maurice F. Wiles (Oxford), Dr David Trobisch (Heidelberg) and Dr Markus Vinzent (Cambridge) for helpful suggestions and criticisms.

[1] W. C. van Unnik, 'Ἡ καινὴ διαθήκη—A Problem in the Early History of the Canon', in: *StPatr* I, Berlin 1961, pp. 212–227; also in: id., *Sparsa Collecta*, vol. II, Leiden 1980, pp. 157–171 (quoted thereafter), p. 159.

[2] Cf. Philipp Vielhauer, *Geschichte der urchristlichen Literatur: Einleitung in das Neue Testament, die Apokryphen und die Apostolischen Väter*, Berlin 1975, pp. 775–777; Wilhelm Schneemelcher, art. 'Bibel III', in: *TRE* VI, 1980, pp. 22–48, 27 f.; id. in: Edgar Hennecke/Wilhelm Schneemelcher, *Neutestamentliche Apokryphen in deutsche Übersetzung*, fifth ed., 2 vols., Tübingen 1987/89, I, pp. 4 f.; Bruce M. Metzger, *The Canon of the New Testament: Its Origin, Development and Significance*, second ed., Oxford 1988, p. 106. Cf. also the remarks by van Unnik, art. cit., p. 159.

[Journal of Theological Studies, NS, Vol. 45, Pt. 2, October 1994]

equal contracting partners, but, rather, means a 'unilateral "ordinance", "obligation"—as an obligation imposed by oneself or by somebody else'.[3] Kutsch's thorough analysis has shown that this is also the meaning of the Greek translation of the term (διαθήκη) in the Septuagint and in the literature influenced by it. Originally, however, διαθήκη means primarily 'last Will and Testament' and is, therefore, also translated *testamentum* in the *Vetus Latina*. Thus the theological concept behind these various terms underwent a considerable transformation, by which the ultimate character of the ordinance was emphasized. At the same time, however, the original meaning of διαθήκη ('last Will and Testament') by no means disappeared. Already in the Greek New Testament διαθήκη was not only used in the sense of 'ordinance' (בְּרִית) but was also understood to mean 'last Will and Testament' (cf. Gal. 3: 15,17; Heb. 9: 16 f.). This shift of the meaning of בְּרִית in Greek from 'ordinance' to 'last Will and Testament' initiated a whole new series of theological metaphors and associations.[4] In what follows, I shall use the established translations 'testament' and 'covenant' which, however, are meant to include the modifications mentioned.

The relevant research may be quickly summarized. The seminal study of the problem is found in Theodor Zahn's monumental *Geschichte des Neutestamentlichen Kanons*.[5] Zahn analysed the various designations of the Bible in the first to third centuries and emphasized that, in the event, 'Old' and 'New Testament' had prevailed. In Zahn's opinion, however, the titles did not correspond to the original meaning of these biblical terms. For 'in the Bible διαθήκη meant the covenant established by God, the order of the relationship between God and the community given by Him and καινὴ διαθήκη a re-organization of this relationship by Christ which was reserved for the end of times, hence not the *document* of the revelation, but *revelation* itself.'[6] For Zahn, there-

---

[3] Cf. Ernst Kutsch, *Neues Testament—Neuer Bund? Eine Fehlübersetzung wird korrigiert*, Neukirchen-Vluyn 1978, p. 85. Moreover, id., art. 'Bund', in: *TRE* VII, 1981, pp. 397–410, 397 ff.; Erich Gräßer, *Der Alte Bund im Neuen: Exegetische Studien zur Israelfrage im Neuen Testament*, Tübingen 1985 (WUNT 35), pp. 1–7.

[4] Cf. Kutsch, *Neues Testament—Neuer Bund?*, op. cit., pp. 100–102, 136–142; Gräßer, op. cit., pp. 56–69, 98 f. I have studied those passages in early Christian literature where, in theological discourse, διαθήκη is understood to mean 'last Will and Testament' in my book *Erbin Kirche: Die Auslegung von Psalm 5,1 in den Psalmenhomilien des Asterius und in der Alten Kirche*, Heidelberg 1990 (AHAW.PH 1990/2), pp. 78–96. Cf. also below.

[5] 2 vols., Erlangen 1888/92, I/1, pp. 85–111.

[6] 'Bezeichnete doch διαθήκη in der Bibel den von Gott gestifteten Bund, die von Gott der Gemeinde gegebene Ordnung ihres Verhältnisses zu ihm, und καινὴ

fore, the titles 'Old' and 'New Testament' for the two parts of the Christian Bible are ultimately a popular misunderstanding of the theological term, a misunderstanding which 'sensitive' theologians such as Origen and Augustine still objected to.

Zahn's hypothesis, however, is unsatisfactory, since, as Kutsch and others have shown, διαθήκη does originally designate a written document—namely 'last Will and Testament', a point, to which I shall return below. Moreover, I shall attempt to demonstrate in this paper that Origen and Augustine did not object to the use of 'Old' and 'New Testament' because it was theologically imprecise—or at least not in the sense presupposed by Zahn, namely that διαθήκη did not mean the written document of 'revelation', but 'revelation' itself.

In the ensuing decades interest in the problem subsided. It was not until W. C. van Unnik's study of 1961 that it received renewed attention. Van Unnik painted quite a different picture from Zahn. In his opinion the title under discussion prevailed because it was a consequence of the theology of the covenants as developed towards the end of the second century. Some years later, Hans von Campenhausen argued in his book *The Formation of the Christian Bible* that the titles 'Old Testament' and 'New Testament' prevailed over all others because of the very nature of the Bible as a book in two parts: 'They denoted a comprehensive and theologically very significant dual concept, in which nevertheless each group of Scriptures had its clearly defined place.'[7] This argument alone, however, did not suffice. In addition, therefore, von Campenhausen adopted van Unnik's results and also emphasized that the book title 'New Testament' was a consequence of the covenantal theology which was developed at the same time. He was not interested, however, in the question as to when and how exactly the New Testament came to be called 'New Testament', but resigned himself to saying: 'It is a matter of a gradual process, which cannot be pinpointed with precision; but for understanding what is involved in practice this is not important.'[8]

However, given the various designations for the Holy Scriptures which were in use at this time, the question as to why precisely διαθήκη prevailed does not appear to me to be trivial. Moreover,

---

διαθήκη eine der Endzeit vorbehaltene, durch Christus gestiftete Neuordnung dieses Verhältnisses, also nicht Offenbarungsurkunde, sondern Offenbarung' (ibid., p. 103; my italics).

[7] Hans von Campenhausen, *The Formation of the Christian Bible*, London 1972. p. 263.

[8] Ibid., p. 264.

in my opinion von Campenhausen's case (and by implication, therefore, van Unnik's position, too) is not very strong. Von Campenhausen's argument based on the 'suitability' of the terms does not carry much weight, because it implicitly presupposes that only the most suitable terms could and did survive, which is by no means certain. As regards his second point (the point which he shares with van Unnik), it is no doubt correct to assume that there is a close relation between 'New Testament' as a book title and the theology of the time. In the second half of the second century the theological concept of God's covenant with his people enjoyed renewed currency among Christians. The coming of Christ was now regarded as the establishment of the 'new convenant' prophesied in Jer. 31: 31–34. Even though Paul and the author of the Epistle to the Hebrews had already developed this concept, in subsequent Christian literature it is not found until Justin, who took it up in his *Dialgoue with Trypho*.[9]

Even though, therefore, the development of this type of theology is one of the necessary preconditions for the emergence of the title under discussion, it would be rash to draw the converse conclusion, namely that because of a theology based on the idea of two covenants of God with his people the title would automatically follow. First, even after 'Old' and 'New Testament' came into use as titles, the other titles by no means disappeared. Even authors who championed the theology of the covenants, such as Justin, Irenaeus, Tertullian or Clement,[10] continued to speak of the 'Prophets and the Apostles' or used similar terms when referring to the two parts of the Christian Bible.[11] As I shall show below in more detail, there was even a tendency within the *Église savante* to avoid the use of this title.[12] Secondly, in the literature of the second and third centuries we do not only find the idea of *two* covenants ('old' and 'new'), but also of *three* and even of *four*. Clement of Alexandria, for example, thought that in addition to the covenant with Israel God had given philosophy to the Greeks

---

[9] I have discussed this phenomenon *in extenso* in my book *Novitas Christiana: Die Idee des Fortschritts in der Alten Kirche*, Göttingen 1994 (FKDG 58), pp. 111–116 on Paul and Hebrews; pp. 122–140 on the later development. Cf. also Kinzig, *Erbin Kirche*, pp. 78–96.

[10] Cf. Kinzig, *Novitas Christiana*, pp. 128–132, 210–279, 284–297.

[11] Cf. e.g. the references given by Zahn, op. cit., I/1, pp. 85–111, esp. 101, n. 2; von Campenhausen, op. cit., p. 257, n. 257; J. E. L. van der Geest, *Le Christ et l'Ancien Testament chez Tertullien: Recherche terminologique*, Nijmegen 1972 (LCP 22), pp. 3–62; René Braun, *Deus Christianorum: Recherches sur le vocabulaire doctrinal de Tertullien*, second ed., Paris 1977 (EAug), pp. 455–473, 716 f.

[12] Cf. below pp. 11 f., 14–16, 21–25.

'as a kind of covenant peculiar to them'.[13] Both covenants were superseded by the covenant in Christ.[14] In a passage, the text of which is somewhat corrupt, Irenaeus mentions four covenants, namely either with Adam, Noah, and Moses, and the covenant in Christ (in the Latin version of *Adversus haereses*) or with Noah, Abraham, and Moses, and the covenant in Christ (in a Greek fragment from the same work preserved by Anastasius the Sinaite).[15]

In other words, this type of theology was quite flexible and by no means centred on the idea of just two convenants. Hence the development of this theology alone, important though it is, does not fully account for the formation of the title. It appears, therefore, that we have to look for a more precise *Sitz im Leben* for the title. The evidence which I have gathered suggests that there was a deliberate attempt to distinguish a body of writings called the 'New Testament' from a body of writings termed 'Old Testament'.

II

There was nothing unusual about the use of the term διαϑήκη as title for a book. In the Judaeo-Christian tradition there was a whole series of writings bearing this name, the best known example being the *Testaments of the Twelve Patriarchs*.[16] It is not clear, however, whether or not we are in fact dealing here with a distinct literary genre.[17] If so, then according to the comprehensive

[13] Cf. *str.* 6,67,1; cf., moreover, 1,80,5 f. and 6,42,1–3; Kinzig, *Novitas Christiana*, pp. 154–157, 290.

[14] Cf. esp. *str.* 3,70; 7,107,3–6; Kinzig, *Novitas Christiana*, pp. 155, 291 f.

[15] Cf. *adv. haer.* 3,11,8 and the comments ad loc. in the edition by Rousseau *et al.*; cf., moreover, Clem. Alex., *str.* 5,34,4 and *ecl. proph.* 51,1 (Adam, Noah, Abraham and Moses); also Origen, *comm. Matt.* 15,32 (Adam, Noah, Abraham, Moses, Christ; Origen, however, does not explicitly speak of four (five) covenants, but mentions a covenant only as regards Noah). Furthermore Kinzig, *Novitas Christiana*, p. 221 n. 65.

[16] Cf. the extensive study by Eckhard von Nordheim, *Die Lehre der Alten, I. Das Testament als Literaturgattung im Judentum der hellenistisch-römischen Zeit, II. Das Testament als Literaturgattung im Alten Testament und im alten Vorderen Orlent*, 2 vols., Leiden 1980/85 (Arbeiten zur Literatur und Geschichte des hellenistischen Judentums 17–18). As regards later Christian works bearing this title, cf. e.g. the *Testament of Our Lord Jesus Christ* or the *Testament of the Forty Martyrs*; cf. Berthold Altaner/Alfred Stuiber, *Patrologie: Leben, Lehre und Schriften der Kirchenväter*, ninth ed., Freiburg etc. 1980, pp. 257, 93. On book titles in classical antiquity and early Christianity, cf. e.g. Martin Hengel, *Die Evangelienüberschriften*, Heidelberg 1984 (SHAW.PH 1984/3), pp. 28–33 who lists the relevant literature.

[17] Cf. M. de Jonge's critical review of Nordheim's first volume in *JSJ* 12 (1981), pp. 112–117; J. J. Collins, 'Testaments', in: Michael E. Stone (ed.), *Jewish Writings*

524   WOLFRAM KINZIG

study by Eckehard von Nordheim, it derives from Israelitic wisdom and its main purpose is ethical teaching and admonition. It is, therefore, quite distinct from most writings in the New Testament or from the New Testament as a whole.[18] In pagan literature the title occurs occasionally as well. Yet in those cases where any remains of these writings have been preserved, διαθήκη means first and foremost 'last Will and Testament'.[19] At first glance, however, it is difficult to see how such an understanding could apply in the case under discussion, since none of the writings in the New Testament is stylized as a testament in the legal sense of the term.

Nevertheless, as already mentioned, the translations διαθήκη and *testamentum* for בְּרִית lent themselves to such a legal interpretation and could be understood in this sense. This phenomenon already occurs in Philo's writings.[20] In Christian literature we find quite frequently the view expressed that after the death of Christ a 'new Testament' was opened, the Jews disinherited and the

of the Second Temple Period: Apocrypha, Pseudepigrapha, Qumran Sectarian Writings, Philo, Josephus, Assen 1984 (Compendia Rerum Iudaicarum ad Novum Testamentum II/2), pp. 325–355, 325 f.; Klaus Berger, Formgeschichte des Neuen Testaments, Heidelberg 1984, S. 75–80; H. W. Hollander/M. de Jonge, *The Testament of the Twelve Patriarchs: A Commentary*, Leiden 1985 (Studia in Veteris Testamenti Pseudepigrapha 8), pp. 29–41, esp. 32 f.; James H. Charlesworth, in: id. (ed.), *The Old Testament Pseudepigrapha*, 2 vols., London 1983/85, I, p. 773; R. P. Spittler, in: ibid., pp. 831 f.; E. P. Sanders, in: ibid., pp. 879 f.

[18] Cf. Nordheim, op. cit., I, esp. pp. 229–242. As regards 2 Timothy and 2 Peter, it is a matter of controversy whether or not these writings belong to the genre of 'testament'. Cf. e.g. Richard J. Bauckham, '2 Peter: An Account of Research', in: *ANRW* II/25,5, 1988, pp. 3713–3752, esp. 3734 f.; Berger, op. cit., p. 79.

[19] Both Theophilus of Antioch (*ad Autol.* 3,2) and the author of the treatise *De monarchia* which has been preserved under the name of Justin (2,4) quote an Orphic work entitled Διαθῆκαι which argued for the existence of one God only (=*frgg.* 245–247 Kern). Cf. also Nordheim, op. cit., I, pp. 241 f. Christoph Riedweg has now seriously questioned the authenticity of this title. In his view, the fragments in question do not stem from a 'Testament', but form part of an imitation of an Orphic hieros logos. Cf. his study *Jüdisch-hellenistische Imitation eines orphischen Hieros Logos: Beobachtungen zu OF 245 und 247 (sog. Testament des Orpheus)*, Tübingen 1993 (Classica Monacensia 7), esp. pp. 44–55.

[20] Cf. Annie Jaubert, *La notion d'alliance dans le judaïsme aux abords de l'ère chrétienne*, Paris 1963 (PatSor 6), pp. 414–416; Kutsch, *Neues Testament*, pp. 81–83. On what follows cf. also Dirk van Damme, *Pseudo-Cyprian, Adversus Iudaeos. Gegen die Judenchristen. Die älteste lateinische Predigt*, Freiburg, Switzerland 1969 (Par. 22), pp. 27–30, 46–50; Vincenzio Loi, 'L'interpretazione giuridica del *testamentum* divino nella storia della salvezza (dalla *Vetus Latina* a Lattanzio)', *Aug.* 16 (1976), pp. 41–52; Josef Fellermayr, *Tradition und Sukzession im Lichte des römisch-antiken Erbdenkens: Untersuchungen zu den lateinischen Vätern bis zu Leo dem Großen*, Munich 1979, esp. pp. 24 ff.; id., art. 'Hereditas', in: *RAC* XIV, 1988, cols. 626–648, 633 and Kinzig, *Erbin Kirche*, *passim*.

Christians instituted as the new heirs. In the first three centuries this understanding occurs not only in Gal. 3: 15, 3: 17 and Heb. 9: 16 f., but also, for example, in the *Epistle of Barnabas*,[21] in the homily *Adversus Iudaeos* by Pseudo-Cyprian,[22] in Irenaeus,[23] Tertullian,[24] Origen,[25] Commodian,[26] and Victorinus of Pettau.[27] Like Paul and the author of Hebrews, these later theologians, too, did not always clearly distinguish between the meaning of διαθήκη as 'covenant' and its use as a legal metaphor. Irenaeus, *adv. haer.* 5,9,4 provides an example:

Therefore Christ died that the open testament (will) of the Gospel read in the wide world should first set his servants free, and then should make them heirs of all his possessions, the Spirit inheriting them, as we have shown. For he who lives inherits, and it is the flesh which is acquired as inheritance.

It appears as if Irenaeus were speaking here of a *real* will which Christ had composed before his death and which was then opened and read to the world. Hence to call a body of writings 'New Testament' was not necessarily surprising, but must be understood against this background in which the meanings 'covenant' and 'will' were strangely intermingled.

III

If, therefore, the title 'New Testament' can be explained on the basis of contemporary theology, we must next ask whether we have some indication of when and how quickly it came into use. This question could be answered more easily if we had some Bible manuscripts at our disposal which date back to the period in question. Unfortunately, however, our oldest majuscule codices, the famous *Sinaiticus* and the *Vaticanus*, were copied in the fourth century, that is at a time when the title 'New Testament' had already been well established.[28] Owing to their fragmentary state the papyri, though considerably older, do not help us either. If I am not mistaken, none of them contains διαθήκη in its Christian

---

[21] Cf. Kinzig, *Erbin Kirche*, pp. 80–83.
[22] Cf. Kinzig, *Erbin Kirche*, pp. 83–92.
[23] Cf. van Damme, op. cit., pp. 46–50.
[24] Cf. van der Geest, *Le Christ et l'Ancien Testament*, p. 32, n. 2; Loi, art. cit., pp. 46–49.
[25] Cf. e.g. *comm. Matt.* 14,19.
[26] Cf. Loi, art. cit., p. 49.
[27] Cf. Loi, art. cit., pp. 49 f.
[28] On the dates, cf. e.g. Kurt and Barbara Aland, *The Text of the New Testament: An Introduction to the Critical Editions and to the Theory and Practice of Modern Textual Criticism*, second ed., Grand Rapids/Leiden 1989, pp. 107–109.

usage, let alone as a title for a collection of writings. In general, the practice of the production and distribution of books in late antiquity does not yield any clues which bear upon our problem. As is well known, the use of the papyrus codex instead of the scroll is one of the distinctive features of the transmission of Christian literature from its beginnings.[29] As Colin H. Roberts and T. C. Skeat have emphasized, however, 'so universal is the Christian use of the codex in the second century that its introduction must date well before AD 100', that is, at a time when the title in question was not yet used.[30]

This observation appears to be contradicted by the fact that the apostle Paul refers to a collection of writings called 'the Old Testament'. In 2 Cor. 3: 12–16 he says:

Since we have such a hope, we are very bold, not like Moses, who put a veil over his face so that the Israelites might not see the end of the fading splendour. But their minds were hardened; for to this day, that same veil remains on the old covenant when it is read, and it is not taken away, because in Christ (the covenant) is abolished. Yes, to this day whenever Moses is read a veil lies over their minds; "but when a man turns to the Lord the veil is removed" [Exod. 34: 34] (tr. RSV; altered).

'Old Testament' here probably means the Law, the Torah which is read in the synagogue.[31] In calling the Torah διαθήκη Paul clearly follows a long-established Jewish usage.[32] He seems, however, to be the first to add the adjective παλαιός which he probably uses *ad hoc* to emphasize the distinction between the old covenant of the letter and the new covenant of the Spirit which the

[29] Cf. Colin H. Roberts/T. C. Skeat, *The Birth of the Codex*, second ed., London 1985 (=first ed. 1983), *passim*.

[30] Roberts/Skeat, op. cit., p. 45; cf. also pp. 62–66, esp. 62: 'As regards the Christian Bible as a whole, any possible influence of the codex on its contents can be immediately dismissed'.

[31] Cf. e.g. Ernst Lohmeyer, *Diatheke: Ein Beitrag zur Erklärung des neutestamentlichen Begriffs*, Leipzig 1913 (UNT 2), p. 130, n. 1; Rudolf Bultmann, art. 'ἀναγινώσκω, ἀνάγνωσις', in: *ThWNT* I, 1933, p. 347; Gottfried Quell/Johannes Behm. art. 'διατίθημι, διαθήκη', in: *ThWNT* II, 1935, pp. 105–137, 133; Heinrich Seesemann, art. 'πάλαι κ.τ.λ.', in: *ThWNT* V, n.d. (1954), p. 713–717, 716; van Unnik, ''Η καινὴ διαθήκη', pp. 164 f.; von Campenhausen, *The Formation of the Christian Bible*, p. 264, n. 283; Rudolf Bultmann, *Der Zweite Brief an die Korinther*, ed. by Erich Dinkler, Göttingen 1976 (KEK Sonderband), ad loc.: Gerhard Schneider, art. 'παλαιός', in: *Exegetisches Wörterbuch zum Neuen Testament* III, 1983, cols. 15–17, 16; Gräßer, *Der Alte Bund im Neuen*, 1985, p. 91. *Pace* Johannes Behm, *Der Begriff* ΔΙΑΘΗΚΗ *im Neuen Testament*, Leipzig 1912, pp. 53–55.

[32] Cf. e.g. Exod. 24: 7; 4 Kgs. 23: 2, 21; 2 Chr. 34: 30; Sir. 24: 23; 1 Macc. 1: 57; moreover Quell/Behm, art. cit., pp. 128–131, 133; Kutsch, *Neues Testament—Neuer Bund?*, pp. 63, 66; Gräßer, *Der Alte Bund im Neuen*, p. 91 n. 377.

Christians serve (cf. v. 6).[33] Even though, therefore, the Torah was often called διαθήκη by Greek-speaking Jews, the Christians at the time of Paul hardly spoke of the Law and/or the Prophets as 'the Old Testament'.

Another passage often quoted as proof for the use of παλαιὰ διαθήκη as a book title is found in the only extant fragment of the *Extracts* by Melito of Sardis, a fragment preserved by Eusebius (*h.e.* 4,26,13 f. = fragment 3 [Perler; Hall]). The passage quoted by Eusebius comes from the beginning of the work which was probably written around 170.[34] Onesimus, the addressee of the work, who is otherwise unknown, had asked 'to be made possessor of extracts from both the law and the prophets concerning the Saviour and all our faith' and, moreover, 'to be precisely informed about the ancient books, both as to their number and as to their arrangement'. Melito then goes on to claim that he went 'to the east' and 'reached the place where it was proclaimed and done'. There he got 'precise information about the books of the Old Testament' about which he sends Onesimus a list. Finally, Melito concludes by saying that he composed a collection of extracts from these works which he divided into six books.

We are not so much concerned here with the precise contents of this list which correspond rougly to the canon of the Hebrew Bible (omitting Esther).[35] Instead the expression 'the books of the Old Testament' (τὰ τῆς παλαιᾶς διαθήκης βιβλία) needs further examination. Two questions need to be answered in this respect. First, is 'Old Testament' the title of the collection of books in question? And secondly, if this is the case, can we conclude from this that there was a corresponding collection of writings called 'the New Testament'?

As regards the first question, if Melito had said something like 'it is written in the Old Testament', an answer would have been easy. Unfortunately, however, he uses the genitive τῆς παλαιᾶς διαθήκης. It is, then, not clear whether he does this, because in

[33] Cf. Quell/Behm, art. cit., p. 133; Seesemann, art. cit., p. 716; H(arald) Hegermann, art. 'διαθήκη', in: *Exegetisches Wörterbuch zum Neuen Testament* I, 1980, cols. 718–725, 723; Gräßer, *Der Alte Bund im Neuen*, pp. 91 f.

[34] Melito's *Easter Homily* was probably written sometime between 160–170 (cf. Hall 1979, pp. XXI–XXII), the *Apology* in 170 (cf. Wolfram Kinzig, 'Der "Sitz im Leben" der Apologie in der Alten Kirche', ZKG 100 (1989), pp. 291–317, 297 and n. 16).

[35] Cf. Stuart George Hall, *Melito of Sardis—On Pascha and Fragments. Texts and translations*, Oxford 1979 (OECT), note ad loc. As regards the reasons cf. van Unnik, Ἡ καινὴ διαθήκη, pp. 163 f.; Adolf Martin Ritter, 'Zur Kanonbildung in der alten Kirche', in: id., *Charisma und Caritas: Aufsätze zur Geschichte der Alten Kirche*, Göttingen 1993, pp. 265–280, 273 f.

what follows he is going to give a list of the books called 'The Old Testament', or whether by 'Old Testament' he means a theological concept and, therefore, refers to those books that *contain* the Old Testament, i.e. the old covenant, the covenant of God with Israel as opposed to the new covenant with the Church.[36] Since, therefore, Melito's expression is ambiguous, we do not know whether or not there was a collection of writings called the 'New Testament'.[37]

We obtain the same negative result when we analyse a quotation from an anonymous anti-Montanist writer, preserved in Eusebius (*h.e.* 5,16,3). He says that he initially shrank back from writing a treatise against the Montanists 'from fear and extreme caution, lest perchance I might seem to some to be adding a new article or clause to the word of the New Covenant of the Gospel, to which no one who has purposed to live according to the Gospel may add, from which no one may take away' (tr. van Unnik). As van Unnik, partly retracting his earlier opinion,[38] has argued, by speaking about 'the word of the New Covenant of the Gospel' the unknown author 'has in mind the total message', 'the Christian era marked as a καινὴ διαθήκη stamped by the Gospel' and not a collection of books with this title.[39] I have nothing to add.

In Justin's works the opposition between the old and the new διαθήκη plays a prominent role.[40] It is, therefore, surprising to see that he never uses the term as a book title. The same is still true for Irenaeus, whose anti-heretical work was composed around 180.[41] Given the high number of biblical quotations in the works

[36] Cf. also the references given above n. 9. Moreover Gottlob Schrenk, art. 'βίβλος, βιβλίον', in: *ThWNT* I/1, 1933, pp. 613–620, 616 f.; Zahn, *Geschichte des Neutestamentlichen Kanons*, I, p. 104: 'Eine Benennung des jüdischen Kanons als AT und vollends der apostolischen Schriften als NT ist damit ebensowenig gegeben, als wenn wir von Schriften des alten Bundes oder von Thatsachen und Zuständen reden, welche unter dem alten oder im neuen Bunde stattgefunden haben oder stattfinden.'

[37] Cf. also van Unnik, 'Η καινὴ διαθήκη, pp. 163 f.; Harry Y. Gamble, *The New Testament Canon: Its Making and Meaning*, Philadelphia 1985, p. 20; Metzger, *The Canon of the New Testament*, p. 123.

[38] Cf. W. C. van Unnik, 'De la regle Μήτε προσθεῖναι μήτε ἀφελεῖν dans l'histoire du canon', *VigChr* 3 (1949), pp. 1–36; also in: id., *Sparsa Collecta*, vol. II, Leiden 1980, pp. 123–156 (quoted thereafter), p. 155.

[39] Cf. van Unnik, 'Η καινὴ διαθήκη, pp. 162 f. The quotations are found on p. 163. Cf. also von Campenhausen, *The Formation of the Christian Bible*, pp. 265 f.; Gamble, op. cit., p. 20; *Metzger, The Canon of the New Testament*, pp. 103 f.

[40] Cf. Behm, *Der Begriff ΔΙΑΘΗΚΗ im Neuen Testament*, pp. 102–106; Kinzig, *Novitas Christiana*, pp. 128–132.

[41] Cf. Zahn, *Geschichte des Neutestamentlichen Kanons*, I/1, p. 104 and n. 3; Ellen Flesseman-van Leer, *Tradition and Scripture in the Early Church*, Assen 1953, pp. 128 f.; Kinzig, *Novitas Christiana*, pp. 210–238. On the date of the

of both these authors this has some significance, and could mean either that they did not know these titles yet or that for some reason they disapproved of them. We shall return to this problem later.

The first unequivocal testimonies are found around the year 200 in the writings of Clement of Alexandria. In Clement's theology, too, the idea of God's covenant with His people plays a major role.[42] The term διαθήκη itself occurs 63 times. In one case διαθήκη refers to the original legal meaning 'last Will and Testament'.[43] Ten references come from biblical quotations.[44] The vast majority of references (41) refer to the theological meaning of διαθήκη.[45] Even though the boundaries between διαθήκη as a theological term and as a book title are blurred,[46] in a significant number of cases (5) διαθήκη does appear to have the technical meaning in which we are interested here.[47]

A little later we find the first evidence that Tertullian, too, knew this book title. Tertullian is a particularly interesting case, since, as van der Geest has shown, in his work a development can be observed: whereas in the writings which he wrote before *Adversus Marcionem*, *testamentum* means God's 'ordinance' (the meaning 'covenant' is virtually absent from his works[48]), with his work

Adversus haereses, cf. Hans-Joachim Jaschke, art. 'Irenäus von Lyon, in: *TRE* XVI, 1987, pp. 258–268, 258. Even though, as bishop of Lyon, Irenaeus lived in a somewhat remote area of the Roman Empire, he was well acquainted with the theological literature of his predecessors and contemporaries, both 'heretical' and 'orthodox'. In other words, we may assume that, if καινὴ διαθήκη was used at that time to designate the writings of the second part of the Bible, he must have known it. On the sources of Irenaeus cf. e.g. Jaschke, art. cit., p. 259.

[42] Cf. Kinzig, *Novitas Christiana*, pp. 284–297.

[43] *Str.* 5,55,4: Clement is referring here to a *testamentum per aes et libram*; cf. Max Kaser, *Das römische Privatrecht*, 2 vols., second ed., Munich 1971/75 (HAW III,3,1/2), I, pp. 41–48, 107–109, 678–680.

[44] *Protr.* 23,2; *paed.* 1,56,3; 1,86,1; *str.* 1,125,5; 2,29,1; 4,33,1; 4,100,2; 6,41,5; 6,44,2; 7,88,2.

[45] *Protr.* 94,1; *paed.* 1,20,2; 1,33,4; 1,59,1 (*bis*); *str.* 1,28,2; 1,182,2 (*quater*); 2,28,6; 2,29,2; 2,47,3; 4,130,4; 4,149,5; 5,3,3; 5,34,4; 5,38,5; 5,61,1; 5,62,2; 6,42,1; 6,42,2; 6,63,3; 6,64,4; 6,67,1; 6,106,3; 6,120,3; 6,134,1; 6,161,5; 7,34,2; 7,69,5; 7,107,5 (*bis*); *ecl. proph.* 43,1; 51,1 (*bis*); 51,2; 59,1; *qu. div. salv.* 3,6; 37,4; *exc. ex Theod.* 1,24,2.

[46] In my opinion, in the following cases διαθήκη may refer to the biblical books: *paed.* 1,59,2; *str.* 3,54,4; 3,82,4; 3,108,2; 4,134,2; 6,125,3.

[47] *Str.* 1,44,3; 3,71,3; 4,134,4; 5,85,1; 7,100,5 (cf. also the context). Cf. also Zahn, *Geschichte des Neutestamentlichen Kanons*, I/1, p. 105, n. 2; von Campenhausen, *The Formation of the Christian Bible*, pp. 266 f.

[48] Cf. van der Geest, *Le Christ et l'Ancien Testament chez Tertullien*, p. 30, n. 2: "'Règlement" rend mieux qu'"alliance" ce que Tertullien entend par *testamentum*: l'idée d'une alliance, dans le sens de בְּרִית, joue à peine pour lui. *Testamentum* est la réglementation que Dieu a établie avec Israël et renouvelée dans le Christ. *Ordo*

against the great heretic, i.e. between 207 and 211/12,[49] a new phase begins. Now occasionally passages are found in which *testamentum* undoubtedly refers to the biblical books. The first example is *adv. Marc.* 4,1,1 to which I shall return below.[50] At the same time, however, the older meaning 'ordinance' by no means disappears. Moreover, Tertullian does not often use *testamentum* as a title for the biblical books[51] and continues to refer to the Bible with other expressions.[52]

As regards Origen, von Campenhausen, following Zahn, claimed that for him '*diatheke* in the sense of "book" was a perfectly normal usage'.[53] In reality, the picture is more complex. Unfortunately, a thorough analysis of the use of διαϑήκη by Origen is complicated by the fragmentary preservation of his writings and problems of authenticity which make it impossible to give precise overall figures. In what follows, I shall, therefore, leave aside these problematic cases. Moreover, I shall pass over those works which have been preserved in Rufinus' Latin translation only. In *Contra Celsum*, for example, διαϑήκη occurs ten times. In four cases the word is mentioned in quotations from the Bible.[54] In five instances Origen's choice of the word is clearly influenced by Eph. 2: 12 (ξένοι τῶν διαϑηκῶν τῆς ἐπαγγελίας) and does not primarily express Origen's own theological views.[55] Origen uses διαϑήκη just once to express his own views about God's second 'legislation and covenant in Christ' (2,75). The word is never used, however, as a book title.

Given the fact that we are dealing with an apologetic work addressed to a pagan audience, this result may not come as a surprise. When we turn to the exegetical works, the numbers are different. In the bulky *Commentary on John* (including the fragments) διαϑήκη occurs 33 times. In three instances Origen quotes

---

et *dispositio* expriment la même chose.' On what follows, cf. ibid., pp. 29–35; Braun, *Deus Christianorum*, pp. 470, 716 f.

[49] On the date, cf. René Braun, *Tertullien—Contre Marcion*, Tome I (Livre I). Introduction, texte critique, traduction et notes, Paris 1990 (SC 365), pp. 17–19.

[50] Cf. van der Geest, *Le Christ et l'Ancien Testament chez Tertullien*, pp. 31 f.

[51] According to van der Geest out of 60 references for *testamentum* in Tertullian's writings only 7 (10) apply to the biblical books: *adv. Marc.* 4,1,1; *adv. Prax.* 15,1; 31,1; *pud* 1,5; 6,5; *mon.* 6,3; *cast.* 10,4 (cf. moreover *pud.* 12,10; *adv. Prax.* 20,2; *iei.* 11,1)! Cf. ibid., pp. 31–34. For reasons explained below, I should like to add *adv. Marc.* 4,6,1; 5,11,4; *praescr. haer.* 30,9. Just as in *adv. Marc.* 4,1,1, however, in these three passages Tertullian quotes Marcion's terminology.

[52] Cf. ibid., p. 34.

[53] Von Campenhausen, *The Formation of the Christian Bible*, p. 267. Cf. also Zahn, *Geschichte des Neutestamentlichen Kanons*, I/1, p. 103.

[54] Cf. 1,53; 4,44; 6,70; 8,10.

[55] Cf. 2,78; 5,33; 8,5 (*bis*); 8,43.

directly from the Bible.[56] In four cases Origen is strongly influenced by 2 Cor. 3: 6 (διακόνους καινῆς διαϑήκης)[57] and twice by Eph. 2: 12.[58] Twice he uses διαϑήκη in the technical sense of 'ark of the covenant' (κιβωτὸς τῆς διαϑήκης),[59] whereas in just 11 cases he uses the term largely independently of the Bible in the sense of 'covenant'.[60] This last figure is surprisingly low, given the length of this commentary, and indicates that the concept of 'covenant' does not play a major role in Origen's thought. But that is not the subject of the present paper. There remain 11 cases. Seven times, διαϑήκη quite clearly means the biblical books;[61] in the remaining four cases such an interpretation is at least possible.[62]

We get similar results when we look at his *Commentary on Matthew*. Among the 26 occurrences of διαϑήκη (including the *Commentariorum series* and the *Fragmenta*) there are five quotations,[63] two occurrences deriving immediately from quotations;[64] eight times διαϑήκη is used in a theological sense,[65] five times perhaps as a book title[66] and six times definitely as a book title.[67] In the *Homilies on Jeremiah*, διαϑήκη occurs in ten quotations,[68] three times as a theological term,[69] once possibly as a book title[70] and four times certainly as a book title.[71]

We can conclude from this that Origen knew the title 'Old and New Testament' very well. Given the number of biblical quota-

---

[56] 2,154; 13,451; 32,334.

[57] 1,64; 4,1; 5,1; 5,8.

[58] 6,27; 10,193.

[59] 6,231; 10,280.

[60] 1,36 (*ter*); 1,80; 1,85; 2,198; 6,90; 6,117; 6,230; 10,174; 10,271.

[61] 1,19; 1,228; 2,197; 5,8 (cf. also below n. 74); 20,297; 32,8 (cf. also *frgg. in Lucam* 209 and 210 (Rauer²); cf. below n. 75); *frg.* 49 (cf. also below n. 125). On the authenticity of the fragments cf. CPG I, no. 1453 and the literature listed there.

[62] 1,82 (cf. also below n. 125); 10,175; *frgg. Ioh.* 57; 92.

[63] *Comm. Matt.* 15,13; 16,20 (*bis*); 16,14; 16,15.

[64] *Comm. Matt.* 10,16 (Eph 2: 2); 17,33 (Luke 22: 2).

[65] *Comm. ser. Matt.* 54 (Klostermann 122,15); *comm. Matt.* 14,19 (here διαϑήκη clearly means 'last Will and Testament' and is used metaphorically; cf. above n. 25); 15,22; 15,32; 15,34 (*bis*); 17,2 (*bis*).

[66] *Comm. Matt.* 10,14; 14,4 (*bis*); 17,18; *frg.* 382 *in Matt.* (authenticity uncertain).

[67] *Comm. Matt.* 12,3; 14,14; 14,23; 15,1; 15,2; 15,14.

[68] *Hom. Ier.* 4,2; 9 t.; 9,1; 9,2 (*quater*); 9,4 (*ter*).

[69] *Hom. Ier.* 4,5; 9,2 (*bis*).

[70] *Hom. Ier.* 8,5.

[71] *Hom. Ier.* 1,7 (*bis*); 4,6 (τὰ βιβλία τῆς διαϑήκης; even though, just as in the quotation from Melito cited above, διαϑήκη is in the genitive depending on τὰ βιβλία, in my opinion, owing to its being parallel to τὰ παλαιὰ a little earlier, it is here a book title.); 5,8.

tions in his works, however, it is surprising that he does not use it more frequently. To this observation we may add another one, which has already been made by other scholars, namely that in some places Origen explicitly qualifies his use of the term. In his *De principiis* 4,1,1 he emphasizes that in order to examine the divine character of the Holy Scriptures he wants also to draw on 'testimonies from those writings which we believe to be divine, that is the so-called Old Testament and the so-called New Testament'.[72] In his book *On Prayer*, when dealing with the address of the Lord's Prayer he admonishes 'to have a careful look through the so-called Old Testament, whether in it a prayer can be found by someone who calls God "Father"'.[73] And in his *Commentary on John*, Origen praises 'the sublimity of the evangelical message, filled with the harmony of the teachings common to both the so-called Old Testament and the so-called New'.[74] It is quite striking, therefore, that Origen appears to use the terms with some hesitation.[75]

A quick look into some later authors reveals a similar picture. In Hippolytus' works, διαθήκη appears to be relatively rare.[76] Cyprian uses *testamentum* just twice in the *capitula* of his

---

[72] ...τῆς τε λεγομένης παλαιᾶς διαθήκης καὶ τῆς καλουμένης καινῆς ... (Görgemanns/Karpp 668,12).

[73] ... τὴν λεγομένην παλαιὰν διαθήκην... (22,1 [Koetschau 346,13]).

[74] ... τὸ ὕψος τοῦ εὐαγγελικοῦ κηρύγματος, πεπληρωμένον συμφωνίας δογμάτων κοινῶν τῇ καλουμένῃ παλαιᾷ πρὸς τὴν ὀνομαζομένην καινὴν διαθήκην (5,8 [Preuschen 105,14–16]). Cf. also *comm. Matt.* 14,4 on Matt. 18: 19 (20); *exh. mart.* 12.

[75] Cf. also *philoc.* 6,2 where Origen enumerates a whole series of designations for the Bible and its constituent parts, among which also 'Old' and 'New Writings' (not *Testaments*): ... οὕτως οἱ μὴ ἐπιστάμενοι ἀκούειν τῆς τοῦ θεοῦ ἐν ταῖς ἱεραῖς γραφαῖς ἁρμονίας οἴονται ἀνάρμοστον εἶναι τῇ καινῇ τὴν παλαιάν, ἢ τῷ νόμῳ τοὺς προφήτας, ἢ τὰ εὐαγγέλια ἀλλήλοις, ἢ τὸν ἀπόστολον τῷ εὐαγγελίῳ ἢ ἑαυτῷ ἢ τοῖς ἀποστόλοις (Harl 310,50–9). Cf. moreover *frg.* 209 *Lc.* (on Luke 14: 12): »Ἄριστον« [cf. Luke 14: 15 v.l.] μὲν γὰρ οἱ εἰσαγωγικοὶ λόγοι ἢ ἠθικοὶ ἢ τὰ παλαιὰ λόγια, »δεῖπνον« [cf. Luke 14: 16] δὲ οἱ ἐν προκοπῇ λόγοι μυστικοὶ ἢ οἱ τῆς νέας διαθήκης (Rauer² 317,20 f.). In what follows I give some further examples for the use as a book title. Not in all cases is the authenticity of the quotations beyond doubt: *princ.* 3,1,16; *philoc.* 27,8; *frg. I Cor.* 37,16–18 on 1 Cor. 7: 18–20 (ed. Claude Jenkins, 'Origen on I Corinthians', *JTS* 9 (1908), pp. 231–247, 353–372, 500–514; 10 (1909), pp. 25–51; here: p. 506); *frg. Eph.* 30,15 f. on Eph. 5: 31 (ed. J. A. F. Gregg, 'The Commentary of Origen Upon the Epistle to the Ephesians', *JTS* 3 (1902), pp. 233–244, 398–420, 554–576, here: p. 567); *comm. Rom.* (Scherer 220,5–8); *ep. Afric.* 15; *sel. Ies. Nav.* (PG 12,824B).

[76] It does not, for example, occur in the *Refutation* at all. This is not least, because he does not have a concept of *Heilsgeschichte*. Cf. my remarks in *Novitas Christiana*, pp. 297–302, where further references are given.

Testimonies, but not as a book title.[77] In this sense it is also absent from the sermon *Adversus Iudaeos* preserved under Cyprian's name, even though here *testamentum* occurs very often.[78] Methodius mentions the term rarely[79] and perhaps just once as a book title.[80] Lactantius, it is true, explicitly mentions that 'all Scripture is divided into two Testaments', and goes on to say: 'That which preceded the advent and passion of Christ—that is the law and the prophets—is called the Old; but those things which were written after His resurrection are named New Testament'.[81] Yet this passage notwithstanding, he hardly ever uses the term and never as a book title.[82] An exception to this rule is Novatian, who not only knows the book titles *Vetus* and *Novum Testamentum,* but also uses the terms fairly regularly in this sense. He may even be the only author so far in whose works the term occurs only as book title.[83]

This hesitation is still found as late as the fifth century: in the second book of his *De doctrina christiana,* Augustine gives a list of writings belonging to the 'canon of Scriptures' (*canon scripturarum*). He concludes the enumeration of the books of the Old Testament by saying: 'The authority of the Old Testament is contained within the limits of these forty-four books.'[84] In his *Revisions* Augustine comments on this use of 'Old Testament' by saying: 'In calling (these books) "Old Testament" I have followed the usage with which the Church speaks. The Apostle, however, seems to call "Old Testament" only what was given on Mount Sinai' (*retr.* 2,4,3). Augustine here appears to allude either to 2 Cor. 3: 14 or to Gal. 4: 24, where Hagar is identified with the covenant 'from Mount Sinai', or to a combination of both

---

[77] Cf. 1,11; 1,18.

[78] Cf. van Damme, *Pseudo Cyprian,* p. 30; Kinzig, *Erbin Kirche,* pp. 83–92.

[79] *Symp.* 19; *res.* 1,56,5; *frg. 2 in Iob* 9,5 in the sense of covenant.

[80] *Symp.* 260.

[81] *Inst.* 4,20,4; tr. ANCL.

[82] Cf. *inst.* 4,11,2; 4,20,2f.10; 5,9,16; *mort. pers.* 2,2. Here *testamentum* always means 'last Will and Testament'. Cf. the discussion in Joseph Fischer, 'Die Einheit der beiden Testamente bei Laktanz, Viktorin von Pettau und deren Quellen', *MThZ* 1/3 (1950), pp. 96–101; Loi, 'L'interpretazione giuridica', pp. 50 f.; Pierre Monat, *Lactance et la Bible: Une propédeutique latine à la lecture de la Bible dans l'occident constantinien,* 2 vols., Paris 1982 (EAug), I, pp. 72 f. and Kinzig, *Erbin Kirche,* pp. 88 f., 92–96.

[83] In *trin.* 7,5 (*bis*); 9,2 (*bis*); 10,1; 10,2; 18,10; 26,20; 30,1 *testamentum* quite clearly refers to the Bible; in 17,3; 17,5 (*quater*) and 17,6 (*bis*) possibly so. There are no further occurrences in his writings. Cf. also van Damme, *Pseudo-Cyprian,* p. 28; Loi, 'L'interpretazione giuridica', p. 42, n. 9.

[84] 'His quadraginta quattuor libris testamenti ueteris terminatur auctoritas' (2,13 [CChr.SL 32,40,47 f.]).

passages. We may conclude from his remark that, at the time of Augustine, *Vetus Testamentum* as a title for the books of the first part of the Christian Bible was common in the Church at large, which is quite in line with the results of our investigation so far. Owing to the brevity of the remark, however, it is more difficult to say why precisely Augustine feels uneasy about applying this title to the Old Testament as a whole and why, following the apostle Paul, he wants to restrict it to the Pentateuch.[85]

Our analysis of the usage of διαθήκη/*testamentum* as a book title has yielded some surprising results: Διαθήκη and/or *testamentum* are not attested as book titles before the end of the second century, but then appear almost simultaneously in Alexandria (Clement and, a little later, Origen) and North Africa (Tertullian), and soon occur in Rome (Novatian) also. At the same time, leading theologians both in the East and in the West caution against the unqualified use of the terms in this sense. It looks, therefore, as if these titles had become popular among simple believers. Thus, pressure was exerted on the leading theologians in the Church to take them over, which they did with some hesitation. This reserve calls for an explanation.

IV

At this point, it may be useful to recall that two facts had to be established before the expression 'New Testament' could be used as a book title. First, there must have been a corpus of writings which was perceived as a unity. Secondly, this corpus of writings as a whole must have been seen in opposition to those writings which so far had been considered as the only Holy Scriptures (i.e. our 'Old Testament' which, however, had probably not yet been termed thus in the Church at large). In other words: the development of a specifically Christian canon of Holy Scriptures as opposed to the Judaeo-Christian canon of Holy Scriptures must have preceded or accompanied the spread of the titles 'Old Testament' and 'New Testament' respectively.[86] Now, in current research on the history of the canon there is wide agreement that

---

[85] As regards Augustine's attitude towards the O.T. canon, cf. Ralph Hennings, *Der Briefwechsel zwischen Augustinus und Hieronymus und ihr Streit um den Kanon des Alten Testaments und die Auslegung von Gal. 2,11–14*, Leiden/New York/Cologne 1994 (Supplements to Vigiliae Christianae 21), pp. 200–216, esp. 206–209.

[86] This is one of the principal reasons why the new book by Geoffrey Mark Hahneman, *The Muratorian Fragment and the Development of the Canon*, Oxford 1992 (OTM), which argues *inter alia* that the idea of a Christian canon of Scriptures did not come into existence before the fourth century, must be treated with some caution.

one of the most important people in this process was Marcion.[87] As far as we know, he was the first to form a canon of Christian sacred writings. This new canon consisted of the Gospel of Luke and ten of Paul's Letters, namely Galatians, 1 Corinthians, 2 Corinthians, Romans, 1 Thessalonians, 2 Thessalonians, Laodiceans (= Ephesians), Colossians, Philippians, and Philemon, all in an expurgated version.[88] Scholars are divided, however, over the question of whether our present canon is a direct reaction by the Greater Church to Marcion's collection[89] or whether Marcion's canon was just one step in a longer process towards the formation of the canon of the New Testament as we know it.[90] As regards our question, however, this debate is not very significant. It suffices to say that Marcion did play an important role in the process. If this is the case, then, there is the possibility that

[87] On the present state of research on Marcion cf. Barbara Aland, art. 'Marcion (ca. 85–160)/Marcioniten', in: *TRE* XXII, 1992, pp. 89–101.

[88] Cf. Adolf von Harnack, *Marcion: Das Evangelium vom fremden Gott. Eine Monographie zur Geschichte der Grundlegung der katholischen Kirche*, second ed., Leipzig 1924, pp. 35–73; Beilagen III and IV.

[89] Cf. e.g. Adolf von Harnack, *Neue Studien zu Marcion*, Leipzig 1923, pp. 20–23; id., *Marcion*, p. 151; Robert Smith Wilson, *Marcion: A Study of a Second-century Heretic*, London n.d. (1933), pp. 153, 160–164; John Knox, *Marcion and the New Testament: An Essay in the Early History of the Canon*, Illinois 1942, esp. pp. 19–38; von Campenhausen, *The Formation of the Christian Bible*, p. 148; Vielhauer, *Geschichte der urchristlichen Literatur*, p. 783.

[90] Cf. e.g. Ellen Flesseman-van Leer, 'Prinzipien der Sammlung und Ausscheidung bei der Bildung des Kanons', *ZThK* 61 (1964), pp. 404–420, 410; Werner Georg Kümmel, *Einleitung in das Neue Testament*, twenty-first ed., Heidelberg 1981, p. 431; Schneemelcher, 'Bibel III', p. 38; cf. also Andreas Lindemann, *Paulus im ältesten Christentum: Das Bild des Apostels und die Rezeption der paulinischen Theologie in der frühchristlichen Literatur bis Marcion*, Tübingen 1979 (BHTh 58), pp. 381 f.; R. Joseph Hoffmann, *Marcion: On the Restitution of Christianity. An Essay on the Development of Radical Paulinist Theology in the Second Century*, Chico, Calif. 1984 (American Academy of Religion/Academy Series), p. 107 and n. 29 (with further literature); Gamble, *The New Testament Canon*, p. 62; Metzger, *The Canon of the New Testament*, p. 99; F. F. Bruce, *The Canon of Scripture*, Glasgow 1988, p. 144; Schneemelcher in: Hennecke/Schneemelcher, *Neutestamentliche Apokryphen*, I, p. 17; Adolf Martin Ritter, 'Die Entstehung des neutestamentlichen Kanons: Selbstdurchsetzung oder autoritative Entscheidung?' in: Aleida and Jan Assmann (eds.), *Kanon und Zensur: Beiträge zur Archäologie der literarischen Kommunikation II*, Munich 1987, pp. 93–99, 95 f.; A. F. J. Klijn, 'Die Entstehungsgeschichte des Neuen Testaments', in: *ANRW* II/26,1, 1992, pp. 64–97, 83–86; Ritter, 'Zur Kanonbildung in der Alten Kirche', pp. 266 f. For entirely different views cf. Isidor Frank, *Der Sinn der Kanonbildung: Eine historisch-theologische Untersuchung der Zeit vom 1. Clemensbrief bis Irenäus von Lyon*, Freiburg 1971 (FThSt 90), esp. p. 207; Franz Stuhlhofer, *Der Gebrauch der Bibel von Jesus bis Euseb: Eine statistische Untersuchung zur Kanonsgeschichte*, Wuppertal 1988, pp. 69–76; Hahneman, *The Muratorian Fragment*.

it was this arch-heretic who first used the title 'New Testament' for his canon.

Distinguished scholars, however, have denied that this was the case. Von Harnack himself, even though he attributed to Marcion the decisive role in the formation of the canon, thought that there had been no overall name for Marcion's canon, but added cautiously: 'At least there is no evidence as regards this question'.[91] Knox argued that the idea of a 'New Testament' was already present in Marcion, but left the question open as to 'whether Marcion used that phrase or not'.[92] Von Campenhausen observed: 'Even Marcion, despite his pronounced sense of canonicity, apparently still had no common name for his Gospel and Apostle'.[93] Van der Geest, too, considered this possibility 'unlikely', since the new meaning of *testamentum*, as it is found in Tertullian, 'would not have failed to provoke lively resistance'.[94] Other authors, such as Lindemann, Schneemelcher, Metzger and Bruce, adopted this general view.[95] I beg to differ. In my opinion there is strong evidence pointing to the conclusion that Marcion gave his Gospel and *Apostolos* the overall name 'New Testament'.

In this regard, a passage in Tertullian which has not so far received sufficient attention deserves further examination. In *adv. Marc.* 4,6,1 Tertullian writes, as regards Marcion's gospel:

Certainly the whole of the work he has done, including the prefixing of his *Antitheses*, he directs to the one purpose of setting up opposition between the Old Testament and the New, and thereby putting his Christ in separation from the Creator, as belonging to another god, and having no connection with the law and the prophets.[96]

From this we learn that Marcion's version of the Gospel (which, as I have mentioned above, was an 'expurgated' version of the Gospel of Luke) was introduced by his work *Antitheses*, the basic

[91] Cf. von Harnack, *Marcion*, p. 441*.

[92] Knox, *Marcion*, p. 21.

[93] Von Campenhausen, *The Formation of the Christian Bible*, p. 262. Cf. also ibid., p. 163, n. 67 where he adds: 'This appears surprising, but ceases to be strange when we realize that at that time no exact designation for the O.T. as a whole was current either'.

[94] Van der Geest, *Le Christ et l'Ancien Testament chez Tertullien*, p. 32. Cf. also p. 61, n. 1.

[95] Cf. Lindemann, *Paulus im ältesten Christentum*, p. 379; Schneemelcher, 'Bibel III', p. 36; Metzger, *The Canon of the New Testament*, p. 98; Bruce, *The Canon of Scripture*, p. 137. Cf. also Stuhlhofer, *Der Gebrauch der Bibel von Jesus bis Euseb*, p. 75.

[96] 'Certe enim totum quod elaboravit etiam Antitheses praestruendo in hoc cogit, ut veteris et novi testamenti diversitatem constituat, proinde Christum suum a creatore separatum, ut dei alterius, ut alienum legis et prophetarum' (*adv. Marc.* 4,6,1 [Evans II,274]; tr. Evans).

outlines of which have been reconstructed by Adolf von Harnack.[97] According to von Harnack, however, 'in the *Antitheses* no catchword appears to have occurred more frequently than "new"'.[98] According to Marcion, the unknown God is a God of mercy who is diametrically opposed to the God of justice of the Old Testament.[99] In Marcion's view this can especially be seen from the 'new doctrines of the new Christ':[100] Christ himself distinguished that which is 'new' from that which is 'old'. In this respect Marcion referred to Luke 5: 36–38 which he quoted omitting verse 39 ('And no one after drinking old wine desires new; for he says, "The old is good."').[101] Christ proclaimed a 'new kingdom' (cf. Luke 10: 9).[102] His proclamation itself was 'a new manner of speaking', since it consisted in parables and answering of questions.[103] This proclamation, however, was also materially new, because it announced the forgiveness of sins and the love of one's enemy, which were both, in Marcion's view, unknown to the Old Testament (cf. Luke 5: 18–26 and 6: 27–31). This teaching was the result of a 'new kind of mercy of the new Christ' and a 'new kind of patience' respectively.[104] This 'new' message was confirmed by his deeds. Marcion sees in Jesus' raising of the young man of Nain from the dead (Luke 7: 11–17) a *novum documentum*;[105] the same is true for Christ's attitude towards observing the sabbath (Luke 6: 1–5)[106] and his calming the storm on the Lake of Gennesaret (Luke 8: 22–25).[107]

[97] Cf. von Harnack, *Marcion*, pp. 74–92, 256*–313*. Cf. also *adv. Marc.* 4,1,1, where Tertullian calls the *Antitheses* the 'dowry' (*dotem quandam*) of the Gospel. I do not see why it follows from this passage that Marcion's canon and his book were separate, as von Harnack (and, following him, Bardy) claim *pace* Hahn and Ritschl. Cf. von Harnack, *Marcion*, p. 82f.; G(ustave) Bardy, art. 'Marcion', in: *DBS* V, 1957, cols. 862–877, 875.

[98] Von Harnack, *Marcion*, p. 87. On what follows cf. ibid., pp. 87 f.; 126 f.; id., 'Die Neuheit des Evangeliums nach Marcion', *ChW* 43 (1929), cols. 362–370; also in: id., *Aus der Werkstatt des Vollendeten*, ed. by Axel von Harnack, Gießen 1930 (Reden und Aufsätze 5), pp. 128–143 (quoted thereafter).

[99] Cf. Adam., *dial.* 2,16; moreover Gerhard May, 'Marcion in Contemporary Views: Results and Open Questions', *The Second Century* 6 (1987/88), pp. 129–151, 144–146.

[100] Tert., *adv. Marc.* 4,28,8: *novae doctrinae novi Christi*; cf. 3,3,4: *documenta nova*; 4,12,2: '... nec posse retorqueri ex ipsa novitate institutionis cuiusque satis aliam a Christo demonstratam divinitatem' (Evans II, 310). As regards the expression 'new Christ' cf. also 4,10,4; 4,18,5; 3,4,1 (*novus filius*).

[101] Cf. ibid. 4,11,9–11; Adam., *dial.* 2,16.

[102] Cf. Tert., *adv. Marc.* 3,24,13; 4,24,5.

[103] Cf. ibid. 4,11,12: *nova forma sermonis*; moreover 4,19,1.

[194] Cf. ibid. 4,10,4: *nova Christi novi benignitas*; 4,16,2: *nova patientia*.

[105] Cf. ibid. 4,18,2.

[106] Cf. ibid. 4,12,2: *nova institutio*.

[107] Cf. ibid. 4,20,1: Christus als *novus dominator atque possessor elementorum*.

Given the importance, therefore, which the Marcionite definition of Christianity as a 'new' religion played in the *Antitheses*, it
appears to me quite likely that the 'opposition between the Old
Testament and the New' in this work to which Tertullian refers
was not only one of content, but also of terminology. Hence
Marcion himself probably spoke explicitly of the opposition of the
'New Testament' and the 'Old'. Now one of the main characteristics of Marcion's exegesis was its literalism.[108] And since, as
pointed out, the original sense of διαθήκη was 'Will' and referred,
therefore, to a written document, there is a strong case for suggesting that Marcion would have understood the word in that
sense and thought of the collection of writings compiled by himself
as such a document.[109]

Other passages taken from Tertullian's writings may serve to
strengthen this point. One of the principal characteristics of his
refutation of Marcion's ideas is his insistence on God's oneness,
which was denied by the heretic. In his discussion of the correct
interpretation of 2 Corinthians 1–4, the rhetor from Carthage
argued that Marcion could only call his recently revealed God
merciful, if there was any previous evidence:

Only if his existence were previously acknowledged could attributes be
attached to him. That which is alleged as an attribute is ⟨in logical terms⟩
an accident, and accidents are preceded by evidence of the object to which
they occur,—and especially so when someone else is already in possession
of that which is being ascribed to him of whose existence there has been
no previous evidence.[110]

Tertullian goes on to say:

So also the New Testament will belong to none other than him who
made that promise: even if the letter is not his, yet the spirit is: herein
lies the newness. Indeed he who had engraved the letter upon tables of

---

[108] Cf. von Harnack, *Marcion*, pp. 66 f., 259 f.; id., 'Die Neuheit des
Evangeliums nach Marcion', pp. 136 f.; Edwin Cyril Blackman, *Marcion and His
Influence*, London 1948, pp. 114 ff.; P. G. Verweijs, *Evangelium und neues Gesetz
in der ältesten Christenheit bis auf Marcion*, Utrecht 1960 (STRT 5), pp. 273–289;
Lindemann, *Paulus im ältesten Christentum*, p. 389; Hoffmann, *Marcion*, p. 228,
287 f.
[109] Van der Geest, *Le Christ et l'Ancien Testament chez Tertullien*, p. 31, leaves
the possibility open whether or not *novum testamentum* in *adv. Marc.* 4,6,1 means
'"ordonnance" de Dieu' or 'dénomination de l'Écriture'.
[110] 'Non potest igitur aliquid ei adscribere quem tunc ostendit cum aliquid ei
adscribit. Si enim prius constaret eum esse, tunc et adscribi ei potest. Accidens
enim est quod adscribitur, accidentia autem antecedit ipsius rei ostensio cui acci-
dunt, maxime cum iam alterius est quod adscribitur ei qui prius non sit ostensus.
Tanto magis negabitur esse, quanto per quod affirmatur esse eius est qui iam
ostensus est' (*adv. Marc.* 5,11,3 [Evans II, 578]; tr. Evans).

stone is the same who also proclaimed, in reference to the Spirit, »I will pour forth of my Spirit upon all flesh« [Joel 2: 28].[111]

Tertullian's remark *etsi non littera, at eius spiritus* in relation to the *testamentum novum* alludes, of course, to 2 Cor. 3: 6. Yet it is no true reproduction of Paul's argument. Whereas Paul proclaimed that Christians 'were competent to be ministers of a new covenant, not of the letter but of the spirit', Tertullian appears to presuppose that the New Testament is a written document and concedes to his opponent that its wording may not be from the creator God, but insists that its spirit is.[112] This is why Tertullian refers to Joel 2: 28: what is new about the New Testament is not that its words were written by the creator God, but that its spirit is his. Tertullian's argument only makes sense, if he was aware of the existence of two bodies of writings called 'Old Testament' and 'New Testament'. He feels uneasy about these designations, because they seem to imply a difference in authorship (as Marcion indeed claimed). Here, however, he could not avoid dealing with them (as he does in so many other places when referring to the Bible) because *Marcion himself* spoke of his canon as a '*New Testament*' to underline the gulf which separated the creator God from the God of Christ.

In *adv. Marc.* 4,1,1 Tertullian says:

Besides that, to work up credence for it [sc. his gospel] he [sc. Marcion] has contrived a sort of dowry, a work entitled *Antitheses* because of its juxtaposition of opposites, a work strained into making such a division between the Law and the Gospel as thereby to make two separate gods, opposite to each other, one belonging to one instrument (or, as it is more usual to say, testament), one to the other, and thus lend its patronage to faith in another gospel, that according to the *Antitheses*.[113]

Among scholars there is a consensus that *testamentum* here has to be identified with *instrumentum* and refers to the biblical books.[114]

---

[111] 'Sic et testamentum novum non alterius erit quam qui illud repromisit; etsi non littera, at eius spiritus; hoc erit novitas. Denique qui litteram tabulis lapideis inciderat, idem et de spiritu edixerat, Effundam de meo spiritu in omnem carnem' (5,11,4 [Evans II, 578]; cf. also 5).

[112] *Pace* van der Geest, *Le Christ et l'Ancien Testament chez Tertullien*, p. 32 n. 2 who counts this passage among those 'where *testamentum* refers undoubtedly to God's ordinance'.

[113] 'Et ut fidem instrueret, dotem quandam commentatus est illi, opus ex contrarietatum oppositionibus *Antitheses* cognominatum et ad separationem legis et evangelii coactum, qua duos deos dividens, proinde diversos, alterum alterius instrumenti, vel, quod magis usui est dicere, testamenti, ut exinde evangelio quoque secundum *Antitheses* credendo patrocinaretur' (Evans II,258; tr. Evans).

[114] Cf. Zahn, *Geschichte des Neutestamentlichen Kanons*, I/1, p. 106; von Campenhausen, *The Formation of the Christian Bible*, pp. 267 f.; van der Geest, *Le Christ et l'Ancien Testament chez Tertullien*, pp. 31 f. (cf., however, his note 1 on p. 32); Braun, *Deus Christianorum*, pp. 470, 716 f.

The qualifying expression *quod magis usui est dicere* is then usually understood to mean that Tertullian is here referring to a popular expression for the Bible which he, however, disapproves of because it is not as accurate as *instrumentum*, but which he adopts, precisely because it is more common.[115] This interpretation is, of course, not impossible, but it fails to explain why Tertullian adds this more popular expression here, whereas in all the other cases where he uses *instrumentum* in this sense he does not feel the need to express himself more clearly. I should, therefore, like to suggest that Tertullian adds this remark because Marcion used *testamentum*, i.e. διαθήκη, as designation for the Scriptures and that *quod magis usui est dicere* has to be referred to Marcion: *he* is the one who usually calls his Bible *testamentum*. It can hardly be coincidence that, as pointed out before,[116] Tertullian never used *testamentum* in this sense before he wrote his anti-Marcionite work. This is precisely, because he adopted this manner of referring to the Bible from the great heretic.

One last passage from Tertullian's writings, this time from the *de praescriptione haereticorum*, may serve to underline this hypothesis. In chapter 30 he attempts to show that in the beginning there was unity within the Church and that the heresies, such as Marcion's, crept in only much later. He says:

But, in fact, by their own works they are convicted, as the Lord said [cf. Matt. 7: 16]. For since Marcion separated the New Testament from the Old, he is (necessarily) subsequent to that which he separated, inasmuch as it was only in his power to separate what was (previously) united. Having then been united previous to its separation, the fact of its subsequent separation proves the subsequence also of the man who effected the separation.[117]

Opera here undoubtedly refers to *written* works. (In 30,11, immediately following this passage, Tertullian mentions Valentinus and his exegesis and revision of the Bible.) The passage, therefore, refers to Marcion's New Testament.[118] In my opinion, the passage is most easily understood if Marcion himself called his canon

[115] *Usui esse* is used here in the sense of *in usu esse*. Cf. Braun, *Deus Christianorum*, pp. 716 f.

[116] Cf. above pp. 11f.

[117] 'Quamquam et de operibus suis, ut dixit Dominus, reuincuntur. Si enim Marcion novum testamentum a vetere separavit, posterior est eo quod separavit quia separare non posset nisi quod unitum fuit. Vnitum ergo antequam separaretur postea factum separatum posteriorem ostendit separatorem' (*praescr. haer.* 30,8–10 [CChr.SL 1,211,27–32]; tr. ANF; slightly altered). Cf. also Knox, *Marcion and the New Testament*, p. 31, n. 18.

[118] Cf. also van der Geest, *Le Christ et l'Ancien Testament chez Tertullien*, p. 31 who, however, appears to be too cautious.

'New Testament'. (Tertullian's claim that there was just *one* canon before Marcion's 'separation' is no doubt fiction.) In his later works Tertullian occasionally uses *testamentum* as the title for the parts of the Bible, quite independently of his campaign against the great heretic.[119] This is because, owing to the influence of the Marcionite church in North Africa,[120] it was now quite common also within the Greater Church.

When we finally turn to Origen, here, too, we may now see some passages in a different light. In his exposition of Num. 16: 46, the great Alexandrine theologian polemicizes against heretics who claim 'that the God of Law is not good, but just and that the law of Moses does not contain goodness, but justice'.[121] Origen is, therefore, probably writing against Marcionites, since the distinction between the just God of the Old Testament Law and the good God of Jesus is a typically Marcionite idea.[122] Origen objects that Moses, too, had obeyed the commandment of the love of one's enemies (Matt. 5: 44) and goes on to say:

The power of the gospel is, therefore, also found in the Law and it becomes clear that the Gospels are based on the foundation of the Law. And I do not call the Law 'Old Testament', when I try to understand it spiritually. The Law becomes the Old Testament only to those who try to understand it carnally. And to those it has necessarily become old and outdated, because it cannot retain its strength. To us, however, who understand and interpret it spiritually and in an evangelical way, it is always new; and both are for us a 'New Testament', not in the sense of temporal age, but because of the novel understanding.[123]

The opponents are obviously still the Marcionites who interpreted the Jewish Bible literally or, in Origen's terminology, *carnaliter* (σαρκικῶς).[124] It seems, therefore, that the Marcionites called the Law, i.e. the Torah, 'Old Testament'. This Paulinian expression could well have been taken up for polemical purposes by Marcion

[119] Cf. above n. 51.
[120] On the influence and spread of the Marcionite Church in the West cf. Harnack, *Marcion*, pp. 153–155.
[121] '...illis dicentibus quoniam Deus legis non est bonus, sed iustus, et Moysi lex non bonitatem continet, sed iustitiam' (*hom. Num.* 9,4 [Baehrens 58,30–59,2]).
[122] Cf. e.g. Adam., *dial.* 2,16; May, 'Marcion in Contemporary Views', pp. 144–146.
[123] 'Sic ergo invenitur et evangelii virtus in lege et fundamento legis subnixa intelliguntur evangelia; nec vetus testamentum nomino ego legem, si eam spiritaliter intelligam. Illis tantummodo lex vetus efficitur testamentum, qui eam carnaliter intelligere volunt; et necessario illis vetus effecta est et senuit, quia vires suas non potest obtinere. Nobis autem, qui eam spiritaliter et evangelico sensu intelligimus et exponimus, semper nova est; et utrumque nobis novum testamentum est, non temporis aetate, sed intelligentiae novitate' (Baehrens 59,7–15).
[124] Cf. above n. 108.

who saw his 'New Testament' canon in opposition to the outdated 'Old Testament' of the Jews.

This suggestion is confirmed in one of the fragments of Origen's *Commentary on John* where the 'heretics' (Origen seems to have primarily Marcionites in view) are criticized for 'dividing the godhead and, therefore, saying that the old scripture was of one god, and regarding the New Testament as of another'.[125] The parallelism of 'old scripture' and the 'New Testament' makes it quite clear that the latter expression refers to the biblical books and, given the large number of similar passages in this and other authors, there is a strong case for claiming that Marcion did indeed speak of his canon as 'New Testament'.

V

In conclusion, what did Marcion mean when he called his canon 'New Testament'? Apparently, these terms would have meant the written διαθῆκαι of the creator of God and the new, alien God respectively, which have to be understood in a literal sense. In terms of Marcionite theology they were, therefore, two separate, unlinked entities.[126] According to Tertullian, that was even the principal subject of the *Antitheses*, in which Marcion tried to prove the 'conflict and disagreement of the Gospel and the Law, so that from the diversity of principles between those two testaments they may argue further for a diversity of gods'.[127]

The Marcionite church exerted a great influence upon the Greater Church and was, therefore, perceived as an immediate threat. This can be seen from the vigour with which the latter

---

[125] ... διαιροῦντες τὴν θεότητα καὶ διὰ τοῦτο τὴν παλαιὰν γραφὴν ἑτέρου λέγοντες θεοῦ καὶ ἑτέρου τὴν καινὴν διαθήκην τιθέντες ... (*frg. Ioh.* 49 [Preuschen 523,24 f.]).

Cf. also *comm. Ioh.* 1,82; furthermore *frg. in Ps.* 77: 10–12 (Pitra III,114 f.); *en. in Iob* on Job 21: 11 f. (PG 17,80A); *princ.* 3,1,16 (cf. above n. 75).

[126] Cf. also Kinzig, *Novitas Christiana*, pp. 138 f. and n. 256.

[127] 'Nam hae sunt Antitheses Marcionis, id est contrariae oppositiones, quae conantur discordiam evangelii cum lege committere, ut ex diversitate sententiarum utriusque testamenti diversitatem quoque argumententur deorum' (1,19,4 [Evans I, 48]; tr. Evans).

Cf. also ps.-Tert., c. *adv. Marc.* 2,20–22: '... Adversum sese duo testamenta sonare, / Contra prophetarum domini committere uerba // Dissimili longe sententia uelle probare ...' (CChr.SL 2,1427). Greg. Naz., c. *de vita sua* 1160 f., 1169 f.: Οἱ τὴν παλαιὰν καὶ νέαν δύω θεοῖς/νείμαντες, αὐστηρῷ τε κἀγαθωτάτῳ (Jungck 110); cf. Christoph Jungck, *Gregor von Nazianz—De Vita Sua.* Einleitung, Text, Übersetzung, Kommentar, Heidelberg 1974 (WKLGS), p. 200.

attacked the movement.[128] On a more practical level the spread of the Marcionite canon (and, consequently, also of the title of the new creation) could have been considerably facilitated if Marcion's New Testament was circulated in one single codex—as opposed to the canon of the Greater Church which was too bulky.[129] Yet since no such codex survives, this remains speculation.

The Greater Church did not take over Marcion's canon. It did, however, adopt its name: Καινὴ διαθήκη. Owing to Marcion's influence, the term had probably become popular in the Church at large, before the 'orthodox' canon took its final shape. The *Église savante* initially tried to fend off this new designation. This explains why it is found neither in Justin nor in Irenaeus. At a later stage it was adopted by theologians such as Tertullian, Origen and Augustine only with considerable reluctance—precisely because they were unaware of its origin. The theology behind this designation, however, was taken over already by Justin, because it suited him well in his own controversy with Judaism.[130] Only later, the theologians of the Greater Church realized that the Marcionite division of the Bible into Old and New Testaments came in handy because, ironically enough, it could be understood not only in an anti-*Jewish*, but also in an anti-*Marcionite* sense, once the concept of a bipartite canon had been developed. The concept allowed for an emphasis both on the continuity between the old covenant and the new (against Marcion)[131] and on the

---

[128] Cf. von Harnack, *Marcion*, pp. 154 f.; cf. also Gilles Pelland, art. 'Marcion', in: *DSp* X, 1980, cols. 311–321, 318 f.; B. Aland, art. 'Marcion', pp. 98–100. This hypothesis of the influence of the Marcionite canon on the Church could be strengthened, if, as von Harnack and others have claimed, the prologues to the Pauline Epistles and the pseudo-Pauline *Epistle to the Laodiceans* were indeed Marcionite fabrications. This remains, however, uncertain. Cf. the controversial discussion in: Jürgen Regul, *Die antimarcionitischen Evangelienprologe*, Freiburg 1969 (VL/AGLB 6), pp. 84–94; Nils A. Dahl, 'The Origin of the Earliest Prologues to the Pauline Letters', *Semeia* 12 (1978), pp. 233–277 (who gives a summary of the previous debate); Karl Th. Schäfer, 'Marius Victorinus und die marcionitischen Prologe zu den Paulusbriefen', *RBen* 24 (1970), pp. 7–16; id., 'Marcion und die ältesten Prologe zu den Paulusbriefen', in: Patrick Granfield/Josef A. Jungmann (eds.), *Kyriakon: Festschrift Johannes Quasten*, vol. I, Münster, Westf. 1970, pp. 135–150; Gamble, *The New Testament Canon*, p. 61; W. Schneemelcher in: Hennecke/Schneemelcher, *Neutestamentliche Apokryphen*, II, pp. 42 f.; Metzger, *The Canon of the New Testament*, pp. 94–97, 182 f.; Bruce, *The Canon of Scripture*, pp. 141–144; Hahneman, *The Muratorian Fragment and the Development of the Canon*, pp. 111–115, 196–200.

[129] Cf. Roberts/Skeat, *The Birth of the Codex*, p. 48.

[130] Cf. Kinzig, *Novitas Christiana*, pp. 128–132.

[131] This becomes especially clear from Orig., *sel. in Deut.* on Deut. 24: 6: Ἐπεὶ οὖν καὶ Ἰουδαῖοι μίαν διαθήκην ἔχουσιν· ὁμοίως δὲ καὶ πᾶσα αἵρεσις δοκοῦσα ταύτην τὴν καινὴν μόνην ἔχειν, οὐκ ἀληθοῦσι ἐν τῷ μυλῶνι τούτῳ, ἵνα γεύσωνται τοῦ ἐπουρανίου ἄρτου· ἐὰν γάρ, φησί, μὴ συντριβῇ καὶ ἀληθῆ ὁ σῖτος, ἄσιτοι

544 WOLFRAM KINZIG

discontinuity (against the Jews).[132] Hence the Jewish Bible which Marcion had downgraded to be the 'Old Testament' and which had been superseded by the 'New' was not abandoned, but retained and reinterpreted in the light of the revelation in Christ as contained in the Gospels and the Epistles which now formed the New Testament.

WOLFRAM KINZIG

μένουσιν. Ἐκ τούτου οὖν καὶ αὐτὸς ὁρμώμενος τὸν προκείμενον σαφηνίζω νόμον· »οὐκ ἐνεχυράσεις μύλον«, τουτέστιν, οὐ μὴ βεβηλώσεις τὴν παλαιὰν καὶ οὐ μὴ ἀπώσεις αὐτὴν τῆς σῆς οἰκίας· »οὐδὲ ἐπιμύλιον·« ἀντὶ τοῦ, τὴν καινήν, »ὅτι ψυχὴν οὗτος ἐνεχυράζει«, τουτέστι τούτοις τρέφεται ἡ ψυχὴ ἀπολαύουσα νοητῶν ἐδεσμάτων (PG 12,813D–816A).
[132] As regards this dual opposition, cf. also Gerd Lüdemann, *Paulus der Heidenapostel*, 2 vols., Göttingen 1980/83 (FRLANT 123/130), II. p. 210. Similarly, the distinction between Gospel(s) and *Apostolikon* as written corpora within the New Testament was no doubt taken over from Marcion by the Greater Church. To my knowledge, prior to Irenaeus it is found for the first time in Marcion; cf. Kinzig, *Novitas Christiana*, p. 139, n. 258 where references and literature are given.

Similar attempts both to emphasize continuity and discontinuity may be observed in the Epistle to the Hebrews. Cf. Susanne Lehne, *The New Covenant in Hebrews*, Sheffield 1990 (Journal for the Study of the New Testament, Supplement Series 44), esp. pp. 119–124.

Clement of Alexandria as a Witness to the Development of the New Testament Canon

JAMES A. BROOKS

Clement made no explicit statements about the canonicity of individual books or about the content of the New Testament. It is necessary, therefore, to approach the subject indirectly by, first, examining his knowledge and use of early Christian writings; second, considering various terms and ideas which reveal something about his concept of canonicity; and, third, comparing him with his contemporaries.

I

CLEMENT'S KNOWLEDGE AND USE OF CHRISTIAN WRITINGS

By way of introduction to this division, there is some value in briefly surveying Clement's use of Old Testament writings. An examination of the index of citations in the standard critical edition of Clement's works reveals that he makes reference to all the books in the Hebrew canon except Ruth, Song of Solomon, and Obadiah.[1] The omissions are insignificant. It is probable that there was no occasion for him to cite such brief and comparatively unimportant writings, although the omission of the Song may be due to his negative attitude toward romantic love. That he knew Obadiah may be inferred from his specific reference to "the Twelve."[2] As one would expect he also refers to various "outside books": 1 and 2 Esdras, Tobit, Judith, the Additions to Esther, the Wisdom of

---

JAMES A. BROOKS is a professor at Bethel Theological Seminary, 3949 Bethel Drive, St. Paul, MN 55112.

[1]Otto Stählin (ed.), *Clemens Alexandrinus*, 4 vols., vols. 12, 15, 17, and 39 of Die griechischen christlichen Schriftsteller der ersten drei Jahrhunderte (Leipzig: J. C. Hinrichs'sche Buchhandlung, 1905–36). The index appears in vol. 4, pp. 1–59, and these and the following statistics have been gathered from it. See below for some additional comments on the index and the statistics.

[2]*Str.* 1.21.122.

Solomon, Sirach, 1 Baruch, Susanna, Bel and the Dragon, and 2 Maccabees among those now in the (Protestant) Apocrypha: and *1 Enoch*, the *Assumption of Moses*, and the *Sibylline Oracles* in the Pseudepigrapha.

Writings Now Classified as Canonical

It would appear that Clement divided the New Testament into the Gospel and the Apostles.[3] His knowledge and use of individual books are as follows.

Matthew,[4] Mark,[5] Luke,[6] and John[7] are quoted by name and in such a way as to indicate that they possessed the highest authority for him. Their authority is also seen in the statement, "We do not have this saying in the four Gospels which have been handed down to us but in the one According to the Egyptians."[8] Eusebius claimed that Clement provided some information about their order of writing: "The earliest Gospels were those containing the genealogies."[9]

Acts is quoted by name and is attributed to Luke.[10] It has been questioned, however, whether Clement attached scriptural authority to Acts.[11] It is true that he does not quote it often, but neither does he often quote the historical books of the Old Testament, which certainly he accepted as scripture. The probable reason for such neglect is that his interests were predominantly theological and philosophical.

Romans,[12] 1 Corinthians,[13] 2 Corinthians,[14] Galatians,[15] Ephesians,[16]

---

[3]In *Str.* 6.11.88 he sees a parallel between the Gospel and the Apostles and the Law and the Prophets.

[4]Ibid., 1.21.147.

[5]*Quis dives salvetur?* 5.

[6]*Str.* 1.21.145. The quotation is introduced with "It is written."

[7]*Paed.* 1.6.38.

[8]*Str.* 3.13.93 (translation mine). Unless otherwise indicated the translation is that in vol. 2 of Alexander Roberts and James Donaldson, ed., *The Ante-Nicene Fathers*, rev. A. C. Coxe, 10 vols. (reprint edition; Grand Rapids: Eerdmans, 1962).

[9]*H. E.* 6.14.5 (translation mine). There follows an account of the writing of Mark in which Mark is described as the follower of Peter, who was urged by Peter's hearers in Rome to record Peter's teaching. Eusebius adds that Peter neither opposed nor encouraged the work. See also H. Merkel, "Clemens Alexandrinus über die Reihenfolge der Evangelien," *Ephemerides Theologicae Lovaniensis* 60 (1984): 382–5.

[10]*Str.* 5.12.82.

[11]E. J. Goodspeed, *Formation of the New Testament* (Chicago: University of Chicago Press, 1926) 87; Adolf von Harnack, *Origin of the New Testament*, trans. J. R. Wilkinson (London: Williams and Norgate, 1925) 110; J. Leipoldt, *Geschichte des neutestamentlichen Kanons* (Leipzig: J. C. Hinrichs'sche Buchhandlung, 1907) 1:200.

[12]*Str.* 3.11.75.

Philippians,[17] Colossians,[18] 1 Timothy,[19] 2 Timothy,[20] and Titus[21] are quoted directly by name and attributed either to Paul or "the apostle." 1 Thessalonians[22] and 2 Thessalonians[23] are quoted directly and attributed to "the apostle" but are not referred to by name. There is no trace of Philemon.

Hebrews is quoted directly by name and attributed to Paul.[24] Eusebius indicates that Clement also claimed that Hebrews was written in Hebrew and translated by Luke and that Paul omitted his name to avoid prejudicing Jewish readers against the writing.[25]

There are no certain or even probable references to James. Stählin lists twenty-one possible allusions, but accompanies all with a question mark. Individual examination confirms that none is probable. 1 Peter is twice quoted directly with the formula "Peter in his Epistle."[26] The implication is that Clement knew only one letter bearing the name of Peter. Stählin lists eight questionable allusions to 2 Peter, but again examination results in rejection. 1 John is quoted directly and attributed to "John . . . in his larger Epistle."[27] Presumably the smaller one is 2 John.[28] This is confirmed by the survival of fragments of Clement's commentary on 1 and 2 John in a Latin translation by Cassiodorus. There is not even a possible

---

[13]*Paed.* 1.6.33.

[14]*Str.* 4.14.100.

[15]Ibid., 3.15.99.

[16]*Paed.* 1.5.18.

[17]*Str.* 4.13.92.

[18]Ibid., 5.10.60.

[19]Ibid. 3.6.51 and 2.11.52.

[20]*Prot.* 9.87. Actually neither 1 or 2 Timothy is quoted by name, but in *Str.* 3.6.53 Clement refers to a passage in 1 Timothy as being in "the other epistle . . . Paul wrote to Timothy," and in ibid. 2.9.52 he states that "the heretics reject the Epistles to Timothy."

[21]*Str.* 1.14.59.

[22]Ibid., 1.1.6.

[23]Ibid., 5.3.17.

[24]Ibid. 6.8.62.

[25]*H. E.* 6.14.2. In the same passage Eusebius also records Clement's own quotation of the "blessed presbyter" (almost certainly his teacher Pantaenus) that Paul the apostle to the Gentiles omitted his name out of reverence to Christ the apostle to the Jews.

[26]*Str.* 3.18.110; 4.20.129.

[27]Ibid. 2.15.66.

[28]Stählin, *Clemens Alexandrinus*, 4:25, lists six possible allusions, but none is convincing.

allusion to 3 John. Jude is quoted directly and attributed to that person.[29]

Before leaving the subject of the General Epistles, however, reference must be made to an enigmatic statement by Eusebius: "In the *Hypotyposes* . . . [Clement] has made brief explanations all the canonical Scripture, not omitting the disputed books—I mean the one of Jude and the other General Epistles, the one of Barnabas, and the so-called Revelation of Peter."[30] Inasmuch as Eusebius certainly knew all the General Epistles, inasmuch as there is no reason why he would have misrepresented Clement, and inasmuch as he seems to have had a firsthand knowledge of the *Hypotyposes*, the statement would seem to indicate that Clement knew and used as scripture and even wrote a commentary upon all the General Epistles. Nevertheless, it is difficult to explain the absence of at least James and 2 Peter (3 John is too brief to be significant) from Clement's extant writings in Greek and from the Latin translation of the *Hypotyposes* known as the *Adumbrationes*. The only safe conclusion is that it is uncertain whether Clement knew James, 2 Peter, and 3 John.

Revelation is quoted rarely, but it is quoted directly by name and attributed to John without further qualification.[31]

To summarize, Clement knew and used, almost certainly as scripture, twenty-three out of the twenty-seven books now in the New Testament. He probably recognized Philemon as well but had no occasion to refer to it. It is most uncertain whether he knew James, 2 Peter, and 3 John.

Writings Now Classified as Patristic or Apocryphal

Clement knew other gospels besides the four. According to Stählin there are nine references to the *Gospel of the Egyptians*, four to the *Gospel of the Hebrews*, one to the *Protevangelium of James*, and two to the *Traditions of Matthew*—although some of these are doubtful. The *Gospel of the Egyptians* is quoted by name but evidently is given a different status from the four.[32] And the *Gospel of the Hebrews* is quoted directly with the formula "it is written." Not much significance should be attached to the citation formula, however, because it will be shown below that Clement used it loosely and even to refer to secular writings.

In recent years a question has arisen whether Clement knew and perhaps recognized as scripture another gospel, a *Secret Gospel of Mark*. In 1958 Prof. Morton Smith discovered at the monastery of Mar Saba near Jerusalem a fragment of a letter written in an eighteenth-century hand in

---

[29]*Paed.* 3.8.44.

[30]*H. E.* 6.14.1 (translation mine).

[31]*Str.* 6.13.106 and *Paed.* 2.10.108.

[32]*Str.* 3.13.93 quoted above.

the back of a seventeenth-century book.[33] The heading of the letter reads, "From the letters of the most holy Clement, the author of the Stromateis. To Theodore" (who is otherwise unknown). After relating something about the composition of the canonical Gospel of Mark, the letter goes on:

> He [Mark] composed a more spiritual Gospel for the use of those who were being perfected. Nevertheless, he did not divulge the things not to be uttered . . . [Upon] dying, he left his composition to the church in Alexandria, where it even yet is most carefully guarded, being read only to those who are being initiated in the great mysteries.
>
> . . . Carpocrates . . . so enslaved a certain presbyter of the church in Alexandria that he got from him a copy of the secret Gospel, which he both interpreted according to his blasphemous and carnal doctrine and, moreover, polluted, mixing with spotless and holy words utterly shameless lies.[34]

Two quotations follow from the copy of the *Secret Gospel* possessed by the church at Alexandria and one from the version used by the Carpocratian heretics. Also, Clement advises Theodore to deny with an oath that Mark wrote the *Secret Gospel*.

The first question is whether the letter is genuine. Most, but by no means all, of those who have reviewed the book or studied the matter further have agreed that it is. It is beyond the scope of the present study to deal with the matter of authenticity. The best procedure will be to affirm uncertainty but to proceed on the assumption of authenticity.

If in fact the letter comes from Clement, what was his attitude toward the *Secret Gospel*? Despite his admonition to Theodore to deny that Mark wrote it, Clement himself seems to have believed that Mark did so and that it contained authentic traditions which, however, were of such a nature that they should be revealed only to advanced Christians. The fact that Clement nowhere quotes from it—unless some of the unidentified agrapha are from it—and his statement quoted above about "the four Gospels which have been handed down to us" make it doubtful that he put much stock in it. It would appear that he did not know what to make of it, that his position was ambiguous. The *Secret Gospel* existed; it bore the name of an evangelist; it contained much that was recognized as authoritative by all; yet it had been misappropriated by heretics and was of such a nature that it should be withheld from the Christian public. So well did Clement and his associates maintain silence that there is no other reference to it in early Christian literature. The evidence does not support the view that Clement accepted the *Secret Gospel* as scripture. At the most it was one among a large number of writings Christian, Jewish, and

---

[33]Morton Smith, *Clement of Alexandria and a Secret Gospel of Mark* (Cambridge: Harvard Univ. Press, 1973).

[34]Ibid., 446–7.

pagan in which this open-minded Alexandrian found something of value. Clement's low opinion of apocryphal gospels in general may be seen from the fact that Stählin's index has only nineteen references to them (plus thirty-one unidentified agrapha[35]) against 1,579 from the canonical Gospels.

Clement also knew several apocryphal acts: the *Acts of John*,[36] the *Preaching of Peter*,[37] and possibly the *Acts of Paul*.[38]

Eusebius's statement that Clement commented upon the *Epistle of Barnabas* has already been noted. Clement himself quotes it directly and attributes it to the apostle Barnabas.[39] There is a question, however, about the authority Clement attached to this work. In one passage he quotes *Barnabas*'s explanation of Psalm 1 and then indicates that he prefers another interpretation.[40] *1 Clement* is cited by name and attributed to Clement of Rome,[41] who is called an apostle,[42] but there is no further indication of scriptural status. It is difficult to determine what authority it held for the Alexandrian. Stählin lists six possible allusions to the letters of Ignatius and two possible allusions to Polycarp's *Letter to the Philippians*, but none is very likely.

As indicated above, the *Apocalypse of Peter* was included in the *Hypotyposes*, and it is quoted several times in Clement's work *Eclogae Propheticae*.[43]

The *Didache* is not quoted by name, but "Son, be not a liar; for falsehood leads to theft" seems to be from it.[44] The *Shepherd* of Hermas is quoted directly by name and is attributed to Hermas and to divine power

---

[35]See J. Ruwet, "Les Agrapha dans les oeuvres de Clément d'Alexandrie," *Biblica* 30(1949): 133–60.

[36]*Adumb.* 3.87 on 1 John 1:1. The allusion—not a quotation—is introduced with "It is related in the traditions that John . . ."

[37]*Str.* 6.6.48. Stählin lists ten references to this work. Indeed Clement is the principal source of knowledge of it.

[38]Stählin, *Clemens Alexandrinus*, 2:453, has conjectured that the statement, "Take also of the Hellenic books, read the Sibyl, how it is shown that God is one, and how the future is indicated," is from the *Acts of Paul*.

[39]*Str.* 2.6.31.

[40]Ibid., 2.15.67–8.

[41]Ibid., 1.7.38.

[42]Ibid., 4.17.105.

[43]One quotation in sec. 48 is introduced with "Peter says in the Apocalypse," and another in sec. 41 is introduced with, "The scripture says."

[44]*Str.* 1.20.100; cf. *Didache* 3.5. The quotation is preceded by the statement, "It is such an one that is by scripture called a 'thief'," but it is uncertain whether the word "scripture" refers to the *Didache* or to John 10:8.

and revelation.[45] A passage is commented upon as though it were scripture.[46]

It is difficult to decide how much authority Clement attached to the above writings. Only the *Apocalypse of Peter* is certainly called scripture. The fact that Clement included the *Epistle of Barnabas* and the *Apocalypse of Peter* in a biblical commentary may indicate that he regarded them as scripture. The description of the *Shepherd* as having been given to Hermas "by revelation" may indicate the same status for it. The number and nature of the quotations from the *Preaching of Peter* indicates a very high regard for it. Therefore it is possible—even probable—that Clement recognized as scripture four or five early Christian writings which ultimately failed to find a place in the canon.

Before concluding the first division of this study, there may be some value in considering some further statistics from Stählin's index. He lists 1,842 references to the Old Testament (including the "outside" books), 3,279 to the New Testament, 71 to New Testament apocrypha, 258 to patristic writings, 126 to other Christian sources including heretics, and 3,162 to classical and other non-Christian writings—a total of 8,612. The New Testament can be broken down into Gospels—1,579, Acts—57, Pauline Epistles (including Hebrews)—1,372, General Epistles—237, and Revelation—34.[47]

Several conclusions can be drawn from the above statistics. First, more than a third of Clement's quotations and allusions are from pagan writers. This shows how thoroughly Hellenized was his brand of Christianity. He was a liberal thinker and perhaps the first churchman to see a preponderance of good in the world and to attempt to reconcile Christianity and culture. This should be kept in mind in attempting to ascertain his attitude toward the New Testament canon, especially his inclusion of books which later were rejected.

Second, he quoted New Testament writings almost twice as often as

---

[45]*Str.* 1.29.181; 2.12.55.

[46]Ibid., 6.6.46.

[47]Several things need to be said concerning these statistics. First, all figures are approximate. Every attempt was made to count accurately, but in view of the vast number of references exact accuracy cannot be guaranteed. Second, many are references to possible allusions rather than certain quotations. Most contemporary scholars would be reluctant to accept many of Stählin's references. Third, there is some overlapping. For example in the case of parallel passages in the Gospels, where it is impossible to determine from which Gospel Clement is quoting, Stählin usually indexes the passage for all the possibilities. A comparison of the above statistics with those of Hermann Kutter, *Clemens Alexandrinus und das Neue Testament* (Giessen: J. Ricker, 1897), 99–100, will reveal that in every instance his numbers are smaller.

Old Testament ones. This is quite significant in view of the fact that he unquestionably accepted the Old Testament as sacred scripture. Was the emerging New Testament even more weighty for him?

Third, his citation of New Testament books is approximately proportionate to their length and enduring significance. Approximately forty-five percent are from the Gospels and forty percent from Paul. Among the larger and more important books, only Acts and Revelation are in any way neglected.

Fourth, it is revealing that so liberal a thinker as Clement quoted books now in the New Testament about sixteen times more often than apocryphal and patristic writings which for a while in one place or another contended for a place in the canon.

II
CLEMENT'S CONCEPT OF CANONICITY

The purpose of this section will be to investigate various topics and terms which shed light on Clement's concept of canonicity as opposed to his use of particular books.

His View of Inspiration and Authority

There can be no doubt that Clement accepted as inspired and authoritative a body of writings both Jewish and Christian in origin.

[God] leads us in the inspired Scripture.[48]

I could adduce ten thousand Scriptures of which not "one tittle shall pass away" without being fulfilled; for the mouth of the Lord the Holy Spirit hath spoken these things.[49]

. . . the Lord Himself speaking in Isaiah, in Elias—speaking himself by the mouth of the prophets.[50]

. . . the prophets of God Almighty becoming the organs of the divine voice.[51]

We have, as the source of teaching, the Lord, both by the prophets, the Gospel, and the blessed apostles . . . He . . . who . . . believes the Scripture and the voice of the Lord . . . is . . . faithful.[52]

It would appear therefore that Clement like many of the Fathers believed in verbal inspiration of both the Old and New Testament. Nevertheless there is a problem about his view of inspiration and authority. It is the contention of Dausch that Clement makes little distinction between

[48]*Str.* 7.16.101.
[49]*Prot.* 9.82.
[50]Ibid., 1.8.
[51]*Str.* 6.18.168.
[52]Ibid., 7.16.94.

the inspiration of Christian and heathen, orthodox and heretical, authentic and apocryphal writings. He further says that Clement knows of but one revelation which sometimes comes to light in biblical and sometimes in classical writings.[53] Harnack takes a similar position when he says that Clement viewed as inspired any literature dealing with morals and religion.[54]

There is some truth in these claims. Clement does indeed use such words as prophet, inspiration, scripture, and "it is written" in a wider as well as in a more restricted sense. For example he refers to the Sibyl as a prophetess[55] and ascribes inspiration to philosophers.[56] His cosmopolitan mind found truth in many different sources, and whatever he found he used. Nevertheless two things must be noted. The first is that he appeals to scripture to settle any controversy. This practice implies that he had a higher view of the authority of scripture than of other writings. Perhaps even more significant is his claim that the truth which is in the writings of the philosophers was plagiarized from the Hebrew scriptures.

> There is then in philosophy, though stolen as the fire of Prometheus, a slender spark, capable of being fanned into flame, a trace of wisdom and an impulse from God. . . . "the thieves and robbers" are the philosophers among the Greeks, who from the Hebrew prophets . . . received fragments of the truth, not full knowledge, and claimed these as their own teachings.[57]

No matter how ridiculous Clement's view of the source of philosophical truth may be, it clearly shows that he considered the inspiration and authority of the scripture to be primary and that of the philosophers to be secondary and derived. For him Holy Scripture was the final authority.

His Knowledge of an Old and New Testament

Clement ordinarily employed the word διαθήκη to mean a covenant or agreement between God and human beings. There are several instances, however, when he used it to refer to a collection of writings which embodies the covenant.

> The law and the prophets should be placed beneath the Lord's head, because in both Testaments mention is made of the righteous.[58]

---

[53]Petrus Dausch, *Der neutestamentliche Schriftcanon und Clemens von Alexandrien* (Freiburg: Herder, 1894), 51–2.

[54]Adolf von Harnack, *History of Dogma*, 7 vols., trans. N. Buchanan et al. (Boston: Little, Brown, and Co., 1907), 2:157–8.

[55]*Prot.* 2.27.

[56]*Str.* 5.14.138.

[57]Ibid., 1.17.87. See also 6.3.28–34.

[58]*Str.* 5.6.38.

Does he not lay down the same principle in the Old Testament?[59]

[Paul's] writings depend on the Old Testament, breathing and speaking of them.[60]

From the beginning the law commanded, "You shall not covet your neighbor's wife." This was long before the Lord's similar saying in the New Testament . . .[61]

Therefore, there is no question that Clement used the word διαθήκη to refer to a group of books, and in this he represents an advance beyond the use of the Septuagint, the New Testament (but cf. 2 Cor. 3:14), and most earlier Christian writers. "The use of word διαθήκη by Clement indicates therefore a transition from the old abstract meaning to the new concrete one, which later became the predominant use."[62] Whether Clement himself had in mind a definite number of books—either Old or New Testament books—is quite doubtful, but today one can look back and see that he was on the way toward having a New Testament with a fixed number of books.

Just as important as the fact that Clement had an Old and New Testament is his idea of their relationship. Like many of the Fathers he claimed that the Old Testament was the rightful possession of the church. For example he frequently wrote of "our scriptures."[63] It has already been pointed out that he attributed the same authority to both. Also he believed in the unity of divine revelation.

The true church, that which is really ancient, is one. . . . We say that the ancient and the catholic church is alone, collecting as it does into the unity of the one faith—which results frrm the peculiar Testaments, or rather the one Testament in different times by the will of the one God, through one Lord—those . . . whom God predestinated.[64]

Just as Clement viewed the economy of the Old Covenant and that of the New as being essentially one, he also looked upon the books associated with these dispensations as being essentially one. As has been seen, he quoted indiscriminately from the books in both divisions and attached the same authority to both. Within the Old Testament he made no distinction between the authority of the Law and the Prophets. It is the position of this study that within the New Testament he made no distinction between the Gospels and the Epistles. Harnack, however, claimed that Clement considered only the Gospels to possess the same scriptural au-

---

[59]Ibid., 3.6.54 (translation mine).

[60]Ibid., 4.21.134.

[61]Ibid., 3.111.171 (translation mine).

[62]Hermann Eickhoff, *Das Neue Testament des Clemens Alexandrinus* (Schleswig: Buchdruckerei der Taubstummen-Anstalt, 1890), 7. Translation mine.

[63]*Str.* 2.1.1; 5.4.25; 6.3.29–30.

[64]Ibid., 7.17.107. It is uncertain, however, whether the word διαθήκη refers to the Old and New Testament (books) or the Old and New Covenant (compacts).

thority as the Old Testament.[65] It is true that Clement's canon of the Gospel exhibited a greater degree of fixity than that of the Epistles, but this has nothing to do with the authority he attached to the Epistles. It must be remembered that he quoted from the Epistles almost as many times as from the Gospels. Decisive is the passage which has already been cited in another connection: "We have, as the source of our teaching, the Lord, both by the prophets, the Gospel, and the blessed apostles."[66]

His Use of the Word γρηφή

Clement used the word γραφή more times than can be conveniently counted in Stählin's index/concordance. It has both a comprehensive use and a restricted one. In the former sense it is applied to pagan writings[67] and even to his own.[68] Nevertheless the predominant use is to refer to the inspired, biblical writings of the Old and New Testaments. One finds in Clement's works such expressions as "our scriptures,"[69] "the scriptures of the Lord,"[70] "the collected scriptures,"[71] and "the Old Scripture"[72] (referring to the Old Testament and clearly implying a New Testament). Although Clement's use of the term "scripture" is neither completely defined nor accurately limited, one begins to see in it a concept of a group of books possessing unique authority. What has been said about γραφή can also be said about γέγραπται and φησί.

His Emphasis upon Apostolic Tradition

Clement looked upon tradition, παράδοσις, as being a primary source of authority. It was because of tradition that he accepted only four Gospels.[73] The heretics are those who have "rejected the ecclesiastical tradition."[74] The importance of apostolic tradition can be seen from what Clement says about some of his teachers: "They preserving the tradition of the blessed doctrine delivered from the holy apostles . . . the sons receiving it from the father . . . [This] will be agreeable to a soul desirous of preserving . . . the blessed tradition."[75]

---

[65]*History of Dogma*, 2:58.

[66]*Str.* 7.16.95.

[67]Ibid., 1.16.78.

[68]Ibid., 6.15.131.

[69]Ibid., 4.17.44.

[70]Ibid., 6.11.91.

[71]*Prot.* 9.87.

[72]*Str.* 6.15.119.

[73]Ibid., 3.13.93.

[74]Ibid., 7.16.95.

[75]Ibid., 1.1.11–12.

Of what significance is Clement's view of tradition for his concept of canonicity? Does he identify tradition solely with oral teaching or does he also include written documents? Kutter claims: "παράδοσις in its essential meaning for Clement lies only in the Holy Scriptures themselves."[76] The statement claims too much. The oral and esoteric aspect of tradition comes out in the following:

> The Lord . . . allowed us to communicate of those divine mysteries, and of that holy light, to those who were able to receive them. He did not certainly disclose to the many what did not belong to the many; but to the few of whom he knew that they belonged, who were capable of receiving and being molded according to them. But secret things are entrusted to speech, not to writing.[77]

The esoteric element of tradition comes out again in Clement's exegesis of scripture. Well known is his allegorical method, which was based on the presupposition that there is a hidden meaning which may be discovered only by the elite. This concept of hidden meaning, however, leads to the idea that Clement in some sense also associated tradition with the written word. It thus becomes clear that tradition is embodied in scripture as well as oral teaching. Consider the following:

> Our Gnostic then alone, having grown old in the Scriptures, and maintaining apostolic and ecclesiastical orthodoxy in doctrines, lives most correctly in accordance with the Gospel, and discovers the proofs . . . from the Law and the Prophets. For the life of the Gnostic . . . is . . . the deeds and words corresponding to the tradition of the Lord.[78]

The fact that Clement found tradition to be embodied in that which is written is one explanation for his acceptance and use of many writings which did not in the end gain admission to the canon.

His Exegetical Work

Since Clement attaches so much importance to the very words of scripture, one might expect that his quotations would be precise and exact. Such is not the case. The majority of his quotations are from memory, and as a result he sometimes blends two or more passages into a single quotation,[79] sometimes expresses the sense of a passage in different words,[80] and sometimes attributes to one writer a passage from another.[81] This practice, however, does not in any way diminish his respect for biblical

---

[76]*Clemens Alexandrinus und das N.T.*, 148. Translation mine.

[77]*Str.*, 1.1.13.

[78]Ibid., 7.16.104. By "Gnostic" Clement means, not a heretic, but an *enlightened*, orthodox Christian.

[79]For example in *Prot.* 8.78 Isa. 51:6 and 40:8 are combined.

[80]In quoting 1 Cor. 13:8 in *Q.D.S.* he substitutes "gifts of healing shall fail on earth" for "where there is knowledge it will cease."

[81]In *Prot.* 8.79 he attributes Amos 4:13 to Hosea.

writings. Loose quotation was simply a contemporary practice and is widely found in the New Testament itself. Nor does his practice of allegorical interpretation in any way detract from his high view of scripture and tradition. Quite to the contrary, it shows how highly he did regard them. In them were concealed the deep mysteries of God.

Also of importance is the commentary he wrote. Commentary probably implies canonical status, certainly authoritative status. Eusebius's famous statement has already been cited. It would seem to indicate that Clement commented on "all canonical Scripture," including the disputed General Epistles and the *Epistle of Barnabas* and *Apocalypse of Peter*. Photius, however, seems to indicate that Clement dealt only with Genesis, Exodus, the Psalms, Ecclesiastes, the Epistles of Paul, and the General Epistles.[82] And Cassiodorus's translation contained only the commentaries on 1 Peter, 1 and 2 John, and Jude. On the one hand, it seems improbable that Clement could have written even a brief commentary[83] on the entire Bible. On the other, large portions could have been lost before it reached Cassiodorus and Photius. The exact content of the *Hypotyposes* cannot be determined, but the fact that Clement wrote a commentary demonstrates that he had a meaningful concept of canonicity.

His Opposition to Heretics

It has often been pointed out that the controversies with heresies forced the church to define carefully her authority and thus to formulate a canon of scripture. This formulation may be seen in progress in Clement. Even a casual reading of his works will show how deeply he was involved in combating heresy. He defined heretics as those who "will not make use of all the Scriptures."[84] The exact influence of heresy is difficult to trace, but there is good reason to conclude that it was at work in the formation of Clement's concept of canonicity.

His Use of the Word κανών

Clement uses the word κανών twenty-one times.[85] Invariably the word means *a standard or rule by which something is measured or judged*. He speaks of the "canon of the church"[86] and an "ecclesiastical canon,"[87] by which he means the inner principle of authority which the church possesses in the areas of doctrine and conduct. Likewise he speaks of a "canon

---

[82]*Bibliotheca* 109 (MG 103:381–384).

[83]ὑποτύπωσις means *an outline, a pattern*.

[84]*Str.* 7.16.96.

[85]Stählin, *Clemens Alexandrinus*, 4:494.

[86]*Str.* 7.16.105.

[87]Ibid., 7.17.41.

of truth"[88] and a "canon of faith."[89] None of these, however, has anything
to do with books. That use of the word did not emerge for another century. Although Clement did not use the word, the evidence collected in
this study shows that he did have a concept of what is now called canonicity and an indefinite and fluid group of books which nevertheless
constituted a provisional canon.[90]

III

CLEMENT AND HIS CONTEMPORARIES[91]

To the extent that he does not have a canon list or a fixed number of
books, Clement does not exhibit the degree of development as does Marcion
or the Muratorian Canon.[92] Clement's unofficial or fluid canon is of course
much more extensive than the eleven books in the canon of Marcion. In
some instances Marcion's mini canon may be due to the lack of knowledge of books, but for the most part it is due to dogmatic bias. Therefore,
it is difficult to compare him and Clement. Marcion's heresy, but not his
canon, is condemned by Clement.[93]

The content of Clement's New Testament is quite similar to that of the
Muratorianum. Whereas Clement has no reference to Philemon, the Mur-
atorian list certainly affirms it. Whereas Clement affirms Hebrews and 1
Peter, the Muratorian list does not mention them. Neither has James, 2
Peter, or 3 John. Both accept Jude and Revelation. Both accept the
Apocalypse of Peter. Clement may accept Hermas; the Muratorian list
certainly rejects it. And the Muratorian Canon accepts the Wisdom of
Solomon, whereas Clement shows no knowledge of it. One may conclude

[88]Ibid., 7:16.94.

[89]Ibid., 4.15.98.

[90]In addition to the articles and monographs mentioned above, and in addition to the
treatments in introductions to the canon (cf. the following note), see also J. Ruwet, "Clément
d'Alexandrie Canon des Écritures et Apocryphes," *Biblica* 29 (1948): 391–408; and G.
Brambillasca, "Citations de l'Écriture Sainte et des auteurs classiques dans le Protreptikos
pros Ellenas de Clément d'Alexandrie," *Studia Patristica* 11:2 (1972): 8–12.

[91]Information about Marcion, the Muratorian Canon List, Irenaeus, and Tertullian has
been gleaned from B. M. Metzger, *The Canon of the New Testament* (Oxford: Clarendon,
1987); F. F. Bruce, *The Canon of Scripture* (Downers Grove, IL: Inter Varsity, 1988);
and the present writer's own research.

[92]It is assumed that this list comes from Rome about 180. It is not possible to discuss
here the question of date and provenance. For another view see A. C. Sundburg, Jr.,
"Canon Muratori: A Fourth-Century List," *HTR* 66 (1973): 1–14. For a reaffirmation of
the traditional view see E. Ferguson, "Canon Muratori: Date and Provenance," *Studia
Patristica* 18 (1982): 677–83.

[93]*Str.* 3.3.12ff; 5.1.4; 7.17.102; 7.17.107–8.

that Clement and the Muratorian list are at about the same stage of development of the canon. The only point at which Clement may lag behind the Muratorianum is in seeming to accept additional works which were later rejected.

Irenaeus, like Clement, makes no reference to Philemon. Clement accepts Hebrews and Jude, but Irenaeus makes no certain reference to them. Neither reveals a knowledge of James, 2 Peter, or 3 John. Both accept Revelation. Both appear to accept Hermas as scripture. Both cite Clement of Rome favorably but probably do not accept his writing as scripture. Clement and Irenaeus therefore also attest a similar level of development. Although both refer to a four-Gospel canon, Irenaeus's adamant affirmation may indicate a slight advance at that point. And Clement's high regard for additional outside books may also indicate that Irenaeus was slightly further along toward a limited canon.

Whereas Clement evidently had no occasion to mention Philemon, Tertullian accepted it. Clement certainly and Tertullian probably accepted Hebrews, although Tertullian ascribed it to Barnabas. Both accepted Jude and Revelation, although Tertullian made even less use of the latter than Clement. Neither has any references to James, 2 Peter, and 3 John, and Tertullian has no references to 2 John either. Tertullian goes beyond his contemporaries in accepting no book into the New Testament which did not later become canonical. Therefore, Clement and Tertullian are not far apart in the content of their New Testament.

The differences among Irenaeus, the Muratorian Canon, Clement, and Tertullian are minor. They represent approximately the same level of canonical development. A preliminary and provisional canon consisting of the four Gospels, Acts, thirteen letters of Paul, 1 Peter, 1 John, and Revelation[94] had clearly evolved. Some books which were later rejected were still contending for a place, and some which were later accepted were apparently unknown to these writers. No book which was ultimately accepted was explicitly rejected by any of the four. The period 180–220 therefore is probably the most significant in the history of the New Testament canon.

---

[94]Revelation, however, later came under heavy fire in the East. Furthermore, although Irenaeus has no certain reference to Jude, the Muratorian none to 1 Peter, and Tertullian none to 2 John, there is no indication that these were disputed at the time.

Irenaeus' Use of Paul
in His Polemic
Against the Gnostics

RICHARD A. NORRIS, JR.

Not a great deal has been written, of a systematic sort, about Irenaeus' use or interpretation of Paul since the influential 1889 monograph of Dr. Johannes Werner.[1] Such work as has appeared, moreover, has most often touched on Irenaeus' part in the reception of the Pauline corpus as an element in the emerging New Testament canon; and in this connection a great deal of stress has been laid on his role as a legitimizer or domesticator of the Pauline and deutero-Pauline letters at a time when, as it has seemed, their principal advocates and exponents were followers of Marcion or of Valentinus.[2] By contrast, less attention has been directed to the question of what sense Irenaeus himself made of the apostle's writings. Even when this task has been undertaken, moreover, the method adopted has as often as not been, in effect, that of testing Irenaeus' understanding of Paul by reference to Luther's, or Calvin's, or even F. C. Baur's.[3]

It seems apparent, however, even from a cursory reading of the treatise *Adversus haereses*, that Irenaeus, as he cites, alludes to, and muses over Paul's writings, is not merely engaged, as Werner thought, in an unwelcome apologetic task that circumstance had more or less forced on him. To be sure, he is committed to establishing the thesis that the Apostle Paul was neither an explicit Marcionite nor a concealed Valentinian. If, however, one surveys Irenaeus' references to the Pauline corpus, it quickly becomes apparent that the majority of them serve no merely defensive purpose. No doubt they function—at least as we encounter them— in the setting of a polemical enterprise; and the agenda of that enterprise must be expected to provide the framework within which we see Irenaeus reading Paul. For this reason if for no other, it is useless to inquire whether Irenaeus' Paul conforms to the image of the apostle that was later unveiled by the interests and perceptions of evangelical Protestantism. His concerns and questions—and those of his opponents—were of a different order. To say this, however, does not entail the conclusion that Irenaeus cared nothing for, and made nothing of, the Pauline corpus. Hence it is reasonable to ask how Irenaeus himself reads the letters associated with the name of Paul—or, in other words, to ask whether, and how, they contribute positively to his own theological vision.

The aim of this study, then, will be a simple one: to trace or indicate the outlines of what I shall call Irenaeus' "reading" of Paul. To this end it is important to distinguish the different purposes for which Irenaeus appeals to Paul in the course of his polemic against his opponents—and in particular to distinguish the cases in which he is controverting his opponents' exegesis of Paul from those in which he is using Paul either to refute their general position or to build and support his own. On the basis of such an analysis, it should be possible to identify Pauline texts or passages—or combinations of them—that feed Irenaeus' own theological vision, and so to suggest what Paul "meant" to a bishop of Lyons around the end of the second century. In pursuing this general aim, I shall be much less interested in questions about Irenaeus' exegetical methods, or about the "correctness" of his interpretation of Paul, than simply in the sort of thing he discovers in Paul's letters. And since Irenaeus was unaware of any distinction between "Pauline" and "deutero-Pauline" works, I shall, for the purposes of this investigation, mean by the expression "Paul's letters" just what Irenaeus would have meant by it: the entire Pauline corpus with the exception of Hebrews and (probably) Philemon.

The first—and no doubt most obvious—manner in which Irenaeus treats of Pauline texts is in the narrowest sense controversial. I refer to those cases in which he seeks directly to controvert what he regards as a wrongheaded reading of some particular verse or passage.

On several occasions in Book 1 of the *Adversus haereses*, Irenaeus indicates the drift of Valentinian exegeses of particular Pauline texts. His opponents saw, for example, a reference to the pleromatic savior in Colossians 3:11 and 2:9, where the apostle states that Christ is "all things" and that "in him the whole fulness of deity dwells"; and they saw a similar confirmation of their teaching that the Savior is the "All" in Ephesians 1:10 with its reference to the "summing up" of all things "in Christ" (*AH* 1.3.4). In Paul's references to the cross at 1 Corinthians 1:18 and Galatians 6:4, the disciples of Ptolemy found an allusion to the eon "Limit," to which they also gave the name "Cross." The Valentinians further took the assertion of Colossians 1:16—"in him all things were created"—to mean that the Savior is respon-sible for the chain of events that led to the formation of the visible cosmos (*AH* 1.4.5). Later on (*AH* 1.8.3), Irenaeus also notes that his adversaries supported or derived their distinction between hylic, psychic, and pneumatic persons out of various texts in the Pauline letters. They appeal not only to statements in which Paul opposes "pneumatic" to "psychic" (1 Cor. 2:14) and "earthy" to "heavenly" (1 Cor. 15:48), but also to Romans 11:16, asserting that the sanctification of the "whole lump" by the "firstfruits" signifies the relation between pneumatics and psychics (i.e., between themselves and the ordinary Christians) in the church. Above all, they characterize their own status by cit-ing Paul's assertion that "the pneumatic person judges all things, but is himself judged by no one" (1 Cor. 2:15). Finally, Irenaeus notes that the Marcosians apply the words of Psalm 14:2,[4] as quoted by Paul in the third chapter of Romans, to ignorance of the ultimate Depth (*AH* 1.19.1), and that one group of heretics—traditionally identified as the "Ophites"—quote the words "Flesh and blood do not grasp the kingdom of God" (cf. 1 Cor. 15:50) to show that the disciples of Jesus were deceived in think-ing that he was raised up in *corpore mundiali*. Later in his treatise, however, Irenaeus says that "all the heretics" appeal to this text, not with reference to Jesus' resurrection but to prove that the *plasmatio* of God is not saved (*AH* 5.9.1).

In Book 1—Irenaeus' *narratio*—none of these exegeses are controverted, save perhaps by a rhetorical lifting of the eyebrow.

Clearly, they are submitted principally by way of illustration; and in some cases at least, one suspects that Irenaeus does not regard them as worthy of attention. Some of them, however, recur for extended discussion in later books of *Adversus haereses.* In Book 4, Irenaeus offers his own lengthy account of the identity of the *pneumatikos* who "judges all things" (AH 4.33.1–15), and he devotes a significant section of Book 5 to developing his own understanding of the difference between "psychics" and "pneumatics."[5] In these cases, however, his attention is focused less on a particular text than on the general outlook that informs Valentinian exegesis of the Pauline statements in question. The same appears to be true in the case of Ephesians 1:10. Irenaeus has—as I need hardly observe—his own way of understanding what it means that "all things" are "summed up" in Christ, and in articulating it he is clearly aware of his opponents' way of handling this text,[6] but he does not address the text, or their exegesis of it, directly, perhaps because his difference with them in fact lies at the deeper level of the assumptions with which the text is approached. The expression "all things," he says significantly (AH 3.16.6), includes in its denotation the visible and tangible *plasmatio Dei* that is humanity. Hence he concludes that "things visible and corporeal" too are necessarily incorporated in what the Christ "sums up."

But if, in these cases, Irenaeus in effect replies to his opponents simply by employing a controversial Pauline text in the exposition of his own beliefs, there are also a number of instances in which he addresses their exegesis of a text directly. The most notorious of these, perhaps, is the case of 2 Corinthians 4:4, which contains the phrase *Deus saeculi huius* ("the god of this world"). Plainly Irenaeus' opponents—or some particular group of them—appealed to this expression to justify their belief in a second, cosmic deity hostile to, or ignorant of, the supreme Father. Irenaeus' reply takes the form of a verbal quibble that serves to display his rhetorical learning, in which he no doubt took great pride. Paul, he says, *propter velocitatem sermonum suorum* (AH 3.7.2), was in the habit of using the rhetorical device of *hyperbaton,* inversion of words. To understand the text properly, therefore, one must take the phrase "of this world" not with "God" but with "unbelievers." In that way one obtains the true sense: "God blinded the minds of the unbelievers of this world" (AH 3.7.1).[7] Irenaeus takes a less high-handed way with his adversaries when, in dealing with the same range of issues, he urges that the phrase "every so-called god" at 2 Thessalonians 2:4 cannot be referred to the creator, on the ground that "the Father of all things" can scarcely be regarded as a member of a class of "so-called gods" (AH 3.6.5); and again when he argues that 1 Corinthians 8:5, in referring to "so-called gods whether in heaven or on earth," does not mean *mundi fabricatores* but "the moon and the stars" to which Moses referred in Deuteronomy.[8]

But the instance of heretical exegesis that he takes the greatest pains to refute is the Gnostic handling of 1 Corinthians 15:50 ("Flesh and blood cannot inherit the kingdom of God"). His adversaries of course saw in this text a denial that the material shell of the human person can share in salvation, that is, in the resurrection. Irenaeus devotes, in all, six chapters of Book 5 to an exposition of these words. His objections to the interpretation proposed by his adversaries are carefully summarized in *Adversus haereses* 5.13.2–3. His fundamental negative point is that they take the expression "flesh and blood" *nude*—which means, presumably, "in its most obvious and ordinary sense"— and hence fail to grasp the true force of the words or the intent of the apostle (AH 5.13.2). Irenaeus thinks (AH 5.13.3) that 1 Corinthians 15:53–55, where among other things it is said that "this mortal thing must put on immortality" and that "death is swallowed up in victory," provides a clear indication that Paul did not mean what the Valentinians had taken him to mean—as, for that matter, does Philippians 3:20–21.[9] Their exegesis, he asserts, makes Paul appear to contradict himself. As to the correct exegesis, he wants to insist on two points. In the first place, he concludes that "flesh and blood" refers here primarily to "the works of the flesh" and not to materiality as such; but then, in the second place, he wants to argue that flesh—taken now to mean precisely the physical dimension of the human constitution— *does* "inherit the kingdom of God" in the sense that "death is swallowed up in victory" and that flesh *is inherited* by the Spirit. These two contentions he has already defended at greater length.[10] They depend, as we shall see, on Irenaeus' assessment of the general "drift" of Pauline theology.

From this brief and summary examination—no doubt in-complete—of heretical exegeses that Irenaeus sets out to contro-vert, two tentative conclusions seem to emerge. First, it is only on occasion that he directly and deliberately notes and seeks to refute a Valentinian—or possibly, in some cases, a Marcionite—interpretation of Paul. In many instances he simply "re-handles" the text in question; that is, he "exhibits" what he takes to be its meaning by letting it speak within the frame of his own theologi-cal understanding or argument.[11] Second, all of the exegeses that he *does* attack in a direct way concern one or the other of two broad sets of issues: the distinction between an ultimate God and a cosmic demiurge, or the Valentinian understanding of human nature and its redemption. If, as I suspect, this circumstance provides a clue to the themes that dominated his opponents' interpretation of the Pauline letters,[12] it may also, in the end, provide a useful backdrop against which to measure Irenaeus' own way of reading Paul.

There is, however, a second manner in which Irenaeus uses the Pauline letters in his polemic, one that defines a much more numerous class of citations and allusions. I refer to those passages in which Irenaeus appeals to a Pauline text in order to refute not a contrary exegesis of the text itself but some teaching that he takes to be an integral part of his opponents' *hypothesis*, whether or not that teaching has any relation to their interpretation of Paul.

The first issue concerning which Irenaeus appeals to Paul is—inevitably—that constituted by the Valentinian and Marcionite distinction between the cosmic creator and the supreme Father. Irenaeus, as one need hardly say, is determined to show that Paul affirmed *one* God—God the creator. We have already seen how, in *Adversus haereses* 3.6.5 and 3.7.1, he contradicts the Valentinian (?) exegesis of certain Pauline texts that had been taken to support this distinction. His primary appeal, however, is to texts in which Paul deprecates pagan polytheism. In particular, he cites Galatians 4:8-9 (with its contrast between "God" and "beings that by nature are no gods") and, of course, 1 Corinthians 8:4-6, with its assertion of "one God, the Father, from whom are all things"—a passage that, taken in its full extent, seems to have dictated, among other things, the basic outline of Book 3 from the sixth chapter on. In this connection—and, interestingly enough, in this connection alone—Irenaeus also appeals to two speeches attributed to Paul in the Acts of the Apostles (although only in a section of his argument that is devoted exclusively to the evidence of that work).[13] He does not raise the issue of whether these denials of polytheism are in fact relevant to the sort of question with which both he and his opponents were concerned; he simply assumes that they are.

A second issue on which Irenaeus appeals to the authority of Paul against the teaching of his heretics is, of course, that of the person of Christ. In accordance with the language of 1 Corinthians 8:6, Irenaeus wants to maintain that there is "one Lord Jesus Christ" just as there is "one God the Father"; and this against views which separated the pleromatic "Christ" from the cosmic "Jesus" in such wise as to deny that the former suffered or was born—or, indeed, shared in any way in the human condition as Irenaeus understood the human condition. In opposition to such views, he wanted to assert that Jesus and the Christ are *unus et idem*, a phrase that echoes back and forth through three chapters (16–18) of Book 3. Needless to say, this precise issue was, again, not one to which Paul had ever bent his mind, but Irenaeus' invocation of the two texts in which the apostle happens to attach the epithet "one" to the style "Jesus Christ"[14] may be less contrived than it appears at first sight to a modern reader. His point seems to be merely that in Paul's habitual usage, "Jesus" and "Christ" denote the same person and not two separate beings.

Closely related to this is Irenaeus' citation of Pauline texts to show that the apostle ascribed death to the one he referred to as "Christ" or "Jesus Christ" or "Son of God"—and not only death but also birth and resurrection from the dead.[15] Here the issue is not so much the unity of the person of Christ as it is whether that unity encompasses what Irenaeus understands humanity to be— that is, flesh, the *plasmatio* of God that is subject to birth, suffering, and death. The fact that he does not distinguish these two questions very clearly in his mind no doubt lends an air of imprecision to his argument, but the point is clear. He makes it positively at the very beginning of his christological disquisition, where, after submitting the teaching of the Fourth Gospel by title and passing on to Matthew, he arrives finally at Paul, quoting Romans 1:1-4 at length and then Galatians 4:4-5. Both texts speak of "the Son of God"—whom Irenaeus, following the lead of John 1:1-14 and Colossians 1:15,[16] understands to be that "Word" who is "the first-born of all creation"—and at the same time characterize him as human: he is "of the seed of David according to the flesh" and he is "born of a woman." This of course is what Irenaeus wants to argue: that Paul, unlike the Valentinians, speaks of Christ as one person who is God's "Son . . . born of a woman."

A third issue on which Irenaeus appeals to Paul against his opponents is the complex and difficult one of the continuities and discontinuities between the new covenant in Christ and the covenants with Abraham and Moses. In the first instance, this issue was one that concerned Christian use and interpretation of the Jewish scriptures; but it also touched, for Irenaeus, on two more general but not less central matters: the question of the unity of humanity's history with God and, underlying that, the funda-mental question of the unity of God. Furthermore, this issue was rendered the more complex by the fact that Irenaeus saw himself confronted by two distinct groups of opponents: the followers of Marcion, who simply repudiated the Jewish scriptures, and the Valentinians, who, if Ptolemy's *Letter to Flora* can be taken as representing their general outlook, saw themselves as occupying a middle ground, at least on the subject of the law.

By contrast both to Marcion and to the Valentinians, Ire-naeus argues that the same God who "sent his Son" into the world is the author of the Mosaic law. To support this thesis, he cites (*AH* 4.2.7) Paul's statement that the law was *paedagogum nostrum in Christum Jesum* (Gal. 3:24). He appeals not only to Jesus' summary of the law but also (*AH* 4.12.2) to Paul's statement that "love is the fulfilling of the law" (Rom. 13:10). His aim here is to argue that it is not the legislation of Moses as such but the human "tradition" of the elders that the gospel repudiates.[17] The essential law—which Irenaeus, not unlike Ptolemy, clearly identi-fies with the *moral* injunctions of Moses—is fulfilled in Christ. Paul's assertion that Christ is the *telos* of the law (Rom. 10:4) thus means, for Irenaeus, not that Christ simply abolishes the law but that he is the goal toward which it points and moves. Hence, as he sees it, the apostle's assertion also entails the proposition that Christ is the *arche* of the law (*AH* 4.12.3)—presumably because that which functions as the end or goal of something must, in Irenaeus' mind, serve also as its ultimate and original explanation. He of course agrees with Ptolemy that the ceremonial laws of the Mosaic covenant are—for Christians if not for those who originally received them—simply "types"; and to this point he cites, one need hardly add, 1 Corinthians 10:11 (*AH* 4.14.3). He also agrees with Ptolemy that, as the Lord himself said, some laws were given to the Israelites by Moses in his own right "on account of the hardness of their heart" (Mk. 19:7f.); but Irenaeus is swift to note that such regulations exist even under the new covenant, since Paul too, in 1 Corinthians 7, gives instructions on his own authority by way of concession to human weakness (*AH* 4.15.2). Irenaeus further (*AH* 4.16.4) counters the suggestion that the Mosaic legislation was given by the demiurge out of self-regarding motives by repeating the commonplace that God stands in need of nothing; in fact, he argues, it was given out of love, as the apostle suggests, and for the benefit of human beings, because they "fall short of the glory of God" (Rom. 3:23). Thus the same God is the author of both covenants, and Irenaeus makes this point against Marcion by firmly quoting Romans 3:21: the righteousness of God is indeed manifested "apart from the law," but it is nevertheless attested by the law and the prophets (*AH* 4.34.3). The brightness of Moses' face, which because of its splendor the Israelites could not gaze upon (2 Cor. 3:7), was the glory of "the person who loves God" (*AH* 4.26.1). As such, it was a foreshadowing of the destiny that God wills for all human beings.

Irenaeus also makes great play with Paul's treatment of Abraham in Romans and Galatians. For him, however, the point is not primarily that the "father" of Israel was reckoned acceptable to God on the basis of faith rather than on the basis of observance of the Mosaic covenant. Instead it is that Abraham represents both a foreshadowing and a beginning of the life of the church.[18] The promise to Abraham was that his seed should be *quasi stellas caeli*. The fact that Paul refers to his congregation at Philippi as "lights in the world" (Phil. 2:15) and to believers as "children of Abraham" (Rom. 4:12f.) indicates, on the one hand, that the community of believers fulfills that promise (AH 4.5.3) and, on the other, that Abraham himself was "a follower of the Word" (AH 4.5.4)—the same Word who said, "Abraham rejoiced to see my day" (Jn. 8:56). It is John, then, who teaches Irenaeus to envisage Abraham as a prophet who saw what was coming in God's *oikonomia*; Paul's Abraham stands rather as an attestation of the fact that God's way of dealing with humanity has not changed in substance even if it has changed in the manner of its administration. *Una et eadem illius et nostra sit fides* (AH 4.21.1).

The fact is, of course, that Irenaeus is fairly sure that God's way of dealing with humanity has not changed in every respect. This attitude emerges in his treatment of arguments—quite probably Marcionite in origin[19]—that denigrated the Jewish scriptures by dwelling either on the reprehensible deeds of ancient kings, judges, and patriarchs or on the creator's unfortunate habit of imposing peremptory demands and punishments. Irenaeus points out, referring to 1 Corinthians 10:1–12, that Paul himself does not bother to condemn the sins of the Israelites but envisages the sins—and the punishments they evoked—as warnings to us (AH 4.27.3). This means, however, that the apostle saw Christian believers as standing in the presence of the same God, the same moral demand, and the same judgment as had their forebears in faith (AH 4.27.4). Did he not say that *all* "fall short of the glory of God" (Rom. 3:23)? The situation in that respect has not changed. Nor is it true that the God of the elder covenant was a God of judgment while the God revealed by Christ is purely a God of grace. Following his nameless presbyter, Irenaeus alludes to a whole catena of Pauline texts that speak of the judgment or the wrath of God, leading off with the question (1 Cor. 6:9), "Do you not know that the unrighteous will not inherit the kingdom of God?" He concedes, indeed, that there is, in at least one respect, a significant difference between the Christian and the Mosaic dispensations. In the former the promise is greater; hence its demand for righteousness of life is more thoroughgoing and the punishment it threatens more lasting (AH 4.28.2). But neither sin nor its judgment is a speciality of the old covenant.

Here, then, we have Irenaeus using the Pauline corpus to attack his adversaries on central points of their teaching. The greatest mass of Pauline evidence is marshaled to contradict Valentinian and Marcionite estimates of the Jewish scriptures—estimates that subserved their contention that there is a difference between the creator God of the old covenant and the Father of Jesus Christ. By the same token, Paul's writings are used to criticize this latter contention directly and also to controvert Valentinian christology, both in its dualism and in its refusal to incorporate humanity as "flesh" in the person of Christ. If, as I suggested earlier, Irenaeus reflects the agenda of a "Gnostic" reading of Paul when he attacks Valentinian exegesis of particular texts, his agenda in these forays manifests rather his own notion of the issues on which his opponents' *hypothesis* went systematically wrong. His use of Paul, in other words, is governed by his determination to defend the three basic—and related—principles of one God, one Christ, and one providentially ordered history. And while this polemical agenda may, as I suspect, have been suggested to him in part by a Pauline text (i.e., 1 Corinthians 8:6), the issues are clearly not Paul's own; and Irenaeus' use of the apostle, whether apt or not, can therefore project no clear "picture," no "reading," as I have called it, of the thematic structures of Paul's teaching. For that, we must look further—not at Irenaeus' polemics but at the theological vision he articulates when he is suggesting how and why his three principles make coherent sense.

To see how—and to what extent—a reading of Paul contributes to this theological vision, one can do worse than begin with a Pauline text whose language is not only intermittently quoted by Irenaeus[20] but seems, as a matter of fact, to have become part and parcel of his own vocabulary. "But when the fulness of time arrived, God sent his Son, born from a woman, born under the law, to redeem those who were under the law, in order that we might receive the adoption of sons. And because you are sons, God sent the Spirit of his Son into our hearts" (Gal. 4:4-6). The phrases "fulness of time" and "adoption of sons"[21] (or simply "adoption") recur regularly in Irenaeus' writing, regularly enough to indicate that the thought—or better, perhaps, the picture—that he culled from these verses was, for him, a central and thematic one. Therefore, it is worth seeing not only how Irenaeus uses this text itself but also how he connects its language and the ideas he finds in it with other Pauline passages.

We can begin our inquiry by asking how Irenaeus understands the words "God sent his Son, born of a woman." As we have already seen, *Adversus haereses* 3.16.3 sets them alongside Romans 1:1-4 and Colossians 1:15ff., and together the three passages interpret one another for Irenaeus. The mention of "God" in Galatians is given precision by the passage from Romans: the "God" in question is the one who "promised" good news "beforehand through his prophets in the holy scriptures" (Rom. 1:2). This God is, in short, the creator God of the Jewish scriptures. In a similar way, the meaning of "Son" is specified by Colossians 1:15ff. The Son in question is "the first-born of all creation," whom Irenaeus, as we have seen, identifies, not imperceptively perhaps, with the *Logos* of John 1:1-14. Hence the words "born of a woman"—in effect reiterated and confirmed by the expression "of the seed of David according to the flesh" (Rom. 1:3)—represent a restatement of the Johannine "became flesh." Paul in Galatians, then, is locating the central redemptive event in the incarnation of the divine Son or Word. But more than that, he is presenting this event as the outcome of an initiative on the part of the God of the prophets—the God who spoke in the Jewish scriptures and who, indeed, *promised* this redemption *ahead of time* in those very scriptures. How, then, do Pauline texts and ideas figure in Irenaeus' development and expansion of these two themes that he sees adumbrated in Galatians, the themes of redemption as worked (a) by the creator God revealed in law and prophets, and (b) through the incarnation of God's Son?

Where the first of these themes is concerned, we do well to attend, at least initially, to another phrase from the text in Galatians: "in the fulness of time." What it conveys to Irenaeus in the first instance is nicely suggested in *Adversus haereses* 3.16.7. There he is, in effect, explaining what it means that there is a divine *oikonomia* that embraces everything (*universa dispositio*: *AH* 3.16.6) and culminates in the enfleshing of God's Son. It

means that "all thing are foreknown by the Father and carried out
by the Son . . . at the moment that is appropriate (*apto tempore*)." God, then, has a *history* with humanity, and humanity with
God, and in that history different things happen at different
times. The phrase "fulness of time" itself, of course, refers to one
moment in that history, the time of the Word's being made flesh
(*AH* 3.17.4), but it also implies for Irenaeus that there are other
"times" that have their place in the same divine scheme. This
conclusion is confirmed for him, moreover, by a variety of Pauline
texts. He notes, no doubt recalling Galatians 4:21ff., that the one
divine householder "who brings out of his treasure what is new
and what is old" (Mt. 13:52) had one commandment for "slaves,"
the old covenant, and another for those who have been liberated
by faith—the latter of which Irenaeus sums up in the words of
Psalm 96:1: "Sing to the Lord a new song" (*AH* 4.9.1). By the same
token, when Paul says (1 Cor. 13:9–10) "We know in part and we
prophesy in part, but when that which is perfect comes, the
imperfect will pass away," he testifies that the history of God with
humanity is still not completed (*AH* 4.9.2).[22] Indeed Irenaeus
thinks that the spelling-out of the story of humanity's creation
and salvation in time is implied not only by Paul's insistence that
the race moves from the "psychic" to the "spiritual" (1 Cor. 15:46)
but also by his statement "I fed you with milk, not solid food;
for you were not ready for it" (1 Cor. 3:2).[23] Irenaeus is very
conscious, then, that Paul sees God's dealings with humanity to
be susceptible of analysis in terms of "befores" and "afters"; and
to him this means not only that humanity's history with God is
a story of change and growth but also that at any "time" one
can name—including the moment that he refers to as "the fulness of time"—there is always a "more" that God has to give and a
"more" that humanity has to receive.[24]

It seems to be Paul, moreover, who supplies Irenaeus with a
way of envisaging the unity of this history in all its variety.[25] The
bishop's basic theme, of course, is simply that the one God is
the single source of all things. This he seeks to establish, at the
opening of his little treatise on the prophets, by referring not only
to Paul[26] but also to Hermas' *Shepherd* and to the prophet
Malachi. He further argues that since Christ said "All things are

delivered to me by my Father" (Mt. 11:27), it is the one Son, the Word, in whom God must be understood to carry out the works of creation, revelation, and salvation (AH 4.20.2). But even when he has established these points to his satisfaction, Irenaeus remains grimly aware of his opponents' delight in exploiting whatever evidence the scriptures contain of discontinuity between the Mosaic and the Christian dispensations. Accordingly, he must somehow show that the presence of variety and change in the *oikonomiai* of God is not in itself inconsistent with the operation of a single divine initiative and purpose in all of them. To this end, he transfers—interestingly and oddly—Paul's image of one body with many members to the history of God's self-revelation. He speaks of the *integrum corpus operis Filii Dei* (AH 4.33.15), different aspects or traits of which the different prophets manifested by their words (or actions); and in another place he explains that the prophets were "members of Christ" and that their prophecies therefore make up a whole, even though each prophesied in accordance with his individual calling as a member (AH 4.33.10). In 4.20.6, he alludes directly to 1 Corinthians 12:4-7. The saying that there are "diversities of operations, but the same Lord" Irenaeus applies to the different ways in which the prophets were led to understand and express the truth that human beings should come to the vision of God and to immortality; but this leads him, in 4.20.7, to go further and to suggest that the different *oikonomiai* of the divine Word must be conceived on the analogy of the successive notes that constitute a single melody. Paul's image for the church thus becomes Irenaeus' image for the history of creation and salvation as a single organic whole constituted of a variety of differing "parts"; and the connection between the two uses of this image lies, one suspects, in Irenaeus' perception of the history of salvation as, so to speak, the variegated spectrum that articulates in the medium of time the *integrum corpus operis Filii Dei*. And with this idea Irenaeus brings us back to the theme of the "fulness of time" and to the fleshly advent of the Son of God that constitutes that fulness.

For, of course, it is notorious that Irenaeus envisages God's "Son . . . born of a woman" as being, in accordance with Ephesians 1:10, one in whom all things are "summed up." In the first instance, Irenaeus develops this notion, as we have seen, along lines suggested to him by Colossians 1:15ff. The Word who is "first-born of all creation" takes flesh, dies, and becomes "first-born from the dead." In thus recapitulating humanity in himself and raising it, Christ becomes the one in whom God and creation, invisible and visible, meet (AH 3.16.6). He is the "summing up," then, and the unification of what we may, in un-Irenaean language, call the orders of being. But there is yet another dimension, as Irenaeus sees it, to this "summing up" of things in Christ. When, at *Adversus haereses* 3.18.1, Irenaeus faces the objection of people who say that if Christ was born at a particular time, then "he did not exist beforehand," his reply is twofold. He of course refers back to his development of the idea that the Son of God is, as Galatians puts it, *sent*, and sent "in the fulness of time" (AH 3.17.4). This clearly implies (for Irenaeus) that "the Son of God did not begin to be at that point, since he always exists with the Father" and so has always dwelt with the human race. But then, if the occurrence of the incarnation at a particular time is thus part of a providential divine scheme whose executive, so to speak, is the Logos, what the sending of God's Son fulfills and so "sums up" is, as Irenaeus now argues, the *longam hominum expositionem*, the "narrative"[27] or history of the human race in its relation with God. And this idea, in turn, Irenaeus works out in terms of the Pauline contrast between the disobedient Adam and the obedient Christ (AH 3.18.2).[28] The incarnation of the Logos encompasses and embraces the disobedient Adam in the victory of the Son of God, who was—as the apostle explains in Philippians—obedient even to the point of death on the cross (Phil. 2:8). Thus it "fulfills the scheme (*oikonomia*) of our salvation." The source, then, of Irenaeus' notion of recapitulation as "reversal" or "inverse repetition" appears, in the end, to be Romans 5:12ff., which portrays the "logic" of humanity's *longa expositio* as one of an inclusive sin reversed by an equally inclusive righteousness. Naturally enough, therefore, it is Paul whom Irenaeus quotes to explain the "reason" (*ratio*) of this act: "For to this end Christ died and lived again, that he might be Lord both of the dead and of the living" (Rom. 14:9). The "summing up" that occurs in the incarnation of the Son whom God sent "in the fulness of time" embraces and joins not

merely the visible and invisible orders, as Colossians suggests, but
humanity's past, its present, and (one supposes) its future. The
"summing up" exhibits humanity as created "after the image and
likeness of God"—that is, it exhibits the finished, the "second"
Adam, of whom the apostle speaks in 1 Corinthians 15.

So far, however, in this attempt to understand Irenaeus'
Paul through the lens of Galatians 4:4-6, we have virtually ignored what, for Irenaeus, is the second central theme of this
passage: its assertion that the purpose of God's sending his Son
"in the fulness of time" was to confer on humanity the
"adoption of sons." What Irenaeus understands by this phrase is
evident from a number of texts. The adoption of sons, he tells
us, depends on humanity's *koinonia* with the Son of God (*AH*
3.18.7)—on the fact that, as a result of the incarnation, humanity "bears and grasps and embraces the Son of God" (*AH* 3.16.3).
This notion in its turn, however, is closely bound up with Irenaeus' reading of 1 Corinthians 15:53-54. There Paul speaks of
the corruptible "putting on" incorruption and the mortal
"putting on" immortality, and drives his point home by quoting
a form of Isaiah 25:8: "Death is swallowed up in victory." Irenaeus seizes upon this image of "swallowing up," which Paul
also uses at 2 Corinthians 5:4.[29] For him, the "putting on" of
immortality and incorruption defines the *filiorum adoptio*, but it
comes about because in Christ "that which was corruptible is
swallowed up (*absorberetur*) by incorruption" (*AH* 3.19.1) and
because humanity—which for him of course means "flesh," the
plasmatio of God—is "swallowed up . . . in the victory and
the patience . . . and the resurrection" of the Son of God
(*AH* 3.19.3).[30]

Behind this picture, however—which is a picture of the humanity both of Christ and, by implication, of Adam—there lies yet
another Irenaean excursion through Pauline thought. The fact
that humanity's "adoption" comes about through a "putting on" of
immortality and through a "swallowing up" of death in victory
means for Irenaeus that it comes about through a gift of God,
through the power of God. This is—and must be—the case,
moreover, because the human being in itself is "flesh," as Paul
among others suggests, and because flesh in itself is weak. Indeed

the apostle says as much at Romans 7:18: "I know that no good
dwells in my flesh" (*AH* 3.20.3). What Paul means, however, is not
that flesh is beyond salvation but that "the good thing which is our
salvation is not from us but from God." For what Paul teaches is
that God's "power is made perfect in weakness" (2 Cor. 12:9)—a
text on which Irenaeus dwells at *Adversus haereses* 3.20.1, and then
again at 5.3.2–3, and which seems to define a thematic element in
his anthropology. In both passages he connects this idea with 1
Corinthians 15:53: the perfecting of power in weakness *is* for him
the conferring of incorruptibility on what is corruptible. The
phrase "power . . . made perfect in weakness" therefore describes both the incarnation of the Son of God and the redemption of humanity through its *koinonia* with him, that is, the
filiorum adoptio (cf. *AH* 3.20.2). It also leads Irenaeus to reflect on
the meaning of Paul's statement that "God has consigned all to
disobedience that he may have mercy upon all" (Rom. 11:23). As
Irenaeus sees it, the point of this assertion is that God permits
human beings to experience their own mortality and weakness so
that they may the better appreciate the grace and power of God
(*AH* 3.20.2).[31] The apostle makes the same point, Irenaeus notes, at
1 Corinthians 1:29, where he says that God chose what is "low and
despised . . . lest any flesh should glory before the face of God."
The truth is, Irenaeus insists a bit later on, that flesh has nothing
of its own to glory in: "the glory of a human being is God."

But how does a human being participate in this glory—in
the "adoption of sons," "the redemption of our bodies" (Rom.
8:23), incorruptibility? It is, we have said, through a sharing,
a *koinonia* with Christ (*AH* 3.18.7). And in characterizing this
sharing, Irenaeus draws on the whole array of Pauline language
that describes believers' unity with Christ. He uses the language
of membership in Christ (*AH* 5.2.3). He appeals to 1 Corinthians
15:20, where Christ is characterized as "the first fruits of those
who have fallen asleep." His understanding of this text is manifest
from the fact that he almost immediately turns to the head-and-
body image in Ephesians 1:22 and Colossians 1:18 and then develops it by allusion to Ephesians 4:16: the resurrection of the head
brings with it, in the end, that of "the rest of the body" as it is
"strengthened by the growth that comes from God" (*AH* 3.19.3).

Believers are to be "conformed to the image of [God's] Son," as
Paul says in Romans 8:29 (AH 5.6.1, cf. 4.37.7); that is yet another
aspect of what is meant by "adoption of sons."

But if one asked Irenaeus *how* this sharing in Christ comes
about, he would doubtless appeal, as he does in Book 5, to the
work of God's other "hand," the Spirit. Irenaeus notes (AH 5.6.2)
the passage in which Paul speaks of the body as the temple of
God's Spirit (1 Cor. 3:16). He also notes (AH 5.7.1) Romans 8:11:
"If the Spirit of him who raised Jesus from the dead dwells in you,
he who raised Christ Jesus from the dead will give life to your
mortal bodies also through his Spirit which dwells in you." In
Book 5, this text is employed by Irenaeus primarily to argue that it
is indeed "mortal bodies" that are raised; but it is also closely connected in his mind with his exegesis of 1 Thessalonians 5:23, where
Paul speaks of "spirit and soul and body," apparently as constituents of the human person. Irenaeus' idea is that "spirit" in the
text from Thessalonians in fact refers to that same *divine* Spirit
which is mentioned not only in Romans 8:11 but also in Ephesians
1:13f., where the apostle says that believers are "sealed with the
promised Holy Spirit"[32] and that this gift is "the guarantee of our
inheritance" (AH 5.8.1). The complete or "perfected" human being therefore is, as Irenaeus sees it, one who has received the Holy
Spirit—one who is not "unclothed, but . . . further clothed"
(2 Cor. 5:4) with the "wedding garment" of the Holy Spirit (AH
4.36.6) or, in another image, "flesh possessed by Spirit" (AH 5.9.3)
and inherited by Spirit. And this conclusion, he thinks, agrees
with what Paul says in 1 Corinthians 15:42–50. There a distinction
is made between body enlivened by soul, which corresponds to the
"first Adam," the "earthy one," and body enlivened by Spirit, the
"final Adam" and "the human being from heaven." And the perfection of humanity occurs as the transition is made from a state in
which people bear "the image of the earthy one" to a state in which
they bear "the image of the heavenly one." But this transition,
Irenaeus thinks, is to be understood in the light of 1 Corinthians
6:9–11, with its reference to the washing of baptism in which the
gift of the Spirit is conveyed and people put off "the works of
the flesh" (AH 5.11.2). The adoption of sons, then, in which believers receive the gift of incorruption and are conformed to the

image of God's Son, is the doing of the Spirit, in whose power "the works of the flesh" are put aside and humanity is "adjusted to God" (*aptare Deo*; cf. *AH* 3.17.2).

All this, furthermore, connects back with Irenaeus' understanding of the person and work of Christ, with which we started these explorations. It helps us, in fact, to understand why, in Book 3, Irenaeus takes time out to make a direct attack on the idea that it was the Christ from the pleroma who descended on Jesus at his baptism in the Jordan. The motive of this attack is not so much— as in the rest of this section of Book 3—to insist on the *unity* of the Christ. Rather it is to insist that *as a human being* the Christ was endowed with the Spirit—was indeed, as 1 Corinthians 15:45 suggests, a "lifegiving Spirit," a *sōma pneumatikon*—and this apparently for two reasons. In the first place, Irenaeus is eager to maintain the analogy—indeed the commonality of nature— between the Christ and believers that is presupposed by his understanding of the adoption of sons.[33] If only for this reason, Christ's humanity must be a Spirit-endowed humanity: in Christ, the Spirit becomes "accustomed . . . to dwell in the human race" (*AH* 3.17.1). But in the second place, Christ for Irenaeus is the *source* of the Holy Spirit for the rest of the human race. When Paul, at Romans 12:5, speaks of believers as "one body in Christ," what he says is strictly incomprehensible, Irenaeus thinks, apart from the gift of the Spirit in baptism; and this, in turn, "the Lord . . . gives to those who have a share in him (*qui ex ipso participantur*), sending the Holy Spirit into the whole earth."

But what are we to make of all this? There are at least two places in *Adversus haereses* where Irenaeus sums up what he takes the essential message of Paul to have been.[34] In both passages the summary follows the outline suggested by 1 Corinthians 8:6 but in each case with significant importations and additions. Paul is said first to have taught that there is one God—an element that, Irenaeus argues, was necessary in the preaching of one who brought the gospel to Gentiles uninstructed in the first principle of Jewish faith. Second, Paul is said to have taught the doctrine of the incarnation of the (preexistent) Son or Word of God. This is, no doubt, Irenaeus' interpretation of the phrase "one Lord Jesus

Christ"—an interpretation that is indebted, as we have seen, to
Galatians 4:4–6 read in conjunction with John 1:1–14 and certain
other Pauline passages. But to this Irenaeus adds, in each case, a
statement of the aim or purpose of the incarnation, which turns
out to be not only the conquest of Satan, the *inimicum hominis*,
but also the re-formation of the human race (*AH* 4.24.1) or "the
adoption of sons" (*AH* 3.16.3).

We have seen how Irenaeus develops these three themes and
weaves them together. The first—the principle of monotheism—
functions exclusively in Irenaeus' directly polemical use of Paul—
as indeed does the second to the extent that "one Lord Jesus
Christ" is taken by Irenaeus simply to register the fact that for Paul
there are not different Christs at different levels of being. Insofar,
however, as this second theme incorporates, in Irenaeus' mind, the
picture of God's dealings with humanity that he sees focused in
Galatians 4:4–6, it immediately spills over into the third—the
theme of adoption and renovation—which, as we have seen, Irenaeus develops on the basis of a reading of 1 Corinthians 15, Romans 5, and a variety of other Pauline passages. And this, I would
argue, is the area in which one must look to discern what it is that
Irenaeus himself takes to be the burden of Paul's teaching in his
letters. In the first instance, what he sees there is an account of
human salvation that is centered in the work of God's "Son . . .
born of a woman," who through the pouring out of the Spirit
brings human persons to share in his divine sonship—which to
Irenaeus means a sharing in the incorruption promised in Christ's
resurrection. But he also finds in Paul intimations of a theology of
history that turns not only, or even primarily, on controversial
questions about the status of the law and the prophets in God's
purposes, but more particularly on the movement from Adam
to Christ, from the first to the ultimate humanity. And in the
same assemblage of Pauline passages Irenaeus finds the outline
of his anthropology, which appeals not only to Paul's language in
1 Corinthians 15 and 1 Thessalonians 5:23 but also to the thematic
idea of power made perfect in weakness. Irenaeus' Paul is less interested in justification than in the transfiguration of humanity after
the image of God's Son.

IRENAEUS' USE OF PAUL IN HIS
POLEMIC AGAINST THE GNOSTICS

1. Johannes Werner, *Der Paulinismus des Irenaeus*, Texte und Unter-
    suchungen 6.2 (Leipzig, 1889). See also, for example, J. Hoh, *Die Lehre
    des Hl. Irenäus über das Neue Testament* (Münster, 1919); John H.

Lawson, *The Biblical Theology of Saint Irenaeus* (London, 1948); J. Ben-
tivegna, "Pauline Elements in the Anthropology of St. Irenaeus," *Studia
Evangelica 5* [= Texte und Untersuchungen 103] (1968): 229–33; Elio
Peretto, *La lettera ai Romani cc. 1–8 nell' Adversus Haereses d'Ireneo*
(Bari, 1971), which I have not been able to consult; John S. Coolidge,
The Pauline Basis of the Concept of Scriptural Form in Irenaeus, Center
for Hermeneutical Studies in Hellenistic and Modern Culture, Berkeley,
Calif., Protocol of the Eighth Colloquy: 4 November 1973 (Berkeley,
Calif., 1975); François Altermath, *Du corps psychique au corps spirituel:
Interprétation de 1 Cor. 15,35–49 par les auteurs chrétiens des quatre
premiers siècles*, Beiträge zur Geschichte der biblischen Exegese 18 (Tübingen, 1977); and also the brief notes in André Benoit, *Saint Irénée:
Introduction à l'étude de sa théologie* (Paris, 1960); Hans von Campenhausen, *The Formation of the Christian Bible*, trans. J. A. Baker (Philadelphia, 1972); Ernst Dassmann, *Der Stachel im Fleisch: Paulus in der
frühchristlichen Literatur bis Irenaeus* (Münster, 1979); and Andreas Lindemann, *Paulus im ältesten Christentum: Das Bild des Apostels und die
Rezeption der paulinischen Theologie in der frühchristlichen Literatur bis
Marcion*, Beiträge zur historischen Theologie 58 (Tübingen, 1979).

2. On this point, see Werner, 47; Adolf Harnack, *History of Dogma*, trans.
    Neil Buchanan, 7 vols. (reprint: New York, 1961), 2:48 n. 2, 51. For a
    different view, see Lindemann, 390.

3. For example, see Lawson, 74: "S. Paul gave the great historic witness to the
    futility of religion based upon the hope of man earning forgiveness and
    righteousness in the sight of God by his own efforts. It is disappointing to
    find that S. Irenaeus made so little of this vital element in Romans"; also
    Werner, 49.

4. "No one understands, no one seeks for God."

5. *AH* 5.6.1–8.3. This section opens with a quotation of 1 Cor. 2:6, which
    raises the question of what Paul means by "the perfect"; it proceeds,
    alluding to 1 Cor. 2:15 and 1 Thes. 5:23, to consider the identity of the
    pneumatikos and closes off with an allusion to 1 Cor. 2:14.

6. See, in particular, *AH* 3.16.6. Here Irenaeus, like his opponents, develops
    the sense of Eph. 1:10 in conjunction with a reading of the christological
    hymn of Col. 1:15ff., and the recapitulation in Christ is envisaged pri-
    marily in cosmic terms.

7. It is worth noting that Irenaeus takes this interpretation quite seriously.
    AH 4.29.1 quotes the text again, in connection with a quite different issue,
    but in the course of an argument that makes it plain he is not taking "of
    this world" with "God."

8. Cf. Dt. 4:19 and 5:8. The difficulty with this argument, of course, is that
    Irenaeus' opponents may have thought exactly the same thing but referred
    the creation of the cosmos to these heavenly powers.

9. "But our *conversatio* is in the heavens, whence also we await a savior, the
    Lord Jesus, who will transfigure the body of our lowliness to be like
    the body of his glory. . . ."

10. See *AH* 5.10.1–11.2 and 5.9.2–4.

11. Thus at *AH* 3.20.3, Irenaeus cites Rom. 7:18 ("I know that no good dwells in my flesh") and 7:24 ("Who will free me from the body of this death?") and, without allusion to any Valentinian reading of the texts in question, simply asserts that Paul's point is that *non a nobis sed a Deo est bonum salutis nostrae.*

12. Even a cursory reading of Elaine H. Pagels, *The Gnostic Paul: Gnostic Exegesis of the Pauline Letters* (Philadelphia, 1975), seems to confirm this suggestion.

13. See *AH* 3.12.9. The references are to the Areopagus speech (Acts 17:22ff., especially vv. 24–28) and to Acts 14:6–13.

14. 1 Cor. 8:6, already referred to, and Rom. 5:17 (*tou henos Iesou Christou*), which Irenaeus cites at *AH* 3.16.9.

15. See *AH* 3.16.9, where Irenaeus cites Rom. 6:3–4, 5:6, 8–10, 8:34, and 8:11 to this effect.

16. Irenaeus clearly takes the christological hymn of Col. 1:15ff. itself to make the very point he is interested in. The description of Christ as the "first-born of all creation . . . in [whom] all things were created" is balanced by the description of him as "first-born from the dead." This can only mean that the Christ is the one Son of God become a human being. Thus in *AH* 4.2.4, the phrase "first-born from the dead" entails the belief that Moses, the prophets, and the Lord himself are *ex una substantia.*

17. Cf. *AH* 4.12.3, where Rom. 10:3–4 is quoted to the same point.

18. See *AH* 4.25.1, where Abraham is described as *princeps et praenuntiator . . . nostrae fidei.*

19. I am inclined to think that the exegesis of Irenaeus' presbyter, which Irenaeus makes his own, is in fact directed against Marcionites primarily if not exclusively.

20. I count thirteen occasions—all save one in Books 3 and 4 of *Adversus haereses*—on which Irenaeus cites one or another expression from Gal. 4:4–6.

21. It should be noted that this expression occurs also at Rom 8:23 and in association with ideas ("first fruits of the Spirit," "redemption of our bodies") that are basic to Irenaeus' theology.

22. To this point Irenaeus also cites Phil. 3:12, where Paul insists that he has not yet received "the prize."

23. See *AH* 3.22.3 and 4.38.2.

24. See, for example, *AH* 4.9.2.

25. On what follows, see also Coolidge's important essay, especially 4 and 12ff.

26. Eph. 4:6 ("One God and Father of us all, who is above all and through all and in all").

27. On this point, see Adelin Rousseau's note in *Irénée de Lyon: Contre les hérésies, Livre III*, ed. Rousseau and Louis Doutreleau, vol. 1: *Introduction, notes justificatives, tables*, Sources chrétiennes 210 (Paris, 1974), 332.

28. Needless to say, this is not the only way in which Irenaeus characterizes that history. He also appeals to the Pauline image of "psychic" first and

"spiritual" second (1 Cor. 15:45–46), which suggests to Irenaeus that the history of humanity with God can be conceived not only as Christ's reversal of Adam's disobedience, but also as a process of maturation or growth. Thus it is Paul who lies at the root of the apparent conflict in Irenaeus' thought between a picture of human history as an affair of fall and restoration and a picture of it as a movement from small beginnings to realized likeness to God.

29. ". . . not that we would be unclothed, but that we would be further clothed, so that what is mortal may be swallowed up by life."

30. See the Greek of the fragment preserved in Theodoret *Eranistes* 3: *en tō nikan kai hypomenein . . . kai anistasthai . . .* (*Irénée de Lyon: Contre les hérésies, Livre III*, ed. Rousseau and Doutreleau, vol. 2: *Texte et traduction*, Sources chrétiennes 211 [Paris, 1974], 378).

31. And cf. 5.3.1: *per suam infirmitatem cognoscit virtutem Dei*.

32. Again compare Rom. 8:23.

33. See, for example, the well-known passage at AH 3.18.7, where it is said of the Christ: *haerere . . . fecit et adunivit . . . hominem Deo*; the possibility of this work of mediation (cf. 1 Tm. 2:5) is seen to depend in part on his being what a human person is.

34. See AH 3.16.3 and 4.24.1.

The Use and Interpretation of Paul in Irenaeus's Five Books *Adversus Haereses*

DAVID L. BALÁS, O. Cist

As the title indicates, the present paper limits itself to the use and interpretation of Paul in Irenaeus's main work, *Adversus Haereses* (AH) or—according to the more complete title—"The Refutation and Overthrow of the Knowledge Falsely So Called." Even so, the topic would be too large even for a full dissertation (see, *e.g.*, Peretto's sizable book on just Romans 1–8 in AH).[1] All that a brief paper can hope to do is to make a modest contribution, and to elicit further discussion, reflection, and research.

Thanks to a team of scholars led by Adelin Rousseau, we have finally a complete critical edition of AH in the series *Sources Chrétiennes*.[2] This edition of the complete Latin text with facing French translation, giving not only all the extant Greek fragments but reconstructing for AH 3–5 the Greek text and providing also substantial introductions and copious notes, has truly renewed the state of Irenaean studies. It has, in turn, encouraged a whole series of monographic investigations, many of them relevant to our topic.[3]

The present paper grew out of a brief response to Professor Richard Norris's paper on the same topic at the recent international conference

DAVID L. BALÁS, O. Cist. is Profesor and Chairman, Department of Theology, University of Dallas, Irving, Texas 75062-4799.

[1]E. Peretto, *La Lettera ai Romani cc. 1–8 nell'Adversus Haereses d'Ireneo* (Bari: Istituto di Letteratura Cristiana Antica, 1971).

[2]Irénée de Lyon, *Contre les Hérésies*, édition critique par A. Rousseau, *et. al.* = *Sources Chrétiennes*, vols. 100, 152–153, 210–211, 263–264, 293–294 (Paris: Cerf, 1965–1982). For a brief account of the history of this edition see "Avant-Propos" of AH 2 = SC 293, pp. 7–14.

[3]See the valuable survey of M. A. Donovan, "Irenaeus in Recent Scholarship," *The Second Century* 4(1984):219–241.

on "Paul and the Legacies of Paul" held at Southern Methodist University.[4] After a brief report on his paper (1), its main section (2) investigates the place and role of Paul within the structure of AH. After a final section on the main characteristics of the interpretation of Irenaeus (3), some concluding remarks are made on the role of Paul in Irenaeus's theological synthesis.

I
A BRIEF REPORT ON PROFESSOR NORRIS'S PAPER

Whereas the fact that Irenaeus used Pauline texts (quoting them or alluding to them) extensively has been universally recognized, there has been, nonetheless, a widespread view that he did so reluctantly and that his interpretation of Paul is generally characterized by misunderstanding or even distortion.[5] As several other scholars in more recent times,[6] so also Professor Norris takes, in my judgment correctly, a much more positive view: "It seems apparent that Irenaeus, as he cites, alludes to, and muses over Paul's writings, is not merely engaged, as Werner thought, in an unwelcome apologetic task that circumstances have more or less forced upon him."[7] His paper, therefore, addresses the positive task of investigating "how Irenaeus himself reads the letters associated with the name of Paul—or, in other words, to ask whether, and how, they contribute positively to his own theological vision."[8]

Irenaeus's treatment of Pauline texts is then analyzed under three headings.

(1) Instances when Irenaeus directly controverts an—in his judgment—wrong interpretation of Pauline texts by the heretics.[9] Professor Norris concludes that this happens only occasionally,

---

[4]R. A. Norris, Jr., "Irenaeus' Use of Paul in His Polemic Against the Gnostics," in *Paul and the Legacies of Paul*, ed. by W. S. Babcock (Dallas: Southern Methodist University Press, 1990) 79–98, notes on pp. 337–340. The responses to the papers were, as a rule, not published in the volume.

[5]Good survey in E. Dassmann, *Der Stachel im Fleisch: Paulus in der frühchristlichen Literatur bis Irenäus* (Münster i. W.: Aschendorff, 1979) 305–307.

[6]See, *e.g.* B. Aland, "Fides und Subjectio: Zur Anthropologie des Irenaeus," in *Kerygma und Logos: Festschrift für Carl Andresen*, ed. by A. M. Ritter (Göttingen: Vandenhoeck & Ruprecht, 1979) 9–28; C. Andresen, ed. *Handbuch der Dogmen- und Theologiegeschichte I* (Göttingen: Vandenhoeck & Ruprecht, 1982) 79–98 (by Andresen); Dassmann, op. cit. (n. 5), pp. 292–315; A. Lindemann, *Paulus im ältesten Christentum* (Tübingen: J. C. Mohr, 1979); Peretto, op. cit. (n. 1. above).

[7]Norris, art. cit. (n. 4), p. 79.

[8]Ibid., p. 80.

[9]Ibid., pp. 80–84.

and when it happens it is in opposition to the distinction of the true God from the cosmic Demiurge (Gnostics, Marcion) or to the Valentinian understanding of human nature and its redemption.

(2) Appeals to Pauline texts in refuting heretical teachings. The first main doctrine, rejected by Irenaeus, is the Valentinian and Marcionite distinction between the cosmic Creator and the supreme Father. The second issue is the unity of Jesus Christ as the incarnate Son (Logos) of God, the third is the unity of salvation history (esp. Old Testament and New Testament).[10]

(3) How the Pauline texts contributed to Irenaeus's own theological vision. Professor Norris investigates in particular Irenaeus's use and interpretation of Galatians 4:4–6. He shows how Irenaeus interprets the Pauline texts with the help of others, taken practically from the whole Pauline corpus (esp. Romans and 1 Corinthians).[11] As a result, we can see how Irenaeus's vision of the unity of salvation history (One and the same God the Father, one eternal Logos incarnate in Christ, one Spirit, one progressive plan—involving both restoration and continuous growth) is based on Pauline texts and theology.

Professor Norris concludes that Irenaeus sees the essential message of Paul as centered on the unity of God, the unity of Jesus Christ, and the unity of the divine "economy," in which, through the one Spirit, human persons are brought to share in the divine sonship of Christ.[12]

Both the analyses and the conclusion of Professor Norris's paper command my substantial agreement. The points which follow are not brought forward as contradictions to, not even as criticism of, Professor Norris's paper, but rather as complements.

II
THE PLACE OF PAULINE TEXTS IN THE STRUCTURE OF AH

Whereas, as we have seen, there were many disagreements on the value of Irenaeus's theological contribution, there reigned—until quite recently—a virtual agreement on the low quality of the composition of AH. The words of Professor Johannes Quasten's *Patrology*, otherwise most sympathetic to Irenaeus, can be quoted as characteristic:

[10]Ibid., pp. 84–89.
[11]Ibid., pp. 89–97.
[12]Ibid., pp. 97–98.

The whole work suffers from a lack of clear arrangement and unity of thought. Prolixity and frequent repetition make its perusal wearisome. . . . Evidently he did not have the ability to shape his materials into a homogeneous whole. The defects of form which offend the reader are the result of his lack of synthesis.[13]

This consensus, however, has been now strongly challenged by the monumental new edition of the work. Adelin Rousseau has given us in the introductory volumes preceding each one of the volumes containing the text a series of increasingly detailed analyses of the content and plan of each book. In the chronologically first of these he gives only a brief "Analysis of Book IV,"[14] which serves also as a table of contents—otherwise absent—of the corresponding text volume. As Rousseau himself remarks, this analysis reproduces essentially that of A. Benoît in his *Saint Irénée: Introduction a l'étude de sa théologie*. It seems, however, that in the process of preparing the edition and translation of AH 5 Rousseau's views substantially developed. The introduction to AH 5 includes a long chapter on the "Plan of Book V,"[15] in which—in conscious opposition to A. Benoît and the tendency of prevalently German *Quellenforschung* as represented *e.g.* by Loofs—Rousseau insists on the "powerful unity which organizes, from within, the complex collection of the biblical texts and of the various arguments. . . ."[16] The introductions to the subsequently edited books further confirm this view.[17]

Even if Rousseau in his (understandable) enthusiasm for his author may have exaggerated the logic and artfulness of the plan of AH, his detailed analyses provide convincing evidence that the above described consensus on the shortcomings of Irenaeus's composition needs to be revised.

If this is so, then an investigation on the use and interpretation of Pauline texts in AH should, it seems to me, raise a fundamental and yet thus far generally neglected question: What are the place and role of Pauline texts in the very structure of AH?

In what follows I would like to give a brief and necessarily provisional answer to this question primarily on the basis of the SC edition and its introductions.

AH 1[18] contains primarily an exposition of the Gnostic doctrines (of Ptolemy, of Marcus the Magician and the Marcosians, of the Valentinians

---

[13]J. Quasten, *Patrology*, I (Utrecht: Spectrum, 1953) 289.

[14]Intr. to AH 4 = SC 100, T.1, pp. 341–343.

[15]Intr. to AH 5 = SC 152, pp. 166–191.

[16]Ibid., p. 167; see also ibid., pp. 189–90.

[17]See especially AH 1 = SC 263, p. 115, p. 132, n.1.

[18]See SC 263, pp. 113–164: "Contenu et plan du livre I" and SC 264, pp. 393–394: Table of Contents.

and their ancestors), and, in contrast, a brief presentation of the unity of the church's faith (10 and 22). The sacred scriptures enter into the constitution of the book isofar as Irenaeus, after exposing the Gnostic speculations, repeatedly consecrates a shorter or longer section to the Gnostic exegeses of biblical texts in which they pretend to find support for their teachings. In giving these examples, Irenaeus usually starts with the synoptic gospels, but exegeses of Pauline texts are adduced too (e.g., in 3; 8–9) as well as texts from the "The Law and Prophets." AH 1.8.5 quotes at length Ptolemy's exegesis of the Prologue of John. The Marcosian speculations seem to be based primarily on an esoteric exegesis of the Old Testament (1.18–19), and the Gospels (20), whereas their peculiar rite of "redemption" appeals also to some Pauline texts (21.1–2). In the section on the ancestors of the Valentinians, Irenaeus speaks also of Cerdon, who opposed the just God of the Old Testament to the good God of the New Testament, and of Marcion, who according to Irenaeus has developed these doctrines further and reduced the sacred scriptures to the Gospel of Luke and the letters of Paul—mutilating them, however, of all passages where the apostle affirms the identity of the Creator with the Father of Jesus Christ (27.2).

Summarizing our findings as to the use and interpretation of Paul in Book I we can say the following: Irenaeus does not perceive the teaching of the Gnostics as being based on Paul in any particular way. The examples of Gnostic exegesis given include Pauline texts but they do not seem to have had a more important role for the Gnostics than, e.g., the synoptic gospels, John, or the Old Testament. Marcion has been the only one, as Irenaeus emphatically affirms, to mutilate openly the sacred scriptures (27.4), and thus even though Irenaeus considers him as one of the Gnostics in the wider sense, he also observes that Marcion will have to be refuted "from those words of our Lord and of the Apostle which he himself uses." Irenaeus gives certainly no indication that he would see in Paul the source of Marcion's errors. Furthermore, the brief, but important, summaries of the faith of the universal Church (10.1 and 22.1) contain a fair proportion of Pauline teaching and language, as does also the interesting list of legitimate questions for theological reflection given by Irenaeus (10.3).

AH 2[19] contains the refutation of the principal theses of the Valentinians (1–30) and of some non-Valentinian Gnostics (31–35). Since Irenaeus argues here primarily from what he considers to be the intrinsic absurdities and contradictions of the Gnostic teachings, scriptural exegesis plays no major role in parts one and two of the Book (1–11; 12–19). Part three

[19]See SC 293, pp. 117–195 and SC 294, pp. 369–372.

(20–28), refuting the Valentinian speculations concerning numbers (20–24), confronts explicitly the scriptural exegeses on which such speculations claim to be based; none of these, however, involves Pauline texts, but rather those of the gospels. Paul is mentioned here once, interestingly, because Irenaeus adduces him, "Apostle" additionally to the twelve, as one of the refutations of the correspondence between twelve *Aeons* and the twelve apostles (21.2). Reflecting, then, on the wrong attitudes which led the Gnostics away from the rule of truth (25.1–2) Irenaeus finds their root in pride. In this context, he appeals especially to Paul:

> It is therefore better and more profitable to belong to the simple and unlettered class, and by means of love to attain to nearness to God, than, by imagining ourselves learned and skillful, to be found [among those who are] blasphemous against their own God, inasmuch as they conjure up another God as the Father. And for this reason Paul exclaimed, "Knowledge puffs up, but love edifies:" not that he meant to inveigh against a true knowledge of God, for in that case he would have accused himself; but, because he knew that some, puffed up by the pretence of knowledge, fall away from the love of God, and imagine that they themselves are perfect, for this reason that they set forth an imperfect Creator, with the view of putting an end to the pride which they feel on account of knowledge of this kind, he says, "Knowledge puffs up, but love edifies." Now there can be no greater conceit than this, that any one should imagine he is better and more perfect than He who made and fashioned him, and imparted to him the breath of life, and gave him this very existence. It is therefore, better, as I have said, that one should have no knowledge whatever of any one reason why a single thing in creation has been made, but should believe in God, and continue in His love, than that, puffed up through knowledge of this kind, he should fall away from that love which is the life of man; and that he should search after no other knowledge except [the knowledge of] Jesus Christ the Son of God, who was crucified for us, than that by subtle questions and hair-splitting expressions he should fall into impiety. (26.1)[20]

In the fourth part of the book (29–30) there is again an appeal to Paul (2 Cor. 12:2–4) against the Valentinians' identification of the third heaven with the psychic Demiurge (30.8–9).

The fifth part (31–35), important as it is not only for the refutation of certain Gnostic theses but also for Irenaeus's theology, contains no major references to Pauline texts.

AH 3[21] begins Irenaeus's "demonstration" of the teaching of the church from the sacred scriptures. After a brief preface, a substantial preliminary section on the one gospel, received and transmitted by the apostles in the form of preaching and then also in writing, describes the relationship between the one public tradition of the universal church, consonant with the apostolic scriptures, and the variety of the contradictory secret tra-

---

[20]ANF, vol. I, p. 397, modified according to the critical edition.
[21]See SC 210, pp. 171–205 and SC 211, pp. 493–495.

ditions claimed by the heretics (AH 3.1–5). Irenaeus then treats the witness of the scriptures (primarily of the New Testament on the one God, Creator of all (AH 3.6–15) and then on Christ, Son of God, who became man in order to recapitulate in himself the whole of humanity (16–23). The conclusion returns again to the unity of the truth preserved in the church by the Holy Spirit and the unity of God (24–25).

In this context the apostle Paul and Pauline texts are referred to repeatedly. In the preliminary section, speaking of the four written gospels, Irenaeus affirms that "Luke, the companion of Paul, wrote down in a book the gospel preached by this latter" (AH 3.1.1). Then, insisting that the one apostolic tradition can be found most certainly in the churches where it has been preserved by the successors of the apostles to the present, Irenaeus chooses to report the succession of bishops in the church of Rome, the pre-eminence of which he seems to attribute to its "most excellent origin," i.e. to the fact that it was "founded and established by those two most glorious apostles Peter and Paul."

In the first part (AH 3.6–15) Irenaeus presents first the global testimony of the scriptures on the one true God (6–8), and within this section, after the testimony of the Old Testament, Irenaeus quotes several Pauline texts where the one true God is opposed to the false gods (AH 3.6.5). He then devotes several pages to a text which causes him real embarrassment: 2 Corinthians 4:4 (*In quibus Deus saeculi huius excaecavit mentem infidelium*). Irenaeus, rather artificially sees here an inversion of words: It is the unbelievers who are of this world (AH 3.7.1). Paul "because of the velocity of his speech and the impetus of the Spirit present in him" often speaks this way, and Irenaeus illustrates this with examples from other letters of Paul (7.2).

After having surveyed the testimony of Christ himself (8.1) and then, at length, of the four evangelists (9–11), Irenaeus returns again to the testimony of the (other) apostles (12) following, essentially, the Acts of the Apostles. After Peter (12.1–7) and Philip (12.8), Irenaeus quotes from Paul's teaching as found in Acts, with occasional references to the Pauline epistles (12.9). This section concludes with the affirmation that Irenaeus "will show how all the letters of Paul concord with these sermons (from Acts) using these letters themselves when presenting the teaching of the apostle" (12.9). Irenaeus continues with the witness of Stephen (12.10–13) and then treats the Council of Jerusalem (12.14–15). At the end of this section there is a brief reference to Peter's behavior described in Galatians 2:12–13; Irenaeus emphasizes how all this manifests the apostles' convicton that the Father proclaimed by Jesus has been also the author of the Old Testament.

It is, I think, not by chance that Irenaeus includes here an excursus, of special interest for our topic, on the value of the witness of Paul (AH 3.13–15).

First, he argues againt "those who hold that Paul alone has known the truth" (13.1). These are refuted by Paul himself (Gal. 2:8; Rom. 10:15; 1 Cor. 15:11), and the gospels, where Christ is affirmed to have revealed to the apostles the Father who is truth (13.2). The correspondence between Acts 15 and Galatians 2 shows that Luke and Paul are in agreement (13.3).

Luke's close association with Paul is evident, according to Irenaeus, from his first-person accounts of events in Acts and Paul's testimony in 2 Timothy 4:10–11 (AH 3.14.1). Acts (*e.g.* 20:17–28) also show that Paul has taught the same message openly to all (14.2). If one rejects Luke, one has to reject a large part of the events and sayings of Christ which are found only in Luke and are retained also by the heretics (14.3). Therefore, they should accept the whole testimony of Luke or reject the whole: In the latter case the Marcionites will have no gospel at all, and the Valentinians will lose one of their principal sources (14.4).

To those who do not recognize Paul (one wonders which category of the Gnostics Irenaeus has in view),[22] Irenaeus repeats the same argumentation. Either they should also reject that part of the gospel which we know only through Luke, or accept also Luke's testimony (in Acts) on Paul's conversion and vocation as an apostle (15.1).

The second part of AH 3 (16–23) deals with the oneness of Christ and with his mission. That the Son of God did truly become man (16–18) is proven against the heretics by the testimony of the evangelists, and also that of Paul (16.3; 16.9; 18.1–3). The sections dealing with the descent of the Holy Spirit upon Jesus (17) and the soteriological significance of the incarnation (18.7) contain, too, numerous Pauline refernces.

The next section of the second part (19–21.9) affirms—against, it seems, Ebionite tendencies—that Jesus was not merely a man but truly the Son of God, incarnate and born of a virgin. Understandably, Irenaeus argues here prevalently from the messianic prophecies of the Old Testament though often presenting also the New Testament fulfillment, and here some Pauline texts, too, come into play (cf., *e.g.*, 20.2).

The last section deals with the purpose of the coming of Christ, the "recapitulation" of the first Adam (21.10–23.8). Of course, Romans 5:11–21 and Ephesians 1:10 are here key texts, but the section uses several other non-Pauline scriptural texts as well.

The conclusion (24–25) insists again on the preservation of the truth

---

[22]Probably the Ebionites.

preached in the church by the Spirit: both the creation and the economy of salvation come from the same God who (in opposition to the error of Marcion) is both good and just.

AH 4,[23] according to the preface, wants to confirm from the words of Christ himself what AH 3 has proved from the teaching of the apostles.

The first part (1–19) argues for the unity of the two Testaments (or, rather, the identity of the God of both economies) from the teachings of Christ found in the gospels—even though, of course, also some Old Testament and Pauline texts are embodied in the discourse. The second part (20–35) shows especially how the Old Testament is a prophecy of the New Testament and thus uses primarily Old Testament texts in combination with texts of the gospels. But here, too, Irenaeus refers repeatedly to Paul as well.

Within this second part Irenaeus has an opportunity to explain why Paul could rightly say that he labored more than all others (1 Cor. 15:1): the Gentiles, viz., had not been prepared by the Old Testament for the teaching of Christ (24.1–2).

In a later section (27.1–32.1) Irenaeus reports the teaching of a certain presbyter, disciple of the apostles, on the two Testaments. In this context several Pauline quotations are adduced to show that the Old Testament had been written for our instruction, and 1 Corinthians 10:1–12 is quoted at length (27.2–4).

Of special interest for our topic is the section commenting on 1 Corinthians 2:15 (33.1–8) and explaining how a truly "spiritual" disciple, i.e. one who receives the Spirit of God who was at work already from the beginning and thus also in the Old Testament, "judges all and is not judged by any." Irenaeus shows how such a one can judge, i.e. convict of error, the Jews (33.1), Marcion (33.2), the Valentinians (33.3), the Ebionites (33.4), the Docetists (33.5), the false prophets (33.6), the schismatics (33.7), i.e. "all those who are outside the truth, i.e. outside the church" (33.7).

The third and last part of AH 4 shows the unity of the two Testaments from the parables of the Lord (36–41). Included within this part is a sizable section treating of human freedom (37.1–7), proving its existence from the words of the Lord and also from the various moral imperatives of Paul's letters (see *e.g.* 1 Cor. 9:24–27 in 37.7). Irenaeus continues

---

[23]The analysis in SC 100, Tome 1 is insufficient, but see Ph. Bacq, *De l'ancienne à la nouvelle alliance selon S. Irénée: Unité du livre IV de l'Adversus Haereses* (Paris: Lethielleux, 1978).

with a section on progressive divine pedagogy, adapted to the changeable
and free nature of man (38–40.2).

The conclusion of AH 4 is at the same time an anticipation of book
five:

> But it is necessary to subjoin to this composition, in what follows, also the doctrine
> of Paul after the words of the Lord, to examine his teaching, to expound the Apos-
> tle, and to explain whatsoever [passages] have received other interpretations from
> the heretics, who have altogether not understood what Paul has spoken, . . . and
> to demonstrate from that same Paul, from whose [writings] they press questions
> upon us, that they are indeed utterers of falsehood, but that the apostle was a preacher
> of the truth, and that he taught all things in agreement with the message of the truth,
> [i.e. that there is] one God the Father who spoke with Abraham, who gave the law,
> who sent the prophets beforehand, who in the last times sent his Son, and conferred
> salvation upon his own handiwork—that is the substance of the flesh. Arranging,
> then, in another book the rest of the words of the Lord, which he taught concerning
> the Father not by parables but directly [*simpliciter ipsis dictionibus*], and the ex-
> position of the Epistles of the blessed apostle, I shall, with God's help, furnish you
> with the complete work of the exposure and refutation of knowledge falsely so
> called. (AH 4.41.4).[24]

AH 5,[25] part one, in accordance with the preceding quote, deals with
the resurrection of the body (flesh), proven primarily from the epistles of
Paul (1–14). It starts with a section showing how the resurrection of the
flesh is a necessary consequence of the incarnation (1–2). As Rousseau
has shown, even though Irenaeus does not quote here Paul explicitly,
certain Pauline texts are alluded to and are presupposed by his argumentation (Eph. 3:19—Pref., end; Col. 1:14 and 1 Tim. 2:6—1.1; 1 Cor.
10:16—2.2–3). Section two (3–5) shows the resurrection to be a work
of God's power. Irenaeus starts with an explicit quotation of 2 Corinthians
12:7–9; especially verse eight (*virtus in infirmitate perficitur*) dominates
the argumentation. The third section (6–8), consists of a series of Pauline
texts commented upon by Irenaeus: 1 Thessalonians 5:23, referring to
spirit, soul, and body as to be preserved without blemish for the day of
the Lord (6.1); 1 Corinthians 3:16 and 6:15: the body is a temple of God
and a member of Christ (6.2); 1 Corinthians 6:13–14 and Romans 8:11:
the resurrection of Christ assures our bodily resurrection (6.2–7.1); 1
Corinthians 15:42–44: the body will rise in incorruptibility, as "spiritual"
(7.1–2); 1 Corinthians 13:9–12 and Ephesians 1:13–14: the Holy Spirit
is an earnest of our resurrection (7.2–8.1). At the end of the section
Irenaeus explains in what sense Paul speaks of spiritual and carnal men
(1 Cor. 2:15; 3:1, 3) and shows the continuity of his teaching with the
Old Testament (8.2–3).

---

[24] ANF, vol. I, p. 525—modified according to the critical edition.
[25] See SC 152, pp. 166–191 and SC 153, pp. 469–472.

Section four (9–14) treats 1 Corinthians 15:50 ("flesh and blood cannot inherit the kingdom of God") often quoted by the Gnostics against the resurrection of the body. Quoting, and commenting upon, a series of Pauline texts (and a few others) Irenaeus explains his understanding of the true meaning of the passage: the one who does not partake of the Spirit but lives according to the flesh cannot share in eternal life.

The second part of book five (15–24) returns to the affirmation of the unity of God the Creator and the Father, arguing from three events of Christ's life: the healing of the man born blind (John 9:1–7—15.2–16.2); the crucifixion (where, besides the gospels, also Phil. 2:8 is used—16.3–20); and the temptation of Christ (21–24).

The third part of book five (25–36) continues to prove the identity of God the Creator and God the Father using the teaching of the scriptures on the end of times. Irenaeus's method here is to show the agreement of the teaching of the apostles (Paul, John), of Christ, and of the prophets (i.e, of scriptures as a whole)[26] on two issues: the Antichrist (25–30) and the resurrection of the just (31–36). The use of Pauline texts is less prominent here. In the first section (25–30) Irenaeus refers repeatedly to 2 Thessalonians 2. As to the millennial kingdom of the just on earth, Irenaeus appeals primarily to Old Testament prophecies, the teaching of Jesus in the (synoptic) gospels and, naturally, to the book of Revelation (31–35). The earthly Jerusalem, however, will be followed, after the general resurrection and judgment, by the descent of the heavenly Jerusalem. In this section (35.2–36.2), besides the Old Testament, synoptic gospels, and Revelation, Irenaeus uses also Pauline texts (e.g. Gal. 4:26; 1 Cor. 7:31). He quotes in particular 1 Cor. 15:25–28 to show how the just are progressively led by the Spirit to the Son who, in turn, submits his kingdom to the Father (36.2).

Book five, and the whole work, concludes with a reaffirmation of the harmony between the prophets, Christ, and the apostles (Irenaeus mentions explicitly John and "the apostle" = Paul), and of the unity of God and of the divine economy (36.3).

The preceding survey of the place and role of Pauline texts book by book is not a sufficient basis for definitive conclusions. One can say, however, at a minimum the following: Irenaeus did not write in a haphazard way but followed a careful and complex plan. Within this the place and role of Paul is both quantitatively[27] and qualitatively impres-

---

[26]See D. Farkasfalvy, "Theology of Scripture in St. Irenaeus," *Revue Bénédictine* 78 (1968): 319–333.

[27]For comparative statistics see Paretto, op. cit. (n. 1.), pp. 51 ff. and Dassmann, op. cit. (n. 5), pp. 295–297.

sive. This is due primarily, it seems to me, to Irenaeus's own conviction (received from an already existing tradition but clarified and strengthened further by him) that the witness of Paul is an integral and substantial part of the apostolic witness to Christ (see especially AH 3.13–15). Irenaeus is conscious also of the importance of the Pauline writings for the heretics (see, *e.g.*, AH 1.27.2 and AH 3.13–15 for Marcion; AH 4.41.4 and AH 5.9–14 for the Gnostics in general). The source of their errors, however, is—according to Irenaeus—not Paul; they misinterpret the apostle because of preconceived doctrines rooted, ultimately, in their pride (see, *e.g.* AH 2.26.1 quoted above).

III
CHARACTERISTICS OF IRENAEUS'S INTERPRETATION

What characterizes Irenaeus's use and interpretation of Paul? Two major traits are, I think, most prominent:

(1) His conviction—in theory and in praxis—of the unity of the scriptures. The prophets (Old Testament) are fulfilled in Christ (see, *e.g.*, AH 4.33.10–15). The apostles (and that comprehends directly or indirectly the whole New Testament, since also Mark and Luke depend on apostolic preaching: see, *e.g.*, AH 3.1.1), in turn, preach the same Christ (the same God the Father, Son, and Spirit and the same economy of salvation). The heretics, on the contrary, pick and choose—according to Irenaeus—from the whole of scripture what seems to them to support their particular doctrines, *e.g.*, one gospel from among the four (see AH 3.11.7—Ebionites: Matthew; Marcion: amputated Luke; Docetists: Mark; Valentinians: John), or Paul against all other apostles (see AH 3.13—Marcion) or the other apostles against Paul (see AH 3.15—probably the Ebionites). But, as Irenaeus shows again and again, because of the unity of the underlying message, their errors can be refuted even from their own restricted scriptures themselves.

(2) The normative role of the apostolic tradition preserved in the church. In this connection we can understand better the meaning and function of Irenaeus's famous "rule of truth." In various wordings, but essentially with the same content, this rule occurs again and again in AH and has an important place within its argumentative structure (see, *e.g.*, AH 1.10 and 22; AH 2.25; AH 3.4.2). It contains, in summary form, the fundamentals of the apostolic preaching which is preserved, one and the same, by the succession of bishops in the whole church. It does not add to the content of scriptures, since the same teaching is found in both; actually it is from the scriptures that it can be unfolded in detail (see AH 3–5). It can and does function, however, as a criterion against the misinterpretations of the scriptures by the heretics. This function could be further

illustrated by a comparison of Irenaeus: the heretics are like the one who takes apart an artful mosaic of precious stones representing the image of a king (= scriptures) and composes, with the same pieces, an inferior picture of a fox (AH 1.8.1—cf. also AH 1.9.4). Extending this comparison beyond its explicit use by Irenaeus one can say: the "rule of truth" gives us with a few lines the original image or outline (i.e. the essential content of the Christian message transmitted by the apostolic preaching and writings) and thus enables us to recognize any heretical distortion, in spite of its use of the same stones (i.e. bits and pieces of scriptures) for what it is: a distortion.

* * *

The preceding considerations have established, I hope, some of the essential presuppositions for assessing correctly the place and role of "Paul" in the *theology* of Irenaeus. First of all, one has to recognize, I think—in agreement with a growing number of recent scholarly investigations of Irenaeus's thought—that he is not a servile compiler of borrowed materials, but a genuine theologian. He is not interested, however, in reconstructing Paul's theology, and even less that of a particular epistle (legitimate as such an interest may be). He not only interprets any Pauline text in the light of other texts taken from the whole Pauline (and deutero-Pauline) corpus—as Prof. Norris has rightly observed—but also with the use of texts taken from the whole New Testament (and the Old Testament as well).[28] Nor is his theology simply a presentation of biblical faith, for he does elaborate a deeper understanding of this faith to a remarkable extent.[29] But the place and role of "Paul" (i.e. of Pauline texts, terms, images, ideas, and teachings) in Irenaeus's theological synthesis is—regrettably—beyond the limits of this paper.

---

[28]On the influence of Johannine terminology and theology on Irenaeus's interpretation of Paul see, *e.g.*, Dassmann, op. cit., pp. 310–314.

[29]See, *e.g.*, R. Tremblay, *La manifestation et la vision de Dieu selon saint Irénée de Lyon* (Münster i. W.: Aschendorff, 1978) and R. Berthouzoz, *Liberté et Grâce suivant la théologie d'Irénée de Lyon* (Fribourg, Suisse: Editions Universitaires, 1980).

In novissimis diebus: *Biblical Promises, Jewish Hopes and Early Christian Exegesis*

ROBERT L. WILKEN

The phrase "in these last days" (*novissimis diebus*) occurs in Isaiah 2 and Micah 4. This article discusses how this expression was interpreted in early Christian commentaries on Isaiah and Micah. It shows that the Christian interpretation of Isaiah 2 and Micah 4 is best seen in the context of a rival Jewish understanding of the text. Jews interpreted the passage not to refer to the exile in Babylonia but to the future coming of "their" Messiah. The question, then, for early Christian exegetes was not whether the text was to be taken "historically," but to which later events was it to be applied, those that defined the Jewish people or those that gave rise to the Church.

Michael Wyschogrod, the Jewish philosopher, has observed that the State of Israel is a theological as well as a political problem for Christians. Some Christians, he wrote, find little difficulty in "validating the Jewish right to the land of Israel on the basis of biblical promises," but others (Wyschogrod has in mind the Vatican), by ignoring the Biblical roots of the ancient promises of return to the land, "err in the other direction". Unless Christianity is to repudiate the ancient decision to "make the Hebrew Bible its own," it must realize that these promises are part of the Scriptural tradition, and hence of concern not only to Jews, but "something the Church must struggle with." Nevertheless, many Christians, he writes, "persist in spiritualizing the promises of the land, an ancient strategy not easy to defend in the new theological climate of Jewish-Christian dialogue."[1]

The "ancient strategy" of which Wyschogrod speaks is already evident in the New Testament but it received its classical expression in the commen-

1. Michael Wyschogrod, "The Bishops and the Middle East," *First Things* (April, 1990), 16.

Journal of Early Christian Studies 1:1, 1–19 © 1993 The Johns Hopkins University Press

taries on the Septuagint as well as in exegetical and theological treatises written during the patristic period. From the *Epistle of Barnabas* and Justin's *Dialogue with Trypho* to the commentaries of Jerome and Cyril of Alexandria and Theodoret of Cyrus on Isaiah or the Minor Prophets one can discern, in the midst of different social settings and among a variety of exegetical techniques, wide agreement that the promises of the Jewish Scriptures are to be understood "spiritually." Even Theodore of Mopsuestia, who was critical of the indiscriminate application of prophetic texts to the life of Christ, recognized that several psalms (2, 8 and 45) and some passages from the prophets, e.g. Joel 2.28, Zech 9.9, Mal 4.5–6, et al. and the book of Jonah referred to Christ.

Early Christian "spiritual" interpretation of the prophets has of course been challenged by historical criticism. As A. Merx observed over a hundred years ago in a study of the interpretation of the prophet Joel in the early church: "Where allegory and its deviations, anagogy and moral interpretration make their appearance, understanding of the text is destroyed."[2] As historical criticism has extended its hegemony over every aspect of scholarly exegesis, similar views have achieved the status of an *opinio communis*. What is, however, noteworthy about Wyschogrod's objection to patristic exegesis is that it springs not so much from historical-critical exegesis as it does from Jewish interpretation of the prophets. Wyschogrod suggests, perhaps inadvertently, that the exegesis of biblical promises about the Land of Irael turns not so much on a "historical" versus a "spiritual" interpretation of the prophets but on how "later" events bear on the understanding of the text. By posing the question in this way he helps us to appreciate features of early Christian exegesis that have been ignored or forgotten.

Without appealing to the Hebrew prophets it would have been impossible for early Christian thinkers to formulate, much less defend, the claim that Jesus of Nazareth was the Messiah of the Jews. That is apparent in the early decades when most Christians were Jews and supported their conviction that Jesus of Nazareth was the promised Messiah by reference to the Septuagint. "All this took place to fulfil what the Lord had spoken by the prophet: 'Behold, a virgin shall conceive and bear a son, and his name shall be called Emmanuel'" (Matt 1.22–23). But even when Christians moved into the larger society and addressed their message to Greeks and Romans they appealed to the testimony of the prophets. In I Apology Justin wrote: "There were among the Jews certain men who were prophets of God,

2. A. Merx, *Die Prophetie Joel und ihre Ausleger* (1879), 112.

through whom the prophetic Spirit announced in advance events that were to occur. . . . We find predicted in the books of the prophets that Jesus our Christ would come, born of a virgin . . . crucified, dying and rising again and ascending into heaven. . . ." (*1 apol.* 31).

From the beginning Jews challenged Christian interpretation of the prophets. The locus classicus is book 4 of Origen's *Peri Archōn* where he discusses (according to Photius), "how the divine scriptures are to be read and interpreted" (*princ.* 4.1.1). The first topic Origen addresses is Jewish objections to Christian interpretation of the prophets. The Jews do not believe in "our savior," writes Origen, because "they think that one must follow the 'letter' when the prophets speak about him and because they are not able to see with their eyes (*aisthētos*) that the things proclaimed about him have happened." As illustration of the Jewish argument Origen cites a number of passages from the prophets: Isaiah 61.1 "liberty to captives"; Ezekiel 48.15 and Psalm 46.4 the "building of a genuine city of God;" Zachariah 9.10, "cutting off the chariot from Ephraim and the war horse from Jersualem," i.e. the shattering of Israel's enemies; and Isaiah 11.6–7, "the wolf shall dwell with the lamb, and the leopard shall lie down with the kid. . . ."

In this debate the matter at issue is the character of the Messianic age, and hence of the community that will come into being at that time; for the prophets proclaim a future marked by untroubled joy and gladness, the end of war and strife, an age of peace and harmony among the nations of the world, of wealth and prosperity, a time when the people of God will serve God with their whole hearts and the Law will be observed perfectly.[3] Origen's Jewish critics make the reasonable argument that these things have not happened, hence the Messianic age has not yet arrived. Therefore Jesus cannot be the Messiah.

The Christian claim that Jesus is the Messiah was based on the correspondence between the historical events of Jesus' life and Resurrection and a series of oracles from the Hebrew prophets.[4] Among the many texts that made up this building, the famous passage in Isaiah 2 was one of the cornerstones: "It shall come to pass in the latter days (*in novissimis diebus*)

3. For a useful survey of Jewish Messianic expectations, see Emil Schuerer, *The History of the Jewish People in the Age of Jesus Christ*, ed. G. Vermes, F. Millar, M. Black (Edinburgh, 1979), 2:524–554.

4. There were other arguments: the events announced by the prophets had not happened in Jewish history (Origen and Theodoret of Cyrus); the prophets would not have continued to repeat their oracles of restoration if the events they prophesied had come to pass. "If these things had happened to someone who lived long ago (*in veteribus*), those prophets who came later would not have prophesied that these things were going to happen in the latter days (*in novissimis temporibus*)" (Irenaeus, *haer.* 4.34.3).

that the mountain of the house of the Lord shall be established as the highest of the mountains, and shall be raised above the hills; and all the nations shall flow to it, and many peoples shall come and say: 'Come, let us go up to the mountain of the Lord, to the house of the God of Jacob; that he may teach us his ways and that we may walk in his paths.' For out of Zion shall go forth the law and the word of the Lord from Jerusalem" (Isaiah 2.2–4; par. Micah 4.1–3)[5].

This passage is not cited in the New Testament, but it is alluded to on several occasions, most notably in the opening words of the book of Hebrews: "In many and various ways God spoke of old to our fathers by the prophets; but in these last days he has spoken to us by a Son. . . ." (Heb 1.1)[6] The phrase "in these last days," is also cited in Acts 2 at the beginning of Peter's sermon on Pentecost. In this case it is the prophet Joel who is cited but the text is conflated with the words of Isaiah 2. "In the last days it will be, God declares, that I will pour out my Spirit upon all flesh."

Just how important the phrase "in these last days" was to become can be illustrated by two well known passages. It is quoted at the very beginning of Origen's *Peri Archōn*. The God of Adam, Abel, Noah, Abraham, Isaac, Jacob, Moses and the prophets "in these last days, according to the previous announcements made through his prophets, sent the Lord Jesus Christ. . . ." (*princ.* 1.pref.4) And it occurs, significantly, in the decree of the Council of Chalcedon: "We confess one and the same our Lord Jesus Christ . . . begotten before ages of the Father in Godhead, the same *in the last days* for us. . . ." It is also cited early in Christian literature by Justin Martyr and Irenaeus and is used by Tertullian at key places in his *Adversus Iudaeos* and *Adversus Marcionem*.[7] So I need not belabor the point that "in these last days" played a key hermeneutical role in early Christian thinking.

In this article I am less interested in tracing the phrase in early Christian

---

5. For modern discussion of Isaiah 2 and Micah 4 and a survey of proposals concerning the literary relation between the two passages, see J. Vermeylen, *Du Prophète Isaïe à l'Apocalyptique. Isaïe I–XXXV* (Paris, 1977), 1:113–133.

6. See also Heb 9.26, 1 Cor 10.11.

7. Justin, *dial.* 109; Tertullian, *Iud.* 3. Note that Tertullian says the prophecy refers to "us" who have been taught by the new law. Also in *Marc.* 3.21 where Tertullian discusses biblical promises concerning the Land of Israel. Irenaeus says that if the things announced by the prophets had happened to those who lived in former times the prophets who lived later would not have said that these things "were going to happen in the last days (*in novissimis temporibus*)" (*haer.* 4.34.3–4). For Origen, the phrase "*in novissimis diebus*," cited in the first line of his *Homilies on Leviticus*, provided the hermeneutical key to his interpretation of the book (*Hom. in Lev.* 1.1). Jerome, in his letter to Dardanus (*Ep.* 129.8) on the meaning of the phrase "land of promise," alludes to 1 Cor 10.11, "*in quos fines saeculi decurrerunt*."

literature than in examining it within the context of commentaries on the book of Isaiah. For it is one thing to extract the phrase from the Scriptures and use it in a theological argument, something else to expound the text in a line by line biblical commentary. For in that genre historical and hermeneutical issues put a different kind of pressure on the interpreter. In a commentary, as Origen observed, it was not possible "to leave anything unexplained."[8] The length of his commentaries—thirty on Isaiah, twenty-five on Ezekiel, thirty-two on the Gospel of John—gives a clue as to what he meant.

The first Christian commentary on the book of the prophet Isaiah was a massive work of Origen in thirty books. Unfortunately it is no longer extant.[9] Dionysius of Alexandria is reported to have written a commentary on Isaiah but that too is lost.[10] The earliest extant commentary on Isaiah was written by Eusebius of Caesarea who was a disciple of Origen and drew extensively on his commentary.[11] When Eusebius reaches chapter 2 in his commentary he observes that this passage, which follows oracles critical of the "people of the circumcision,"[12] inaugurates a section on the calling of the gentiles. The prophet "gives a perspicacious sign of the time in which these things will take place."[13] It will be an age of peace when there will no longer be "toparchy and polyarchy, nations will not rise up against each other nor cities make war on each other. . . ." In Eusebius' view this can only mean the time of the Roman empire after the coming of Christ. In this period the word of the Lord has gone forth from the "land of the Jews and from Zion itself" into all the world.[14]

Jews, however, apply the prophecy to the "people of the Jews" as though it referred to "their land."[15] They take the passage "in a bodily sense"

8. Origen, *Hom. 14.1 in Numeros.* For the difference between the scholia, homilies and commentaries among Origen's exegetical works see E. Klostermann, "Formen des exegetischen Arbeiten des Origenes," *Theologische Literaturzeitung* 72 (1947):203–208.

9. For discussion see Pierre Nautin, *Origène. Sa vie et son oeuvre* (Paris, 1977), 247–248; also Ziegler's remarks in the introduction to Eusebius' *Commentary on Isaiah* (see note 11), xxxi–xxxiv. However, nine homilies on Isaiah by Origen exist in a Latin translation prepared by Jerome (PG 13.219–254; critical ed. by W. A. Baehrens in GCS 33 [1925]).

10. This information comes from the twelfth century collection of commentaries on the prophet Isaiah by Nicolas Mouzan. See Jean Dumortier and A. Liefooghe, ed. *Jean Chrysostome. Commentaire sur Isaie,* SC 304 (Paris, 1983), 9–10.

11. Text ed. Joseph Ziegler, *Der Jesajakommentar,* in *Eusebius Werke 9,* GCS (Berlin, 1975).

12. Eusebius, *Comm. in Isaiam* (GCS, *Eusebius Werke* 9:14, 16).

13. Ibid. (GCS, *Eusebius Werke* 9:14, 32–15, 2).

14. Ibid. (GCS, *Eusebius Werke* 9:15, 13).

15. Ibid. (GCS, *Eusebuis Werke* 9:15, 31–32).

(sōmatikoteron) to signify the "land of Palestine".[16] What Eusebius means by this term is that the Jews take the prophecy as a promise that will be fulfilled politically among the Jewish people, namely that the Jews would once again possess Jerusalem and Judea, the exiles will return, and a Jewish kingdom will be established in the land of Israel.[17] In Eusebius' day, Jews continued to anticipate the time when Jerusalem would again be the capital of a Jewish kingdom. In his discussion of Isaiah 5.1, "Let me sing for my beloved a love song concerning his vineyard . . . ," Eusebius remarks: "Some say that this passage refers to the land of Judea." They offer this interpretation because Judea is "fertile and fruitful," and they take the reference to a hill in the text to signify "the royal metropolis that will be established in this same Jerusalem."[18]

For Eusebius the key to understanding Isaiah 2.1–4 is the phrase "in the last days" which is to be interpreted in light of passages from the New Testament that speak of the "the end of the age," as for example Hebrews 9:26: Christ "appeared once for all at the *end of the age* to put away sin by the sacrifice of himself." The "last days" refers to the calling into being of a new community which is the offspring of the "Jerusalem above the mother of us all" (16.15–16).[19]

Two other commentaries from the fourth century, John Chrysostom's *Homilies on Isaiah* and the *Commentary on Isaiah* 1–16 attributed to Basil of Caesarea, interpret Isaiah 2 along the lines set down by Eusebius. Each takes the phrase "last days" to be a key to understand the passage and relate it to texts in the New Testament that speak of the "time" of Christ's coming. Pseudo-Basil alludes to Hebrew 9.26 which had been cited by Eusebius [20] and John cites the phrase "fullness of time" in Galatians 4:4 and Ephesians 1.10.[21]

16. Ibid. (GCS, *Eusebius Werke* 9:16, 12–13).

17. See also his commentary on Isaiah 4.2, "The fruit of the land shall be the pride and glory of the survivors of Israel." (Eusebius, *Comm. in Isaiam* [GCS, *Eusebius Werke* 9:26, 36–27, 5]).

18. Eusebius, *Comm. in Isaiam* (GSC, *Eusebius Werke* 9:9, 14–17). The Jews, says Eusebius, understand the term "Judea" to mean "nothing more than the land of Palestine," and consider "earthly Jerusalem God's dwelling place": *Comm. in Psalmos* (PG 23.876d).

19. A similar argument appears at Isaiah 4.2, "the fruit of the land shall be the pride and glory of the survivors of Israel." This text, says Eusebius, speaks of the "entire earth and the whole world." The "survivors" who will be called "holy" (4.3) are those who are worthy to "be recorded for life eternal in the 'heavenly Jerusalem' (Heb 12.22)": *Comm. in Isaiam* (GCS, *Eusebius Werke* 9:26, 36–27, 5)

20. Ps.-Basil, *Comm. in Isaiam*, ed. Sac. Pietro Trevisan, *San Basilio. Commento al Profeta Isaia* (Torino, 1939), 1:195–8.

21. John Chrysostom, *Hom. in Isaiam* (PG 56, 29a).

John is particularly conscious of the hermeneutical significance of the references to time in the book of Isaiah. He observed that chapter two begins with a superscript that suggests a kind of second beginning or at least a shift of subject matter from chapter one. Chapter one begins: "The vision of Isaiah son of Amoz which he saw against Judah and against Jerusalem in the days of Uzziah, Jothan, Ahaz, and Hezekiah, kings of Judah" (LXX). Chapter two begins: "The word that came to Isaiah son of Amoz concerning Judah and concerning Jerusalem" (LXX). Why, asks John, does the text repeat that Isaiah had a vision concerning Judah and Jerusalem? He replies that the book of Isaiah is composed of oracles that were pronounced "at different times," and that they were only later collected together in a book. In this respect the book of Isaiah differs from the letters of Paul or the gospels which were composed at one time. This means that different sections composed at different times often refer to different topics, and because these texts include prophetic oracles, to different times in the future. Chapter two then has a different "hypothesis," another central theme than chapter one, indeed it deals with "more sublime matters." Its subject is "the calling of the gentiles, the showing forth of the gospel, the knowledge of God extending throughout the whole world. . . ." [22]

With the meaning of "in these last days" clarified by reference to the New Testament, fourth century Christian exegetes were able to give the details in the text a specifically Christian interpretation. Thus the phrase "all the nations" is taken to refer to the preaching of the gospel in all the world.[23] Similarily the phrase "on the highest mountain" was applied to the church which is "visible to all human beings" not to the "temple of the Jews" which did not rest on the highest mountain. Mt. Zion was overshadowed by Mt. Olive from which one looked down on the temple mount.[24] Further the clause "out of Zion shall go forth instruction" cannot apply to Moses for he received the Law not on Mt. Zion but on Sinai and he did not himself enter into the land of promise. Hence Zion, which means Jerusalem, refers to the gospel which began at Jerusalem and from there went into all the world.[25]

Now all this is familiar terrain and needs little elaboration. What I wish to note is that Eusebius, as well as other commentators on Isaiah, give their intepretation of this text a polemical cast and direct their observations against Jewish views of the text. Which is to say that the exegesis of the

22. Ibid. (PG 56, 27b).
23. Ps.-Basil, *Comm. in Isaiam* (Trevisan, 1:202–206).
24. John Chrysostom, *Hom. in Isaiam* (PG 56, 29b).
25. Ps.-Basil, *Comm. in Isaiam* (Trevisan, 1:212); John Chrysostom, *Hom. in Isaiam* (PG 56, 32a).

prophets did not take place in a vacuum; Christian interpreters had to defend their views in the face of rival claimants to the meaning of the text.[26] Hence the importance of the phrase "in these last days"; it gave a foothold for a Christian interpretation. In the words of the commentary Pseudo-Basil the passage is to be interpreted in light of the "great and exalted economy for the salvation of all human beings."[27]

Of course there are nuances of interpretation and different ways of rendering the specifics of the text, but Eusebius and John Chrysostom and Pseudo-Basil can be taken to reflect the central exegetical tradition up to the middle of the fourth century, which is to say before Theodore of Mopsuestia. For, as is well known, Theodore refused to give the text a Messianic interpretation.[28]

Theodore was of course aware that this text had been interpreted christologically. He writes (in his commentary on Micah, the commentary on Isaiah is not extant): "I am amazed at those who say that these things spoken by the prophets about the Israelites when they were about to return from Babylon, are a kind of type that refers to what will happen at the time of the Lord Christ. Those who say that the return of the people from Babylon is signified by these things, I praise as speaking beautifully; but I do not know how one could be brought to say that this is a type of the events that took place at the time of the Lord Christ. For it is clear that every type has a correspondence (*mimēsis*) to the thing of which it is a type." [29]

Theodore's principle is that the words of the prophets must be interpreted within the context of the time the prophet wrote unless there is "correspondence" between the text and the later events or the New Testament applies the text to later events.[30] In his view Micah 4 (and presumbly Isaiah 2) fall in that category even though certain passages in the New Testament use its language of "last days" to refer to the coming of Christ. Accordingly Micah is to be understood in the context of the events surrounding the captivity of the Israelites, first at the hands of the Assyrians, later by the Babylonians and their hope of return and restoration. The text

26. On Eusebius's commentary and the Jews see Michael Hollerich, "The Godly Polity in the Light of Prohecy. A Study of Eusebius of Caesarea's Commentary on Isaiah," unpublished Ph.D. dissertation, University of Chicago, 1986.

27. Ps.-Basil, *Comm. in Isaiam* (Trevisan, 1:199).

28. Theodore's observations occur in his commentary on Micah 4, the parallel to Isaiah 2. See *Theodori Mopsuesteni Commentarius in XII Prophetas,* ed. Norbert Sprenger (Wiesbaden, 1977), 206–213. From Theodore we have no commentary on Isaiah.

29. Theodore of Mopsuestia, *Comm. in Michaeam* (Sprenger, 206ff.)

30. Joel 2.28, Amos 9.11–12, Micah 5.1, Zach 9.9, Mal 3.1 (to John the Baptist), and the book of Jonah.

announces that there will be a "transformation of this place [Jerusalem] and the mount in which God commanded them to dwell will be stand out above all mountains. . . ." On that day the exiles will be gathered from many places as well as foreigners, God will be glorified in Jerusalem, and the Law will be observed. Theodore reasons as follows: "The phrase 'the law will go forth from Zion and the word of the Law from Jerusalem, stands far from the dispensation at the time when Christ the Lord spoke clearly to the Samaritan woman. 'Believe me woman, the time is coming, and now is, when the true worshipers will worship the Father in spirit and truth. . . .'" The words of Jesus show that when Christ comes God will be not be worshipped in a particular place. In that day "preoccupation with places" will be eliminated and no preference will be shown to Jersualem over other places. Micah, on the other hand, said that the Law will go forth "from Zion," and the word of the Lord "from Jerusalem." Hence the prophecy cannot be a type of Christ.

Theodore ignores the phrase "in these last days," the one feature of the text that other exegetes took to be the key to its interpretation. The only temporal reference that he discusses is the term "forever." Micah wrote: "And the Lord will reign over them in Mount Zion from this time forth and for evermore." Theodore realized that this phrase posed a problem for his reading of the passage, because no matter how one interpreted the prophecy, the deliverance of which it spoke had not lasted forever. After the return from exile Judea was a province of the Persian Empire, and later the city came under Ptolemaic and Seleucid rule. And of course Jerusalem was destroyed by the Romans in the first century of the common era, and in Theodore's day the Jews were still in exile. Furthermore Jerusalem was becoming a Christian city. Accordingly he interprets the phrase "forever" to mean "for a very long time."[31]

Why Theodore would depart from traditional exegesis of the prophets, even in cases where the New Testament guided that interpretation, has been a matter of continuing discussion among scholars. With the publication of Christoph Schaeublin's book *Untersuchungen zu Methode und Herkunft der antiochenischen Exegese*[32] almost two decades ago, it is

31. Theodore of Mopsuestia, *Comm. in Michaeam* (Sprenger, 209, 27).
32. Christoph Schaeublin, *Untersuchungen zu Methode und Herkunft der antiochenischen Exegese* (Koeln-Bonn, 1974). Many reasons have been proffered to explain Theodore's exegesis: a reaction against the arbitrariness of the Alexandrian exegetes, notably that of Origen; the result of Jewish influences; the application of "rational" principles learned from Aristotle to literary texts. Schaeublin's work builds on the latter position. The traditional view is that Theodore practiced a kind of Jewish interpretation. This opinion is stated already in the 11th century by Nicetas of Heracleon who says he does not include Theodore and Apollinaris in his catena because "they interpret in a

evident that the grammatical and literary techniques used to interpret classical authors influenced Theodore's exegesis of the Bible.[33] In this tradition the first question to be asked of any literary work concerned the "hypothesis" or *skopos* of the text as this was shaped by the historical setting, the author's intention, and literary character of the work.[34] But consideration of grammatical and literary questions was not unique to Theodore. Similar techniques were used by other writers, Diodore of Tarsus, John Chrysostom, Jerome, Cyril of Alexandria, and Theodoret of Cyrus, to mention the more obvious exegetes from the fourth and fifth centuries.[35]

Theodore has been singled out, however, because he applied the principles of grammatical and literary analysis more rigorously and seems to

---

Jewish fashion." See G. Karo and I. Lietzmann, "Catenarum graecarum catalogus" in *Nachrichten von der koeniglichen Gesellschaft der Wissenschaften zu Goettingen*, Phil.-hist. Kl. (1902), 34. It is also possible that Theodore was responding to Jewish criticism of Christian exegesis of the psalms and the prophets. It was reported about Theodore (at the Council of Constantinople in 553) that he said Christians "make themselves a laughing stock to Jews" when they apply passages from the prophets to Christ (*Acta Conciliorum Oecumenicorum*, ed. E. Schwartz and J. Straub [Berlin, 1971], 4, 1:53). For survey of the different ways of explaining Antiochene exegesis see Schaeublin, *Untersuchungen*, 24–33.

33. Besides Schaeublin see the discussion of Theodore's exegesis in Sprenger's edition, 84–110 and Robert Devreesse, *Essai sur Théodore de Mopsueste* (Vatican City, 1948).

34. Besides general consideration about the *skopos* of a book and its literary form, the grammarians, e.g. Dionysios Thrax, according to Schaeublin also provided a set of critical questions that could be addressed to each text: how to read it correctly, analysis of "literary expressions," explanation of mythological and historical details, explanation of difficult words, consideration of analogies, and evaluation of the aesthetic quality of the text (34–35). For recent discussion of the techniques of the grammarians as applied to classical texts, see David Cassel, "Cyril of Alexandria and the Science of the Grammarians: A Study in the Setting, Purpose, and Emphasis of Cyril's *Commentary on Isaiah*," Unpublished Ph.D. dissertation, University of Virginia, Charlottesville, Va., 1992.

35. Schaeublin's approach was influenced by Wilhelm Dilthey who believed that there were two conflicting hermeutical trends in the ancient world, one deriving from Aristotle and the other from the Stoics, and it is this division that was replicated in the Christian biblical interpretation. Cassel is critical of the assumptions behind this argument. He shows that the techniques of the grammarians were not an end in themselves. Rather they provided interpreters with the data necessary to interpret a text but did not in themselves determine what kind of interpretation was appropriate (see Cassel, *Cyril of Alexandria*, 217–224). What determined the interpretation of a text, one might add, was the audience one addressed and the use one was expected to make of the text. At the beginning of the *De doctrina Christiana* Augustine observes that there are two things necessary in interpreting the Scriptures: there is a way of "discovering" (*modus inveniendi*) those things which are to be understood and a way of "presenting" (*modus proferendi*) what we have learned (*doct.* 1.1).

conform more closely to what contemporary scholars consider proper exegesis. A common observation about Theodore is that he practiced "sober, historical exegesis",[36] the term "sober" serving as a kind of code word to set Theodore apart from other ancient commentators who practiced allegory or other forms of, shall we say, "inebriated" exegesis. Sprenger, in the introduction to his edition of the commentary on the Minor prophets, praises Theodore's for his criticism of "mythologizing" exegesis that "falsified the characteristic meaning of the Biblical text." In his view the presupposition for "good exegesis of the biblical text," i.e. "historical-grammatical" exegesis, was knowledge of the historical circumstances.[37] Hence the Old Testament must be interpreted in its own setting, not in relation to the N.T.

It is easy, especially in the twentieth century, when biblical scholarship has been dominated by the techniques of grammatical and historical criticism, to understand why Theodore has been lionized by scholars. He seems so much like ourselves. No less an exegete than Rudolf Bultman wrote his Habilitationsschrift on Theodore of Mopsuestia, *Die Exegese des Theodor von Mopsuestia*.[38] In this work Bultmann praised Theodore not only for his interest in the historical setting of the prophets, but also because he did not inject homiletical comments in his exegesis or use the text as a basis for dogmatic assertions.[39] Theodore possessed, it seems, that quality which is necessary for historical criticism: distance from the text. He realized that the text belonged to a different historical epoch (the LXX was an ancient book) and the task of the exegete was to interpret the text within its own original context. What had happened between the writing of the text and the interpreter was irrelevant to its interpretation. As Mariès put it early in this century in his study of Diodore of Tarsus, he brought to his task "the good sense of a reasonable man in the face of any text."[40] Before joining this chorus of praise for Theodore, it may be useful to look again at his exegesis in relation to *his* context and to the work of those he ridicules.

36. Maurice Wiles in *The Cambridge History of the Bible*, ed. P. R. Ackroyd and C. F. Evans (Cambridge, 1970), 1:490.

37. Sprenger, *Theodori Mopsuesteni Commentarius*, 109.

38. Ed. Helmut Feld and Karl Hermann Shelkle (Stuttgart, 1984). For Theodore, writes Bultman, the text is not "Mittel zum Zweck, sondern Selbstzweck" (27).

39. When I read Bultmann's book on Theodore, I was reminded of Maurice Wiles' observation on Theodore: "Fourth-century Antioch was an outstanding centre of biblical scholarship and of ecclesiastical confusion. The former was not the primary cause of the latter, but the two were not wholly unconnected." (*Cambridge History of the Bible*, 1:489).

40. L. Mariès, *Études préliminaires à l'édition de Diodore de Tarse sur les Psaumes* (Paris, 1933), 129.

Theodore of course recognized the Holy Scriptures are not only documents from the ancient Near East but also a book of the church. Certain passages of the prophets must be interpreted with reference to later events, more specifically with reference to the coming of Christ, at least in a secondary sense.[41] What he does not seem to take into consideration in his exegesis is that the words of prophets were a book of the synagogue as well as a book of the church. For the Jews the oracles of the promises were not moribund oracles about the distant past. They were also voices of hope and expectation. Which is to say that in antiquity there was a third claimant on the meaning of the Jewish Scriptures besides that of history and Christology, namely the hopes of the Jews.

To be sure in disputes between Jews and Christians, Jews sometimes challenged Christian views by appealing to the historical setting in which the prophecies were written. For example, in the prologue to his *Commentary on Zachariah* Jerome said that he had "combined the historical views of the Hebrews with our spiritual exegesis."[42] And in his actual exegesis he often reports that Jewish interpreters refer the oracles of the prophets to the time of the captivity in Babylon or the period of return late in the sixth century B.C.E. Commenting on Ezekiel 28.25–26, "Thus says the Lord God: when I gather the house of Israel from the peoples among whom they are scattered . . . ," Jerome says that the Jews take this passage to be referring to the "time of Zerubbabel, Ezra and Nehemiah when the Jews returned from exile in Babylonia to dwell in the land of Judea."[43]

But the appeal to the original historical setting is only one side of Jewish exegesis of the prophets, and that the least important. Again Jerome is instructive. As often as he says that Jews interpret the prophetic oracles in the context of the exile and return from Babylon, he also reports that they refer the texts to the Messianic age which is yet to come. In his commentary on the passage from Ezekiel cited above Jerome goes on to say that other Jews believe Ezekiel is referring to something that has not yet happened and will be fulfilled "in the last time." [44] At Isaiah 58, "Your ancient ruins shall

41. For example, Joel 2.28–32 (Theodore of Mopsuestia, *Comm. in Ioelem* [Sprenger, 95–98]). His principle seems to be that this and similar texts, e.g. Amos 9.11–12 (Theodore of Mopsuestia, *Comm. in Amos* [Sprenger, 155]) or Psalm 2, are given a Christological interpretation in the New Testament. For Theodore's comments on Psalm 2 (where he cites Hebrews 1.5), see Robert Devreesse, *Le Commentaire de Théodore de Mopsueste sur les Psaumes (I-LXXX)*. Studi e Testi 93 (Città del Vaticano, 1939), 7–8.
42. Jerome, *Comm. in Zachariam* (CChr 76a, 748). On this point see Pierre Jay, *L'exégèse de Saint Jérôme d'après son 'Commentaire sur Isaïe'*, Etudes Augustiniennes (Paris, 1985), 194–200.
43. Jerome, *Comm. in Hiezechielem* 28.20–26 (CChr 75, 400).
44. Ibid.

be rebuilt . . . ," the Jews "claim either that this took place under Zerub-babel and Ezra and Nehemiah *or* they refer it to the end of time, to the reconstruction of Jerusalem and the laying of deep foundations around the cities and the building of walls so high that no enemy can enter and all foes will be barred from them."[45] In short the Jews, like the Christians, saw the oracles of the prophets as *promises*, hence like the Christians they were as much interested in their bearing on events that were subsequent to the prophets as they were in the original historical setting. Indeed here is where the real dispute was to be found.

There seems to have been a genre of early Christian literature dealing with biblical promises, e.g. Tertullian's lost work *De Spe Fidelium*, Dionysius of Alexandria's work *On Promises*, or book 2.11 of Origen's *Peri Archōn* which is entitled "De Repromissibus."[46] The works of Origen and Dionysius were directed against chiliastic interpretation of the biblical promises; Tertullian's work, however, was a defense of chiliasm along the lines set down by Irenaeus in the latter chapters of his *Adversus Haereses.*[47] In his *Commentary on Ezekiel* Jerome mentions Tertullian's *De Spe Fidelium* along with the writings of other chiliasts, Lactantius, Victorinus of Petau, Irenaeus and Apolinaris.[48] In the same passage he also says that on the basis of this oracle Jews (and judaizing Christians) are hoping for the day "when the city of Jerusalem and the temple will be rebuilt."[49] Ezekiel is a book of promises that have not yet been fulfilled.

The prophecy from Isaiah 2 was also such a promise.[50] According to the Jews, Isaiah spoke not only to his time, but also of a future that was yet to come. The evidence for this can be found in Jewish and Christian sources. In the second century Justin cited Micah 4.1–7 in his *Dialogue with Trypho*. He says to Trypho: "I am aware, that your teachers, sir, acknowledge that all the words of this passage were spoken of the Messiah."[51] Both Trypho and Justin agreed that the text was Messianic; the question was whether it had been fulfilled. For both Jews and Christians it was assumed

---

45. Jerome, *Comm. in Esaiam* 58.12 (CChr 73a, 672–73). On this topic see Robert L. Wilken, *The Land Called Holy. Palestine in Christian History and Thought* (New Haven, 1992), 133–137. Also Jay, *L'exégèse*, 198, who observes that the division between Jews and Christians was over the "import" of the text. The Jews sought a meaning in an "event beyond" the historical setting of the prophets and which had not yet taken place.

46. Tertullian, *Marc.* 3.24; Dionysius in Eusebius, *h.e.* 3.24.

47. Irenaeus, *haer.* 5.31–36.

48. Jerome, *Comm. in Hiezechielem* 36.1–15 (CChr 75, 500).

49. Ibid. (CChr 75, 499).

50. See Jerome's comments on the passage in Micah 4.

51. Justin Martyr, *dial.* 110.

that the meaning of Micah 4 is to be found not in the return from captivity in Babylonia but in the future Messianic age. Neither Jew nor Christian was interested in a strictly historical reading of the text.

Jews realized that the ancient prophecies to the Israelites during the Assyrian and Babylonian captivities had not come to perfect fulfilment during the period of the second temple. Jonathan Goldstein writes: "Those unfulfilled prophecies each promised one or more of the following: the permanent liberation of the Jews from exile, from foreign rule, and from all mishap; the erection at Jerusalem of a temple more magnificent than Solomon's, which God Himself would choose as His own place, glorifying it and making it secure from desecration and destruction; the rule over the Jews of a great and just king from the dynasty of David; their exaltation to imperial primacy among the nations; the conversion of the gentiles to follow the ways of the true God; the coming of a permanent era of peace; the resurrection of the righteous dead; and the punishment of all the wicked, past and present."[52] Though the temple had been rebuilt and some of the exiles had returned, the Jews remained subject to foreign powers. Hence they looked to a more complete restoration, in the words of Tobit, "when the times of the age are completed . . . just as the prophets said . . ." (14.5).[53]

The hope of restoration was intensified after the destruction of Jerusalem by the Romans and Isaiah 2 came to be one of the arsenal of texts from the prophets cited in support of the hope of rebuilding the temple. At the end of *Tractate Menacoth* (meal offerings) in the Tosefta, there is a discussion about the reasons why the several temples of the Jews were destroyed, the temple at Shiloh, Solomon's temple, and Herod's temple. Then the text asks: "What of the final building which is destined to be built—may it be in our lifetime and *in our days*." In answer *Tractate Menacoth* cites Isaiah 2.2–3: "It shall come to pass in the latter days that the mountain of the house of the Lord shall be established as the highest of the mountains. . . ."[54] This tradition continued into the middle ages as can be seen

52. Jonathan Goldstein, "How the Authors of 1 and 2 Maccabees Treated the Messianic Promises," in *Judaism and Their Messiahs at the Turn of the Christian Era*, ed. J. Neusner, W. Green, and E. Frerichs (Cambridge, 1987), 69.
53. In the fragmentary *pesharim* on Isaiah found at Qumran the phrase "in the last days" refers to what is happening in the present and future. 4Q161 and 4Q163 in *Discoveries in the Judaean Desert or Jordan Qumran Cave 4*, ed. John M. Allegro and A. A. Anderson (Oxford, 1968), 13–14, 24.
54. T. Klauser writes: "When the Messianic expectations were not fulfilled in the time of Hezekiah, the nation—and perhaps also the prophet himself—postponed the fulfillment to a later time. Such postponement was natural and necessary. It was also proper. For the basic principle of the Messianic expectation is nothing else than the

from David Kimchi's commentary on Isaiah. Commenting on Isaiah 2 he writes: "When the Scripture use the phrase 'at the end of the ages' it refers to the days of the Messiah."[55] The Jews, it seems, were no more interested in the historical meaning of Isaiah 2 than were the Christians.[56] That Jews would sometimes urge a historical interpretation against the Christians was a polemical strategy used to discredit Christian claims on the text.

Once the biblical prophecies are viewed in light of Jewish hopes and are transplanted from the serene solitude of the scholar's study to the tumultuous arena of religious controversy, questions of interpretation take a quite different form. In that setting the issue becomes: which events qualify as a likely fulfilment of the text? To which future do they belong or to which community are they to be applied. The Jews applied them to the future of the Jewish people and the reestablishment of a Jewish kingdom in the land. Christian commentators, in response, insisted that they refer to the church. This is evident in a poignant and arresting passage in the *Dialogue with Trypho*. Justin had cited a number of passages that refer to Israel, e.g. "Israel my inheritance" (Isa 19.24) and "I will let men walk upon you, even my people Israel. . . ." (Ezek 36.12). Trypho realized that Justin was claiming that references to Israel in the prophets (and one might add in the psalms and elsewhere) applied to Christians: Hence he asks: "What is this? Are *you* Israel and is he speaking these things *about you*?" Justin answers: "Yes." [57]

This exchange tells us as much about Jewish self-understanding as it does about Christian exegesis. For Trypho the term "Israel" and its many biblical cognates is univocal. It applied only to the people who were descendants of Abraham. This was an acute problem for the early Christians. Is the new community born *within* Israel continuous with the Israel spoken of in the Scriptures, the "us" mentioned in Isaiah 2. "Let *us* go up to the

---

longing for the Golden Age in the future, whether near or distant. . . . And this basic principle is the secret of the eternal endurance of the Messianic expectations." (*The Messianic Idea in Israel* [New York, 1955], 57).

55. *The Commentary of David Kimhi on Isaiah*, ed. Louis Finkelstein (New York, 1966), 11. See Jerome, *Comm. in Michaeam*: Jews refer the text to a thousand year reign.

56. Isaiah 2 is cited, along with a series of other prophetic oracles, in an apocalyptic poem written shortly after the Muslim conquest of Palestine. The poet anticipates the day when the exiles would return and Jerusalem would be rebuilt as a Jewish city. See Joseph Yahalon, "On the Value of Literary Works as Sources to Elucidate Historical Questions," *Cathedra* 22 (1979):133 (in Hebrew). The phrase "in the last days" is cited in the apocalyptic work *Book of Zerubbabel* which was written (or re-edited) at the time of the Persian conquest of Jerusalem in the early seventh century. The book's theme is: when will the time of deliverance come? See Even Shmuel, *Midreshei Geulah* (Jerusalem and Tel Aviv, 1954), 73, ln.45.

57. Justin Martyr, *dial.* 123. See also *dial.*11.

mountain of the God of Jacob that he may teach *us* his ways and that *we* may walk in his paths"? Already in the song of Mary at the Annunciation, such an identification is made. "He has helped his servant *Israel*, in remembrance of his mercy, according to the promise he made to *our* ancestors, to Abraham and to his descendants forever" (Lk 1.55). But the point had to be reiterated as Christian thinkers sought to provide a credible interpretation of the Septuagint as a whole. In an offhand comment on the Annunciation to Mary, Eusebius of Caesarea grasped the essential point. The name Jacob or Israel "does not designate the Jewish people alone but all those from among all the nations have been who given the status of children of God when called by the Savior."[58]

With these considerations in mind let us turn finally to the commentaries on Isaiah (and Micah) written in the fifth century by Jerome, Cyril of Alexandria and Theodoret of Cyrus. For these expositors, though cognizant of Theodore's criticism, reaffirm that the key to understanding the text is not place, i.e. to say Mt. Zion, but time, the phrase "in these last days." And like earlier commentators their interpretation has a polemical edge. The Jews, says Jerome, take the "last days" to refer to the Messianic age, the "rule of the Messiah," which has not yet taken place and will occur at the "end of the ages."[59] At other places in his commentaries, in a similar context, he speaks of the Messianic age as the coming of "their Messiah," i.e. the Messiah of the Jews, in contrast to the Christ of the Christians.[60]

In response Jerome argues that Isaiah 2 refers to the church, which had its origins in the coming of Jesus of Nazareth, not the Messianic age which is anticipated by the Jews. He notes that the term "house" used in Isaiah, "the mountain of the Lord's house," designates the church in the New Testament, for example in 1 Timothy: "You may know how one ought to behave in the household of God, which is the church of the living God, the pillar and bulwark of truth" (3.15). And to respond to the Jewish view that in the Messianic age the nations will come to Jerusalem to do homage to the God of Israel, he argues that this text says that "instruction *shall go forth* out of Zion, and the word of the Lord *from Jerusalem*." In his view this refers to the spreading of the Gospel which began with the apostles.[61]

58. Eusebius of Caesarea, *Comm. in Lucam* (PG 24, 532c). A similar identification is made in the song of Zechariah in Lk 1.68.
59. Jerome, *Comm. in Michaem* 4.1–7 (CChr 76, 472).
60. See Jerome, *Comm. in Hiezechielem* 16:55 (CChr 75, 210, 1ns. 805–806; *Comm. in Hiezechielem* 40.5–13 (CChr 75, 557, 1n.165). Here he refers to Christ as "Salvator Noster" (467, 1n.57).
61. Jerome, *Comm. in Esaiam* 2.3–4 (CChr 73, 29, 1ns.40–43). Like Chrysostom, Jerome noted that the break between chapters one and two of Isaiah, but because he read the Hebrew text as well as the LXX he also realized that the LXX translators had

Cyril of Alexandria also believed that the key to interpreting the text is the phrase "in the last days" which is to say the "time" to which the text refers. Like John Chrysostom he observes that there is a clean break between the first and second chapters of Isaiah. When the prophet begins chapter two he makes clear that the "vision" of chapter one has come to an end. Now as he records a "second vision" he "designates the time" and that is signified by the phrase "in the last days." The "time" to which the prophet refers is an age in which the power of the devil will be overcome "not in one country and city . . . but in every place under the heavens."[62] Because this prophecy has been fulfilled in the birth and expansion of the church into the whole world, the text must be interpreted in light of events that have already taken place. "This [the oracle in Isaiah 2] has been accomplished among those who were on earth in the last days, i.e. at the last times of the present age, in which the only begotten son of God the Word shined forth, born of a woman. . . . Christ showed forth the church of the nations, as it were in the last time, that is at the end of this age (Heb 9.26).[63]

Finally Theodoret of Cyrus. Like Chrysostom he notes that chapter two serves almost as "another preface" to the book of Isaiah. The prophet wishes to introduce a different subject from that of chapter one and he signals this by the phrase "in these last days." He observes that the phrase occurs in the New Testament in two key passages. The first is Acts 2.17 where the writer cites Joel 2.28–32, "I will pour out my Spirit on all flesh, and your sons and your daughters shall prophesy . . . . Then everyone who calls on the name of the Lord shall be saved." But in citing the prophet Joel Acts replaces the opening phrase "then afterward" with the words of Isaiah "In these last days." Secondly Theodoret cites Hebrews 1.1 "In many and various ways God spoke to our ancestors by the prophets, but *in these last days* he has spoken to us by a Son."[64]

Accordingly Theodoret interprets the passage with respect to the church, citing Hebrews 3.6, "Christ was faithful over God's *house* as a son, and we are his house" to be a reference to the "Lord's house" in Isaiah 2.2.

---

mistranslated the prepositions in 1.1 and 2.1. In Hebrew the preposition in the phrase "concerning Judah and Jerusalem" is *al*. But in the Septuagint 1.1 is rendered "against" (*kata*) and 2.1 "concerning" (*peri*). Jerome comments: "*Miror cur LXX interpretes in illa dixerint: contra Iudaeam et Hierusalem; et in hac: de Iudaea et de Hierusalem. . . .* " (*Comm. in Esaiam* 2.1 (CChr 73, 26).

62. Cyril of Alexandria, *Comm. in Isaiam* 2.1 (PG 70, 68b).

63. Ibid. (PG 70, 68c). Cyril gives a similar interpretation, citing Hebrews 9.26, in his *Commentary on Micah*. The text refers to the calling of the "church from the gentiles" and to things that happened "among us": *Comm. in Michaeam* 4.1–2 (Pusey, 657).

64. Theodoret of Cyrus, *Comm. on Esaiam* 2.1–2 (SC 276, 188–190).

He also criticizes a purely historical interpretation of the passage. "I am amazed at those who insist on interpreting this passage otherwise and who think that through these words the return from Babylon was prophesied."[65] Though these observations may have been directed at Jews, it is more likely, as Guinot observes, that Theodoret's has in mind Christian interpreters, notably Theodore of Mopseustia who, as we have seen, gave the text a strictly historical interpretation.[66] In some places in his commentaries he criticizes Jews who give the prophetic oracles a historical interpretation,[67] but he is more critical of Jews and judaizing Christians who took the restorationist passages of the prophets to be referring to the rebuilding of Jerusalem as a Jewish city.[68]

The ancient oracles of the prophets will inevitably look different when the interpreter is faced with actual events that seem to correspond, however unexpectedly, to what the prophets envisioned.[69] That is true of Jews as well as of Christians. History, even sacred history, seldom follows a predetermined pattern. When the Persians conquered Jerusalem in the seventh century, Jews in Palestine saw the defeat of the Byzantines, i.e. the Christians, as a fulfilment of the prophecies about the restoration of Jerusalem. They discerned a close correspondence between the name of the Sassanid Chosroe II and the ancient Persian king Cyrus who had delivered the Jews from the Babylonians.[70] And they saw the words of the prophet coming to fulfilment in their own time.

It is one thing to anticipate a Messianic age at some time in the distant future, something else to claim that it has begun to appear. When that occurs the words of the prophets may not mean what they seem to mean, a point that Maimonides understood well. In his view the Messianic age may not be marked by catastrophic events that make all sit up and take note. When the Messiah comes, he writes, "the world will follow its normal course." For this reason, he says, the words of the prophets, e.g. about a peaceable kingdom in Isaiah 11, "the wolf shall live with the lamb, the leopard shall lie down with the kid," are to be taken "figuratively" and

65. Ibid. (2.4) (SC 276, 192–194).

66. On this point see Jean-Noël Guinot, *Théodoret de Cyr. Commentaire sur Isaïe* (SC 276, 193, n.3).

67. See, for example, Theodoret of Cyrus' *Comm. in Michaeam* 4.1–4 (PG 81, 1760d-1761a).

68. See Theodoret of Cyrus, *Comm. in Hiezechielem* 48.35 (PG 81, 1248–1256).

69. As Irenaeus puts it: Christ "brought something wholly new (*omnem novitatem*) offering himself who had been announced." To which he adds a few paragraphs later: "For it can be said that none of these things has properly speaking actually happened to any of the fathers or prophets or ancient kings" (*haer.* 4.34.1–3).

70. See the Jewish apocalypse *Book of Elijah* in *Midreshei Geulah*, ed. Shmuel, 42.

"similar expressions used in connection with the Messiah" are to be understood "metaphorically." [71] The meaning of the ancient oracles will only be apparent when the Messianic age has come.

That, finally, was the argument Christian interpreters gave to their critics. They have a much too restricted view of what it means for the prophecies to be fulfilled. Origen cheerfully acknowledged that the words of the prophets have not been fulfilled in the way they were thought to take place. "None of these things that have taken place can be seen with the senses" (*princ.* 4.2.1). Yet something had happened (and was seen) and it had occurred in space and time. The first Christians did not bear witness to an apparition. As Origen put it: "The Word of God itself, that Wisdom of God . . . came to exist within the circumscribed limits of a man who *appeared* in Judea . . ." (*princ.* 2.6.2).

Early Christian interpreters did not impose an evanescent superstructure on the text without root in history or experience. Most Christian exegetes repudiated a literal or historical reading of the prophets, not because they preferred allegory or anagogy to history, but because they were attentive to a new set of historical events. If Jesus of Nazareth was the Messiah, as the Scriptures taught, the prophecies about the Messianic age had already been fulfilled, and it was the task of biblical interpreters to discover what the scriptural promises meant in light of this new fact. Paradoxically, in the language of early Christian exegesis, the spiritual sense *was* the historical sense.

Robert L. Wilken is the William R. Kenan, jr., Professor of the History of Christianity

---

71. Maimonides, *Mishneh Torah*, Book Fourteen, Book of Judges, Treatise Five, Kings and Wars, chapter 12.

Chalcedon Revisited:
A Historical and Theological Reflection

RICHARD NORRIS, JR.

The *Definition* of the Council of Chalcedon — a relatively brief para-graph appended to the conciliar decree as its conclusion — has always been a focus for controversy. Historically speaking, it perches, placidly and perhaps rather quizzically, at the center of a storm. Penned under the pressure of a passionate doctrinal debate to which was wedded an equally passionate power-struggle, it was no sooner promulgated than it gave rise to a new series of controversies, which for two centuries and more disturbed the peace of the early Byzantine Empire, frustrated the hopes and policies of a whole series of emperors, and in the end left the churches of the East divided by schisms that have endured to the present day. And as if that were not enough, it has now once again become a focus of criticism and debate, this time in the theological academy. After centuries during which, at least in the West, it enjoyed the obscurity that comes of success and served as the unexamined basis of an elaborate tradition of discourse on the person of Christ, the Chalcedonian *Definition* is at length paying the price of that success. It is now being called to account for that entire tradition, in the light of more recent readings both of the New Testament and of the philosophical heritage of the past.

The Chalcedonian *Definition*'s language and thought, then, are closely and intricately woven into the tradition of Christian teaching and specu-lation about the person of Christ, and for that reason there is no way of isolating it either from the debates that led up to it or from the criticisms and interpretations it has evoked: like some other focal texts of Christian history, it belongs to more than one place and time. Nevertheless one is bound to inquire what the original burden of the *Definition* was and what, in the light of an answer to that question, it may have to say about the very controversies to which it has given rise. In the end, one might hope to allow the *Definition* to comment on its commentators, and thus to bring it back into dialogue both with its critics and with its admirers.

I

The bishops assembled at Chalcedon were not, as modern interpreters have tended to make them out, professional philosophers or even, in the contemporary sense, professional theologians. In their day, academic theology did not exist (there appear to have been no *periti* in attendance at the Council), and the only "schools" with which they were concerned were those in which catechesis occurred. They would have been startled, then, to know that their statements have latterly been read as propounding some particular, theoretically devised "christology" (a useful modern term with which they were not familiar). In their view, after all, it was even questionable whether they had any business to go beyond the statements made in what, by their time, was the normal basis of doctrinal catechesis, namely, the Nicene faith in its several versions.[1] "This wise and saving symbol of the divine grace," they said,

> should have been sufficient for the knowledge and support of true religion, for it gives the complete teaching about the Father and the Son and the Holy Spirit, and to those who receive it faithfully it interprets the Lord's becoming human.[2]

Hence they understood their *Definition,* as its opening phrase "Following the holy Fathers" indicates clearly enough, to be little more than an exegetical note calculated to render the teaching of the Nicene faith on "the Lord's becoming human" explicit.

---

1. The principle of the sufficiency of the Nicene "creed," which seems to have been assumed in the controversy between Cyril of Alexandria and Nestorius, was explicitly enjoined by the Council of Ephesus in 431.
2. For the translation, see R. A. Norris, *The Christological Controversy* (Philadelphia, 1980), p. 157.

What is more, the exegetical note itself is essentially a pastiche of allusions and quotations. It drew its language from writers as far back as Irenaeus and Tertullian, but the immediate sources of the formulas it employs were texts whose phraseology was shaped in the course of the Nestorian and Eutychian controversies. It echoed Leo the Great's *Tome* and certain of Cyril of Alexandria's letters. It repeated the language of the Formulary of Reunion, which Cyril had applauded in his letter *Laetentur caeli* to John of Antioch, and of Flavian's profession of faith before the Home Synod at Constantinople.[3] For the use of "one hypostasis" in conjunction with "in two natures," it seems to have drawn on the usage of Proclus of Constantinople.[4]

Thus the *Definition* presents itself tacitly both as a consensus document and as a reiteration of tradition. It aims to exhibit an underlying and substantive agreement among the great sees of Rome, Constantinople, Alexandria, and Antioch and therefore among the traditions they represent — even though certain of their prominent representatives, like Nestorius and Eutyches, might in the past have departed from this broad consensus and even if certain ways of speaking about Christ that one or more of these traditions had found acceptable in the past needed to be set quietly aside as inconsistent with the wider consensus.

By their very attempt to put this consensus — this *traditional* consensus, as they saw it — into words, however, the bishops at Chalcedon were condemned to at least a modest originality. Even though their language was deliberately and systematically unoriginal, even though their grasp of its sense was merely "intuitive," and "none of them could have given a definition of the concepts"[5] that they were using, they were bound, not only because of the issues immediately before them but also because of the very language of the Nicene faith, to tackle one central problem.

That problem was to explicate the Nicene symbol's statement that there is "one Lord Jesus Christ," identified as "true God from true God" who "became incarnate" *(sarkōthenta)* and "became human" *(enan-*

---

3. On this point see A. Grillmeier, *Christ in Christian Tradition*, vol. I (2nd ed., Atlanta, 1975), p. 544; and R. V. Sellers, *The Council of Chalcedon: A Historical and Doctrinal Survey* (London, 1953), pp. 210ff.

4. See Jean Galot, "'Une seule personne, une seule hypostase,'" in *Gregorianum* 70 (1989), esp. pp. 257-65.

5. Grillmeier, *Christ in Christian Tradition* I, p. 545.

thrōpēsanta), and indeed "was crucified for us . . . and suffered . . . and rose on the third day." These words of the creed take the form of a brisk narrative account whose subject is the "Lord Jesus Christ"; and they speak of this Christ first as God and then as a human being, while conveying the unmistakable impression that he retains his fundamental identity throughout, since there is only one *subject* to whom the narrative attributes both sets of epithets, divine and human.[6] The bishops' problem, then, was to find a way of making sense of the basic assumption of this narrative: the assumption, namely, that an individual identified as "God from God" can also — and truly — be a human being without ceasing to be one and the same individual. And this of course was precisely the problem that had been raised in an acute form by both Nestorius and Eutyches and that had taken the form of a political confrontation that embroiled all the great sees of the Church.

In the text of their *Definition*, the bishops begin, therefore, with what they are confident everyone is prepared to agree on. They present what amounts to a transposition of the creedal narrative into a new form. Where the symbol of faith tells what happens to its subject, the *Definition* gives an account of how, in the light of that narrative, its subject is to be characterized. The result, naturally enough, is a resounding affirmation of the *oneness* of the Christ, a statement that can be read simply as a rhetorically enhanced analysis of what the creedal account of the incarnation directly implies about Christ's person. The bishops speak of "one and the same Son, who is our Lord Jesus Christ"; and they then proceed to reiterate the phrase *ho autos* ("the very same") five times, in each case predicating of this one subject, the Christ, a double set of attributes. He is "complete *(teleios)* in his deity and . . . complete in his humanity," "coessential *(homo-ousios)* with the Father . . . and coessential with us." Here, then, there is stated — no doubt in a form calculated in principle to frustrate the errors of Nestorius and Eutyches alike — what the bishops took to be the heart of God's *oikonomia* of salvation, the Incarnation.

This paraphrase, however, for all its illumination of the unity-in-duality of Christ, did not directly address the burning issue of the time, which turned on the mode — or at any rate on the proper mode of expres-

6. Compare Leo's *Tome* 2 (Norris, *Christological Controversy,* p. 146), where Leo appeals in a similar fashion, and to the same end, to the language of the traditional Roman baptismal symbol.

sion — of Christ's unity. Accordingly, in the second part of the *Definition*, which also opens with a ringing affirmation of "one and the same Christ," the bishops offer what amounts to a tacit criticism of the ways in which the terms "subject" *(hypostasis)* and "nature" *(physis)* had been employed in the controversies evoked by the teaching of Nestorius and, later, Eutyches. On both sides of that debate, "subject" and "nature" had been used, if not as synonymous in their connotation, then at any rate as synonymous in their reference. The affirmation of two natures was taken, in the tradition of the school of Antioch, to entail that of two hypostases, presumably on the assumption that there can be no real nature save in the form of a complete and concrete existent;[7] and similarly, in Alexandrian circles, "one hypostasis" was widely taken to imply "one nature," even if Cyril of Alexandria had, though subtly and seldom, intimated the contrary.[8]

The *Definition*, however, drew on the language of Proclus of Constantinople and Basil of Seleucia[9] to make a distinction between hypostasis and nature. If it were granted that this "one and the same Son" is at once complete in deity and complete in humanity (a proposition to which all would presumably subscribe), sharing the *ousia* of God on the one hand and of human beings on the other — and if, as was generally understood, *ousia* ("essence") and *physis* ("nature") meant roughly the same thing, then it made perfect sense to summarize the teaching of the opening section of the *Definition* in the words "one and the same Christ, Son, Lord, Only-begotten, acknowledged [to be] . . . *in two natures.*" This crucial and controverted phrase, then, appears in the text of the *Definition* as nothing more than a summary transcription of what had already been said in its first section, as, that is, a reasonable and indeed almost inevitable way of putting what everyone was already agreed about. To be sure, one had to remember that each nature was "complete" (or "perfect": *teleios*) and thus continued, even in the incarnation, to be itself, distinct from the other, even though it did not exist apart from the other. Hence the bishops added to this phrase their four famous adverbs — "unconfusedly, unalterably, undividedly, inseparably" — to guarantee just these points.

7. See, e.g., L. Scipioni, *Richerche sulla cristologia del 'Libro di Eraclide' di Nestorio* (Fribourg, 1956), pp. 45ff.

8. On this point see the complex discussion of Grillmeier, *Christ in Christian Tradition* I, pp. 480ff.

9. See Galot, " 'Une seule personne, une seule hypostase,' " n. 4; Grillmeier, *Christ in Christian Tradition* I, p. 548.

And having thus — as they thought — reiterated in different terms the affirmations of the opening section of the text, they proceeded to do so once more, but with a different emphasis. Their first transcription had started with the "one and the same" Son and gone on to affirm that he is "acknowledged" (or perhaps "recognized") "in two natures." The second transcription, intended further to clarify the first, starts out with the two natures and moves thence to the ground of their unity.

> . . . the difference of the natures is not destroyed because of the union, but on the contrary, the character of each nature is preserved and comes together in one person *(prosōpon)* and one hypostasis.[10]

The interesting circumstance here is the substitution of "one person and one hypostasis" for "one and the same Christ." Once again, the *Definition* works by rephrasing, or paraphrasing, its basic affirmations. Just as one can use "nature" as a convenient and plausible term to refer summarily to the respects in which Christ is twofold (as being "complete" both in deity and in humanity), so one can employ "person" or "hypostasis" to denote that "one and the same" to whom these "natures" are attributed. This legitimizes the traditional Antiochene use of *prosōpon* to refer to the one Christ, but at the same time insists that the term be regarded as an equivalent for *hypostasis* — which was by no means an outrageous demand, since the two words had been employed in this way in discourse about the Trinity since the last quarter of the previous century.

The Chalcedonian *Definition*, then, though not without some precedent, intimates a distinction of meaning as between "nature" and "hypostasis" — a distinction that would allow one to speak of Christ as *one hypostasis in two natures.* It must be noticed, however, that the Council never uses this expression nor, what is more important, defines these terms. They had been delivered to it, to be sure, as part of the idiom in which a burning theological and political controversy was being conducted. In the *Definition*, however, the terms in question derive their sense not from any explicit delimitation of meaning that might elevate them to status as technical terms, nor even from the ways in which they had been used in earlier stages of the controversy,[11] but strictly from the way they

10. Norris, *The Christological Controversy,* p. 159.
11. While the Council employs the terms "nature," "person," and "hypostasis," it is a point insufficiently stressed that it uses them in a way that does not appear to

are employed *in this text,* that is, from the fact that they transcribe, in a generalizing and abstract fashion, what had been directly said in the opening section of the *Definition.* "Hypostasis" is short for "one and the same Christ, Son, Lord, Only begotten," and "two natures" transcribes, with useful brevity, the fact that this hypostasis is regularly characterized — not only in the *Definition* itself, but in the Nicene symbol — by two different *sets* of predications, distinguishable because one set contains the sorts of things one normally says about God, and the other, the sorts of things one normally says about human beings. The formula affirms, then, that there is a case, the case of Jesus Christ, in which "one and the same" reality *(hypostasis)* is properly characterized at once as a divine reality *(physis)* and as a human reality *(physis).*

Now it is arguable that a formula like this, apart from any clear specification of the meanings of the terms it employs, represents not so much a solution of the problem as it does a mere statement of it. Such a judgment, moreover, is entirely consonant with the real, if commonly unacknowledged, modesty of the Fathers of Chalcedon. Nevertheless, the judgment needs some qualification, for the *Definition's* "statement of the problem" accomplished precisely what it set out to accomplish and thus did not leave the christological state of affairs unaltered. First, it clearly excluded, on the one hand, the Nestorian doctrine of "two sons" and, on the other, the view — intimated in the public testimony of Eutyches at his trial — that the human "nature" of Christ is somehow fused into, or absorbed by, his divine "nature." But second, it accomplished these ends not by writing a new and freshly inspired "christology," but by teasing out certain assumptions that it saw underlying the Nicene symbol's account of the divine *oikonomia* of salvation and by phrasing them in the established idiom of the disputes about the person of Christ that had been rumbling since the days of Apollinaris of Laodicea. Hence the bishops' "statement of the problem" was also a bit more than just that. It was also a ruling that

---

correspond with the usages of Apollinaris, Theodore of Mopsuestia, and Nestorius, or even of Cyril of Alexandria (as Severus of Antioch was quick to insist). "Nature" in particular was a term of plastic sense. Leo I's use of it, for example, seems to involve a reminiscence of Tertullian's *substantia* (see Tertullian, *Adversus Praxean* 27). On Cyril's understanding of Christ's humanity (which he did not like to call a nature), see the learned and helpful article of Ruth M. Siddals, "Logic and Christology in Cyril of Alexandria," *Journal of Theological Studies* n.s. 38 (1987), pp. 341-67.

excluded certain teachings and at the same time a definition of what one might call the agenda of christological inquiry: an agenda determined by the grammatical and logical structure of the narrative of the second article of the Nicene symbol. Thus the bishops at Chalcedon did not, even in the end, fail to keep faith with the Ephesian Council of 431, nor did they waver in their conviction that the *Definition* ought to be, even if it was not, superfluous.

II

How wrong they were in this conviction was to be demonstrated by the two great spates of criticism that their *Definition* evoked in the course of the later history of the Christian movement. The first of these, of course, was the critique mounted by the Monophysites, who, out of loyalty to Cyril of Alexandria, and also eventually no doubt out of distaste for Byzantine hegemony, sought to maintain, in opposition to the language of two natures, the formula *One incarnate nature of the divine Word*.[12] The second is a debate that is still going on — a debate stimulated in part by modern critical interest in the figure of "the historical Jesus," with its concomitant delight in "christology from below," but also by severe doubts about the utility and coherence of the traditional discourse about natures and hypostases. In what follows, I will hope to indicate that there is a connection between these criticisms of the Chalcedonian *Definition*, a connection that brings into bold relief the virtues of the modesty with which the Council did its business.

The struggle between defenders of Cyril of Alexandria's formula, "One incarnate nature of the divine Word," and later proponents of the Chalcedonian "in two natures" turned essentially on the issue of the sense in which the humanity of Christ represented an independent or self-standing factor in the economy of salvation. To be sure, there were Monophysites and

---

12. Here one ought of course to mention also the ill-fated attempt at compromise with Monophysitism that goes under the name of Monothelitism. The controversy over the issue of "one will" or "one energy" in Christ touched on a central issue in the debate between Chalcedonians and Monophysites; but the formula cannot be described with strict accuracy as a product of the Monophysite camp and was in fact inspired by a desire to evade use of the expression "one nature."

Monophysites, just as there were Chalcedonians and Chalcedonians. A Monophysite thinker and leader like Severus of Antioch objected strongly to the Eutychianism or "synousianism" of those who interpreted "one nature" to mean that Christ was some sort of unprecedented "cross" between humanity and divinity. But he objected just as strenuously to the Nestorian hypothesis of two hypostases or subjects in Christ; and it was Nestorianism that he discerned in the language of Leo the Great's *Tome,* with its assertion that

> Each "form" [cf. Phil. 2:6-7] carries on its proper activities in communion with the other. The Word does what belongs to it, and the flesh carries out what belongs to it. The one shimmers with wondrous deeds, the other succumbs to injury and insult.[13]

To Severus and those who thought like him, this suggestion that "the flesh" of Christ "carries on its own proper activities" implied that it belonged ultimately to itself and not to the divine Word; and this contention they took to constitute the heart of the Nestorian error. Yet the Council of Chalcedon had not merely used the phrase "in two natures;" it had canonized this *Tome* of Leo's and thus indicated that Leo's views were consistent with its *Definition.* To be sure, it had also, to use its own words,

> received . . . the synodical letters of the blessed Cyril . . . to Nestorius and the Orientals, for the sake of refuting the follies of Nestorius and for the instruction of those who, in religious zeal, seek understanding of the saving Symbol.[14]

But the contention, thus embodied in conciliar action, that "Leo agrees with Cyril" (as the Council Fathers had even shouted at one point) was at the very least difficult to sustain; and this was precisely the point of the Monophysite polemic. The conciliar *Definition,* it argued, was for all practical purposes a Nestorian document.

At the base of this Monophysite polemic, then, there lay a straightforward loyalty to the views and insights of Cyril of Alexandria. Monophysitism arose out of a belief that the Council of Chalcedon had betrayed both Cyril and the Ephesian Council of 431, which was associated with

---

13. *Tome* 4, in Norris, *The Christological Controversy,* p. 150.
14. Ibid., p. 158.

Cyril's name. Essential to this belief, however, was a further conviction, quite correctly noted by John of Damascus, that the words "hypostasis" and "nature" (to which list "person" might also be added) "mean the same thing";[15] for given this conviction, it was impossible for a teacher like Severus of Antioch not to descry Nestorianism in any assertion of two natures. On the other hand, this Cyrillian Monophysitism was just as resolutely opposed to any notion that the humanity of Christ ceased to be humanity or the divinity, divinity. The "union" *(henōsis)* or "composition" *(synthesis)* through which the Word became flesh created a single individual subject, just as the union or composition of soul and body in a human person creates a single individual subject. Nevertheless the defining "what" of these elements is not altered: there is no confusion of divinity and humanity in Christ, any more than soul ceases to be soul or body ceases to be body in the human individual.[16] The important point for someone like Severus of Antioch is by no means that the humanity should cease to be human, but that it should be a humanity that *belongs to* the Word (even as a body is said to belong to its soul) and in that sense is completely at one with the Word and expressive of the divine and salvific purpose that the incarnation enacts.[17]

The odd thing is, then, that a Monophysite like Severus of Antioch in the end constructed an account of the person of Christ that, in spite of its refusal of the language of "two natures," *says* more or less exactly what the Council of Chalcedon had insisted upon. Like the bishops of the Council, Severus sees himself beset on the one hand by a Nestorian dualism and on the other by a synousianism that cannot tell, or refuses to maintain, the difference between humanity and divinity in Christ. Like the bishops of the Council again, Severus responds by insisting upon "one and the same Christ" in whom deity and humanity are united in one reality while remaining distinct in the "what" that each is. If one were to institute a search for the real difference between them, it would be hard to identify, apart from Severus's refusal to employ the term *physis* to denote the "what" of

15. *To auto legein: De fide orthodoxa* 3.3 (*Patrologia Graeco-Latina* [hereafter *PG*] 94:992A). See also the remarks of J. Lebon, "La christologie du monophysisme syrien," in A. Grillmeier and H. Bacht, eds., *Das Konzil von Chalkedon* (Würzburg, 1951) I, pp. 461-67, with the references there.

16. See Lebon, "La christologie du monophysisme syrien," 472-77.

17. For this point, see the important discussion in I. R. Torrance, *Christology after Chalcedon* (Norwich, 1988), pp. 82ff.

divinity on the one hand and of humanity on the other; and this difference, it seems, is not substantive but turns merely on the matter of how each party stipulated the sense of a particular term.

But is this conclusion justified? Surely in the end there *is* a significant difference between the two parties — a difference apparent on the one hand in Severus's early polemic against Leo's *Tome* and on the other in the orthodox view, represented much later by Maximus the Confessor and John of Damascus, of the relation between nature and will *(thelēma)* or energy *(energeia)*. In the words of the Damascene:

> Since . . . Christ has two natures, he also has two natural wills and two natural energies. But since there is one hypostasis of his two natures, we say that it is "one and the same" who wills and energizes naturally in accordance with both of the natures out of which, and in which, and which Christ our God is; and [we say] that he wills and energizes not dividedly but in a unified manner. For he wills and energizes in each "form" [cf. Phil. 2:6-7] in union [*koinônia*] with the other. For things that have the same essence have the same will and energy; but things whose essence is different have a different will and energy.[18]

Here John is asserting the principle, long established in trinitarian discourse, that activity *(energeia)* is a function of essence *(ousia)* or of nature, not of subject. That is, the way something acts depends on its "what" and not on its "who." Therefore the humanity of Christ, if it is real and distinct from his divinity, will retain its own ways of acting (and hence its own will, since humanity is rational) in the incarnation. This statement of John's, though, is a reiteration of the very idea, and indeed embodies a reminiscence of the very passage, in Leo's *Tome* that had most offended Severus; and it seems to justify entirely his belief that Chalcedonians were wedded to some idea of the *independence* of Christ's human nature. For to speak of a human will in Christ is, surely, to repeat the error of Nestorius, since it inevitably makes the Lord's humanity a free-standing agent and reduces the unity of God and humanity in Christ to the level of a friendly alliance.

John of Damascus, of course, would regard such an accusation as false. He makes it perfectly plain that the *subject* of Christ's human acting and willing is the Word, and that the human nature in Christ is, as we might say, perfectly

18. *De fide orthodoxa* 3.14 (*PG* 94:1033BC).

in tune with the divine since it is in a natural and not a sinful state, as the Third Council of Constantinople (680) had insisted. John's "neo"-Chalcedonianism, then, intends — or at least manages — to accommodate both Leo the Great and Severus on this issue: to intimate that Leo's concern for the reality and fullness of Christ's human nature is not inconsistent with Severus's insistence that after all the work of human salvation has God, in the person of the Word, not merely as its "subject" but as its primary agent. Furthermore, if my account of the Chalcedonian *Definition*'s sense is correct, then John is right to take this line, since it accords exactly with Chalcedon's rule for discourse about the person of Christ: that "one and the same" Christ, who is in the first instance understood and spoken of as God, is also, in virtue of the incarnation, truly understood and spoken of as a human being.

III

The interesting difference to be noted, then, is not the difference of emphasis between John of Damascus and Severus, or for that matter between Leo and Cyril, but a more subtle one between Chalcedon itself and the positions of all or any of these contributors to the great christological controversy. To define this difference, moreover, is to discern the source of much modern skepticism about traditional talk of "natures" in christology — and also, at the same time, the degree to which contemporary theology perpetuates, in its own characteristic way, the very incoherence it criticizes in the tradition.

The Chalcedonian *Definition*, as I have indicated, offers little more than a paradigm. It does not explicitly explain or define what "nature" and "hypostasis" mean, save by tacit reference to the way in which the Nicene symbol *speaks* of Christ; and to that extent, what it provides is essentially a transcription and an account of a pattern of predication. By contrast, the contributors to the debates that surrounded Chalcedon take another course. Even when their language conforms to this paradigm, they interpret the two sets of predicates as referring to things or substances of the sort that occur in the normal world of human experience. The "natures," in short, are reified. Thus these thinkers discern an analogy to the incarnation in the wedding of soul and body in the human individual (as we have seen in the case of Severus of Antioch);[19] or they exploit the well-known image of the

19. John of Damascus used the same image to his own purposes (see *De fide*

"mixture" of iron and fire[20] and speak of "putting together" *(synthesis)* and "unification" *(henōsis)*, not to mention the Antiochene "indwelling." John of Damascus conceives of human intellect (or rational soul), in view of its being the image of God, as "in the border-area between God and flesh" and thus envisages it as the "medium" *(mesos)* through which the Word was united to or mingled with flesh.[21] In other words, the interpreters and critics of Chalcedon employed what one might call "physical" models to convey the virtues or limitations of the Council's paradigm.

Now each of these models depends on the plausibility of an analogy. Each amounts, for all practical purposes, to a *metaphor* for the relation between Word and flesh. So much is apparent from the very manner in which the models in question are handled. Thus the fundamental analogy of synthesis or mixture appeared, on examination, to have certain disadvantages. It seemed to presuppose the existence of two distinct and parallel "somethings" that "come together" in the incarnation. Such an image, however, might well suggest the need for a third, external factor to function as the agent or agency by which the union of the two is effected; and it certainly intimates that each of things that are united *preexist* their "coming together." All parties to these controversies, however, were instant to repudiate any such suggestions as these (for reasons I have already indicated); and so they set about the business of controlling or qualifying this particular range of metaphors by another. They turn from analysis of the constituents of Christ's person to narrative discourse about the incarnation; and by doing so they intimate that the "natures" that are brought together are not related symmetrically. Thus Leo the Great describes the incarnation by reference to Proverbs 9:1 ("Wisdom has built herself a house"), taking this text to mean that "lowliness is taken on by majesty, weakness by power, mortality by eternity."[22] It is the divine Word, then, who by a self-emptying that takes the form of an act of appropriation, *makes humanity his own* — brings into being his own particular humanity. This shift of metaphor

---

orthodoxa 3.16), as indeed Theodore of Mopsuestia had used it to his very different purposes (H. B. Swete, ed., *Theodori Episcopi Mopsuesteni in Epistolas B. Pauli Commentarii* [Cambridge, 1882] II, p. 318).

20. See, e.g., John of Damascus, *De fide orthodoxa* 3.15 (*PG* 94:1053CD).

21. Ibid., 3.18 (*PG* 94:1073A), 6 (*PG* 94:1005B). The idea is no doubt derived from Gregory of Nazianzus.

22. *Tome* 3 (in Norris, *The Christological Controversy*, p. 148).

makes it plain that the agent or agency of the "union" is not external to it, but is one of the "somethings" involved in it; and this revision changes the picture in a significant way because it implies that the "somethings" are neither parallel nor equal — are not "factors" in the same sense. The one — humanity — is real only *in* the reality of the other *(enhypostasia)*, being the "own" humanity — the ensouled body — of the divine Word.[23] The incarnation, then, is understandable only as a salvific act of God designed for the liberation and elevation of human nature "in Christ": it cannot rightly be pictured as a "convergence" of otherwise independent elements.

Now let there be no doubt that such an account of the incarnation accords admirably, as I have indicated, with the language of Chalcedon. Indeed the strategy of introducing the metaphor of "appropriation" has precisely the effect of conforming the original metaphor of "union" or "synthesis" or "mixture" to the Chalcedonian paradigm. To be sure, in doing so, it shores up the conception of christology as an analysis of the makeup of Christ's person, that is, as a kind of sacred physics; but this, after all, is no more than natural. The difficulty in this discourse lies elsewhere — namely in the fact that the sort of christological discourse pursued by Leo, Severus, and John of Damascus tends to misunderstand its own modus operandi. It resorts systematically to analogy and metaphor to convey the meaning of the incarnation — that is, to be specific, it explains the relationship of divine Word and human flesh by reference to a variety of *other* relationships, of the sort that obtain between realities *within* the created order. Nevertheless, this discourse fails in practice to acknowledge its own radically improper and metaphorical character.[24] By taking themselves quite literally, these accounts forget that the divine "nature" of which they speak is no part of the natural order — that is, that it is not of the same order as the human "nature"; and therein they run the risk of reducing themselves to incoherence.

The reason for this can best be grasped by taking a closer look at the term "nature." For commonsense purposes, "nature" meant, then as now,

---

23. See John of Damascus, *De fide orthodoxa* 3.9 (*PG* 94:1017AB), 12 (*PG* 94:1029B).

24. There is a further difficulty to be noted in the fact that many of these metaphors cease to illuminate when the relationships to which they allude are no longer recognized. The ancient Stoic theory of mixture *(krasis)*, for example, fails to provide moderns with an illuminating metaphor for much of anything, any more than does an ancient understanding of the relation of soul to body.

"what something is," or "the state of being (a) something." Thus the expression "human nature" connoted, for Christians of the fifth and following centuries, the state of being a created composite of rational soul and body; and this characterization qualified as normal, literal language. It was this state upon which the divine Word entered when he assumed the "measures," as Cyril of Alexandria might have put it, of human existence. Furthermore, such an act of incarnation, while surely not itself a "natural" occurrence, made a degree of sense if one acknowledged the truth that humanity, as the creature fashioned "after the image" of God, bears a certain analogy to the divine Word; for in that case the person of Christ would seem to embody a drawing of like together with like.

On the other hand, this happy analogy seemed to dissipate once one attempted to indicate, in similarly ordinary and literal language, the meaning of the expression "divine nature." For while it is possible to distinguish the nature of humanity from that of other sorts of beings within the created order by the enumeration of a few significant *differentiae,* the contrast between a creature — even a rational creature — and the Uncreated could in the end, it seemed, be expressed only by a systematic exclusion of all creaturely characteristics from the divine nature. Thus "divine nature" had to connote that which is non-mutable, non-temporal, non-material, non-passible — and the like; and such language, calculated as it is to stress the logical contrariety of the divine and human "natures," would appear to render the incarnation not so much implausible as inconceivable, and any statement of it an oxymoron. Classical christology thus appears to insist upon a synthesis or union of *incompatibles* — precisely because it takes its physical models too seriously.

One might of course contend that much of such negative language is, for practical purposes, little more than rhetorical in its function. It is intended to evoke the wonder, the mystery, and the exaltedness of God, much as Leo the Great does when he speaks of "lowliness . . . taken on by majesty, weakness by power. . . ."[25] But this response, while not false in what it asserts, is far too easy. The language of classical christology, which emerged precisely in the disputes of which the Chalcedonian *Definition* was the focus, was most commonly employed, as I have said, to serve as the idiom of a kind of sacred physics. Hence even if this language did serve the legitimate purposes of rhetoric — that is, the purposes of evocation and

25. See n. 22 above.

persuasion — that was not its primary intent. Its primary intent was to *explain* or to *show* how it is possible to speak consistently of the divine Word's appropriation of the human way of being: to construct, as it were, an analysis of the constituents of the Christ. It was to this end, accordingly, that the discourse about natures was shaped. And for these purposes, it seemed necessary both to *say* what one meant by "divine nature" and to take the definition that one produced with complete and literal seriousness, as though the two "natures" were entities *on the same level,* different locations, as it were, on the same map — and this even though the *relation* between the two natures could be conveyed only by a series of highly, and admittedly, improper analogies. Thus, for example, one was put in the position of using the analogy of total mutual interpenetration *(krasis)* to describe the relation of two substances one had previously defined as mutually opposed in nature.

Such a procedure is, to say the least, perplexing; and for just this reason, most modern students of the classical discourse about the person of Christ have been disposed to discount that entire earlier enterprise. This reaction, however, while understandable, has itself failed to deal with the problem that evoked it. In simply dismissing the christology that grew up in the course of the period between, roughly, 375 and 700, modern theology does not appear to have questioned or reexamined the sense of the radical inconsistency between God and humanity that informed the accepted version of the doctrine of two natures. Even if it has not attempted the same sort of sacred physics, it seems even more obsessed than the ancients with a sense of the incompatibility, not so much between human and divine "natures," as between discourses in which God is cast as an actor and those in which human beings are the agents. Moreover, it is less disposed than were the shapers of the classical style in christology to tolerate, and even sometimes to learn wisdom from, its own moments of incoherence. Consequently it struggles, in a contest of uncertain issue, with a new type of Monophysitism — a tendency, in the face of its own strong sense of the incompatibility of divine and human agencies, to reduce the Christ not to a God fitted out with the vestiges of humanity but to a human being adorned with the vestiges of divinity.

What classical and contemporary christologies have in common, then, is a tendency — to use the familiar vocabulary of the ancients — to imagine that in speaking of a divine and a human "nature" one is speaking of two *interchangeable contraries* — not unlike a Queen and a Knight which, if they

173

sit on the same chessboard, cannot, given the rules of the game, inseparably occupy the same square at the same time. Indeed, the one that moves "takes" the other, performing even as one or the other "nature" does in a Monophysite christology. One might of course, with the problems of christology in mind, invite people to *imagine* a Queen and a Knight occupying the same square on the same board; and one might hope, in doing so, that the very oddity of the notion would, in the manner of all startling metaphors, trigger insight into the meaning of the incarnation. Indeed I venture to think that this is precisely the force of christologies like those of Leo, Severus, or John of Damascus: by the elaborate lengths to which they go in the effort to say something that is, in the end, unsayable under the tacit rules of their game, they evoke a vision of the unity of Word and flesh, God and humanity, that pierces beyond the limitations of their discourse. The trouble is that they would be bound to repudiate any such account of their enterprise, for the good enough reason that they seem, in spite of themselves, to think that the word "nature" can be used of God in the same sense that it is used of humanity.

This belief, though, which lies at the root of the picture of God and humanity as interchangeable contraries, is precisely what needs to be examined critically. Apples and oranges are interchangeable contraries — mutually inconsistent because of their differences, but interchangeable in that both can be assigned to the category of edible fruits. Creator and creature, however, are neither different in this sense nor interchangeable in this sense, since *there is no overarching category in which both can be classified.* "God," if the monotheistic hypothesis is correct, does not fall into any class, even if human beings do; and that circumstance, while it certainly marks a difference between God and *any* creature, does not mark the sort of difference that is discerned between people and trees, apples and grapes, or (in chess) Queens and Knights. And to the extent that this is true, then the sort of incompatibility that obtains between contraries cannot be thought to obtain between God and creatures. It is in failing thoroughly to explore this vertiginous thought that both classical and modern christologies have, as it were, spiked the gun of their sacred physics.

Further reflection, then, is needed on the force of the "negative" theology — that is, on the force of expressions like "non-mutable," "non-passible," "non-temporal," and "non-spatial" when they are applied to God. The general assumption, no doubt stemming from the very use of physical models for the incarnation, seems to have been that such terms actually do serve to *put God in a category* of some sort. Occasionally, however — and most notably perhaps in the case of the Cappadocian response to neo-Arianism — they have in effect been taken to intimate instead that God is *apeiros* — infinite, not capable of being categorized — and hence not capable of being grasped in human concepts. This interpretation, moreover, is commended by the consideration that a strictly negative theology, if it is, *per impossibile*, construed to classify God, can do so only by marking God off as, so to speak, not an ordinary contrary but as the *contradictory* of any creaturely reality; and this would seem to imply in turn the paradox that one can only speak of the Creator in the absence of creatures. In fact, however, as both classical and modern christological discourse testify, it is of the essence of Christian faith — and not of Christian faith alone — that one speaks of God conjointly with creatures, as, for example, "with us." Thus it would seem that a negative theology is best interpreted as saying precisely that the *difference* between God and humanity is à matter neither of contrariety nor of contradiction, that God is not related to us as an element or factor or reality that is either interchangeable with the creature as a contrary (i.e., a different thing of the same general sort) or incompatible with the creature as its utter negation.

IV

And curiously enough it is the Council of Chalcedon's *Definition* — as distinct from most of the christologies it has generated — that allows room for such a conclusion and for the rethinking to which it might lead. If, as I have suggested, the Chalcedonian discourse about natures and hypostases provides what is essentially a rule of predication, a reflective formulation of the way in which the traditional narrative about Christ speaks of him, then it is has to be construed as noncommittal with regard to the logical relation between the set of "God-befitting" predicates (which it fails in any case to enumerate) and those that construct the meaning of "human nature." What it insists upon is a threefold scheme.

First, it insists that there can be no reason to talk about a "Christ" (and *a fortiori* an "incarnation") save as an event which, being salvific, can only be construed as a self-manifestation of God in the Word. Whatever species of sacred physics one may happen to favor, ancient or modern, the impulse for indulging in it in the first place is faith's acknowledgment that in Christ *God* is with us — that a relation with Christ entails and is an encounter with God. The ultimate subject of christological predication is, then, a divine subject, spoken of in the way that people normally speak of God.

But in the second place it insists that to talk about Christ is to talk about one whose being humans share, and therefore one whose calling and destiny they *may* share. That is, to talk about Christ is to talk about him in straightforwardly human terms.

Finally, it insists that these ways of talking are indeed different, and not to be confused. It does not, however, define the *nature of this difference:* and it is in that sense that the *Definition* of Chalcedon can be judged merely to have stated the terms of the christological problem. If interpreters of Chalcedon, friendly and unfriendly, have tended, by reason of a misapprehension of the status and function of their sacred physics, to render this difference as a relation of logical contrariety, thus tacitly making of God and humanity differing items of the same order, that is understandable, but neither it nor the confusion it entails is requisite.

In stating the "terms of the christological problem," Chalcedon, wittingly or not, defined an agenda and thus posed a question. And the question — the challenge — was not how to fit two logical contraries together into one, as its ancient and modern interpreters have all but uniformly supposed, but how to dispense with a binary logic in figuring the relation between God and creatures. Maybe after all, suggests Chalcedon, God and humanity are not related as "yes" and "no" or "off" and "on." And this *theological* issue is the real agenda item it defines.

Journal of Ecclesiastical History, Vol. 44, No. 3, July 1993

Diogenes Laertius and the Apostolic Succession

by ALLEN BRENT

The cultural and historical location of the concept of διαδοχή in second century claims about the apostolic succession has been widely debated. In England, under the influence of Ehrhardt, the term is generally taken to be used by analogy with the sacerdotal succession of Jewish high priests, and to derive from the influence of James the Just on Jewish Christianity.[1] In Germany, on the other hand, following Campenhausen, διαδοχή has been understood in terms of continuity of doctrine, in which references to James in the sources are regarded as pure legend constructed to make the point of such continuity in a picturesque way.[2] Both Ehrhardt and Campenhausen, and their respective followers, regard the διαδοχή of teachers in the literature of the Hellenistic philosophical schools as quite incidental, without any close relation to the Christian usage. In this article I will argue the contrary, that there are in fact integral connections between the Hellenistic literature of the philosophical successions, and the development of the idea of the apostolic succession in the late second century, where perhaps the true origin of the Christian concept is to be found.

Ehrhardt argued cogently for the influence of the apocalyptic concerns of the late second century upon the development of the Eusebian succession lists, which he associated with the hieratical succession of the Maccabees.[3] Both Hippolytus and Eusebius were influenced by that tradition in the emphasis on the bishop as high priestly successor to the

---

A first draft of this paper was read to Professor C. Stead's seminar at Cambridge in 1989. I acknowledge with thanks the contributions of Dr Ernst Bammel, Dr Caroline Bammel, and Dr Lionel Wickham.

[1] A. A. J. Ehrhardt, *The Apostolic Succession in the First Two Centuries of the Church*, London 1953; W. Telfer, *The Office of a Bishop*, London 1962.

[2] H. von Campenhausen, 'Der urchristliche Apostelbegriff', *Studia Theologica* i. fasc. I–II (1947), 96–120 and 'Die Nachfolge des Jakobs', *Zeitschrift für Kirchengeschichte* lxiii (1952–3), 133–44.

[3] Ehrhardt, *Apostolic Succession*, 44–61, cf. Telfer, *Office of a Bishop*, ch. iv.

apostles in the former,[4] and in the appearance of James at the head of all succession lists in the latter.[5] Both reflect the Christianising of apocalyptic themes latent in Josephus.[6] A parallel influence on both is to be seen, moreover, in Julius Africanus, like Hippolytus an early third-century author of a chronicle of world history the significance of which was eschatological, anxious to show in such a context that the priestly and royal lines of the Maccabees continued in Christ.[7]

Ehrhardt, however, mistakenly reads back into the second century the influence of the lists of high priests as critical both on Irenaeus and Hegesippus, and on Clement (I Corinthians xliv. 3), in the development of their concept of succession, and so ignored the influence of διαδοχή in the Greek philosophical schools. His position is summed up in the questionable statement: 'the main purpose of Sotion in establishing the heads of philosophical sects was the elucidation of the progress of philosophical research. No such intention can be proved for the episcopal lists, and therefore such similarities as exist are on the whole superficial.'[8] I will argue that the concept of διαδοχή and the historiographic form adopted in that *genre* of literature of which Diogenes Laertius' *The Successions of the Philosophers*,[9] is our surviving representative, are far more important for our understanding of the development of the idea of apostolic succession than Ehrhardt admitted. A careful analysis of Diogenes as representative of a whole *genre* of historiography about philosophers and their schools will reveal certain specific and fundamental connections between such historiography and Justin, Irenaeus, Hegesippus, Hippolytus, and the Clementine literature, which have been overlooked in the discussion dominated, at least in English-speaking quarters, by Ehrhardt's thesis. We will see that Hippolytus' extraneous idea of a specifically sacerdotal succession has been falsely imposed upon the essentially scholastic view of succession in these earlier writers.

The Roman community in the second century

The Church of Rome of the mid- to late second century resembled a collection of philosophical schools, whilst no doubt emphasising the religious and liturgical basis for the community's life more than was usual for such schools. Though Hippolytus may associate the 'grace of teaching'

---

[4] *Apostolica Traditio* 3. 2–4.   [5] Ehrhardt, *Apostolic Succession*, 63–5ff.

[6] *Antiquitates Judaicae* xiii. 11. 301 cf. 20. 10.   [7] *Ad Aristidem* iv.

[8] Ehrhardt, *Apostolic Succession*, 44.

[9] I prefer the title *Successions* to the Byzantine *Lives* (βιῶν) employed by R. D. Hicks in his edition, Diogenes Laertius, *Lives of Eminent Philosophers*, Cambridge, Mass. 1925. I show below that, in the Severan age in which he lived (c. AD 205) the *genre* in which he wrote would have suggested the title διαδοχαί, as is clear from the titles used by his predecessors.

(διδασκαλίας) with that of 'high priesthood' (ἀρχιερατείας), in which, as one of the successors (διάδοχοι) of the apostles, he claims to share,[10] we shall show cause to question any such previous sacerdotal association in Clement, Hegesippus, or Irenaeus. For the moment, let us trace in greater detail the scholastic rather than sacerdotal descriptions in the surviving, fragmentary, evidence. Hippolytus attended Irenaeus' lectures and made a summary (σύνταγμα) of them in the form of a small book (βιβλάριδιον).[11]

Irenaeus' community had every appearance of a school, even though he reserves the terms σχολαί or διδασκαλεῖα for heretical groups who had 'left'. Cerdon had his 'school' in which the Marcion who 'succeeded' him was a pupil.[12] Valentinus, who arrived under Hygenus and left under Anicetus, founded a school.[13] Thus we find in numerous passages close association between such terms as διαδεξάμενος, αἱρέσεως τὰς ἀρχάς, and διδασκαλεῖον. Diogenes also sought to give, not only an account of διαδοχή, but also of the ἀρχή of an αἵρεσις, used non-pejoratively, of a philosophical group following 'a certain principle in their treatment of the visible (τὴν λόγῳ τινὶ κατὰ τὸ φαινόμενον ἀκολουθοῦσαν)' or 'with a bias for coherent positive doctrines (πρόσκλισιν δόγμασιν ἀκολουθίαν ἔχουσιν)'.[14]

Although Hippolytus develops this Irenaean attack upon heresy as being merely a school of (Greek) philosophy, in contrast with the Catholic Church, his corporate description of his own group in contrast with that of Callixtus gives the game away. In his *Refutatio Omnium Haeresium* ix. 12. 20, 25 Hippolytus records how his arch-rival Callixtus 'founded a school (συνεστήσατο διδασκαλεῖον) having taught against the church (κατὰ τῆς ἐκκλησίας διδάξας)', whose members 'presume (ἐπιχειροῦσι) to call themselves the Catholic Church (καθολικὴν ἐκκλησίαν ἀποκαλεῖν)'. Callixtus, and not 'presbyter' Hippolytus, however, was to appear later in the Liberian list as the bishop of Rome and successor of St Peter, despite the latter's claim to apostolic succession.[15]

Thus we see that there are few objective facts to which appeal might be made in the light of which a community that is the Catholic Church could be distinguished from a heretical school. Such a description as συνεστήσατο διδασκαλεῖον is not value-free, nor would the heretics or schismatics themselves have accepted it as a tribute to their gnostic learning in comparison with the psychics. Rather διδασκαλεῖον and σχολή

---

[10] *Ap. Trad.* 3. 2–4, cf. proem. 6: οἱ ἀπόστολοι... ὧν ἡμεῖς διάδοχοι τυγχάνοντες τῆς τε αὐτῆς χάριτος μετέχοντες ἀρχιερατείας τε καὶ διδασκαλίας. [11] Photius, *Bibliotheca* 121.

[12] *Adverses Haereses* i. 27. 2: Διαδεξάμενος δὲ αὐτὸν Μαρκίων ὁ Ποντικὸς αὔξησε τὸ διδασκαλεῖον, cf. *Ref.* x. 19.

[13] *Adv. Haer.* i. 11. 1; *Ref.* vi. 38. 2; *Adv. Haer.* i. 13. 1 (ὁ μὲν γὰρ πρῶτος ἀπὸ τῆς λεγομένης Γνωστικῆς αἱρέσεως τὰς ἀρχὰς εἰς ἴδιον χαραχτῆρα διδασχαλείου μεθαρμόσας Οὐαλεντῖνος οὕτως ὡρίσατο); *Ref.* vi. 39. 1; Tertullian, *De Praescriptione Haereticorum* 42.

[14] *Succ.* i. 20.

[15] J. B. Lightfoot, *The Apostolic Fathers*, I: *Clement of Rome*, London 1890, 255.

are prescriptive and pejorative, like σχίσμα and αἵρεσις, at least in the sense in which these terms are used by Christian writers though not by Diogenes. 'School' and 'Church' are simply value judgements applied to what in appearance and organisation are very similar institutions, with, at their head, similar officials, who by this time were claiming to stand in the apostolic teaching succession.

Thus we are in no position to claim as part of any objective historical analysis that the catholic διαδοχή is to be understood in a sacerdotal as opposed to a scholastic sense, as Ehrhardt claimed. From Hippolytus' schismatical point of view what later will be regarded as the one true Catholic Church is a διδασκαλεῖον or a σχολή. But his opponents, such as Callixtus, will for their part regard Hippolytus' community in such terms.

Bardy, in the generation prior to Ehrhardt, contributed to the mistake of granting to the sacerdotal/scholastic distinction an objective reference. Only one part of his picture of the Roman community in the second century is accurate. Roman Christianity would indeed have appeared from the standpoint of Graeco-Roman culture as a collection of different philosophical schools.[16] But Bardy's further contention, that there existed a hierarchy alongside the teachers in the schools, approving some and judging the excesses of others, and finally formalising everything in the pontificate of Victor, goes way beyond the evidence.

The model of Justin Martyr's orthodox community was predominantly that of a school.[17] He disputes with Trypho at Ephesus. He founds a school at Rome, in the house of a certain Martin, by the bath of Timothy.[18] His method is that which was general in the pagan schools. But we should beware of regarding Justin's school as a catechetical institution to provide converts for a quite different, sacerdotally and hierarchically governed Church. From Acts we can discover disciples' names: Evelpiste (born in Cappadocia, slave of Caesar); Hierax (born in Iconium in Phrygia); and a lady named Charito. But they were not all converted by his lectures since Pean declares that his parents had been believers.

Furthermore, the gathered school and the gathered Church in the liturgy would be one and the same. It is not insignificant in this context that Justin's famous description of the eucharist calls the 'president' by the term ὁ προεστώς,[19] which is used most frequently in Diogenes for the

<hr/>

[16] G. Bardy, 'Les écoles romaines au second siècle', *Revue d'histoire ecclésiastique* xxviii (1932), 501–32. See also G. La Piana, 'The Roman Church at the end of the second century', *Harvard Theological Review* xviii (1925), 201–77. For a more recent analysis see also P. Lampe, 'Die stadtrömischen Christen in den ersten beiden Jahrhunderten', *Wissenschaftliche Untersuchungen zum Neuen Testament* ii (1987), 18, where order is correctly seen as more fluid before the pontificate of Victor. [17] *Dialogus* 1. 2; 3. 1; 9. 1.
[18] *Acta Justina* 3. 3, ed. Knopf-Krüger, Tübingen 1929, 16. Cf. the study of the organisation of Greek philosophical schools as arising within the ambience of the Greek house in R. E. Wycherley 'Peripatos: the ancient philosophical scene', *Greece and Rome* viii (1961); ix (1962). [19] 1 *Apologia* 65, 66.

head or founder of a philosophical school: ''Ακαδημαϊκῆς μὲν οὖν τῆς ἀρχαίας προέστη Πλάτων, τῆς μεσῆς 'Αρχεσίλαος, τῆς νέας Λακύδης (Plato founded the Old Academy, Archesilaus the Middle, and Lakudes the New)', and so on for the 'founders' of other schools.[20] Thus it is arguable that he who celebrates Justin's eucharist is regarded more like the founder of a philosophical school, and derives his presidency from that fact rather than from a hierocratically conceived authority.[21]

It is of course important not to secularise the Graeco-Roman philosophical school. As the genuine account in Diogenes of Theophrastus' will shows, there is a temple connected with Aristotle's school, into which his statue is to be put along with other consecrated objects (ἔπειτα τὴν τοῦ 'Αριστοτέλους εἰκόνα τεθῆναι εἰς τὸ ἱερὸν καὶ τὰ λοιπὰ ἀναθήματα ὅσα πρότερον ὑπῆρξεν ἐν τῷ ἱερῷ).[22] The altar is to be repaired (ἐπισκευασθῆναι δὲ καὶ τὸν βωμόν). Furthermore, the property of the school is to be held 'in joint possession, like a temple' (ἀλλ' ὡς ἂν ἱερὸν κοινῇ κεκτημένοις).[23] A Christian community organised on the pattern of a philosophical school, however reversed some of the analogies might be, could therefore have its cultic moments. The 'founder' or προεστώς of the school might offer the 'pure sacrifice' of Malachi, as Justin describes the eucharist,[24] as part of the liturgy of the school, just as offering a cock to Aesclepius might be part of the ritual of a Socratic school, however loath the early Fathers may have been to make verbally explicit such eucharistic analogies with pagan cultic acts.

Our picture of the Roman community, conceived on the model of a philosophic school, now invites us to compare more closely the text of Diogenes Laertius and its encoded historiographic message about the true character of the schools of Greek philosophers and their successions, and the literature of the apostolic succession in Hippolytus, the Clementines, Irenaeus and Hegesippus. We shall draw₁ out formal correspondences between the former and the latter.

[20] *Succ.* proem. 19.

[21] For a recent serious challenge to my argument, published too late for the more detailed consideration that it deserves, see E. Bammel, 'Sukzessionsprinzip im Urchristentum', *Studia Ephemeridis 'Augustinianum'* xxxi (1990), 63–72. Bammel argues, on the basis of an inscription published by Schubart in 1917, that the original significance of διαδοχή was juridicial, and was the means by which pagan priests established the regularity and good order of their cult in the eyes of the Roman emperor. Thus its Christian use was primarily sacerdotal but also apologetic. My reply, briefly, would be in line with that of J. Gluckner, 'Antiochus and the late academy', *Hypomnemata: Untersuchungen zur Antike und zu ihrem Nachleben* lvi (1978), 149–58ff., who argues the essential distinction between διάδοχος as the heir to the teaching of a set of ideas and the possession of διάδοχα or the property of a school as such. The critical text here is the *Epistula Plotinae* in *Inscriptiones Graecae*, ed. J. Kirschner, ii, iii, Berlin 1913, 1099.

[22] *Succ.* v. 51–2.   [23] Ibid. v. 52–3.

[24] *Dial.* 117.

Diogenes Laertius and the Successions of the Philosophers

In his *Successions of the Philosophers*, Diogenes Laertius writes in an existing tradition of historiography that charts the inter-relationships between systems of philosophical thought in terms of relations between persons rather than abstract ideas. A modern but equally historiographical account would, in almost complete contrast, describe ideas apart from the human beings who conceive them in a depersonalised, ideal perspective, as though concepts in such an ideal form could enjoy relations with each other apart from their human agents. Thus the notion of the διαδοχή is fundamental as a description of how one named individual succeeds another as head of a school, and how a philosophical system itself grows.

Diogenes mentions as his sources such men as Sotion (200–170 BC), Sosicrates of Rhodes, and Heraclides of Callatis or Alexandria, Antisthenes of Rhodes, Lembus (181–146 BC), and Alexander (viii. 24). Sotion's book was entitled *Successions of the Philosophers* (Διαδοχαὶ τῶν φιλόσοφων) and is regularly cited by Diogenes as ἐν Διαδοχαῖς,[25] as is Sosicrates' work.[26] As a variant, Sosicrates' book is on one occasion described as 'the Successors' (ἐν τρίτῃ Διαδοχῶν),[27] and Callatis is described as having written the 'Succession' (Διαδοχὴν).[28] As these works have not survived, it is not evident how Diogenes' historiographic method in describing the philosophical schools was different from theirs. If we can discover how he differed from them, we will be able to discern the specific purpose with which he wrote, and his own individual concept of what philosophy was. Diogenes' work has been convincingly dated at *c.* AD 217, and was therefore contemporaneous with the conflict between Callixtus and Hippolytus. Thus there can be no direct dependence between them, but both draw on a common historiographical tradition about philosophic διαδοχαί.[29]

What is to our purpose, however, in view of his likely dating, is the fact that Diogenes ends his succession of the philosophers effectively with Epicurus (341–271 BC) and Chrysippus (282–206 BC). Any later Greek writers that he mentions (Plutarch,[30] Epictetus,[31] Sextus Empedokles)[32] are thus treated as commentaries in footnotes to a phenomenon that has taken place but which is to all intents and purposes completed. Latin writers such as Lucretius, Cicero and Seneca are completely ignored. Clearly Diogenes is a cultural purist who believed that only Greek was cultural, and that the golden age was past.

In Diogenes' scheme there are two origins or ἀρχαί of philosophy, one from Anaximander, and the other from Pythagoras: 'They are called the Ionic and the Italic. The former ends with Cleitomachus and Chrysippus

---

[25] *Succ.* ii. 12.   [26] Ibid. i. 107; vi. 80; viii. 8.   [27] Ibid. vi. 13.   [28] Ibid. v. 94.
[29] For a full discussion of the dating, see M. Trevissoi, 'Diogene Laerzio: L'età in cui visse', *Rivista di Storia Antica* xii (1908), 482–505. See also R. Hope, *The Book of Diogenes Laertios: its spirit and its method*, New York 1930, 6–7.   [30] *Succ.* ix. 60.   [31] Ibid. x. 6.
[32] Ibid. ix. 87, 116.

and Theophrastus, the latter with Epicurus.'³³ Such a method of classification, however, leads to disparate systems of thought being classed together, as when Anaximander, Anaximenes and Archelaus are associated as a single succession with Socrates and Plato.³⁴ Indeed, the Ionic succession has to be given three concluding philosophers: Clitomachus, who descends from Plato through Speusippus and Xenocrates; Chrysippus, who descends through Antisthenes; and Theophrastus, who concludes the Aristotelian line. Pherekydes, by contrast, has a unilinear succession from Democritus to Epicurus. The links in the chain of succession are weakly drawn (οὗ Δημόκριτος, οὗ πολλοὶ μέν, ἐπ' ὀνόματος δὲ Ναυσιφάνης καὶ Ναυκύδης, ὧν 'Επίκουρος).³⁵ Thus emerge the four great schools of Diogenes' time, the Academic, Stoic, Peripatetic, and Epicurean.³⁶

The description of the relationships between members of the διαδοχαί are not consistently drawn by Diogenes. The successions, as the books proceed, do not correspond precisely with the outline given in the prologue. Telauges is the son of Pythagoras, and in the prologue he is described as the teacher of Xenophanes,³⁷ although in the latter's *Life* he is not mentioned as such.³⁸ In the *Life* of Empedocles he does not appear as the subject's teacher,³⁹ though that is his description in the *Life* of Pythagoras.⁴⁰ In ix. 21 Parmenides is considered the pupil of the Pythagoreans and not Xenophanes as we would expect from i. 15.⁴¹

Undoubtedly these, along with other features of his account, indicate Diogenes' work to be a 'compilation very carelessly thrown together by a collector...not only the materials of others, but also fragments of their outlines'.⁴² But there remains nevertheless a further question, namely whether his use of the concept of διαδοχή as such did not serve a definite purpose. It is arguable that it was necessary for his purpose to establish that there was a διαδοχή, even though the precise details of its members and their chronological relationship were relatively unimportant, and could therefore be left so haphazardly drawn in his text.

Diogenes writes with one obvious and incontestable purpose, and that is to demonstrate, in opposition to his predecessors who wrote Διαδοχαί in the same literary *genre*, that philosophy had its origin wholly within Greek culture. His thesis is that Sotion, as well as Aristotle in the *Magicus*, had been quite wrong in beginning the διαδοχαί of the philosophers with Persian or Babylonian and Assyrian magicians, with Indian gymnophysists, or with the Holy Ones of the Druids. Instead, Diogenes asserts: 'They ignore the achievements of the Greeks from whom not only philosophy but the human race itself begins, when they attribute them to the barbarians.'⁴³

³³ Ibid. proem. 14.　　　³⁴ Ibid.　　　³⁵ Ibid. 15.
³⁶ Hope, *The Book of Diogenes Laertios*, 133–4.　　³⁷ *Succ.* i. 15.　　³⁸ Ibid. ix. 21.
³⁹ Ibid. viii. 50.　　　⁴⁰ Ibid. viii. 42.
⁴¹ For a full discussion of these see Hope, *The Book of Diogenes Laertios*, 133–9.
⁴² Ibid. 138.　　　⁴³ *Succ.* i. 3.

To support this claim, Diogenes advances three arguments. The first, involving an appeal to Greek mythology, uses the fact that Musaeus, amongst the Athenians, wrote a cosmology and constructed a sphere, and Linus, amongst the Thebans, wrote on creation, the sun and moon, and the growth of animals and plants. Musaeus was son of Eumolpus, and Linos was the son of Hermes and the Muse Ourania, so that both the human race and philosophy begin together with the Greeks, in the age when the gods consorted with humans.[44]

His second reason is to claim that 'philosophy' as a Greek word, could not be translated into any barbarian language, and was first used by Pythagoras.[45] His third reason is, I would claim, the one that he finds personally the most cogent. He anticipates the objection that Orpheus the Thracian should be regarded as the first philosopher and thus a non-Greek. Diogenes now uses neither an objection from Greek mythology nor from philology but one which involves what he holds to be the true nature of philosophy itself: 'I do not know if he ought to be called a philosopher who speaks publicly such things about the gods, nor what he must be described as who does not scruple to attribute (προστρῖψαι) to the gods every human condition (πᾶν τὸ ἀνθρώπειον πάθος)'.[46] In view of the late second- to early third-century historical context in which Diogenes writes, this would appear to be his real objection to ideas which he would consider both 'barbarian' and 'non-philosophic'. We have here the very same sort of objection as that which Celsus made against the claims of Christianity to the status of real philosophy.[47] Thus Diogenes reflects, and contributes to, the currents of opinion in which Irenaeus and Hippolytus, and their contemporaries, were themselves involved.

Diogenes regards his succession lists as establishing the coherence of Hellenistic civilization in terms of a common philosophical culture. Similarly Irenaeus, before Hippolytus, had used the historiographical method of establishing a διαδοχή between a series of teachers as a guarantee of the coherence of a common Christian doctrine, untainted culturally by paganism. He drew up the episcopal succession list for the see of Rome, and claimed that it was typical of similar lists for other sees.[48] And he did so in a context in which Christian communities, as we have seen, resembled conflicting philosophical schools. But Hippolytus uses somewhat differently the historiographic method to which Diogenes attests.

He draws the διαδοχαί, the successions of the heretics, and not as Irenaeus had done, of named apostles and bishops, to show that they derived their origins from Greek philosophers and not from Judaeo-Christian culture. His claim is that the ultimate origin of heresy does not lie, as Irenaeus had asserted, behind a succession of teachers beginning with those, such as Simon Magus, who opposed the apostles in their day. Rather the heretical schools are the descendants of pagan philosophical

[44] Ibid. [45] Ibid. i. 4, 12. [46] Ibid. i. 5.
[47] Origen, *Contra Celsum* i. 69–70; ii. 30–1; iv. 18 etc. [48] *Adv. Haer.* iii. 3. 2–4.

schools in disguise, which in turn go back to the snake-worship of the Naasenes.[49] Thus he parallels Diogenes' scheme in which there are two origins or ἀρχαί of philosophy, one from Anaximander, and the other from Pythagoras. The diverse antecedents of heresy must be shown to emanate from a common ἀρχή in pagan culture.

Thus we find Diogenes' historiography reflected in Hippolytus' methodology in the *Refutatio*. The schema of succession is, in critical parts, highly artificial yet as a historiographical device it serves the author's purpose. Diogenes, writing in the mid-third century AD, brought his διαδοχαί to an end in the mid-second century BC. For him the philosophical possibilities were exhausted and philosophy brought to its most developed form with Platonism, Stoicism, Aristotelianism, and Epicureanism. There is to be no further development, since as Plato claimed, change is an illusion, and as Aristotle held, development has a final end. So too with Hippolytus Christian heresies are διαδοχαί from pagan philosophers. So the διαδοχή of Valentinus from Plato and Pythagoras, Justin from Herodotus, Marcion from Empedokles, Basilides from Aristotle, and Noetus from Heracleitus. The connections are highly tendentious. Empedokles' first two principles, Strife and Love, for example, are equated with Marcion's two Gods by a tortuous discussion intended to show that Marcion is a 'stealer of [his] arguments' (κλεψιλόγος).[50] There are no new heresies and no new orthodoxy for Hippolytus, any more than there are for Diogenes, even though the latter may understand 'heresy' in a less pejorative sense.

Diogenes' historiographical tradition is reflected, although in a different way, in another group of second century writings on the theme of succession, namely in the Clementines. To this we now turn.

Succession in Diogenes and in the Clementines

Diogenes presented, not a historical argument, but a historical myth: his purist thesis of culture is hence encoded in mythopoeic logic. He asserts that philosophy is a wholly Greek cultural phenomenon which reached its natural completion with Chrysippus, Theophrastus, and Epicurus. The legend of the seven sages or wise men of Greece is taken and reshaped in order to argue his point mythopoeically. Beginning with the usual seven wise men of Greek antiquity, Thales, Solon, Periander, Cleobulus, Chilon, Bias, Pittacus, he brings their number up to eleven or twelve by claiming that 'with these are numbered (τούτοις προσαριθμοῦσιν) Anacharsis the Scythian, Myson of Chen, Pherecydes of Syros, Epimenides the Cretan; and by some even Pisistratus the tyrant'.[51]

---

[49] In *Ref.* v. 6. 3 the claim αἴτιος τῆς πλάνης ὄφις indicates that, convinced by his new discovery of gnostic texts, Justin (1 *Apol.*) was wrong in ascribing to Simon Magus the origin of all heresy, as was Irenaeus (*Adv. Haer.* i. 22. 2–23, 1–4): M. Marcovich, *Hippolytus' Refutatio Omnium Haeresium*, Berlin–New York 1986, 34–5.

[50] *Ref.* viii. 29–30.   [51] *Succ.* i. 13.

These eleven or twelve wise men or σοφοί are kept quite distinct from the φιλοσοφοί. They exist for Diogenes, as it were, in the *Urzeit* of Greek civilization. Their unity in a common Greek civilization is not established by a comparison of the distinctiveness of the philosophical ideas which they shared in contrast to the barbarians, any more than the relationship between the succession of philosophers was drawn as a succession of ideas rather than of persons. The wise men write letters to each other, and by means of this literary fiction, their unity, and thus the coherence of Greek civilization, is represented in the *Urzeit*. Thales writes to Pherekydes, and then to Solon, and Pherekydes replies.[52] Solon writes to Periander, then to Epimenides, to Pisistratus and to Croesus. Pisistratus also writes to Solon.[53] Throughout the list runs a similar chain of epistolary inter-relations.[54]

A direct parallel to this is to be found in the contemporary development of episcopal succession lists witnessed by Irenaeus and Hippolytus where the apostles are outside the succession itself in the Christian *Urzeit*. Both Pherekydes and Thales initiate their respective successions, though they are not the first members. These two wise men of Greece, like the apostles, stand outside the succession from which the two separate successions of Anaximander and Pythagoras, like those of Linus or Clement from Peter, begin. Thus Thales communicates with Pherekydes and Pherekydes communicates with Thales. Anaximenes, 'pupil of Anaximander' (ἤκουσεν Ἀναξιμάνδρου),[55] who begins one philosophical succession, writes to Pythagagoras who begins the other,[56] and Anaximenes replies.[57] Thus the two rival successions maintain the unity of a common philosophical and Greek culture as philosophers, just as the wise men did in the *Urzeit*. Most of the wise men of the *Urzeit* of Hellenistic culture have no role other than to personify the beginnings of cultural identity. The majority of the apostles perform the same function. Only Thales and Pherekydes, amongst the wise men, produced successions of philosophers through Anaximander and Pythagoras; only Peter and James amongst the apostles and their associates produce successions through Clement and the Roman list, and through the Jerusalem list.

The Pseudoclementines do not refer directly to any successions of bishops like the successions of philosophers in Diogenes and his predecessors. Indeed such direct reference is excluded by the conditions of pseudonymity. The scene depicted to give credence to the pseudonymic device is in past time, where any mention of successors would destroy the impression that we are in the presence of the pristine ἀρχαί of the succession lists. In the *Urzeit* we see only the relationship of St Peter with his immediate successor, Clement, and with James the Lord's brother.

[52] Ibid. i. 43–4, 122.   [53] Ibid. i. 53, 64–7.

[54] Chilon to Periander (i. 73); Pittacus to Croesus (i. 81); Bias none; Cleobulus to Solon (i. 93); Periander to the wise men and then to Procles, with a letter from Thrasybulus to him (i. 99–100); Anacharsis to Croesus (i. 105); Myson none; Epimenides to Solon (i. 113–15).   [55] Ibid. ii. 3.   [56] Ibid. ii. 4.   [57] Ibid. viii. 49.

Such literature therefore envisages a Christian *Urzeit*, which parallels Diogenes' *Urzeit* inhabited by the wise men, from whom the philosophers ultimately derived the wisdom which they loved. In the Christian *Urzeit*, the place of the seven, eleven, or twelve 'wise men', is taken by the twelve apostles. The philosophers' place is taken by the bishops. The apostles begin the succession, but are not included in it. Though the number and the names of the twelve wise men, like the twelve apostles, are important for the encoded message they carry about a united and uncontaminated culture from which doctrine derives its ἀρχή, only two of the wise men (Pherekydes and Thales) and only one or perhaps two (Peter, perhaps James) of the apostles actually initiate teaching successions.

It is true that though Thales and Pherekydes do not communicate by letter with those who begin the philosophic succession, Peter the apostle does communicate by letter with James, 'Lord and bishop of the Holy Church'.[58] But James's position, whether he ranks with the bishops or with the apostles, was always ambiguous, as was Paul's, since before Luke–Acts the apostolic ministry of the Church was not limited to the Twelve. Both James and Paul prefigure as apostles in the list of eyewitnesses in 1 Cor. xv. 3–9. Clement, unambiguously a bishop, is instructed to write to James 'Lord and bishop of bishops who rules the Holy Church of the Hebrews at Jerusalem, and the churches everywhere founded in the foreknowledge of God'.[59] But there is no pseudepigraphic attempt to produce a letter of James in reply to Clement. Furthermore, a pseudepigraphic reply in the form of a letter from Peter would be too incongruous. Clement, after all, is writing to James after Peter's death, which in itself is incongruous in view of the fact that James's martyrdom probably took place before that of Peter.

James does not reply to Clement's letter, according to the conventions of Diogenes' *genre*, because Peter and James (albeit ambiguously) are, like Thales and Pherekydes, inhabitants of the *Urzeit*, outside the successions they founded, but of which they do not form part. Peter communicates by letter with James – as Pherekydes the ἀρχή of one succession does with Thales as ἀρχή of the other – regarding the preservation of his books of teaching and its true interpretation.[60] But neither from the Christian *Urzeit* communicates directly by letter with Clement. Granted Clement writes to James after Peter's death, on the latter's instruction, setting out the details of his consecration as bishop,[61] while Pythagoras and Anaximander as φιλοσοφοί had no such communication with Pherekydes and Thales as σοφοί. But this simply confirms James's ambiguous status as apostle, corresponding to σοφός, and bishop, corresponding to φιλοσοφός. Indeed there was a further and unrelated early catholic motive which had, as it were, a vested interest in such an ambiguity: James the brother of the Lord must be given apostolic status in recognition of the catholicity of the Jacobean congregations. Such an

---

[58] *Epistula Petri ad Iacobum* 1. 1.
[59] *Epistula Clementis ad Iacobum* 1. 1.
[60] *Epist. Pet. ad Iac.* 2–3.
[61] *Epist. Clem. ad Iac.* 1. 19.

additional motive at work in second-century Christian reflection has therefore distorted the neatness of Diogenes' scheme when applied to the Christian διαδοχή.

But Clement's communication with James can be paralleled from Diogenes if it is regarded as another instance of James as bishop and not as apostle. Pythagoras, the first member of the succession whose ἀρχή was Pherekydes, wrote to Anaximenes, second member of the other succession whose first member was Anaximander and whose ἀρχή was Thales.[62] Thus there was direct communication between the two successions. Likewise Peter, outside the succession, does not communicate by letter directly with Clement third bishop in the succession according to Irenaeus but first according to the Liberian catalogue. Rather he instructs Clement to communicate with James and thus these two successions are also shown to be twin features of a common, early catholic orthodoxy. But the author of the two pseudepigraphic letters that preface the Clementine *Homilies*, whilst operating within the kind of historiographic perspective to which Diogenes bears witness, wished to make a somewhat different point from that of the unity of Greek culture in diversity. Early Catholicism demanded a far more homogeneous unity than that. 'Clement', or the Roman community, is demanding unqualified recognition from 'James', or his Palestinian or Syrian one. Peter is ὁ διὰ τὴν ἀληθῆ πίστιν καὶ ἀσφαλεστάτην αὐτοῦ τῆς διδασκαλίας ὑπόθεσιν τῆς ἐκκλησίας θεμέλιος, and described as κλητός, ἐκλεκτός, ὁ καλὸς καὶ δόκιμος μαθητής, ὁ τῶν ἀποστόλων πρῶτος, etc.[63] For early Catholicism, Christianity, unlike Greek culture, cannot have two ἀρχαί but only one.

We can now see why James is so significant a figure in the two pseudepigraphic epistles. It is that he plays a key literary role in a description of the Christian *Urzeit*. That he played this part because he was 'the Lord's brother' is mentioned,[64] but never emphasised, nor is any putatively sacerdotal authority which may be derived from that relationship. Indeed, throughout the Clementines, the authority of the ministry is as a teaching authority, and presidency at the eucharist is not mentioned. It is the teaching authority and the transmission of right doctrine that is emphasised.

Peter has sent James the books of his preaching,[65] whose contents he is to commit to examined and approved men 'according to the educational method (τότε αὐτῷ κατὰ τὴν ἀγωγὴν παραδοῦναι) that Moses handed on to the seventy who had received his chair (τοῖς τὴν καθέδραν αὐτοῦ παρειληφόσιν)'.[66] The elders, to appear in the later context of Hippolytan sacerdotalism as sharers with the bishop in the high priesthood (ἀρχιερατεία),[67] have no priestly role in the Clementines.[68] Rather, 'by

[62] *Succ.* ii. 3–4; viii. 49. [63] *Epist. Clem. ad Iac.* 1. [64] Ibid. 19. 2.
[65] *Epist. Pet. ad Iac.* 2. 1. [66] Ibid. 1. 3. [67] *Ref.* i proem. 6, cf. *Ap. Trad.* 7.
[68] For a detailed summary of research on the Clementines, see F. Stanley Jones, 'The Pseudo Clementines: a history of research', *Second Century* ii (1982), 1–33, 63–96. Although the Clementines in their final form may be mid-third century and subsequent to

188

reason of the rule delivered to them (κατὰ γὰρ τὸν παραδοθέντα αὐτοῖς κανόνα)', they seek to correct scriptural discrepancies.[69] The authority of the bishop over such elders is a teaching authority. They will only examine others and transmit the books in accordance with the 'mind of the bishop (ταῦτα ἐπὶ τῇ τοῦ ἐπισκόπου γνώμῃ ποιησάμενος)'.[70] The bishop receives the books when they would otherwise be left unattended.[71]

At Clement's consecration too the emphasis is on the succession of teaching. Peter, with foreknowledge of his death, takes Clement by the hand in the presence of the church and says: 'I ordain Clement here your bishop (Κλήμεντα τοῦτον ἐπίσκοπον ὑμῖν χειροτονῶ) to whom I entrust the chair of my discourse (ᾧ τὴν ἐμὴν τῶν λόγων πιστεύω καθέδραν).'[72] Furthermore, the gift of binding and loosing has to do with ruling and interpreting, and not with the forgiveness of sins, as later in the *Didascalia Apostolorum* where the removal of sin in absolution is associated with Christ's priestly role in removing sin by the sacrifice of himself.[73] Hence when Peter gives to Clement authority to bind and loose, he assures him that 'whatever you ordain (χειροτονήσῃ) on earth will have been decreed (δεδογματισμένον) in heaven because you know the rule of the church (ὡς τὸν τῆς ἐκκλησίας εἰδὼς κανόνα)'.[74]

Thus the binding and loosing retains its rabbinic sense of harmonising a body of doctrine. Clement as bishop is not high priest but the elder in the succession of Mosaic teachers who 'is pre-eminent in truth (τὸν ἀληθείας προκαθεζόμενον)'.[75] This teaching theme is further emphasised when Clement tries to refuse τὴν τῆς καθέδρας τιμήν τε καὶ ἐξουσίαν.[76] Peter is pleased because the *cathedra* is not for anyone who desires the chair 'but one whose conversation is pious and who is learned in argument (ἀλλ᾽ εὐλαβοῦς τὸν τρόπον καὶ πολυμαθοῦς τὸν λόγον)'.[77] Salvation is through the hearing of 'lifegiving words', and the connection between ζωοποιοὺς λόγους, 'the rule of the church' (ἐκκλησίας κανόνα), and the καθέδρα held in trust is underlined.[78]

We see therefore that in the Clementines there are certain parallels with the kind of historiography of the succession of philosophical schools represented later by Diogenes Laertius, who drew on his predecessors

Hippolytus, it has been argued that a common and early liturgy underlines both the report of Clement's consecration in *Epist. Clem. ad Iac.* and in *Homilies* 3. 62–71, with the epistle's account as the more original. Furthermore, such an account must underlie the *Grundschrift*, since the passages in the *Homilies* are paralleled in the *Recognitions* (3. 65–6) too: G. Strecker, 'Das Judenchristentum in der Pseudoclementinen', *Texte und Untersuchungen* lxx (1958), 97–115. Such a liturgy would, according to my argument, originate in Irenaeus' time, and predate Hippolytan sacerdotalism. [69] *Epist. Pet. ad Iac.* 1. 3–4.
[70] Ibid. 3. 1. [71] Ibid. 3. 3. [72] *Epist. Clem. ad Iac.* 2. 2. [73] *Ap. Cons.* 2. 25. 9–13.
[74] *Epist. Clem. ad Iac.* 2. 4, cf. for this phrase, Origen *De Principiis* 4. 9: ἐχομένοις τοῦ κανόνος τῆς Ἰησοῦ Χριστοῦ κατὰ διαδοχὴν τῶν ἀποστόλων οὐρανίου Ἐκκλησίας.
[75] *Epist. Clem. ad Iac.* 2. 5, cf. 6. 2–4; 17. 1. I translate τὸν ἀληθείας προκαθεζόμενον as 'pre-eminent' rather than 'preside' here as well as in the Ignatian passages, as far more natural. See A. Brent 'The relation between Ignatius of Antioch and the *Didascalia Apostolorum*', *Second Century* viii (1991), 129–56. [76] *Epist. Clem. ad Iac.* 3. 1.
[77] Ibid. 3. 2; cf. 4. 4; 13. 3. [78] Ibid. 19. 3; 6. 2.

both substantively and formally in the literary *genre* in which he wrote. Whilst there is clearly a rabbinic influence at work too in the reference to the Mosaic elders and their rule of interpretation, the Clementines cannot be analysed purely in those terms. The emphasis on a teaching succession and an educational procedure (ἀγωγή) is also reflected in Greek philosophical schools, as the disputations between Peter and Simon Magus in the house of Zacheus show.[79] The *Grundschrift*, of which the letters form part, is contemporaneous with the age of Hippolytus, and was dated by Strecker at *c.* 220, although they represent, we have argued, a liturgy which predates Hippolytan sacerdotalism. The provenance has been argued to be Roman, though the modern consensus has focused upon Syria.[80] Certainly the rabbinic influence upon the text would support this though the predominantly Hellenistic and 'school' model, presupposed by the texts, should not therefore be ruled out. After all, Lucian, who wrote the *Passing of Peregrinus*, was a citizen of Antioch in Syria.

But let us now re-examine the key texts from Irenaeus, Hegesippus, and Clement, in the light of the argument that the introduction of sacerdotal images into both the idea of succession and the ordination liturgies themselves came comparatively late.

Irenaeus and the διαδοχή

Irenaeus concentrates upon a succession of teachers. He records of the Roman succession list that it is but an example of the διαδοχαί for all the churches ('omnium ecclesiarum...successiones').[81] That succession, moreover, is a teaching succession, for it is about 'that tradition and faith which it has from the apostles and which is proclaimed to mankind and which reaches up to our time through the successions of bishops (per successiones episcoporum)'. At Rome 'the tradition which is from the apostles' is preserved. The point emphasised throughout Irenaeus' comments on the individual names in his list, such as that of Clement, is that the succession marks the reliability of what is taught. Clement 'saw and consorted with the apostles' so that 'the preaching of the apostles was ringing (insonantem) in his ears and the tradition was before his eyes – not alone; since many then survived who had been taught by the apostles'. At the conclusion, with Eleutheros, it is emphasised that through 'this very succession (τῇ αὐτῇ διαδοχῇ ἥ τε τῶν ἀποστόλων) the tradition of the apostles in the Church and the preaching of truth has come down to us'.[82]

Any hierocratic and cultic understanding of the succession is absent from Irenaeus, notwithstanding his use of the Old Testament *cultus* to explain two New Testament passages about the *disciples*, one of which is

[79] *Hom.* 29–58; *Recog.* 19–70. [80] Strecker, 'Das Judenchristentum', 259–70.
[81] *Adv. Haer.* iii. 3. 2. [82] Ibid. iii. 3. 3.

the Last Supper. Firstly, *Adversus Haereses* iv. 8. 3, notwithstanding Telford's interpretation of this passage to mean 'all the apostles of the Lord are priests',[83] is a commentary on Matt. xii. 3–5 and refers throughout to the disciples as they appear on the pages of the gospel. Irenaeus says nothing to associate the levitical priesthood of the disciples here with the apostles, whom he does not mention, let alone assigning to them, as his pupil Hippolytus was to do, the ἀρχιερατεία. The disciples are priests because: (1) all the just have the order of priesthood ('omnes enim justi sacerdotalem habent ordinem');[84] and (2) the disciples had forsaken all their property and family ties to follow Christ. It is because of this material sacrifice that, figuratively, the disciples can be said to 'always serve the altar and God'. Their act places them in the same position as the Levites.[85] They are not doing secular but religious duties in plucking the corn on the sabbath, in the service of their Lord ('dominica perficient ministeria'). Thus they fulfil the law ('legem adimplentes').

Secondly, in iv. 17. 5–18. 1 the words of consecration at the Last Supper are given as the fulfilment of the 'pure sacrifice' which Malachi prophesied.[86] But once again Irenaeus does not associate this with any sacerdotal conception of the apostolic office as such. Christ 'gives counsel to his disciples to offer to God the first fruits of what he has created'. It is this oblation, given to the disciples at the Last Supper, that the Church offers, having received it from the apostles ('confessus est et novi Testamenti novam docuit oblationem; quam Ecclesia ab Apostolis accipiens in universo mundo offert Deo'). The statement that it is the Church's offering (not the bishop's) is repeated twice more.[87] No connection is made here, therefore, between high priesthood and the office of bishop as apostolic successor, as occurs later in Hippolytus. Moreover, both these passages occur quite outside the earlier context of apostolic succession. In both we have an exposition of the New Testament, not in support of church order but in refutation of Marcion's theology of the two Gods of the two Covenants. The passages occur in two of a series of chapters dealing with the relationship between the law and the gospel following Marcion's attack.[88] For example, in the case of the gospel account of the woman with the issue of blood,[89] Irenaeus claims that Christ was not destroying the law but fulfilling it – 'Non enim solvebat sed adimpleat legem' – and acting as high priest ('summi Sacerdotis

---

[83] My italics: W. Telfer, 'Was Hegesippus a Jew?', *Harvard Theological Review* liii (1960), 143–53. Cf. also 'It is thus the sacerdotal character of the bishop which Irenaeus sees as passing from the order of the apostles to the order of bishops': idem, *Office of a Bishop*, 115.

[84] The text of this sentence is problematic. The alternative, Greek reading from John Damascene, *Sacra Parallela* (Holl edition), 61 is πᾶς βασιλεὺς δίκαιος ἱερατικὴν ἔχει τάξιν. In that case, it was the character of Christ as priest that constituted the real justification for the disciples' act rather than their own righteousness. See Irénée de Lyon, *Contre Les Hérésies*, in A. Rousseau and others, *Sources Chrétiennes* C, Paris 1965, Livre IV, 472–3.

[85] *Deut.* xxxiii. 9; x. 9; xviii. 1.   [86] *Mal.* 1. 10–11.   [87] *Adv. Haer.* iv. 17. 6; 18. 1.

[88] Ibid. iv. 2. 2; vi. 2. 4; 8. 1.   [89] Luke xiii. 10–13.

operam perficiens').[90] Thus the law cannot be framed by an evil God and does not resist Christ's work as Marcion would have had to argue. Likewise, it was necessary to argue that Jesus did not allow the disciples to break the sabbath as an act of opposition to an imperfect God whose work required correction in Matt. xii. 3–5. So too at the Last Supper the Jewish sacrifices were not abrogated but completed and fulfilled in the pure sacrifice of the Church throughout the whole world.

If, therefore, Irenaeus was influenced by Hegesippus, as seems likely, and if, as a result of his Palestinian travels, Hegesippus was influenced by the Jacobean succession lists, the allegedly sacerdotal character of those lists have left little trace on Irenaeus. But recent studies, as we shall now see, have seriously questioned the sacerdotalism of Hegesippus on which Ehrhardt's argument rests.

Hegesippus and the Jacobean succession

There is an obstacle to linking Hegesippus' use of διαδοχή with that of Irenaeus, granted the background of the latter's usage in the philosophical schools. Examinations of the fragments of Hegesippus in Eusebius have led many scholars to conclude that Hegesippus' use of the term must be Palestinian-Jewish, must be associated with the alleged 'caliphate' of James, of which some fragments speak at length, and must therefore be within the literary context of the priest–king succession list of the Maccabees. Even Schmittals persisted in following Ehrhardt, about whom he expressed reservations, in concluding that Hegesippus was influenced by the Maccabean lists of priest–kings which 'are the only type that can have been followed by the episcopal succession lists'.[91]

But Hegesippus' Palestinian-Jewish background has not gone un-challenged. Telfer argued that Eusebius was misled; that Hegesippus could not have been of the 'first, sub-apostolic generation',[92] since Eusebius' account shows that he wrote after the time of Eleutheros AD 175–89).[93] Thus he is dependent on a written source for his account of James, on one which uses LXX. Furthermore, this written source has no direct historical memory of the *cultus* before AD 70, since allusions to it are based on garbled interpretations from the Old Testament, as when it is concluded that the 'sons of Rechab' were a group of priests at James's stoning, because in Jer. xxxv the Rechabites are brought into a priest's chambers.[94] It should be noted that Telfer nevertheless holds that the succession lists derive from Jewish–Christian communities in Palestine

[90] *Adv. Haer.* iv. 8. 2.

[91] He uses this quote from Ehrhardt (*Apostolic Succession*, 82) against Campenhausen: W. Smittals, *Office of Apostle in the Early Church*, trans J. E. Steely, London 1971, 288. Cf. von Campenhausen, 'Der urchristliche Apostelbegriff', 96–120, and 'Die Nachfolge des Jakobs', 133–44.   [92] *HE* ii. 23. 3.   [93] Ibid. iv. 22. 4, 3.

[94] Telfer, 'Hegesippus', 143–56.

who traced their episcopate through a Jacobean succession based upon a blood relationship with Christ. If this is the case, it is difficult to see how Hegesippus' references to James's cultic functions can be reliable. The fragment of Hegesippus found in Eusebius, *HE* ii. 23. 4–7, often advanced to support James's sacerdotal position and the succession from him as correspondingly sacerdotal, has been convincingly shown by Zuckschwert to point to exactly the opposite conclusion. James's life of prayer, his abstinence from wine and living flesh, his linen as opposed to woollen clothes, his forgoing the use of the razor, oil, and bath all point to his right to enter the sanctuary as a Nazirite rather than as a priest. The legend reflects movements within the Judaeo-Christian community that were opposed to the priestly conception of ministry through its underlying anti-highpriestly and anti-sacerdotal conceptions of holiness.[95]

Indeed, the hierocratic influence upon the Palestinian tradition, allegedly emanating from the Jacobean community after James's martyrdom, has been exaggerated. Telfer himself, though maintaining that Hegesippus was not a Jew, believed that he had travelled amongst Jewish–Christian communities, refugees after AD 135, in the eastern part of the empire, and 'found the Judaeo-Christians whom he encountered orthodox by his own standards. And he discovered that they attributed their orthodoxy to the fact that, down to their dispersal, they had had a succession of desposyni (kinsmen of Christ) as heads of their church, for most of the time'.[96] Thus Telfer was able to maintain his allegiance to Ehrhardt's thesis. But there are good grounds for questioning the existence of a caliphate derived from James the Lord's brother, and hence from his kinship with Christ, and legitimating a succession of bishops by analogy with the line of blood-related high priests.

A caliphate is a system of government in which, as with the heirs of the Macabees, power and authority are legitimated solely in terms of blood relationship to the charismatic founder of the dynasty.[97] But the Hegesippus fragments do not support this interpretation of the form of church government over which James presided. In *HE* iii. 11, the strong notion of 'caliphate' as involving a blood relationship indispensable to holding office simply does not apply. Symeon is elected unanimously, yet it is mentioned only incidentally that he was the Lord's cousin since his

<hr />

[95] E. Zuckschwerdt, 'Das Naziraät des Herrenbruders Jakobus nach Hegesippus', *Zeitschrift für die neutestamentliche Wissenschaft* lxviii (1977), 276–87: 'die Tradition des lebenslangen Nazirtums...wurde durch den Gegensatz zu dieser priesterlichen Konzeption und durch die sich heraus ergebenden, im Lauf der Zeit zunehmend verschärften Antithesen, die Wiederspeigelungen geschichtlicher Spannungen und hieraus erwachsender Gegensätze zum priesterlich bestimmten' (p. 287).

[96] Telfer, 'Hegesippus', 149.

[97] J. Coulsen, *Les functions ecclésiales aux deux premiers siècles*, Paris 1956, 117–19: 'ces juifs convertis de Jérusalem avaient choisi...celui qui était le plus proche par le sang du "Fils de David." Ainsi, à la morte de Judas Macchabée...s'était continuée la "dynastie" macchabéenne.... Sans doute "la chair et le sang" trouvent encore leur compte dans une telle mentalité'.

father Clopas was Joseph's brother. In *HE* iv. 22. 4–5 Symeon must therefore have been chosen because he was the most suitable and not merely because of his blood line. Thebouthis began the line of heretics because he was not elected in succession to James. If the Jerusalem church had a succession-principle which required a blood-relationship with the Lord, then Thebouthis's candidature would have been ruled out from the start. This does not of course mean that Symeon may not have benefited from his family connections in winning the election, but Ehrhardt's thesis requires that the form of government itself demanded Maccabean blood-relationships, which was clearly not the case.[98]

Stauffer would no doubt cite in his defence, *HE* i. 7. 14 where the δεσπόσυνοι are related to the σωτηριὸν γένος. But Eusebius is quoting verbatim from Julius Africanus' *Ad Aristidem* at this point. I have no doubt that Africanus, like Hippolytus, did hold a belief about the eschatological significance of the σωτηριὸν γένος, whether that phrase be translated 'saving lineage', thus endowing the blood-line with a redemptive significance, or simply as 'Saviour's lineage'.[99] But I question the existence of such a view before Hippolytus' time.

Furthermore, Stauffer also appeals to *HE* i. 7. 1–2 where three bishops are mentioned in Seleucia on the Tigris in the third century who 'nacheinander regiert, die ihren Stammbaum auf den Vater Jesu zurückführten'.[100] But there is no claim here to a succession before these three bishops in a blood relationship. The importance of such a lineage is clearly a new one, arising out of the apocalyptic concerns of the early third century, which Africanus and Hippolytus shared; it is not a time-honoured tradition.[101] At all events, as with Polycrates and the seven bishops in his family before him, family influence in a weak sense is fully consistent with church government, which nevertheless does not require such qualifications.[102] It is equally vain to appeal to the δεσπόσυνοι in the fragment from Hegesippus. Hegesippus had apologetic intentions in showing that Christianity made no political claims when he records the legend of Domitian's contemptuous dismissal of the δεσπόσυνοι.[103]

Moreover Josephus, the near contemporary witness, never connects James's primacy over the church at Jerusalem with a caliphate in the strong sense nor does he support the later identification of both Levitical and Davidic lines necessary if James had been regarded as atypical of the

---

[98] E. Stauffer, 'Zum Kalifat des Jacobus', *Zeitschrift für Religions und Geistesgeschichte* iv (1952), 193–214, in reply to von Campenhausen, 'Die Nachfolge des Jakobs'. The most recent historical study supporting the caliphate view is M. Hengel, 'Jacobus der Herrenbruder – der erst Papst?', in *Glaube und Eschatologie, Festshrift für W. C. Kümmel zum 80 Geburtstag*, Tübingen 1985, 71–104. [99] *HE* i. 6. 11.
[100] Stauffer, 'Kalifat des Jacobus', 200. [101] Ibid. 199–200.
[102] Eusebius, *HE* v. 24. 6, cf. Stauffer, 'Kalifat des Jacobus', 200.
[103] Eusebius, *HE* v. 3. 20, cf. N. Hyldahl, 'Hegesipps Hypomnemata', *Studia Theologica* xiv (1960), 87: 'Die Fragen des Domitian an die Nachkommen Davids...sind Fragen die nur innerhalb einer ganz bestimmten Problemstellung einen Sinn hatten, nämlich bei der Frage nach dem Verhältnis der Christen und der Kaisermacht zueinander.'

Maccabees. James is 'the brother of Jesus' but is nowhere described as a Levitical priest. Moreover, James and his Jewish–Christian community could not have claimed for himself and for his successors the Messianic tradition to which Josephus is held to have appealed in *Antiquitates Judaicae* xx. 200. In such a case, Josephus would have regarded James's position as comparable with that of both Judas of Galilee and the Maccabees.[104] He could not then have been so sympathetic to James, given his desire to rehabilitate main-line Judaism with the Roman government. James is martyred between the death of Festus and the arrival of Cestius Florus. Ananus, the Sadducean high priest, is deposed by Agrippa II for the illegal stoning as the result of the protest of the 'fair-minded' amongst the citizens. Any suggestion that James was a Davidic and priestly figure whose authority derived from a caliphate based upon these two qualifications would have made him far more akin to the Zealots in Josephus' eyes and a definite *persona non grata* given his apologetic concerns.

Regardless of such apologetics, it is a historical fact that Ananus proceeded against James on a purely religious charge, which is why he was stoned and not crucified. The latter would have been his fate, with Florus' consent, if political charges could have been made to stick.[105] In this respect, Josephus' narrative must also count against there being any historical basis to Hegesippus' legend of the δεσπόσυνοι, which was itself an apologetic fiction refuting political charges against Christianity after Domitian's time. There is, therefore, no regal/sacerdotal context in terms of which we can interpret what Hegesippus has to say on episcopal succession. But let us now look specifically at the passage in which he has been held to speak of his composition of the archetype of Irenaeus' Roman succession list.

Hegesippus' use of διαδοχή has been interpreted in two different ways.[106] The first, according to Lightfoot, Turner, Caspar, and Herzogs, was to translate διαδοχὴν ἐποιησάμην μέχρις 'Ανικήτου as 'I composed a succession-list as far as Anicetus', thus beginning the list which Irenaeus was to complete down till the time of Eleutheros. The second, according to Hyldahl, was that there was no list of names and that what Hegesippus established was a succession of doctrine. At Rome he did no more than at Corinth where he observed that, until Primus' time (μέχρι Πρίμου), orthodox doctrine had prevailed.[107] Thus his words are to be translated 'I established a succession [of doctrinal orthodoxy] at Rome until

---

[104] See e.g. Stauffer 'Zum Kalifat des Jacobus', 119–200, 202, 206; S. C. F. Brandon, *Jesus and the Zealots*, Manchester 1967, 28–32, 115–25; Telfer, *Office of a Bishop*, 11–12.

[105] Brandon finds this passage most embarrassing to his case for the political messianism of both Jesus and the Jacobean Church: *Jesus and the Zealots*, 119–21, where he tries to associate the present, allegedly corrupt text of Josephus with doubts about the *Testimonium Flavianum* and possible Christian insertions and editing. For a contrary view, see E. Schürer, *The History of the Jewish People in the Age of Jesus. (17 B.C.–A.D.)*, ed. G. Vermes, F. Millar and M. Black, Edinburgh 1979, i. 428–41.   [106] *HE* iv. 22. 2–3.

[107] Ibid. iv. 22. 2.

Anicetus' time'. Thus he can conclude that, as his travels have shown him, 'In each succession (ἐν ἑκάστῃ διαδοχῇ) and in each city it is the case that the law is preached with the prophets and the Lord'.[108]

Hyldahl's interpretation must be rejected. Hyldahl believed that he had been able to do justice to the objections of Harnack and Zahn that διαδοχή could not mean 'list' or 'catalogue', but avoided having to explain the word as a textual corruption of διατριβήν.[109] This interpretation is, however, anachronistic for the second century. It reflects a historiography, an extreme form of which is to be found in contemporary analytic philosophy, where the history of ideas is written in isolation from the human beings who formulated them. Neither Hegesippus nor Irenaeus would have understand a system of thought in which διαδοχή could refer to disembodied doctrine alone. We have demonstrated by means of Diogenes and his sources, and the connection of those sources with Irenaeus' and especially Hippolytus' use of διαδοχή that it would be quite wrong to interpret this term as referring to a doctrinal succession existing in a conceptual vacuum without any reference to the human participants in that succession. διαδοχή has a quite specific meaning as a *genre* of literature in which the coherence of a system of ideas is charted over time and in which named lists of successors play a role in that description.

Diogenes spoke of a διαδοχή, in the singular, of a work that describes named philosophers in a relation of succession with each other, in combination with epitomes of what they taught. Such a διαδοχή is not unlike the succession list which Irenaeus gives us, interlaced as are the names of Clement and Linus with incidents from their lives, and with, in Clement's case, a credal synopsis of what he taught on the oneness of the Creator who addressed both Abraham and Moses.[110] There is an intimate connection in Greek historiography of ideas between relations between systems of thought and the head of the philosophical school, eponymous or otherwise, who is responsible for transmission. Thus a διαδοχή was never a list or catalogue of names *per se* but a literary *genre* which would include such lists, as is shown in the work of Diogenes and his predecessors.

Let us now turn to the final link in the chain of witness to an alleged sacerdotal succession.

[108] Ibid. iv. 22. 3, cf. Hyldahl, 'Hegesipps Hypomnemata', 100–3. See also H. von Campenhausen, 'Lehrerreihen und Bishofsreihen im 2. Jahrhundert', in *In Memoriam Ernst Lohmeyer*, Stuttgart 1953, 247: 'Daher verzichtet sie auf die Datierung und überhaupt auf jede historische Auswertung und zählt die Apostel nicht etwa selbst schon also das erste Glied sondern nur den jeweiligen Abstand, in dem die späteren Bischofe also Erben ihrer Lehre in dem Zusammenhang der διαδοχή erscheinen.'
[109] Hyldahl, 'Hegesipps Hypomnemata', 101.
[110] *Adv. Haer.* iii. 3. 3, cf. *Succ.* proem. 1; v. 94.

Clement of Rome

Ehrhardt cited various passages in 1 Clement xl–xliv to support his case that the apostolic succession was primarily understood as a sacerdotal succession list.[111] *Prima facie* it is of course possible that Hegesippus' and Irenaeus' conception of the διαδοχή as primarily a succession of teachers is idiosyncratic. In that case, Hippolytus would have derived his sacerdotal perspective, integrated with their teaching model, from Clement and Josephus, even though the latter may not have originally seen the Judaeo-Christian Jacobean community in that light. It might be argued that Hippolytus' emphasis on a teaching succession derived from his attendance at Irenaeus' lectures, especially since the concept of διαδοχή, derived from the schools of philosophers, was used by him to fashion his own method of refuting heresy. According to this view, his hierocratic emphasis continued that of Clement, which Irenaeus, and hence Hegesippus, had excluded. Let us examine Clement's statements to see if they support such a view.[112]

Clement speaks of the apostles making provision in the event of their deaths that 'other approved men (ἕτεροι δεδοκιμασμένοι ἄνδρες) might succeed (διαδέξωνται) to their ministry (or liturgy, λειτουργίαν)'.[113] Should we interpret their ministry (λειτουργία) specifically in terms of the cultic function of eucharistic presidency, as, in other words, their 'liturgy', a term which is reiterated throughout xliv. 2–6? In xliv. 4, after all, strongly cultic language is used: 'For it would be a great sin on our part if we were to cast out of the bishop's office (τῆς ἐπισκοπῆς) those who had blamelessly and holily offered the gifts (προσενεγκόντας τὰ δῶρα).'

It is possible to connect this passage with xl and xli where an unfavourable comparison is drawn between the state of affairs in Corinth due to the deposition of the presbyters, and the Old Testament *cultus*. But it is questionable how far the analogy is to be drawn between the high priest, priests, levites, and laity mentioned there,[114] and cultic functions within the Roman community. There was as yet no single bishop to correspond with the high priest, so that priests and levites alone could correspond with bishop–presbyters and deacons. Furthermore, ἴδιαι λειτουργίαι are connected with the high priest alone, whereas 'to the priests are assigned an individual place, and upon the levites are laid their individual services (ἴδιαι διακονίαι)'. The comparison is not with cultic functions but with the order and discipline of the Old Testament *cultus* in which no group goes beyond 'the appointed rule of its ministry (τὸν ὡρισμένον τῆς λειτουργίας αὐτοῦ κανόνα)', and pleases God in 'its own

---

[111] *Apostolic Succession*, 77–80, 121–2.

[112] von Campenhausen, 'Lehrerreihen und Bishofsreihen', 242: 'An den person-lichen, rechtlichen oder sakramentalen Zusammenhang mit den Aposteln ist ebenfalls noch nich gedacht, und der Gedanke an eine Lehre und Lehrüberlieferung bleibt völlig beiseite'.   [113] 1 Clement xliv. 2.   [114] Ibid. xl. 5.

rank (ἐν τῷ ἰδίῳ τάγματι)'.[115] Indeed, the apostolic function that is emphasised is that of preaching the gospel that Christ received from God, and which the apostles received from Christ and passed on to the bishops and deacons 'in good order (εὐτάκτως) according to the will of God'.[116]

It might however be misconceived to include Clement in this discussion since he has no succession list as such and never uses the noun διαδοχή and the verb διαδέξωνται once only.[117] Undoubtedly Josephus uses this term frequently for the succession of the high priests, and, according to Ehrhardt, did have such a list. How can we decide therefore whether Clement's use of this term should be located in Irenaeus' matrix of the historiography of Greek philosophical schools because of his emphasis on the apostles as teachers, or should instead be interpreted in terms of Josephus' high-priestly succession?

Josephus himself may have adopted the language of the philosophic school to describe Jewish institutions as part of his apologetic purpose. But Clement's use of διαδέξωνται is not the only clue in this passage to the true matrix in which the conceptualisation of ecclesial order was taking place. Those who succeed are also ἐλλόγιμοι ἄνδρες. Now although the verb may be ambiguous as between a scholastic and philosophical *milieu* and a sacerdotal one, the subject of the verb as it is qualified adjectively is not. We find the term ἐλλόγιμος used frequently to describe heads of the philosophical schools in Diogenes.[118] While Josephus, Ehrhardt's principal alleged source for archierocratic succession lists, uses διαδοχή in the required sense,[119] he only uses ἐλλόγιμος of cities and temples in two places in one passage.[120]

Conclusion

We have thus established a clear connection between the διαδοχὴ τῶν ἀποστόλων and the διαδοχὴ φιλοσόφων. The historical *genre* of writing διαδοχαί, the descriptions of the schools as σχολεῖα or σχολαί, with the verb συστῆναι, as well as the use of προεστώς and cognates for presidency of the school or academy, all pointed to that connection. In both cases, moreover, tracing descent, however artificial, between schools of opinions seemed necessary for the demonstration of the truth or falsity of the enterprise, or at least its validity. In the case of both apostolic and philosophic succession the literary form expressed cultural identity by positing an *Urzeit*, whether populated by twelve apostles, or seven, eleven, or twelve wise men, and by the literary and legendary device of establishing an epistolary network between them. The successions, in both cases, outside the *Urzeit*, are themselves fused into one. The correspondence between James and Peter in the Clementines establishes the

---

[115] Ibid. xli. 1–2.   [116] Ibid. xlii. 2.   [117] Ibid. xliv. 2.
[118] *Succ:* viii. 50. 91; ix. 1; x. 21. 25.
[119] *Ant. Jud.* xx. 16. 103, 197, 213, 229, 235 etc.   [120] Ibid. xv. 297–8.

succession, but in this case Clement as first on one succession list intervenes to combine the two lines by writing to James at Peter's instruction. Likewise Anaximenes, pupil of Anaximander with first place in one succession list, writes to Pythagoras who has first place in the other thus establishing the coherence of philosophical schools within a common Hellenistic culture. Finally, we have seen that the philosophic view of succession is of a piece with the character of the Hippolytan community as a Christian, philosophic school.

We have furthermore examined the evidence for the existence of a hierocratic succession before Hippolytus and found it wanting.

POSITION AND PATRONAGE IN THE EARLY CHURCH: THE ORIGINAL MEANING OF 'PRIMACY OF HONOUR'

'The Bishop of Constantinople shall have the primacy of honour after the Bishop of Rome, because Constantinople is new Rome.' This terse sentence, tantalizing both in what it implies and in what it leaves unexplained, is the full text of canon 3 of the First Council of Constantinople (381), as it is usually translated into English.[1] Like the six other canons attributed to that Council (three of which are probably the work of later gatherings), it seems to have had only limited authority in the early Church, until a caucus of the Eastern bishops participating in the Council of Chalcedon seventy years later appealed to it in the famous resolution that came to be known as that Council's 28th canon—a text that set out to define the primacy of the see of Constantinople more closely, among the churches of the Eastern Empire.[2] Yet in the centuries that followed, as both the Eastern and the Western Churches struggled to identify and shape, theologically and canonically, the structure and norms of ecclesial authority, this third canon of Constantinople I, along with its interpretation in the 28th canon of Chalcedon, has remained fundamentally important, both for defining the terms of Church leadership and for identifying the relationship of its traditional centres.

To most people today, a 'primacy of honour' doubtless suggests a status of eminence and a role of leadership that is purely ceremonial: a mark of public recognition without practical rights or

---

[1] The translation here is that of W. A. Hammond, in *Creeds, Councils and Controversies*, J. Stevenson (Seabury: New York, 1966), 148. For the Greek text, see Centro di Documentazione, Istituto per le Scienze Religiose (Bologna), *Conciliorum Oecumenicorum Decreta* (Freiburg, etc., 1962) (hereafter: COD) 28, ll. 14–19. This collection has newly been republished with facing English translation: N. P. Tanner (ed.), *Decrees of the Ecumenical Councils*, 2 vols., (London and Washington, 1990) (hereafter: Tanner). For can. 3 of Constantinople in this collection, see p. 32.

[2] The Papal delegates at Chalcedon first responded to the use of can. 3 of Constantinople by suggesting it did not form part of the received collection of conciliar decisions: ACO II, 1, 453 f. For the history of the text of the canons of Constantinople I, and of their later inclusion in canonical collections of the Eastern and Western Churches, see A. Michel, 'Der Kampf um das politische oder petrinische Prinzip der Kirchenführung', in *Das Konzil von Chalkedon 2*, A. Grillmeier and H. Bacht (Würzburg, 1953), 495–99; I. Ortiz de Urbina, *Nicée et Constantinople* (Paris, 1963), 206; A. M. Ritter, *Das Konzil von Konstantinopel und sein Symbol* (Göttingen, 1965), 92; 'Il secondo concilio ecumenico e la sua recezione. Stato della ricerca', *Cristianesimo nella storia* 2 (1981), 341–65.

© Oxford University Press 1993
[Journal of Theological Studies, NS, Vol. 44, Pt. 2, October 1993]

duties, much like honorary citizenship, an honorary fellowship in a college, or an honorary degree. So most modern authors who discuss these early canons tend to assume that a 'primacy of honour' is a position of moral leadership: a sign of traditionally recognized *auctoritas* or prestige, as distinguished from effective decision making or juridical power within the structures of Church institutions—in other words, as distinguished from jurisdiction.[3]

This also seems to have been what it suggested, first of all, to the great twelfth-century Byzantine canonists. Joannes Zonaras, for instance, in arguing that the placing of the Bishop of Constantinople 'after the Bishop of Rome' cannot have a simply chronological meaning (as Alexios Aristenos and others argued), but that it must refer in some way to their relative rank in the universal Church, observes that it would be impossible for both 'thrones' to possess exactly equivalent honour (τιμή): someone, after all, must be named first in the Eucharistic anaphora and sit in the first place at synods, and someone's name must appear first on conciliar documents.[4] And Theodore Balsamon, in a comment on canon 28 of Chalcedon, lists as the privileges (προνόμια) of the Bishop of Rome several of the ceremonial distinctions accorded the Pope in the ninth-century 'Donation of Constantine': the right to wear a Phrygian cap and a chain of office, for instance, or to carry a sceptre and walk in procession preceded by banners, or to ride a horse—all quasi-imperial honours Balsamon wistfully wishes his own Patriarch might be allowed to claim as well.[5] By modern standards, these clearly fall into the category of 'purely honorary' privileges.

As always, however, there is a danger here of reading back into the decisions of the fourth and fifth centuries distinctions that are meaningful only in the context of a later Church and a later civil society. However important it may be to distinguish between

---

[3] See, for example, the classic statement of J. Meyendorff: 'L'autorité de ces Eglises [i.e., those recognized in these canons as having a 'primacy of honour'] ne comportait pas, par elle-même, de pouvoir juridique: la distinction entre cette *autorité* et ce *pouvoir* est essentielle pour comprendre l'organisation de l'Eglise ancienne et son évolution.' ('La primauté romaine dans la tradition canonique jusqu'au Concile de Chalcédoine', *Istina* 4 (1957), 481.) Among Roman Catholic authors the same assumption tends to be made; see, for instance, G. Jouassard, 'Sur les décisions des conciles généraux des IVe et Ve siècles dans leur rapports avec la primauté romaine', *ibid.* 490; and more recently, A. de Halleux, 'Le décret chalcédonien sur les prérogatives de la Nouvelle Rome', *Ephemerides theologicae Lovanienses* 64 (1988), 300, 308.

[4] Commentary on can. 3 of Constantinople I (*PG* 137. 325 C2–7).

[5] Ibid. 488 A3–B11. For the corresponding text in *Donatio Constantini* 14–16, see C. Mirbt and K. Aland (eds.), *Quellen zur Geschichte des Papsttums und des Römischen Katholizismus* (Tübingen, 1967), 254 f.

personal or moral 'authority' and canonical or structural 'jurisdiction' in the Churches and constitutional republics of today, one cannot simply assume that such distinctions hold good for the traditions and legislation of the Patristic age. I believe, in fact, that in the mind of the ancient Hellenistic and Roman world, 'honour' and actual influence on the course of events within society were not so easily separated from each other, and that the 'primacy' these canons ascribe to the bishops of both Rome and Constantinople among their episcopal colleagues must be understood, in their original context, as having clearly practical, even juridical implications.

I. THE MEANING OF THE TERMS

In ancient Mediterranean societies, the respect of one's neighbours was a prime criterion for determining the value of a person's life. 'Honour' (*honos*), for the Romans of Republican times, was not simply an internal sense of human dignity, an attitude of respect, or an awareness of one's own or another's worth; it was understood to be essentially something *bestowed* by other members of the body politic in recognition of a person's intrinsic virtue and meritorious public actions, in other words, the result of a public judgement about someone's value to society.[6] Honour was the grateful recognition not only of political goodness but of political service; and the normal means ancient societies had for expressing it was through the bestowal of office: an institutionalized position of political responsibility. A city without the ability to elect public officials, in Cicero's view, was crippled, because it had no way of stimulating generous displays of public service: 'Where honour is not publicly given, there can be no desire for glory.'[7] So both *honos* and *dignitas*—which suggested the long-term status of a person who is continually given honour—came to be used, by the Romans, to mean political *office* itself: the elected position of influence and power that was a mark of public recognition. Thus the ideal career of a Roman male, who had enough wealth and social connections to realize it, was conceived of as a kind of spiral of generous actions and resulting civic responsibilities: personal excellence (*virtus*) showed itself in virtuous public deeds, which were recognized by election to office; good performance there led to the more profound recognition of higher offices. 'Honour',

[6] See the interesting reflections, with abundant sources, of F. Klose, 'Altrömische Wertbegriffe (*honos* und *dignitas*)', *Neue Jahrbücher für Antike und deutsche Bildung* 1 (1938), 268–78.

[7] *De lege agraria* 2.91, speaking of the political paralysis of the city of Capua.

habitualized as 'dignity', meant both society's approval and the position of leadership, or even legal jurisdiction, through which that approval was normally expressed.

Classical Greece seems to have shared the same basic assumptions about virtue and its rewards. Τιμή, which we usually translate as 'honour' or 'esteem', was also used to mean the prerogative of a king[8] or an elected office within a democracy. In arguing that only virtuous people (οἱ ἐπιεικεῖς) should actually rule (ἀρχεῖν, κυρίους εἶναι) in society, Aristotle concludes: 'Therefore the rest must necessarily be without honour (ἀτίμους), since they are not given the honours of political office; for we call positions of rule (ἀρχάς) "honours", and if these are the ones who always rule, the rest must necessarily be "those without honour".'[9] The peak of honour, clearly, was to win first prize in a game or political contest, or to hold first place (τὸ πρωτεῖον): this was once Athens' role among the cities of the Greek world,[10] and was, analogously, the mind's role among human powers.[11] It was natural for a Greek, then, to equate 'first place' (τὰ πρωτεῖα) with 'honour' (τιμή) and 'glory' (δόξα),[12] and also to refer to the leading figures of a city, when exercising their civic functions, as 'the first people' or 'primates' (οἱ πρωτεύοντες).[13] And it was natural, too, for early Christian writers to use this same term for the 'headship' of Christ in the universe,[14] or for the role of the bishop as 'head' of the local church.[15]

[8] E.g., Herodian, *Historiae* 7.10.5 (2nd cent. CE).

[9] *Politics* 3.6.3 (1281a 30–33).

[10] Demosthenes, *Fourth Phillippic*, Or 10.74.   [11] Plato, *Philebus* 22e, 33c.

[12] For a revealing discussion using all these terms, see Diodorus Siculus, *Bibliotheca Historica* 1.1.4–1.2.2; Diodorus suggests that the 'first place' of honour should really be given to history itself, for making the healthy desire for lasting civic honour capable of realization.

[13] E.g., Herodian, *Historiae* 8.7.2.

[14] A striking example is a passage in the third book of Irenaeus' *Adversus Haereses*. The Word of God became visible, comprehensible, even passible, Irenaeus writes, 'so that, as the Word of God has first rank (*princeps est*; πρωτεύει) in things that are above the heavens, in spiritual and invisible things, so also he might have first rank (*principatum*; πρωτεύσῃ) in visible and corporeal things, and that, by taking primacy (*primatum*; τὰ πρωτεῖα) to himself and making himself head of the Church, he might draw all things to himself in the proper time' (3.16.6). For a perceptive study of the ecclesiological implications of this whole family of expressions, see H. Holstein, '"Propter potentiorem principalitatem" (Saint Irénée, *Adversus Haereses* III, 3, 2)', *Recherches de science religieuse* 36 (1949), 122–35.

[15] Cyprian, for instance, seems to use *primatus* not just to mean 'firstness' in temporal sequence or ceremonial seniority, but to imply some claim to a 'prior' authority to preach, baptize, and judge within the Churches; this, at least, seems to be its implication in Epp. 69.8 and 71.3—otherwise there would be no cause for argument. See J. Le Moyne, 'Saint Cyprien est-il bien l'auteur de la rédaction

Πρεσβεία, too, was an important term for the position that served as the basis for practical leadership. Related to the adjective 'old' (πρεσβύς), it meant, first of all, 'seniority', and then 'precedence'—authority based on age, which Aristotle suggests is one of the main sources of parental authority, as well as 'the form of royal rule'.[16] Plato uses this notion of precedence in parallel to 'power' (δύναμις), when speaking of the 'super-essential' position and causal role of the Form of the Good[17]—a passage Origen alludes to in discussing the essence of God.[18] Similarly, the neuter form of the related adjective (τὸ πρεσβεῖον, τὰ πρεσβεῖα) is regularly used to mean the rights and privileges that come with seniority: the authority to judge (ἐπιδιακρίνειν)[19] or to rule as king.[20] Like other expressions of 'firstness', πρεσβεία and τὰ πρεσβεῖα clearly imply, for classical Greek authors, a primacy of position that is assumed to have practical results in terms of social authority: prerogatives that are not *merely* honorary in modern terms— but are also real. Rank and power are, for the ancient Mediterranean mind if not for our own, inseparable from each other.

II. The Prerogatives of 'Old' and 'New' Rome

It is always a risky business to base the interpretation of historical events and institutions on the study of words, especially since the meanings of words evolve in ways that can only be determined from the context of a previously understood history. Making precise judgments about the meaning of Greek words in the later Patristic period is especially difficult, because the lexical and grammatical features of the language in the early Christian centuries have, until now, been only sketchily and inconsistently studied. Still, our knowledge of Greek literary style and usage in the fourth and fifth centuries—particularly in the imperial capital—suggests

brève de "De Unitate" chapitre 4?' *Revue Bénédictine* 63 (1953), 107–11. Opposed to this understanding, however, is M. Bévenot, "'Primatus Petri Datur". St. Cyprian on the Papacy', *JTS* 5 (1954), 22–25, esp. 24: 'That [*primatus*] should have the meaning of "power" in general, or of "episcopal power", seems to have no roots anywhere in Cyprian.' Bévenot's later interpretation of *primatus* in Cyprian's works, however, is more cautious: it 'need not mean "the primacy", with all its modern overtones. It could imply no more than a certain priority, usually in time' (*Cyprian, De Lapsis and De Ecclesiae Catholicae Unitate* (Oxford, 1971), xiv).

[16] *Politics* 1.5.2 (1259b 12).   [17] *Republic* 6.19 (509b).
[18] *Commentary on John* 13.21 (123): SC 222.95 f.
[19] Plato, *Gorgias* 79 (524a).
[20] Sophocles, *Aegeus*, Fragment 1 (from Strabo 9.601): 'My father decided to go away …, Giving me authority over the land (γῆς πρεσβεῖα).'

that one is justified in looking to the classical form of the language, rather than later Byzantine idiom, for help in understanding the nuances of official proclamations. It was, after all, the language of Libanius and the Emperor Julian, of the great fourth-century grammarians and lexicographers, as well as the language of the Cappadocian Fathers—a language that was normally intended to be classical when used before a discerning world. For this reason, I suggest that a more natural translation of the third canon of Constantinople, in the context of classical usage, would be the following: 'The Bishop of Constantinople shall have the prerogatives of office (τὰ πρεσβεῖα τῆς τιμῆς) after the Bishop of Rome, because it [i.e., Constantinople] is a new Rome.' And I believe that a careful reading of the documents that form the broader context of this legislation—particularly the acts of the Council of Chalcedon, where the meaning and implications of the Bishop of Constantinople's privileges were discussed and specified in clear, practical terms—confirms the intuition that a 'purely honorary' primacy for the Bishop of either 'Old Rome' or 'New Rome' was not at all what the early councils meant to define and confirm.

The development of Church office in the early Christian community, as well as the events and implications of the early councils, have been discussed in almost overpowering detail; we cannot and need not do more here than highlight a few aspects of that development, and of the discussions that surrounded it, which may shed light on our argument.

    1.   The Council of Nicaea (325), that first world-wide gathering of Christian bishops which remained, for later councils, the norm of authoritative proclamation and legislation, itself took important steps to regulate and define the relationships of the major sees. Canon 6 of Nicaea laid down, as consistent with 'the ancient customs' of Egypt and Libya, 'that the bishop of Alexandria should have authority (ἐξουσίαν) over all these [churches], since this is likewise the custom for the bishop in Rome'.[21] Similarly, the Council ordains, 'the prerogatives (πρεσβεῖα) are to be preserved for the Churches in Antioch and in the other provinces'. Apparently, a first attempt was being made here to define canonically the precedence or 'seniority' of metropolitan sees: the churches in the capital cities of civil provinces, with particular reference to the church of Alexandria, the centre of both theological and jurisdictional crisis in 325. The normal Christian practice, as reflected here and in the preceding canon, was for the

---

[21] COD 8; Tanner 8 f.

bishops of the local churches to gather for common concerns in synodal groupings parallel to each civic province (ἐπαρχία), under the presidency of the bishop of the province's major city or metropolis; but the Bishop of Alexandria is recognized here as having, by force of ancient custom, a wider jurisdiction: a seniority and an authority over the four provinces of eastern North Africa that comprised most of the civil 'diocese' of Egypt.[22] The model given by the canon, in confirming this extraordinary role for the Alexandrian bishop, is the authority of the Bishop of Rome—presumably in his role in the provinces of central Italy.

The canon then ordains, more generally, that 'in Antioch and the other provinces, the prerogatives (πρεσβεῖα) of the Churches are to be preserved', and gives, perhaps simply as a classic example, at least one important way in which the normal pattern of super-episcopal authority is to be understood: if someone is made bishop without the approval of the metropolitan bishop, 'the great synod'—presumably the full assembly of the bishops of the province, meeting twice a year and presided over by the metropolitan, as decreed in canon 5—is to decide by vote whether or not he is to be recognized. 'The πρεσβεῖα of the Churches', and of metropolitans within them, both in Alexandria and elsewhere, clearly has a juridical application here, precisely in the often contentious question of confirming the appointment of local bishops.

Canon 7 of Nicaea is also interesting as an illustration of how this same range of terms is used in an ecclesial context. 'Since the custom and the ancient tradition still holds good', it decrees, 'that the bishop in Aelia [Jerusalem] should have rank (τιμᾶσθαι: lit., 'be honoured'), let him possess the consequences of that rank (τὴν ἀκολουθίαν τῆς τιμῆς), while the proper dignity (ἀξίωμα) of the metropolitan [of Caesaraea] is preserved'.[23] The ancient status of the see of Jerusalem—insignificant since the early second century,

[22] Since well before the time of Nicaea, the bishops of Alexandria apparently exercised extraordinary 'patriarchal' power in the provinces of Upper and Lower Egypt, Libya, and the Pentapolis, monitoring all episcopal elections and ordaining all the bishops of the region, as well as virtually controlling the doctrinal and liturgical life in these provinces. See E. Wipszycka, 'La chiesa nell' Egitto del IV secolo: le strutture ecclesiastiche', *Miscellanea Historiae Ecclesiasticae VI: Les transformations dans la société chrétienne au IVe siècle* (Congress of Warsaw, 1978; Brussels, 1983), 182–201; cf. R. Williams, *Arius. Heresy and Tradition* (London, 1987), 42–45, and further references cited there. On the original intent of the sixth canon of Nicaea, see H. Chadwick, 'Faith and Order at the Council of Nicaea: a Note on the Background of the Sixth Canon', *Harvard Theological Review* 53 (1960), 171–95.
[23] COD 8; Tanner 9.

but now regaining its importance as a Christian centre—is to be recognized in a practical way; yet how that role is to be realized concretely is here left undefined, even though the canon obviously foresees a clash between the revived rank of Jerusalem and the privileges of Caesaraea, the metropolitan see of southern Palestine. Despite its vagueness, this canon seems to imply more than the purely ceremonial rank some have seen in it;[24] if the 'consequences of rank' confirmed here were not of some practical import in the life of the Palestinian churches, there would be no need to stress the continuing 'dignity' of Caesaraea as well.

2. The great post-Nicene provincial Synod of Antioch, traditionally dated in 341,[25] carried this definition of the authority of the 'metropolitan' bishop a step further. He is to 'precede the others in rank (τῇ τιμῇ προηγεῖσθαι)', according to canon 9, and to 'bear responsibility (τὴν φροντίδα ἀναδέχεσθαι) for the whole province'; this is interpreted as meaning that bishops within the province are not to do anything 'without him', except what is strictly internal to their own local churches. And the metropolitan, in turn, is not to act—again, presumably, outside the boundaries of his own church—'without the approval of the rest [of the bishops of the province]'.[26] Although his jurisdiction is limited by the obligation to consult the provincial synod, the τιμή of the metropolitan bishop is understood here, once again, to be more than a simply honorary title.

3. The main agenda of the synod that gathered in Constantinople in 381, under the sponsorship of the Emperor Theodosius I, is recognized by scholars today to have been more than simply dogmatic: more than simply the reaffirmation of the faith of Nicaea, through the Trinitarian lens of Cappadocian theology, and the condemnation of the principal heresies of the late fourth century. In the turbulence of the theological conflicts in the capital at the beginning of Theodosius' reign, Maximus 'the Cynic' had managed to have himself ordained bishop of the homoousian community there by a legate of Peter, Bishop of Alexandria—with the long-distance support of Ambrose of Milan—in opposition to Gregory of Nazianzus, homoousian

[24] E.g., Jouassard (above, n. 3), 489.

[25] Eduard Schwartz, however, argued that the canons of Antioch should not be associated with the 'Dedication Synod' of 341 but with an earlier gathering, a few years after Nicaea itself: *Zur Geschichte der Alten Kirche und ihres Rechts* (= *Gesammelte Studien* 4, Berlin, 1960), 163, n. 1; 189–97; 241 f.

[26] G. A. Rhalles and M. Potles, *Syntagma tōn Theiōn kai Hierōn Kanonōn* 3 (Athens, 1853), 140 f.; the medieval Byzantine commentators point out the substantial agreement between this canon and *Apostolic Canons* 34, which probably was formulated later in the century (*ibid.*; cf. 2.45).

Bishop of Constantinople, who was to preside over the synod. Another prime sponsor of the gathering, Meletius of Antioch, had himself struggled for some twenty years with Paulinus, the rival claimant to his see who also had the backing of both the Roman and the Alexandrian Churches. Understandably, this synod seems to have gathered in an anti-Alexandrian (and possibly an anti-Roman) mood, and to have had from the start the clear purpose of reaffirming the principles of non-interference among the regions of Christendom that had been laid down at Nicaea and Antioch earlier in the century, but which had been widely abused in the intervening decades.[27] Gregory was, as always, a reluctant chairman, and Meletius died during the early days of the Council; but the bishops present—mainly from central, northern and eastern Asia Minor, and from Syria and Palestine (all part of the Antiochene and Constantinopolitan spheres of influence)—seem to have been determined to limit the ability of the Alexandrian Church to influence the affairs of the other Eastern Churches in the future.

Canon 2 of Constantinople extended the ancient principle of a territorially limited jurisdiction over groups of local churches, formally enunciated at Nicaea, from the provincial level to that of the civil diocese or region. The canons of Antioch had proposed guidelines for appeals by bishops to 'greater', super-provincial episcopal gatherings if they should be unwilling to accept decisions of their own provincial synods on disputed issues, but they did not define just how those 'greater' gatherings were to be composed.[28] This canon now clarified the same principle, expressly on (civil) diocesan lines, by insisting—doubtless with Alexandria primarily in mind—that no bishop may 'go beyond' his diocese to share in any administrative activity (οἰκονομία) or to participate in ordinations, unless he is specially invited. Explicitly listed here are the five civil dioceses of the Greek-speaking part of the Empire: Egypt (the northeastern corner of Africa), Oriens (including the Levant, Syria, and Palestine), Pontus (northern and eastern Asia Minor), Asia (western and southern Asia Minor) and Thrace (the eastern tip of Europe south of the Danube). Only the diocese of Egypt is spoken of here as having a single bishop as its administrative head; responsibility in the other four is attributed simply to

[27] See esp. Ritter (above, n. 2) 38 ff., 87 ff.; also Metropolitan Maximus of Sardis, *Le Patriarcat oecuménique dans l'église orthodoxe. Etude historique et canonique* (Théologie historique 32, Paris, 1975), 123 f.

[28] Synod of Antioch, cans. 12 and 14: Rhalles and Potles 3.146, 152.

'the bishops', which presumably refers, at least in principle, to new, super-provincial or diocesan synods.[29]

But while the leadership of the Bishop of Antioch in the diocese of Oriens would certainly be felt under such a new, regional system,[30] the three smaller dioceses of the north, of Asia Minor and Greek-speaking Europe, had now been officially recognized as super-provincial ecclesial units without having parallel, traditionally recognized centres of gravity. The implication seems clear enough: Constantinople, the imperial capital on the Bosporus, the 'New Rome' of the Christian Empire, would be expected to fill the vacuum of Church leadership in those regions. Without explicitly defining the terms of Constantinople's influence or focusing it directly on this area, canon 3 of the Council of 381 seems to follow naturally from this line of thought; it not only sets the stage for the development of such a 'northern' centre of authority, but ranks it second after 'Old Rome' in order of importance—ahead of both Alexandria and Antioch. The foundation of the 'patriarchal' system that would be canonized by Justinian in the sixth century had now been laid.

4. After 381, the bishops of Constantinople were not slow to begin using their newly enunciated 'seniority' or 'prerogatives of office' in a practical way.[31] In 394, for instance, Bishop Nectarius of Constantinople presided at a synod in the capital, attended by the bishops of both Alexandria and Antioch, at which the agenda included a discussion of the affairs of the Church of Bosra in Arabia—part of the diocese of Oriens (and therefore in the 'patriarchal' region of Antioch), under the metropolitan jurisdiction of

---

[29] So can. 6 of Constantinople (COD 27 f.; Tanner 33 f.), which may well be the work of a synod held in that same city the following year, defines the 'greater synod' as that of all the bishops in a civil diocese: see Ritter 92, n. 1. Ritter rightly points out here that the interest of the Synod, in can. 2, is not so much to set up new organs of jurisdiction as to draw sharper limits to the spheres of influence in which any bishop may expect to operate.

[30] Depending on how the Greek is punctuated, can. 6 of Nicaea could also be taken as attributing to the Church of Antioch a special role of leadership in the diocese of Oriens, similar to that of Alexandria but not further defined. Constantinople, can. 2, clearly interprets the earlier canon in this sense: '... The bishops of the Orient should administer only the Orient, with the seniority (πρεσβεῖα) given to the Church of Antioch in the canons of Nicaea preserved ...' (COD 27.27–31; Tanner 31). Schwartz saw can. 6 of Nicaea not only as ambiguous, but as deliberately so: 'Der sechste nicaenische Kanon auf der Synode von Chalkedon', *Sitzungsberichte der Preussischen Akademie der Wissenschaften, philosophisch-historische Klasse* 27 (Berlin, 1930), 636 and n. 1. See also Chadwick (above, n. 22), 180–83.

[31] For details of the increasingly active role of the bishops of Constantinople in the affairs of all the Eastern Churches from the 390s onwards, see Maximos of Sardis, 139–53.

Caesaraea, and in the acknowledged sphere of influence of Jerusalem! John Chrysostom, at the start of the next decade, ordained bishops in all three of the 'smaller' dioceses of the north, as did his successors Atticus (406–25) and Proclus (434–46).[32] In a decree of 14 July, 421, the Emperor Theodosius II placed the province of Illyricum (today northern Greece) under the ecclesiastical supervision of the Bishop of Constantinople, even though it had, for some sixty years, been supervised by the Bishop of Rome through his legate, the Bishop of Thessalonica; Theodosius' reason was that Constantinople 'enjoys the prerogatives (*praerogativa* = πρεσβεῖα) of Old Rome'.[33] Pope Boniface I persuaded Honorius, Theodosius' Western colleague, to countermand this decree, but it was clear that the thinking in the Eastern capital, of both bishop and emperor, was moving in the direction of real, formally recognized super-provincial jurisdiction for the see of Constantinople, at least in the matter of episcopal ordinations. The 'office' of being bishop of the imperial city was already understood to have practical consequences far beyond the Bosporus, even before those powers were canonically defined.

5. This definition was begun in earnest at the Council of Chalcedon (451). Doctrinally and politically, that gathering also meant defeat for the Church of Alexandria and its ambitious bishop, Dioscorus. After the completion of the dogmatic statement on the person of Christ, and the enactment of a number of disciplinary canons, a smaller group of 185 Greek-speaking bishops— mainly from the three smaller dioceses of the north[34]—passed a resolution on 29 October, 451, defining more exactly the prerogatives (πρεσβεῖα) of the Bishop of Constantinople in the wider Church.[35] This resolution, which eventually came to be known as

[32] Socrates, *Hist. Eccl.* 7.28. See Emil Herman, 'Chalkedon und die Ausgestaltung des konstantinopolitanischen Primats', *Das Konzil von Chalkedon* II, 472 ff.

[33] *Codex Theodosiana* 16.2.45, T. Mommsen (ed.) I 2, 2nd ed. (Berlin: 1854, 852); cf. *Codex Justiniana* 11.21.1, P. Krueger (ed.): Corpus Juris Civilis II (Berlin: 1888, 434).

[34] For an analysis of the geographical and political significance of the group of bishops who signed the resolution known as canon 28, see Schwartz, 'Der sechste nizänische Kanon' (above, n. 30), 614 f., n. 2.

[35] COD 75 f.; Tanner 99 f.; ACO II, 1, 447, l.28–448, l.17 (Greek); ACO II, 3, 541, ll.3–19 (Latin). This text is referred to in the *Acta* of Chalcedon simply as a 'resolution' (ψῆφος), and probably was not intended to be a formal enactment of the whole synod, but rather a policy decision by the bishops of the dioceses of Asia, Pontus, Thrace, and Oriens, who were principally affected by it. It was not included in sixth-century Greek canonical collections, and was only 'received' as part of the canonical heritage by canon 36 of the Synod 'in Trullo', in 692. See Schwartz, *ibid.* 613. For a very full and nuanced recent discussion of the original intent and importance of this canon, with extensive bibliography, see A. De

the 28th canon of Chalcedon, begins with a declaration of intent to follow both 'the definitions of the Fathers'—a phrase which probably refers to canon 6 of the Council of Nicaea[36]—and the legislation of the Council of Constantinople. 'The Fathers have rightly recognized[37] the prerogatives' of 'the throne of the older Rome' because of the city's imperial status, and the 'hundred and fifty' at Constantinople followed the same reasoning in giving 'equal prerogatives (τὰ ἴσα πρεσβεῖα) to the most holy throne of new Rome': its growth to second status on the political stage calls for it to 'be magnified, as [Rome] is, also in ecclesiastical matters'. The decree then spells out at least two major jurisdictional dimensions of these prerogatives: the bishops of Constantinople shall, from now on, ordain all the metropolitan bishops of the three northern imperial dioceses, leaving it to these metropolitans to ordain the bishops of their own provinces; and the bishops of Constantinople shall also ordain the bishops of the 'barbarian' or mission regions, dependent on these dioceses but outside the borders of the Empire.

Canons 9 and 17 of the council, previously approved by the full assembly, had spelled out another new aspect of Constantinople's super-provincial jurisdiction, by allowing a bishop who had a canonical complaint against the metropolitan of his province to appeal either to 'the exarch of the diocese'—the metropolitan, presumably, of the diocese's main city—or to 'the throne of Constantinople'.[38] It is not clear from the text whether this arrangement is meant simply to apply, like the jurisdictional details of 'canon 28', to the three smaller Eastern dioceses, none of which could claim an ancient ecclesiastical point of reference at its centre with the prestige of an Alexandria or an Antioch, or

Halleux, 'Le décret chalcédonien' (above, n. 3), 288–323. On the dating of the discussion and enactment of the resolution, I have followed Eduard Schwartz; De Halleux (290, n. 9), however, returns to the more traditional dating of 30 Oct. and 1 Nov., 451, following E. Chrysos, 'Ἡ διάταξις τῶν συνεδριῶν τῆς ἐν Χαλκηδόνι Οἰκουμενικῆς Συνόδου', Κληρονομία 3 (1971), 275–81.

[36] So Herman (above, n. 32) 466 ff.; De Halleux 289. Maximos of Sardis prefers to take the phrase simply as a reference to long-standing tradition: Le patriarchat oecuménique (above, n. 27), 269.

[37] The word used here, ἀποδεδώκασι, usually does not simply mean 'give' or 'accord', but suggests the repayment of a debt or the assignment of what is due; the verb used for the granting of 'equal prerogatives' to New Rome a few lines later, however, ἀπένειμαν simply means 'assign', 'apportion'. The framers of the resolution were aware that they were canonizing a new institutional development. See De Halleux 289.

[38] For the text of these canons, see COD 67, ll.18–40; 71, ll.1–24; Tanner 91, 95; ACO II, 1, 356, ll.5–13; 357, ll.17–24 (Greek); ACO II, 3, 533, l.26–534, l.3; 535, ll.19–28 (Latin).

whether it is intended to recognize the see of Constantinople as
at least an alternative court of appeal for bishops throughout the
Greek-speaking world.[39] The result, in any case, of these three
canons of Chalcedon was to provide a first canonical definition of
what would be called, from the sixth century on, the 'Patriarchate'
of the capital city. And Bishop Juvenal of Jerusalem, who, through
private negotiations with the Bishop of Antioch at the time of the
council, succeeded in defining his own see's super-metropolitan
jurisdiction within the three provinces of Palestine,[40] joined with
these three canons in setting the stage for the classical theory of
the Pentarchy, which would begin to be articulated in the time of
Justinian.

6.   In themselves, of course, these jurisdictional measures only
provide us with a sketchy structural outline of the way the 'primacy' of these episcopal sees was meant to function; they tell us
nothing of the motivation behind them, or the fears and expectations they aroused, and give us little information on what contemporaries considered to be their real relevance. Legislation always
needs to be contextualized if its meaning and force is to be understood; and since the Acta of Chalcedon—thanks to Justinian's
apologetic efforts during the following century on behalf of the
Council's Christology[41]—have been preserved with a fulness
unparalleled in ancient or medieval Christianity, they provide the
best contextual guide to how the terminology of 'honour', 'primacy', and 'power' was understood, in Latin and Greek, at the
time of the Council and its reception.

If one compares the Greek and Latin texts of the debates and
documents of Chalcedon on this issue, one cannot help but be
struck by the fluidity with which terms implying rank and honour
are used. The letter of the assembled bishops to Pope Leo at the
end of the Council, for instance, speaks of the πρεσβεῖα or privileges which the Council has accorded to the see of Constantinople,
second now to those of Leo himself; the Latin translation of
Rusticus the Deacon renders this by *honores*, while an earlier Latin
translation speaks instead of *primatus*.[42] When the Roman legates

---

[39] Joannes Zonaras, commenting on can. 17 of Chalcedon, limits the right of
bishops to choose to be judged by the Bishop of Constantinople to those living
within his 'Patriarchal' area: i.e., those in the three 'northern' civil dioceses (*PG*
137.456A 2–11). For arguments of Byzantine and modern Orthodox canonists in
favour of a broader interpretation, see Maximos of Sardis, 191–253.

[40] See S. Vailhé, 'La formation du patriarcat de Jérusalem', *Echos d'Orient* 13
(1910), 325–36; Herman (above, n. 32), 478 f.

[41] On the origin and character of the various versions of the Acta of Chalcedon,
see especially Schwartz, 'Der sechste nicaenische Kanon' (above, n. 30), 615–26.

[42] Greek: ACO II, 1, 477, l.15; Latin: ACO II, 3, 354, l.12; 356, l.40.

and the Greek secretary of the Council each read aloud the text of canon 6 of Nicaea at the start of the debate on the resolution in session 17, the Latin version (which seems to represent a late fourth-century translation of the Nicene canons[43]) translates the original word used there for the rights of metropolitan bishops, πρεσβεῖα, by *primatus*, which in turn is rendered back, in the Greek version of the Acta of Chalcedon, by πρωτεῖα.[44] *Primatus*, in fact, seems to be used rather broadly in the Latin Acta to signify 'chief responsibility', final executive or judicial power: so the imperial letter appointing Dioscorus to preside over the quasi-judicial proceedings of the Synod of Ephesus in 449, and included in the Chalcedonian dossier, grants him 'authority and primacy' (τὴν αὐθεντίαν καὶ τὰ πρωτεῖα = *auctoritatem et primatum*[45]); the monk Eutyches' role, as superior of his community, is also referred to in the Latin translation as *primatus*.[46] Perhaps most significant of all, Rusticus' Latin version of canon 3 of Constantinople, as read by the secretary in session 17, translates the phrase 'primacy of honour' (πρεσβεῖα τῆς τιμῆς) as *primatūs honorem* ('the honour of primacy' or 'the status of seniority'): for this sixth-century Latin writer, at least, the 'precedence' implied in πρεσβεῖα was sufficiently close to the 'honour' it conferred to allow the two terms to be reversed without altering the meaning of the phrase. 'Primacy' and 'honour' seem, for him at least, to be synonyms.

In all this shifting usage of Greek and Latin terms, it is clear that being 'first' implied much more practical consequences for the bishops of the mid-fifth century than wearing a Phrygian cap or riding a horse. In his stern letter of protest on the primacy resolution, written in the spring of 452 to Bishop Anatolius of Constantinople, Pope Leo complained that the new structure infringes the *privilegia honoris* (πρεσβεῖα τῆς τιμῆς) confirmed at Nicaea for the bishops of Alexandria and Antioch: now, in effect, they are deprived of *proprio honore* and 'subordinated to your powers' (*iuri tuo subditi*).[47] To Maximus, Bishop of Antioch, Leo wrote a year later, urging him to take steps to affirm the traditional *privilegia* of his Church. Even if the merits of bishops vary through

---

[43] See Schwartz (above, n. 30), 627–31.

[44] Latin: ACO II, 3, 548, l.24; Greek: ACO II, 1, 454, l.20.

[45] Greek: ACO II, 1, 74, ll.19 f.; Latin: ACO II, 3, 49, l.17. At session 3, Bishop Julian of Hypaipon refers to Dioscorus' authority in 449 as τὸ κῦρος (Latin: *primatum*), and says the papal legate Paschasinus now possesses 'the authority (τὸ κῦρος; *primatum*) of the most holy Leo' (Greek: ACO II, 1, 224, ll.5, 9; Latin: ACO I, 3, 304, ll.4, 7).

[46] ACO II, 3, 173, ll.5, 22 (for Greek ἡγεμονίαν: ACO II, 1, 182, l.24 and 183, l.2); ACO II, 3, 165, l.22 (for Greek προΐστασθαι: ACO II, 1, 176, l.19).

[47] ACO II, 4, 60, ll.6–11 (= Ep. 106.2: *PL* 54.1003 A11–B6).

the years, Leo observes, 'the rights (*iura*) of their sees remain, and the ambitious may perhaps trouble those sees, but cannot lessen their worth (*dignitatem*)'.[48]

For the Eastern bishops who had voted for the resolution on 31 October, and who explained their reasons during the debate the following day, these primatial rights or πρεσβεῖα of the see of Constantinople meant above all the right to *ordain bishops*. So five of the thirteen who spoke on the subject—all from provinces in Asia Minor and all from cities at some distance from the capital—pointed to the fact that they, and in several cases two or three of their predecessors, had been ordained by the Bishop of Constantinople.[49] And the right to ordain clearly implied, for them, not simply a ceremonial custom, but the ability to act as referee—as well as the duty to take unpopular decisions—in the struggles over episcopal succession that racked so many small Hellenistic cities.[50]

What was at stake, in fact, was not simply 'moral authority' in the modern sense, but the relationship of a powerful benefactor to a grateful and dependent protégé, closely analogous to the *patronage* that continued to play an important role in the relationships of both individuals and cities to wealthy senators and officials, even in the fifth and sixth centuries.[51] To have been confirmed as a candidate for Church office and ordained by an

---

[48] ACO II, 4, 74, ll.1–3 (=Ep. 119.3: *PL* 54.1043 A4–7).

[49] These bishops were: Romanus of Myra (Lycia, diocese of Asia); Seleucus of Amasea (Hellenopontus, diocese of Pontus); Peter of Gangra (Paphlagonia, diocese of Pontus); Marinianus of Synadoi (Phrygia Salutaris, diocese of Asia); and Critonianus of Aphrodisias (Caria, diocese of Asia). See ACO II, 1, 455 f. (Greek); ACO II, 3, 550 f. (Latin). Only the first three of these were metropolitan sees; the last two were ordinary bishoprics, in which the Bishop of Constantinople would no longer have ordination rights according to the new resolution.

[50] See the revealing, if rather rambling remarks of Eusebius, metropolitan of Ancyra (and apparently chief metropolitan or 'exarch' of the diocese of Pontus), in the same debate: while insisting that he has never had any desire to get involved in the business of episcopal ordinations personally, because of the conflicts involved, he suggests that the only way to prevent violence and bribery would be to canonize a system that allowed each provincial synod to solve its own problems internally. The agents of the Bishop of Constantinople quickly argue him down. See ACO II, 1, 456, l.31–457, l.31 (Greek); ACO II, 3, 551, l.13–552, l.7 (Latin).

[51] On the continued vitality of the patronage system in the late Roman Empire, both East and West, see F. Tinnefeld, *Die frühbyzantinische Gesellschaft* (Munich, 1977), 42 f.; J.-U. Krause, *Spätantike Patronatsformen im Westen des Römischen Reiches* (Munich, 1987), 8–20 (patronage of private individuals), 68–87 (patronage of cities); A. Demandt, *Die Spätantike. Römische Geschichte von Diocletian bis Justinian (284–565 n. Chr.* (Handbuch der Altertumswissenschaft III/6, Munich, 1989), 286.

544   BRIAN E. DALEY

important metropolitan, especially if the election process had been contentious, put both a bishop and his whole Church in that metropolitan's debt. It made the local bishop his dependent, and so, in a very practical sense, his client, with traditionally understood obligations of loyalty and support. So Critianus of Aphrodisias defends his own support of the Chalcedonian resolution in these terms: 'I gave my signature of my own free will, wanting to follow the intentions of the holy Fathers [i.e., canon 3 of Constantinople] and because I am a debtor (χρεωστῶν) to that throne; I was ordained [by the bishop of Constantinople], and my predecessors were, and our Church received its whole patronage (προστασία) from it.'[52] Romanus of Myra puts the relationship more simply and more forcefully: 'I was not forced to sign [the resolution]; I am glad to be under (ὑπὸ) the throne of Constantinople, since he gave me my position and he ordained me (αὐτός με ἐτίμησεν καὶ αὐτός με ἐχειροτόνησεν).'[53] The one who confers an honour can expect, in the ancient Church as in the ancient world, to receive both deference and higher honour in return.

This does not mean that the bishops assembled at Chalcedon were unable to confer titles and distinctions that were also purely honorary in the modern sense of the term—lacking, that is, both canonical jurisdiction and recognized practical influence. At the end of session 6, for instance, amid the cheers and self-congratulation of the ceremony at which the Emperor and Empress formally received the council's definition of faith, Marcian himself proclaimed that the city in which this definition was forged—simply a small town of Bithynia, across the Bosporus from the capital—should henceforth have honorary metropolitan status: 'In honour of the holy martyr Euphemia and of your holinesses,' he informs the bishops assembled in Euphemia's shrine, 'we have decreed that the city of Chalcedon, in which the holy faith has been confirmed by this synod, shall have the rank (πρεσβεῖα) of a metropolis; but we only wish to honour it with the name (ὀνόματι μόνῳ ... τιμήσαντες), and the proper role (τοῦ οἰκείου ἀξιώματος) of the metropolitan city of Nicomedia is to be preserved.'[54]

[52] Greek: ACO II, 1, 456, ll.24–27 (χρεωστῶν τῷ θρόνῳ τούτῳ ... καὶ πάσης προστασίας ἡ ἐκκλησία ἡμῶν τέτυχεν); Latin: ACO II, 3, 551, ll.1–3 (debitor huius sedis existens...et omne patrocinium nostra ecclesia promeretur). This language of indebtedness for favours from above echoes the classical Roman view of the attitude a client or protégé should show towards his patron: see R. P. Saller, Personal Patronage under the Early Empire (Cambridge, 1982), 15–18.
[53] Greek: ACO II, 1, 455, ll.30–32; Latin: ACO II, 3, 550, ll.8–10.
[54] Greek: ACO I, 1, 353, ll.35–38; Latin: ACO II, 3, 439, ll.1–5.

The brief fourteenth session of the Council was dedicated to solving a jurisdictional dispute between Eunomius, Bishop of Nicomedia, and Anastasius, Bishop of Nicaea, both of whom—on the basis of custom and earlier imperial decrees—claimed metropolitan rank in the province of Bithynia, and the rights of ordination and patronage that flowed from it. The judgment of their fellow bishops was that the Bishop of Nicomedia, the see of more ancient importance, should have 'the full authority (αὐθεν-τία) of metropolitan' in the province, 'and the bishop of Nicaea shall have only the honour (τὴν τίμην μόνην) of metropolitan, but shall be under the authority (ὑποκείμενον) of the bishop of Nicomedia in the same way as all the other bishops of the province'.[55] A 'purely honorary' rank among the churches, in other words, was certainly possible in the fifth century; but the language that recognizes it must be explicitly and rather laboriously nuanced in order to show that the τιμή in question is *not* endowed with its normal powers. In the absence of such periphrasis, it is to be presumed that 'honour' and 'rank' have practical consequences in the structure of authority.

Even a brief look such as this at the language of 'honour' and 'primacy' in the debates of Chalcedon may help us to understand more clearly not only the controversial resolution of 29 October, 451, and the canon of Constantinople which it claimed as its precedent, but also the precisely worded judgement by which the imperial commissioners, who presided at the following day's debate of the resolution, expressed their understanding and approval. From what had been argued in the debate, they concluded 'that according to the canons, the first place (τὰ πρωτεῖα) and the highest rank (τὴν ἐξαίρετον τιμήν) before all others (πρὸ πάντων) is reserved to the archbishop[56] of the older Rome, beloved of God; and that the most holy archbishop of the royal city of Constantinople, New Rome, enjoys the same prerogatives of office (τῶν αὐτῶν πρεσβείων τῆς τιμῆς=*eisdem primatibus honoris*)'.[57] They then proceed to spell out in some detail what these 'prerogatives of office' entail: the Bishop of Constantinople shall have 'full and supreme authority' (ἐξ αὐθεντίας ἐξουσίαν=*potestatem*) to ordain the metropolitans of the three civil dioceses of Asia, Pontus, and Thrace, once they have been duly elected by the 'clerics,

[55] Greek: ACO II, 1, 421, ll.27–30; Latin: ACI II, 3, 509, ll.29–32. On the position of Chalcedon and Nicaea, as well as of Nicomedia, in the official *Notitia Episcopatum* of the Church of Constantinople in later centuries, see H.-G. Beck, *Kirche und Theologische Literatur im Byzantinischen Reich* (Munich, 1959), 165 f.
[56] On the early use of this title, see Maximos of Sardis (above, n. 27) 76 f.
[57] Greek: ACO II, 1, 457, ll.33–36; Latin: ACO II, 3, 552, ll.10–12.

landowners and distinguished men of each metropolis, and then chosen by all or a majority of the reverend bishops of the province ...'.[58] The Bishop of Constantinople is to ordain each metropolitan, either in the metropolitan city or in the capital; and with that right of ordination, as the discussion at Chalcedon and as the practice of the preceding seventy years attests, came the duty of approving the elected candidates for metropolitan sees and of making an authoritative judgement in disputed elections. The commissioners stress, however, that he is not to become involved at all in the elections or ordinations of local bishops—i.e., those *below* metropolitan rank—within these civil dioceses.[59] No further mention is made of the ordination of bishops for 'barbarian' territories, presumably because this was clear in itself and less controversial.

Read in this way, the ψῆφος of 29 October, 451, was both an affirmation and a restriction of the ecclesiastical patronage practised by the bishops of the Eastern capital since the 390s. Like canon 6 of Nicaea, the super-metropolitan rights of Constantinople are defined here with the help of a reference to the older, parallel rights of 'Old Rome', in Italy and the West.[60] In the three northern dioceses of the East, at least, 'New Rome' is to enjoy the same effective status, the same 'prerogatives of office', that the older Rome enjoys in its own geographical sphere of influence. Yet on the wider stage of Christendom, the hallowed traditional 'firstness' of 'Old Rome' is still to be respected; the ἴσα πρεσβεῖα of Constantinople, as defined by this resolution, are in no sense to be seen as a contradiction of the ἐξαίρετος τιμή, the primary position of honour and influence in the world Church, of the Bishop of Rome.

The clarity of the imperial commissioners' reading of canon 28 of Chalcedon helps clarify, in turn, what was and what was not behind Rome's strongly negative reaction to the resolution. As soon as the text was read, on the morning of 30 October, 451, Leo's delegates, Paschasinus and Lucensius, protested that it was both an 'affront' (*iniuria*) to the Roman see and 'a violation of the canons' (*canonum eversio*).[61] Yet the problem cannot have been

[58] Greek: ACO II, 1, 457, ll.36–40; Latin: II, 3, 552, ll.12–15.

[59] Greek: ACO II, 1, 458, ll.4–8; Latin: ACO II, 3, 552, ll.19–22.

[60] For classic discussions of the various levels of patronage or spheres of influence in which the Roman bishops exercised their power in the fourth and fifth century, see P. Batiffol, *Cathedra Petri* (Unam Sanctam 4, Paris, 1938), 41–79; and C. Vogel, 'Unité de l'église et pluralité des formes historiques d'organisation ecclésiastique du IIIe au Ve siècle,' in *L'Episcopat et l'Eglise Universelle*, Y. Congar and B.-D. Dupuy (eds.) (Unam Sanctam 39, Paris, 1962), 591–636.

[61] ACO II, 3, 553, l.3; Greek: ACO II, 1, 458, ll.20 f.

that the resolution had failed to acknowledge the traditional 'first place' of the Roman bishop, or that it canonized the primatial function which the bishops of Constantinople had, in fact, been exercising—with Rome's tacit acceptance—for some seventy years.[62] Both of these primacies, by now, were beyond question.

The problem for the West, apparently, lay both in the resolution's argumentation and in the precedents it cited. By emphasizing the third canon of Constantinople as a normative antecedent, the resolution implied official acceptance, as law, of the canons of a council that had not yet been formally received by the Western Church, and probably not even by the Church of Alexandria. The Western delegates had apparently been prepared to accept the solemn invocation of Constantinople I as a precedent for the Chalcedonian definition of Christological faith, presumably because this was simply a variant of a widely-used Eastern baptismal creed, which reaffirmed the basic teaching of Nicaea and developed it more fully with respect to the Holy Spirit.[63] But they were much more wary of giving official recognition to Constantinople's disciplinary measures.[64] To set it alongside Nicaea as a source of binding canonical tradition, as well as a supplementary witness to right faith, was to alter the perspectives of that tradition, to raise a second episcopal gathering beyond the status of the various synods of the mid-fourth century, and to attribute to it the normative value that until then was attributed

[62] See De Halleux (above, n. 3) 300–304; Maximos of Sardis (above, n. 27) 253. Note Lucensius' sarcastic question, after hearing the draft of the resolution: 'They say this [privilege] was established eighty years ago. If they have made use of its prerogatives for all this time, what more do they need now? If they have never used them, why do they seek them?' see ACO II, 1, 454, ll.3 f. (Greek); II, 3, 548, ll.3–5 (Latin). Leo complained to the Empress Pulcheria, in fact, in July of 451, that Dioscorus and the synod of Ephesus (449) had stripped some people (presumably Flavian of Constantinople above all) of their *privilegium honoris* (ACO II, 4, 51, ll.4–7); at the third session of Chalcedon, the Roman legates charge Dioscorus with having 'taken the primacy into his own hands' (αὐθεντήσας; *praesumens sibi primatum*) in receiving Eutyches into communion, so doing injury to both Leo and Flavian, who had lawfully excommunicated him! See ACO II, 1, 224, l.29 (Greek); ACO II, 3, 304, ll.26–28 (Latin).

[63] See J. Lebon, 'Les anciens symboles dans la définition de Chalcédoine', *Revue d'histoire ecclésiastique* 37 (1936), 809–76, esp. 810 f., 859 ff., 874; J. N. D. Kelly, *Early Christian Creeds* (London, 1950), 299–305, 317 f., 322–31, 344–48.

[64] Rome had been unwilling to recognize the validity of the disciplinary canons of Constantinople I even at the time of their first enactment. The Roman synod of 382, held under Pope Damasus, responded to can. 3 of Constantinople by reaffirming the traditional order of the great sees implied in can. 6 of Nicaea. For the text of this Roman resolution, with commentary, see P.-P. Joannou, *Die Ostkirche und die 'Cathedra Petri' im 4. Jahrhundert* (Päpste und Papsttum 3; Stuttgart, 1972), 285–89.

only to Nicaea. Thus Lucensius' first question, after hearing the text of the resolution, was not simply whether the bishops who had signed it had done so free of compulsion—a question one might well ask when the privileges of the emperor's own city were at stake—but why they 'had been forced to give their signatures to canons not included in the official collection (*non conscriptis canonibus*)'.[65]

Perhaps more serious were the objections Leo and his delegates raised to the way in which the resolution argued for the reasonableness of its measures. The framers of the text clearly went out of their way to suggest that all primacy in the Church, at least in the concrete details of its practice, is founded on political realities, and therefore must be adjusted as those realities change: 'The Fathers rightly recognized the prerogatives of Old Rome because that city reigned supreme; moved by the same purpose, the 150 bishops [at Constantinople, 381], beloved of God, gave the same prerogatives to the most holy throne of New Rome, rightly judging that a city honoured by the imperial rule and by the Senate should enjoy equal privileges with the older royal Rome, and in ecclesiastical matters should be elevated as [Old Rome] is, being second after it ...'[66] Leo's repeated insistence, in the years that followed the Council, that the ancient order of the Churches, officially sealed by canon 6 of Nicaea, could never be changed,[67] seems to have grown out of his sense of the continuity and integrity of apostolic tradition, and of his consciousness of his own role as being, above all, the guardian of that tradition.[68] His 'Petrine' office, as he understood it, was the obligation to be the personal and abiding foundation of a different, more lasting order than that of the Roman Empire. 'May the city of Constantinople have its own glory, as we hope,' he wrote to the Emperor Marcian in 452, 'and by the protection of God's hand may it enjoy your Clemency's

---

[65] ACO II, 3, 547, ll.23 f. (Latin). See Leo's similar remark in his letter to Anatolius of Constantinople of May 22, 452: ACO II, 4, 61, ll.13–18. The Greek text of the discussion of 30 October 451, significantly omits the suggestion that the third canon of Constantinople I was 'not officially received': ACO II, 1, 453, ll.33 ff.

[66] Greek: ACO II, 1, 448, ll.3–9; Latin: ACO II, 3, 541, ll.7–13.

[67] See, e.g., his letters to the Emperor Marcian, of 22 May 452: ACO II, 4, 56, ll.20–27; to the Empress Pulcheria, of the same date: *ibid.* 58, l.33–59, l.2; to Anatolius, of the same date: *ibid.* 60, ll.16–21; 61, ll.1–9; to Julian of Kios, of the same date: *ibid.* 62, ll.14–17; to Maximus of Antioch, of 11 June 453: *ibid.* 73, ll.34 f.; 74, ll.5–9.

[68] On Leo's understanding of his own 'Petrine' office primarily as guardian and proclaimer of the whole Church's continuing tradition, and particularly as defender of the work of earlier councils, see H.-J. Sieben, *Die Konzilsidee der Alten Kirche* (Paderborn, 1979), 124–35.

constant imperial rule; nonetheless, the order (*ratio*) of the things of the world is one thing, and that of the things of God another, nor will there ever be a stable edifice except that built on the rock which the Lord laid as a foundation.'[69] It was not the confirmation of Constantinople's πρεσβεῖα τῆς τιμῆς in themselves, in other words, to which Leo objected in the Chalcedonian resolution— not to the establishment of Constantinople's 'pariarchal' jurisdiction of the northern dioceses and the areas beyond the frontier— but the resolution's attempt to rearrange the global order of precedence among the great sees which had been canonized by ecclesial tradition and the Council of Nicaea, and the subordination of the ecclesial to the political order that such an innovation, in his view, implied. The reasoning of the resolution opened the way to 'dissolving all the Church's rules (*dissolvi omnes ecclesiasticas regulas*)', he wrote to his Eastern representative, Bishop Julian of Kios, and in doing so it ultimately could only mean 'the destruction of the Church's constitution (*excidium ecclesiastici statūs*)'.[70]

7. In the end, Anatolius and the Emperor did not insist on the reception of the Chalcedonian resolution as binding, and good relations between the Churches were restored.[71] Nevertheless, the Bishops of Constantinople continued to make wide use of their ecclesiastical position, in both an 'honorary' and a 'real' way, during the decades that followed Chalcedon. Patriarch Acacius, for instance, himself ordained Calandion, a loyal Chalcedonian, as Bishop of Antioch in 479, during the early struggles over the reception of the Council, despite the accepted canons and the misgivings of Pope Simplicius.[72] These actions may have been canonically irregular, but they were necessary for the continuity of Chalcedonian orthodoxy in those regions, as Simplicius himself conceded, and the Bishop of Constantinople took responsibility for them.[73] A decree of Emperor Zeno of 16 December, 477,

[69] ACO II, 4, 56, ll.13-17.

[70] ACO II, 4, 62, ll.16, 21 (=Ep. 107: PL 53.1009 B13-16). For a revival of A. Wille's suggestion that Julian may be bishop of Kios in Bithynia, not far from Chalcedon and the capital, rather than from the Aegean island of Kos, see W. H. C. Frend, *The Rise of the Monophysite Movement* (Cambridge, 1972), 147, n. 2.

[71] See the letter of Anatolius to Leo, April 454 (Leo, Epist. 132: PL 54.1084 A5-B7), and Leo's reply of 29 May 454 (Epist. 135: ACO II, 4, 88, ll.22-39).

[72] See Simplicius' letters to Emperor Zeno on this issue, *Collectio Avellana* 66 and 67, O. Guenther (ed.), *CSEL* 35 (Vienna, 1895) 148, l.14-149, l.5; 150, ll.1-22.

[73] On the growing dominance and active leadership of the Patriarchate of Constantinople, even in the regions traditionally dominated by Antioch and Alexandria, during the late fifth and sixth centuries, in the face of growing popular dissent against Chalcedonian Christology, see H.-G. Beck, 'Die Frühbyzantinische Kirche', in H. Jedin (ed.), *Handbuch der Kirchengeschichte II/2: Die Reichskirche nach Konstantin dem Grossen* (Freiburg, 1982), 75 ff.

revoking all the ecclesiastical legislation of the usurper Basiliscus during Zeno's forced exile, spoke of the Church of Constantinople as 'mother of our piety [i.e., of the Emperor himself!] and of all Christians of orthodox religion' and restored all the former 'prerogatives and titles (*privilegia et honores*)' which its bishops had 'over the creation of bishops and the right of being seated before others, and all the rest'.[74] During the late sixth century, too, Bishop Acacius of Constantinople was the first to use the title 'ecumenical Patriarch', a title also applied to the bishops of Rome and Antioch in sixth-century imperial correspondence, but later sharply rejected by Gregory the Great.[75] While the title probably denoted simply a Church leader of the highest rank, and of imperial rather than local importance,[76] its use suggests some sense of special pastoral responsibility towards the whole Church, as well as a justification for intervening even in the affairs of other Churches than one's own, in extraordinary circumstances.

The Emperor Justinian was capable of using both the traditional language of Roman 'primacy' and the newer, pragmatic dominance of Constantinople in the Eastern empire as 'second' see in the interests of his own plans for imperial reunification. A letter to Pope John I dated 5 June, 533—at the height of Justinian's attempts to reconcile the anti-Chalcedonian opposition within the Church—assures the Pope that 'we have taken steps that all bishops of the whole Eastern region should be subject to (*subicere*) and united with your holiness' see', and promises that he will keep the Pope informed of 'everything that pertains to the state of the Churches, ... since [your holiness] is head of all the holy Churches'.[77] The purpose of the letter is to win the Pope's seal of approval for Justinian's own reading of Chalcedonian Christology, which strongly emphasized the union of natures in the single divine hypostasis of the Son—a position Pope John was quite ready to confirm. Justinian, in turn, was willing to accord special favours to the Roman See, even in the Eastern empire,

[74] *Codex Justinianus* 1.2.16, P. Krueger (ed.) (above, n. 33), 14B46–51. One should note again the connection here between the power to confirm and confer Church office and the publicly recognized rank or precedence of the one who has that power.

[75] For literature on this title, see Michel (above, n. 2) 494; more recently, see C. Dagens, 'L'église universelle et le monde oriental chez Grégoire le Grand', *Istina* 20 (1975), 457–75; A. Tuilier, 'Grégoire le Grand et le titre de Patriarche Oecuménique', in J. Fontaine, R. Gillet and S. Pellistrandi (eds.), *Grégoire le Grand* (Colloque de Chantilly, 1982; Paris, 1986), 69–81.

[76] So Henri Grégoire, 'Notules II: Patriarche œcuménique', *Byzantion* 8 (1933), 570 f.

[77] *Codex Justinianus* 1.1.8.9, 11, Krueger (above, n. 33) 11 A24 f., 32–38.

such as his extension of the legal privilege of *praescriptio* from 30 to 100 years for Papal properties there.[78] On the other hand, he formally confirmed the legislation of Constantinople I and Chalcedon on the 'second place' of the Bishop of 'New Rome', specifying that the bishop of the Eastern imperial capital should 'have a position of prior honour (προτιμᾶσθαι = *praeferatur*), before all others'.[79] In practice, Justinian tended to treat the bishops of Rome simply as Patriarchs of the West,[80] and was not above changing the boundaries of their super-provincial jurisdiction,[81] or even keeping Pope Vigilius under house arrest to force him to join in condemning the 'Three Chapters'. In matters of authority, the theologian-emperor was above all a politician.

III. CONCLUDING REFLECTIONS

This brief consideration of the origins of the phrase 'primacy of honour', and of its implications in the two centuries that surrounded its first use as a canonical term, raises many more issues than it has been possible even to touch on here: issues of authority and structure in general in the early Church, of the relations of East and West, of the developing roles of Popes and Patriarchs in late antiquity and the early Middle Ages.[82] The purpose here has simply been to illustrate the original point: that what was at stake in these first discussions of 'primatial' privilege and power in the Church was not simply ceremonial practice or even 'moral' authority alone, but jurisdiction—practical leadership—in a very real sense. In fact, it seems that the distinction between authority and

[78] *Nov.* 9, of 13 April, 535, R. Schoell and G. Kroll (eds.), Corpus Juris Civilis III (Berlin, 1912), 91. The reason for this privilege is that Rome is both the 'source of laws' and the 'summit of the high priesthood' (*summi pontificatus apex*); it is only appropriate, then, for that priesthood to receive the law's special favour.

[79] *Nov.* 131.2, of 18 March, 545 (ibid. 655, 9–14).

[80] So Michel (above, n. 2), 494. On the development of the canonical theory of the Pentarchate, and of Patriarchal jurisdiction in general, see Maximos of Sardis (above, n. 28), 288–302. For astute reflections on the conception of Patriarchal jurisdiction in relation to traditional Latin ideas of Papal primacy, see Y. Congar, 'Le Pape comme patriarche d'Occident. Approche d'une réalité trop négligé', *Istina* 28 (1983), 374–90.

[81] See *Nov.* 11, of 14 May 535 (Schoell and Kroll 94), setting up a new, ecclesiastically independent region in the provinces south of the Danube, under the supervision of the bishop of his new city, Justiniana Prima. This limitation of the Roman see's authority came at about the same time as the grant of special privileges for Roman real estate mentioned above!

[82] A concise but classic account of the developing understanding of primacy in the Eastern and Western Churches, until the 'freezing' of positions on both sides in the scholasticisms of the thirteenth century, is F. Dvornik, *Byzantium and the Roman Primacy* (New York, 1965).

jurisdiction, that is between prestige or honour or status, on the one hand, and the ability to make decisions that bind—in other words, to end disputes and ratify elections, and to 'lay down the law'—on the other, was not at this time clearly made in many areas of Roman society, let alone in either the Eastern or the Western Churches.[83] In an age in which the patronage system still functioned, often under other names but nonetheless with reliable consistency,[84] and in an age, too, in which both synods and Patriarchs were struggling to regulate customary procedures and relationships with the limiting tools of canon law, the recognized position of an episcopal see was clearly a matter of effective influence, of 'office', as well as of rank. The reason that the 'primacy of honour' of the great sees, and the sequential ordering of that primacy in the universal Church, was important enough to argue about was precisely because it could—and, in some circumstances, did—make a practical difference.

Our difficulty, as modern Westerners, in grasping the full implications of the phrase 'primacy of honour' is mainly due, no doubt, to the fact that we live in societies in which honour and patronage are carefully distinguished—at least in theory—from the judicial and executive power that are defined by constitutions and realized in the impersonal functioning of bureaucracies. More deeply, perhaps, our difficulty lies in the ambiguity of authority itself. Leadership, influence on decisions that are made, and the role of being a pillar of ultimate recourse in times of crisis are all the charismatic qualities of extraordinary people, as much as they are the juridically definable roles of institutions.

Nevertheless, even this rapid survey of the language and legislation used to describe the developing role of the see of Constantinople among the Eastern Churches, its new 'priority'

[83] So Perikles Joannou suggests that 'primacy' (which he defines as 'allgemeiner Vorrang') meant, in the fourth century, that its possessor was first of all a judge of last resort: 'höchster Richter im Glauben wie in der Disziplin'. Originally a matter of custom and only later codified by imperial legislation, such 'primacy' found its conceptual model in the role of the *paterfamilias*, 'der Vorrang des Familienältesten', *Die Ostkirche und die 'Cathedra Petri'* (above, n. 64), 19. This same model lay behind the traditional understanding of patronage in civil society: see Saller, *Personal Patonage* (above, n. 52), 7–39.

[84] See L. Harmand, *Le Patronat sur les collectivités publiques des origines au bas-empire* (Paris, 1957), especially 467–73 (on the continuation of local and civic clientage in the Eastern empire, from the fourth through the tenth century). For a complete discussion of the ideology and functioning of patronage, both personal and civic, in Roman society, see R. P. Saller (above, n. 52); P. D. Garnsey and R. P. Saller, *The Roman Empire. Economy, Society and Culture* (Berkeley and Los Angeles, 1987), 148–59; and A. Wallace-Hadrill (ed.), *Patronage in Ancient Society* (London and New York, 1989).

and its relationship to the traditionally recognized 'priority' of the older See of Rome, should make it clear that these early councils, bishops and emperors were struggling to define a structure of Church authority that would *not* simply rest on the personal charisms of individuals, or exhaust itself in ceremony alone. When the bishops who were gathered in Constantinople in 381, and in Chalcedon seventy years later, decreed that the bishop of the Eastern capital should have the πρεσβεῖα τῆς τιμῆς directly after the bishop of the older Rome, they were attempting, in a rather daring way, to assure and confirm for both of them a position of eminent and coordinated power within the rapidly evolving institutional structures of the Christian Church. Whatever use the Churches make of this hoary phrase today, in their delicate ecumenical discussions and in their own internal theological and structural renewal, they must also take into account the very concrete ecclesiological implications of its original meaning. If either 'primacy' or 'honour' are to be genuine, they must still imply the ability to make a practical difference.

BRIAN E. DALEY

Augustinian Studies 22 (1991) 7-35
James J. O'Donnell

The 1991 Saint Augustine Lecture

The Authority of Augustine[1]

Augustine speaks: "The thirteenth of November was my birthday. After a lunch (light enough to keep from putting a burden on our mental faculties), I called the whole group that dined together that way every day, to go and sit in the baths, for that seemed a suitably private spot."[2] Some of those present had probably spent the morning reading a bit of Vergil and were now ready for higher and nobler things. What followed was the conversation recorded in the first book of Augustine's *De beata vita*.

And so we are here, 1505 years after that afternoon in the baths, 1537 years after Augustine's birth, speaking of this man long deceased as though we know him. This lecture is about him, it belongs to a series named after him, and it has the sponsorship of a venerable and international order of religious men dedicated to his name and example. I have spent my entire adult life reading him and writing books about him. We live in a time, moreover, in which his words have reached their largest audience (if we count rather than weigh readers), but it is a time that imagines itself more free of his influence than any other since his lifetime, and that views some of his most characteristic ideas as rebarbative. But even hostility is a token of esteem: if you despise Augustine and write or speak about him in that vein, you judge him worth despising somehow; and so even there he hovers over us.

The power of this man's name is much with us. My topic is precisely that power. How did he come to have it? And what are we to make of it? Why have we made of Augustine a saint of this sort? Did he wish to be treated

227

so? What right have we to acclaim him? And what decorum should govern our applause?

For holy men often attract a veneration that they would deprecate. To take an example Augustine could have known, the first paragraph of the ostensibly quite pious *Life of Plotinus* by his chief disciple Porphyry records an act of rebellion against the philosopher and offers a measure of the distance between master and disciples. Porphyry recounts a subterfuge by which the students managed to have an artist create a portrait of the philosopher, despite Plotinus' reluctance.[3] The subterfuge was comical: the painter Carterius attended Plotinus' lectures as if to listen though actually to look, and look hard, at the speaker, then go out to create just the sort of image of an image that Plotinus abhorred. Though the reluctance to face the painter is soundly based in Plotinus' philosophical ideas,[4] and though his disciples could cite nothing in his doctrines in support of their act, they nonetheless overrode his judgment in order to ensure that he was made a plaster (or pigment) sage according to their preconceptions of the role that was his to play.

We leave our holy men no choice: we insist they be saints. One could as easily cite the veneration accorded Socrates or Francis of Assisi. But they did not write, and Plotinus resisted writing, and wrote with difficulty: is it different when we deal with a figure like Augustine, who wrote as though his life depended on it? Does not he at least deserve to become a Great Book? We will return to the difference that his being a writer makes.

To speak circumspectly of the authority of Augustine, it is worth first asking what Augustine's own attitude in the face of authority was, both in theory and in practice; and then how Augustine came to achieve what authority he did; and finally what we can make of that authority today.

Augustine's epistemology is, like so much of his thought, difficult to characterize in a way that avoids misinterpretation. He has the knack, as so often elsewhere, of holding views that seem irreconcilable with each other. The paradox of Augustine's epistemology is that it sometimes sounds completely a prioristic and intellectualist, and at other times it sounds completely ecclesiastical and authoritarian. It is both and in the combination is the genius of it. What I set forth here is a tentative interpretation. It draws on works of the early period, and chiefly on the *De vera religione*: not because that period is to be privileged as authoritatively Augustinian, but because it was at that period that issues of this sort moved him most often to theoretical statement.

In principle, Augustine held that human powers suffice to know, love, and serve God. A purely natural theology approach is possible: Romans 1.20, "for the invisible things of him from the creation of the world are clearly seen, being understood through the things that are made: his eternal power also and divinity: so that they are inexcusable," offers the scriptural warrant. It ought in principle to be possible for a person to look upon a tree, infer from that tree the existence of God, and have not only reached the right conclusion, but have done so in a logically impeccable way. In practice, such natural theology is impossible.[5] In practice, men do not think that way; but, Augustine would argue, they *should* do so, and they are for him, as Paul says, inexcusable if they do not do so. Created nature itself is the source and human reason is the instrument.

In a fallen world, God provides an alternate path. Scripture,[6] the book of God's word, tells a portion of the history of creation, with certain passages underlined. If it is not possible to see God in any tree you happen to gaze upon, it may be possible to see him in a bush that burns and is not consumed. Specific deeds of God and men and specific accounts of those deeds have the effect of calling to human attention the data necessary to come to an adequate and redemptive knowledge of God. But unaided human reason still cannot achieve that goal, even with the help of Scripture; a multiplicity of conflicting opinions, a diversity of heresies, the perversity of men, all conspire to make univocal interpretation difficult to achieve.[7] Here is the place for "authority."[8]

For just as scripture represents the created world with certain passages underlined, "authority" for Augustine represents the world of the working of human reason with certain passages underlined:[9] certain specific acts, certain specific individuals, who have been granted by God to see and know what is divine through the unimpeded working of their rational faculty,[10] have interpreted scripture at crucial points and in essential ways in such a fashion that those who come after, bound together with them in the community of the church,[11] may confidently believe what they have been told.

For scripture and authority are sufficient to engender belief and to guarantee the validity of sacramental initiation into the Christian community. In practical terms, as is well known, what was passed into the hands of the individual baptismal candidate was the simplest and most stripped-down form of Christian doctrine: the Lord's prayer and the creed.[12] Those texts, the first scriptural and the second based on ancient church authority, embodied in practice what new Christians needed to believe and know. The faith they acquired in this way was adequate for salvation.

The genius of Augustine's paradoxical combination of natural reason and authoritative guidance lies in his familiar notion of the relation of faith and understanding, a notion which is fully developed by the time of *De vera religione*. "Faith" is what is achieved by reliance on scripture and authority; "understanding" is the fully autonomous and the paradoxically fully obedient knowledge of God that will in practice for the faithful come in the next life; but movement towards "understanding," the ascent of the mind to God, is a very old theme[13] in Augustine and one that never leaves his works. The straining of belief towards something richer and stronger and more powerful than belief is the most poignant movement in all of Augustine's thought.[14] Augustine the believer, the bishop, the writer, lives in the radically ambiguous time between faith and understanding, *in hoc interim saeculo* as he would call it later,[15] relying on faith and struggling confidently towards an understanding that will not come now, but that is worth struggling towards all the same.

How far Augustine's theory is validated by his practice is a large question in the development of his thought. Does he begin with scripture? How far is he guided by authority? It is notorious that a natural theology does precede the scriptural for Augustine: he believes in "God" before ever he can bring himself to become a baptized Christian, before ever he can achieve an adequate relationship with scripture. I personally incline to think that he could have defended his practice, arguing that his notion of "God" itself came to him mediated by the Christian church of his youth, but he might have a hard time convincing us.[16] I do not then mean here to undertake any comprehensive investigation of how far theory and practice coincide in Augustine. I mean rather to ask the more specific question of the concrete forms "authority" took for him. What "authority" did he know and recognize? There are points of interest.

First, it is easy to forget how thin was Augustine's "library of the Fathers." Most of what Greek thought had produced was still closed off to him for most of his career.[17] The *possible* library of Latin fathers was still thin, and he had some trouble gaining access to it; and the looming figure of Tertullian was hedged away from him by late turning to heterodoxy. In practice, he confronts Cyprian, Hilary, Ambrose, and Jerome, in various degrees and various ways.

I will set aside Hilary, for he appears in Augustine as do many of the Greek writers of whom he knows a little, as a mediator of the teachings of the councils of Nicea and Constantinople; and with them I will set aside the question of conciliar authority. Such authority is relatively unproblematic for Augustine: the universal councils he accepts, and the Nicene (or Niceo-Constantinopolitan) orthodoxy he accepts. (He was fortunate enough not to have lived through the years of Constantius II, when knowing which council to accept was not so simple a matter.) It is worth noting in passing (and we will return to this) that counciliar authority could still be problematic in one way: if you did not know what the council had said, you could go astray. When bishop Valerius set Augustine to preaching while Augustine was still only a presbyter and later ordained him bishop while he himself was still alive, the canons of Nicea itself were violated, and when this later came to light, Augustine could only plead (not to universal credulity) ignorance. That is a worthy reminder that one aspect of "authority" in the early church was always access: texts were hard to come by, and you could very well know of a writer and his wisdom without being able to get at it.[18]

Ambrose came first chronologically. Augustine knew him, and heard him preach. He was a bishop, he baptized Augustine, and if we are to believe the narrative of the *Confessiones* at all, his influence was important in shaping Augustine's own view of scriptural interpretation.[19] Several points merit comment, however. First, the problem of access. In the 390s, Augustine has to make a special effort to gain access to some of Ambrose's works.[20] Second, the problem of accuracy of oral tradition.[21] Third, the place of authority in discourse. For many years even after Augustine acquires some of Ambrose's works, there is little mention of Ambrose as an authority. Augustine works characteristically alone, under the spotlight, and whatever he has learned he makes his own, distinctively. That all changes late in life when Augustine encounters the fierce attacks of the Pelagians. At this point, Ambrose becomes a buckler and shield. Ambrose is *certainly* orthodox, Augustine's reiterated arguments run, so in saying what he said, I am certainly orthodox myself. It is only in this period that we see an abundance of quotations (many of them repeated over and over again) from a wide variety of Ambrose's works.[22] This is appeal to authority not merely to find truth but to win argument. The technique is distinctive.[23]

231

The case of Cyprian is very different. Cyprian was a figure of authority whom Augustine inherited by virtue of their relative positions in the African church. Cyprian had written, not abundantly, and not as an intellectual, but the texts were preserved, and Cyprian's standing as martyred bishop of Carthage gave him incomparable status in the African church. Unfortunately for Augustine and his community, Cyprian was an ambiguous figure. In *the* great controversy of the African church in Augustine's time, that with the Donatists, the authority of Cyprian was on balance more readily cited by the Donatists than by the Christians. Cyprian was one who dealt sternly with those who had lapsed in time of persecution, and he seems to have been in favor of rebaptism — and in favoring rebaptism he was out of touch with his own tradition. This was a source of great awkwardness for Augustine, and it is no coincidence that the most extensive anti-Donatist treatise, the one he had been trying to write for some years,[24] was the *De baptismo*. This treatise, whatever else it is, is an extended exposition of a way to reconcile the available texts regarding Cyprian with the position of the contemporary church. The importance of this example is that it shows Augustine in dialogue with a figure of authority whom in principle he follows wholeheartedly and with whom he has no sound reason for disagreeing; but there is a dialogue here in which Augustine himself "receives" the authoritative in such a way as to shape it carefully.[25] I think it fair to say that there is not in Augustine a theory to justify or explain *this* practice: it represents an instinctive adaptation of technique to hard facts.[26]

What remains remarkable about Augustine's practice, however, is how small a part "authority" appears to play in his texts.[27] Texts are rarely quoted, names infrequently cited. One may explain this in various ways. Part of it is literary style of a sort (quotation of anterior texts is relatively infrequent in discursive, for example philosophical, literature, even when those texts — like the philosophical dialogues of Cicero — are pervaded through and through with the ideas and expressions of anterior texts); part of it is to be explained as a reflection of the specific Christian deference to scripture. Scriptural texts are the waves of the ocean beating on the shore in Augustine's work, while the quotations from the works of the "fathers" are by comparison occasional glasses of tap water. Part *should* be explained in terms of Augustine's own standing as bishop: for the church in front of him, *he* was the living authority, and that standing is explicit in works like *De doctrina christiana* and *De catechizandis rudibus* and implicit everywhere else. In the way he deals with his authorities, Augustine is not untypical: the example of Gregory the Great comes to mind — a writer who has read widely and deeply in the Latin theological tradition available to him, but who nevertheless rarely quotes or cites those texts, while designedly allowing the *ipsissima verba* of scripture to permeate his text as fully as they do that of Augustine.[28]

But part of this independence is Augustine himself. It requires no partisanship and not even any approval of a single word he wrote to stand nevertheless in awe of his independence of mind, his freshness of approach, and the novelty of the questions he asked. It is characteristic of Augustine that each time he takes up the task of writing, he approaches his subject afresh, asking good questions. Where there is repetition in Augustine, it is the repetition of the jazz improvisionalist repeating old themes but never in the same way.[29] Though many themes and expressions and ideas recur in Augustine, few if any of his works may be dismissed out of hand as simple rehash of something that has gone before: every sermon and every work of his that you pick up does something he has not done before, asks some new question, presses some new line of argument. And he is not dependent on others for the questions that press him, though he exploits the curiosity of others with rare resourcefulness. To read the dossier of correspondence with Marcellinus and Volusianus in the early 410s[30] and then to turn to the *De civitate dei* is to see what extraordinary range and power of thought Augustine could bring to bear on pedestrian and really rather thoughtless lines of inquiry. There is a moral elegance to the way in which Augustine continues to ask questions, fresh questions, and to press his inquiries well into late middle age. It is conventional nowadays to decry the turn Augustine's thought took during the Pelagian crisis, and the last works against Julian certainly make for us wearying reading; but the detailed biography of Augustine in these late years still needs writing,[31] and I think that a fair reading of all his late works would show that the strength of mind and the freshness of approach was still there, however the atmosphere had clouded.

The question *how* Augustine emerged as a figure of authority perhaps deserves to be prefaced with the question *whether*: for it is one of the remarkable gaps in our scholarly literature that we have no satisfactory, and really very little unsatisfactory, treatment of the question of the spread of Augustine's influence. It is often assumed that "the early middle ages" were a period profoundly influenced by Augustine, but in just what way this influence was exercised, what its limits were, and how it came to be, these are questions that still deserve attention. Here I will only sketch, by way of suggesting the questions and problems that remain, something of how Augustine's reputation grew in his lifetime, and then how his name survived in the century and a half following his death.

Augustine's authority spread in his lifetime in two ways: ecclesiastical and personal. Both were important, though on Augustine's own theory only the first should have been determinative. The personal influence came through his epistolary contacts with the world outside his native Africa. The correspondence with Paulinus of Nola was a standing link between Augustine and one of the best-placed and best-connected ascetic aristocrats in the Roman world.[32] There is no exhaustive treatment of Augustine's letters, but one would be most welcome. The contact that Augustine had with Melania and Pinianus, by letters and in person,[33] is a reminder that from humble origins Augustine had become himself a well-connected figure: his books would travel and his name would be spoken of where his letters and his correspondents went.[34] What was novel about this was that before the generation of Ambrose and Augustine, Latin bishops tended not to move in those circles.

The case of Jerome is of course important and instructive as well. Jerome was nothing if not well-, if often acerbically, connected, and by coming into communication with Jerome Augustine was linking up with a "textual community"[35] of no small importance. What is most instructive about that relationship is the way in which authority was balanced between the two. On many points, it is easy for us to see Jerome as more authoritative, more scholarly, than Augustine, and Augustine's comparative reluctance to accept Jerome's translations looks a lot like institutional foot-dragging to our eyes. But we should remember that in that correspondence, Augustine was a bishop, Jerome was not. At the most nettlesome moments of their correspondence, Jerome did not forget this. If he expressed himself with irony sometimes[36] and was resourceful enough to cover himself in the authority of a bishop even greater than Augustine,[37] he also knew how to maintain proper protocol;[38] how much genuine deference there is in such texts remains hard to say, but what is important is that both Augustine and Jerome expected the deference and acted, whatever the facts of their respective scholarly authority on given points, with the protocol in mind.[39]

To the wider ecclesiastical world and to the general public, such as it was, Augustine's name first became important in connection with his role in the Donatist controversy.[40] The renown that he achieved at this time was far from unambiguously positive: as he took an increasingly strong part, with Aurelius of Carthage, in attacking the Donatists, the Donatists themselves took advantage of what they perceived to be chinks in his armor to attack him.[41] Augustine came on to the center stage defending himself and his past against various charges; the *Confessions* may very well have reached some of their first audience in the same way and for the same reasons that Newman's *Apologia* reached an unconverted and unconvinced audience. And the *Confessions* were of course not universally well-received.[42] The most famous case is that of Pelagius, not yet then famous but already mingling in Italy in circles that Augustine's name and book reached because of his personal, rather than his ecclesiastical, contacts; and we have the story of how Pelagius was so shocked by some of what he heard that he leapt up and left the room where the text was quoted.[43]

For all that, Augustine's visibility and influence (if not universal acclaim) continued to grow through the early 400s, culminating in his strategic mastery of the politics of the conference of Carthage of 411.[44] That moment represented the high point of Augustine's career as a political bishop: the execution of his friend Marcellinus on trumped-up charges two years later, on the other hand, sent Augustine back to Hippo a changed man; his visits to Carthage — for him the center of action linked to the great world of church and empire — drop off sharply after that date[45] and he was content to work for the most part from his home base in Hippo from then on: at about age 60, one important part of Augustine's career was over.

The Pelagian controversy itself when it erupted about then thrust Augustine into the limelight, but in a different way. From this point on, it was his books that spoke for him; and because books could speak beyond the range of his voice and travels, and because the Pelagian controversy quickly became "international" in scope, it was in the last fifteen years of Augustine's life that he became a figure of truly international reputation.[46] Julian of Eclanum is the appropriate cautionary figure here: he would never have attacked Augustine so vehemently, so copiously, and so often if Augustine were not a figure of commanding presence in his world. At the same time, he would not have attacked him so boldly or in the same way if he did not sense in Augustine vulnerabilities that he could exploit. Augustine's name did not travel abroad from his home during his lifetime except accompanied by this ambiguity. But we run a risk in calculating positive and negative reputations even in our day of public opinion polls, and we have no serious method of balancing the books for a period as far removed as that of

Augustine. The poignant description of the power of the *Confessions* from the *Retractations*[47] tells us something of the praise Augustine must have heard, as for that matter does the long meditation in Book 10 of the *Confessions* on the perils of vainglory to which someone in the exposed and veneration position of bishop was exposed.[48]

Augustine the bishop, of course, was not without some responsibility for assuring his own reputation. We have already seen and will see again the importance in the manuscript culture of late antiquity that attaches to the availability of written works. The most brilliant and uplifting book lying unread in a single copy was far less influential than much more pedestrian works widely disseminated. Augustine, with the help of his discipline Possidius, bishop of Calama, is directly responsible for his own literary success in a way he did not perhaps anticipate. By the preparation of the *Retractations*[49] and by Possidius' authorship of the *Life of Augustine*[50] and his compilation of the little pamphlet we call his *indiculum* of Augustine's writings,[51] Augustine left this world with a more secure claim on future readers' attention than any other writer of his age. The availability of the two comprehensive lists of Augustine's authentic works did more, immediately and throughout the middle ages, than anything else could have to assure that the names of Augustine's books were known; and that knowledge in turn made it easier for readers everywhere to seek out his works, to fill gaps in their collections, and to recognize doubtfully attributed works as authentic.[52]

For all that, it remains remarkable that so much of Augustine's work survived the twin blows that shattered his homeland and the church he had worked for. The Vandal invasion completed shortly after his death (he died, let us not forget, in a city under siege) led to a regime in Africa for a hundred years that was at times fiercely hostile to orthodox Christianity,[53] and if there then followed a century and more of Byzantine interim,[54] the eventual conquest of north Africa by Islam by the end of the seventh century meant the extermination of Augustine's heritage in his native land. We know too little about the movement of his works from Africa to the northern shores of the Mediterranean; but this movement must have been facilitated by the handy index of the *Retractations*, and we surmise that there may have been a systematic movement at some point. The translation of Augustine's body from Africa first to Sardinia and then to Pavia (where it may still be seen) suggests a deliberate and timely withdrawal: if his mortal remains received such attention, it is not unlikely that his literary remains were similarly cared for.

Now for the unwritten history of Augustine's influence after his death, I will sketch here briefly only two important and early episodes. The first shows us how ambiguously he could be received, the second how enthusiastically he could be received in spite of ambiguity.

Already in Augustine's lifetime, his argument with the Pelagians had earned him trouble on another front: in its mildest form, it took the shape of inquiries from monks — still a relative novelty in the Latin west — asking just *what* their numerous privations and disciplines were for, if divine predestination had assorted them their lots long beforehand.[55] The center of the controversy that followed was southern Gaul, and the intellectual master was Augustine's near-contemporary John Cassian.[56] Cassian was less well educated and well connected than the mature Augustine, but he was also in many ways less provincial and more widely sensitive to the varieties of Christianity in his time. He was writing books (the *Institutes* and the *Conferences*) that would be the spiritual charters of monasticism for all the early Latin middle ages. The story of how and why Cassian and his disciples found Augustine's teachings unacceptable has been told, but deserves retelling soon. Suffice it to say that the dangers of elitism and perfectionism that Augustine sensed in a mixed lay community in a provincial city, and against which *his* doctrine militated, were very different from those of indifference that a Cassian sensed and against which *he* wrote. The necessary differences of circumstance taken into consideration, the positions of African and Gaulish churchmen in this period are not so very far apart, perhaps,[57] but at the time what counted were the differences.

Nevertheless, all agree that the remarkable thing about the controversy that flourished in Gaul in the fifth century, and that came to an end only in the early sixth century under the leadership of Caesarius of Arles, is the relatively eirenic tone and the absence of mutual excommunications. Augustine's opponents and defenders all deferred to him. Vincent of Lérins, whose *commonitorium* is rightly taken as the most strident attack on what it saw as the novelty and excesses of Augustinian doctrine,[58] was also the compiler of a respectful anthology of passages from Augustine's own writings.[59] There was remarkably little name-calling, and remarkable circumspection in all the debates. The results of this controversy were scarcely less remarkable: the council of Orange in 529 promulgated what *may* be taken as a reading of Augustine, but at the same time may be taken as a quiet refusal to accept all that Augustine said or seemed to say. The decrees of Orange could be taken by all sides in good part: they represent in many ways the most successful resolution of a doctrinal controversy in all of Christian antiquity. But as one sign of that success, and perhaps one reason for it, the issues and the decrees quickly became a matter of little interest. Serious argument over predestination and free will in the west was put off until the ninth century, and the Augustine who is read and praised in the intervening years is *not* the Augustine of predestination.

The best evidence we have for the way Augustine was really being read in the sixth century is the thousand page anthology of Augustine compiled by Eugippius at the monastery of Lucullanum, near Naples.[60] He is known otherwise mainly for his life of saint Severinus of Noricum, but we have recently been made aware that his monastic and literary endeavors were more extensive than we have previously known and indeed give him reason to be set alongside Cassiodorus as one of the leaders of the monastic/literary life in Italy of his time.[61]

The anthology that Eugippius put together has not yet received an adequate critical edition, and so some conclusions must be drawn with care. In particular, we do not yet know accurately just how large Eugippius's original collection was and how many of the added items in some manuscripts may have come from revision by him or from later accretion elsewhere. The order of excerpts is in the main guaranteed, but there are some problems there too. Some things may, however, be said with fair certainty. First, the "authority of Augustine" in this collection is limited in an interesting way. Eugippius had no idea of producing "The Essential Augustine' with a view to illuminating Augustine's special contributions to Christian thought or his distinctive positions. Rather, the usefulness of Augustine lay in his way of representing the common Christian tradition. What was valuable about Augustine, put another way, was not what was distinctive about him but what he had said that formed a useful part of the common deposit of faith and interpretation. He had acquired his authority not by being unique and brilliant and original, but by accomplishing the common task of interpretation and teaching in a way that others could share wholeheartedly. So we might think that, especially in view of the controversy over grace and free will that had animated Gaul in the fifth century, a reasonable anthology would have a distinct section of clear and concise excerpts from the anti-Pelagian writings, to make *Augustine's* position clear. Those writings are seriously underrepresented in the collection as a whole, and the few excerpts that do appear come near the end, with no special emphasis.[62]

So there is no attempt to represent distinctive Augustinian ideas or works. Passages that we regard as essentially Augustinian are missing, and the organization is at every turn an obstacle to an attempt to see what *Augustine* thought. The extracts from the *Confessions*, for example, show very little interest in the autobiographical element and reflect rather an interest in passages that modern, post-Romantic readers regard as stolidly theological.

So the principle of organization that does obtain is scriptural. The arrangement of excerpts does not follow the order of Augustine's own works, except incidentally, and does follow the order of the books of scripture. What Augustine has to say that can in one form or another illuminate the book of Genesis, for example, leads the collection.[63] Old Testament first, New Testament later. The point is again the effacement of the cult of personality and emphasis on the common task of interpreting scripture. Whatever we may think of the relation of theory and practice in Augustine's own writings, Eugippius is an heir of the theory who *is* determined to put it into practice: the "authority" of Augustine for Eugippius is what there is in Augustine that helps the reader come to a better interpretation and fuller understanding of the scriptural text.

It is on those terms that I think we can best understand Augustine's authority in the sixth century. So when Augustine is quoted by Primasius of Hadrumetum, in the prologue to his commentary on the Apocalypse, or by Pelagius I in his *Defense of the Three Chapters*, there is no special axe to grind, there is no special cult of personality directed towards Augustine being exploited. The Second Council of Constantinople of 553 quotes three Latin authorities only: Hilary, Ambrose, and Augustine. At that moment, it is still clear that one element in the council's choice is the episcopal standing of those it quotes. So in the "sententia synodica" at the end of that council, Augustine is quoted thus: "Letters of Augustine of holy memory, who shone among the bishops of Africa, were read, to the effect that it is necessary that heretics be excommunicated even after death."[64] The recitation took place at the fifth session, with texts put in consideration by Sextilianus of Tunes, representing Primosus bishop of Carthage: *Epistula 185, Contra Cresonium, Epistola ad catholicos, Gesta collationes.* Now the content of the passages quoted is of interest and importance for our theme.

In in every case where he was quoted, Augustine was speaking of affairs in the orthodox controversy with the Donatists in the fourth century; he spoke about words and deeds of the early Donatists as they were reported in *other* texts, but he was not actually talking about excommunicating *texts*; the second council of Constantinople, on the other hand, was the first that sought to excommunicate not men but dead men, which is to say, men represented only by texts, not by their living words. In a city in which the books of long-dead Origen had lately been put under the ban, this was not altogether surprising; but it was unprecedented, as serious observers at the time knew, and as the leaders of the council had to deny. They could not allow themselves to be aware of the difference.

We come closer to the heart of Augustine's reputation in the west with Cassiodorus' *Institutiones*, where Augustine is a regular component of the bibliography,[65] and the object of one of several short paragraphs of eulogy, in praise of Hilary, Cyprian, Ambrose, and Jerome, and is followed by a single chapter praising Cassiodorus's contemporaries, Dionysius Exiguus and Eugippius (n.b.: none of the last three was a bishop). The paragraph[66] on Augustine comes after the numerous paragraphs in which Augustine's works on scripture had been cited (including *De doctrina christiana*), and so the works that remain to be praised there are *Confessiones*, his numerous expositions of the creed (ecclesiastical "authority" of a very specialized and important kind), and his translation and expansion of Epiphanius' work on the heresies. Augustine is praised for his polemical skills and for his mixture of subtlety and accessibility: "what he says clearly, he says sweetly, and what he says darkly is rich and filled with great usefulness."[67] In short, Augustine is useful, but he is no longer an authority because he was a bishop, nor again because he was an especially holy man, but he is an authority because he was a brilliant writer. This marks a sea-change with profound implications for the future. It creates a world quite different from the one in which Augustine lived.

There is still another history to be written here, of the *quality* of Augustine's readership in late antiquity. Cassiodorus offers two cautionary pieces of evidence. One is his revision of Pelagius' commentary on Paul:[68] for all the deference Cassiodorus shows to Augustine, and for all his awareness of Pelagius's problems, the revision of Pelagius's commentary produces a hybrid artifact with which Augustine himself might have been very little satisfied. Similarly, when Cassiodorus talks of original sin, the distance between him and Augustine is, for all that he would have wanted to be completely faithful, very great.[69]

For the point I would make here is that the history of Augustine's rise to widespread acclaim in the fifth and sixth centuries accompanies and exemplifies one of the most important developments in the history of Christianity: the emergence in the Latin west of a distinctively Christian body of religious literature. Now it is conventional in our histories to focus on the producers of a high literature, and so to emphasize what can only be called a golden age: the few decades in which Hilary, Marius Victorinus, Ambrose, Prudentius, Jerome, Ambrosiaster, Jerome, and Cassian, to name only the leading lights, created a body of Latin Christian literature that far outshone all that had come before and that would loom large over all that came after. But in the conditions of a manuscript culture, production was only a part of the story. In their lifetimes, those authors' books had a certain life, but also certain very pronounced limitations. There were no Christian libraries or schools, no established means of distribution, not even any systematic means of disseminating the mere fact that a book existed.

So the second essential stage in the making of Latin patristic literary history is the period from roughly Jerome to Cassiodorus when the *fact* of the literature's existence imposed itself on the minds of an audience. Gradually an ancillary literature began to emerge. Augustine's own *Retractationes* and Possidius' *indiculum* are early examples of texts that helped the reader keep track of other texts. Jerome's *De viris illustribus* marks the first major attempt to gather and disseminate in Latin information about Christian writers generally; Augustine's catalogue *De haeresibus* makes an odd counterpoint to it. But in the course of the fifth century we then get Gennadius,[70] also writing *De viris illustribus*, followed in the early sixth century by the very important "decretum de libris recipiendis et non recipiendis" once attributed to pope Gelasius and now thought to be north Italian in provenance.[71] Eugippius gathering the works of Augustine and indexing them with "chapter headings" represents another stage in the attempt to gather and control the growing body of literature.[72] Dionysius Exiguus' collection of church canons is another such exercise, while at Rome we have evidence of the increasing dependence on texts and the consequent organization of texts of the papacy itself: the library of pope Agapetus[73] was only one example; the first compilations of the *liber Pontificalis* apparently date to the early sixth century,[74] and it is noteworthy that we even have evidence from that period of competing *versions* of the book of Popes being created and disseminated by rival factions in the Laurentian schism that arose from the papal election of 498/9. That schism also the generation of bogus documents from earlier papal history, the so-called Symmachan apocrypha,[75] whose relevance here is that they show that authority by now resided for the Christians of Rome in texts brought forth from an *armarium* and was no longer controlled by the spoken word of the inspired and anointed leader of the community.[76]

The story of the textualization of Latin Christianity deserves to be told at greater length elsewhere; for our purposes, I think it worth rehearsing briefly by way of showing one important reason why, and method by which, Augustine came to the pre-eminent place he held in later Christian thought. He was not only a bishop and a holy man, but he was the preeminent *writer*, his works far outrunning in sheer bulk those of any nearest competitor.[77] His office, his holiness, and his orthodoxy were all factors in claiming his place: but had he not written, had he not written so much, and had his works not survived so consistently (we have already seen some reasons why they did), he would never have become the authority figure that he did become. He was the right man in the right place at the right time.

To explain how Augustine came to his place of pre-eminence is one thing. To know what to make of it now is another. I am not the one to trace the history of Augustine's prestige in later times, and a checkered history it is. The medieval history alone is rich and varied and of great interest; as in so many other areas, the insular, then Carolingian phases seem essential to the shaping of the reputation that emerged,[78] but here again, there have been too few detailed studies and certainly no serious attempt at synthesis.[79] It has generally been recounted in theological terms, and those are terms that are sobering to consider.[80] But even on those terms, there are cautions for us. Surely the reverence for Augustine of a Jansen has something demented about it, and at the same time it has the mad logic of great dementia.[81] If we place Augustine on a pedestal, then why not do the job seriously?

But the twentieth century prestige of Augustine has little to do with old doctrinal quarrels. He benefitted rather from the general revival in prestige of the church fathers that was fueled by the liberal wing of Roman Catholicism in the first half of this century. Augustine was easy and relatively safe to praise, and a collection of cutting-edge scholarly publications could easily be prefaced by nothing less than a papal encyclical;[82] and at the same time,

Augustine and the fathers generally offered a vocabulary and a range of reference quite different from that of the official scholasticism of the time.

But Augustine came to the twentieth century not only as an authority to churchgoers. He has imperceptibly been granted a position of high eminence by scholars of every stripe. There are those who admire him without believing a word he says;[83] and then there are those who do not admire him at all but, believing him to be a powerful influence, feel they must attack him precisely because he embodies all that is wrong with — what? Modern Christianity? Or the society that Christianity shaped? It is often very hard to tell, when Augustine is being attacked,[84] just what his crimes really are, or why he matters so much.

I would argue that we live in an age that has discovered in itself a curious *need* for Augustine's authority, precisely among those who would attack it. We have imperceptibly moved into a post-modern culture, one which is more like a cargo cult than anything else. In such a culture, Augustine becomes a piece of vaguely significant debris from another culture that has washed up on the shore. So he is read in the most strikingly out-of-context ways, though he is known vaguely to be an authority of the highest order and so he may be made, quite arbitrarily, part of the problem. The great Father of the Latin church is just the father that moderns and post-moderns need in their own Oedipal struggles with the past.[85] It is safe to say that Augustine is now more quoted, either to be attacked or to defend something he would never have defended,[86] and read, when he is actually read, in ways that go far astray from the original contexts and purposes of the works. The post-modern version of sanctity is of course celebrity, and Augustine's authority today is often hard to distinguish in effect from that of Mark Twain or Yogi Berra.

Now I say all this conscious that I am speaking to an audience that presumably still respects Augustine (though there may be those here who have a family quarrel with him of one sort or another) but that may find it difficult to express just how that respect is to be managed and displayed in these curious times. My purpose in sketching the story of his authority has been to provoke reflection and give some basis for serious consideration of just how we who are inclined to esteem and admire him should go about that business. I will conclude with a few remarks meant to be anything but prescriptive: here I am genuinely only thinking aloud.

Let me call to mind again the example I instanced at the outset of the disciples of Plotinus making a portrait of the master against his express wishes. Nothing seems clearer to me than that Augustine himself had no intention of ever being made a plaster saint. In his own treatment of the Christian past, he had an absolute respect for and veneration of scripture as the word of God. His veneration for and respect of such intermediate figures as Ambrose, on the other hand, is of quite a different sort. To him, ecclesiastical authority is always *faute de mieux*: contingent and transient, however practically necessary. He does not allow his veneration for another person to *determine* or limit his own spiritual life. He never surrenders that life to another. Augustine's questions remain his own questions; he remains constantly in touch with the text of scripture himself, asking his questions and pressing for answers. That he knows how to accept *no* answer[87] is a sign of his wisdom; but whatever he has received from his teachers, he has received it with all his wit, faithfully but at the same time discerningly. When we read Augustine, we are reading no disciple of any human teacher;[88] what we value in him is the authentic directness of the Christian experience, checked by ecclesiastical authority in some ways, but enlivened and liberated by it in others.

The challenge for the modern disciple of Augustine is to behave towards him in a way that confounds the attacks of his enemies. The anti-Augustinian of our time assumes that Augustine had, and even meant to have, mindless disciples, who would take every word at face value and believe it and repeat it without end. The one thing we can say about such disciples, if any there are, is that they are the people in our midst the most *un*-like Augustine of all. What we can learn from Augustine, it seems to me, is intellectual and spiritual integrity: fidelity to scripture and the church that is at once complete and at the same time resourceful, imaginative, and enriched. To read Augustine is to encounter one who has made of orthodoxy, of "thinking with the church," an adventure that is very like a high-wire act. His Christianity arises from liturgy and scripture, both contributing to a spirituality that is at once fully obedient and at the same time fully personal — private, but at the same time communitarian or, better, ecclesiastical. The authority of those who have gone on before gives him confidence, but in the end it is his *own* faith and courage — not any borrowed bravado — that bears him along.

To put it another way: in Augustine's Christianity there is no vicarious experience; all is immediate. For us to become disciples of Augustine in

244

such a way that we let him live our Christian exploration for us would be to betray him in something essential. What he finally teaches us is Christian freedom.

Notes

1. It is a pleasure to express my gratitude to Villanova University for extending the invitation to deliver the 1991 St. Augustine Lecture; to Fr. Allan Fitzgerald, OSA, for his many kindnesses over the years; to my other Augustinian friends, notably Frs. George Lawless, John J. Gavigan, and Donald X. Burt, OSA, for fruitful conversations and good advice; and to the memory of my first host on the Villanova campus, the late Fr. Richard Russell, OSA, whose spirit animates the whole series of St. Augustine Lectures. I also acknowledge, and the acknowledgement is a pleasure as a duty, that this lecture has been prepared with the assistance of the Augustine Concordance Project of the University of Würzburg, in the copy located at Villanova University. Professor Steven N. Orso read a draft and made an important and welcome suggestion.

This lecture was composed after a very large manuscript was sent to the press but may well appear in print before the resulting book: my edition of and commentary on the *Confessions* will appear under the imprint of Oxford University Press in 1992 or 1993. This lecture represents reflections consecutive to the completion of that large work and the long period of development it represents; but there are some small points of overlap, as I adduce here bits of evidence and argument that may also be found in a different context in the commentary. But the lecture represents in its main lines wholly new work.

2. *De beata vita* 1.6, "Idibus Novembribus mihi natialis dies erat. Post tam tenue prandium, ut ab eo nihil ingeniorum inpediretur, omnes, qui simul non modo illo die sed cottidie convivabamur, in balneas ad consedendum vocavi; nam is tempori aptus locus secretus occurrerat."

3. Porphyry, *Life of Plotinus* 1 (trans. Armstrong), "Why really, is it not enough to have to carry the image in which nature has encased us, without your requesting me to agree to leave behind me a longer-lasting image of the image, as if it was something genuinely worth looking at?"

4. E.g., Plotinus 1.2.7 (trans Armstrong), "For it is to [the gods], not to good men, that we are to be made like. Likeness to good men is the likeness of two pictures of the same subject to each other; but likeness to the gods is likeness to the model, a being of a different kind to ourselves."

5. See G. Madec, "Connaissance de Dieu et action de grâces. Essai sur les citations de l'*Ep. aux Romains*, I, 18-25 dans l'oeuvre de saint Augustin," *Recherches augustiniennes* 2 (1962) 273-309; but I would not follow Madec (and Courcelle, *Recherches sur les Confessions de saint Augustin*, Paris, 1950, p. 177) in seeing *Confessiones* 7.17.23 as a report that Augustine knew and used the verse in this sense

245

already at Milan on the morning after reading the *platonicorum libri*; Courcelle further sees (improbably) an early reference at *quant. an.* 34.77, but the verse only comes into Augustine's works in *De vera religione* 10.19 and 52.101. How and whether it is appropriate to see scholastic natural theology as an attempt to do what Augustine and the early readers of Rom. 1.20 imagined is a good and important question: the best resolution would come through the thorough study of the history of interpretation of that verse in the middle ages, when it was widely cited and used.

6. It is easy for us to take scripture for granted; it is worth remembering that for Augustine, who probably never saw a "Bible" (that is, a single large codex containing all the scriptural books), the matter was not so easy, and his discussion of questions of canon and authority at *De doctrina christiana* 2.8.13 was important for him; consider also the atmosphere of this interesting passage at *De civitate dei* 15.23, "omittamus igitur earum scripturarum fabulas quae apocryphae nuncupantur, eo quod earum occulta origo non claruit patribus, a quibus usque ad nos auctoritas veracium scripturarum certissima et notissima successione pervenit. in his autem apocryphis etsi invenitur aliqua veritas, tamen propter multa falsa nulla est canonica auctoritas. scripsisse quidem nonnulla divine illum Enoch, septimum ab Adam, negare non possumus, cum hoc in epistula canonica Iudas apostolus dicat [Iud. 14]. sed non frustra non sunt in eo canone scripturarum, qui servabatur in templo Hebraei populi succedentium diligentia sacerdotum, nisi quia ob antiquitatem suspectae fidei iudicata sunt, nec utrum haec essent quae ille scripsisset poterat inveniri, non talibus proferentibus qui ea per seriem successionis reperirentur rite servasse."

7. One need only read Augustine's *De haeresibus*, the catalogue he compiled late in life (based on a Greek source) of all the heresies known to him to get a sense of how fragile and threatened was his sense of church unity: so many ways to go wrong, such fine points leading to such disastrous error. But of course, that said, there is also in Augustine what is often for moderns a surprising vein of licit multiplicity of interpretation. For him the *regula fidei* as guide of interpretation was a much less explicit, detailed, and risky matter than it later became for western Christians, and so we get the development at *Confessiones* 12.14.17ff of the idea that an interpretation of scripture may be erroneous as regards the author's intent but correct if it is remains in accord with the will of God; the same idea underlies the generosity that permeates the interpretative precepts of *De doctrina christiana*.

8. In reflection of Augustine's own practice, I will speak of "authority" to mean post-scriptural and ecclesiastical authority. The "authority" of scripture is of course overwhelming in Augustine, but since for him it represents a different discourse entirely from that of churchmen like Augustine himself, it seems appropriate to make a distinction.

In most of Augustine's early works, *auctoritas* appears in benevolent guise (e.g., *De vera religione* 29.52, "auctoritatis beneficentia"), but a particularly clear series of texts revealing ambiguity and marked by the lingering anxiety of the search for authority, appears in *De utilitate credendi*: 9.21-1.25, "nam vera religio . . . omnino sine quodam *gravi auctoritatis imperio* inire recte nullo pacto potest. . . . (11.25) quod intellegimus igitur, debemus rationi, quod credimus, auctoritati, quod opinamur, errori."

9. *Auctoritas* is the crutch that supports the weakened faculty of *ratio*: *De vera religione* 24.45, "auctoritas fidem flagitat et rationi praeparat hominem." See Holte, *Béatitude et Sagesse*, Paris, 1962, esp. 304-10, who measures the extent and limits of Augustine's originality here. The yoking of *ratio* and *auctoritas* (Holte 308) "n'a pas de parfait équivalent chez les théologiens occidentaux antérieurs comme Tertullien, Lactance ou Ambroise, quoique la terminologie elle-même soit attestée chez ce dernier."

The juxtaposition of *ratio* and *auctoritas* is familiar in Cicero, e.g., Cic. *Lucullus* 18.60, "quae sunt tandem ista mysteria, aut cur celatis quasi turpe aliquid sententiam vestram? 'ut qui audient' inquit 'ratione potius quam auctoritate ducantur.' quid si utrumque, num peius est? unum tamen illud non celant, nihil esse quod percipi possit. an in eo auctoritas nihil obest? mihi quidem videtur vel plurimum." At *Contra academicos* 1.3.8, Trygetius seems to share Cicero's preference for *ratio* in claiming to have thrown off the *iugum auctoritatis* in the name of that *libertas* which *philosophia* promises. But a characteristically Augustinian view is also present: *Contra academicos* 3.20.43, "nulli autem dubium est gemino pondere nos impelli ad discendum, auctoritatis atque rationis. mihi autem certum est nusquam prorsus a Christi auctoritate discedere; non enim reperio valentiorem."

10. Just how the fallen reason of the church fathers, or the fathers of an ecumenical council, may be temporarily liberated from the penalties of the fall is a subject that Augustine would understand in terms of the inspiration of the spirit; and the technicalities again he would leave for later generations to worry about.

11. To anticipate, this is how Augustine expects to be read himself: *Confessiones* 10.3.3, "sed quia caritas omnia credit, inter eos utique quos conexos sibimet unum facit, ego quoque, domine, etiam sic tibi confiteor ut audiant homines, quibus demonstrare non possum an vera confitear. sed credunt mihi quorum mihi aures caritas aperit."

12. For the rituals, see best F. Van Der Meer, *Augustine the Bishop*, London, 1961, 347-87.

13. Classic studies include Courcelle, *Recherches sur les Confessions* 147-57; A. Mandouze, *Saint Augustin: L'aventure du raison et de la grâce* (Paris, 1968); Courcelle, *Les Confessions dans la tradition littéraire* (Paris, 1973), 43-58; R. J. O'Connell, *Saint Augustine's Confessions. The Odyssey of Soul*, Cambridge, Mass., 1969; and G. Madec, "La Délivrance de l'Esprit (Confessions VII)", in *'Le Confessioni' di Agostino d'Ippona: Libri VI-IX*, Palermo, 1985, 45-69, the most recent extended statement of Madec's views. To state my own position (fully developed in my commentary) very baldly, I believe that a theory about the ascent of the mind to God derived from neo-Platonism but fully (to Augustine's mind) Christianized is one of the structural principles of *Confessiones* as a whole and a factor that animates much of what he wrote before and after, notably *De Genesi ad litteram* and *De Trinitate*.

14. It is the signal merit of the St. Augustine Lecture for 1984 (R. A. Markus, *Conversion and Disenchantment in Augustine's Spiritual Career*, Villanova, 1989) to have described with compassion and clarity the sea-change of expectations that Augustine underwent in the 390s, resulting in the poignant and rich expression of his new, chastened, expectations in *Confessiones.*

15. *De civitate dei* 11.1.

16. *Confessiones* 1.11.17 reports Augustine's earliest religious awareness, clearly mediated to him by Christianity; *Confessiones* 7.3.4, on the other hand, shows Augustine *before* reading the *platonicorum libri* in possession of a doctrine of God that few of us would find *very* incompatible with Christianity; but I argue in my commentary that one point of *Confessiones* 7 is to show how errors in his view of God that obstructed progress were decisively removed. On the other hand, O. du Roy, *L'intelligence de la foi en la trinité selon saint Augustin: genèse de sa théologie trinitaire jusqu'en 391*, Paris, 1966, 96-106, makes a case that cannot be dismissed out of hand that Augustine's view of a trinitarian God derives from the neo-Platonists; du Roy reproaches him from a theological point of view for this dependance on an extra-Christian source. I discuss du Roy's view further in my commentary.

17. The classic studies are P. Courcelle, *Late Latin Writers and Their Greek Sources*, Cambridge, Mass., 1969; trans. French ed. of 1948, 149-223; and the articles of B. Altaner, collected in his *Kleine Patristische Schriften*, Berlin, 1967, 181-331.

18. So the points where Augustine remarks that some has not yet been dealt with by any authoritative writer *as far as he knew* (e.g., *De libero arbitrio* 3.21.59, on different theories for the origin of the soul); often he was right and his profession of ignorance is a veiled statement of the originality of his own line of inquiry, but the riches of the Greeks could have served him well at many points.

19. See L. F. Pizzolato, *La dottrina esegetica di sant'Ambrogio*, Milan, 1978; since it is unlikely that Augustine and Ambrose ever really sat down to have what Bertie Wooster would call a bit of the old heart-to-heart (as many modern students seem determined to believe that they *must* have done), the question of just how much influence Ambrose exercised is a vexed one, still not satisfactorily studied in detail. As always, Augustine received by transforming.

20. Augustine, *Epistula* 31 to Paulinus of Nola (c. 397?) asks for a copy of the now lost but important work of Ambrose, *De sacramento regenerationis sive de philosophia*.

21. Ten years after leaving Milan, Augustine was sure he had heard Ambrose say that Plato met Jeremiah in Egypt (*De doctrina christiana* 2.28.43); but he was wrong, as he would have learned from the *De sacramento regenerationis sive de philosophia* and as he acknowledges at *De civitate dei* 8.11 and *Retractationes* 2.4 (Mutzenbecher).

22. In the absence of complete critical editions of the works against Julian, any list is provisional, but would have to include Ambrose's *In Isaiam, In Lucam, De sacramento regenerationis sive de philosophia, De Isaac, De arca Noe, Contra Novatianos, De apologia prophetae David, Explanatio super Ps. 48, De Tobia,* and *De paradiso.*

23. Polemically, it was combined with a different appeal to Ambrose's authority: in 422, Augustine patronized the production of Paulinus' of Milan's life of Ambrose, undoubtedly to buttress Augustine's own increasing reliance on Ambrose's views. The later date for Paulinus' *Vita* is preferable in spite of É. Lamirande, *Paulin de Milan et la 'Vita Ambrosii'*, Paris/Montreal, 1983, 214; though Lamirande prefers a date of 412-13, he does not positively rule out 422. More satisfactory is A. Paredi, *Sacris Erudiri* 14 (1963) 212-13 (good on the anti-Pelagian context of the *Vita*).

24. The mid 390s were a time when Augustine fought off a case of writer's block, leaving work after work unfinished, until *Confessiones* brought release and led to a remarkable outpouring of ambitious projects. The lost *Contra epistulam Donati* known from *Retractationes* 2.5 (Mutzenbecher) was his anti-Donatist failure of this period, which *De baptismo* redeemed.

25. To be sure, Augustine quotes Cyprian later in life, e.g., *Contra Julianum* 2.6, 2.25, as a frank "authority" when it suits him, and cf. the unambiguous praise of Cyprian in the sermons preached on his feast day (e.g., *ss.* 309-13).

26. And it perhaps offers a model for our own response to Augustine; see my concluding remarks below.

27. Perhaps it is worth emphasizing that the *platonicorum libri* (*Confessiones* 7.9.13) that played such an important and now controversial part in Augustine's conversion never became "authoritative" in any way in Augustine's writings. Whatever he owes them, he owes implicitly.

28. Thus we have had two books of the first water about Gregory in the last fifteen years (C. Dagens, *Saint Grégoire le Grand: Culture et expérience chrétiennes*, Paris, 1977, and C. Straw, *Gregory the Great: Perfection in Imperfection*, Berkeley, 1988), neither of which more than flirts with the question of the Augustinianism of Gregory.

29. Music offers a good point of comparison: compare the way he treats the subject, both in *De musica* (which never quite gets to technical music) and in remarks elsewhere with the slavishness and scholasticism of Boethius or Cassiodorus.

30. *Epistulas* 128-29, 132-33, 135-39, 143; see M. Moreau, *Recherches Augustiniennes* 9 (1973) 1-181 (also published separately as *Le dossier Marcellinus dans la correspondance de saint Augustin*, Paris, 1973).

31. Peter Brown's biography is a marvel of the nations, but it is now a quarter century old; and it is noteworthy that it does not provide a detailed chronicle or an equally comprehensive and thorough treatment of all periods of Augustine's life. The chronological researches of A.-M. La Bonnardière had to be pursued before any such thing would be possible, and continued work on the *Biblia Augustiniana* will be needed; but sometime in the *next* generation, the avenue will be open for a new, probably multi-volume, biography of Augustine to reshape the landscape once again. It would be interesting to study in detail the effect of Brown's portrayal of Augustine's later years and the quarrel with Julian on the readership of Augustine in the last generation; I do not think a work such as E. Pagels, *Adam, Eve, and the Serpent*, New York, 1988, would have been possible without it.

32. Courcelle, *Les Confessions dans la tradition littéraire* 559-607, is exhaustive and exemplary on epistolary relations with Paulinus of Nola (though Courcelle's intention to link that correspondence closely with the writing of *Confessiones* leads him to pressing his case further than was wise at several points); the studies provoked by the discovery of the Divjak letters (see *Les lettres de saint Augustin découvertes par Johannes Divjak*, Paris, 1983 and the annotated edition/translation in *BA* 46B) offer many points of interest in this regard as well.

33. Augustine, *Epistula* 94; see P. Brown, *Augustine of Hippo*, Berkeley, 1967, 340.

34. Think, for example, of Orosius coming from Spain to make himself Augustine's (occasionally irritating) lapdog (Oros. *hist.* 1.prol.3) or Consentius of Maiorca (see *Epistulas* 119, 120, 205, 11*, 12*, and *Contra mendacium*; discussion now by M. Moreau in *BA* 46B.479-93).

35. The phrase is one I owe to the suggestive volume of B. Stock, *Implications of Literacy*, Princeton, 1982.

36. Augustine, *Epistulas* 75.7.22, "tu qui iuvenis es, et in pontificali culmine constitutus, doceto populos; et novis Africae frugibus Romana tecta locupleta. mihi sufficit, cum auditore et lectore pauperculo in angulo monasterii susurrare."

37. *Epistula* 75.3.6, on the controversy between Augustine and Jerome over the apparent quarrel between Peter and Paul, invokes Chrysostom as holding the same opinion as he, thus, "si igitur me reprehendis errantem, patere me, quaeso, errare cum talibus."

38. *Epistula* 72.1.2, "deinde illud cavebam, ne episcopo communionis meae viderer procaciter respondere, et aliqua in reprehendentis epistula reprehendere; praesertim cum quaedam in illa haeretica iudicarem"; *Epistula* 72.2.4, "non enim convenit ut ab adolescentia usque ad hanc aetatem, in monasteriolo cum sanctis fratribus labore desudans, aliquid contra episcopum communionis meae scribere audeam, et eum episcopum quem ante coepi amare quam nosse, qui me prior ad amicitiam provocavit, quem post me orientem in scripturarum eruditione laetatus sum."

39. One other aspect of Jerome's work is instructive here: his repeated references to and defenses against his critics, usually in the prefaces to his works, are a reminder of the considerable *resistance* to "patristic" authority that such texts found when they first reached the general Christian public. None of the most famous and influential writers of the golden age of patristic Christianity was the object of universal acclaim and all had their enemies and critics.

40. His earliest successes had been against the Manichees (recorded in dialogues like *Contra Fortunatum* and in imposing a stricter discipline on popular customs [see *Epistula* 29]). Both of these contests were played out on parochial stages.

41. *Enarrationes in psalmos* 36 and *Contra litteras Petiliani* 3.25.30, for example, defend against such attacks.

42. Cf. Secundinus the Manichee (*Contra Secundinum* 3), Consentius of Maiorca (*Epistula* 12*.1.3: sympathetic as regards doctrine, but critical of the style), Pelagius (see next note), and Julian (*Contra Julianum* 1.68).

43. *De dono perseverantiae* 20.53, "quae mea verba [*Confessiones* 10.29.40ff, 'da quod iubes et iube quod vis'] Pelagius Romae cum a quodam fratre coepiscopo meo fuissent eo praesente conmemorata, ferre non potuit et contradicens aliquanto conmotius paene cum eo, qui illa conmemoraverat, litigavit."

44. Best in English is still W. H. C. Frend, *The Donatist Church*, Oxford, 1951, 275-89, with which cf. the acts of the Council itself, best read in the *SC* edition of S. Lancel (*SC* 194, 195, 225).

45. See O. Perler, *Les Voyages de saint Augustin*, Paris, 1969, with summary for these years on pp. 462-76.

46. For that controversy in its "international" context, see O. Wermelinger, *Rom und Pelagius*, Stuttgart, 1975. The emperor Theodosius II apparently made a special point of inviting Augustine to attend the council of Ephesus of 431, but Augustine had already died in August 430 when the invitation was issued later that year: see Liberatus, *Breviarium* 5.17 (PL 68.977).

47. *Retractationes* 2.6.1, "confessionum mearum libri tredecim et de malis et de bonis meis deum laudant iustum et bonum atque in eum excitant humanum intellectum et affectum. interim quod ad me attinet, hoc in me egerunt cum scriberentur et agunt cum leguntur. quid de illis alii sentiant, ipsi viderint; multis tamen fratribus eos multum placuisse et placere scio."

48. *Confessiones* 10.36.58ff.

49. Ed. Mutzenbecher, CCSL 57 (1984).

50. Ed. M. Pellegrino, Alba, 1955.

51. Ed. A. Wilmart, in *Miscellanea Agostiniana*, Vatican City, 1931, 2.149-233.

52. Mutzenbecher knows no fewer than 25 manuscripts of *Retractationes* from before 1100 and another 40 from the 12th century alone.

53. The harrowing picture in Victor of Vita's history of persecutions is perhaps overdrawn but not fundamentally inaccurate (see, for example, his account of a veritable shoot-out in church on Easter Sunday morning: Victor Vit. 1.13).

54. See Averil Cameron, "Byzantine Africa: The Literary Evidence," in J. Humphrey, ed., *Excavations at Carthage VIII*, Ann Arbor, 1982, pp. 29-62.

55. Augustine's response is given in *De dono perseverantiae* and *De praedestinatione sanctorum*.

56. A full review of the Gaulish controversy would be welcome; for background, see still O. Chadwick, *John Cassian*, 2nd ed., Cambridge, 1968, and now R. A. Markus, *The End of Ancient Christianity*, Cambridge, 1990, pp. 157-97.

57. See my "Salvian and Augustine," *Augustinian Studies* 14 (1983) 25-34.

58. Carried out, of course, in veiled language, of which the most explicit is perhaps at Vinc. Ler. *comm.* 26.37, "audent etenim polliceri et docere quod in ecclesia sua,

id est, in communionis suae conventiculo, magna et specialis ac plane personalis quaedam sit dei gratia, adeo ut sine ullo labore, sine ullo studio, sine ulla industria, etiamsi nec petant nec quaerant nec pulsent [echoing Mt. 7.7, itself a favorite text of Augustine's], quicumque illi ad numerum suum pertinent, tamen ita divinitus dispensentur, ut angelicis evecti manibus, id est, angelica protectione servati, numquam possint 'offendere ad lapidem pedem suum' [Mt. 4.6], id est, numquam scandalizari."

59. Vinc. Ler., *Excerpta sanctae memoriae Vincentii Lirinensis insulae presbyteri ex universo beatae recordationis Augustini episcopi in unum collecta* (ed. R. Demeulenaere, *CCSL* 64 [1985]); the passages are chosen to express Augustine's orthodox teaching on trinity and incarnation against the Arians, Apollinarians, and Nestorians.

60. Eugippius, *Excerpta ex operibus sancti Augustini* (ed. Knöll, CSEL 9.1 [1885]).

61. I have in mind the important articles of M. M. Gorman, esp. "Eugippius and the Origins of the Manuscript Tradition of St. Augustine's 'De Genesi ad litteram'", *Revue Bénédictine* 93 (1983) 7-30.

62. The arrangement is fundamentally scriptural: approximately 200 of the nearly four hundred excerpts are arranged from Genesis through the gospels. The work begins with excerpts on the four cardinal virtues and ends with two on *caritas*. The anti-Pelagian extracts appear as nos. 305-22 in Knöll's edition, which comprises 384 items in all, and they fill approximately 60 out of the 1100 pages of the printed edition.

The point is important for recent discussions of Augustine's views on sexuality and his influence on the later western tradition. Two Princeton books, P. Brown, *The Body and Society* and E. Pagels, *Adam, Eve, and the Serpent* (both New York, 1988), characterize Augustine's views as the culmination of a late antique development and then leave the story in mid-air (Brown adds a suggestive epilogue, pp. 428-447, but Pagels goes no further). They seem to assume that it may be taken for granted that Augustine's ideas exercised wide influence, but it must be emphasized that neither they nor anyone else has troubled to trace the steps by which that influence was felt. If, as I suspect, the essential development is not medieval at all but modern (here I would follow M. Foucault, *The History of Sexuality, I: An Introduction*, New York, 1978, trans. French original of 1976), then it scarcely matters what Augustine may have said or meant; for if he had not said what the sixteenth and seventeenth centuries wanted him to say, that would scarcely have dissuaded them from imposing the views they had already developed quite without attention to Augustine.

63. The same principle animates the ninth century anthology of Augustinian texts made by Florus of Lyons.

64. *ACO* 4.1.212.4-6: "Augustini religiosae memoriae, qui inter Africanos episcopos splenduit, diversae epistolae recitatae sunt significantes quod oportet haereticos et post mortem anathematizari."

65. And of course Cassiodorus had emulated Augustine in commenting on the whole Psalter, and had used his *Enarrationes in psalmos* wittingly in the process. See inter

alia A. Quacquarelli, "La elocutio di S. Agostino nelle riflessioni di Cassiodoro," *Augustinianum* 25 (1985) 385-403; repr. in *Vetera Christianorum* 25 (1988) 177-98. See n. 68 below.

66. *Institutiones* 1.22.

67. "cuius aperta suavia sunt, obscura vero magnis utilitatibus farcita pinguescunt."

68. It is a pleasure to praise the dissertation of D.W. Johnson, *Purging the Poison: The revision of Pelagius' Pauline Commentaries by Cassiodorus and his Students* (diss., Princeton Theological Seminary, 1989). There are uncertainties because there is no critical edition of Cassiodorus' revision, but the main lines of investigation are sound and I think the conclusions suggestive. I particularly admired the corollary demonstration (at 256-74) that the standard histories of doctrine (e.g., Harnack, Pelikan) are on very shaky ground when they speak of the history of Augustinian influence in late antiquity. See also Johnson, "The Myth of the Augustinian Synthesis," *Lutheran Quarterly* 5.2 (Summer 1991), 157-69, which reached me after this lecture was completed: he shows in both places how Cassiodorus' version of Augustine was not so much unfaithful as simply incoherent, an incoherency arising from the difficulty of the issues and the imperfection of Cassiodorus' own grasp of the positions taken by both Augustine and Pelagius.

69. See J. Gross, "Cassiodorus und die augustinische Erbsündenlehre," *Zeitschrift für Kirchengeschichte* 69 (1958) 299-308: Cassiodorus's Augustinian God winds up foreknowing merits, and in *De anima* goes for a creationist origin of soul, though Augustine had been unable to reconcile that with original sin/predestination.

70. *De viris illustribus*, ed. Richardson, Leipzig, 1896. Gennadius is particularly interesting for his insistence, *De viris illustribus* 4.4, that books have authors' names attached to them in order to be accepted: names are the guarantors of authenticity. (So Paul's name was early attached to the Epistle to the Hebrews, though few ever really accepted that attribution.)

71. See E. von Dobschütz, *Das Decretum Gelasianum de libris recipiendis et non recipiendis*, Leipzig, 1912.

72. See Gorman, *art. cit.* at note 53 above.

73. H.-I. Marrou, "Autour de la bibliothèque du pape Agapit," *MEFR* 48 (1931) 124-69.

74. For demonstration, see the edition of L. Duchesne, Paris, 1886, 1.xxiii-xlviii.

75. These fascinating texts have no adequate editions and must be sought out in eighteenth century texts, one of which is not even in *PL*: for details, see *Clavis Patrum Latinorum* nos. 1679-82.

76. For it is a curious fact that the rise of the papacy is associated with the decline of the charismatic authority of the holder of the chair: the prestige of the institution prevails at the expense of that of the individual who holds the office.

77. Computer checks now make it possible to say that Augustine's surviving works comprise about four times the words of the surviving works of Cicero, and the extant writings of the first generations of Latin Christian fathers down to Augustine,

Jerome, and Cassian — those writings *alone* add up to a corpus larger than all of surviving classical Latin literature.

78. The importance of the Visigothic, and particularly, the Isidoran contribution should not be forgotten. Isidore's Augustine remains a fertile subject for investigation.

79. A good example of the kind of meticulous study required is H. A. Oberman and F. A. James III, edd., *Via Augustini: Augustine in the Later Middle Ages, Renaissance, and Reformation: Essays in Honor of Damasus Trapp, OSA*, Leiden, 1991; cf. esp. Trapp's own "Hitalinger's Augustinian Quotations" reprinted in that volume at 189-220. General studies of the Reformation of course pay much lip-service to Augustine's role, but I do not see that even there do we have a study that approaches the subject with adequate range and attention to detail.

80. For a central part of the history, see N. Abercrombie, *The Origins of Jansenism*, Oxford, 1936, and *Saint Augustine and French Classical Thought*, Oxford, 1938, especially the introductory chapter in the latter work, and revise with reference to the numerous works of Jean Orcibal, most recently his *Jansenius d'Ypres*, Paris, 1989; for the wider theological picture, see H. de Lubac, *Augustinianism and Modern Theology*, London, 1969.

81. J. Orcibal, *Jansenius d'Ypres (1585-1638)*, Paris, 1989, p. 304: "C'est là le point faible de l'*Augustinus*, car cette litanie ne justifie guère le privilège doctrinal exorbitant que l'auteur en accorde à son héros." One need not believe the report that Jansenius had read all of Augustine ten times and the anti-Pelagian parts thirty times to recognize in it a substantial truth about the disorder of his proceedings. (Texts need not always be read to be influential: I have never seen a copy of Jansenius' *Augustinus*, and for good reason. There seems to have been *no* printing of the work from the seventeenth to the twentieth century, and then only a single 1960s-vintage photographic reprint, not abundantly disseminated.)

82. See *Miscellanea Agostiniana*, Vatican City, 1931, 2.ix-xxxvi.

83. This admiration leads to a curious kind of ritual invocation, for Augustine has achieved a place in a kind of multicultural pantheon in which he can be instanced without being read, often in association with Plato. A critic like George Steiner (see his recent *Real Presences*, Chicago, 1989) manages this with an easy dexterity that glibly masks the distortion and misrepresentation of Augustine that necessarily attends the ritual.

84. One thinks of the works of E. Pagels (see above) and Margaret Miles (*Augustine on the Body*, Missoula, MT, 1979; "Infancy, Parenting, and Nourishment in Augustine's 'Confessions,'" *The Journal of the American Academy of Religion* 50[1982], 349-364; and in other works of a more general nature), and the remarkable little book of C. Lorin, *Pour Saint Augustin*, Paris, 1988.

85. One has this impression never so strongly as when reading attempts to interpret Augustine in light of modern psychoanalytic categories. The literature on the subject does not in the main repay reading; pride of place in any catalogue goes to the embarrassingly naive and unscholarly symposium published in the *Journal for the*

Scientific (sic) *Study of Religion* 5(1965/6), 130-52 and 273-89, with articles by D. Bakan, W. H. Clark, J. Dittes, J. Havens, P. J. Pruyser, and P. Woolcott; that journal returned to the subject with a similarly distressing symposium twenty years later (*Jour. Sci. Stud. Rel.* 25 [1986] 57-115). The classic study of Freudian orthodoxy is that of C. Kligerman, "A Psychoanalytic Study of the Confessions of St. Augustine," *Journal of the American Psychoanalytic Association* 5 (1957) 469-84; of interest also is E. R. Dodds, "Augustine's Confessions: A study of spiritual maladjustment," *Hibbert Journal* 26 (1928) 459-73, but to my taste the two most interesting and least personally involved studies are the oldest (W. Achelis, *Die Deutung Augustins*, Prien am Chiemsee, 1921 — very hard to find) and one by a well-regarded student of Augustine who also happens to be a woman and thus not quite so driven to compete with the father-figure: P. Fredriksen, "Augustine and his analysts: The possibility of a psychohistory," *Soundings* 51 (1978) 206-27.

86. I have been told but cannot verify that President Bush at one point in early 1991 invoked the doctrine of a "just war" by explicit reference to "Saint Ambrose Augustine" (sic). I have discussed elsewhere how poor a patron saint Augustine makes for "the just war": see my *Augustine*, Boston, 1985, p. 58.

87. *Confessiones* 1.6.10, "quid ad me, si quis non intellegat? gaudeat et ipse dicens, 'quid est hoc?' gaudeat etiam sic, et amet non inveniendo invenire potius quam inveniendo non invenire te." A similar idea may be found at Cic. *Tusc.* 1.25.60, "nescio, nec me pudet, ut istos, fateri nescire, quod nesciam"; there is a sense in which Augustine became an Academic skeptic in 385 and never really gave up the sect, finding in Christianity the support he needed to live with the philosophical uncertainty to which he found himself driven.

88. This should not be surprising if we consider only what Paul said about those who would make themselves disciples of either Paul or Apollo (1 Cor. 1.12), but it is also the explicit theme of Augustine's *De magistro* and it recurs through *Confessiones* 10.

HTR 84:2 (1991) 163–84

THE EYES INFECTED BY EVIL:
BASIL OF CAESAREA'S HOMILY, *ON ENVY**

Vasiliki Limberis
Temple University

Basil wrote the homily *On Envy* around 364, after he was ordained a pres-byter by Eusebius of Caesarea.[1] He probably intended it as a Lenten ser-mon for his congregation in Caesarea, which was largely composed of catechumens. The homily has received very little attention from scholars, although, along with nine other homilies, it has been classified as one of the moral treatises, rather than as an exegetic or panegyric work.[2] Most recent scholarship has deemed it an authentic homily of Basil's.[3] One can readily see why *On Envy* has been overlooked by historical theologians: the treatise is didactically straightforward, theologically and philosophically unsophisticated, and in no way combats Arian opponents. There are, how-ever, other reasons to find *On Envy* of interest. The treatise documents Basil's attempt to confront a mode of behavior that implicitly questions the church's authority.[4] Simply stated, *On Envy* is Basil's direct effort to wrest

---

*I thank Kelley McCarthy Spoerl, David T. M. Frankfurter, Joseph Russo, and my hus-band, Paul J. Smith, for their critical comments on this paper. I am also grateful to Mrs. Rabia Aksöy for her time.

[1] Paul J. Fedwick, *The Church and the Charisma of Leadership in Basil of Caesarea* (Toronto: Pontifical Institute of Medieval Studies, 1979) 140.

[2] *NPNF* 8. lv.

[3] Fedwick, *The Church and the Charisma*; and Jean Bernardi, *La prédication des Pères cappadociens. Le prédicateur et son auditoire* (Paris: Presses universitaires de France, 1968) 59.

[4] Basil documents this behavior in his *Commentary on Isaiah* and *Homily on Psalm 45*: Νοσεῖ τό παιδίον· Καὶ σὺ τὸν ἐπαοιδὸν περισκοπεῖς, ἢ τὸν τοὺς περιέργους χαρακτῆρας τοῖς τραχήλοις τῶν ἀναιτίων νηπίων περιτιθέντα ἢ τό γε τελευταῖον ἐπὶ τὸν ἰατρόν· ἔρχῃ καὶ τὰ φάρμακα, τοῦ δυναμένου σῴζειν καταμελήσας. Κἂν ἐνύπνιόν σε ἐκταράξῃ, πρὸς τὸν ὀνειροσκόπον τρέχεις. Κἂν φοβεθῇς ἐχθρὸν προστάτην ἕνα τῶν ἀνθρώπων περινοεῖς ("Is the child sick? You look around everywhere for a spell or else you place useless charms around the innocent child's neck. Finally with no hope you run to a doctor and to drugs, since

control over the evil eye for the church. What is significant about the homily is that it demonstrates how Basil continued to work within the indigenous code of Mediterranean social behavior that was dominated by honor, shame, revenge, and envy. Thus what Basil offered his congregation as a solution to the grave problem of envy is really a recasting of the pursuit of virtue, so common to Christian Neoplatonists, into the Mediterranean social code. Virtue is rewarded by the most valued possession: honor.

RECOGNIZING ENVY

Basil begins the homily in no uncertain terms. God authors all good and provides good for deserving people. The devil is evil and works all manner of destruction in creation and people's lives. The most insidious of the evils is envy. Basil states that envy looks insignificant from the outside, but "no suffering more destructive than envy grows in the souls of humanity."[5]

Two metaphors predominate in his description of the malady. The first is that of wasting and rotting. "For just as rust is to iron, so envy exhausts the soul. Just as they say vipers eat up afterbirth after delivery, so does envy grow to consume and destroy the soul in travail."[6] Envy "eats up the intestines slowly."[7] In a parasitical manner it weakens friendship, like "red spots" that ruin grain in the fields.[8] Vigorous health is worn away by envy. Like vultures and flies, envy prefers stench to perfumed meadows in order to consume every last bit of good health in a person.[9]

Basil's second metaphor likens envy's operation to arrows that light upon and attack the victim through optical means. Envy is visually attracted to the

---

you have already neglected the saving power. And if your sleep disturbs you, you run to a dream reader. And if you are frightened by an enemy, you consider a protector from among men.") (*Homily on Psalm 45*, PG 29. 417; Fedwick [*The Church and the Charisma*, 148] dates this commentary to 375 CE); the *Commentary on Isaiah* catalogues dream readers, divining rods, oracle-readers and fortune-tellers, seances, worshiping idols of stone, wood, copper and gold, and reciting the words of the Gospel like incantations (PG 30. 499, 500, 501). This work is considered by Fedwick and others to be spurious, although Fedwick (*The Church and the Charisma*, 154) says, "This is certainly the work of a Cappadocian of the fourth century."

[5]PG 31. 372 (38) Φθόνου γὰρ πάθος οὐδὲν ὀλεθριώτερον ψυχαῖς ἀνθρώπων ἐμφύεται.

[6]PG 31. 373 (41) "Ωσπερ γὰρ ἰὸς σίδηρον, οὕτως ὁ φθόνος τὴν ἔχουσαν αὐτὸν ψυχὴν ἐξαναλίσκει. Μᾶλλον δὲ ὥσπερ τὰς ἐχίδνας φασὶ τὴν κυήσασαν αὐτὰς γαστέρα διεσθιούσας ἀπογεννᾶσθαι, οὕτω καὶ ὁ φθόνος τὴν ὠδίνουσαν αὐτὸν ψυχὴν πέφυκε δαπανᾶν.

[7]PG 31. 373 (45) ἐν τῷ βάθει κατέχει τήν νόσον ὑποσμύχουσαν αὐτοῦ τὰ σπλάγχνα καὶ κατεσθίουσαν.

[8]PG 31. 380 (52) ὥσπερ ἡ ἐρυσίβη ἴδιόν ἐστι τοῦ σίτου νόσημα, οὕτως ὁ φθόνος φιλίας ἐστὶν ἀρρώστημα.

[9]PG 31. 381 (57).

qualities of unsuspecting victims; the envious person "stares" (ἀποβλέπεται), he cannot "bear the vision of another's good," and "envy is hurled (ἐπιβάλλειν) from the eyes."[10] The arrows are violent, striking blows to the hapless target.

There are two victims of this moral disease: the envious and the envied. If envious people could admit their disease, in embarrassment they would morosely confess that they are "envy personified," and among other things, each would say, "My friend's goodness afflicts me, and I complain at the happiness of my brother."[11] But since they cannot speak the truth, they must bear the wretched disease and be consumed by it. The progressive consumption is physically visible to the sensitive observer. The envious bend their heads forward in dejection. Confusion and suffering are their chief characteristics. They have "dry, unlit eyes, sunken cheeks, and contracted eyebrows."[12]

More important are the actions of the envious. They are immediately drawn to successful people, yet they despise their virtues. "They are horrible as they calumniate virtue from their proximity to evil. For although they preach boldness and strength, to them temperance is stupid; justice, crude; prudence, fraudulent."[13] For Basil the reason for this is that evil, the author of envy, has made it impossible for the envious even to understand what virtue is.

The envious have but one relief and goal, the destruction of those they envy. When they see the victim suffering, they will go and "comfort" the victim, not in sympathy, but inwardly gloating. Although never praising a child in life, they are quick to praise it when dead,[14] but will quickly resume their slander once they hear too many people extolling the dead child. In death the envious admire the former beauty, strength, and good health of the deceased.[15]

The last feature of envy that Basil details is that it does not participate in the natural order. Nature and life are God-given gifts, but envy was introduced into the world by the devil, who was "excited" to war with

[10]PG 31. 373 (43); 380 (53); 373 (44) καὶ οὐ φέρω τὴν θέαν τῶν ἀλλοτρίων καλῶν.
[11]PG 31. 373 (44) Βάσκανός εἰμι καὶ πικρός, καὶ ἐπιτρίβει με τὰ τοῦ φίλου καλά, καὶ τοῦ ἀδελφοῦ τὴν εὐθυμίαν ὀδύρομαι.
[12]PG 31. 380 (57) Ὄμμα τούτοις ξηρὸν καὶ ἀλαμπές, παρειὰ κατηφής, ὀφρὺς συμπεπτωκυῖα.
[13]PG 31. 381 (58) Δεινοὶ δὲ... ἐκ τῆς γείτονος κακίας τὴν ἀρετὴν διαβαλεῖν. Θρασὺν μὲν γὰρ λέγουσι τὸν ἀνδρεῖον, ἀνάλγητον δὲ τὸν σώφρονα, τὸν δίκαιον ἀπηνῆ κακοῦργον τὸν φρόνιμον.
[14]PG 31. 373 (45) Τὸ παιδίον μετὰ τὸν θάνατον ἐπαινεῖ.
[15]PG 31. 373-76 (45) Τὸν πλοῦτον θαυμάζει μετὰ τὴν ἔκπτωσιν. Τὴν ὥραν τοῦ σώματος, ἢ τὴν ῥώμην καὶ τὴν εὐεξίαν μετὰ τὰς νόσους ἐπαινεῖ καὶ ἐξαίρει.

humanity. "[Envy] is the corruption of life and the brutal defilement of nature" (λύμη τῆς φύσεως),[16] and "a mixing of laws" (θεσμῶν σύγχυσις).[17] As a result people afflicted with envy act irrationally. For example, when rational people are in difficult straits, they are thankful and gladdened by the help they receive from a wealthier, generous neighbor. But such aid only serves to aggravate envious people: "Dogs which are fed are tamed, lions who are worse become healed; but the envious ones become even wilder with more ministrations."[18]

THE HERMENEUTIC OF ENVY

Basil substantiates his observations on envy with examples from scripture. In his first account, the story of Saul and David (1 Samuel 17–30), Basil stresses how Saul was irrationally possessed by envy. He opens the section with a question, "If you were indignant at having received benefaction, would you not openly slander that help? Such a person was Saul."[19] Basil recounts how jealous Saul became at his people's recurrent acclamation, "Saul has slain his thousands and David his ten thousands" (1 Sam 18:7). Significantly he does not relate that the evil spirit that came upon Saul was from God, although scripture does: "And on the morrow an evil spirit from God rushed upon Saul" (1 Sam 18:10).[20] Rather Basil interprets the account in terms of the honor and shame model pervasive in his society, a model that we shall analyze more fully below as a hierarchy based on the "honor of virtue." When David eschews his chance to kill Saul in the cave, Basil offers an explanation that is at variance with the text's emphasis on David's respect for and submission to the king anointed by God. According to the biblical account, Saul at that moment is overwhelmed by David's goodness and mercy. David has left justice and revenge to God.[21] In contrast, Basil passes over this aspect and remarks that because David spared Saul he demonstrated *virtue*—a virtue that evoked in Saul the *evil* of envy. Basil concludes this didactic section by saying that envy is the most difficult form of enmity to handle.[22]

---

[16]PG 31. 376 (45).

[17]PG 31. 385 (74).

[18]PG 31. 377 (48) Οἱ κύνες τρεφόμενοι ἡμεροῦνται· οἱ λέοντες χειροήθεις γίνονται θεραπευόμενοι· οἱ δὲ βάσκανοι ταῖς θεραπείαις πλέον ἐξαγριαίνονται.

[19]PG 31. 376 (46).

[20]In fact the biblical text relates twice that an "evil spirit from the Lord came upon Saul" (1 Sam 18:10; 19:9).

[21]1 Samuel 24.

[22]PG 31. 376 (48) Δυσμεταχειριστότατον ἔχθρας εἶδος ὁ φθόνος.

On the one hand, it can certainly be argued that there is little difference between goodness, mercy, and virtue; the first two are indeed virtues. On the other hand, this is not what the biblical account states, and Basil's use of the word ἀρετή to describe the biblical terms has a technical, philosophical significance. At this point it is important only to note Basil's distinctive use of the term, consistent with his education and social views, as a hermeneutical device. The meaning of "virtue" in Basil's thought will be discussed below.

The next section of the homily is stylistically powerful. Answering his own series of pithy rhetorical questions, Basil identifies the envy that propelled key biblical events. "What made Joseph a noble servant? Was it not the brothers' envy?"[23] Through the economy of God, however, Joseph was able to ward off the consequences of his brothers' actions. Basil continues in this same section with a brief synopsis of the Savior's mission.

> Why was he [Jesus] envied? Because of the miracles. . . . The dead were raised, and the giver of life was slandered. . . . Demons were destroyed and the smiter was plotted against. And finally they handed the joy of life over to death, and they whipped the liberator of humanity, and they condemned the judge of the universe.[24]

Jesus was the quintessential victim of envy, even though it was part of God's plan.

The only explanation for this divine economy is the cosmological history of the devil's battle with God. Basil implies that the devil was not really capable of carrying out a full-fledged "theomachy," so it consistently co-opts human beings into carrying out its evil intentions. The devil's chief way of "engineering the downfall of the universe" is through the weapon of war (ὅπλον), envy.[25] The first instance is Cain's murder of his brother Abel,[26] who was "the honor of God" (τὴν παρὰ Θεοῦ τιμήν). Because of Abel's honor Cain was "puffed up by jealousy" (καὶ ἐξεκαύθη πρὸς ζῆλον).[27]

---

[23]PG 31. 377 (48) Τί τὸν γενναῖον Ἰωσὴφ δοῦλον ἐποίησεν; Οὐχ ὁ φθόνος τῶν ἀδελφῶν;

[24]PG 31. 377 (48) Διὰ τί ἐφθονεῖτο; Διὰ τὰ θαύματα. . . ἡγείροντο οἱ νεκροί, καὶ ὁ ζωοποιῶν ἐβασκαίνετο· δαίμονες ἀπηλαύνοντο, καὶ ὁ ἐπιτάσσων ἐπεβουλεύετο. . . . Καὶ τὸ τελευταῖον θανάτῳ παρέδωκαν τὸν τὴν ζωὴν χαρισάμενον, καὶ ἐμαστίγουν τὸν ἐλευθερωτὴν τῶν ἀνθρώπων, καὶ κατεδίκαζον τὸν κριτὴν τοῦ κόσμου.

[25]PG 31. 377 (49).

[26]PG 31. 376 (45).

[27]Ibid.

Basil says that envy and murder are "sisters of lawlessness," and he cites Paul's passage in Rom 1:29: "They were filled with all manner of wickedness, evil, covetousness, malice. Full of envy, murder, strife, deceit, malignity. . . ." It is important to note that Basil has inferred the causal effect of envy in this passage.[28] Envy permeates everything and is the pathway to all other sins. Basil's emphasis is on the cosmological level rather than on the personal: the devil is warring with God, and human beings are caught and compelled by the devil to carry out its purpose. Because he overlooks human responsibility for actions, Basil can say that the sins that the devil makes human beings commit as part of its battle plan "damage everything until the end of the ages."[29]

Basil ends this excursus on the devil's role in the universe with one of his most provocative and intriguing warnings. Demons, catching an opportunity to make use of a human being,

> make use of the evil eye for the service of their own will. Would you not shudder at the idea of the service of yourself for the toil of the demon's destruction? Rather would you submit to evil through which you would become the enemy of the sinless person? Would you be the enemy of the God of good and of the absence of envy?[30]

As we shall see shortly, it is no surprise to Basil or the Caesareans that envy's operations culminate in the evil eye. Rather, what Basil is attempting to do is make his congregation aware that this social phenomenon—the process of the evil eye—is connected with an ordered history of creation revealed and documented in scripture, in which the devil ceaselessly seeks the destruction of God's universe. In this passage Basil links the age-old cosmological struggle of the devil and God, the unseen forces of the cosmos, with the day-to-day realities of life in Caesarea. Here he exposes the shocking nexus of the quotidian and the universal. His audience would readily understand the blunt realities of their role in this unseen battle. More importantly, this passage on the evil eye brings to light how Basil

---

[28]Paul (Rom 1:29–30) also included rivalry, treachery, and malevolence.

[29]PG 31. 377 (49) Καὶ ἐνὶ τούτῳ ὅπλῳ ἀπὸ καταβολῆς ἀρξάμενος κόσμου μέχρι συντελείας αἰῶνος πάντας τιτρώσκει.

[30]PG 31. 380 (55–56) Ἐκεῖνο δέ φημι, ὅτι οἱ μισόκαλοι δαίμονες, ἐπειδὰν οἰκείας ἑαυτοῖς εὕρωσι προαιρέσεις, παντοίως· αὐταῖς πρὸς τὸ ἴδιον ἀποκέχρηνται βούλημα· ὥστε καὶ τοῖς ὀφθαλμοῖς τῶν βασκάνων εἰς ὑπηρεσίαν χρῆσθαι τοῦ ἰδίου θελήματος. Εἶτα οὐ φρίσσεις ὑπηρέτην σεαυτὸν ποιῶν δαίμονος ὀλεθρίου, ἀλλ᾽ ὑποδέχῃ κακόν, δι᾽ οὗ ἐχθρὸς μὲν γενήσῃ τῶν μηδὲν ἀδικούντων, ἐχθρὸς δὲ Θεοῦ τοῦ ἀγαθοῦ καὶ ἀφθόνου;

shares and explains the social customs of his day, a set of customs that we can now define as the "Mediterranean code of social behavior."

ENVY AND THE HONOR HIERARCHY

For the last twenty-five years anthropologists such as Julian Pitt-Rivers, Jean Peristiany, John Campbell, Stanley Brandes, and Michael Herzfeld have identified the core of Mediterranean social values.[31] Their work has demonstrated that the Mediterranean region constitutes a cultural unit. With varying degrees of emphasis anthropologists agree that the dyads, honor/ shame and their correlatives, envy/revenge, are the moral principles that provide an "internal cohesiveness" for Mediterranean society.[32] Stanley Brandes points out that "honor and shame are above all mechanisms of social control that operate through the manipulation of personal images and reputations."[33] In an honor/shame society, the community provides the external controls of moral behavior; each member of the community receives either approval or scorn for his or her actions.

Broadly speaking, there are three characteristics of the honor/shame culture that make it unique to the Mediterranean region. First, morality and self-esteem are inextricably connected to gender. According to Brandes, both men and women are "biologically endowed" with gender-specific traits, essentially programming them to behave in certain ways that are virtually beyond their control.[34] Second, because of geography and the kind of agricultural patterns that developed in the Mediterranean, strong nuclear families that tend to be "atomistic and isolated" prevail.[35] Any moral and material support the nuclear family might receive from affines and agnates is not expected and is even viewed with suspicion.[36] The third characteristic is male competitiveness.

[31]Julian Pitt-Rivers, "Honour and Social Status," 19–77; Jean G. Peristiany, "Honour and Shame in a Cypriot Highland Village," 171–90; John K. Campbell, "Honour and the Devil," 139–70; all in Jean G. Peristiany, ed., *Honour and Shame. The Values of Mediterranean Society* (1966; reprinted Chicago: Midway Press, 1974).

[32]David D. Gilmore, "The Shame of Dishonor," in idem, ed., *Honor and Shame and the Unity of the Mediterranean* (Washington, DC: American Anthropological Association, 1987) 3.

[33]Stanley Brandes, "Reflections on Honor and Shame in the Mediterranean," in Gilmore, *Honor and Shame*, 131.

[34]Ibid.

[35]Ibid.

[36]Campbell, "Honour and the Devil," 142–43; see also Jane Schneider, "Of Vigilance and Virgins: Honor, Shame, and Access to Resources in Mediterranean Society," *Ethnology* 10 (1971) 1–24.

What is at stake, of course, is honor. Honor is a quality that each person and family has from the beginning; it is a state of integrity that may be lost, violated, damaged, insulted, or betrayed.[37] Honor must be defended at all costs so that it will remain "untouched." In men honor is "manliness" (ἀνδρισμός); in women it is "propriety" (ἐντροπή).[38] Propriety not only consists of physical virginity before marriage and fidelity afterwards; it is also the guide of female behavior in the marketplace, in her home, and with her relatives and neighbors. Both manliness and propriety are easily lost; they must be "conserved," protected, and guarded. Honor and propriety are reciprocal moral values; throughout the Mediterranean male honor is not solely but in great part derived from the successful protection of the propriety of the women of the family.[39] Thus dishonor for both sexes comes from the males' inability to control women. Power, aggressiveness, precedence, and even physical violence are manifestations of this competition for sexual control. Since honor is always conferred by others in the community, it is fiercely vied for in struggles that turn almost every social interaction into a contest.

Although honor and propriety in the Mediterranean are fundamentally tied to sexuality and all its ramifications, in more recent years anthropologists have refined the model. They have recognized that the gender-based model is heuristically clumsy and reductionistic as an explanation for much of Mediterranean behavior. While retaining the "competitiveness" of the gender-based model,[40] anthropologists of Mediterranean society have sought to explain both male and female behavior with the more subtle notion of "the honor of virtue."[41] Virtues such as honesty, loyalty, hospitality, and concern for reputation form the layers of dutiful obligatory actions (and have nothing to do with preservation of sexual honor) that both men and women participate in to vie for esteem imputed by the community. These virtues are both competitive and cooperative, softening the tensions between competing individuals and families. They also account for the multitude of behaviors that, although not overtly aggressive, nevertheless do

---

[37]Campbell, "Honour and the Devil," 144.

[38]Ibid., 50; and David D. Gilmore, "Honor, Honesty, Shame: Male Status in Contemporary Andalusia," in Gilmore, *Honor and Shame*, 90–103. "Propriety" conveys the positive connotation to the word "shame" in Greek and in other languages of the Mediterranean region.

[39]Gilmore, "The Shame of Dishonor," 4.

[40]See Pitt-Rivers and Peristiany discussed in Gilmore, "The Shame of Dishonor," 5; and Michael Herzfeld, "As in Your Own House," in Gilmore, *Honor and Shame*, 86–87.

[41]Gilmore, "The Shame of Dishonor," 5.

win honor and respect for the person—and are characterstically "Mediterranean." Brandes explains:

> The symbolic emphasis on these harmonious qualities within Mediterranean communities also must have occurred in part as a compensatory response to competitive pressures, as mechanisms through which aggressive tendencies might be ameliorated. In the Mediterranean, historically as well as contemporaneously, there has always existed a tension between cooperation and competition.[42]

Despite the promotion of cooperative virtues to ameliorate the aggressiveness of Mediterranean society, even this pursuit of the "honor of virtue" is fundamentally competitive. Here envy enters the picture, for envy is the underside of honor. Unlike the loss of sexual propriety or manliness, envy does not threaten the family honor, "nor does it conflict with the values of honour and pride."[43] Since honor is controlled by the community, gaining or preserving it entails conforming to a certain idealized type. Those who fall short in any way, or are simply less fortunate, are necessarily less honorable, and they *"must envy* those who surpass them."[44]

It is no surprise that both anthropologists and Basil catalogue the same characteristics as the fruits of envy in social interactions: greed, deceit, cunning, quarrelsomeness, gossip, slander.[45] Envy is the way that inferior members of a society have of fighting for any shred of dignity. They do this not through the "fair fight" of the public arena, but by admiring the person or quality to such a degree that they vicariously share in the honor. Envious people may also seek to demean the honored one in the eyes of the community by continual gossip and slander.

It is important to note that the honor/shame system operates most pervasively in a community where there are no vast gaps between social classes. That is not to say that there are no distinctions between richer and poorer, powerful and dependent, superior and inferior. It means, rather, that honor and shame are proportional to material wealth. A very poor person or family has less honor than the richer neighbors. When tremendous differences in wealth and social status exist, the inferior people act and are treated as though they have no honor at all; they can be insulted with impunity be-

---

[42]Brandes, "Reflections," 132.
[43]Campbell, "Honour and the Devil," 157.
[44]Ibid.
[45]Ibid., 165.

cause they supposedly have no honor to damage.[46] In communities where there are only gradual material differences between families and, as a result, few class distinctions, hierarchies of honor are strongest and begin to operate as class distinction themselves. The anthropologist, John Davis, remarks: "It is characteristic of honor hierarchies that they tend to be absolute: an absolute hierarchy is one in which each ranked unit—a person, family, descent group—occupies or potentially occupies a unique position superior or inferior to each other unit."[47]

Was fourth-century Caesarean society sufficiently homogeneous to spawn an honor hierarchy? The reforms of Diocletian and Constantine suggest that it was. Those reforms were above all attempts to alleviate the fiscal, agricultural, and administrative ailments of the empire. The upkeep of the army and empire required a reliable flow of taxes. If a tax collector met deficits, he had to make up the difference himself. If he could not, the town councillors were responsible for the money. Thus, in order to guarantee its tax revenues the state attempted to freeze its subjects into what were regarded as the more productive occupations. "It is not surprising that the state, in the face of the anxiety of such burdens, now. . . completely developed the hereditary fixation of individuals in a class."[48] Diocletian's policy of increasing military recruitments had a profound effect on landowners. "An indirect form of levy existed to provide recruits, laid upon the landowners by the state, which must have helped not a little to bind the *coloni* to the soil they cultivated."[49] Tenant farmers (*coloni*), the independent peasantry,[50] slaves, those practicing various trades and professions in the towns, and those in municipal service[51] were bound by law to remain in their occupation, as were their descendents.

This effort to freeze the economy led, however, to its deterioration, especially in conjunction with the state's policy on imperial land holdings. We know from Basil's letters and Justinian's continuing attempt at land reform policies in Asia Minor[52] that the imperial land holdings in Cappadocia

---

[46]John Davis, *People of the Mediterranean* (London: Routledge and Kegan Paul, 1977) 91.

[47]Ibid., 77–78.

[48]W. Ensslin, "The Reforms of Diocletian," *CAH* 12. 401.

[49]Ibid., 12. 396.

[50]Ibid., 12. 404.

[51]J. B. Bury, *History of the Later Roman Empire from the Death of Theodosius I to the Death of Justinian* (2 vols.; New York: Dover, 1958) 2. 55–56.

[52]A. H. M. Jones (*Cities of the Eastern Roman Provinces* [Oxford: Clarendon, 1971] 184–90) refers to Basil's *Epistulae* 74–77, and Justinian's *Novella* 30; see also J. S. Reid, "The Reorganisation of the Empire," in *The Cambridge Medieval History* 1. 43–44.

were significant. The greatest number of imperial estates were located in the area surrounding Caesarea, although they were adminstratively completely independent of Caesarea's municipal government. Those farmers renting imperial land were also required by legislation to remain in their positions. Moreover, during Basil's tenure all agricultural tenants, including those on the imperial estates, had to pay the *annona* tax in an attempt "to equalize the burdens of taxation."[53] As a result of these policies,

> the aristocracy of the towns was ruined, and in province after province the free peasants were successively reduced to the position of *coloni*, tied to the soil. . . . Where powerful landed proprietors asserted themselves against the imperial claim it was at the expense of the common good and in selfish isolation.[54]

In Caesarea the rigorous new tax collection and the legislation binding people and their descendents to certain occupations led to a collapse of civic life and a gradual dissolution of the middle class. There were fewer prominent provincial citizens. The government's policies effectively diminished class distinctions. This homogenization was probably further enhanced by the reduction in the variety of local occupations, given the fact that Caesarea was surrounded by so many imperial estates. It is most likely that in Basil's congregation there were only slight differences in class and wealth, which provided a rich environment for the rise of an honor hierarchy.

In detailing exactly how envy works, Basil gives clues as to the social situation of the community. First, he shows that people must be in close proximity to one another for envy to flourish. He asks, "Is the neighbor's field fertile? Does the household thrive in all the needs of life?"[55] Envious people despise their brother's good fortune and their friend's success.[56] Wise people are enjoined to "keep from the company (of envious people) at dinner as well as from the society of all events in life in which there is interchange with them."[57] In his astute assessment of how envious people insinuate their way into the affairs of honored ones, Basil stresses how close in occupation, social class, and familiarity the two must be.

---

[53]Ennslin, "Reforms," 12. 402.
[54]"Epilogue," 12. 708–9. See also Bury, *History*, 2. 58.
[55]PG 31. 373 (42) εὐφόρησεν ἡ χώρα τοῦ πλησίον; εὐθηνεῖται πᾶσι τοῖς κατὰ τὸν βίον οἶκος;
[56]PG 31. 373 (44); see n. 11.
[57]PG 31. 377 (50) ἀπὸ τῆς ἐν τῷ δείπνῳ συνουσίας περὶ πάσης ὁμοῦ τῆς κατὰ τὸν βίον κοινωνίας διαλεγόμενος.

"A man who envies another is a companion of his" [Eccl 4:4; Basil's version is τῷ ἀνδρὶ ὁ ζῆλος παρὰ τοῦ ἑταίρου αὐτοῦ][58] For thus it is. The Scythian does not cast the evil eye at the Egyptian at all, *but at his own kind*. And among those he knows best, he did not envy those he did not know, *but his closest intimates*, his neighbors, and those of the same trade, those of the same age, his relatives, and brothers.[59]

Basil's own observations on envy suggest a community that is relatively close knit, one in which differences in wealth are not so great that they provide a barrier to social contact. Neighbors share the same occupation, farming or a trade, and sometimes have occasion to celebrate at dinners together. Finally, it does not seem far-fetched to say that in Caesarea the nuclear family was stronger than the loyalties to extended family. In three different places Basil mentions that envy grows between brothers and relatives,[60] suggesting that Caesarean society had the conditions that Brandes and Campbell deem conducive to the emergence of an honor hierarchy.

Second, Basil enumerates the kinds of honor that attract envy in his community. Honored people might simply be blessed with the innate qualities of bravery, a healthy body, or a beautiful shape.[61] But more important are the qualities that the honored person cultivates. They are prudence (ἡ φρόνησις), advantages of the soul (προτέρημα τῆς ψυχῆς), and facility at public speaking (ἡ δύναμις λόγων).[62] Above all the envied person practices love of honor (φιλοτιμεῖται λαμπρῶς), a bright, public display of generous financial gifts, and help for the needy that the community acknowledges and by which it benefits.[63] Basil asks, "Is there great approval for him for his benevolence?"[64] Basil implies that there is—and should be—although the approval infuriates envious people more than anything else. The person who practices φιλοτιμία actively seeks honor and gains it. The envious people, however, spurn such magnificence (ἡ

[58]Eccl 4:4 in the LXX reads, ὅτι αὐτὸ ζῆλος ἀνδρὸς ἀπὸ τοῦ ἑταίρου αὐτοῦ, καί γε τοῦτο ματαιότης καὶ προαίρεσις, πνεύματος.
[59]PG 31. 380 (51–52) Οὐχὶ τῷ Αἰγυπτίῳ βασκαίνει ὁ Σκύθης, ἀλλὰ τῷ ὁμοεθνεῖ ἕκαστος· καὶ ἐν τῷ ὁμοεθνεῖ μέντοι οὐ τοῖς ἀγνοουμένοις φθονεῖ, ἀλλὰ τοῖς συνηθεστάτοις· καὶ τῶν συνήθων τοῖς γείτοσι καὶ ὁμοτέχνοις, καὶ τοῖς ἄλλως οἰκείοις κἂν τούτοις πάλιν, ἡλικιώταις καὶ συγγενέσι καὶ ἀδελφοῖς.
[60]Ibid., and see nn. 57, 11.
[61]PG 31. 373 (42–43).
[62]PG 31. 373 (43)
[63]Ibid., καὶ κοινωνίᾳ τῇ πρὸς τοὺς ἐκδεεῖς.
[64]Ibid., καὶ πολὺς αὐτῷ παρὰ τῶν εὐεργετουμένων ὁ ἔπαινος;

μεγαλοπρέπεια) and financial liberality (τὸ ἐλευθέριον) when Basil says they ought to praise (τὸ ἐπαινέτον) them.[65]

This evidence suggests the keen competition for "honor of virtue" present in Basil's parish in Caesarea.[66] All the virtues except "advantages of the soul" put the person in the public eye, since they involve community action. Basil sees striving for honor (φιλοτιμία) positively; the competition itself poses no problem. Rather, it is the envious who skew the fair contest. He poignantly remarks about the competition: "For envy is the sadness that comes from being close to success."[67]

The symptoms of envy, as we have seen, are manifold. One manifestation above all provoked Basil's discomfort: the prevalence in his community of the evil eye. Much as the devil uses envy to manipulate people in its battle with God, people use the evil eye to smite those they envy. Many people in Basil's community considered that the harm they suffered as coming to them "through the eyes alone."[68] "Their good fortune is destroyed at its peak. I for my part dismiss that story as popular, which is spread by women's groups and old ladies."[69]

But Basil's effort to dethrone the evil eye and make the church supreme guardian of the people's welfare was by no means simple, for the evil eye had already enjoyed a long history in the Mediterranean. In order to analyze what the evil eye means for Basil in this tract, we must investigate the presence of the evil eye in the context of late antique society.

THE EVIL EYE IN MEDITERRANEAN SOCIETY

A great deal of literary and archaeological evidence attests to the persistence of the belief in the evil eye (βάσκανος ὀφθαλμός) in the eastern Mediterranean for more than a millennium starting with Hesiod. Callimachus, Plato, Diodorus Siculus, Theocritus, Plutarch, Heliodorus, and Stobaeus are just some of the authors who vividly describe the effects of the evil eye.[70]

---

[65]PG 31. 381 (58–59).

[66]It must be noted that Basil gives no evidence in the treatise for the presence of honor connected to gender.

[67]PG 31. 373 (41) Λύπη γάρ ἐστι τῆς τοῦ πλησίον εὐπραγίας ὁ φθόνος.

[68]PG 31. 380 (53–55) τοὺς δὲ φθονερούς τινες οἴονται καὶ δι' ὀφθαλμῶν μόνων τὴν βλάβην ἐπιβάλλειν· ὥστε τὰ εὐεκτικὰ σώματα, καὶ ἐκ τῆς κατὰ τὴν ἡλικίαν ἀκμῆς εἰς τὴν ἄκραν ὥραν ὑπερανθήσαντα, τήκεσθαι παρ' αὐτῶν καταβασκαινόμενα. . . Ἐγὼ δὲ τοῦτον μὲν τὸν λόγον ἀποπέμπομαι, ὡς δημώδη καὶ τῇ γυναικωνίτιδι παρεισαχθέντα ὑπὸ γραϊδίων.

[69]Ibid.

[70]The more than one hundred references to the evil eye in these authors' works are cited in Peter Walcot, *Envy and the Greeks: A Study of Human Behavior* (Warminster: Aris and Phillips, 1978) 107–15.

Βασκαίνειν most commonly means "to cast the evil eye."[71] Although each author details the causes and effects of this malign power, they all agree on the typical characteristic of the phenomenon of the evil eye:

1. Envy (φθόνος) breeds the evil eye.
2. Those possessing the evil eye do not consciously will harm on those they envy. They are weak people by nature, which allows envy to take over their entire being.
3. The evil eye is transmitted optically or through "infected" air, i.e., air the envious person has breathed.
4. All people are wary of neighbors or relatives who compliment their children, herds, or possessions. The praise is an obvious clue to potential trouble or sickness coming upon the household.
5. Headaches, sudden sickness, or death especially in children or an animal, sudden change in the state of a matrimonial arrangement, and infertility are all common effects of the evil eye.
6. Apotropaic amulets hung around the neck or hidden in clothing attract the evil eye and divert its malignant effects.

Plutarch (ca. 125 CE) writes an account of the operations of the evil eye in *Quaestiones Convivales*, 5.6–7. It is interesting to note that Basil's account of envy and his are almost identical in several instances.

Envy (φθόνος), which naturally roots itself more deeply in the mind than any other passion, contaminates the body too with evil. This is the morbid condition that artists well attempt to render when painting the face of envy. When those possessed by envy to this degree let their glance fall upon a person, their eyes, which are close to the mind and draw from it the evil influence of the passion, then assail that person as if *with poison arrows* (ὥσπερ πεφαρμαγμένα βέλη προσπίπτωσιν); hence I conclude, it is not paradoxical or incredible that they should have an effect on the persons who encounter their gaze [my emphasis].[72]

Plutarch also relates that those infected with envy "are acting as their nature but not as their will directs."[73] They attack their closest friends and

---

[71]Ibid., 79.

[72]Plutarch *Quaestiones Convivales* 5.7.681 in Plutarch *Moralia* (*LCL*; 16 vols.; trans. Paul A. Clement; Cambridge, MA: Harvard University Press, 1969) 8. 425.

[73]Ibid., 8. 429.

family members[74] and he warns, as Hippocrates had, that those in the best of health actually have much to worry about because they are a temptation for the evil eye.[75]

There are two texts discussing the evil eye from the third and fourth centuries CE. In Heliodorus's long novel, *Aethiopica*, the young heroine, Chariclea, is believed by her father to have suffered from the evil eye (βασκανία σου καθήψατο) at a festival at Delphi.[76] He consults a friend about the inner working of βασκανία. The friend's reply only confirms his fears that envy and the evil eye can infect someone through breathing the same air that the envious person exhaled. A letter in the *Papyrus Abinnaeus* (fourth century CE) concludes with the salutation praying that the household and children "be preserved from the evil eye."[77]

More numerous are amulets, seals, coins, weights, and other material testimonies to the belief in the evil eye from late antiquity. James Russell has documented the objects found at Anumerium, a town on the southern coast of Isauria.[78] There are examples from the second to the seventh centuries CE. The majority of those from the third, fourth, and fifth centuries[79] refer to the popular *Testament of Solomon*. According to this text Solomon overpowered evil spirits by his supernatural powers. "King Solomon was able to control and exploit the forces of evil, and thereby built the Temple, only because God had given him a 'little seal ring' with which he could 'lock up all the demons.'"[80] The text gives explicit instructions on how to counter the power of the evil eye; a demon says, "I cast the glance of envy at everyone. My power is annulled by the engraved image of the much-suffering Eye."[81]

---

[74]Ibid.

[75]Ibid.; *LCL*, 8. 431, καὶ τὰ σώματα προελθόντα μέχρι τῆς ἄκρας ἀκμῆς οὐκ ἔστηκεν. Cf. Basil (PG 31. 380 [54]) ὥστε τὰ εὐτικὰ σώματα, καὶ ἐκ τῆς κατὰ τὴν ἡλικίαν ἀκμῆς εἰς τὴν ἄκραν ὥραν ὑπερανθήσαντα, τήκεσθαι παρ' αὐτῶν καταβασκαινόμενα.

[76]Heliodorus *Aethiopica* 4.5.5.

[77]*Papyrus Abinnaeus* 35, 28–29; as quoted in Walcot, *Envy*, 86.

[78]James Russell, "The Evil Eye in Early Byzantine Society," *Jahrbuch der österreichischen Byzantinistik* 32 (1982) 539–50.

[79]Ibid., 540–42, but for the difficulty of dating the Solomon types see also Campbell Bonner, *Studies in Magical Amulets Chiefly Greco-Egyptian* (Ann Arbor: University of Michigan Press, 1950) 211, 214–15, 221: "Whether the simpler Solomon type was used by Christians or not, there is no doubt that a great number of Christian amulets were derived from it" (p. 211).

[80]Gary Vikan, "Art, Medicine, and Magic in Early Byzantium," *DOP* 38 (1984) 80, who quotes Chester Charlton McCown, ed., *The Testament of Solomon* (Leipzig: Hinrichs, 1922) 94.

[81]*T. Sol.* 4.2, as quoted in Russell, "The Evil Eye," 542.

Solomon was popularly represented on amulets as a mounted horse-man.[82] The reverse read σφραγίς θεοῦ ("the seal of God"). Russell lists an amulet with the Trisagion on one side and on the other the inscription, σφραγίς Σολομῶνος ἔχι τὴν βασκανίαν ("the seal of Solomon holds the evil eye"). Two other amulets can be described as typical of many others, "as they are by no means rare."[83] The first has an eye staring at two spears on the left and on the right it is stabbed by a knife. Animals attack it from below. The inscription reads κύρι βοήθι ("Lord, help!") "which gives the piece a Christian association."[84] The second amulet bears the inscription, φεῦγε μεμισιμένι, Σολομῶν σε διόκι ("Flee thou loathsome demoness, Solomon pursues thee"), surrounding the horseman.[85] The reverse reads, σφραγὶς Σολομῶνος· ἀποδιόξον πᾶν κακὸν ἀπὸ τοῦ φοροῦντος ("Seal of Solomon, drive away all evil from him who wears it").[86] The eye is identified by the word, φθόνος.[87]

The most stunning example Russell cites is a mosaic inscription on the floor of a dressing room in a bath house.[88] A στρατηγός ("general") named Mouseos donated the floor sometime in the first half of the fifth century CE. The inscription reads, "let envy keep away from the excellence of the mosaic." Russell's point in including this example is twofold: the wealthier and more educated citizens believed in the evil eye along with "the lower strata of society in Anemurium," and Mouseos's generosity could well attract the evil eye, "hence the need for some prophylactic formula to confront the potential malefactor as he entered the room."[89]

Returning now to Basil's passage on the evil eye, we may note a curious ambivalence that he seems to be expressing about the phenomenon. He has introduced three innovations to the traditional explanation of the evil eye. First, as we have seen, he has linked its operation to the scriptural history of the cosmos. Second, he calls on his parishioners to be aware that they are manipulated by the devil through envy and the evil eye to participate in a profound theomachy. Basil is persuasive when he demonstrates how the

---

[82]Vikan, "Art," 79.
[83]Russell, "The Evil Eye," 540, figs. 1, 2.
[84]Ibid., 540, 541, fig. 5.
[85]Ibid., 541.
[86]Ibid.
[87]Ibid. Many of the amulets of the "much-suffering eye" have been found in Egypt, Syria, and Palestine and are documented in Bonner. Bonner (*Studies*, 99) says, "The Evil Eye is only as a reverse type, the obverse being regularly a figure on horseback marked as saintly or divine by a halo. These Syrian bronzes seem to date from about the third century down into Byzantine times."
[88]Russell, "The Evil Eye," 544.
[89]Ibid., 544–45.

devil uses this common social phenomenon, the evil eye, to ensnare human beings for its own aims. Pagans too knew that they were tricked by "suprahuman agencies in such a way as to bypass the human agent. For pagan and Christian alike, misfortune was unambiguously the work of suprahuman agents, the *daemones*."[90] All members of society knew they bore no responsibility for their malevolent actions; they were co-opted.

Finally, Basil appropriates the power to battle the devil and the evil eye for the church. Peter Brown has aptly called the relationship between the church in the period and "sorcery beliefs" a "détente."[91] He points out that rather than railing against certain "superstitious practices" like the evil eye, "the Christian church offered an explanation of misfortune that both embraced all the phenomena previously ascribed to sorcery, and armed the individual with weapons of satisfying precision and efficacy against suprahuman agents."[92]

This third innovation would explain Basil's apparent equivocation about the evil eye. In contrast to his certainty about the evil eye in the cosmological realm, he simply dismisses the power of the evil eye on the social level. Basil denies specific social groups (among them "women's groups and old ladies") power over the evil eye in two respects. First, his dismissal would serve to discredit parishioners' complaints and accusations against others for the supposed harm they had brought them through the evil eye. This would diffuse the hostility among people in his parish. If the eye had been cast, it was the devil that was operating through a person, and the church had the power and responsibility to remedy the situation. Second, Basil's dismissal would have the effect of divesting the accused person or group of a malevolent supernatural power with which they either intimidated their neighbors or because of which they suffered the stigma of false accusations or ostracism. This would explain why one person's account of misfortune is, according to Basil, a "popular story"; although he strongly declares in the next sentence that the "haters of good, the demons, make use of the evil eye for their own purposes."[93] Basil does not deny that the evil eye has wretched effects on people's everyday lives, but he has transferred the real meaning and emphasis of the destruction from earth to the cosmos. Blame and responsibility belong still, as the pagans would say, to the supernatural realm. But now the evil eye is not simply controlled by

---

[90]Peter Brown, "Sorcery, Demons, and the Rise of Christianity from Late Antiquity into the Middle Ages," in Mary Douglas, ed., *Witchcraft, Confessions, and Accusations* (London: Tavistock, 1970) 28.

[91]Ibid.

[92]Ibid.

[93]PG 31. 380 (55–56); see nn. 30 and 68.

random *daemones*; rather, one identified devil manages the operation of the evil eye. It is the church who has named and personified the devil, given the devil a history, and has been invested with the legitimate power to mediate between heaven and earth for the ultimate victory over the enemy.

"RENDERING ENVY HELPLESS"

Having given graphic descriptions of the envious and their actions, Basil turns to his remedy. He says identification of the problem of envy is only half the cure. What people must realize is that nothing human is of value, not resourcefulness, prestige, or a disciplined body, "for we do not define the good to be in anything that passes away, rather it is the things that last through the ages that we call good and true."[94]

When people stop placing so much value on these transient characteristics, two things happen. The initial pangs of jealousy stop when they see these attributes in others; and, more importantly, they come to understand that wealth, glory, bodily strength, wisdom, and the like are "instruments of virtue" (ὄργανα ἀρετῆς). But "possessing them is not a virtue in itself."[95] A person then has the choice to use these instruments responsibly and reasonably, or "hoard things for his own enjoyment."[96] The praise and love received for using the gifts for the good of the community is justified.

Basil contrasts the person who is "affected by the struggle" to use the gifts responsibly with the person who is oblivious. Providing money for the needy and furnishing services for the sick renders the giver freedom from envy (ἄφθονος).[97] The person "unaffected by the struggle,"[98] on the other hand, is subject to envy's control, is more likely to commit evil deeds, and even worse, casts the evil eye on him or herself.

> If a rich man takes the road of injustice, he is wretched while wealthy;
> if he gives service to virtue, by providing common aid to everyone,
> the evil eye has no space; unless someone were to indulge in the

---

[94]PG 31. 381 (63) οὐ γὰρ ἐν τοῖς παρερχομένοις ὁριζόμεθα εἶναι τὸ ἀγαθόν, ἀλλ᾽ ἐπὶ αἰωνίων ἀγαθῶν καὶ ἀληθινῶν μετουσίαν κεκλήμεθα.

[95]PG 31. 381 (63) οὐκ αὐτὰ ἐν ἑαυτοῖς ἔχοντα τὸ μακάριον.

[96]PG 31. 384 (63) οὐχὶ δὲ πρὸς ἰδίαν ἀπόλαυσιν θησαυρίζει, ἐπαινεῖσθαι καὶ ἀγαπᾶσθαι δίκαιός ἐστι διὰ τὸ φιλάδελφον καὶ κοινωνικὸν τοῦ τρόπου.

[97]PG 31. 384 (68) ὡς τῇ μὲν τῶν χρημάτων χορηγίᾳ ἄφθονος εἶναι τοῖς δεομένοις τῷ σώματι δὲ ὑπερεσίαν παρέχειν τοῖς ἀσθενοῦσι.

[98]PG 31. 384 (68–69) τὸν δὲ μὴ οὕτω πρὸς ταῦτα διακείμενον ἄθλιον τίθεσθαι μᾶλλον ἢ ἐπίφθονον, εἰ μείζονας ἔχει πρὸς τὸ κακὸς εἶναι τὰς ἀφορμάς.

advantages of evil, then he would be casting the evil eye on himself and depriving himself of good things.[99]

What finally "renders envy helpless"[100] is the process Basil describes as "transcending the merely human with reason."[101] Reason leads to the ability to discern "what promotes blessedness and what promotes jealousy" (μακαριστὸν κρῖναι καὶ ζηλωτόν). Another quality of discernment is a steady, passionless state. The human qualities that society values—wealth, prestige, beauty—hold no awe for the discerning person. Rather, Basil says:

> If you strive for [the proper] glory, and you are both eager to be above ordinary people, and because of this will not tolerate being second-rate (for this is an attack of envy), then, like a stream, change yourself by love of honor (τὸ φιλότιμον) towards the acquisition of virtue.[102]

For Basil the attainment of virtue is the goal of the process. By his time the pursuit of virtue was the time-honored goal of the contemplative life, long-established, with varying emphases, by the different traditions of Platonism.[103] According to Basil, virtue will manifest itself concretely in one's daily actions through justice, temperance, prudence, strength, and patience. He startles the audience by simply stating: "In just this way you will save yourself, and the more good you do the more you will have."[104] The person takes on virtue's properties, and virtue is "possessed by love of toil."[105] Consequently, the circumstances of money, elegance of body, or

---

[99]PG 31. 384 (69) Εἰ μὲν γὰρ ἐφόδιον πρὸς ἀδικίαν ὁ πλοῦτος, ἐλεεινὸς ὁ πλουτῶν. εἰ δὲ ὑπηρεσία πρὸς ἀρετήν, οὐκ ἔχει χώραν ἡ βασκανία, κοινῆς τῆς ἀπ' αὐτῶν ὠφελείας ἅπασι προκειμένης. πλὴν εἰ μή τις ἄρα τῇ περιουσίᾳ τῆς πονηρίας καὶ ἑαυτῷ βασκαίνοι τῶν ἀγαθῶν.

[100]PG 31. 384 (71) ἀμήχανόν ποτε παραγενέσθαι τὸν φθόνον.

[101]PG 31. 384 (69) ὑπερκύψας τῷ λογισμῷ τὰ ἀνθρώπινα.

[102]PG 31. 384 (71-72) Εἰ δὲ πάντως δόξης ἐπιθυμεῖς, καὶ βούλει τῶν πολλῶν ὑπερφαίνεσθαι, καὶ διὰ τοῦτο οὐκ ἀνέχῃ δεύτερος εἶναι (ἔστι γὰρ οὖν δὴ καὶ τοῦτο πρὸς τὸ φθονεῖν ἀφορμή) σὺ δὲ ἐπὶ τὴν κτῆσιν ἀρετῆς, ὥσπερ τι ῥεῦμα, μετάθες σεαυτοῦ τὸ φιλότιμον.

[103]See Rowan A. Greer, *The Fear of Freedom* (University Park: Pennsylvania State University Press, 1989) 81–87; John M. Rist, *Plotinus: The Road to Reality* (Cambridge: Cambridge University Press, 1967) 156–57.

[104]PG 31. 385 (72) Οὕτω γὰρ καὶ σεαυτὸν σώσεις, καὶ ἐπὶ μείζοσιν ἀγαθοῖς μείζονα ἕξεις τὴν περιφάνειαν.

[105]Ibid. Ἡ μὲν γὰρ ἀρετὴ ἐφ' ἡμῖν, καὶ δυνατὴ κτηθῆναι τῷ φιλοπόνῳ. ἡ δὲ τῶν χρημάτων περιβολὴ, καὶ ὥρα σώματος, καὶ ὄγκος· ἀξιωμάτων, οὐκ ἐφ' ἡμῖν.

the prestige of dignity do not have room to take hold in the person.[106] Yet, unless the soul is cleansed of all the desires and other passions—especially the evil eye (βασκανία)[107]—virtue cannot grow in the soul.

What Basil has outlined is a plan to overcome envy through Christian Neoplatonism. Basil, true to his philosophic education, believed that human beings were created in the image of God as part of the intelligible world. Only because of the Fall are they mired in the sensible world, victims of time and death, and easy prey for chaos and evil.[108] Basil writes in the *Hexaemeron*:

> The Creator and the Demiurge of the Universe perfected his works in it,. . . intellectual and invisible natures, all the orderly arrangement of pure intelligences who are beyond the reach of our mind. . . . To this world at last it was necessary to add a new world, *both a school and training place* where the souls of men should be taught.[109]

The task of the Christian, as of the Neoplatonic philosopher, is to reverse the downward progression towards matter and ascend to the intelligible world of God. When Basil explained that the first step in overcoming envy is "to transcend the human with reason,"[110] he referred to the one redeeming characteristic that humanity retained after the Fall. Death and sin resulted from the descent from the intelligible world to the sensible, but "the privilege of reason" enables humanity to "raise [itself] to heaven."[111] For both pagan and Christian reason and intellect were means to begin the ascent to God.[112]

Unlike their non-Christian colleagues, Basil and the other Christian Platonists held that both the body and the soul were created and that both needed restoration to eternal life.[113] "This rehabilitation of the body implied a continuity of the sensible and intelligible worlds in the face of a transcendent creator, and this in turn affected the division of all human

---

[106]Ibid.

[107]Ibid.

[108]I. P. Sheldon Williams, "The Greek Christian Platonist Tradition from the Cappadocians to Maximus and Eriugina," in Arthur H. Armstrong, ed., *Cambridge History of Later Greek and Early Medieval Philosophy* (Cambridge: Cambridge University Press, 1967) 438.

[109]Basil *Hexaemeron* 1.5 (*NPNF* 8. 54).

[110]See n. 101.

[111]Basil *Hexaemeron* 6.1 (*NPNF* 8. 82).

[112]Williams, "The Greek Christian," 427.

[113]Ibid., 435.

knowledge into 'praxis and theoria.'"[114] This view of creation accords a great deal of freedom to each person to "move towards virtue."[115] Basil states in *On Envy* that after reason one must begin acquiring virtue by practicing virtue. Doing good works cleanses the body and opens the way for virtue to dwell in the person. As Sheldon Williams eloquently puts it, "action, then, is propaedeutic of contemplation, of which deification is the end."[116]

The soul, however, has a great advantage over the body. Basil writes in the *Hexaemeron* that virtue is known to the soul naturally.

> Virtues exist in us also by nature, and the soul has affinity with them not by education, but by nature herself. . . . Thus, without having need of lessons the soul can attain by herself to what is fit and comfortable in nature.[117]

Basil understands "the natural creation as the setting for human moral and spiritual growth."[118] When not subjected to the random deviations of the body, the soul, innately recognizing virtue, is attracted to it. The training of the body (Basil uses the word ἄθλιον)[119] and the conforming of the soul to virtue result in the attainment of the practical virtues,[120] or "praxis," the first step in the ascent to God.

Although Basil does not use the word διάκρισις, "discernment," his reference to the ability to judge what is useful and what is harmful is just that. In the schematization of Christian Neoplatonism, this ability is wisdom, divinely given, enabling the person to begin the contemplation of God. This is the second step, "theoria," in the ascent to God.

Basil only mentions this "ability to judge" in the end of the tract; it is obviously not his purpose to preach on the pursuit of contemplation in this homily. *On Envy* is solely concerned with the practice of virtue in the community. Thus Basil, after the "acquisition of virtue," merges the schema of divine ascent with the honor/shame code of society. Twice at the end of the tract he says attainment of virtue will make the person "better than" or

[114]Ibid., 426.
[115]Greer, *Fear*, 166.
[116]Williams, "The Greek Christian," 428.
[117]Basil *Hexaemeron* 9.4 (*NPNF* 8. 103).
[118]Greer, *Fear*, 169.
[119]See n. 98.
[120]Williams, "The Greek Christian," 427.

"more famous than" others.[121] He does not instruct his congregation to change themselves towards virtue through the desire for purification, contemplation, and finally union with God in deification. Basil's problem is too concrete and practical for such a sermon to be effective. The operation of envy is creating havoc in his community. He teaches his parishioners to rid themselves of envy and acquire virtue, not through desire for the ascent to God, but through the *love of honor* (ἡ φιλοτιμία), the quality most redolent with social connotations.

By ingeniously linking Neoplatonic virtue with the reward of honor, Basil provides great motivation to his congregation to change behavior. Basil and the Caesareans all knew that there was nothing more valuable in life than gaining and preserving honor, acting with φιλοτιμία, and being acknowledged as doing so. Basil cleverly introduces a tension: he plays on each person's competitive desire for honor, but he removes the contest from the destructive arena of the societal monitors and their effects. Society would (and should, he says) still honor them for their good works, but because of their attainment of the virtues, they would be immune from any attacks of envy or the evil eye, should their neighbors inadvertently be so inclined. Most importantly they are now enlisted in the church's forces—with all its powers to protect—against the devil.

CONCLUSION

On Envy provides a fascinating glimpse into the life of Basil's Caesarean parish. Not only do we see that envy and the evil eye were pervasive problems providing the occasion for the homily, we also notice that the Mediterranean social code provided both the rudimentary basis for such a phenomenon as the evil eye to flourish and the foundation for Basil's remedy for it. Basil attempted to redeem the social code by which he was raised and by which he lived and viewed the world. This characteristic is most obvious in his exegesis of scripture and his positive view of competition. In Basil's schema the church has replaced the devil as the force behind the code of honor. The devil used to enlist unwitting souls in its plans for thwarting the universe; now the church inspires people to pursue virtue in order to gain honor. This pursuit leaves them impervious to attacks of envy or the evil eye. Finally, Basil has successfully synthesized his Christian Neoplatonism with the Mediterranean social code: "Reason, for the discovery of truth, is much surer than the eye."[122]

---

[121]PG 31. 384 (71) and 385 (72); the same root is used in both instances: ὑπερφαίνεσθαι and ἡ περιφάνεια.

[122]Basil *Hexaemeron* 6.11 (*NPNF* 8. 89).

John Chrysostom on Almsgiving and the Use of Money[*]

Blake Leyerle
University of Notre Dame

F ew themes so dominate the homilies of John Chrysostom (ca. 347–407 CE) as the plight of the poor and the necessity of almsgiving. His picture of the poor, however, is always set against the prosperous market-place of late antiquity. It seems therefore scarcely surprising that his sermons on almsgiving resound with the language of investment. With such imagery, Chrysostom tried not only to prod wealthy Christians into acts of charity but also, and perhaps more importantly, to dislodge his rich parishioners from their conviction that an uncrossable social gulf separated them from the poor. The rhetorical strategy he used is typical of all his polemical attacks. On the one hand, he denigrated the pursuit of money and social status as fundamentally unattractive; it is both unchristian and unmasculine. On the other hand, he insisted that real wealth and lasting prestige should indeed be pursued, but more effectively through almsgiving. I shall first examine how Chrysostom effected this recalculation of wealth, and then I shall turn to the question of whether there may have been some advantage for him in pleading so eloquently on behalf the poor.

[*]An earlier version of this paper was presented at the Annual Meeting of the American Academy of Religion, New Orleans, LA in November 1990. I wish to thank John C. Cavadini, Vasiliki Limberis, and Eric A. Plumer for their suggestions and assistance. I also thank Lawrence A. Hoffman for teaching me so much about φιλανθρωπία.

HTR 87:1 (1994) 29–47

■ The Antiochene Social System of Wealth

In the market of fourth-century Antioch, everything that one's heart desired was for sale. Since it was late antiquity, however, it was perhaps less a matter of the heart than of the liver, the organ that brooked no limitation of desire. Libanius described the typical sumptuous array of merchandise.

> What is more inexhaustible, more lasting, than the wealth of goods which we have for sale? These are so distributed through the whole city that no one part of the city can be called the market; neither must those who wish to buy things come together in any one place, but the goods are right before everyone, before their very doors, and everywhere it is possible for one simply to stretch out his hand in order to take what he wishes. . . . for the things which one needed, no one has ever sought in vain. . . . And although the supply of things for sale is brilliant, it is even more a subject for wonder because it is inexhaustible.[1]

Chrysostom recognized in the agora a sensitive index of the city's greatness. When he, for example, considered writing a new sort of encomium on Antioch, he first listed its traditional claims to fame: "Speak to me not of the suburb of Daphne, nor of the size and height of its cypresses, nor of its springs of waters, nor of the great population which inhabits the city, nor of the great confidence with which its marketplace is frequented until even late at night, nor of the abundance of goods for sale."[2] There was, accordingly, no more telling image of the dread that struck the city after the Riot of the Statues in 387 CE than the desolate marketplace:

> If anyone. . . wished to enter the market, he was immediately driven back to his house by the cheerless spectacle—true, he might see one or two people but they were bowed down and creeping about deject-

---

[1]Libanius *Or.* 11.251–55 (ed. Richard Foerster; Stuttgart: Teubner, 1903) 526–27; the translation is that of Glanville Downey, "Libanius' Oration in Praise of Antioch (*Or.* xi)," *The Proceedings of the American Philosophical Society* 103 (1959) 679–80; τῆς δ' αὖ τῶν ὠνίων περιουσίας τί μὲν ἀφθονώτερον, τί δὲ διαρκέστερον; ἃ διὰ πάσης μὲν οὕτω κέχυται τῆς πόλεως, ὡς μὴ μέρος τι τῆς πόλεως ἓν ἀγορὰν κεκλῆσθαι μηδὲ δεῖν εἰς ἕν τι συνελθεῖν ὠνησομένους, ἀλλὰ πᾶσιν ἐν ποσὶν εἶναι καὶ πρὸ θυρῶν καὶ πανταχοῦ χεῖρα ἐκτείναντι λαβεῖν ὑπάρχειν. . . . ὧν δὲ εἰς χρείαν ἦλθε, ταῦτα οὐδεὶς ἐζήτησεν ἀπόντα. . . . λαμπρὰ δὲ οὖσα τῶν ὠνίων ἡ κατασκευὴ τῷ διηνεκεῖ πλέον τεθαύμασται. Libanius also noted that the market was full all day (*Or.* 11.169).

[2]Chrysostom *Ad populum Antiochenum de statuis* 17.14 (PG 49. 179) Ὅταν ἐθέλῃς τῆς πόλεως εἰπεῖν ἐγκώμιον, μή μοι τὴν Δάφνην εἴπῃς τὸ προάστειον, μηδὲ τὸ πλῆθος καὶ μῆκος τῶν κυπαρίσσων, μηδὲ τὰς πηγὰς τῶν ὑδάτων, μηδὲ τὸ πολλοὺς τὴν πόλιν οἰκεῖν ἀνθρώπους, μηδὲ τὸ μέχρι βαθυτάτης ἑσπέρας ἐπὶ τῆς ἀγορᾶς διατρίβειν μετὰ ἀδείας πολλῆς, μηδὲ τῶν ὠνίων τὴν ἀφθονίαν.

edly—whereas only a few days before the crowd had swept along [as imperiously as] the river's currents.[3]

A similar lull in commerce had been provoked by the emperor Julian's attempt to restore the worship of the traditional gods. "Remember," Chrysostom insisted, "how really empty the market was of goods and how the workshops were full of confusion, and how each person fended for himself, snatching up whatever was available before scurrying home."[4]

The importance of the marketplace, however, went beyond the simple transaction of goods. Apart from the wondrous items for sale, the agora also provided a venue for a ware less easily commodifiable. Here money purchased not only tangibilities but also sensibilities, as a certain lavishness with money bought personal reputation, honor, and the status of a patron. Chrysostom was acutely aware of how the market functioned to display social status. He noted dourly that "nothing so leads to a yearning for riches as the passion for glory. . . [the desire to] parade before the multitude"[5] and "the wish to engrave one's name on property, baths, and houses."[6]

Precisely because rich patrons were so crucial in social structuring, both their wealth and the prestige that it betokened demanded display. Chrysostom admitted that "often when we are insulted in a quarrel, we take it well, saying to the one who insulted us, 'What can I do to you? A certain one holds me back—the man who is your patron; he restrains my hands.'"[7] Given that social status was a matter of display, it was also subject to constant reassessment and adjustment.[8] Scrupulous management of the impression one made was thus the rule of the day and could be, apparently, an all-consuming task.[9]

---

[3]Ibid., 2.2 (PG 49. 36) Εἰ δέ τις. . . ἐθελήσειεν εἰς ἀγορὰν ἐμβαλεῖν, ὑπὸ τῆς ὄψεως τῆς ἀτερποῦς εὐθέως εἰς τὴν οἰκίαν εἰσελαύνεται τὴν ἑαυτοῦ, ἕνα που καὶ δύο μόλις ὁρῶν συγκεκυφότας, καὶ μετὰ πολλῆς βαδίζοντας τῆς κατηφείας, ἔνθα πρὸ ὀλίγων ἡμερῶν ποταμῶν ρεύματα τὸ πλῆθος ἀπέκρυπτεν.

[4]Chrysostom Panegyrium in Babylam martyrem 2 (PG 50. 531) Ἴστε γὰρ δήπου καὶ μέμνησθε, πῶς κενὴ μὲν ἦν ὠνίων ἡ ἀγορά, μεστὰ δὲ θορύβων τὰ ἐργαστήρια, ἑκάστου φιλονεικοῦντος τὸ φανὲν προαρπάσαι, καὶ ἀπελθεῖν.

[5]Chrysostom Hom. in Matt. 20.2 (PG 57. 289) Οὐδὲν γὰρ οὕτω χρημάτων ἐρᾶν παρασκευάζει, ὡς ὁ τῆς δόξης ἔρως· . . . ἵνα τοῖς πολλοῖς ἐπιδείξωνται.

[6]Chrysostom Hom. in Gen. 22.7 (PG 53. 195) Ἀλλὰ τῶν κακῶν ἁπάντων τὸ αἴτιον ἡ κενοδοξία, καὶ τὸ βούλεσθαι τὴν προσηγορίαν ἐπικεῖσθαι τὴν αὐτοῦ τοῖς ἀγροῖς, τοῖς βαλανείοις, ταῖς οἰκίαις; see also ibid., 30.2 (PG 53. 275).

[7]Chrysostom Ad populum Antiochenum de statuis 15.7 (PG 49. 161) Πολλάκις γοῦν μάχης γινομένης ὑβριζόμενοι φέρομεν γενναίως, καὶ πρὸς τὸν ὑβρίζοντα λέγομεν· Τί σοι ποιήσω; Ὁ δεῖνά με κωλύει, ὁ προστάτης ὁ σός, ἐκεῖνός μου κατέχει τὰς χεῖρας.

[8]Andrew Wallace-Hadrill, "Patronage in Roman Society from Republic to Empire," in idem, ed., Patronage in Ancient Society (London/New York: Routledge, 1989) 83.

[9]Chrysostom Panegyrium in Ignatium martyrem 1 (PG 50. 587); idem, Hom. in Eph. 20.7 (PG 62. 144).

In Chrysostom's homilies we catch glimpses of these late antique patrons as they swan about the marketplace, drawing all eyes to themselves by their entourage—their "swarms" of eunuchs, "herds" of slaves, bridles spangled with gold, and even their imported shoelaces of silk.[10] The controlling ethic was neatly summed up in a mocking tag drawn from the comic stage, a tag that swept Christians in with their pagan neighbors: "Woe to you, Mammon, [but woe especially] to whoever has not enough of you!"[11] Behind this quip and the social dynamics it represents, we may easily recognize the contours of the classical ideal of *philotimia*, the pursuit of public praise and honor through civic expenditure which had long served to establish the social hierarchy.[12] From Libanius we know that this tradition was still very much alive in the fourth century. The sophist noted with approval that the citizens of Antioch "take greater pleasure in spending for the benefit of the city than others take in amassing wealth. . . . For the feeling which elsewhere follows upon gain is here joined instead to spending."[13]

If for the wealthy few the agora offered the perfect venue for an ostentatious display of patronage, for the many it meant the austere cultivation of the status of client. Differences in status were made apparent not only by the massed attendants upon the rich, but also by the contrast they posed to the destitute, who formed in their pathetic misery something of an antispectacle. Chrysostom's words suggest indeed that the desperation of the poor lent to the ease of the rich a certain piquancy:

> There are other poor people. . . who, when their begging yields them nothing, start to do tricks, some eating the leather from worn out shoes, others driving sharp nails into their heads; still others plunging their naked bodies in water frozen by the cold—or doing other even

---

[10]Chrysostom *Hom. in Eph.* 20.7 (PG 62. 144) οἰκετῶν ἀγέλας ἔχει καὶ εὐνούχων ἐσμόν; idem, *Hom. in Rom.* 11.5 (PG 60. 491) ὁ τοῦ ἵππου χαλινὸς πολλῷ τῷ χρυσῷ; idem, *Hom. in Matt.* 20.2 (PG 57. 289) Διὰ γοῦν τοῦτο καὶ τὰς τῶν ἀνδραπόδων ἀγέλας, καὶ τὸν ἐσμὸν εὐνούχων, καὶ τοὺς χρυσοφοροῦντας ἵππους; idem, *Hom. in Matt.* 49.5 (PG 58. 501) ὅταν γὰρ τὰ νήματα σηρικά, ἃ μηδὲ ἐν ἱμάτοις ὑφαίνεσθαι καλόν, ταῦτα ἐν ὑποδήμασι διαπτάπτητε.

[11]Chrysostom *Hom. in Eph.* 17.2 (PG 62. 120) Καὶ πάλιν ἕτεροί φασιν· Οὐαί σοι μαμμωνᾶ, καὶ τῷ μὴ ἔχοντί σε; idem, *Hom. in Heb.* 15.3 (PG 63. 121) Οὐαί σοι, μαμωνᾶ [sic], καὶ τῷ μὴ ἔχοντί σε!

[12]On the importance of urban munificence, see Evelyne Patlagean, *Pauvreté économique et pauvreté sociale à Byzance* (Paris/The Hague: Mouton, 1977) 182–83; see also Peter Brown, *The Making of Late Antiquity* (Cambridge, MA: Harvard University Press, 1978) esp. 27–55; J. H. W. G. Liebeschuetz, *Antioch: City and Imperial Administration in the Later Roman Empire* (Oxford: Clarendon, 1972) 204.

[13]Libanius *Or.* 11.134–38 (ed. Foerster, 481; trans. Downey, "Libanius' Oration," 667) ἥδιον μὲν δαπανώμενοι περὶ τὴν πόλιν ἢ κερδαίνουσιν ἕτεροι. . . . ὃ γὰρ ἀλλαχοῦ τῷ κερδαίνειν ἕπεται, τοῦτο τῇδε τῷ δαπανᾶσθαι συνέξευκται.

more senseless things in order to present a wretched spectacle. But while these things are going on, you stand there laughing and marveling—being entertained by the miseries of others. . . . And in order that he may perform his tricks better, you give him money more liberally.[14]

The wealthy, however, were not readily abashed. They excused themselves by saying that almsgiving was the church's responsibility—and they had already given to the church—besides, who knew what the priests did with that money.[15] Or, they claimed that the poor were indolent and simply faking their distress.[16] Chrysostom was outraged by such sentiments. To those among his congregation who felt obliged to carry out an interrogation before parting with their cash he insisted, "You must not demand an audit of a person's life—just correct the poverty and supply the need."[17] An example of the kind of interchange he had in mind may inform the dialogue he imagined taking place between Jesus and the paralyzed man of John 5:2–9. Chrysostom was impressed that in response to Jesus' question, "Do you want to be healed?" the sufferer "did not make the usual reply, 'You see that I have been lying here paralyzed for this long time, and you ask me if I want to be healed? Did you come here to insult my sufferings, to reproach, mock, and make a comedy of my misfortune?'"[18] From this

---

[14]Chrysostom *Hom. in 1 Cor.* 21.5–6 (PG 61. 177) Εἰσὶν ἕτεροι πένητες κοῦφοι καὶ μετέωροι τὰς ψυχάς, καὶ οὐκ εἰδότες φέρειν λιμόν, ἀλλὰ πάντα μᾶλλον, ἢ τοῦτο ὑπομένοντες. Οὗτοι πολλάκις ὑμῖν ἐλεεινοῖς καὶ σχήμασι καὶ ῥήμασιν ἐντυχόντες, ἐπειδὴ οὐδὲν ὤνησαν τὰς ἱκετηρίας ἀφέντες ἐκείνας, τοὺς θαυματοποιοὺς ὑμῖν λοιπὸν παρήλασαν, οἱ μὲν δέρματα ὑποδημάτων μασώμενοι πεπονηκότων, οἱ δὲ κατὰ τῆς κεφαλῆς ἥλους ὀξεῖς διαπείροντες, ἕτεροι πεπηγόσιν ὕδασιν ὑπὸ τοῦ κρυμοῦ γυμνῇ τῇ γαστρὶ προσομιλοῦντες, ἄλλοι δὲ ἕτερα ἀτοπώτερα τούτων ὑπομένοντες, ἵνα τὸ πονηρὸν περιστήσωσι θέατρον. (ζ) Σὺ δέ, τούτων γινομένων, ἕστηκας γελῶν, καὶ θαυμάζων, καὶ ἐμπομπεύων τοῖς ἑτέρων κακοῖς. . . . Εἶτα ἵνα προθυμότερον ποιήσῃ ταῦτα, δαψιλέστερον δίδως ἀργύριον.

[15]Ibid., 21.6 (PG 61. 179) Ἀλλὰ τίς ὁ πολὺς αὐτῶν λόγος. . . . Ἔχει τὸ κοινὸν τῆς Ἐκκλησίας, φησί. . . . Ἀλλ᾽ ὑποπτεύεις τὸν ἱερέα; . . . Μὴ δὴ ταύτας προβαλλώμεθα τὰς προφάσεις, μηδὲ ἀπολογίαν εἶναι νομίζωμεν τὸ τὴν Ἐκκλησίαν πολλὰ κεκτῆσθαι.

[16]Ibid., 21.5 (PG 61. 176) Ἀλλὰ προφασίζεται, φησί, τὸν τρόμον καὶ τὴν ἀσθένειαν.

[17]Ibid., 21.5 (PG 61. 177) Τοῦτον εὐθύνας ἀπαιτεῖς ἀκριβεῖς; idem, *In Lazarum* 2.5–6 (PG 48. 989) Τόν γὰρ φιλοφροσύνην ἐπιδεικνύμενον οὐκ εὐθύνας ἀπαιτεῖν δεῖ βίου, ἀλλὰ μόνον τὴν πενίαν διορθοῦν, καὶ τὴν χρείαν πληροῦν. . . . Οὕτω καὶ ἡμεῖς ποιῶμεν, παρακαλῶ, μηδὲν ἀκριβολογούμενοι πέρα τοῦ δέοντος.

[18]Chrysostom *Homilia in paralyticum demissum per tectum* 1 (PG 51. 49) Εἰπόντι γὰρ αὐτῷ, θέλεις ὑγιὴς γενέσθαι; οὐδὲν εἶπεν οἷον εἰκὸς ἦν, ὅτι Ὁρᾷς με παραλελυμένον χρόνον τοσοῦτον κατακείμενον, καὶ ἐρωτᾷς εἰ βούλομαι γενέσθαι ὑγιὴς ἐπεμβῆναί μου τοῖς κακοῖς ἦλθες, ὀνειδίσαι, καὶ καταγελάσαι, καὶ κωμῳδῆσαι τὴν συμφοράν; compare idem, *Hom. in Rom.* 21.5 (PG 60. 608).

perspective, we can see that the concept of philanthropy in late antiquity was less an extension of any concern for the welfare of the destitute, than part of the desire to publicize one's social standing.

It was thus precisely because it was the forum for self-aggrandizement and a display of status that Chrysostom indicted the marketplace. There, any exchange of money was, finally, incidental to the real goal of prestige. This reality did not surprise him, since commerce had been born of envy.

> In the beginning there was no gold, nor was anyone infatuated with it. But if you like, I shall tell you how this evil was introduced: each person by envying the other brought on this disease, and once having caught it, inflamed even those who had no desire [for it]. For when they saw beautiful houses, extensive fields, herds of slaves, silver vessels, and a vast heap of clothes, they were willing to do anything to be preeminent.[19]

In the traditional virtue of *philotimia*, Chrysostom located the source of appetite and root of all evil.[20] Having pinpointed the problem, he launched upon an earnest program of reform.

■ Chrysostom and *Philotimia*

Chrysostom's first tactic is to elaborate upon the commonplace of antiquity that the cultivation of honor inevitably enslaved a person, not, as he himself pointed out, to "one master only, but. . . to two or three thousand masters, all issuing different orders."[21] Even though such submission to the masses was galling enough,[22] there was more. One entered, paradoxically,

---

[19]Chrysostom *Hom. in John* 65.3 (PG 59. 364) ἢ γὰρ ἂν παρὰ τὴν ἀρχὴν ἐνετέθη· νῦν δὲ χρυσίον οὐκ ἦν ἄνωθεν, οὐδὲ ἦρά τις χρυσίου. Ἀλλ' εἰ βούλεσθε, λέγω πόθεν εἰσῆλθε τὸ κακόν. Ἕκαστος τὸν πρὸ αὐτοῦ ζηλοῦντες ἐπέτεινον τὸ νόσημα, καὶ τὸν οὐ βουλόμενον ὁ προλαβὼν ἐρεθίζει. Ὅταν γὰρ ἴδωσιν οἰκίας λαμπρὰς, καὶ πλῆθος ἀγρῶν, καὶ ἀνδραπόδων ἀγέλας, καὶ ἀργυρᾶ σκεύη, καὶ πολὺν ἱματίων φορυτὸν, πάντα πράττουσιν, ὥστε ὑπερβαλέσθαι. The Jews during the Exodus thus had a novel way of life: being fed by manna, they had no commerce or trade or craft (idem, *Quod nemo laedatur nisi a seipso* 13 [PG 52. 473–74]).

[20]Chrysostom *Hom. in John* 28.3 (PG 59. 166). This sentiment is central to Chrysostom's thought; see idem, *Adversus oppugnatores vitae monasticae* 3.6–8 (PG 47. 357); idem, *De laude Maximi et quales ducendae uxores* 3.4 (PG 51. 231); idem, *Hom. in Gen.* 20.5 (PG 53. 173); see also Francis Leduc, "Le Thème de la vaine gloire," *Proche-Orient Chrétien* 19 (1969) 3–32.

[21]Chrysostom *Hom. in John* 42.4 (PG 59. 243) δούλους οὐχ ἑνὶ δεσπότῃ μόνον, ἀλλὰ καὶ δυσὶ καὶ τρισὶ καὶ μυρίοις διάφορα ἐπιτάττουσιν ὑπακούοντας.

[22]Traditional elitist prejudices emerge as Chrysostom glosses "the people" as πρᾶγμα θορύβου γέμον καὶ ταραχῶδες, καὶ ἐξ ἀνοίας τὸ πλέον συγκείμενον, ἁπλῶς φερόμενον, κατὰ τὰ τῆς θαλάττης κύματα ("full of uproar and disorder and for the most part made up of thoughtlessness—just carried along like the waves of the sea"; *Hom. in John* 3.5 [PG 59. 44]).

into a kind of bondage to one's own ostentation. Borrowing from common Stoic philosophy, Chrysostom observed out that although a rich man's servants can go everywhere independently about their business, the one who appears to be their master "does not dare go out into the marketplace without them, nor to the baths, nor into the countryside. . . if he even peeps out of the house by himself, he is sure that he will be a laughingstock."[23]

This suggestion of status reversal, that mastery may take on the lineaments of slavery, however, was blunted by familiarity. To it, therefore, Chrysostom appended a more shocking charge, namely, that these concerns with what we may term personal appearance were hardly masculine. Indeed, the topic of cosmetics had continually fascinated and exercised him. In this context he toyed with the conceit that worldly honor, as a superficial and fleeting amelioration, resembles nothing so much as the feminine use of cosmetics,[24] and where there is heavy use of cosmetics, harlotry cannot be far behind. This point he found well worth elaboration:

> Riches lead those taken in by them into an honor which is the opposite of [real honor], but one painted over with colors so persuasive that they believe it is the same, although it is not really, even if it seems so to the eye. For while the lovely appearance of courtesans made up out of emollients and eyeliners is bereft of real beauty, it

[23]Ibid., 80.3 (PG 59. 436) Οὗτοι δὲ πολλάκις χωρὶς ἐκείνου πανταχοῦ περίιασιν. Ἀλλ' ὁ δοκῶν εἶναι κύριος, ἂν μὴ παρῶσιν οἱ δοῦλοι, οὐ τολμᾷ προελθεῖν οἴκοθεν, ἀλλὰ κἂν προκύψῃ τῆς οἰκίας μόνος, καταγέλαστον ἑαυτὸν εἶναι νομίζει. Compare idem, *Hom. in Matt.* 20.5 (PG 57. 293); and idem, *Hom. in John* 87.3–4 (PG 59. 477–78). One should regard wealth, along with the other passions, "from the position of masters and not slaves, in order to rule them and not be ruled by them, in order to put them to good use and not abuse them" (ἐν τάξει δεσποτῶν, καὶ μὴ δούλων, ὥστε κρατεῖν αὐτῶν, καὶ μὴ κρατεῖσθαι ὑπ' αὐτῶν, ὥστε κεχρῆσθαι αὐτοῖς, καὶ μὴ παρακεχρῆσθαι; idem, *Hom. in John* 19.3 [PG 59. 123]). See also idem, *Hom. in John* 59.4 [PG 59. 326]; idem, *Hom. in 1 Cor.* 19.4 [PG 61. 156]); idem, *Hom. in Col.* 7.3 (PG 62. 347). Chrysostom compared wealthy women who "cannot" go out without their mules to beggars who have had their feet cut off (*De Virginitate* 66.10–12 [SC 125. 334]).

[24]Chrysostom *Hom. in Col.* 7.4 (PG 62. 349). For Chrysostom on cosmetics, see idem, *Adhortationes ad Theodorum lapsum* 1.13 (PG 47. 295–96); compare *Hom. in Matt.* 20.1 (PG 57. 287). By giving alms, a woman beautifies herself far more effectively than with cosmetics (idem, *Hom. in John* 69.3 [PG 59. 380]). Michel Foucault has suggested (*History of Sexuality*, vol. 2: *Use of Pleasure* [trans. Robert Hurley; New York: Random House, 1986] 161) that makeup and adornment formed an important theme in ancient morality texts, precisely because they posed the problem of the relationship between truth and the pleasures. Xenophon noted that women who use makeup "are found out while they are dressing in the morning: they perspire and are lost; a tear convicts them; the bath reveals them as they are" (ἢ γὰρ ἐξ εὐνῆς ἁλίσκονται ἐξανιστάμενοι, πρὶν παρασκευάσασθαι ἢ ὑπὸ ἱδρῶτος ἐλέγχοντι, ἢ ὑπὸ δακρύων βασανίζονται ἢ ὑπὸ λουτροῦ ἀληθινῶς κατωπτεύθησαν; *Oec.* 10.8 [LCL; 7 vols.; trans. E. C. Marchant; Cambridge, MA: Harvard University Press, 1979] 4. 451).

nevertheless makes an ugly and unsightly face appear beautiful and
well-formed to those deceived by it, although it is not so in reality. In
exactly this way riches force flattery to look like honor.[25]

The comparison of public honor to the use of cosmetics should logically
have led Chrysostom to find the man involved in business guilty of a kind
of prostitution. This is in fact the case: warming to his topic, he cried,

What is more disgraceful than a man in love with money? Whatsoever
call girls or women who work the street do not refuse to do, neither
does he refuse. . . . But if prostitutes stand in front of their houses and
are indicted for selling their bodies for money, they have an excuse:
poverty, and driving hunger. . . . But the greedy man stands, not
before his house, but in the middle of the city. . . . And just as harlots
belong to whoever gives them gold—even a slave or a freedman or a
gladiator or anyone at all, if he can meet their price,. . . . [so rich
men] for the sake of gold. . . associate with anyone shamelessly.[26]

It is noteworthy that Chrysostom underscored the economic rather than the
sexual aspect of prostitution.[27] In prostitution, as in business, supply and

[25]Chrysostom *Quod nemo se laedatur nisi a seipso* 9 (PG 52. 470) τὴν δὲ ἐναντίαν
ἐκείνας, τοῖς ἐκείνης χρώμασιν ἀναχρωννύς, καὶ οὕτω προσάγων τοῖς ἠπατημένοις,
καὶ πείθων ταύτην ἐκείνην εἶναι νομίζειν, οὐκ οὖσαν τῇ φύσει, ἀλλὰ τῇ ὄψει
δοκοῦσαν εἶναι. Ͼαθάπερ γὰρ τὰ κάλλη τῶν ἐταιριζομένων γυναικῶν ἐπιτρίμμασι
καὶ ὑπογραφαῖς συγκείμενα, κάλλους μὲν ἀπεστέρηται, τὴν δὲ αἰσχρὰν ὄψιν
καὶ δυσειδῆ καλήν τε καὶ εὐειδῆ εἶναι ποιεῖ παρὰ τοῖς ὑπ' αὐτῆς ἠπατημένοις,
οὐκ οὖσαν καλήν· οὕτω δὴ καὶ ὁ πλοῦτος τὴν κολακείαν βιαζόμενος τιμὴν
δεικνύναι ποιεῖ. Compare idem, *Quod nemo se laedatur nisi a seipso* 6 (PG 52. 467); and
idem, *Ad viduam juniorem* 5.344–63 (SC 138. 142–44). By definition, "a harlot knows not
how to love, but only how to ensnare" (Πόρνη γὰρ φιλεῖν οὐκ ἐπίσταται, ἀλλ' ἐπιβουλεύει
μόνον; idem, *Ad populom Antiochenum de statuis* 14.4 [PG 49. 149]); see also Xenophon
Oec. 1.13–23 (LCL, 4. 369–73).
[26]Chrysostom *Hom. in Heb.* 15.3 (PG 63. 120–21) Τί γὰρ αἰσχρότερον ἀνδρὸς
χρημάτων ἐρῶντος; ὅσα αἱ ἐταιριζόμεναι γυναῖκες, ὅσα αἱ ἐπὶ τῆς σκηνῆς
οὐ παραιτοῦνται ποιεῖν, τοσαῦτα οὐδὲ οὗτος. . .Ἀλλ' ἑστήκασιν ἐπὶ οἰκήματος
αἱ πόρναι, καὶ τοῦτό ἐστι τὸ ἔγκλημα, ὅτι τὸ σῶμα πωλοῦσι χρημάτων
ἕνεκεν· ἀλλ' ἔχουσί τινα ἀπολογίαν, τὴν πενίαν καὶ τὸν καταναγκάζοντα
λιμόν· . . . Ἐνταῦθα δὲ ἔστηκεν ὁ πλεονέκτης, οὐκ ἐπὶ οἰκήματος, ἀλλ' ἐπὶ
τῆς πόλεως μέσης. . . . Καὶ τοῦτο δὲ τῶν πορνῶν ἴδιόν ἐστιν, ὅτι τοῦ τὸ
χρυσίον διδόντος εἰσί· κἂν γὰρ δοῦλος ᾖ, κἂν ἐλεύθερος, κἂν μονομάχος,
κἂν ὁστισοῦν, προτείνῃ δὲ τὸν μισθόν, καταδέχονται·. . . διὰ τὸ χρυσίον, καὶ
ἀσχημόνως συγγίνονται. Similar imagery is used of the eunuch Eutropius after his fall;
Chrysostom thus described his face: "denuded of its enamel and pigments by the action of
adversity as by a sponge" (καθάπερ σπογγιᾷ τινι τῇ μεταβολῇ τὰ ἐπιτρίμματα καὶ
τὰς ἐπιγραφὰς ἐκμάξασαν, *In Eutropium eunuchum* 1.3 [PG 52. 394]).
[27]Elizabeth Clark has pointed out ("Friendship Between the Sexes: Classical Theory and
Christian Practice," in idem, *Jerome, Chrysostom and Friends. Essays and Translations*

demand create and service a market, and money changes hands. The point that drove Chrysostom's comparison, however, is the product purchased. Whereas the wealthy man in the agora transacts his dealings in the confidence that expenditure buys honor, Chrysostom would have him stand corrected: like the prostitute, he sells himself and accrues only dishonor. This is a deft rhetorical touch. Likening the prosperous male business of the agora to the ignoble work of women in commerce not only carries the emotional shock of gender inversion, but also relegates, at a single stroke, what is in the economic mainstream to the margins of society.[28]

We ought, however, to return to the central issue of money. To the regular and considerable expense entailed by *philotimia*, Chrysostom presented an alternative. He pointed out that heavenly favor can be obtained remarkably cheaply, indeed for free. One need only ask. In his sermons, however, it becomes embarrassingly clear that divine favor is, after all, to be secured by entirely traditional means. He thus rebuked those who said, "I can make a friend without mammon, and a rather better one than with mammon."[29] In spiritual matters also, he insisted, "no revenue comes without expenditure, nor wealth without outlay."[30] Christ, like the vulgar masses, stands ready to reward with honor—indeed, with heavenly acclamations—

[Lewiston, NY: Mellen, 1979] 57–58) that, as with the related issue of ornamentation of dress, Chrysostom is chiefly concerned not with the enhancement of sexual appeal but with the issue of expense and misuse of money. As modern analyses suggest, the attraction of prostitution lies in the high earnings per hour. "Women enter the market willingly, for the money. . . . They think of themselves as business women" (Helen Reynolds, *The Economics of Prostitution* [Springfield, IL: Thomas, 1986] 4, 6). As dancers were linked with prostitution in Chrysostom's mind, he suspects, "If I ask him, 'Why ever have you given up other trades to go into this polluted and abominable one?' He will say that in it it is possible for one to gain much by doing little" (Κἀκεῖνον μὲν ἐὰν ἔρωμαι, τί δήποτε τὰς ἄλλας τέχνας ἀφεὶς, ἐπὶ ταύτην ἦλθες τὴν ἐναγῆ καὶ μιαράν· ἐρεῖ, ὅτι ἔξεστιν ὀλίγα πονοῦντα, πολλὰ καρποῦσθαι; *Hom. in John* 42.4 [PG 59. 244]).

[28]Gayle Rubin ("The Traffic in Women," in Rayna R. Reiter, ed., *Towards an Anthropology of Women* [New York: Monthly Review, 1975] 174) points to the difference between men as transactors and women as transacted bodies in kinship networks. See also the remarks of Alain Corbin (*Women for Hire* [trans. Alan Sheridan; Cambridge, MA: Harvard University Press, 1990] 5–7) on the nineteenth-century French regulationist Alexandre-Jean-Baptiste Parent-Duchâtelet, who built up an anthropology of the woman belonging "to the class of public prostitution"; she symbolized "disorder, excess and improvidence" and was defined chiefly by marginality.

[29]Chrysostom *In Lazarum* 3.10 (PG 48. 1006) Δύναμαι χωρὶς τοῦ μαμμωνᾶ ποιῆσαι φίλον, καὶ σπουδαιότερον μᾶλλον, ἢ διὰ τοῦ μαμμωνᾶ. Almsgiving is proof of Christian profession (idem, *Hom. in John* 20.3 [PG 59. 128]).

[30]Chrysostom *Hom. in John* 19.3 (PG 59. 124) Οὐδὲ γὰρ ἔνι γενέσθαι πρόσοδον δαπάνης χωρὶς, οὐδὲ πλοῦτον ἄνευ ἀναλωμάτων.

the lavish spender.[31] The question becomes a simple one of venue. "If you wish your property to rest secure and indeed for it to increase," Chrysostom advised, "invest in heaven. . . where no thief, schemer or any destructive thing will be able to pounce upon it."[32] Timid investors should know that "Christ stands ready to receive and to keep a close watch over your deposits for you—and not only to keep a close watch, but even to augment them, and pay them back with a lot of interest!"[33] In this venture, just as in any ambitious deal, "it is possible to lose by being sparing, and by not being sparing, to gain."[34]

Where does this canny opportunity for investment lie? Chrysostom located it at the very bottom of the socioeconomic ladder, in the antispectacle of the market, among the poor and the destitute. To invest in these people was to lay up "gain and good merchandise" in heaven, whereas "to encircle slaves and mules and horses with golden collars, but to let the Lord walk around naked"[35] marked not only a terrible hardness of heart, but also a

---

[31]Acclamations were an intrinsic part of the patronage system (Liebeschuetz, *Antioch*, 218); see also Chrysostom *De inani gloria et de educandis liberis* 4.167–84 (SC 188. 74–78). Although Chrysostom deplored almsgiving done for worldly show (*Hom. in John* 28.3 [PG 59. 166]), he was quite content to summon up an impressive heavenly audience: "In short, if you want to love glory, love glory, but let it be the immortal sort. For its theater is more brilliant and its profit greater" (Ὅλως δὲ εἰ βούλει δόξης ἐρᾶν, ἔρα δόξης, ἀλλὰ τῆς ἀθανάτου. Καὶ γὰρ λαμπρότερον αὐτῆς τὸ θέατρον, καὶ μεῖζον τὸ κέρδος; *Hom. in John* 42.4 [PG 59. 243]; see also 38.5 [PG 59. 218–19]). God's reward is not some "small, low-class theater" (μικρὸν καὶ ταπεινὸν καθίζω θεάτρον; idem, *Hom. in John* 4.4 [PG 59. 51]; see also 3.6 [PG 59. 45]).

[32]Chrysostom *Ad viduam iuniorem* 7.447–52 (SC 138. 152) Ὅλως δὲ εἰ βούλει καὶ τὰ χρήματά σοι μένειν ἐν ἀσφαλείᾳ καὶ αὔξεσθαι πάλιν, ἐγώ σοι καὶ τὸν τρόπον ὑποδείξω καὶ τὸν τόπον, ἔνθα οὐδενὶ τῶν ἐπιβουλευόντων θέμις εἰσελθεῖν. Τίς οὖν ἐστιν ὁ τόπος; Ὁ οὐρανός. Ἀπόστειλον αὐτὰ πρὸς τὸν καλὸν ἐκεῖνον ἄνδρα, καὶ οὔτε κλέπτης, οὔτε ἐπίβουλος, οὔτε ἄλλο τι τῶν λυμαινομένων αὐτοῖς ἐπιτηδῆσαι δυνήσεται.

[33]Chrysostom *Ad populum Antiochenum de statuis* 2.5 (PG 49. 41) ἕστηκεν ὁ Χριστὸς ἕτοιμος ὑποδέξασθαι, καὶ τηρῆσαί σοι τὰς παρακαταθήκας, οὐχὶ τηρῆσαι δὲ μόνον, ἀλλὰ καὶ πλεονάσαι, καὶ μετὰ πολλῆς ἀποδοῦναι τῆς προσθήκας. See also idem, *Hom. in Gen.* 20.5 (PG 53. 174). Not only are we promised a hundredfold return, but even if a thief steals our investment, Christ says, "Set that down to my account" (Ἀπόθεσθε αὐτὰ παρ' ἐμοὶ; idem, *Hom. in 1 Tim.* 11.2 [PG 62. 555]). Money lenders prefer to lend to those who will take a long time to repay, thus making the interest greater (idem, *Hom. in Rom.* 7.8 [PG 60. 451]).

[34]Chrysostom *Hom. in Matt.* 5.5 (PG 57. 61) καὶ οὐκ ἐννοεῖς ὅτι ἔστι φειδόμενον ἀπολέσαι, καὶ μὴ φειδόμενον κερδάναι. See also idem, *Hom. in Gen.* 55.5 (PG 54. 4).

[35]Chrysostom *Hom. in John* 27.3 (PG 59. 161) ἀλλ' οὕτως ἐσμὲν ἀγνώμονες, ὡς οἰκέταις μὲν καὶ ἡμιόνοις καὶ ἵπποις περιδέραια χρυσᾶ περιτιθέναι, τὸν δὲ Δεσπότην γυμνὸν περιϊόντα; see also 25.3 (PG 59. 152); idem, *Hom. in Matt.* 66.3–4 (PG 58. 629–30).

culpable failure to appreciate the volatility of fortune.[36] When preaching on Lazarus and the rich man, Chrysostom scrupulously emphasized the lesson that all worldly wealth must come to an end in death, if not before:

> Do not, beloved, skip lightly over that [phrase], "He was buried." By it you should understand that the silver-wrapped tables, couches, rugs, tapestries, all manner of household furnishings, scented oils, perfumes, a great quantity of undiluted wine, dainty dishes in variety, rich sauces, cooks, flatterers, body guards, domestic slaves, and all the rest of his impressive front have been quenched and turned wholly into ashes.[37]

Heavenly deposits had the advantage of resting beyond any risk of failure, corruption, or reversal, in a security that promised even to fend off the "excessive sadness" to which the rich were of all people especially prone.[38] Chrysostom noted, moreover, that when you give to the poor "you do not have to pay for transport."[39] Such treasure also escaped envy's malicious eye, for the invidiousness felt by the poor when confronted by the spectacle of the idle rich was all too well known.[40] Chrysostom thus spoke approv-

---

[36]Fine houses will become one's greatest accuser on the day of judgment (Chrysostom *Hom. in John* 47.5 [PG 59. 268–69]); it is far better to build splendid houses in heaven (idem, *Ad populum Antiochenum de statuis* 2.16 [PG 49. 41]).

[37]Chrysostom *In Lazarum* 2.3 (PG 48. 985) Μὴ ἁπλῶς παραδράμῃς, ἀγαπητέ, τό, ἐτάφη ἀλλ᾽ ἐνταῦθά μοι νόει τὰς τραπέζας τὰς περιηργυρωμένας, τὰς κλίνας, τοὺς τάπητας, τὰ ἐπιβλήματα, τὰ ἄλλα τὰ κατὰ τὴν οἰκίαν ἅπαντα, τὰ μύρα, τὰ ἀρώματα, τὸν πολὺν ἄκρατον, τῶν ἐδεσμάτων τὰς ποικιλίας, τὰ καρυκεύματα, τοὺς μαγείρους, τοὺς κόλακας, τοὺς δορυφόρους, τοὺς οἰκέτας, τὴν ἄλλην ἅπασαν φαντασίαν κατεσβεσμένην καὶ καταμαρανθεῖσαν. According to Palladius, John Chrysostom is said to have remarked, "This life is a bazaar. We finish our buying and selling and we move elsewhere" (πανήγυρις τὰ παρόντα· ἠγοράσαμεν, ἐπωλήσαμεν, καταλύομεν; *Dialogus* 8.119–20 [SC 341. 166]; the translation is that of Robert T. Meyer, *Dialogue on the Life of St. John Chrysostom* [ACW 45; New York: Newman, 1985] 53). See also Chrysostom *Hom. in John* 47.5 (PG 59. 268); idem, *Ad populum Antiochenum de statuis* 13.2 (PG 49. 138); idem, *In Lazarum* 6.1 (PG 48. 1028–29); idem, *Hom. in John* 44.2 (PG 59. 250); idem, *Adhorationes ad Theodorum lapsum* 1.9 (PG 47. 288); idem, *De virginitate* 68.45–51 (SC 125. 340–42).

[38]On the ravages of moths, rust, and robbers, see Chrysostom *Hom. in Matt.* 47.4 (PG 58. 486); idem, *Hom in Rom.* 30.1 (PG 60. 662); idem, *Hom. in Gen.* 37.5 (PG 53. 349–50); idem, *Hom. in 1 Cor.* 21.5 (PG 61. 176). On the sadness of the wealthy, see idem, *Ad populum Antiochenum de statuis* 18.1 (PG 49. 181–82); idem, *Hom. in Matt.* 68.3 (PG 58. 643); idem, *Hom. in Gen.* 59.2 (PG 54. 515).

[39]Chrysostom *Hom. in Matt.* 66.5 (PG 58. 631) Οὐκ ἔστιν ἐνταῦθα δοῦναι μισθὸν τῆς μετακομιδῆς τῶν εἰσφερομένων. See also idem, *Hom. in Gen.* 20.5 (PG 53. 174) οὐκ ἔστιν ἐνταῦθα καμεῖν ἐξαργυρίζοντας.

[40]Chrysostom *Adversus oppugnatores vitae monasticae* 2.5 (PG 47. 338); idem, *Hom. in John* 44.2 (PG 59. 250); idem, *Homilia in paralyticum demissum per tectum* 1 (PG 51. 49); idem, *Quod nemo laedatur nisi a seipso* 10 (PG 52. 471); idem, *Hom. in 1 Cor.* 12.7 (PG 61. 106).

ingly of Lazarus, as one who "did not question the providence of God as many do today, saying, 'To this one who squanders all he has on parasites, flatterers, and drunkenness, everything flows as if from fountains, whereas I lie here, an object lesson to on-lookers of disgrace and ridicule.' "[41]

Chrysostom knew his congregation. He suspected that they would respond to his advice to "invest in God" by murmuring about how "slowly" God pays back investment.[42] To them any expenditure on the poor represented the senseless cultivation of people from whom no reciprocal good could be expected. Chrysostom countered this prevailing opinion with a longer view of social interaction. Almsgivers would find on the day of judgment that they had secured for themselves the most effective of patrons.[43]

Chrysostom's trenchant appeal to both shame and self-interest marked a strenuous effort to redirect the wealth of his congregation. Why, then, was this such a pressing concern? To be sure, he recalled and could remind his congregation in uncomfortably pointed language with the hard sayings of the gospel: "'Woe to you who are rich.' But you do everything so that [your sons] might enrich themselves. 'Woe to you when everyone speaks well of you.' But you frequently deplete your entire economic base for the praise of the people."[44] Aside from this spiritual peril, however, Chrysostom recognized how conspicuous displays of wealth created fissures in his own

---

[41]Chrysostom *In Lazarum* 1.9 (PG 48. 975) Ἀλλὰ τούτῳ μὲν εἰς παρασίτους καὶ κόλακις καὶ μέθην τὰ ὄντα ἅπαντα δαπανῶντι, ὥσπερ ἐκ πηγῶν ἅπαντα ἐπιρρεῖ ἐγὼ δὲ παράδειγμα τοῖς ὁρῶσι κεῖμαι καὶ αἰσχύνη καὶ γέλως λιμῷ τηκόμενος. See also idem, *Hom. in 1 Cor.* 27.4–5 (PG 61. 230–31); idem, *Hom. in 2 Cor.* 19.3 (PG 61. 533).

[42]Chrysostom *Hom. in 1 Tim.* 11.2 (PG 62. 555) Ἀλλὰ βραδέως μοι, φησὶν, ἀποδίδωσι.

[43]Chrysostom *Ad populum Antiochenum de statuis* 2.6 (PG 49. 42–43); see also idem, *Adversus Judaeos* 7.6 (PG 48. 926). John Chrysostom suggested that we look on the poor "as our benefactors" (καθάπερ εὐεργέτας; *Hom. in Gen.* 34.3 [PG 53. 315]). Personal almsgiving is vastly more effective than an easy reliance upon the patronage of charitable relatives or even churchly connections (idem, *In Lazarum* 3.9 [PG 48. 1005–6]). Monks may also exercise patronage (idem, *Adversus oppugnatores vitae monasticae* 2.7 [PG 47. 342]; idem, *Hom. in Gen.* 21.3 [PG 53. 179]); see also the classic study by Peter Brown, "The Rise and Function of the Holy Man in Late Antiquity," *JRomS* 60–61 (1970/71) 80–101. Chrysostom asserted, however, that it is Bishop Flavian who was the truly effective patron of the city (*Ad populum Antiochenum de statuis* 21.1–4 [PG 49. 211–20]); see also A. Natali, "Eglise et évergétisme à Antioche à fin du siècle d'après Jean Chrysostome," *StPatr* 17 (1982) 1177–78.

[44]Chrysostom *Adversus oppugnatores vitae monasticae* 3.7 (PG 47. 359) Οὐαὶ τοῖς πλουτοῦσιν, ὑμεῖς δὲ ὅπως χρηματίσαιντο, πάντα πράττετε· Οὐαὶ ὅταν καλῶς εἴπωσιν ὑμᾶς πάντες οἱ ἄνθρωποι· ὑμεῖς δὲ καὶ οὐσίας ὁλοκλήρους ὑπὲρ τῆς τῶν δήμων εὐφημίας ἐκενώσατε πολλάκις. See Rudolf Brändle, "Jean Chrysostome— l'importance de Matt. 25, 31–46 pour son éthique," *VC* 31 (1977) 47–52.

community.[45] For the marketplace, as the venue where social status was brokered, showed a disturbing tendency to infiltrate the church. Through Chrysostom's eyes, we can see it happening:

> Has a rich man entered here, or a rich woman? She does not think about how to listen to the words of God but rather how to display herself—how even her sitting can be a boast and an honor—how she can surpass all other women in the costliness of her clothes. In her appearance, aspect, and gait, she strives to make herself august. Indeed her whole preoccupation is, "Didn't that woman see me? Surely she admired me? Isn't my beauty handsomely set off?". . . In just the same way the rich man enters, displaying himself to the poor man, instilling awe in him with his sartorial equipment and his many slaves surrounding him to shoo away the crowd. . . indeed, [the wealthy man] considers that he has graced us and the people—and perhaps even God—because he has come to church.[46]

Chrysostom's congregation agreed all too readily that "the poor man is an object of ridicule, even if he is virtuous."[47]

Against the ostentatious display that was both the basis and the articulation of status, therefore, Chrysostom sketched an alternative economic system in which the rich had to acknowledge their indebtedness precisely to those who were poor and insignificant in the eyes of the world. His message was one of mutuality. He obtained this mutuality by investing the very poor, who had previously been excluded from patron-client relations because they had nothing to contribute, with a valuable commodity, namely, special access to God.[48] "Do you contribute money?" Chrysostom asked the

---

[45]Robert Browning has noted ("The Riot of A.D. 387 in Antioch: The Role of the Theatrical Claque in the Later Roman Empire," *JRomS* 42 [1952] 19) the tension in these years between the rich and the poor. Leduc points out ("Vaine gloire," 15–16) the clarity with which John saw that vainglory was an obstacle to harmonious relations with others.

[46]Chrysostom *Hom. in 2 Thess.* 3.3 (PG 62. 484) Εἰσῆλθε πλούσιος ἐνταῦθα, ἢ καὶ πλουτοῦσα γυνή, οὐ φροντίζει πῶς ἀκούσει τῶν λογίων τοῦ Θεοῦ ἀλλὰ πῶς ἐπιδείξεται, πῶς μετὰ κόμπου καθίσει, πῶς μετὰ δόξης πολλῆς, πῶς πάσας τὰς ἄλλας ὑπερβαλεῖται τῇ τῶν ἱματίων πολυτελείᾳ, καὶ σχήματι καὶ βλέμματι καὶ βαδίσματι σεμνοτέραν ἑαυτὴν ἐργάσεται, καὶ πᾶσα ἡ φροντὶς καὶ ἡ μέριμνα αὐτῇ, ἆρα εἶδεν ἡ δεῖνα; ἆρα ἐθαύμασεν; ἆρα καλῶς κεκαλλώπισμαι;. . . Ὁμοίως καὶ ὁ πλουτῶν ἀνὴρ εἰσέρχεται δείξων ἑαυτὸν τῷ πένητι, καὶ εἰς φόβον καταστήσων διὰ τῆς περιβολῆς τῶν ἱματίων, διὰ τοῦ παῖδας ἔχειν πολλούς· καὶ παρεστήκασιν ἀποσοβοῦντες. . . νομίζει χαρίζεσθαι καὶ ἡμῖν, καὶ τῷ λαῷ, τάχα δὲ καὶ τῷ Θεῷ, ὅτι εἰσῆλθεν εἰς τὸν τοῦ Θεοῦ οἶκον. See also idem, *Hom. in Heb.* 28.14 (PG 63. 200).

[47]Chrysostom *Hom. in John* 76.3 (PG 59. 413) Ἀλλὰ καταγελᾶται ὁ πένης κἂν ἐνάρετος ᾖ, φησιν.

[48]Duncan Cloud, "The Client-Patron Relationship: Emblem and Reality in Juvenal's First

wealthier members of his congregation; "[the poor] contribute freedom of speech before God."[49] He hoped that he would no longer hear voiced the dissociated view that distanced the wealthy from the poor: "What is it to me? . . . The one who perishes, let him perish! The one who is saved, let him be saved! Nothing of this is my concern."[50]

This vision of a new Christian community based on mutuality arises, in part, from Chrysostom's appreciation for the lowly background of the first Christians. When pagans said that the apostles were boorish and lowborn, Chrysostom advised, "Let us follow up that remark, and say that they were also untaught and unlettered and poor and of no account and stupid and unknown."[51] To such people, emperors in purple had been pleased to go as clients. "In Rome, that most imperial of cities, even emperors, generals, and the elite abandon everything and run to the tombs of the fisherman and tentmaker. . . thus have emperors become doorkeepers for fishermen."[52]

Book," in Wallace-Hadrill, *Patronage in Ancient Society*, 210. See Frances Young, "John Chrysostom on 1st and 2nd Corinthians," *StPatr* 18 (1985) 446; and compare Francis Leduc, "L'Éschatologie, une préoccupation centrale de saint Jean Chrysostome," *Proche-Orient Chrétien* 19 (1969) 125.

[49]Chrysostom *Hom. in Rom.* 21.3 (PG 60. 606) Εἰσφέρεις σὺ χρήματα; Εἰσφέρουσί σοι παρρησίαν ἐκεῖνοι τὴν πρὸς τὸν Θεόν. See also G. J. M. Bartelink, "Παρρησία dans les oeuvres de Jean Chrysostome," *StPatr* 16 (1985) 441–48.

[50]Chrysostom *Adversus oppugnatores vitae monasticae* 3.2 (PG 47. 350) Τί μοι, καὶ τῆς τῶν ἄλλων προνοίας; ὁ ἀπολλύμενος ἀπολλύσθω, καὶ ὁ σωζόμενος σωζέσθω· οὐδὲν τούτων πρὸς ἐμέ, τὰ ἐμαυτοῦ σκοπεῖν ἐπιτέταγμαι. See also idem, *Adversus Judaeos* 4.7 (PG 48. 881); idem, *Ad populum Antiochenum de statuis* 1.12 (PG 49. 33); idem, *Hom. in Gen.* 7.5 (PG 53. 63); idem, *Contra eos qui subintroductas habent* 3.20–22 and 4.7–9 (in Jean Dumortier, ed., *Saint Jean Chrysostome: les cohabitations suspectes; comment observer la virginité* [Paris: Belles Lettres, 1955] 53, 56). Peter Brown describes (*The Body and Society: Men, Women, and Sexual Renunciation in Early Christianity* [New York: Columbia University Press, 1988] 306) this appeal as preaching "a solidarity of bodies at risk."

[51]Chrysostom *Hom. in 1 Cor.* 3.4 (PG 61. 28) Καὶ ὅταν εἴπωσιν ἐκεῖνοι, ὅτι ἄγροικοι ἦσαν οἱ ἀπόστολοι, προσθῶμεν ἡμεῖς, καὶ εἴπωμεν, ὅτι καὶ ἀμαθεῖς καὶ ἀγράμματοι καὶ πένητες καὶ εὐτελεῖς καὶ ἀσύνετοι καὶ ἀφανεῖς. Οὐκ ἔστι βλασφημία τῶν ἀποστόλων ταῦτα, ἀλλὰ καὶ δόξα. Chrysostom recognized the social calculus of manual labor, saying of Peter and Paul, "Although the tentmaker has more prestige than the fisherman, he is less esteemed than all other artisans" (τοῦ μὲν γὰρ ἁλιέως ὁ σκηνοποιὸς τιμιώτερος, τῶν δὲ ἄλλων χειροτεχνῶν εὐτελέστερος; *Panegyrium in Babylam martyrem* 3 [PG 50. 538]).

[52]Chrysostom *Contra Judaeos et gentiles Quod Christus sit Deus* 9.6 (PG 48. 825) Ἐν τῇ βασιλικωτάτῃ πόλει Ῥώμῃ, πάντα ἀφιέντες, ἐπὶ τοὺς τάφους τοῦ ἁλιέως καὶ τοῦ σκηνοποιοῦ τρέχουσι καὶ βασιλεῖς καὶ ὕπατοι καὶ στρατηγοί. . . καὶ γεγόνασι θυρωροὶ λοιπὸν τῶν ἁλιέων οἱ βασιλεῖς. Compare idem, *Hom. in 2 Cor.* 26.5 (PG 61. 582); no empress was more conspicuous or celebrated than the tentmaker's wife (idem, *Hom. in Rom.* 30.3 [PG 60. 665]); and Mary's low social status should abash the rich (idem, *Hom. in John* 53.3 [PG 59. 296]).

It is important to note, however, that the new social viability of the poor has been achieved principally through social rather than economic negotiation. The traditional system has undergone some inversion but has not been supplanted. Wealth continues to undergird patron-client relations, but now it is the rich who are to take upon themselves the role of clients and court the poor, who can secure for them valuable patronal services with God.[53] Because the poor, however, could now participate in the system of gift and countergift that structured society, Chrysostom's view of the city shifted. No longer arising from greed, commerce now underscored humanity's mutual need.

> For this reason we have built cities and markets and houses, in order that we may be united with each other—and not just in our houses, but also in the bond of love. Since our nature was created needy by the one who made us, and not self-sufficient, God has advantageously arranged that the help derived from living with each other should supply whatever we need.[54]

In the sense that need does underscore commonality, Chrysostom could even call the church a "spiritual market."[55]

---

[53]"The rich man is a kind of treasury official of goods owed for distribution to the poor" (οὕτω δὴ καὶ ὁ πλούσιος, ὑποδέκτης τίς ἐστι τῶν τοῖς πένησιν ὀφειλομένων χρημάτων διανεμηθῆναι; Chrysostom *In Lazarum* 2.4 [PG 48. 988]; see also 2.1 [PG 48. 992]). In his strongest language, Chrysostom was able to assert that an almsgiver "has God as a debtor" (ὀφειλέτην ἔχει τὸν Θεόν; *Hom. in Gen.* 31.1 [PG 53. 283]). See also idem, *Hom. in Rom.* 7.9 (PG 60. 453); and *Hom. in Matt.* 85.4 (PG 58. 809). Rabbinical homilies of this same time stressed that one should place one's trust in a divine rather than a human patron; see Daniel Sperber, "Patronage in Amoraic Palestine (c. 200–400)," *Journal of the Economic and Social History of the Orient* 14 (1971) 234.
[54]Chrysostom *Hom. in John* 19.1 (PG 59. 119–20) Διὰ τοῦτο καὶ πόλεις ἐδειμάμεθα, καὶ ἀγορὰς καὶ οἰκίας, ἵνα ὁμοῦ καὶ μετ᾿ ἀλλήλων ὦμεν, οὐ κατὰ τὴν οἴκησιν μόνον, ἀλλὰ καὶ κατὰ τὸν τῆς ἀγάπης σύνδεσμον. Ἐπειδὴ γὰρ ἐνδεὴς ἡμῖν ἡ φύσις παρὰ τοῦ πεποιηκότος ἐγένετο, καὶ οὐκ αὐτάρκης ἐστὶν ἑαυτῇ, συμφερόντως ᾠκονόμησεν ὁ Θεὸς τὴν ἐντεῦθεν ἔνδειαν λοιπὸν ἐκ τῆς κατὰ τὴν σύνοδον παρ᾿ ἀλλήλων γινομένης ὠφελείας διορθωθῆναι. Compare idem, *Ad populum Antiochenum de statuis* 16.6 (PG 49. 172) Διὰ τοῦτο μετ᾿ ἀλλήλων ἐσμὲν, καὶ πόλεις οἰκοῦμεν, καὶ ἐν ἐκκλησίαις συναγόμεθα, ἵνα τὰ ἀλλήλων βάρη βαστάζωμεν, ἵνα τὰ ἀλλήλων ἁμαρτήματα διορθώμεθα.
[55]*Hom. in Gen.* 32.1 (PG 53. 293) Καὶ γὰρ πανήγυρίς ἐστι πνευματικὴ τοῦ Θεοῦ ἡ ἐκκλησία. . . καὶ δεῖ καθάπερ εἰς πανήγυριν παραγενομένους, πολλὴν τὴν εὐπορίαν ἐντεῦθεν συλλέξαντας, οὕτως ἐπανιέναι. When Chrysostom was restored to the pulpit after his first brief exile, he thus cried in joy, "The sea has become a city. . . . The market has become church everywhere among us" (τὸ πέλαγος πόλις ἐγίνετο. . . . Γέγονεν ἡ ἀγορὰ ἐκκλησία, τὰ πανταχοῦ δὲ ἡμᾶς; *Homilia post reditum ab exilio* 3 [PG 52. 445]).

293

▌Clergy and Almsgiving

The advantages of Chrysostom's economic vision, however, were not exhausted by the creation of solidarity among the congregation. There was also a direct benefit for Chrysostom himself. To assess this, let us return briefly to his concern over the ways in which displays of status divided his congregation. The ways of the church stood in complete contrast with those of the marketplace. If Christ says,

> "Give to the needy." The other [says]: "Snatch from those in need."
> Christ says, "Forgive those who plot against you and wrong you."
> [Mammon], in return: "Lay snares for those who have done you no
> wrong." Christ says, "Be humane and gentle." He, to the contrary: "Be
> savage and harsh and reckon as nothing the tears of the poor."[56]

There was, accordingly, no greater contrast to the world of business than that of the perfect Christians, the monks, who were defined precisely as those who had "chosen that life which is free from all business."[57]

Wealthy members of the congregation, in contrast, were difficult to assimilate into Christian community.[58] To Chrysostom's intense annoyance, they regularly gave themselves permission to forego church obligations:

> If those absent make the summer season their excuse, saying, "the
> present stifling heat is excessive, the scorching sun intolerable, we
> cannot bear being trampled and crushed in the crowd, and being
> drenched all over with perspiration and oppressed by the heat and
> confined space". . . . Yet in the marketplace, where there is such
> turmoil and crowding, and both scorching heat and wind, how is it

[56]Chrysostom Hom. in John 40.4 (PG 59. 234) Ὁ μὲν γὰρ λέγει, Δίδου τοῖς δεο-μένοις· ὁ δὲ, Ἅρπαζε τῶν δεομένων. Ὁ Χριστὸς λέγει, Καὶ τοῖς ἐπιβουλεύουσι καὶ ἀδικοῦσι συγχώρει· οὗτος ἔμπαλιν, Κατασκεύαζε πάγας κατὰ τῶν οὐδὲν ἀδικούντων. Ὁ Χριστὸς λέγει, Φιλάνθρωπος ἔσο καὶ ἥμερος· οὗτος ἀπ' ἐναντίας, Ὠμὸς ἔσο καὶ ἀπηνής, καὶ μηδὲν εἶναι νόμιζε δάκρυα πενήτων; see also 8.2 (PG 59. 68); and idem, Hom. in 1 Cor. 36.6 (PG 61. 314).

[57]Chrysostom Ad populum Antiochenum de statuis 1.2 (PG 49. 18) Εἰ μὲν γὰρ εἰς ἐκείνων ἦν τῶν εἰς τὰς κορυφὰς τῶν ὀρέων ἀνακεχωρηκότων, καὶ τῶν ἐπὶ τῆς ἐρημίας καλύβην πηξαμένων, καὶ τῶν ἀπράγμονα τοῦτον ἀνηρημένων βίον. See also idem, Hom. in Matt. 68.3 (PG 58. 643–44); and 68.5 (PG 58. 646).

[58]As Elizabeth Clark has pointed out, "the description of all human relationships in the language of political power is especially pronounced in the writings of John Chrysostom"; see Elizabeth A. Clark, "The Virginal Politeia and Plato's Republic: John Chrysostom on Women and the Sexual Relation," in her Jerome, Chrysostom, and Friends, 1; see also William Countryman, The Rich Christian in the Church of the Early Empire (New York/Toronto: Mellen, 1980) esp. chapters 1 (pp. 47–68) and 3 (pp. 103–30).

that you do not plead suffocation and heat as an excuse for absenting yourself?[59]

The rich also wanted to control how the money they donated to the church was spent—a demand which seemed to them, of course, quite reasonable. Worst of all, according to Chrysostom, they asserted a right to appoint and dismiss clerics.[60] Indeed, they made their claim to patronal status only too plain by expecting their bishop to number among their daily clients.[61] Of this, Chrysostom wanted no part. To the contrary, the rich were to recognize their subordination to the clergy. Chrysostom corrected them strenuously, "You believe that it is sufficient to say that you are orthodox, while you deviate from or oppose the hierarchy."[62]

The clergy's position, however, was most delicate; they were aware of their need for the wealthy. Chrysostom knew of some clerics who, when they had been unable to find adequate patronage, had gone into business and "made a shipwreck of their faith."[63] The livelihood of clerics lay in the gifts of their wealthy congregants, as Chrysostom's unusual and pointed praise of the Jews makes clear:

> Consider how great were the things the Jews gave—tithes, first-fruits, tithes again, and again other tithes, and besides this thirteenths, and the shekel—and not one of them said, "The priests are rapacious". . . .

[59]Chrysostom Si esurierit inimicus 2 (PG 51. 174–75) Εἰ δὲ τὸ θέρος προβάλλοιντο· καὶ γὰρ καὶ ταῦτα ἀκούω λεγόντων, ὅτι Σφοδρὸν τὸ πνῖγος νῦν, τὸ καῦμα ἀφόρητον οὐκ ἰσχύομεν στενοχωρεῖσθαι καὶ θλίβεσθαι ἐν τῷ πλήθει, ἱδρῶτι πάντοθεν περιρρεόμενοι καὶ ἀχθόμενοι τῇ θέρμῃ καὶ τῇ στενοχωρίᾳ. . . . ἐπὶ δὲ τῆς ἀγορᾶς, εἰπέ μοι, ἔνθα τοσοῦτος θόρυβος καὶ στενοχωρία καὶ πολὺς ὁ καύσων, πῶς οὐ προβάλλῃ πνῖγος καὶ θέρμην;
[60]Chrysostom Sacerdot. 3.9.32–36 (SC 272. 162–64).
[61]Ibid., 3.14.19–21 (SC 272. 220). For this reason, Chrysostom had also complained earlier in this text, "Whereas Christ called fishermen and tentmakers and tax collectors to this office, these people spit on those who support themselves by daily labor" (Καὶ ὁ μὲν Χριστὸς ἁλιεῖς καὶ τοῦτο ὑποπτεύσων ἦν. ταύτην ἐκάλεσε τὴν ἀρχήν· οὗτοι δὲ τοὺς μὲν ἀπὸ τῆς ἐργασίας τῆς καθημερινῆς τρεφομένοις διάπτουσιν; 2.7.41–43 [SC 272. 132]).
[62]Chrysostom Hom. in Eph. 11.5 (PG 62. 86) Ἀρκεῖν τοῦτο ἡγεῖσθε, εἰπέ μοι, τὸ λέγειν, ὅτι ὀρθόδοξοί εἰσι, τὰ τῆς χειροτοίας δὲ οἴχεται καὶ ἀπόλωλε. See also idem, Hom. in 1 Thess. 2.4 (PG 62. 404). Priests are not to be judged by those subject to them, "and especially by those of quite exceptional simplicity" (καὶ μάλιστα τῶν πάνυ ἀφελεστέρων; idem, Hom. in John 86.4 [PG 59. 472]; compare idem, Salutate Priscillam 2.6 [PG 51. 205]).
[63]Chrysostom Sacerdot. 3.14.7–9 (SC 272. 218) ἤδη γάρ τινες τῶν ἀσθενεστέρων πράγμασιν ἐμπεσόντες, ἐπειδὴ προστασίας οὐκ ἔτυχον, ἐναυάγησαν περὶ τὴν πίστιν.

Nor did they say, "They get too much; they stuff their bellies," as I hear some saying now. While the [rich] are building houses and buying estates for themselves, they still think that they have nothing; but if any priest is wearing better clothes than usual and enjoys more than what is absolutely necessary for his sustenance or has an attendant,. . . they chalk it up as riches. . . . In a word, if you did give it, why do you scold him? You have already borne witness to his poverty by noting that what he has are in fact gifts from you. . . . If he has enough to support himself, is he therefore doing wrong? Would you have him lead a vagabond life and beg? Wouldn't you then, as his disciple, be put to shame?[64]

In sum, the position of the clergy was fraught with ambivalence. On the one hand, it resembled that of the wealthy, since the bishop, dispensing the considerable resources of the church, came "not so much to rule as to be a slave to a thousand masters."[65] On the other hand, the clergy's position also resembled that of the poor. Even while they received material goods from the rich, the clergy remained superior to them, since they were able to convey unspecified and potentially unlimited supernatural goods.

■ Conclusion

Chrysostom's overall message is therefore one that stresses mutuality. The wealthy who were accustomed to showcasing their high status in the marketplace should subordinate themselves in the Christian community. They should know at all times their inferiority to the poverty-striken and indigent in the world. In the eyes of God, which are, after all, the only eyes that truly matter, the poor are the patrons of the rich. Between the poor and the God who is their special patron, however, another figure is interposed, namely, that of the clergy in general and Chrysostom in particular. If it is true, as Peter Brown has remarked, that Chrysostom "saw himself as the

---

[64]Chrysostom *Hom. in Phil.* 9.4 (PG 62. 251) Ἐννόησον ὅσα Ἰουδαῖοι ἐδίδοσαν, δεκάτας, ἀπαρχάς, πάλιν δεκάτας, καὶ πάλιν ἄλλας δεκάτας, καὶ πάλιν ἑτέρας τρισκαιδεκάτας, καὶ τὸ σίκλον· καὶ οὐδεὶς ἔλεγεν, ὅτι πολλὰ κατεσθίουσιν. . . . Οὐκ ἔλεγον, Πολλὰ λαμβάνουσι, γαστρίζονται, ἃ νῦν ἀκούω λεγόντων τινῶν. Καὶ οἱ μὲν οἰκοδομοῦντες οἰκίας, καὶ ἀγροὺς ὠνούμενοι, οὐδὲν ἡγοῦνται ἔχειν· ἂν δέ τις τῶν ἱερέων λαμπρότερον ἱμάτιον περιβάληται, ἢ τῆς ἀναγκαίας εὐπορήσῃ τροφῆς, ἢ τὸν διακονούμενον ἔχῃ, ἵνα μὴ ἀναγκάζηται αὐτὸς ἀσχημονεῖν, πλοῦτον τὸ πρᾶγμα τίθενται. . . . ὅλως δὲ εἰ σὺ ἔδωκας, τί ἐγκαλεῖς; Πρότερον μὲν οὖν αὐτῷ πενίαν ἐμαρτύρεις, λέγων ἅπερ ἔχει δεδωκέναι αὐτός· . . . . Εἰ δὲ ὅτι τῆς ἀναγκαίας εὐπορεῖ τροφῆ, διὰ τοῦτο ἀδικεῖ· ἀλλὰ περιιέναι ἐχρῆν αὐτὸν, καὶ προσαιτεῖν; καὶ οὐκ ἂν σὺ κατη σχύνθης, εἰπέ μοι, ὁ μαθητής;

[65]Chrysostom *Hom. in Titus* 1.3 (PG 62. 668) οὐκ ἐπὶ ἀρχὴν ἔρχεται ὁ τοιοῦτος, ἀλλὰ δουλεύει μυρίοις δεσπόταις.

ambassador of another city. . . the ambassador of the poor,"[66] we should appreciate how this state was not one without privilege. Its median position, however, is instructive. If the clergy are, in important ways, superior to the wealthy, they are also dependent upon them. This dependency, according to Chrysostom, fostered a beneficial humility among the clerical hierarchy which was all too prone to vainglory.[67] Chrysostom thus can even claim that giving alms is like celebrating the eucharist, and that it "makes one holier than priests"[68] and "equal to God."[69] If this promise of prestige through expenditure seems underemphasized within Chrysostom's vast corpus, it may have been too obvious, too well known, to merit mention.

In conclusion, therefore, Chrysostom's advice to the wealthier members of his congregation on wealth and almsgiving deftly bound together two poles of desire in the late antique world. On the one hand was the yearning to make a splash by lavish expenditure—a broadcasting of wealth the precise social valence of which everyone knew, as Chrysostom's own disingenuous remark attests. He averred, with the distinctive ring of a truism, that "to be tight-fisted is servile, but to spend freely is the action of a master and of one with great power."[70] On the other hand was the strong but cautious desire to exercise foresight and prudence by laying up resources in a secure investment. A generous program of almsgiving, as sketched by Chrysostom, answered both of these desires. It also gave Chrysostom a theoretical basis not only for the ascendency of clerical authority over rich parishioners, but also for the construction of a theology of real mutuality, which might serve to bind together a congregation divided by displays of wealth and status.

---

[66]Chrysostom *De eleemosyna* 1 (PG 51. 261) Πρεσβείαν. . . τῶν δὲ τὴν πόλιν οἰκούντων ἡμῖν πτωχῶν ἐπὶ ταύτην με χειροτονησάντων; Brown, *Body*, 309.

[67]Chrysostom *Hom. in Matt.* 40.4 (PG 57. 443); idem, *Hom. in Titus* 1.2–3 (PG 62. 668); idem, *Hom. in Acts* 3.4–5 (PG 60. 39–41); idem, *Hom. in 2 Tim.* 2.2 (PG 62. 610); idem, *Hom. in 1 Cor.* 21.7 (PG 61. 180); 8.1 (PG 61. 69); see also Palladius *Dialogus* 15.21–26 (SC 341. 292); Jerome, *Epistulae* 22.28.

[68]Chrysostom *Hom. in 2 Cor.* 20.3 (PG 61. 539–40) Καὶ ἱερέας καθίστησι καὶ ἱερωσύνην πολὺν φέρουσαν τὸν μισθόν. Ὁ γὰρ ἐλεήμων. . . ἀναβέβληται μὲν τῆς φιλανθρωπίας στολήν, τῆς ἱερᾶς ἐσθῆτος ἁγιωτέραν οὖσαν.

[69]Chrysostom *Hom. in Titus* 6.2 (PG 62. 698) Τοῦτο ὁμοίους ποιεῖ τῷ Θεῷ.

[70]Chrysostom *Hom. in John* 19.3 (PG 59. 123) δούλου, τὸ τηρεῖν, τὸ δὲ ἀναλίσκειν, κυρίου καὶ πολλὴν ἔχοντος τὴν ἐξουσίαν. Elsewhere he noted, "O senseless people, who even curse the poor, saying that both their houses and their life are put to shame by poverty" ('Αλλ' ὦ τῶν ἀνοήτων ἀνθρώπων, οἱ καὶ καταρῶνται τοῖς πένησι, καὶ φασι καταισχύνεσθαι καὶ οἰκίας καὶ βίον ὑπὸ πενίας; idem, *Hom. in Matt.* 83.4 [PG 58. 750]).

Journal of Ecclesiastical History, Vol. 48, No. 2, April 1997
Copyright © 1997 Cambridge University Press

Jerome and the Sham Christians of Rome

by JOHN CURRAN

Be not led by the multitude of those who sin, neither let the host of those who perish tempt you to say secretly: 'What? Must all be lost who live in cities? Behold, they continue to enjoy their property, they serve churches, they frequent baths, they do not disdain cosmetics, and yet they are universally well spoken of.'[1]

This rhetorical question was posed by Jerome in AD 411 to challenge a young man of good family from Toulouse who was contemplating the responsibilities of monastic life. The old man of Bethlehem wrote on city life with some authority; he had achieved fame and notoriety simultaneously at the court of Pope Damasus in Rome in the 380s.[2] And yet, as both men knew well, the moral and physical dangers of the city, the latter resoundingly demonstrated by the Gothic capture of Rome in the previous year, had not prompted the rejection of urban life by western Christians, save by a small and eccentric group of extreme ascetics. Jerome's praise for this group is well known, and his criticism of less committed Christians in Rome is legendary. But when one examines the uniquely vivid testimony of Jerome's letters, one can detect beneath the praise and polemic a vigorous struggle for the support of the

CIL = *Corpus inscriptionum latinarum*; *Codex Theodosianus* = *Codex Theodosianus*, ed. C. Pharr, Princeton 1952; *ICUR* = *Inscriptiones Christianae urbis Romae*, ed. A. Silvagni, Rome 1922; *ILCV* = *Inscriptiones Latinae Christianae veteres*, ed. E. Diehl, Berlin 1924–31; *PLRE* = *The prosopography of the later Roman empire*, ed. A. H. M. Jones, J. R. Martindale and J. Morris, Cambridge 1971; *RC* = Ch. Piétri, *Roma Christiana*, Paris–Rome 1976.

I should like to acknowledge the kindness of my colleagues Professor Brian Scott and Dr Brian Campbell, and the advice of readers appointed by the editors of this JOURNAL for their comments on earlier drafts of this paper.

[1] 'Neque vero peccantium ducaris multitudine et te pereuntium turba sollicitet, ut tacitus cogites: "Quid? Ergo omnes peribunt, qui in urbibus habitant? Ecce illi fruuntur suis rebus, ministrant ecclesiis, adeunt balneas, unguenta non spernunt et tamen in omnium [f]ore versantur"': Jerome, ep. cxxv. 17 (CSEL lvi. 136). Where quotations are made from Jerome's works, I provide full CSEL details; cross references will merely indicate the relevant titles. All translations from Jerome, except where indicated, are those of *The library of Nicene and post-Nicene Fathers of the Church*.

[2] For Jerome and city life generally see P. Antin, 'La ville chez S. Jerome', *Latomus* xx (1961), 298–311.

city's elite. The social background to the struggle as revealed in Jerome's writings is the subject of this article. What emerges is a complex, contradictory and divided Christian community which Jerome unsuccessfully attempted to influence, a failure that brought final and ignominious exile from Rome.

The sociable world

> It is true that Rome has a holy church, trophies of Apostles and martyrs, a true confession of Christ. The faith has been preached there by an apostle, heathenism has been trodden down, the name of Christian is daily exalted higher and higher. But the display, power and size of the city, the seeing and the being seen, the paying and receiving of visits, the alternate flattery and detraction, talking and listening, as well as the necessity of facing so great a throng even when one is least in the mood to do so – all these things are alike foreign to the principles and fatal to the repose of the monastic life.[3]

Jerome's stinging denunciation of upper-class Christian society, written to his friends and fellow ascetics Paula and Eustochium from Bethlehem in 386, concentrated on a vibrant social life as one of the greatest threats to ascetic Christianity. Some well-born Christians at Rome were conspicuously sociable, laying on receptions and banquets for their friends, compelling Jerome repeatedly to urge his correspondents to resist the temptations offered by good food and drink.[4]

As Ammianus confirms, such gourmandism was characteristic of the upper stratum of Roman society, irrespective of religious inclination. In the first of his Roman digressions the luxury of banquets among the wealthy was deemed too outrageous for detailed comment, while in the second the historian satirised the exotic menus and criticised the exaggerated importance of giving and attending dinners.[5]

This common pursuit of the pleasures of the dining table drove Jerome for his part to complain that some Christians compounded the sin of gluttony with idolatry: 'Have *I* ever embellished *my* dinner plates with engravings of idols? Have *I* ever, at a Christian banquet, set before the

---

[3] 'Est quidem ibi sancta ecclesia, sunt tropea apostolorum et martyrum, est Christi vera confessio et ab apostolis praedicata fides et gentilitate calcata in sublime se cotidie erigens vocabulum Christianum, sed ipsa ambitio, potentia, magnitudo urbis, videri et videre, salutari et salutare, laudare et detrahere, audire vel proloqui et tantam frequentiam hominum saltim invitum pati a proposito monachorum et quiete aliena sunt': ep. xlvi. 12 (CSEL liv. 342).

[4] Ep. xxii. 8, 13, cf. liv. 7, 9, 10, Note ep. xxii. 32: '...cum ad agapen vocaverint, praeco conducitur'.

[5] 14. 6. 16; 28. 4. 13, 17 (Loeb edition). See R. Pack, 'The Roman digressions of Ammianus Marcellinus', *Transactions of the American Philological Association*, lxxxiv (1953), 181–9, and J. F. Matthews, *The Roman empire of Ammianus*, London 1989, 414–16.

eyes of virgins the polluting spectacle of satyrs embracing bacchanals?'[6] The transgression was only possible, however, because those in error had whole-heartedly embraced the principles of upper-class Roman hospitality. And as Jerome was uncomfortably aware, his closest friends had come from the same background. Although the responsibility was laid implicitly at the door of Toxotius, Paula's husband, Jerome remembered a time when their daughters had been 'given to the world'.[7] Paula herself, even after Toxotius' death and her own adoption of the ascetic life, felt pressurised into participating in the busy round of visits and receptions.[8] Her eventual rejection of this hectic society was a decisive moment in the development of her own austere Christianity.

With Paula's daughter Eustochium, however, Jerome needed to be particularly vigilant. She was advised not to visit the houses of the high born and encouraged, if she wanted to seek the martyrs, to pray to them in the peace and privacy of her own room.[9] Jerome mistrusted the confident and wealthy Christians who toured the shrines of the martyrs and did not shun crowded churches.[10] But Flavia Eustochium took time to understand how hostile Jerome was to Christian good manners at Rome. On St Peter's feastday in AD 384, she sent him some cooked doves and a bracelet with her note, earning a gentle rebuke from her mentor: 'we must be careful to celebrate our holy day not so much with abundance of food as with exultation of spirit'.[11]

Given the pressures on those actually *disposed* to the ascetic life, there is little surprise that those Christians of Rome less enthusiastic about renunciation should so readily have endorsed the major venues of public recreation in the city. Jerome knew Christians who believed that it was perfectly acceptable for Christian virgins to visit the baths, stipulating only that they should do so in the company of married women and eunuchs, a reference to their elevated social status.[12]

Urban patronage

> Many build churches nowadays; their walls and pillars of glowing marble, their ceilings glittering with gold, their altars studded with

---

[6] 'Numquid in lancibus idola caelata descripsi? Numquid inter epulas Christianas virginalibus oculis baccharum satyrorumque conplexus?': ep. xxvii. 2 (CSEL liv. 225), a striking illustration of Jerome's sensitivity to images in domestic contexts. See K. J. Shelton, *The Esquiline treasure*, London 1981, for a confusion of symbols on fourth-century vessels.   [7] Ep. lxvi. 13.   [8] Ep. cviii. 6.   [9] Ep. xxii. 17.
[10] Deducible from epp. xxii. 17; cvii. 8; cxxviii. 3a. Praise was offered to Asella because she had concealed her identity as she performed acts of devotion: ep. xxiv. 4.
[11] 'Unde nobis sollicitius providendum, ut sollemnem diem non tam ciborum abundantia quam spiritus exultatione celebremus...': ep. xxxi. 3 (CSEL liv. 251). See also ep. lii. 5 (to Nepotian).
[12] Ep. cvii. 11, cf. xlv. 4 for Christian widows attending the baths. Note again the parallel with Ammianus, 28. 4. 9.

JOHN CURRAN

jewels... Let us, therefore, think of His cross and we will count riches to be but dirt.[13]

In the early years of the century the patterns and pace of monumental patronage had been laid down by the imperial family, but increasingly as the century progressed, the wealthy of Rome expressed their Christianity confidently in their own monumental terms.[14] Nobles made gifts of prestige objects to Christian churches in Rome, like the marble pillar donated to the high altar of the church now known as Sant' Anastasia beside the Circus Maximus by Clodius Adelfius, ex-Prefect of the City, some time in the 350s.[15] Others had grander visions. Another Prefect, Longinianus, is reported to have furnished Sant' Anastasia with a baptistery early in the fifth century,[16] and tradition attributed the foundation of two new parish churches, or *tituli*, to aristocrats: Vestina (*titulus Vestinae*) and Pammachus (*titulus SS Johannis et Pauli*).[17] Above all, however, the tomb of Peter, marked by Constantine with a grand basilica, drew new patrons to itself. In the 380s Damasus, bishop of Rome, joined wealthy Christians in improving the drainage of the basilica and ornamenting it with marble.[18] The status of the great church and the rising number of visitors compelled the emperors to provide a new *porticus* to serve the complex of buildings on the Vatican. Running from the Theatre of Balbus in the densely populated Campus Martius region to the Pons Aelius, the only bridge over the Tiber at this point, the Porticus Maximus adorned impressively the arterial route from the city centre to the Apostle's grave.[19] At its northern *terminus*, Gratian, Valentinian and Theodosius erected a great triumphal arch, conspicuously visible to the pilgrims and pious visitors.[20]

The basilica of Peter also attracted the elite dead. The sarcophagus of Junius Bassus, who died in office as Prefect of the City in 359, was

[13] 'Multi aedificant parietes et columnas ecclesiae subtrahunt: marmora nitent, auro splendent lacunaria, gemmis altare distinguitur... cogitemus crucem et divitias lutum putabimus': ep. lii. 10 (CSEL liv. 431–2).
[14] See Ch. Piétri, 'Evergétisme et richesses ecclésiastiques dans l'Italie du ive à la fin du ve siècle: l'exemple romain', *Ktema* iii (1978), 317–37.
[15] *CIL* 6. 1712 = *ILCV*, no. 1850. See J. F. Matthews, 'The poetess Proba and fourth-century Rome: questions of interpretation', in M. Christol, S. Demougin, Y. Duval, C. Lepelley and L. Piétri (eds), *Institutions, société et vie politique dans l'empire romain au IVe siècle a. J.-C. (Collections de l'École française de Rome 159)*, Paris 1992, 277–304 at pp. 299ff.
[16] *ICUR* ii. 150, 19, although there is still some discussion over precisely where this inscription belongs: *RC* i. 490 n. 2. For Longinianus see A. Chastagnol, *Les fastes de la préfecture de Rome au bas-empire (études prosopographiques 2)*, Paris 1962, 255ff.
[17] *Titulus Vestinae: le Liber pontificalis: texte, introduction et commentaire*, ed. L. Duchesne, Paris 1955, i. 220–1; *Titulus Johannis et Pauli: ICUR* ii. 150, 20 with *RC* i. 481ff.
[18] A. Ferrua, *Epigrammata Damasiana*, Rome 1942, 3, 4, 4(1).
[19] *A topographical dictionary of ancient Rome*, ed. S. B. Platner and T. Ashby, London 1929, 423–4. See also L. Reekmans, 'Le développement topographique de la région du Vatican à la fin de l'antiquité et au début du moyen age (300-850)', *Mélanges d'archéologie et d'histoire de l'art offerts au Professeur Jacques Lavalleye*, Paris 1970, 202.
[20] *CIL* vi. 1184.

302

recovered from under the floor of the apse behind Constantine's *confessio* of Peter.[21] Even more impressive was the mausoleum constructed for Sextus Petronius Probus, site of a long epitaph praising the great courtier's deeds, which abutted directly onto the apse.[22]

The ever-growing importance of the shrine of Peter was thus achieved in part by the monumental patronage of wealthy Roman Christians. But upper-class *patroni* also legitimised the practice of Christian charity in a characteristically public manner. Their self-conscious generosity irritated Jerome:

> I lately saw the noblest lady in Rome – I suppress her name because I am no satirist – with a band of eunuchs before her in the basilica of the Blessed Peter. She was giving money to the poor, a coin apiece; and this with her own hand, that she might be accounted the more religious. Hereupon a by no means uncommon incident occurred. An old woman 'full of years and rags' ran forward to get a second coin, but when her turn came she received not a penny but a blow hard enough to draw blood from her guilty veins.[23]

Jerome dissembled in depicting such charity as merely hypocritical; what he observed was a public act entirely consistent with the obligations of high Christian status. St Peter's basilica was well known even to pagans as a site where aristocratic patronage could be exercised. C. Ceionius Rufius Volusianus, a Prefect of the City in 365, petulantly demonstrated his own generosity to the poor on the Vatican Hill as a deliberate slight to an ungrateful race-going public.[24] Jerome's friend Pammachius, 'the commander-in-chief of all the monks', himself staged a huge banquet in the basilica of Peter in the early 390s after the death of his wife Paulina, laying on tables and abundant food for a throng of the poor which Paulinus says crowded the church.[25]

We need not doubt the sincerity of these patrons as they did not doubt it themselves; their outlay could be extensive and costly. But above all, their physical and personal patronage of sites such as that of St Peter's basilica helped fix the church as a major focus for Roman Christianity.

---

[21] For a full discussion of this object see E. S. Malbon, *The iconography of the sarcophagus of Junius Bassus*, Princeton 1990.

[22] *ICUR* ii. 347f. See also J. F. Matthews, *Western aristocracies and imperial court A.D. 364–425*, repr. Oxford 1990, 195–7, 400–1. For a translation of the epitaph see B. Croke and J. Harries (eds), *Religious conflict in fourth-century Rome*, Sydney 1982, 117.

[23] 'Vidi nuper – nomina taceo, ne saturam putes – nobilissimam mulierum Romanarum in basilica beati Petri semiuiris antecedentibus propria manu, quo religiosior putaretur, singulos nummos dispertire pauperibus. Interea ut usu nosse perfacile est – anus quaedam annis pannisque obsita praecurrit, ut alterum nummum acciperet; ad quam cum ordine pervenisset, pugnus porrigitur pro denario et tanti criminis reus sanguis effunditur': ep. xxii. 32 (CSEL liv. 193–4), quoting Terence, *Eunuchus* 236 (ed. A. Fleckeisen).   [24] Ammianus, 27. 3. 6; Chastagnol, *Fastes*, no. 67; *PLRE* i. 978–80.

[25] Paulinus, ep. xiii. 11–15 (ed. G. de Hartel). The description of Pammachius is Jerome's: ep. lxvi. 4.

Christians, 'holy men' and theological controversy

Increasingly in the fourth century, clerics and monks came to be numbered among the *clientes* and *amici* of the great houses of Rome. This network of relationships between upper-class families and 'holy men' was the battleground for a series of bitter and dangerous theological contests in the later years of the fourth century.[26] The *Letters* of Jerome reveal the extent of the influence of individual 'holy men' on upper-class Christians and the degree to which the major theological disputes of the period were themselves coloured by an upper-class social agenda.

Marcella, for example, was warned of Novationists and Montanists; Jerome was clearly afraid that she might fall prey to door-to-door religious callers:[27] 'Certain persons have devoted the whole of their energies and life to the single object of knowing the names, houses and characters of married ladies.'[28] The worst offender was a 'troublesome old man' who had charmed his way into the homes of wealthy Romans only to steal household items.[29] Elsewhere, courtyards of wealthy houses could be found thronged with kissing clergy who accepted gifts of cash from the pious owners.[30] In one highly satirical passage, Jerome denounced Christian widows who associated with teachers and spiritual advisers. Calling them 'widows of necessity and not choice', they had not welcomed the opportunity to lead a continent life when it had been offered to them:

They, meanwhile, seeing that priests cannot do without them, are lifted up with pride and as, having had experience of both, they prefer the licence of widowhood to the restraints of marriage, they call themselves chaste livers and nuns. After an immoderate supper they retire to dream of the apostles.[31]

[26] The Pelagian controversy had a Roman dimension to its early phase but insufficient traces remain in the sources to reconstruct the important social connections confidently. Augustine, ep. clxvii. 2 (ed. A. Goldbacher), refers to Pelagius' life in Rome, and G. De Plinval, *Pélage: ses écrits, sa vie et sa réforme*, Lausanne 1943, 51–5, tentatively identifies one of Jerome's opponents as Pelagius: '...si c'est de lui qu'il s'agit...' (p. 54). Certainly the *kinds* of charges made against him are familiar from elsewhere: ep. l. 3–5. For the later period of Pelagius' career see P. Brown, 'The patrons of Pelagius: the Roman aristocracy between east and west', in his *Religion and society in the age of Saint Augustine*, London 1972, 208–26.

[27] Epp. xli, xlii. Among trustworthy holy men recommended by Jerome: 'Domnio' (xlvii. 3); 'Exuperius' (liv. 11); 'Theodore' (lxxxix).

[28] 'Quidam in hoc omne studium vitamque posuerunt, ut matronarum nomina, domos moresque cognoscant': ep. xxii. 28 (CSEL liv. 185).

[29] Ibid. which also names 'Antimus' and 'Sophronius' as bogus callers. For imperial suspicion of monks see *Codex Theodosianus* 16. 3. 1–2 (AD 390, 392).

[30] Ep. xxii. 16. Young Ambrose was first introduced to the deference of the world's powerful towards God's elect by watching his own widowed mother kissing the hands of visiting clerics at her Roman *palatium*: Paulinus, *Vita Ambrosii* (ed. M. Pellegrino), 4.

[31] 'Illae interim, quae sacerdotes suo vident indigere praesidio, eriguntur in superbiam et, quia maritorum expertae dominatum viduitatis praeferunt libertatem, castae vocantur et nonnae et post cenam dubiam apostolos somniant': ep. xxii. 16 (CSEL liv. 164).

Some women even lodged with clerics and called themselves 'agapetae'.[32]

Evidence from other sources complements Jerome's concern about Christian 'teachers'. Valentinian, Valens and Gratian wrote to Bishop Damasus in July 370 to complain about the number and behaviour of Christian holy men.[33] The emperors issued instructions that kinsmen of widows and wards could have clerics banned from seeing their relatives. Clerics were, additionally, not permitted to receive property from women unless they were kin and if illegal bequests were attempted, then the fisc would confiscate the property involved.[34] Unease persisted into the papacy of Damasus' successor Siricius (AD 384–99) who expressed his own doubts about wandering monks whose theological credentials were unknown.[35]

It is important to realise, however, that the Roman elite was not passive in its relationship with Christian holy men. According to Jerome, asceticism arrived among the aristocrats of the city when Bishop Athanasius and Bishop Peter came from Alexandria and made contact with the young Marcella, telling her of the extraordinary life of St Anthony.[36] Some years later, coming to attend the council summoned by Damasus in Rome in 382, Paulinus of Antioch and Epiphanius of Salamis actually lodged with Paula.[37] Seen in this context, Jerome's friends had played a significant role in cementing relations between aristocratic families and visiting clerics and he was himself a learned beneficiary of wealthy patrons. He was therefore well placed to describe the unique responsibilities of a cleric with aristocratic contacts: 'It is your duty to visit the sick, to know the homes and children of ladies who are married, and not to be unaware of the secrets of noblemen.'[38] And the prize of aristocratic friendship prompted some bitter criticisms of Jerome and his friend, Pope Damasus: the bishop was denounced, memorably, by the authors of a petition to the emperors as 'the ear tickler of matrons'

---

[32] Ibid. 14. For the scandal of *subintroductae* see E. A. Clark, 'Ascetic renunciation and feminine advancement: a paradox of late antique Christianity', *Anglican Theological Review* lxiii (1981), 240–57, repr. in her *Ascetic piety and women's faith*, New York 1986, 175–208 at p. 183; cf. *Codex Theodosianus* 16. 2. 44 (dated 8 May 420).   [33] Ibid. 16. 2. 20.

[34] Cf. ibid. 16. 2. 27 (June 390) and 28 (August 390). Jerome claims, at ep. lii. 6, that this law was circumvented by a fiction of 'trusteeship'.

[35] 'Quantum illicitum sit illud, aestimari non potest, ut transeuntes (sive simulent, sive sint monachi, quod se appellant), quorum nec vitam possumus scire nec baptismum quorum fidem incognitam habemus nec probatam, nolint sumptibus adjuvare, sed statim aut diaconos facere, aut presbyteros ordinare festinent, aut, quod est gravius, episcopos constituere non formident. Charius apud illos dari sumptum est transeunti, quam sacerdotium. Non retenti, inde in superbiam exaltantur, inde insuper ad perfidiam cito corruunt; quia fidem veram in ecclesiasticis toto orbe peregrini discere non asseruntur': PL xiii. 1165–6.   [36] Ep. cxxvii. 5.   [37] Ep. cviii. 6.

[38] 'Officii tui est visitare languentes, nosse domos, matronas ac liberos earum et nobilium virorum non ignorare secreta': ep. lii. 15 (CSEL liv. 438). Some manuscripts replace 'non ignorare' with 'custodire'.

('auriscalpius matronarum'), while tongues wagged over Jerome's relationship with Paula and her daughters.[39]

The desirability of contact with aristocratic families lay in the receptivity of upper-class lay Christians to theological ideas. Palladius reports that Melania the Elder, one of the first senatorial ladies to renounce the city of Rome, had read three million lines of Origen and two and a half million of other Christian writers.[40] But extreme ascetics were far from being the only students of theology. By the middle of the fourth century, a strong lay interest in theological matters had emerged. Among elite Romans, Firmicus Maternus and Marius Victorinus were distinguished, and if the poetess Proba was not, her *cento* nevertheless reveals an educated, sincere and humane exploration of the life of Christ.[41] Jerome complained that the works of Origen had been rejected at Rome by a group of *literati* whose jealousy had been aroused by his brilliance.[42] The same group may well have been behind criticisms of Jerome's Latin edition of the New Testament.[43]

Thus, when major theological disputes broke out in Rome late in the century, an intellectually- and theologically-informed elite looked on. In the 380s a certain Helvidius presented a compelling analysis of the virginity of Mary, mother of Christ.[44] The debate provoked by the work clearly had significance for the status of Christian virgins at Rome and in 383, when Bishop Damasus approached Jerome to commission a refutation of Helvidius' tract, the wider issue of the Christian ascetic life was uppermost in his mind.[45] Helvidius had argued that Mary enjoyed a full and normal married life after the birth of Jesus. The importance of virginity thus became less significant for ordinary Christians and the married life was no longer clearly inferior to virgin celibacy. Jerome's skilful and tendentious rebuttal included a powerfully polemical passage drawn from St Paul's first letter to the Corinthians: 'She that is unmarried is careful for the things of the Lord.... But she that is married is careful for the things of the world, how she may please her husband.'[46] To illustrate the point, Jerome set out the kind of distractions and

---

[39] Damasus: *Collectio Avellana* i. 9 = CSEL xxxv. 4; Jerome, ep. xlv. 2.

[40] *Historia Lausiaca* (ed. G. J. M. Bartelink) 55. 3.

[41] For Firmicus Maternus see R. Turcan, *Firmicus Maternus: l'erreur des réligions païennes*, Paris 1982; for Marius Victorinus, P. Hadot, *Marius Victorinus: récherches sur sa vie et ses oeuvres*, Paris 1971; for Proba, E. A. Clark, 'Faltonia Betitia Proba and her Virgilian poem: the Christian matron as artist', in her *Ascetic piety*, 124–52.   [42] Ep. xxxiii.

[43] Ep. xxvii. 1.

[44] In response to a tract written by a monk called 'Carterius': *Contra Helvidium* (ed. J. P. Migne = PL xxiii. 193–126) 4, 16.

[45] Jerome, ep. xlviii. 18. See Gennadius, *De viris illustribus* (ed. W. Herting) 33, who describes Helvidius' motives as sincerely religious, and also J. N. D. Kelly, *Jerome: his life, writings and controversies*, London 1975, 104–7.

[46] '...et virgo, quae non est nupta, cogitat quae sunt Dei...nam quae nupta est, cogitat, quae sunt mundi, quomodo placeat viro': *Contra Helvidium* 20; cf. 1 Cor. vii. 32–5.

disappointments which married life could bring to young women.[47] The lifestyle which he summarised was unquestionably that of the elite bride. She was to be found in her house surrounded by the burdens of domestic administration. These included seeing to slaves, cooks and weavers. Her children would receive an education which she would want to oversee. Her husband would want to entertain his friends at home and she would be forced not only to provide for them but also, perhaps, to put up with the indignity of having half-naked dancing girls in the house, an entertainment, incidentally, which Ammianus recorded as notoriously popular with upper-class Romans.[48] Like a number of his letters, Jerome's *Contra Helvidium* constituted a blow in the contest for the allegiance of well-off Christians in Rome.

The same readership continued to be the seed-bed of theological controversy in Rome after the publication of the *Contra Helvidium*. In 385 Jerome wrote to Marcella about another of his opponents, Onasus of Segesta. The details of Onasus' attack cannot be known since Jerome's letter was taken up chiefly with personal insults. He was, however, clearly a well-educated and capable speaker. There may be a reference to high-born friends on Onasus' side in the jibe: 'I say that certain persons have by crime, perjury and false pretences, attained to this or that high position. What is it to you who know that the charge does not touch you?'[49] Jerome hints, perhaps, that Onasus was one of the wandering Christian teachers who ingratiated themselves with certain noble families. He plucked an appropriate barb from Perseus: 'May you be a catch for my lord and lady's daughter'[50] – thus condemning the close contacts between preacher and a worldly elite.

Jovinianus, however, was the most important of a number of new theologians who sought upper-class support.[51] In the early 390s he offered a powerful response to the extreme asceticism which had convulsed the senatorial order.[52] He rejected the distinction and ranking of married, widowed and virgin Christians; those who abstained from food were not superior to those who consumed with thanks; husbands and wives ought not to abandon each other, even if only one was a believer.[53]

[47] A common theme: see R. Lizzi, 'Una società esortata all'ascetismo: misure legislative e motivazioni economiche nel IV–V secolo d.c.', *Studi storici* i (1989), 129–53.

[48] *Contra Helvidium* 20; Ammianus, 14. 6. 19.

[49] 'Dico quosdam scelere, periurio, falsitate ad dignitatem nescio quam pervenisse: Quid ad te, qui te intellegis innocentem?': ep. xl. 2 (CSEL liv. 310).

[50] 'Te optent generum rex et regina, puellae te rapiant'. Cf. Perseus, *Satires* (ed. W. V. Clausen) 2. 37–8: 'Hunc optet generum rex et regina, puellae hunc rapiant.'

[51] See D. G. Hunter, 'Resistance to the virginal ideal in late fourth-century Rome: the case of Jovinian', *Theological Studies* xlviii (1987), 45–64; Kelly, *Jerome*, 180ff., and the excellent discussion by P. Brown, *The body and society*, London 1988, 359ff.

[52] We are dependent on hostile sources for the substance of Jovinian's ideas: Siricius, ep. vii (PL xiii. 1168–71); Jerome, *Adversus Jovinianum* (PL xxiii. 221–352); Augustine, *De peccatorum meritis et remissione* 3. 7 (PL xliv. 193–4). See also F. Valli, *Gioviniano*, Urbino 1953.

[53] *Adversus Jovinianum* 1. 10. Cf. Jerome, ep. xlviii. 5, for his hostility to mixed marriages.

Jerome's friend Pammachius drew the attention of Pope Siricius to the controversial works and after the condemnation of the heretic, Jerome was asked to write a detailed refutation of these ideas.[54] Among Jovinianus' teachings had been the suggestion that although widows and virgins would do well to adopt the ascetic life, they could certainly also marry with clear consciences; the position of Christian virgins was not superior to that of married women.[55] He had acknowledged that Christian women were married to non-Christian husbands but suggested that such unions should not be dissolved on sectarian grounds. Jerome replied: 'Yet at the present day many women, despising the Apostle's command, are joined to heathen husbands and prostitute the temples of Christ to idols.'[56] Although Jerome knew that 'crowds of *matronae*' would be furious with him, he stated that such women belonged to Belial, not Christ.

Jovinian had argued that the status of Christian virgin or widow was nothing without good works.[57] Jerome's response was to tell the story of Jacob's dream at Bethel and to ridicule the worldliness of Jovinianus' supporters: 'There are angels who descend from Heaven; but Jovinianus is sure that they retain their inheritance.'[58] In a bitter crescendo to the tract, Jerome pressed home the attack: 'You have, moreover, in your army many subalterns, you have your guardsmen and your skirmishers at the outposts, the round-bellied, the well-dressed, the exquisites, the noisy orators... The nobles make way for you, the wealthy print kisses on your face.'[59]

When Pammachius received his copy of Jerome's text, he made a desperate attempt to stop it circulating. Not only was Jerome's defence of virginity widely interpreted as an indictment of marriage, but the contemptuous references to Jovinianus' friends and supporters wounded a class of Roman citizens whom Pammachius knew only too well.[60]

Jerome's attack upon marriage provoked an outcry and he wrote another letter to Pammachius to clarify his position.[61] He made reference to the traducers of his work: 'They are educated; in their own eyes no mean scholars; competent not merely to censure me but to instruct me.'[62] Those to whom he referred were the senior clergy and laymen of Rome.

---

[54] Jerome, ep. xlviii. 2.   [55] *Adversus Jovinianum* 1. 9.
[56] 'At nunc pleraeque contemnentes apostoli jussionem, junguntur gentilibus, et templa Christi idolis prostituunt': ibid. 1. 10 (PL xxiii. 234).   [57] Ibid. 1. 11, 13.
[58] 'Angeli de coelis descendunt, et Jovinianus de eorum possessione securus est': ibid. 2. 27 (PL xxiii. 338).
[59] 'Habes praeterea in exercitu plures succenturiatos, habes scurras et velites in praesidiis, crassos, comptos, nitidos, clamatores... tibi cedunt de via nobiles, tibi osculantur divites caput': ibid. 2. 37 (PL xxiii. 352).   [60] Jerome, ep. xlix. 1–2.
[61] Ep. xlix.
[62] 'Norunt litteras, videntur sibi scioli: Possunt me non reprehendre, sed docere': ep. xlviii (xlix). 3 (CSEL liv. 348).

Jerome recalled bitterly how Bishop Damasus had not reproached him for his *Contra Helvidium* or *Letter* 22 to Eustochium. He was disappointed that the clerics of Rome, who themselves were celibate, had not backed his ideas in support of Christian virginity: 'Thus, while I try to protect myself on one side, I am wounded on the other. To speak more plainly still, while I close with Jovinianus in hand-to-hand combat, Manichaeus stabs me in the back.'[63] The *Adversus Jovinianum* did not enjoy Siricius' support.[64] The bishop was profoundly suspicious of ascetics whom he did not know and he therefore refused to endorse Jerome's robust defence of general asceticism.[65] Even the blue-blooded Paulinus, a convert to Christian asceticism, found himself unexpectedly refused access to the bishop of Rome in the summer of 395.[66]

Jerome's letters reveal that he was one of a number of Christian 'holy men' in Rome who actively sought the support of literate upper-class Christians in the city. The theological disputes which Jerome witnessed were, in part, a contest for the hearts and minds of this powerful stratum of lay Christians and Jerome's occasional polemical references to the patrons of his theological adversaries show them to have been an important factor in the contests. But the coherence and sincerity of their views are clear above all from the considerable effort expended by Jerome in publishing refutations. And one can appreciate the difficulty of his task further by examining the pervasive influence of aristocratic *mores* on a subject which Jerome considered his own: Christian asceticism.

Sex and marriage

The renunciation of sex, along with the rejection of the urban world, constituted one of the clearest signals of the ascetic life according to Ambrose and Jerome.[67] The most praiseworthy were Christian virgins, like Asella and Flavia Eustochium, who had eschewed earthly suitors to be brides of Christ.[68] Next in sanctity came women like Paula, Blesilla and Lea, living out a devout and continent widowhood.[69] Jerome dismissed as

[63] '...dum unum latus protego, in altero vulneratus sum atque, ut manifestius loquar, dum contra Jovinianum presso gradu pugno, a Manicheo mea terga confossa sunt': ep. xlix (xlviii). 2 (CSEL liv. 352). For Manicheism and the debate on sexuality see Hunter, 'Resistance'. [64] Jerome, ep. xlviii. 18.
[65] The important passages in Siricius are epp. vi. 2. 4 (PL xiii. 1165); i. 6. 7 (PL xiii. 1137); i. 13. 17 (PL xiii. 1144); cf. *Liber pontificalis* i. 216, which alleges that Siricius used monasteries as prisons for ascetics. See also RC i. 642f.
[66] Paulinus, ep. v. 13–14, with P. G. Walsh, *Letters of Saint Paulinus of Nola*, Washington 1967, 221 with n. 46. [67] See Brown, *Body and society*, chs xvii, xviii.
[68] Asella: ep. xxiv. 2; Eustochium: ep. xxii. 16: 'Why do you, God's bridge, hasten to visit the wife of a mere man? Learn in this respect a holy pride [superbia sancta]; know that you are better than they.'
[69] Paula: ep. cviii. 15; Blesilla: epp. xxii. 15; xxxix. 3; Lea: epp. xxiii, xxiv.

frauds a number of other Christians in Rome who claimed to be leading ascetic lives but there is evidence to suggest that elements of ascetical conduct, and in particular sexual renunciation, had been adopted by upper-class Christians.

Jerome knew women from impeccable families who called themselves Christian virgins. He saw them abroad in the streets of the city, surrounded by 'troops' of young men, who were probably among the families' *clientes*.[70] And when Jerome suggested in his widely read *Letter* 22 that they ought not to spend time in such company '... by this I have made the whole city look scandalised and caused everyone to point at me the finger of scorn'.[71] The reality was that although some upper-class Christians and their families had embraced elements of the ascetical regime, their commitment to it was not unconditional. In particular, they or their families were not prepared to see such devotion ruin a great family's fortune: 'Men who pride themselves on their religion give to their daughters scarcely sufficient for their maintenance and bestow the bulk of their property upon sons and daughters living in the world.'[72] Happy to have one daughter a virgin, and often a virgin dedicated to the Church at birth, such families became disturbed if other female children adopted the ascetic life.[73] This 'conditional' virginity is a strikingly persistent theme in the ascetic literature of the period: Ambrose knew of Christian widows who had opposed the wishes of daughters to become virgins; others had been refused access to family resources originally destined to be their dowries; some were threatened with disinheritance.[74] And Augustine had heard of a woman who had dedicated a sick daughter as a Christian virgin only to take her back when her only son died, leaving the family without heirs. The mother dedicated herself as a Christian widow in exchange.[75]

Jerome offers a tantalising anecdote in his tribute to the virgin Asella,

---

[70] Ep. xxii. 13.

[71] 'Unum miser locutus sum, quod virgines saepius deberent cum mulieribus esse, quam cum masculis: Totius oculos urbis offendi, cunctorum digitis' notor': ep. xxvii. 2 (CSEL liv. 225).

[72] '...certe, qui religiosiores sibi videntur, parvo sumptu et qui vix alimenta sufficiat virginibus dato omnem censum in utrosque sexus saecularibus liberis largiuntur': ep. cxxx. 6 (AD 414) (CSEL lvi. 182).

[73] The practice of dedicating children as virgins of the church at birth was so established that a major debate took place during the fourth century on the stage at which the (male) children were to be admitted to clerical orders. See Siricius, ep. i. 9. 13 (PL xiii. 1142); Innocent, ep. iii. 6. 10 (PL xx. 492); Zosimus, ep. ix. 1. 2. 3, 5 (PL xx. 669–72). See also *RC* i. 691f. for the suggestion that the practice actually originated in Milan.

[74] *De virginitate* (ed. E. Cazzaniga) 1. 11. 58; 1. 12. 62; 1. 12. 63, although Ambrose admits that he knew of no parents who had actually *carried out* the threat, testimony of strong parental affection.

[75] Augustine, ep. iii*. 1. 3 in *Sancti Augustini opera, epistulae ex duobus codicibus nuper in lucem prolatate*, ed. J. Divjak, Vienna 1981, 22. See also Brown, *Body and society*, 261 n. 10.

one of the most prominent and respected women in his circle.[76] Dedicated as a virgin when scarcely ten years old, a clear indication of the Christianity of her parents, she came into conflict with her mother Albina when she spontaneously chose to assume the ascetic dress.[77] Albina, however, had never intended Asella's virginity to be of this type, hoping rather that she might reflect the piety and status of the family as a 'public' virgin. And if the opportunity for an advantageous marriage presented itself, the family could probably bear the disappointment of denying Christ another bride. The great Asella seems to have begun her career as one of Jerome's sham Christians.

The connection between Jerome's circle and those he dismissed can be seen more clearly in the case of the Christian widows of Rome. Jerome satirised what he saw as the moral feebleness of this group by putting into the mouth of 'a little widow' ('adulescentua vidua') the sentiments:

'My little patrimony is daily decreasing, the property which I have inherited is being squandered, a servant has spoken insultingly to me, a maid has neglected my orders. Who will appear for me to the authorities? Who will be responsible for the rents of my estates? Who will see to the education of my children and the upbringing of my slaves?' Thus, shameful to say, they put that forward as a reason for marrying again which alone should deter them from so doing.[78]

As with Christian virginity, property again influenced the attitudes of Jerome's sham Christians to continent widowhood. But some of Jerome's paradigmatic Christian women were and remained close to the values of this world. Marcella, for example, renounced the society of Rome in clear defiance of her parents' wishes. As we saw, her sister Asella had been designated a Christian virgin at the tender age of ten. Marcella married, but on becoming a widow after only seven months, she decided to remain celibate.[79] This led to conflict with her mother Albina. The family seem to have had only two daughters and Marcella's parents were determined that she should take a second husband. An enviable match was found in the form of the former consul Naeratius Cerealis, but Marcella scorned the old man and entered upon a distinguished ascetic career.[80]

More significant is the case of Paula and her daughter Blesilla. The latter's husband died early in 384 and after a short illness herself, Blesilla decided to become an ascetic widow.[81] Jerome himself admitted that Christians close to her (propinqui) objected strongly, prompting him to declare, in a letter to Marcella: 'The Christian must rejoice that it is so,

---

[76] Ep. xxiv. [77] Ibid. 3.
[78] 'Patrimoniolum meum cotidie perit, maiorum hereditas dissipatur, servus contumeliose locutus est, imperium ancilla neglexit. Quis procedet ad publicum? Quis respondebit pro agrorum tributis? Parvulos meos quis erudiet? Vernulas quis educabit?' – et hanc – pro nefas! – causam opponunt matrimonii, quae vel sola debuit nuptias inpedire': ep. liv. 15 (CSEL liv. 481–2). [79] Jerome, ep. cxxvii. 2.
[80] For Cerealis see *PLRE* i. 197–9. [81] Ep. xxxviii. 2.

and he that is vexed must admit that he has no claim to be called a Christian.'[82] Who were these indignant *propinqui*? When Blesilla died after enduring the ascetic regime for only four months, the funeral held for her was typically aristocratic: public, processional and splendidly ornate. So conventional was the ceremony that Jerome in a letter to Paula added: 'But I seemed to hear a voice from Heaven saying: "I do not recognise these trappings; such is not the garb I used to wear; this magnificence is strange to me."'[83] But the real point of Jerome's letter was to rebuke Paula for her behaviour at the funeral:

I cannot say what I am about to say without a groan. When you were carried fainting out of the funeral procession, whispers such as these were audible in the crowd: 'Is it not what we have often said? She weeps for her daughter, killed with fasting. She wanted her to marry again, that she might have grandchildren .... They have misled this unhappy lady; that she is not a nun from choice is clear. No heathen mother ever wept for her children as she does for Blesilla.'[84]

Jerome reproached Paula by suggesting that she was of the same mind as the sham Christians. Yet the funeral arrangements can only have been in the hands of Paula and, as we saw, they were held in customary fashion. Additionally, the charge that Paula wanted grandchildren fits plausibly into the pattern we have seen above: Paula's daughter Eustochium had already been dedicated as a Christian virgin; her sister Paulina was living continent and childless with her husband Pammachius. The only hope of the smooth succession of family property lay with Blesilla. Several lines after admonishing Paula, Jerome called on Blesilla: '...to pardon my sins in return for the warnings and advice that I bestowed on her, when to assure her salvation I braved the ill-will of her family'.[85] This circumstantial evidence suggests that *Paula* had sought to make the kind of disposition of property that Jerome had remorselessly criticised in others. Only after the death of Blesilla did Paula begin to contemplate a complete withdrawal from Rome.

[82] 'Qui Christianus est, gaudeat; qui irascitur, non esse se indicat Christianum': ibid. (CSEL liv. 290).

[83] 'Videbatur mihi tunc clamare de caelo "non agnosco vestem; amictus iste non meus, hic ornatus alienus est"': ep. xxxix. 1 (CSEL liv. 295). Cf. the funeral of Junius Bassus, Prefect of the City of Rome AD 359: *Mélanges d'archéologie et d'histoire de l'école française de Rome* lxxiv (1962), 607ff; *PLRE* i. 155.

[84] 'Non possum sine gemitu eloqui, quod dicturus sum. Cum de media pompa funeris exanimem te referrent, hoc inter se populus mussitabat: "Nonne illud est, quod saepius dicebamus? Dolet filiam ieiuniis interfactam, quod non vel de secundo eius matrimonio tenuerit nepotes...matronam miserabilem seduxerunt, quae quam monacha esse noluerit, hinc probatur, quod nulla gentilium ita suos umquam filios fleverit"': ep. xxxix. 6 (CSEL liv. 306).

[85] '...veniam inpetrat peccatorum, quod monui, quod hortatus sum, quod invidiam propinquorum, ut salva esset, excepi': ibid. 7 (CSEL liv. 308). See A. Yarborough, 'Christianisation in the fourth century: the example of Roman women', *Church History* xlv (1976), 149–65 at p. 155.

A contempt for property?

The careful management of property above all else impinged on the relationship between those Christians whom Jerome dismissed as 'sham' and the ascetic life. In contrast, he characterised the asceticism of his friends as ruinously charitable. Asella, for example, had revealed a precocious otherworldliness when barely in her teens, selling off a valuable necklace without consulting her parents.[86] Paula's generosity on the death of her husband had robbed her children: '...and when her relatives remonstrated with her for doing so, she declared that she was leaving to them a better inheritance in the mercy of Christ'.[87] And Pammachius was conspicuous by the poverty of his dress, even in his public duties as a senator.[88]

But despite the impression created by this stirring rhetoric, the *disposal* of property by extreme ascetics seems to have been anything but careless.[89] Melania the Elder, who was the first noblewoman in Rome to leave the city in pursuit of ascetic fulfilment, made careful arrangements before her departure to ensure that her son Valerius Publicola would win wordly success and a good marriage. No less a person than the Prefect of the City himself was called upon to administer the considerable properties left to the young man.[90] In Palladius' words: 'Thanks to [Melania's] prayers, the young man attained a high standard of education, a good character and an illustrious marriage; and participated in the honours of the world.'[91] But as Melania well knew, more than prayers had enabled Publicola to enter upon a public career; she had herself laid the foundations of secular success with some shrewd property management. This same aristocratic astuteness with property also sustained her own life of charity. Palladius affirms that her family resources were not liquidated at a single stroke but financed thirty-seven years of good works; her estates were finally sold off in forty days in 399.[92]

Jerome certainly understood this 'tenacious presence of property'; he had seen it directly in his own friends.[93] Paula's departure for the east was accompanied by a careful disinheritance in favour of her children rather

---

[86] Ep. xxiv. 3.

[87] 'Expoliabat filios et inter obiurgantes propinquos maiorem se eis hereditatem Christi misericordiam dimittere loquebatur': ep. cviii. 5 (CSEL lv. 310).

[88] 'Quis hoc crederet, ut consulum pronepos et Furiani germinis decus inter purpuras senatorum furua tunica pullatus incederet': ep. lxvi. 6 (CSEL liv. 654).

[89] I leave out of consideration here the case of Melania the Younger and Pinianus which merits special treatment. See D. Gorce, *Sainte Mélanie*, Paris 1962.

[90] Palladius, *Historia Lausiaca* 54. 3; cf. Jerome, ep. xxxix. 4.

[91] 'ἀλλὰ ταῖς προσευχαῖς αὐτῆς ὁ νεώτερος εἰς ἄκρον παιδείας καὶ τρόπων ἤλασε καὶ γάμον τὸν ἐπίδοξον, καὶ ἐντὸς τῶν κοσμικῶν ἀξιωμάτων ἐγένετο.': *Historia Lausiaca* 54. 3.

[92] Ibid. 54. 2; 6. See also Paulinus, ep. xxix.

[93] The phrase quoted is Jill Harries's: '"Treasure in heaven": property and inheritance among senators of late Rome', in E. M. Craik (ed.), *Marriage and property*, Aberdeen 1984, 54–70 at p. 56.

than the reckless generosity suggested by Jerome.[94] In 394 he urged Paulinus of Nola to sell up his estates and join the small band of ascetics living in Bethlehem. Jerome gave voice to what he knew were Paulinus' misgivings: 'You are all for delay, you wish to defer action: unless – so you argue – unless I sell my goods piecemeal and with caution, Christ will be at a loss to feed his poor.'[95] Properties held by men like Paulinus had traditionally fuelled a civic pride, embodied in the provision of amusements and amenities for the city-dwellers of the empire. It is significant that Jerome should have chosen to depict Pammachius, one of the brightest of his ascetic 'stars', casting a family fortune from himself, as a great urban patron: 'Thus he speeds his way to Heaven beneficent as a giver of games to the poor and kind as a provider of shows for the needy.'[96] And Jerome deployed the language of aristocratic competition to refer to the provision by Pammachius and Fabiola of a Christian hostel at Portus, a project that had occurred to them independently and had perhaps led to some friction, before they combined forces:

A man and a woman contended for the privilege of setting up Abraham's tent in the harbour of Rome; and this was the struggle between the two, who should be first in that contest of kindness. Each won and each lost. Both confessed themselves victors and vanquished, for what each desired, they carried out together. They join forces and combine their plans that harmony might increase what rivalry would have wasted.[97]

Conclusion

When one examines the references in Jerome's letters to upper-class Christians, it is possible to distil from the polemic some important details of the social world of privileged Christian Rome. Those whom Jerome attacked lived comfortably and sociably as followers of Christ; they expressed their devotion in a wide range of activities, from charitable works to civic patronage; they actively sought out the company of holy men and some of the major theological disputes of the period reflect the interest of elite Romans in Christian thought. Much of the vigour of Jerome's criticism of 'sham' Christians came from the uncomfortable knowledge that his friends were from, and in certain ways remained close

[94] 'Fateor, nulla sic amavit filios, quibus, antequam proficisceretur, cuncta largita est exheredans se in terra, ut hereditatem inveniret in caelo': ep. cviii. 6 (CSEL lv. 312). See also Harries, '"Treasure"', 61.

[95] 'Scilicet, nisi tu semper recrastinans et diem de die trahens caute et pedetemptim tuas possessiunculas vendideris, non habet Christus, unde alat pauperes suos': ep. liii. 11 (CSEL liv. 465).

[96] '...munerarius pauperum, egentium candidatus sic festinat ad caelum': ep. lxvi. 5 (CSEL liv. 653). Cf. J. Labourt, Saint Jérôme lettres, Paris 1953, iii. 171, 230n.

[97] 'Vicit uterque et uterque superatus est. Ambo se victos et victores fatentur dum, quod alter cupiebat, uterque perfecit. Iungunt opes, sociant voluntates, ut, quod aemulatio dissipatura erat, concordia cresceret': ep. lxxvii. 10 (CSEL lv. 47).

to, this world. The skill and piquancy of Jerome's assaults, however, left him open to counter-attack when his patron and protector, Bishop Damasus, died on 11 December 384.

Damasus' successor, Siricius was less indulgent with the irascible scholar. An accusation against Jerome, alleging impropriety, probably in his relationship with Paula, was brought to the court of the bishop.[98] In the investigation which followed, Jerome could not muster sufficient support to save himself from an ignominious censure.[99] His criticism, ridicule and satire had alienated many Roman Christians and persuaded others that Jerome was simply too controversial to be defended. Although acquitted on the most serious charge, Jerome was humiliatingly invited to leave the city of Rome forthwith.[100]

Within months, Paula, the most devoted of Jerome's Roman circle, made her way to Palestine and a new life of ascetical service. But paradoxically, at this moment of greatest renunciation, the values of an ancient elite surfaced once more. When she founded a monastery in Bethlehem, she turned away the servants who had followed some virgins but carefully segregated off from the others those women who had, like herself, come from the noblest families into the ascetic life.[101] Even God could be expected to observe the most fundamental social distinctions.

---

[98] Ep. xlv. 6: 'infamiam falsi criminis inportarunt'.

[99] *Translation of Didymus on the Holy Spirit*, pref. (PL xxiii. 105).

[100] See Kelly, *Jerome*, 113–14.

[101] Ep. cviii. 20; cf. *Vita Olympiadii* (ed. A. Malingrey) 6, for a similar regime in fifth-century Constantinople. See also the important articles by F. E. Consolino, 'Modelli di comportamento e modi di sanctificazione per l'aristocrazia femminile d'Occidente', in A. Giardina (ed.), *Società romana impero tardoantico: istituzioni, ceti, economie*, Rome–Bari 1986, 273–306, and E. A. Clark, 'Authority and humility: a conflict of values in fourth-century female monasticism', in her *Ascetic piety*, 210ff.

Augustinian Studies 21 (1990) 67-81

The Morality of Lying in St. Augustine

Thomas Feehan

College of the Holy Cross

This is a sequel to our article in the 1988 issue of Augustinian Studies.[1] In that article based on Augustine's two opuscula, *De mendacio* and *Contra mendacium*[2], we concentrated exclusively on his philosophical description of lying. Here we shall discuss his normative analysis.

There are two distinguishable questions we can ask on Augustine's strong moral belief about lying: First, "Why did Augustine embrace such an absolute condemnation of lying?" and Secondly, "How did he justify that rigorous moral belief?"

We will argue that the answer to the first factual question is primarily theological while the answer to the second logical question is more philosophical in nature. Hence this article is divided into two parts: the first, *Augustine's view and its theological underpinning;* the second, *the ethical grounds for his strong claim.*

I. Augustine's moral view and its theological underpinning

It is beyond all doubt that Augustine did, in fact, espouse the strong thesis that lying is intrinsically evil and therefore always to be avoided. We see this in his famous quotation from the *De mendacio*, which is so typically Augustinian in style:

> Whoever thinks, moreover, that there is any kind of lie which is not a sin deceives himself sadly when he considers that he, a deceiver of others, is an honest man.[3]

He equates any modification of this doctrine with an approval of evil itself: "Everyone who lies acts unjustly, and if lying ever seems useful to anyone, it is possible that injustice sometimes seems useful to him.[4] This view, of course, is not so all embracing that all lies are of equal malice as he says in *Faith, Hope and Charity*:

> It is my opinion, however, that every lie is a sin, though it makes a great difference with what intention and in what matter the lie is uttered.[5]

In spite of this pastoral concern for those who told lies in our imperfect world, [6] he never varied from his universal condemnation of all lies in themselves. Our question now is why he held such an extreme opinion. And I argue that it was primarily for theological reasons.

Trinitarian Foundation

First of all we have Augustine's doctrine on the triune nature of God. His tract, *De Trinitate* , is one of his greatest theological works and what he has to say in it on the nature and origin of the second person of the Trinity, the Logos or Word, is one of his most fully developed insights.

The trinitarian concept posits three persons in one, three persons who are really distinct yet identical in nature. This *Mysterium Fidei* has been a challenge to the understanding of Christian believers from the beginning. Augustine was able to show by analogy that at least it is not openly contradictory. His contribution consisted in making sense of the "procession" or generative process of the second person from the first and the third person from the first and second. Our interest is in the former process in so far as he compares it to the generation of thought within the human mind.

His fully developed doctrine looks upon the second person as an internal word (logos) spoken (thought) by the first person. As Augustine explains in his own words: "As though uttering himself, the father begot the word."[7] This obviously is an attempt to show how the second and first persons are identical in nature for he states:

The word, therefore, the only-begotten Son of God the Father, is like and equal in all things to the Father, God of God, light of light, wisdom of wisdom, essence of essence; He is wholly the same as the Father...For He would not have uttered Himself completely and perfectly, if there were anything less or more in His word than in Himself.[8]

God the father then is the first and supreme exemplar of truthfulness. Augustine's second move is to consider the truthfulness of the second person, the Word, thus:

And therefore this Word is really truth, whatever is in that know-ledge from which it is born is also in itself and whatever is not in that knowledge is not in the Word. And this Word can never have anything false, because it is unchangeable, as He is from whom it is.[9]

So far then, Augustine has presented what he considered the primordial, originative pattern of truth as found in God Himself; in fact it is considered identical with the very life of God.

Incarnational Element

To this he added the doctrine of the Incarnation, i.e., the belief that the second person or Word took upon himself human nature in the person of Jesus Christ. Christ then is viewed as the external manifestation of God in the world, the witness to truth,[10] in fact as truth itself.[11]

Christian faith, for Augustine, consists in giving assent to truth in Christ and as revealed by Christ. It is easy to see that with such theological beliefs, Augustine would not accept any act contrary to truth as good, especially the lie which he considered as directly and per se opposed to truth.[12] Conversely, truthfulness or veracity is accorded a privileged status among the Christian virtues as so directly paralleling the divine life and character of God as seen in Christ.

319

Divine Illumination

If we add to this Augustine's theory of divine illumination, his case becomes even stronger. Although we have neither the time nor space here to go into this rather obscure doctrine in any detail, we must at least recall his belief that in some sense or other the ultimate source of human wisdom is a kind of interior illumination of the mind which is divine in origin. Whether he meant some kind of direct divine revelation or some intuition we possess of God's essence or, finally, a reference to the natural light of reason as God-given is irrelevant to the point we are trying to make here. Our belief is that Augustine thought that if truth in human knowledge has God as its source, then he would believe that any sort of external, deceptive manifestation of such knowledge, as instantiated above all in lying, would be a sin against God Himself.

Little wonder Augustine would condemn all lying. Since God has spoken truthfully to us through some illumination or other and we in turn have spoken truthfully to ourselves in accepting this illumination, think how wrong it would be for us in turn to speak nontruthfully to another, to deceive another by lying. Lying, in this context, is seen as a denial of that revelation of truth we have enjoyed from a divine source. Hence we must always be, as Augustine says: "...advocates of truth.[13]

Transition

I believe that these theological tenets of Augustine are the real engine which moved him to hold the absolute condemnation of all lies under all circumstances. This strong moral disapproval of lying rooted in his theology explains the apparent weakness of many of his ethical arguments we are about to consider. We mean weak here in the sense that his prior theological convictions, basically founded on revelation and scripture, tended to blind him to the fact that he was guilty of hasty generalizations and in some cases begging the question. He certainly is on to something significant in the reasons he cites for the prima facie evil character of the lie in general, but it is not so clear that he proves his universal thesis that every lie of every sort and in every circumstance is per se evil. But let his arguments speak for themselves.

II. The ethical grounds he offers for his strong claim

There are eight philosophical arguments I have found in these two books on lying, and they seem to fall into two categories: four arguments which purport to support his thesis directly and four which support that thesis indirectly through some sort of *reductio ad absurdum* or *redargutio*. We will now deal briefly with both kinds of arguments.

Direct Arguments

The first class of direct arguments can be further subdivided into (a) those which directly trade on the intrinsic nature of the lie and (b) those which are based on certain natural consequences of lying. There are two arguments of the first class and two of the second.

a. From the Nature of Lying

First Argument: From the Lie as Speech Contrary to the Mind

We are offering this argument first since it is the one later stressed by Thomas Aquinas. Augustine was convinced that human speech existed for the sole purpose of the communication of thought. In his *De magistro* Augustine emphasized that the very nature of external speech was such that it should mirror the internal speech or thought of the agent and thus serve simply to manifest the speaker's mind to others.

Since lying has as one of its necessary conditions an opposition between this external and internal speech, it directly negates the primary purpose of human speech. Thus it constitutes a perversion of that faculty and as such is wrong simpliciter.

As Augustine himself so succinctly put it:

Whoever lies speaks ... contrary to what he thinks in his heart. Speech was instituted...that each might bring his own thoughts to the knowledge of another. Hence, to use speech for deception, contrary to the purpose of its institution, is always a sin.[14]

Second Argument: From the Lie as Deceptive

For Augustine the intention to deceive is also a necessary condition for lying.[15] Whether it be the intention to deceive with respect to the statement uttered or with respect to the speaker's belief in that statement, one or the other is always involved in lying.

He admits that some errors resulting from deception are accompanied by only slight evil or even some measure of good.[16] He cites an example in his own life where he took the wrong road by mistake, i.e., as a result of an error, but by this felicitous false belief was saved from an armed band of heretics waiting on the right road.[17]

After building up such a convincing case for believing that some kinds of error may be good, he goes on to show that on the contrary, every case of error is in fact evil. His first step is to extricate himself from this muddle by distinguishing the error itself and the good consequence it brought. As he says:

> ... it is one thing to think that a road, which is not the right one, is, and another to derive from this error, which is evil, some good, for example, to be delivered from the plotting of wicked men.[18]

He then goes on to say that error in itself is "... ugly and unbecoming in the soul in proportion as we perceive it to be fair and seemingly when we utter it or assent to it.[19] Hence, he admits that error sometimes appears to be good but this is because of our imperfect state here in this life where error at times seems helpful.

Augustine appeals to our natural aversion to error, to show that it is evil and not good at all. Thus he writes "...to this extent does a rational nature shrink from the false and, so far as possible, shun error, that even those who love to deceive (i.e., the liars) choose not to be deceived.[20]

He goes on to conclude with the rhetorical question:

... is there anyone, except through error, who would deny that it is evil to accept the false as true, or to reject the true as if it were false, or to hold what is uncertain as certain or what is certain as uncertain?[21]

b. From the Consequences of Lying

Third Argument: Based on The Breaking of Faith in Lying

This argument is only briefly stated in Augustine but contains its own degree of cogency distinct from the last two. As Augustine writes in his *De mendacio*, "...whoever pronounces any statement gives testimony to his own mind."[22] He explicates this even further in his *De Magistro*, where he writes that:

... when words are heard by one who knows them, he can also know that the speaker has thought these things which the words signify.[23]

Obviously, the speaker who is involved in lying has an added reason to count on the faith of the listener, for the very success of his lie depends on that belief.

Augustine spells out the entire argument quite clearly in his *Christian Instruction*:

No liar preserves faith in that which he lies. He wishes that he to whom he lies may have faith in him, but he chooses not to preserve this faith by lying to him. Every breaker of faith is unjust. Hence, either injustice is sometimes useful (a thing which is impossible) or lying is always hurtful.[24]

Fourth Argument: From the Lie as Harmful to the Liar

In his *De mendacio*, Augustine poses the question of "...whether this violation of truth harms him who, by means of the lie, brings help to another,[25] and then answers in the affirmative. His reasoning is that since the lie is contrary to truth, it is harmful to the liar for "...he violates truth when he affirms something is or is not as his mind, senses, opinion or faith report it to be.[26]

Later in his *Contra mendacium*, he raises the same question and answers again in the affirmative but for another reason. He states: "...there are certain lies which it is not prejudicial to believe, although even in such lies...it is harmful to the liar to have wanted to deceive.[27] So he bases his argument here solely on the intention as involving deception.

Admittedly this argument is not so clearly distinguishable from the first and second types above but worthy of a separate category, since it addresses those cases in which although a given lie has no injurious effects on others whatsoever, it is still harmful to the liar and as such not to be allowed. This obviously has a certain contemporary relevancy, since it answers many counterarguments still raised today.

Indirect Arguments

When we address the indirect arguments, we find that there are again four such arguments. In each, Augustine tries to prove that the acceptance of a doctrine allowing lies of any kind will lead us to an absurdity, i.e., some state of affairs which is simply impossible or at least morally untenable or unacceptable. These states are the following: 5th argument: a society without trust; 6th argument: a deluge of lies; 7th argument: A deluge of all sorts of evil acts and the 8th argument: a contradiction in terms.

Fifth Argument: As Undermining Trust in Society

Augustine claims that allowing any lies would undermine the trust and confidence necessary for a well functioning society. He says, for example:

> ... if (any) lie is accepted and approved, the whole discipline of faith is completely destroyed...if an opportunity be afforded anywhere a so-called serviceable lie, all teaching of truth is lost, as it gives way to most harmful falsehood.[28]

Again he claims that if lying is permitted "...it leads...to make every brother suspect to every other brother ...the result is that faith is accorded to no one."[29]

This argument is one of Augustine's fundamental responses to those who would argue for allowing some lies at some times. We can sum his view up in his own words from the *De mendacio* where he argues:

> Wishing to be helpful by lying, he is held unreliable when he speaks the truth."

Therefore

> ... either (a) the good are not to be believed or (b) they are to be believed who hold the lie is sometimes necessary or (c) it is not to be believed that the good ever lie." But "... of these three possibilities, "a" is dangerous, "b" is foolish. The conclusion is, then, that the good never lie.[30]

Sixth Argument: As Letting in All Sorts of Lies

In his *Contra mendacium*, Augustine baits those who contend that some lies are just by asking them to suggest definite rules and limits to what cases they will allow. As he says: "Let the advocates ...of lies look to what kind of lying it pleases them to justify.[31]

His contention is that once we let in any kind of lies it becomes impossible to set any limit. Things tend to get out of hand, we open up the floodgates and all sorts of permissible lies pour through. As Augustine himself says:

> ... if we grant that we ought to lie (in any cases) ... little by little and bit by bit this evil will grow and by gradual accessions will slowly increase until it becomes a mass of evil lies, it will be utterly impossible to find any means of resisting such a plague of such high proportions through small additions.[32]

Seventh Argument: As Letting in All Sorts of Other Evils

Augustine's idea here is that if we allow lying for any over-riding good purpose, even when there seem to be some lesser evil consequences, then we must extend this utilitarian view to cover almost any kind of heinous act. We do not mean to treat here the usual broad objections to utilitarianism. Rather we intend to concentrate on the specific evils Augustine saw as occasioned by such a doctrine admitting some lies as licit. As Augustine writes:

> If this is so, then the individual ought to benefit himself by a lie which brings harm to no one. But there are inevitable consequences of this action...[33]

He suggests as consequences:

> And so, not about lying alone, but about all works of men...we must consider what opinion we ought to hold, lest we open the door to not only some small sins, but to all kinds of wickedness, and there remain no crime, no outrage, no sacrilege for which circumstances could not arise when it seems right to commit. We must take care lest this opinion subvert the whole righteousness of life.[34]

The kinds of examples he gives speak for themselves. He says that if one can lie to ameliorate the state of another then the following cases also must be condoned. First, if a man were to come to you with a rope and threaten to commit suicide unless you give in to his sexual advances, then you ought to submit willingly to avoid this harm to your neighbor.[35] Again, if you could help the poor by stealing from the rich, that ought to be done with impunity.[36] Finally, adultery as well becomes morally acceptable. Think of the case, he says, where: "...a woman seems certain to die of love unless we consent to her..." (Ibid.) or a woman who is willing to pay you well for your favors so that you might help the poor.[37]

Some of these examples might seem ludicrous but that is Augustine's point. The view of his opponent leads to absurdity.

Eighth Argument: From Its Self-Contradictory Character

What Augustine is attempting to do in this argument is rather subtle and intriguing. He is, in fact, trying to reduce the statement" "Some lies are just" to the logically contradictory statement: "Some unjust acts are just." He presupposes that his adversary begins by accepting the fact that lies are sinful, and then goes on to say, in spite of that fact, that some lies can be told in certain circumstances. He takes two different tacks to prove his point. The argument in its first form is:

> Every lie is a sin. But a sin is always unjust.Hence, to assert that there are some just lies is to assert that there are some just sins and this is equivalent to asserting that "... things which are unjust are just and what could be more absurd."[38]

The second form of his argument is more interesting and affords an added reason to accept the premises of the first:

> The law of God ... is the truth. Those things that are done against the law of God cannot be just. All lying is contrary to truth. Therefore, no lie is just (i.e.,) ... he who says that there are some just lies must be regarded as saying nothing else than ... that some things which are unjust are just.[39]

The first premise here is taken in the natural law sense: if there is a law (i.e., rational order) of God, it pre-eminently deserves to be called The Truth. The second premise simply defines as "unjust" acts contrary to some law. He already proved the truth of the third premise.[40] So he does seem to have constructed a forceful argument here.

CONCLUSION

This brings to a close our consideration of Augustine's views on the morality of lying. We have posited his commitment to certain Trinitarian and Incarnational beliefs, influenced by his Neo-Platonic doctrine of divine illumination, as the driving force behind his adamant stand for truth and against lying.

We have isolated eight ethical arguments directly or indirectly supporting his extreme view. Augustine never wavered in his total condemnation of lying, although he considered numerous counter-examples undermining the universality of his claim. In fact in these two books alone, the *De mendacio* and *Contra mendacium*, I have found at least eighteen such cases he created. But that is subject matter for yet another article, perhaps in the 1991 issue.

Suffice it to say now that (i) many of these examples are convincingly stated and surprisingly similar to those still being raised today and (ii) he answers each of them in an appropriate and decisive manner. That is why I believe that our definitive critique of Augustine's ethical grounds for his universal condemnation of lying must be put off until all the evidence is considered.

NOTES

1. "Augustine on Lying and Deception," Thomas D. Feehan, in *Augustinian Studies*, Vol. 19, 1988, pp. 131ff.

2. All citations in English of Augustine's writings have been taken from *The Fathers of the Church*, ed. Roy Ferrari (Catholic University of America Press, Washington, D.C., 1952). The Latin citations below were taken from *Oeuvres de Saint Augustine* Texte de L'Edition Benedictine, Traduction, Introduction et Notes, 2ème edition, Textes Complets, *Bibliothèque Augustinienne*, (Desclee, de Browwer et cie, Paris, 1949). If other sources are used, it will be so noted.

3. *De Mendacio*, c. XXI, p. 109, *Fathers of the Church*, Vol. 14. "Quisquis autem esse aliquod genus mendacii quod peccatum non sit putaverit decipiet se ipsum turpiter, cum honestum se deceptorem arbitratur aliorum." *Oeuvres*, V. 2 p. 340.

4. *De Doctrina Christiana*, bk. I, c. XXXVI, p. 57, *Fathers of the Church*, Vol. 4: "...omnis autem qui mentitur, iniquitatem facit; et si cuiquam videtur utile aliquando esse mendacium potest videri utilem aliquando esse iniquitatem." *Oeuvres*, Vol. 11, p. 232.

5. *Enchriidion de fide, spe et caritate*, c. VI, p. 383, *Fathers of the Church*, Vol. 4, "Mihi autem videtur peccatum quidem esse omne mendacium, sed multem interesse quo animo et quibus de rebus quisquis mentiatur." *Oeuvres*, Vol. 9, p. 134.

6. Cf. *Contra mendacium*, c. XVI pp. 167-8 and c. XXI, p 178, *Fathers of the Church*, Vol. 14.

7. *De Trinitate*, bk. XV, c. XIV, p. 486, *Fathers of the Church*, Vol. 45. "Proinde tanquam se ipsum dicens Pater genuit Verbum..." *Oeuvres*, Vol. 16, p. 488.

8. *Ibid, eo loco*. "Verbum ergo Dei Patris unigenitus Filius, per omnia Patri similis et aequalis, Deus de Deo, lumen de lumine, sapientia de sapientia, essentia de essentia; est hoc omnino quod Pater...Non enim se ipsum integre perfecteque dixisset, si aliquid minus aut amplius esset in ejus Verbo quam in ipso." *Oeuvres*, Vol. 16, p. 488.

9. *Ibid, eo loco*. " Et ideo Verbum hoc vere veritas est; quoniam quidquid est in ea scientia de qua genitum est et eo in ipso est; quod autem in ea non est, nec in ipso est. Et falsum habere aliquid hoc Verbum numquam potest: quia immutabiliter sic se habet, ut se habet de quo est. *Oeuvres, ibid*.

10. Cf. John 1.14, 8.40.

11. Cf. John 14.6.

12. Thomas Feehan, *opus citatum*, pp. 133-5.

13. *Contra mendacium*, c. II, p. 129 *Fathers of the Church*, Vol. 14. "...non mendacii doctor sed veritatis assertor." *Oeuvres*, Vol. 2, p. 356.

14. *Enchiridion*, c. VII, p. 389 *Fathers of the Church*, Vol. 4. "Omnis autem qui mentitur, contra id quod animo sentit loquitur voluntate fallendi. Et utique verba sunt propterea sicut instituta, ...per quae in alterius quisquis notitiam cogitationes suas perferat. Verbis ergo uti ad fallaciam, non ad quod instituta sunt, peccatum est." *Oeuvres*, Vol. 9, p. 146.

15. Cf. *De mendacio*, pp. 54-6, *Contra mendacium*, pp. 130 and 160 *Fathers of the Church*, Vol. 14.

16. *Enchiridion*, c. VI, p. 385 *Fathers of the Church*, Vol. 4. "In quibusdam ergo rebus magno, in quibusdam parvo, in quibusdam nullo malo, in quibusdam nonnulla etiam bono fallimur." *Oeuvres*, Vol. 9, p 136.

17. *Ibid*, c. V, p. 382 *Fathers of the Church*, Vol. 4. Cf *Oeuvres*, Vol. 9, pp. 129-132.

18. *Ibid*, c. VI, p. 386 *Fathers of the Church*, V4. "Itemque aliud est ipsam viam putare, quae non est ipsa; et aliud est ex hoc erroris malo aliquid boni consequi, velut est ab insidiis malorum hominum liberari." *Oeuvres*, Vol. 9, p. 138.

19. *Ibid*, c. V, p. 382 *Fathers of the Church*, Vol. 4. "...tam sit in animo deforme atque indecens, quam pulchrum et decorum esse sentimus..." *Oeuvres*, Vol. 9, pp. 130-132.

20. *Ibid*, c. V, p. 383 *Fathers of the Church*, Vol. 4. "Usque adeo tamen rationalis natura refugit falsitatem, et quantum potest devitat errorem, ut falli nolint etiam quicumque amant fallere." *Oeuvres*, Vol. 9, p 132.

21. *Ibid*, c. VI, pp. 384-6, *Fathers of the Church*, Vol. 4. "Quis enim nisi errans malum neget, approbare falsa pro veris aut improbare vera pro falsis, aut habere incerta pro certis, vel certa pro incertis?" *Oeuvres*, Vol. 9, p 138.

22. *De mendacio*, c. V, p. 61 *Fathers of the Church*, Vol. 14. "...quisquis enim aliquid enuntiat testimonium perhibet animo suo." *Oeuvres*, Vol. 2, p. 254.

23. *De magistro*, p. 39 as it is translated by J.H.S. Burleigh in *Augustine: Earlier Writings* and appears in *Medieval Philosophy* ed. Herman Shapiro, (Random House, 1964). "...cum verba ejus auditu cui nota sunt accepta fuerint posse illi esse notum de iis rebus quas significant, loquentem cogitavisse..." *Oeuvres*, V6, p. 116.

24. *De Doctrina Christiana*, bk. 1, c. XXXVI, p 57 *Fathers of the Church*, Vol. 2. "Nemo enim mentiens, in eo quod mentitur servat fidem; mam hoc utique vult ut cui mentitur fidem sibi habeat, quam tamen ei mentiendo non servat; omne autem fidei violator, iniquus est. Aut

igitur iniquitas aliquando utilis est, quod fieri non potest; aut mendacium semper inutile est." *Oeuvres*, Vol. 11, p. 232.

25. *De mendacio*, c. XI, p. 80 *Fathers of the Church*, Vol. 14. "...utrumne sibi obsit qui sic prodest alteri ut faciat contra veritatem." *Oeuvres,* Vol. 2, p. 288.

26. *Ibid, eo loco*. "...contra verum tamen facit, qui dicit aliquid ita esse vel non ita, quod ei nec mens, nec senus, nec opinatio sua, fidesve renuntiat." *Oeuvres*, eo loco.

27. *Contra mendacium*, c. III, pp. 129-130, *Fathers of the Church*, Vol. 2. "Verumtamen sunt quaedam mendacia quae credere nihil obsit, quamvis etiam tali mentiendi genere fallere voluisse, mentienti sit noxium, non credenti." *Oeuvres*, Vol. 2, p. 358.

28. *De mendacio,* c. VIII, p. 71 *Fathers of the Church,* Vol. 2. "Quo genere admisso atque approbato, omnis omnino fidei disciplina subvertitur...atque ita omnis doctrina veritatis aufertur, cedens licentiosissimae falsitati si mendacio vel officioso alicunde penetrandi aperitur locus." *Oeuvres*, Vol. 2, pp. 270-272

29. *Contra mendacium*, c. IV, p. 134 *Fathers of the Church*, Vol. 2. "...tendat ut...omnis frater omni fratri non immerito videatur esse suspectus. Atque ita dum per mendacium tenditur ut doceatur fides, id agitur potuis ut nulli habenda sit fides." *Oeuvres*, Vol. 2, p. 366.

30. *De mendacio*, c. VIII, p. 71, *Fathers of the Church*, Vol. 2. "...volens enim cum mentitur esse aptus, fit cum verum dicet incertus. Quamobrem aut non est credendum bonis, aut credendum est eis quos credimus debere aloquando mentiri: aut non est credendum bonos aliquando mentiri: horum trium primum perniciosum est, secundum stultum; restat ergo ut munquam mentiantur boni." *Oeuvres*, Vol. 2, p 272.

31. *Contra mendacium*, c. XVIII, p. 173, *Fathers of the Church*, Vol. 2. "Viderint enim assertores defensoresque mendacii quale genus vel qualia generea mentiendi eos justificare delectet..." *Oeuvres*, Vol. 2. p. 440.

32. *Ibid.*, p. 172. "...quod si concesserimus ... mentiendum ita paulatim minutatimque suc-crescit hoc malum et brevibus accessibus ad tantum acervum mendaciorum sceleratorum sensim subintrando perducitur, ut numquam possit penitus inveniri, ubi tantae pesti per minima additamenta in immensum convalescenti possit obsisti." *Oeuvres*, Vol. 2, pp. 439-40.

33. *De mendacio,* c. VII, p. 80, *Fathers of the Church*, Vol. 2. " Si ita est consequenter etiam sibi prodesse, debet per memdacium quod mulli obest. Sed ea connexa sunt, et istis concessis mecessaria trahuntur quae multum conturbant." *Oeuvres*, Vol. 2, p. 288.

34. *Contra mendacium*, c. XIV, p. 164, *Fathers of the Church*, Vol. 2. "Non de solo itaque mendacio, sed de omnibus operibus...considerandum est quam sententiam proferre debe-amus; ne aperiamus aditum non tantum parvis quibusque peccatis, verum etiam sceleribus cunctis, nullumque remaneat facinus, flagitium, sacrilegium, in quo causa non possit existere qua recte videatur esse faciendum, universamque vitae probitatem opinio ista subvertat." *Oeuvres*, Vol. 2, p. 424.

35. *De mendacio*, c. VI, p. 68, *Fathers of the Church* Vol. 14. "Nesciunt enim ad hoc se cogere ut si loqueum ferat homo et stuprum petat, confirmans quod sibi collum ligabit nisi ei concedatur quod petit, consentiatur propter animan, sicut ipsi dicunt, liberandum." *Oeuvres,* Vol. 2, p. 266.

36. *Enchiridion*, c. VII, p. 390, *Fathers of the Church*, Vol. 4. "Possumus enim et furando, si pauper cui palam datur, sentit commodum, et dives cui clam tollitur, non sentit incommodum: nec ideo tale furtum quisquam dixerit non ess peccatum." *Oeuvres*, Vol. 9, p. 146.

37. *Contra mendacium*, c. VII, p 144, *Fathers of the Church* Vol. 2. "Jam vero si aliquae immundae et divites feminae videantur amatores et stupratores suos insuper ditaturae, cur non et has partes atque artes suscipiat vir misericors quibus pro tam bona causa utator ut habeat unde indigentibus largiatur..." *Oeuvres,* Vol. 2, p. 386.

38. *Contra mendacium*, c. XV, p. 164, *Fathers of the Church*, Vol. 2. "...per hoc aliqua justa esse quae injusta sunt: quo quid absurdius dici potest?" *Oeuvres*, Vol. 2, p. 424.

39. *Ibid.* pp. 164-5 *Fathers of the Church*, Vol. 2. "Lex tua veritas. Ac per hoc quod est contra veritatem, justum esse non potest. Quis autem dubitet contra veritatem esse mendacium omne? Nullum ergo justum esse potest mendacium." *Oeuvres*, Vol. 2, p. 424-26.

"Nihil autem judicandus est dicere, qui dicit aliqua justa esse mendacia, nisi aliqua justa esse peccata, ac per hoc aliqua justa esse quae injusta sunt..." *Ibid.*, p. 424.

40. *Cf.* Thomas Feehan, *opus citatum, eo loco.*

Augustinian Studies 22 (1991) 165-190

Thomas Feehan

Augustine's Own Examples of Lying

Having completed our consideration of Augustine's philosophical understanding of the nature of lying[1] and its moral evaluation,[2] as presented mainly in his *De Mendacio* and *Contra Mendacium*, we can now consider his third move in these opuscula. After committing himself to an absolute moral condemnation of lying of all kinds, he turns his attention to certain seemingly plausible exceptions to the universality of his own ethical thesis.

Augustine is enough of a logician to realize that his position, that every lie in every circumstance is morally evil, is vulnerable to what is now known as the counter-example technique of criticism. That is to say, since according to Augustine: "All lies are intrinsically evil" it follows that if we can conceive of a single case of lying which is not morally evil, Augustine's principle falls.

He is honest enough to admit this and resourceful enough to offer innumerable cases[3] which seem to be such exceptions to his strong claim. He does this although he knows full-well that he can only respond to each of these cases by proving either (1) that it is not a case of lying, thus defusing the objection itself or (ii) that, if it is indeed a lie, then it is also morally evil.[4]

The sheer number of his creative counter-examples to be found in these two treatises alone, makes this matter difficult to handle in an article of this limited length. If we were to list all of them, with their full explanations and his complete responses to each, it would be much too lengthy for a single article. On the other hand, it would be a mistake not to treat them at all, both because Augustine is most ingenious and exhaustive in this matter and also because even a brief acquaintance with these objections and his answers is extremely helpful in our understanding of both Augustine's grasp of the subject of lying as well as his style of moral reasoning.

Finally there is the matter of the contemporary relevance of his examples. There is hardly any sort of counter-example offered in today's literature or discussions on lying which is not clearly included in those offered by Augustine over sixteen hundred years ago.

In this article we will, in Part One, list most of the significant objections Augustine raised with a brief explanation of each. Then in Part Two, we shall present his principle ethical responses to each of these counter-examples. Finally, in Part Three, we will conclude with several brief observations on the nature and significance of Augustine's work on lying.

Part One: Augustine's Own Counter-Examples

Limiting ourselves only to his *De Mendacio* and *Contra Mendacium*, we have distinguished at least eighteen such counter-examples and they fall into three different categories, each containing exactly six objections. Thus, the *first class* of objections takes in *six individual cases* in which it seems morally permissable to lie, namely: (1) to avoid endangering the sick, (2) to hide a fugitive, (3) to keep another from sinning, (4) to save someone from rape, (5) to trap liars and finally (6) to save someone from eternal damnation.

The *second class* of objections includes those which are based on *some general principle*, the six are: (7) the Lesser Evil Principle, (8) the Only For the Perfect Principle, (9) the Violated Right to the Truth Principle, (10) the End Justifies the Means Principle, (11) the Only Helpful and Non-Injurious Principle, and (12) the Keeping Truth in The Heart Principle.

The *third class* of objections takes in *six cases from Scripture* in which the just appear to be lying. These include: (13) Christ's pretenses, and the cases of (14) Sara, Jacob, and the Midwives, the lies of (15) Abraham and Sara, the case of (16) Rahab, that of (17) Jehu and finally of (18) Peter and Barnabas.

For brevity's sake, we will simply list these eighteen objections with only as much comment as is necessary to make them intelligible and persuasive. In place of the descriptive titles just used, we will substitute titles which are expressed in today's vernacular. However, each adheres to the substance of what Augustine himself wrote.

These new titles suggest that each objection is a dialectical antithesis to Augustine's thesis: "All lies in all circumstances are wrong." This brings out clearly the dialectical character of Augustine's thought.

He began with a strong universal condemnation of lying. It wasn't gratuitous, he offered multiple arguments supporting it. It was a reasonable and well-reasoned moral judgment. However, he then bombarded it with counter-examples or antithetical cases. Finally he answered each one in turn, sometimes with three or four arguments, never budging from his original moral position. The actual cases he considered were the following.

Six Individual Cases

1. "But the Truth Would Kill Him."

In his *De Mendacio*, Augustine asks:

> If *a sick person* should ask you for information that it is not expedient for him to have, and if he will be more grievously afflicted if you do not reply, who will dare either to tell the truth at the risk of his life or to be silent rather than by an honorable and merciful lie to minister to his health?[5]

Later in his *Contra Mendacium* he goes into a little more detail, speaking of a man "... whose life is endangered by a serious illness and whose strength will not hold out any longer if he is told of the death of his dearly beloved only son." Augustine says, that, when asked about the son, you must say something: but if you say: "He is alive" or "I don't know," you will be lying and if you say "He is dead" it would kill the poor man. His final remark is a strong one: "Who can bear to hear them exaggerate the evil of avoiding a beneficial lie and of loving homicide as truth?"[6]

2. "But the Enemy is at the Door."

Again in his *De Mendacio*, he asks: "If anyone should flee to you for protection and you were able to free him from death by a single lie, would you not tell that lie?"[7] He elaborates this case further on by stressing the fact that often it is a real dilemma, for if an interrogator asks you point-blank where someone is, you cannot even remain silent without tipping your hand, and if you tell the searcher where he is, you are betraying the one who came to you for help. In fact, as he says, even if you say: "I do not know," (which in itself is a lie), the searcher will surmise that you have something to hide. Therefore, it seems that the only way out is the outright lie: "He is not here."[8]

3. "But You Can't Let Him Do Wrong."

Augustine exemplifies this objection by referring to the case of the serviceable lie being used so ". . . that a man who has been terrified by a false story may be restrained from an act of lust" and asks us if it is not true ". . . that by lying in this manner, he (the liar) is looking out for the spiritual interest of the individual?"[9] This case becomes even more convincing when we consider the situation where the person involved is about to injure another seriously and a simple lie on our part would ". . . deter (that) person from harming others whom he seems intent upon harming unless prevented by our lies."[10]

4. "But He's Going to Rape Her."

This case is stated in Augustine's own words:

> To save a person's bodily chastity seems of such honorable character that it may demand the telling of a lie and that a lie should be told without hesitation if, by means of it, a person attacking another with evil intent may be thwarted.[11]

This is of course, a sub-species of the previous case but since he has a distinct way of answering this particular problem, we have made it an objection in its own right.

5. "But It Takes a Liar to Catch One."

This is the view of the antagonists in his tract *Contra Mendacium*. Since the Priscillianists used lies to conceal their identity, certain Catholics, who were anxious to find them out, thought that in this circumstance it was morally permissible to lie themselves.[12] It sounds like a case of over-anxious zealots adopting the very evil they condemn in others in order to destroy them, as for example violating the rights of defendants because they have violated the rights of others.

6. "But We Have To Save His Soul."

Here Augustine is considering the case in which ". . . we are confronted . . . with a danger to eternal welfare itself, which . . . must be averted by our lying if it is not possible otherwise."[13] The imagined case he envisions is of one who desires baptism (necessary for salvation) but is incarcerated by infidels. If his friends fail to reach him in order to baptize him, he will be executed and will not be saved. Hence if a lie is the only way to deceive the prison guards, and get to him, then a lie should be told and can be told with no moral blame.

B. Six Exceptions on Principle

7. "But Which is Worse?"

The principle itself, Augustine states in his *De Mendacio*: "Now those must be heard carefully who say that there is no evil so great that it may not be done in order to avoid a greater evil."[14] He applies this to our problem in his other treatise: ". . . sometimes a result must be accomplished by a lie, which one detests, in order that something more detestable may be avoided."[15]

The sort of case this refers to, he illustrates in the man who is forced either to offer sacrifice to an idol (a great evil for Augustine) or to suffer defilement (a much greater evil). Such a one, the objector continues, should offer sacrifice, since it is of lesser blame than suffering defilement. Augustine concludes by remarking that it seems true then to say: "How much more readily then, should he have chosen to lie, if by a lie he had been able to ward off so great a crime from his holy body."[16]

8. "But We Are Not all Angels."

Hidden in a long, convoluted exegesis of a scriptural text is the statement ". . . perchance, the precept never to lie at all and not even to wish to lie is intended only for the perfect, while the custom of lying is not permitted to those striving for perfection."[17] Augustine, of course, gives this as the opinion of an adversary and rejects it. The idea behind it is rather subtle. Such antagonists are objecting that the universal precept never to lie is so demanding that it is only incumbent upon the perfect, whereas ordinary people who are still struggling to be good can lie now and again, as long as they do not accept it as a general practice.

9. "But It Doesn't Violate Any Right to the Truth."

If the Decalogue be the only basis for a universal condemnation of lying, then every lie must be considered as a strict case of bearing "false witness." However, even Augustine himself thought that this is not in fact the case. He says: "We are not witnesses to whomever we happen to speak, but we

337

are witnesses (only) to *those who have a right* and who ought to know or to receive the truth through us."[18]

His examples of such persons with the "right to truth" are those such as judges or persons who are instructing others in the faith. The point of the objection is that in the case where, as Augustine says, ". . . a person seeks knowledge which does not concern him or is not expedient for him to have . . ." a lie can and ought to be told. The reasoning behind this is that the lie is evil only because of the false witness involved and if one can eliminate that element in a given case, then the lie is no longer evil and to be shunned.

10. "But It's For a Good Purpose."

Even by way of objection, Augustine could find little which seems to substantiate the principle that evil be done to accomplish some good end. But we do find mention of the principle itself: "Let us sin in order to do good" and again "Why should we not do evil that good come of it."[19]

11. "But It Didn't Hurt Anyone."

Augustine here refers to ". . . some (who) may think . . . that an exception should be sanctioned whereby certain lies which not only injure nobody but are even helpful to some might be considered honorable."[20] The example he offers of this is of a man whose friend hides his money in your presence to protect it from theft. If someone is seeking that money to steal it and asks you where it is, it is perfectly permissible (morally) to lie about its whereabouts. As he says in the same place: "No one sins by hiding his own property." The conclusion is that ". . . such a lie should not be considered reprehensible."[21]

12. "But It's What's in Your Heart That Counts."

This objection comes directly from the beliefs of the Priscillianists. They consider that all that is absolutely necessary is that we keep the truth within, i.e., that we give internal assent to the truth. When it comes to expressing that truth externally, it depends on the circumstances whether it is to be considered good or evil and it is particularly relevant whether we are speaking to friends or strangers. As Augustine says: ". . . this great evil they deem just, for they say that what is true must be kept in the heart, but it is no sin to utter what is false with the tongue to strangers."[22]

C. Six Objections from Scripture

13. "But The Lord Himself Did It."

Augustine admits that a strong case for excusing lying can be made by reference to at least three instances in which Christ himself seems to be telling lies or engaging in lying pretenses. The first two examples occur when he asks of a woman who touched him in a pressing crowd: "Who touched me?"[23] and of Lazurus: "Where have you laid him?"[24] The inference here is that he lied by implication, since being all knowing, his very questions presupposed an ignorance which was not the case, i.e., that he pretended ignorance. The third case is his pretending to go on to a certain village, when he, in fact, did not.[25]

14. "But God Rewarded Them."

Augustine here refers first to the obvious case of Jacob who responded to his father's question: "Who art thou, my son " by replying: "I am Eseu thy firstborn."[26] Then we have Sara stating to her Angelic Visitors that she had not laughed when, in fact, she had. The last case Augustine cited was that of the Egyptian mid-wives who lied in order to save Hebrew children.[27] All three were blessed or rewarded for their actions.

15. "But Even Abraham Wasn't Above It."

Augustine in this objection is referring to Abraham's seemingly blatant lie to protect himself and his wife Sarah. "While in the region of Negeb, . . . he said of his wife Sarah, 'She is my sister.'"[28] The lie did not help in the long run, but he was not reprehended for it, but rather rewarded.

16. "But What of the Biblical 'Jews in the Attic Case'?"

The Biblical account of this story is given in some detail. It seems that two Israelitic spies were sent into an alien country and hid themselves in the home of a certain harlot named Rahab. When the authorities learned of their whereabouts, they came to her house and demanded to know where they were. She then proceeded to tell several lies: (i) that she did not know now where they came from (when she did) (ii) that she did not know now where they were (when she had herself hidden them) and finally later (iii) that they had fled already (when they were, in fact still with her).[29]

339

17. "But They Are Only Satanists."

This is a scriptural example of a lie supposedly perpetrated to accomplish a good end. In order to gather all the worshippers of Baal (presumed enemies of the state) in one place so as to be able to slay them, King Jehu is said to have told them that he himself was one of them (which he was not) and that he wished to worship with them (which he did not). The lie worked and he was able to destroy a great number of this sect.[30]

18. "Et Tu, Sancte Petrus?"

This is a rather complex case he cites. There was a charge of dissimulation leveled against Saint Peter and Barnabas by Saint Paul.[31] In order to save them from this allegation, some authors claim that Paul was the one who had lied when he wrote accusingly: "When I saw that they (Peter and Barnabas) were not walking uprightly according to the truth of the gospel."[32] However either Paul's or Peter's lying in Scripture is hardly exemplary.

Part Two: Augustine's Responses to the Counter-Examples

In view of the great number of counter-examples, we will reduce his responses to their bare essentials only indicating the directions which the responses take, rather than explaining them in detail. We can't ignore them all together since Augustine does have some important additional points to make here as corollaries to his eight principle ethical arguments.[33]

We will divide these responses exactly as we did the counter-examples to allow for easy cross-reference. Hence, "A" will contain the answers to the first six objections based on particular cases, "B" those to the objections founded on principle and "C" those taken from Scripture.

A. Responses to Objections 1 To 6

1. Protecting the Sick

His first reaction to the case of lying to the elderly patient is a sympathetic one: "...I am moved by these arguments..." but then he proceeds to qualify this by saying that he was moved "... more powerfully than wisely."[34] He goes on at some length to explain why truth cannot possibly be viewed as "homicide" and why his first reaction was too hasty.

His first argument is an appeal to Christ as the author of truth; his second is a warning that if lying in such circumstance is considered homicide, then the refusal to make love to a woman who is dying for it (literally!) is likewise homicide. The third response he makes is an appeal to his belief that to let in one lie is to let in all lies[35] and his fourth, the fact that even if we held such a doctrine, we could not teach it to others.[36]

2. Hiding the Fugitive

Augustine's first response to the objection about the man who flees to you for protection, is that there is no comparison between his physical life, lost through the discovery, and your spiritual life, destroyed by your lie. He concludes saying: ". . . does he not speak perversely who says that one person ought to die spiritually so that another may live corporeally?"[37] Then he backs this up with his conviction that if we admit that we should lie to save a life, then we should have to admit we should steal, commit adultery and even suffer defilement for the same reason.[38]

3. Keeping Him From Sinning

He interprets this case of lying to keep someone from sinning as allowing us to perform a lesser evil act, lying, to keep another from committing a greater evil act, e.g., sodomy. He answers with his argument about thus opening the floodgates to all sorts of heinous crimes[39] saying: "When it is established that a man ought to sin less to keep someone else from sinning more, then our thefts will forestall other people's debaucheries, and our debaucheries their incest."[40] He also remarks slyly that it will eventually lead to committing ". . . fewer sins for more, if we are measuring very slight sins of ours and great sins of the other." His idea is that we might come, for example, to a point where we commit two thefts to keep another from committing one sacrilege. He concludes: "What is such wisdom as this if not folly or rather madness?"[41]

4. Saving Her From Rape

He answers this objection about saving someone from rape, by reminding us that chastity of the body cannot be violated against one's consent. Thus a woman who is raped unwillingly is not to be morally condemned in the least (ceteris paribus). His point is that: "In no way, therefore, should the soul defile itself by a lie for the sake of its body."[42] This last leads him into a comparison between the soul and the body claiming that: ". . . no one doubts the soul is to be preferred to the body . . ." (*Ibid.*) Hence, it would seem that even if the violation of the body were imputable to the victim, we should still refrain from injuring our soul by lying to prevent that case of rape.

5. Trapping Liars

Augustine's entire second treatise, *Contra Mendacium*, is on this subject of Catholics lying to trap the deceitful Priscillianists, so he has a host of answers for this objection. For one thing, he says that perhaps it might even be better to leave them alone and undetected than to lie to find them out.[43] He gives a number of different reasons why lying to catch liars will be self-defeating and evil in itself. First he reminds the objectors that the whole idea of discovering the heretics is to teach them the truth and he held that one who has lied will not be accepted as a teacher.[44] Secondly, Augustine says that if we use lies to catch liars then why not: ". . . robbers be proceeded against by means of robbery, sacrilege by sacrilege and adultery by adultery?"[45]

His third argument is that if this case is accepted, then the Catholic liar will be in a worse state than the heretic. The reason for this is that while the heretic lies by expressing other than what is in his mind, at least what he says is true; the Catholic liar, on the other hand, not only expresses something other than that which is in his mind, but also what he says he knows to be objectively false. So the second blasphemes knowingly while the first tells the truth thinking it to be false.[46]

Fourthly, he says that if such blasphemous lies become acceptable because they are uttered for a good purpose (i.e., to detect heretics) then adultery could be sanctioned as well. For example, he asks us to think of the case in which a loose living Priscillianist woman offered to turn over a nest of heretics for a few nights of sexual companionship with a catholic named Joseph (sic). According to the objector's principle, he ought to accept the offer and accommodate her.[47] Here Augustine is following his usual method of reductio based on his assumption that everyone will agree that at least a sin such as adultery is always evil.

6. Saving His Soul.

This lying to save a soul from damnation is the very last objection he considers in his *Contra Mendacium*, the implication being that it is one of the hardest to answer. That seems to be the case, for even if we ought not to sin to save a mere human life, it seems that when eternal salvation is concerned, we should pull out all the stops and at the very least be prepared to tell a lie to save another's soul. Augustine, however, builds a good argument to the contrary. He plays on the fact that his listeners will agree that sensual sins are always wrong and argues thus:

> If we lie to get by the guards, i.e., in order to baptize the prisoner, then why not suffer defilement for the same end, or why not have a woman seduce the guard?[48]

After this, he gives a subtle argument why the lie should no more be told than a sinful sexual act performed. He begins by reminding the listener that truth (God-Christ) teaches us not to sin against chastity and we do not (i.e., without at least realizing that we are doing wrong) but if that is the case "... how can truth command us to lie?"[49]

He even attempts to explain why we have a more natural aversion to evil sensual acts than to acts against truth,[50] appealing to chastity as a virtue illuminated by truth (his metaphor of the divine source of truth as light) whereas truth is God Himself and too dazzling (as illuminating not illuminated) to behold in itself. Although this is more poetic perhaps than convincing, he does have a point. At least in this sense he is right, that men do tend to lie with less provocation and less self-recrimination than they do in the case of blatantly offending against chastity. He is simply trying to give an explanation of this fact.[51]

B: Responses to Objections 7 to 12

7. The Lesser Of Two Evils

Augustine begins to chip away at the Lesser Evil Principle by warning the objector that just because one evil act is less evil than another, it does not follow that the first becomes "good." As he says: "... the former is not good because the latter is worse![52] Then he reminds us again that our inquiry is about whether when "... a man does this or that, he sins or not; it is not whether he sins more or less seriously.[53]

343

He then answers the objection directly by saying that once this principle is accepted, one ends up abandoning all objective norms and classifying various evil acts as it suits him. The result is that the evils we naturally abhor become the worst in our scale of values although in themselves they may not be any more serious than certain evils we find it easier to accept. The point is that it becomes impossible to judge objectively in individual cases. As he explains it himself:

> ... when it has been granted that a certain evil may be done in order to avoid a greater evil, then each one proceeds to measure evil, not according to the norm of truth, but according to his own desire and habit. Hence he considers that evil greater which he himself dreads more, not that which actually should be avoided more ... hence, they hate thieves, robbers, abusive persons, torturers . . . more than libertines, drunkards and profligates, if the latter are not annoying to anyone.[54]

Augustine says that the missing element here that accounts for this muddle is the fact that such people, as the objector, do not consider that in every evil act they are ". . . doing an injury to God."[55] This is his last ditch defense, i.e., even if a lie harms no one directly, and its harm to the liar is problematic, it does offend God and as such ought not be told.

8. Prescribing For The Perfect.

This objection proscribing all lies only for the perfect is, I believe, one which Augustine never explicitly answers. He is quite clear and convincing, I might add, in explaining how this view seems to be based on scriptural texts.[56] A lie might well be entirely prohibited for the ". . . perfect, spiritual persons ..." while for ". . . persons striving for perfection. . . lies ... constitute a duty of mercy."[57] When it comes to refuting this position, he falls back on some very general arguments and never addresses himself specifically to the objection as such.

9. Violating The Right To Truth.

Augustine briefly considers this objection which attempts to equate lying with the violation of a definite right to truth by simply detaching the lie from the false witness. Thus, in effect, he says that the untruth might well not constitute a case of false witness at all but it will still be a lie and thus reprehensible on that account. He concludes: "Hence, if you lie to him (i.e., to one without a right to truth) you will, perhaps, be exonerated from false witness but certainly not from telling a lie."[58]

10. Justifying The Means By The End.

When Augustine turns to the consideration of the principle that one ought to do evil to accomplish some good, he is on firmer ground and answers the objection in detail. First of all, he states his own position unequivocally:

> Of course, it makes a difference for what reason, for what end, with what intention anything is done. But, those things that are clearly sins ought not to be done under any pretext of a good reason, for any supposedly good end, with any seemingly good intention.[59]

He tries to prove this contention by distinguishing morally indifferent acts from morally evil acts. He gives examples of acts such as feeding others or marital intercourse which he says, will be good or bad according to the intention involved.[60] Then he lists cases such as theft, impurity and blasphemy which ". . . are already sins . . ." and claims that to say that these could be done for a good reason, is to say that there are some ". . . just sins. . . ." He thus leads us into the contradiction: "Some just acts are unjust" which we treated elsewhere.[61]

He is perhaps more convincing when he takes a second tack and explains how this principle itself, as utilitarian in nature, leads to many acts contrary to the common wisdom of moral people. Thus, for example, he says that if we ought to perpetrate evil for good then: (a) we ought to steal from the rich, (b) sell testimonies to save the guilty as he says, facetiously: ". . . two goods result from this sale of a lie: money would be obtained whereby to sustain the needy and a judge would be fooled out of punishing a man,"[62] and (c) supplant authentic wills by false ones, so as to direct the money more equitably towards the more deserving (a classical objection to utilitarianism).[63]

These and all other sorts of evils are let in by following such a principle of morality. As he says, it is the result of allowing that ". . . in all the evil work of men we are not to ask what is done, but merely why it is done, so that whatever is found to have been done for a good reason is not judged to be evil in itself."[64] His whole idea here, of course, is that such a denial of the wrong-headed principle itself will separate the objection from its foundation and make an explicit defense of his position on lies unnecessary.

11. Helping Others, Injuring No one.

Augustine dispenses with this objection about benevolent lies quickly and decisively. The objection claims that lies are to be permitted if they harm no one but are of benefit to all. What he asks is that we not cloud the issue by considering accidental circumstances but rather concentrate on ". . . what must we consider about the sin of lying looked at in itself?"[65]

His point is that lying is forbidden by God (eighth commandment) to the same extent that stealing is forbidden (fifth commandment). And he asks why the evil of lying should depend on its consequences and content ". . . although theft and other sins are reprehensible in themselves?"[66] In substance, this response almost amounts to the same as the preceding one but is even stronger as dependent directly on his thesis banning all lies as in se evil.

12. Keeping Truth Within

This objection of keeping truth in the heart, we find correctly answered by Augustine. He attacks those who say an untruth can be told, if we only preserve the truth in our hearts, in two ways. First, he says that if what they claim is so, then why do we condemn those Catholics who ". . . disowned Christ in the presence of their persecutors. . . ." Since they kept the faith within[67] and why did Saint Peter weep so bitterly after his denial of Christ, certainly he ". . . kept the truth within . . ."?[68]

His second response is a negative one in so far as he attempts to explain what that phrase about "keeping the truth in the heart" really signifies. He says it:

> . . . is not to be taken to mean that if the truth is preserved in the heart, a lie may be told with the tongue. The meaning is that it is possible for a man to speak with his tongue a truth that profits him not, if he does not hold it also in his heart, that is to say, if he does not believe what he speaks.[69]

So he turns the objection against the objector and ends up corroborating his own concept of the nature of the lie as well as the root of its evilness.

13-18 Purported Lies In Scripture.

I believe that this last section would be better covered in a more general way, both because I prefer to downplay the role of Scripture and Theology in his philosophical evaluation of lying and because he does have one

346

tripartite approach to all problems that are scripturally based.[70] His answers to these difficulties were always founded on one of the following principles: either:

I. The act described in Scripture was not, in fact, a lie at all (e.g., because it must be taken in a figurative sense).[71]

or:

II. If the act were a lie, than either (A) it is not to be imitated or (B) at least should not bc imitated in religious matters.[72]

The fact that some persons described in Scripture might have, in fact, lied did not greatly disturb Augustine for as he says:

They ought not to be thought worthy of imitation simply because they are found in those books which are justly called sacred and divine. For, those writings contain both the evil actions of men and the good; the former should be avoided; the latter, followed.[73]

In fact, he even goes further and says that we should not, in principle, try to imitate all the actions even of the best of men: "Hence, it is clear that we should not make part of our manners everything that we read as done by righteous and just men."[74] So he is, then, reminding us that the morally good does not depend on what has bccn done, even by the just, but on what ought to be done.[75]

Applying his two general principles then, to the specific objections mentioned above, we can state the following: Objections No. 13,[76] No. 14b (i.e., Jacob) and No. 15 fall under principle number I; Objections no. 14c (the midwives), No. 16, No.17, and No. 18, fall under principle II,A.

We have omitted any reference to Sara's seeming deception for Augustine does not seem to treat it as such, I presume that it would fall under principle II, A. Of the other objections which come under principle II,A, the first two (No. 14c and No. 16) have to do with non-Israelites and Augustine says that they might be expected to lie; the third, No. (17) involves an Israelitic King whom he says is not described as a righteous man in Scripture anyway[77] and the last deals with Saint Peter and Barnabas whom he feels forced into judging strictly for Scripture itself ". . . reproves and corrects them."[78] These failures of Paul or Peter only remind us of the fallibility of the best of men.

He explains the approval of the lie of the Egyptian midwives (Objection No. 14c) as directed not to their lying but to their merciful intention. As he says: "... it was not their deception which was rewarded but their benevolence...."[79] Then he wisely cuts off any misapplication of this doctrine by distinguishing clearly between: saying: "Because we have already sinned, let us do good ... and ... Let us sin in order to do good ... for it is one thing to say 'I ought not to have sinned but I shall perform works of mercy by which I may efface my former sin' and another to say: 'I ought to sin because I cannot otherwise show mercy.'"[80]

His strict view on the evilness of all lies is most obvious when he is judging the case of Rahab. Her lies saved the lives of several Israelite spies. So Augustine sees her's as a seemingly good case for the opposition, and asks accordingly: (would) "... Rahab ... have done better if (she) had shown no mercy being unwilling to lie?"[81] Then he pushes this objection as far as he can and persists in answering in his usual unwavering way.

First, he remarks that if Rahab did not lie but rather told the truth, wouldn't she be betraying her guests? He answers, that she could have said: "I know where they are, but I fear God and will not betray them"[82] thus avoiding a lie and betrayal. Then he objects, to his own response, by saying that if this were the case, the searchers would in all probability kill her and search the house anyway, thus defeating the whole purpose of her concealment. He answers this by saying that she had hid them well and probably they would not be found and as regards her death: "... she would have ended her petty (!) life by a death precious in the sight of the Lord."[83]

Then further on he again objects to himself: "... but what if they did find them?" Augustine turns this around and asks "... what if they didn't believe the lie in the first place because she was a woman of mean reputation already, and they were to go on to kill her and to find them?"[84] Wouldn't this state of affairs be much worse than the other on all counts? Finally as a coup de grace, he asks: "Where are we putting the will and power of God?"[85] Of course before an all powerful and literal deus ex machina such as this, who has a chance?

Part Three: Conclusion

I have included this last narrative of Augustine's treatment of Rahab as an illustration of the way Augustine thinks ethically and the absolutist attitude he has in the specific matter of the morality of lying of which this dialogue is paradigmatic. I would like to make two final observations on the significance of the Augustine's dialectic on lying.

First, this dialectic never got off the ground. It never produced its usual result which is that the thesis- proposer, Augustine, after hearing the antithesis, an Augustinian mock objection, never produced a new synthesis. He did not tighten up his first claim, refining it by delition of some elements or an addition of new qualifiers. This guaranteed that there would be no new thesis to continue the process.

Hence, Augustine, by defending his initial thesis so forcefully, defeated the very purpose of the dialectical process. This brings up our second and final observation.

No matter how we feel about evaluating lies, we have to admire (1st) Augustine's openness in confronting his opposition, listening to their best arguments and answering them. We have to admire (2ndly) his moral fortitude in standing his ground, defending himself on all sides and always remaining firm in his belief that there is something morally wrong with lying. Augustine argued that there is something wrong with misrepresenting the truth, with misleading others, with intentionally implanting false beliefs in the minds of others, with breaking faith with your fellow humans, misusing your God-given faculty of speech and finally undermining the trust and confidence so necessary in forming community and nurturing human relationships, communication and society itself.

At least in a W. D. Rossian sense, isn't there a prima facie duty not to lie to others based on a corresponding prima facie right, not to the truth, but a right not to be lied to? If this is so, and I believe it is, we must count Augustine as one of the principle thinkers over time who has helped us to understand just what is morally wrong with lying and liars.

NOTES

1. "Augustine on Lying And Deception," Thomas D. Feehan, in *Augustinian Studies*, Vol. 19, 1988, pp. 31ff.

2. "Augustine's Moral Evaluation of Lying," Thomas D. Feehan, in *Augustinian Studies*, Vol 21, 1990, pp. 67ff.

3. The large number of these counter-examples, Augustine had ready at hand, bespeaks the fact that his adversaries were numerous and their view excusing some kinds of lies was well thought out and widely accepted.

4. *Contra Mendacium*, c. XVII, pp. 170-171, *Fathers of the Church*, Vol. 14. All citations in English of Augustine's writings have been taken from the *Fathers of the Church*, ed. Roy Ferrari (Catholic University of America press, Washington, D.C., 1952). The Latin citations following were taken from *Oeuvres* de Saint Augustine Texte de L'Edition Benedictine, Traduction, Introduction et Notes, 2ieme edition, Textes Complets, *Bibliotheque Augustine*, (Desclee, de Browwer et cie, Paris, 1949). ". . . ad hanc regulam mihi videntur non solum ista, verum etiam si qua sunt talia redigenda, ut AUT quod esse creditur ostendatur non esse mendacium. . . . AUT quae convincuntur esse mendacia, non esse imitanda monstrentur, ut si qua nobis ut alia peccata subrepserint, non esse tribuendam justitiam, sed veniam postulandum." *Oeuvres*, Vol. 2, p. 436.

5. *De Mendacio*, c. V, pp. 60-61, *Fathers of the Church*, Vol. 14. "Si aliquid aegrotus interroget quod si scire non expedit, qui etiam te non respondente possit gravius affligi, audebisne aut verum dicere in perniciem hominis aut silere potiusquam honesto et misericordio mendacio valetudini ejus opitulari?" *Oeuvres*, Vol. 2, p. 252.

6. *Contra Mendacium*, c. XVIII, pp. 171-172, *Fathers of the Church*, Vol. 14. "Et quis ferat homines exaggerantes quantum sit mali salubre mendacium devitari et homididam diligi veritatem?" *Oeuvres*, Vol. 2, p. 438.

7. *De Mendacio*, c. V, p. 60, *Fathers of the Church*, Vol. 14. "Si quis ad te confugiat, qui mendacio tuo possit a morte liberari, non es mentiturus?" *Oeuvres*, Vol. 2, p. 252.

8. *De Mendacio*, c. XIII, pp. 82-83, *Fathers of the Church*, Vol. 14. "Quid ergo, si ad Christianum homicida confugiat aut videat quo confugit et de hac re interrogetur ab eo qui ad supplicium quaerit hominis interfectorem, mentiendum est? . . . An quia non de peccato quis interrogatur sed de loco ubi lateat? . . . Quid si ad judicem ductus de ipso loco ubi se ille occultet interrogeris, dicturus es aut ibi est ubi eum scis esse, aut non novi et non vidi quod nosti et vidicti?" *Oeuvres*, Vol. 2, pp. 292 and 294.

9. *De Mendacio*, c. VIII, p. 71, *Fathers of the Church*, Vol. 14. ". . . sicut ipse putat, officiosi mendacii, existimans falsa narratione hominem territum posse a libidine cohiberi atque hoc modo etiam si spiritualia se consulere mentiendo arbitretur?" *Oeuvres*, Vol. 2, p. 270.

10. *Contra Mendacium*, c. X, p. 151, *Fathers of the Church*, Vol. 14. ". . . aut ne aliis noceat qui nociturus videtur, nisi mendaciis evitetur." *Oeuvres*, Vol. 2, p. 400.

11. *De Mendacio*, c. VII, pp. 68-69, *Fathers of the Church*, Vol. 14. "Pudicitiae quippe corporis quia multum honorabilis persona videtur occurrere et pro se flagitare mendacium, ut sine dubitatione mentiendum sit, facile responderi potest. . . ." *Oeuvres*, Vol. 2, pp. 266 and 268.

12. *Contra Mendacium*, c. VI, pp. 137-141; c. XI, pp. 156-157, *Fathers of the Church*, Vol. 14. ". . . quos pro magna venatione mendaciis nostris capere malimur? Priscillianistarum est enim, sicut ipse monstrasti, ista sententia . . . Redarguenda sunt ista, non imitanda. . . ." *Oeuvres*, Vol. 2, pp. 352 and 354. "Nos contra, ut se nobis aperiant, si hoc quasi justum mendacium fallendis eis capiendisque. . . ." *Ibid*, p. 372. "Sed

occultos lupos, inquies, indutos pellibus ovium et dominicium gregem latenter qraviterque vastantes aliter vivenire non possumus." *Ibid*, pp. 372 and 374. ". . . multo facilius, inquies, eorum latibula penetramus si quod sunt nos esse mentiamur." *Ibid*, p. 376.

13. *Contra Mendacium*, c. XX, p. 176, *Fathers of the Church*, Vol. 14. ". . . nobis ipsius quoque salutis aeternae periculum, opponitur, quod nostro mendacio si aliter non potest. . . ." *Oeuvres*, Vol. 2, p. 446.

14. *De Mendacio*, c. IX, p. 71, *Fathers of the Church*, Vol. 14. ". . . sed adhuc diligenter audiendi sunt qui dicunt nullum esse tam malum factum quod non in pejoris devitatione faciendum sit. . . ." *Oeuvres*, Vol. 2, p. 272.

15. *De Mendacio*, c. XVII, pp. 101-102, *Fathers of the Church*, Vol. 14. ". . . interdum mentiendo faciendum esse quod oderis ut quod amplius detestandum est devitetur." *Oeuvres*, Vol. 2, p. 328.

16. *De Mendacio*, c. IX, p. 72, *Fathers of the Church*, Vol. 14. "Quanto igitur mendacium proclivius elegisset, si mendacio posset a sancto corpore tam immane flagitium removere." *Oeuvres*, Vol. 2, p. 272.

17. *De Mendacio*, c. XVIII, p. 97, *Fathers of the Church*, Vol. 14. ". . . forte ita perfectorum praeceptum sit, omnino nunquam non solum mentire, sed vel velle mentiri, assiduitas vero mentiendi nec proficientibus permittatur." *Oeuvres*, Vol. 2, p. 320.

18. *De Mendacio*, c. XVII, p. 99, *Fathers of the Church*, Vol. 14. "Non enim aqud quoscumque loquimur, testes sumus, sed apud eos quibus expedit et debetur per nos cognoscere aut credere veritatem." *Oeuvres*, Vol. 2, p. 322.

19. *Contra Mendacium*, c. XV, p. 166, *Fathers of the Church*, Vol. 14. "Peccemus ut benefaciamus . . . faciamus mala, ut veniant bona (Roman, 3.8)." *Oeuvres*, Vol. 2, p. 290.

20. *De Mendacio*, c. XII, p. 81, *Fathers of the Church*, Vol. 14. "Sed fortassis exceptionem addendam quis putet ut sint quaedam honesta mendacia quae non solum nulli absunt sed etiam nonnulli prosunt. . . ." *Oeuvres*, Vol. 2, p. 290.

21. ibid, eo loco. "Non enim quis quam peccat abscondendo rem suam . . . turpe non esset." *Oeuvres*, Vol. 2, p. 290.

22. *Contra Mendacium*, c. II, p. 127, *Fathers of the Church*, Vol. 14. ". . . atque hoc tam magum malum ideo justum existimare quia dicunt in corde retinendum esse quod verum est, ore autem ad alienos proferre falsum nullum esse peccatum. . . ." *Oeuvres*, Vol. 2, p. 354.

23. Luke, 8.45.

24. John, 11.34.

25. Luke, 24.28 in *Contra Mendacium*, c. XIII, p. 161, *Fathers of the Church*, Vol. 14. ". . . Dominum Jesum, posteaquam resurrexit, ambulasse in itinere, cum duobus discipulis, et propinquantibus eis castello quo ibant, illum longius se ire fixisse; ubi evangelista dicens: Ipse autem se finxit longius ire (Luc. XXIV, 28); etiam ipsum

verbum posuit, quo mendaces nimium delectantur, ut impune mentiantur; quasi mendacium sit omne quod fingitur . . ." *Oeuvres*, Vol. 2, p. 418.

26. Genesis, 27.16-19 For this "lie," he seems to have been blessed.

27. Genesis, 18.15. While hiding behind a curtain, she heard the angels tell her husband that she was going to become pregnant. Being an elderly woman, she could not help but laugh. The problem was that when asked, she denied that she laughed at all. Although she was accused of lying (Genesis, 18.15) God still blessed her with child. (Genesis, 21.1.). Exodus, 1.17-20. Here it is clearly stated that "Therefore God dealt well with the midwives. . . ." (Exodus, 1.20).

28. Genesis, 20.1-2.

29. Josue 2 in *Contra Mendacium*, cc. XV, XVI, XVII, pp. 165-168, *Fathers of the Church*, Vol. 14. Cf. infra. footnotes 80-85.

30. 2 Kings, 10. and in *Contra Mendacium*, c. II, p. 128, *Fathers of the Church*, Vol. 14. "Si enim Jehu quem sibi inter cacteros ad exemplus mentiendi prudenter videntur intueri, servum Baalis se esse mentitus est ut servos ejus occideret (IV *Reg.* X). quanto justius, secundum istorum perversitatem, tempore persecutionis servos daemonum se mentirentur servi Christi, ne servi daemonum servos occideret Christi et sacrificarentur idolis ne interficerentur homines. . . ." *Oeuvres*, Vol. 2, p. 356.

31. Galatians, 2.14.

32. *De Mendacio*, c. XXI, p. 109, *Fathers of the Church*, Vol. 14. ". . . si dicamus quaedam Mendacia non esse peccata, nisi etiam in quibusdam peccatum dicunt esse, si mendacio recusemus; eoque perducti sunt defendendo mendacium ut etiam primo illo genere, quod est omnium sceleratissimum, dicant usum fuisse apostolem Paulum. Nam in Epistola ad Galatas, quoe utique sicut caeterae ad doctrinam religionis pietatisque conscripta est, illo loco dicunt eum esse mentitum ubi ait de Petro et Barnaba: 'Cum vidissem quia non recte ingrediuntur ad veritatem Evangelii'. . . ." *Oeuvres*, Vol. 2, p. 340.

33. "Augustine's Moral Evaluation of Lying," Thomas D. Feehan, in *Augustinian Studies*, Vol. 20, 1990.

34. *Contra Mendacium*, c. VIII, p. 172, *Fathers of the Church*, Vol. 14. "Moveor his appositis vehementer . . . sed mirum si etiam sapienter." *Oeuvres*, Vol. 2, p. 438.

35. *Contra Mendacium*, c. VIII, p. 172-173, *Fathers of the Church*, Vol. 14. First Argumemtum: "Cum enim proposuero ante qualesque ocolos cordis mei intelligibilem illius pulcheritudinem, de cujus ore falsi nihil procedit; quamvis ubi radians magis magisque clarescit veritas, ibi palpilans mea reverberator infirmitas; tamen sic amore tanti decoris accendor, ut cuncta quae inde me revocant humana contemnam. Sed multum est ut iste in tantum perseveret affectus, ne in tentatione desit effectus." *Oeuvres*, Vol. 2, pp. 438-440.

Second Argumentum: " Nec me movet contemplantem luminosum bonum, in quo mendacii tenebrae nullae sunt, quod nobis mentiri nolentibus et hominibus vero audito morientibus homicida dicitur veritas. Nunquid enim stuprum appetet inpudica et te non consentiente saevo armore consumpta moriatur homicida erit et castitas?" *Ibid*, eo loco.

Third Argumentum: " Huc accedit, ubi miserabilis ejulandum est, quod si concesserimus pro salute illius aegri de vita filii ejus fuisse mentiendum, ita paulatim minutatumque seccrescit hoc malum et brevibus ascessibus ad tantum acervum mendaciorum sceleratorum sensim subintrando perducitur, ut nunquam possit penitus invenire, ubi tanta pesti minima additamenta in immensum convalescenti possit obsisti." *Ibid*, eo loco.

36. "Augustine on Lying and Deception," Thomas D. Feehan, in *Augustinian Studies*, Vol. 19, p. 133.

37. *De Mendacio*, c. VI, p. 67, *Fathers of the Church*, Vol. 14. "Quomodo ergo non perversissime dicitur ut alter corporaliter vivat debere, alterum spiritualiter mori." *Oeuvres*, Vol. 2, p. 264.

38. *Ibid*, pp. 67-68. "Enim vero isti qui stomachanter et indignatur si nolit aliquis mendacio perimere animan suam ut alius senescat in carne, quid si etiam furto nostro, quid si adulterio liberari possit aliquis de morte, ideone furandum est aut moechandum?. . . cur animam suam quisque mendacio corrumpat ut alter vivat in corpore, cum si suum corpus propterea corrumpendum daret, omnino judicio nefariae turpitudinis damnaretur?" *Oeuvres*, Vol. 2, p. 266.

39. *De Mendacio*, c. VIII, pp. 70-71, *Fathers of the Church*, Vol. 14. ". . . nullum esse flagitium quod non eadem conditione suscipere cogatur, sicut jam superius demonstratum est . . . ." *Oeuvres*, Vol. 2, p. 270.

40. *Contra Mendacium*, c. IX, p. 147, *Fathers of the Church*, Vol. 14. "Sed si hanc peccatis aperuerimus viam, ut committamus minora ne aliis majora committant lato limite, immo nullo limite, sed convulsis et remotis omnibus terminus infinito spatio cuncta intrabunt atque regnabunt. Quando enim fuerit definitum peccandum esse homini minus ne aluis peccet amplius, profecto et furtis nostris cavebuntur aliena et incesta stupris." *Oeuvres*, Vol. 2, p. 392.

41. *Ibid*, p. 148. ". . . non solum minora pro majoribus, verum etiam . . . pauciora pro pluribus; si se ita rerum verset incursus, ut aliter alii non se absteneant a peccatis, nisi minus aliquanto sed tamen peccantibus nobis. . . . . . . Hoc sapere quid est, nisi desipere, vel potius insanire?" *Oeuvres*, Vol. 2, pp. 392 and 394.

42. *De Mendacio*, c. VII, p. 69, *Fathers of the Church*, Vol. 14. "Nullo modo igitur animus se mendacio corrumpat pro corpore suo, quod scit manere incorruptum si ab ipso animo incorruptio non recedat." *Oeuvres*, Vol. 2, p. 268.

43. *Contra Mendacium*, c. VII, p. 142, *Fathers of the Church*, Vol. 14. "Sed si aliter omnino non posset educi de cavernis suis haeretica impietas nisi a tramite veritatis lingua catholica deviaret, tolerabilius occultaretur quam ista praecipitaretur, tolerabilius in suis foveis delitescerent vulpes quam propter illas capiendas in blasphemiae foveam caderent venatores, tolerabilius perfida Priscillianistarum veritatis velamine tegeretur quam fides catholicorum ne a Priscillianistis mentientius laudaretur a catholicis credentibus negaretur." *Oeuvres*, Vol. 2, p. 382.

44. *Contra Mendacium*, c. I, p. 126, *Fathers of the Church*, Vol. 14. "Ut quid enim tanta cura vestigare atque indagere conamur nisi ut captos in apertumque productos, aut etiam ipsos veritatem doceamus, aut certe veritate convictos nocere aliis non sinamus ad hoc ergo ut eorum mendacium deleatur, sive caveatur, Dei autem veritas augeatur. Quomodo igitur mendacio mendacia vecte potero persequi!" *Oeuvres*, Vo. 2, pp. 350 and 352.

45. *Ibid*, eo loco. "An et latrocinio latrocinia et sacrilegio sacrilegia et adulterio sunt adulteria persequenda." *Oeuvres*, Vol. 2, p. 352.

46. *Contra Mendacium*, c. VI, p. 139, *Fathers of the Church*, Vol. 14. "Si enim ut capiatur qui blasphamet nesciens, blasphemabo sciens, pejus est quod facio quam quod capio. Si ut inveniatur qui Christum negat nesciens, ego Christum negabo sciens, ad perditionem me secuturus est quem sic invenero, siquidem ut ullum inveniam prior pereo." *Oeuvres*, Vol. 2, p. 376.

47. *Contra Mendacium*, c. VI, p. 142, *Fathers of the Church*, Vol. 14. "Quid si enim ex numero Priscillianistarum impudicarum aliqua femina injuciat oculum in catholicum Joseph eigue promittat proditdram se latebras eorum si ab illa impetraverit stuprum certumque sit eam, si ei consensum fuerit, quod pollicita est impletruram, faciendumne censebimus...." *Oeuvres*, Vol. 2, p. 382.

48. *Contra Mendacium*, c. XX, pp. 176-177, *Fathers of the Church*, Vol. 14. "...velut si qusquam babtizandus in potestate sit impiorum atque infidelium constitutus ad quem perveniri non possit ... nisi deceptis mentiendo custudibus. Ab hoc invidiosissimo elamore, quo cogimur ... pro aeterna hominis salute mentiri ... Cur enim si custodes isti, ut nos ad babtizandum hominem admittant, stupro illici possunt, non facimus contraria castitate...?" *Oeuvres*, Vol. 2, p. 446.

49. *Ibid*, eo loco. "... quo confugiam, nisi ad te, Veritas et mihi abs te proponitur castitas ... cum procul dubio nulli esset fideliter amabilis castitas, si non eam praeciperet veritas." *Oeuvres*, Vol. 2, p. 446.

50. *De Mendacio*, c. XVIII, p. 102, *Fathers of the Church*, Vol. 14. "Sed in hoc errant homines quod subdunt pretiosa vilioribus. Cum enim concesseris admittendum esse aliquod malum ne aliud gravius admittatur, non ex regula veritatis sed ex sua quisque cupiditate atque consuetudine metitur malum, et id putat gravius quod ipse amplius exhorrescit, non quod amplius re vera fugiendum est." *Oeuvres*, Vol. 2,p. 328.

51. *Contra Mendacium*, c. XX, pp. 176-177, *Fathers of the Church*, Vol. 14. "Cur enim si custodesisti... stupro illici possunt, non facimus contraria castitati, et si mendacio decipi possunt, facimus contra veritati? ... sed sicut oculi ad intuendum solem parum firmi ea tamen quae a sole illustrantur, libenter intueretur: sic animae jam valentes delectari pulchritudine castitatis, non tamen continuo per seipsam considere veritatem unde lucet castitas possunt, ut cum ventum fuerit ad aliquid faciendum quod adversum est veritati ita refugiant et exhorreant, si faciendum quod proponatur quod adversum est castitati." *Oeuvres*, Vol. 2. pp. 446 and 448.

52. *Ibid*, c. VIII, p. 145, *Fathers of the Church*, Vol. 14. "... aequandus est fur quilibet ei furi qui misericordiae volunte furatur: Quis hoc dixerit? Sed horum duorum non ideo est quisquam bonus quia pejor est unus." *Oeuvres*, Vol. 2, p. 390.

53. *Ibid*, p. 146, *Fathers of the Church*, Vol. 14. "Nunc autem quaerimus, si hoc aut illud quisque fecevit, quis non peccabit, sive peccabit, non quis gravius leviusque peccabit . . . Neque nunc agitur quid sit levius sive gravius, sed quae sint peccata vel non sint." *Oeuvres*, Vol. 2, p.390.

54. *De Mendacio*, c. XVIII, p. 102, *Fathers of the Church*, Vol. 14. Cf. supra, footnote #50 coupled with: "Itaque fures et raptores et contumeliosos et tortores atque interfectores magis oderint quam lascivos, ebriosus, luxurioso, si nulli molest sint." *Oeuvres*, Vol. 2, p. 328.

55. *Ibid*, eo loco. "Non enim intelligunt aut omnino curant quod isti Deo faciunt injuriam . . . cum dona ejus in se corrumpunt etiam temporalia atque ipsis corruptionibus aversanter aeterna." *Oeuvres*, Vol. 2, p. 328.

56. Cf. Ecclesiastes, 7.14, "Be not willing to make any kind of lie . . ." coupled with: ". . . for the custom thereof will not lead to good."

57. *De Mendacio*, c. XVII, pp. 96-97, *Fathers of the Church*, Vol. 14. "Et id quod sequitar 'assiduitas evim ejiis non proficiet ad bonum' (Eccli. VII, 14) ita sonat, quasi non a mendacio, sed ab asiduo mendacio, id est, a consuetudine atque amore mentiendi prohibere videatur . . . sed usque adeo esse omme mendacium malum, et perfectis atque spiritualibus animis omni modo fugiendum, ut nec ipsis proficientibus assiduitas ejus permittenda sit." *Oeuvres*, Vol. 2, p. 320.

58. *De Mendacio*, c. XVII, p. 99, *Fathers of the Church*, Vol. 14. "Cum autem ille te interroget aut vult ex te aliquid nosse, qui eam rem quaerit quae non ad eum pertineat aut quam ei nosse, non expedit; non testem sed proditorem requirit. Itaque si ei mentiaris, a falso fortasse testimonio alienus eris, sed a mendacio profecto non eris." *Oeuvres*, Vol. 2, pp. 322 and 324. It must be mentioned that he also held the strong view that all lies are in a sense cases of false witness in so far as with each speech-act we are witnesses to what is in our own minds. In the response in our text, he is taking witness in the strict sense of corresponding to some strict right of the listener, e.g., by reason of his being a judge or the like. Cf. "Augustine's Moral Evaluation of Lying," *Augustinian Studies*, Vol. 21, 1990 p. 73.

59. *Contra Mendacium*, c. VII, p. 143, *Fathers of the Church*, Vol. 14. "Interest quidem plurimum qua causa, quo fine, qua intentione quid fiat: sed ea quae constat esse peccata, nullo bonae causae obtentu nullo quasi bono fine, nulla velut bona intentione, facienda sunt." *Oeuvres*, Vol. 2, p. 384.

60. *Ibid*, eo loco. "Ea quippe opera hominum, sicut causas habuerint bonas seu malas nunc sint bona, nunc mala, quae non sunt per se ipsa peccata: sicut victum praebere pauperibus bonum opus est si fit causa misericordiae cum recta fide, sicut concubitus conjugalis, quando fit causa generandi, si ea fide fiat ut gignantur regenerandi. Haec atque hujusmodi secundum suas causas opera sunt bona vel mala, quia eadem ipsa si habent malas causas in peccata vertuntur, velut si jactantiae causa pauper pascitur, aut lasciviae causa cum uxore concumbitur, aut filii generantur non ut Deo sed ut diabalo nutriantur." *Oeuvres*, Vol. 2, pp. 384 and 386.

61. Cf. "Augustine's Moral Evaluation of Lying," *Augustinian Studies*, Vol 21, 1990, pp. 76-77 and *Contra Mendacium*, c. XV, pp. 164-165, *Fathers of the Church*, Vol.

14. "Nihil antem judicandus est dicere, qui dicit aliqua justa esse mendacia, nisi aliqua justa esse peccata, ac per hoc aliqua justa esse quae injustae sunt." *Oeuvres*, Vol. 2, p. 424.

62. *Contra Mendacium*, c. VII, p. 143, *Fathers of the Church*, Vol. 14. "Duo enim fiunt hujus venditione memdacii ut, et pecunia sumatur unde inops alatur et judex fallatur ne homo puniatur." *Oeuvres*, Vol 2, p. 386.

63. *Ibid*, p. 144. "Testamenta etiam, si possumus, ut haereditates vel legata non habeant indiqui qui nihil ex eis operantur boni, sed hi potius quibus esurientes pascuntar, nudi vestiuntur, peregrini suscipiuntur, captivi redimuntur, ecclesiae construuntur?" *Oeuvres*, Vol. 2, p. 386.

64. *Ibid*, eo loco. ". . . si semel concesserimus in omnibus malis operibus hominum ideo non quid fiat, sed quare fiat esse quaerendum ut quaequam propter bonas causas fact a inveniuntur, nec ipsa mala esse judicentur?" *Oeuvres*, Vol. 2, p. 388.

65. *De Mendacio*, c. XII, p. 81, *Fathers of the Church*, Vol. 14. ". . . quid agimus de ipso peccato mendacii?" *Oeuvres*, Vol. 2, p. 290.

66. *Ibid*, eo loco. ". . . cum ipsum furtum per se culpabile sit, et caetera peccata. An occultare peccatum non licet, facere licet?" *Oeuvres*, Vol. 2, p. 292.

67. *Contra Mendacium*, c. VI, p. 139, *Fathers of the Church*, Vol. 14. "Nonne pere omnes qui Christum coram persecutoribus negaverint quod de illo credebant corde tenuerunt et tamen ore ad salutem non confitendo perierunt nisi qui per poenitentiam revixerunt?" *Oeuvres*, Vol. 2, p. 378.

68. *Ibid*, eo loco. "Quis ita evanescat ut existimet Apostalum Petrum hoc habuisse in corde quod in ore, quando Christum negavit? (Matt. XXXI, 69) Nempe in illa negatione intus veritatem tenebat et foris mendacium proferebat." *Oeuvres*, Vol. 2, p. 378.

69. *Ibid*, p. 140. "Quapropter illud quod scriptum est: 'Qui loquitur veritatem in corde suo' (Ps. XIV, 3) non sic accipiendum est quasi retenta in corde veritate loquendum sit in ore mendacium. Sed ideo dictum est quia fieri potest ut loquatur quisque ore veritatem quae nihil ei prosit si eam in corde non teneat, id est si quod loquitur ipse non credat." *Oeuvres*, Vol. 2, p. 378.

70. *Contra Mendacium*, c. XI, p. 157, *Fathers of the Church*, Vol. 14. ". . . aportet ut dicam cur ista mihi videatur tripartitia ratio disputandi adversus eos qui patronas mendaciis suis volunt adhibere divinas Scripturas: ut prius ostentamus nonnulla quae ibi putantur esse mendacia non esse quod putantur, si recte intelligantur; deinde si qua ibi mendacia manifesta sunt, imitanda non esse; tertio, contra omnes omnium opiniones quibus videtur ad viri boni officium pertinere aliquando mentiri omni modo tenendum, in doctrina religionis nullo modo esse mentiendum." *Oeuvres*, Vol. 2, p. 410.

71. *Ibid*, c. XII, p. 157. "Ad ostendenda ergo quae putantur in Scripturis esse mendacia; non ea esse quod putantur, si recte intelligantur: . . . de propheticis Litteris inveniunt velut exempla mentiendi. Illa quippe omnia quae nominatim commemorant ubi sit quisque mentitus, in eis Libris leguntur, in quibus non solum

dicta, verum facta multa figurata conscripta sunt, quia et figunate gesta sunt. In figuris autem quod velut mendacium dicitur bene intellectum verum invenitur." *Oeuvres*, Vol. 2, p. 412.

72. *Ibid*, pp. 156 and 157. "Ad te igitur pertinet sectam detestabilem cum refellis, sic accienda monstrare ista testimonia Scripturarum ut vel doceas . . . imitanda non esse etiam quae manifestum est esse mendacia, vel certe ad extremum de his saltem rebus quae ad doctrinam religionis pertinent, nullo modo esse mentiendum' Oeuvre, Vol. 2, p.410.

73. *Ibid*, c. XIV, p. 163. ". . . sine dubitatione mentitiae sunt. Sed non ideo debent imitanda existimare, quia in eis reperiuntur libris qui sancti ct divini merito nominatur. Habent enim conscripta et mala hominum et bona; illa vitanda, ista sectanda. . . ." *Oeuvres*, Vol. 2, p. 422.

74. *Ibid*, c. IX, p. 150. "Unde constat quod non omnia quae a sanctis vel justis viris legimus facta, transferre debemus enim mores. . . ." *Oeuvres*, Vol. 2, p. 400.

75. *Ibid*, p. 148. "Haec quando in Scripturis sanctis legimus non ideo quia facta credimus etiam faciendo credamus. . . ." *Oeuvres*, Vol. 2, pp. 394 and 396.

76. The following numeration corresponds to what we used earlier when explicating the six objections from scripture. cf. Supra.

77. *Contra Mendacium*, c. II, p. 129, *Fathers of the Church*, Vol. 14. "Illum vero Jehu mendacio impio et sacrificio sacrilego accidendo impios . . . non imitarentur nec si de illo qualis fuisset eadem Scriptura tacuisset. Cum vero scriptum sit eum rectum cor non habuisse cum Deo (IV *Reg*. X, 29). . . ." *Oeuvres*, Vol. 2, p. 356.

78. *Contra Mendacium*, c. XII, p. 158, *Fathers of the Church*, Vol. 14. "Quando quidem illa Petri et Barnabae simulatio quo gentes judaizare cogebant, merito reprehensa atque correcta est. ne tunc noceret et ne posteris ad imitandum valeret." *Oeuvres*, Vol. 2. p. 412.

79. *Contra Mendacium*, c. XV, p. 165 and *De Mendacio*, c. IV, p. 62, *Fathers of the Church*, Vol. 14. "Sed quod scriptum est bene Deum fecisse cum Haebreis obstretricibus (Exod. I, 17-20) . . . non ideo factum est quia mentitiae sunt, sed quia in homines Dei misericordes fuerunt. Non est itaque in eis remunerata fallacia, sed benevolentia, beniquitas mentis, non iniquitas mentientis." *Oeuvres*, Vol. 2, p. 426.

80. *Contra Mendacium*, c. XV, p. 166, *Fathers of the Church*, Vol. 14. ". . . verumtamen aliud est dicere: Peccare quidem non debui, sed opera misericordiae faciam, quibus deleam quod ante peccavi; et aliud est dicere: Peccare debeo, quia non possum aliter misereri. Aliud est, inquam, dicere: Quia jam peccavimus, benefaciamus, et aliud, est dicere: Peccemus ut benefaciamus. Ibi dicitur. Faciamus bona, quia fecimus mala, hic autem faciamus mala, ut veniant bona." *Oeuvres*, Vol. 2, pp. 426 and 428.

81. *Ibid*, p. 168, *Fathers of the Church*, Vol. 14. ". . . ergone . . . Raab melius fecissent si nullam misericordiam praestitissent, nolendo mentiri?" *Oeuvres*, Vol. 2, pp. 430 and 432.

82. *Ibid*, p. 169, *Fathers of the Church*, Vol. 14. "An posset (Raab) interrogantibus dicere: Scio ubi sunt, sed Deum timeo, non eos prodo." *Oeuvres*, Vol. 2. p. 432.

83. *Ibid* Eo loco. "Ita et illa, si tamen a suis civibus esset occisa pro misericordiae opere, vitam istam finiendam pretiosa in conspectu Domini morte finisset (Psal. CXV, 15) et ergo illos ejus beneficium inane non fuisset." *Oeuvres*, Vol. 2, p. 432.

84. *Ibid* eo loco. "Sed, inquies quid, si et ad illum locum ubi eos occultaverit ii a quibus quaerebantur, perscrutando omnia pervenissent? Isto modo dici potest: Quid si mulieri vilillemae atque turpissimae, non solum mentienti, verum etiam pejeranti credere nuluissent? Nempe etiam sic consecutura fuerant quae timendo mentita est." *Oeuvres*, Vol. 2, p. 432.

85. *Ibid* Eo loco. "Et ubi ponimus voluntatem ac potestatem Dei?" *Oeuvres*, Vol. 2, p. 432.

Acknowledgments

Stanton, Graham N. "The Fourfold Gospel." *New Testament Studies* 43 (1997): 317–46. Reprinted with the permission of Cambridge University Press.

Hill, C.E. "The Debate over the Muratorian Fragment and the Development of the Canon." *Westminster Theological Journal* 57 (1995): 437–52. Reprinted with the permission of the Westminster Theological Seminary.

Horbury, William. "The Wisdom of Solomon in the Muratorian Fragment." *Journal of Theological Studies*, n.s. 45 (1994): 149–59. Reprinted with the permission of Oxford University Press.

Kinzig, Wolfram. "Καινὴ διαθήκη: The Title of the New Testament in the Second and Third Centuries." *Journal of Theological Studies* 45 (1994): 519–44. Reprinted with the permission of Oxford University Press.

Brooks, James A. "Clement of Alexandria as a Witness to the Development of the New Testament Canon." *The Second Century* 9 (1992): 41–55. Reprinted with the permission of Johns Hopkins University Press.

Norris, Richard A., Jr. "Irenaeus' Use of Paul in His Polemic Against the Gnostics." In *Paul and the Legacies of Paul,* edited by William S. Babcock (Dallas: Southern Methodist University Press, 1990): 79–98, 337–40. Reprinted with the permission of Southern Methodist University Press.

Balás, David L. "The Use and Interpretation of Paul in Irenaeus's Five Books *Adversus Haereses.*" *The Second Century* 9 (1992): 27–39. Reprinted with the permission of Johns Hopkins University Press.

Wilken, Robert L. "*In novissimis diebus*: Biblical Promises, Jewish Hopes and Early Christian Exegesis." *Journal of Early Christian Studies* 1 (1993): 1–19. Reprinted with the permission of Johns Hopkins University Press.

Norris, Richard, Jr. "Chalcedon Revisited: A Historical and Theological Reflection." In *New Perspectives on Historical Theology: Essays in Memory of John Meyendorff,* edited by Bradley Nassif (Grand Rapids: William B. Eerdmans Publishing Company, 1996): 140–58. Reprinted with the permission of William B. Eerdmans Publishing Company.

Brent, Allen. "Diogenes Laertius and the Apostolic Succession." *Journal of Ecclesiastical History* 44 (1993): 367–89. Reprinted with the permission of Cambridge University Press.

Daley, Brian E. "Position and Patronage in the Early Church: The Original Meaning of 'Primacy of Honour.'" *Journal of Theological Studies*, n.s. 44 (1993): 529–53. Reprinted with the permission of Oxford University Press.

O'Donnell, James J. "The Authority of Augustine." *Augustinian Studies* 22 (1991): 7–35. Reprinted with the permission of *Augustinian Studies*.

Limberis, Vasiliki. "The Eyes Infected by Evil: Basil of Caesarea's Homily, *On Envy*." *Harvard Theological Review* 84 (1991): 163–84. Copyright 1991 by the President and Fellows of Harvard College. Reprinted by permission.

Leyerle, Blake. "John Chrysostom on Almsgiving and the Use of Money." *Harvard Theological Review* 87 (1994): 29–47. Copyright 1994 by the President and Fellows of Harvard College. Reprinted by permission.

Curran, John. "Jerome and the Sham Christians of Rome." *Journal of Ecclesiastical History* 48 (1997): 213–29. Reprinted with the permission of Cambridge University Press.

Feehan, Thomas. "The Morality of Lying in St. Augustine." *Augustinian Studies* 21 (1990): 67–81. Reprinted with the permission of *Augustinian Studies*.

Feehan, Thomas. "Augustine's Own Examples of Lying." *Augustinian Studies* 22 (1991): 165–90. Reprinted with the permission of *Augustinian Studies*.